A Concise Survey of Western Civilization

A Concise Survey of Western Civilization

Supremacies and Diversities throughout History

BRIAN A. PAVLAC

ROWMAN & LITTLEFIELD PUBLISHERS, INC.
Lanham • Boulder • New York • Toronto • Plymouth, UK

Published by Rowman & Littlefield Publishers, Inc.
A wholly owned subsidiary of The Rowman & Littlefield Publishing Group, Inc.
4501 Forbes Boulevard, Suite 200, Lanham, Maryland 20706
http://www.rowmanlittlefield.com

Estover Road, Plymouth PL6 7PY, United Kingdom

British Library Cataloguing in Publication Information Available

Library of Congress Cataloging-in-Publication Data

Pavlac, Brian Alexander, 1956–
    A concise survey of western civilization : supremacies and diversities throughout history / Brian A. Pavlac.
        p.   cm.
    Includes bibliographical references and index.
    ISBN 978-1-4422-0554-3 (cloth : alk. paper)—ISBN 978-1-4422-0555-0 (pbk. : alk. paper)—ISBN 978-1-4422-0556-7 (electronic)—ISBN 978-1-4422-0781-3 (cloth v. 1 : alk. paper)—ISBN 978-1-4422-0782-0 (paper v. 1 : alk. paper)—ISBN 978-1-4422-0783-7 (electronic v. 1)—ISBN 978-1-4422-0784-4 (cloth v. 2 : alk. paper)—ISBN 978-1-4422-0785-1 (paper v. 2 : alk. paper)—ISBN 978-1-4422-0786-8 (electronic v. 2)
    1. Civilization, Western.   I. Title.
CB245.P38   2011
909′.09821—dc22

                                                                    2010039286

♾ ™ The paper used in this publication meets the minimum requirements of American National Standard for Information Sciences—Permanence of Paper for Printed Library Materials, ANSI/NISO Z39.48-1992.

Printed in the United States of America

Brief Contents

Contents

Diagrams, Figures, Maps, Tables, and Timelines

DIAGRAMS

FIGURES

MAPS

TABLES

TIMELINES

Acknowledgments

I was interested in history from a young age, as most kids are. Too often, as they grow older, kids lose their fascination with the past, partly because it becomes another something they have to learn rather than a path of self-understanding or even just "neat stuff." Wonderful teachers taught me history through the years, and partly inspired by them, I foolishly went on to study history in college. Before I knew it, history became my intended profession; and I have been fortunate to make a living from history.

In teaching courses over the years, I found my own voice about what mattered. Instead of simply sharing my thoughts in lectures, I produced this book. Former teachers, books I have read and documentaries I have viewed, historical sites I have visited, all have contributed to the knowledge poured into these pages. Likewise, many students, too many to be named, have sharpened both words and focus. I owe thanks to the many readers whose suggestions have improved the text. For their help to me in getting this project as far as it has come, I have to thank a number of specific people. I appreciate my editor, Susan McEachern, who gave the book her time and consideration, and her associate, Carrie Broadwell-Tkach, as well as Michele Tomiak and Jehanne Schweitzer. Various people have read drafts and offered useful suggestions: Mark Reinbrecht, Linae Steitz Marek, Megan Lloyd, and especially Jean O'Brien. I thank Cristofer Scarboro, Charles Ingram, Nicole Mares, and Ada Borkowski-Gunn for their feedback from teaching. Helping me with reviewing and editing have been my daughters, Helen K. Pavlac and Margaret Mackenzie Pavlac. Finally, most of all, my spouse, Elizabeth Lott, has sustained me through it all. Her skills in grammar, logic, and good sense have made this a far better book.

The final version is never complete. Every new history source I read makes me want to adjust an adjective, nudge a nuance, or fix a fact. With every reading of this text, I find room for improvement. I have made a great effort for accuracy. Should any errors have crept in, please forgive the oversight and contact me with your proposed corrections.

How to Use This Book

Learning is difficult. If it were easy, everyone would be educated. In this age of multimedia, reading still remains one of the best ways to learn something. Of course, reading well is not always easy. You cannot read a nonfiction informative work such as this in the same way as you would a Harry Potter novel. Those novels, though, are full of information with strange new terms, from *muggles* to *Hogwarts*, that people learn easily and absorb into their knowledge. The same could be true of learning history if you loved it as much as historians do.

I hope to make learning history as enjoyable as possible, even to those who are not historians, not in love with the past. Even as a survey, this book offers one person's opinion about what is good, bad, useful, and wasteful to know about our wider civilization. As it is meant to be a concise book, I have tried to keep it brief. This book covers the minimum historical information that educated adults should know, in the author's opinion, while also providing a tightly focused narrative and interpretive structure. This approach applies major themes of conflict and creativity. Other approaches might be equally as valuable. Indeed, to be truly educated, you should be looking at a variety of views about the past. History is rarely simple. This version provides a foundation for learning more.

The phrase "supremacies and diversities" describes the unifying theme through which this text evaluates the past. "Supremacies" focus on the use of power to dominate societies, ranging from warfare to ideologies. Supremacy seeks stability, order, and amalgamation. "Diversities" encompass the creative impulse that creates new ideas as well as people's efforts to define themselves as different. Diversity creates change, opportunity, and individuality. A tension, of course, arises between the "supremacy" desire for conformity and the "diversity" idea of individuality. This interaction has clearly driven historical conflict and change.

Fulfilling the survey function, this narrative develops political, economic, technological, social, and cultural trends, depending on the historical period. The book does not much emphasize the everyday-life aspects of people in the past. While lifestyle can offer an interesting reflection of larger issues, it in itself rarely promotes change. Five main topical themes regularly inform how this text looks at change: technological innovation, migration and conquest, political and economic decision making, church and state, and disputes about the meaning of life. These topics have significantly altered history and are still influential in the present.

How could you best learn from this book? Read well. This time-tested advice applies to anything you might want to learn thoroughly for the rest of your life. Here are a few steps:

1. Read the text in a space and at a time conducive to reading—not in the few minutes before class, not with television and music blaring.

2. Prudently mark up, underline, highlight, and otherwise annotate your text as you study. Use the margins for notes, questions, comments, and marks to remind you of some important point.

3. Critique the book as you read; enter into its conversation. You might comment in the margins on the following points:

   Connections between themes, ideas, or subjects
   Ideas you agree with
   Ideas you disagree with
   Reactions provoked by the text
   Points or subjects of particular interest to you
   Points or subjects you would like to know more about

4. At the end of each section, jot down notes or write a brief essay about what you read. The review question at the end of each section and the open space there provide a useful opportunity.

5. Use the timelines to review and structure your knowledge according to theme or time period. The most important terms in the text appear in **boldface** and are listed in the timelines. Additionally, definitions for important terms, which appear in ***boldface italics*** in the text, are given in the glossary.

6. If you wish to deepen your experience with the past, try the "Suggested Readings" listed at the end of the book. They provide essential points of view or capture the spirit of their times, sometimes at great length. For other useful and concise sources and study information, see the website.

Finally, connect what you learn here to the rest of your experience. The more you know, the more you can know. And, according to the liberal arts credo, the more you know, the better will be your decisions about your life.

CHAPTER 1

History's Story

N ow" can never take place again. Each moment is surrendered to the past, to be forgotten or to be remembered. In our personal lives, we treasure or bury memories on our own. Our larger society, however, entrusts historians with preserving and making sense of our collective existence. Historians recapture the past by applying particular methods and skills that have been nurtured over the past few centuries. Although such processes are not without problems, the work done by historians has created the subject known as **Western civilization**.

THERE'S METHOD

"How do we know anything?" is our starting point. As **humans**, some of our knowledge comes from instinct; we are born with it, beginning with our first cry and suckle. Yet instinct makes up a small portion of human knowledge. Most everything we need to know we learn in one way or another. First, we learn through direct experience of the senses. These lessons of life can sometimes be painful (fire), other times pleasurable (chocolate). Second, other people teach us many important matters through example and setting rules. Reading this book because of a professor's requirement may be one such demand. Third, human beings can apply reason to figure things out. This ability enables people to take what they know, then learn and rearrange it into some new understanding.

The discipline of ***history*** is one such form of reasoning. History is not just knowing something—names, dates, facts—about the past. The word *history* comes from the Greek word ιστορία for "inquiring," or asking questions. The questioning of the past has been an important tool for gaining information about ourselves. Indirectly, it helps us to better define the present.

Quite often authorities, the people in charge, have used history to shape groups whose shared identities bonded them together into a community. Sharing a view of history can forge social bonds and justify a particular place in the world. For many peoples, history has embodied a mythology that reflected their relationship to the gods. Or history chronicled the deeds of kings, justifying royal rulership. History also sanctioned domination and conquest of one people over another. Most people are raised to believe that their own country or nation is more virtuous and righteous than those beyond their borders. The history of Western civilization abounds with examples of these attitudes.

Then, about two hundred years ago, several men began to try to improve our understanding of the past. Historians began to organize as a profession based in the academic setting of universities. They imitated and adapted the scientific method (see chapter 10) for their own use, renaming it the **historical method** (see table 1.1). In the scientific method, scientists pose hypotheses as reasonable guesses about explanations for how nature works. They then observe and experiment to prove or disprove their hypotheses. In the historical method, historians propose hypotheses to describe and explain how history changes. The two main problems historians have focused on are **causation** (how something happened) and **significance** (what impact something had). Unlike scientists, historians cannot conduct experiments or run historical events with different variables.[1] Historians

Table 1.1.   The Historical Method

1. Find a problem.

2. Form a hypothesis.

3. Conduct research.

Questions to ask of sources:

A.   External: Is it genuine? Is it what it says it is?
     When and where was it made?
     How did it get from its original recording to the present?
     Who is the author?
     What is the author's opportunity for making the source? Is it his/her own eyewitness information or an indirect report? Is it consistent with his/her known character?
     Any interpolations, emendations, or insertions by others?

B.   Internal: What is its meaning? How is it significant?
     What is the source's ostensible or intended purpose?
     How accurate is the author (any competence, bias, prejudice)?
     What is the source's content?
     How does it compare with what else is known or written by the author and/or with other reliable sources?
     What do modern scholars say about the source?

4. Make the argument and conclusions, usually in written form.

5. Share the knowledge, usually through publication.

Note: The step-by-step process of the historical method rigorously questions sources in order to reconstruct the best version of the past.

---

1. Alternative histories are an increasingly popular genre of fiction. Similar to science fiction's guesses about the future, alternative histories are based on "what if" issues of the past: what would have happened differently if, for example, some leader had not been killed or some nation had not lost a war? Reading good examples can help you learn history.

cannot even obtain direct observational evidence—there are no time machines. Instead, historians have to pick through whatever evidence has survived. They call these data **sources**.

At first, historians sought out sources among the written records that had been preserved over centuries in musty books and manuscripts. Eventually historians learned to study objects, ranging from needles to skyscrapers, made by people. Obviously, not all sources are of equal value. Those sources connected directly with past events are called **primary sources**. These are most important for historical investigation.

When evaluating these sources, historians face two problems. For one, evidence for many events has not survived at all or survives only in fragments. For another, some people have forged sources. Much of historical research involves questioning human character, deciding who is honest or deceitful, trustworthy or undependable. Then, through careful examination and questioning, historians try to write the most reliable and accurate explanation of past events, carefully citing their sources.

As the last and most important part of the historical method, professional historians have shared their information with one another. They produce **secondary sources**, usually books and articles. At academic conferences and in more books and articles, historians learn from and judge one another's work. They debate and challenge one another's arguments and conclusions. Often a consensus about the past emerges. Generally, agreed-on views begin to appear in **tertiary sources**, such as encyclopedias and handbooks. Although tertiary sources are several steps removed from the past, they are often the best place for a novice to begin research about a subject since they offer convenient summaries and overviews.

Because the past is so vast and its sources so numerous, historians have always divided it up into smaller, more convenient chunks. All history is about selection, choosing what to examine. Professional historians usually specialize, become experts, in one small slice of the past. Since so many historians publish books today, hardly anyone can ever read all that has been written about any single subject. New books and articles emerge each year, especially about popular topics such as the American Civil War or Hitler. The history of even one day covered in any detail would be long and confusing; the novel *Ulysses* by James Joyce, about the events of 16 July 1904, is an interesting example. Whether writing many volumes or a slim book, it is impossible to cover every detail on even a small subject. Something is always left out.

Therefore, historians prioritize to make the past manageable. They select some events or places as more important than others in answering questions about the past. For example, in one person's life, a one-time decision, such as which college to attend, would probably be more essential to include in her biography than a description about what she chose to eat for breakfast on the day the decision was made. The former probably deserves more attention, since that choice can change a life. The quality of a unique, decisive historical moment is usually more interesting than the quantity of mundane events. However, the description of breakfast choice might be valuable, if, for example, years of eating too much bacon and eggs led to heart disease or a dose of poison killed a person. Few readers, though, would want to read a close description of every repeated meal. Selection and generalization prevent us from becoming overwhelmed.

Historians can select only a few bits of the past, leaving out the vast majority of human activities. They then categorize or organize their selections into sensible stories and arguments. For example, eating breakfast differs a lot from choosing a college or waging a war. Fighting battles and engaging in politics were once considered by historians to be the only important human activities worthy of investigation. Politics—kings, wars, treaties, and rebellions—once dominated historical writing. Within the past century, however, historians have broadened their interests to include a wider range of human activities. These days, many historians examine social matters: family, sex roles, food, and fashion. Even a shift in breakfast habits from waffles and bacon cooked by Mom to drive-in processed portions of an Egg McMuffin® can illustrate something about a **society**, a coherent group of people.

Historians categorize the past in three main ways. The first and most obvious division is **chronological**, using time as a dividing point. The most natural division of time is the day, with its cycle of sunlight and darkness. This cycle regulates us all. Some particular days, like those on which battles are waged or a notable inspiration is put to paper, can change the course of history. A larger natural unit of time is the year, especially important for people in temperate climates who experience the change of seasons. Finally, the basic human experience stretches, for each of us, over a lifetime. Some lives are short, others seem long, but all are finite and end in death. Yet history marches on.

Aside from natural portions of time, historians divide up history into manageable blocks. In the largest artificial division, historians split the past into two periods: **prehistory** and history. Prehistory includes everything humans did up to the first invention of writing, about five thousand years ago in the Middle East and East Asia. We can examine human activity before writing only through physical remains and artifacts, such as bones and shaped stones.

Technology (use of raw materials to make tools), ideology, and narrower political movements also define different eras. The names for the Stone Age or the Iron Age are based on the use of those materials for making tools during those times. The term *Middle Ages* draws on the perceptions of politics and culture that fall between the ancient and modern epochs. The titles of the ages of Renaissance or Enlightenment derive from artistic and intellectual achievements. Sometimes a country's dynasty or ruling family provides a useful marker. Given our preference for round numbers, a century fits into historical schemes, especially the more recent nineteenth or twentieth centuries. Many of the commonly used historical labels, terms such as *antiquity*, *medieval*, and *Renaissance*, were not drawn from the sources and lives of past people; instead, historians later coined those terms. Historians apply such divisions to the past to show both what the people within a period shared in common and what they have to teach us.

While chronology applies time to divide up the past, **geographical** divisions, where events took place on our planet, are equally as common. The largest unit is world or global history. Historians are increasingly finding connections and continuities among civilizations around the planet. By the twentieth century, people were clearly bound together worldwide. At the opposite end of size, the smallest unit could be a town, a college, or even a home. Historians usually focus somewhere between these two extremes, most frequently dealing with a country, nation, or state. Indeed, history became a profession in modern times as academics constructed national stories for the modern nation-states.

The third method that historians use to slice up the past is a **topical** approach, separating the wide range of human activities into smaller groupings of human enterprise. For example, historians today often specialize in areas of intellectual, social, constitutional, gender, literary, diplomatic, or military history.

The timelines in this book apply six main divisions. First is *science* and technology: how we understand the universe and build tools to cope with it. Second is **economics**: how we create and manage the distribution of wealth. Third is **politics**: how people create systems to organize collective decisions. Fourth is **social structures**: the units and hierarchies (such as families and communities) within which people place themselves and the humble activities of daily life. Fifth is **culture**, especially those works and activities that people fashion in order to cope with, understand, or simply share their experiences of the world. Culture includes **art** (largely visual creations), **literature** (compositions of words to be read or performed), and recreation (acts ranging from sports to hobbies). Finally are both *philosophy* and *religion*: how people understand the purpose of life and the meaning of death, which usually involves the supernatural, or beliefs in a reality beyond our senses. These six topics essentially embrace all human accomplishments. Human creativity, though, has led to a wide variety of approaches to these six topics. Collections of people, called societies, have formed and dissolved throughout human history, in various times and places, each living according to its own unique mixture of scientific, economic, political, social, cultural, and religious attitudes. Historians describe and explain these societies in and of themselves and in their conflicts with neighboring peoples. Encounters between people from different cultures have driven change, violent through war, profitable by trade and technology, inspiring from ideas.

Historians, and this text, define certain coherent large collections of peoples as civilizations, especially when they structure significant political, social, and cultural life around cities. The term *civilization* has too often conveyed a sense of sophisticated superiority of the so-called civilized over those who do not belong (see chapter 2). Try to avoid such labeling.

Even when civilization merely defines a collection of people and their practices and ideas, it remains a fluid concept. Where any civilization began (or ended), whether in time, geographic boundary, or membership, depends on who defines it or how. What makes one civilization distinct from another is the degree to which sufficient numbers of its people adopted particular attitudes. No civilization has existed in isolation. Political borders did not prevent people from bringing different beliefs and products into contact with one another. One people might change by free choice, force, or gradual assimilation, or they might continue in their traditional habits. Civilizations do not need to progress or decline (although most have). Progress reflects more power and complexity, while decline involves more disorder and vulnerability to enemies.

Most people have historically tended to view the world from their own vantage points. Historians naturally tend to focus on their own national history. Whether in America, Europe, Asia, or Africa, historians have too rarely gazed across borders and boundaries to see how often and in what ways people have acted and believed in common. This particular text reviews the rise of the society known to many historians as Western civilization. As an academic subject it originated about one hundred years ago, after the United States had risen to become a world power. Many American historians saw a shared Western past with other European nations that had also risen to global-power status. If Americans learned only U.S. history without understanding how it fit into the larger culture of competing European powers, Americans would misunderstand their own heritage and the challenges of the future. The founders of the study of Western civilization consciously tried to weave together American with European history, showing the common origins of so much that Americans, and Europeans, took for granted. Thus Western civilization courses and texts began to multiply.

Western civilization is worth studying because it organizes a large portion of interrelated history. The West is not necessarily better in creativity or virtue than many other civilizations that arose around the world, although many past historians have thought so. This review will often point out where the West borrowed knowledge and when its moral virtue fell short of its proclaimed ideals. Undoubtedly, the West became more powerful. Western civilization also became the dominant society of the modern world. To understand it is to comprehend how many of the globe's institutions, practices, and ideologies came to function as they do, for good or ill.

The word *Western* obviously reveals a strong geographical component. The name separates it from what might be considered northern, southern, or Eastern civilizations. While historians have not created a category for northern or southern civilizations, the term *Eastern* (or *oriental*, from the Latin for where the sun rises) used to be applied to what historians now prefer to call Asian civilizations (China and India, for example). Just as the Orient comes from the place of the rising sun over the Eurasian landmass, the Occident derives from where it sets. As this book will show, the self-defined Western civilization began in the specific geographical area of **western Europe**, the northwestern extension of land from the vast landmass of Eurasia and Africa, bordered by the North Sea, the Western Mediterranean Sea, and the Atlantic. Sometimes the West ranges over much larger territory, however. Its first inspirations lay in the Middle East, the region including the river systems of the Tigris and Euphrates and the Nile. The core of its culture then developed around the Mediterranean Sea until it shifted toward western Europe. About five hundred years ago, bearers of Western civilization began to conquer much of Eurasia and many overseas territories. Today, Western civilization dominates societies around the whole world and is, in turn, being transformed by them. Where the West begins, endures, or ends are some of the vital questions in the world today.

Just as geography defines the West, so does its chronology. Setting an exact starting date presents as many difficulties as setting its contemporary borders. One self-defining moment in Western tradition appears in its calendar, today accepted by many people around the world. The Western chronology divides history into two periods, labeled with the initials B.C. and A.D. These large periods mark the founding of Christianity by Jesus of Nazareth about two thousand years ago (see chapter 6). Most people can readily say B.C. means "before Christ," but fewer can explain that A.D. is the abbreviation for "anno Domini," which means "in the year of the Lord" and refers again to Jesus of Nazareth. Many current history writers, apparently uncomfortable with the religious roots of our calendar, have switched to using the terms B.C.E. and C.E., meaning "before the common era" and "common era." Nevertheless, no other event changed history around two thousand years ago to make any civilization more "common." This book's use of the terms B.C. and A.D. is not intended to privilege Christianity but merely to recognize its traditional usefulness in understanding our dating system.

Rather than this simple duality centered on Christianity, historians more sensibly divide the Western past into three or four periods. Ancient history (which includes prehistory) usually ends around A.D. 500. The Middle Ages then follow, ending any time between 1300 and 1789, depending on the historical point of view. Then early modern history might begin as early as 1400 or as late as 1660 and last until either the modern or contemporary periods take over in the past few centuries. The year 1914 seems useful as a starting point for contemporary history because of the first modern world war. To make the past still more manageable, this narrative divides up the past into fifteen parts, or chapters (with an epilogue to both sum up and point forward). The above dates and eras, of course, make sense only in relation to the history of Europe. Other civilizations need other markers, although historians often try to impose Western categories on world history.

This survey assigns the beginning of Western civilization to between fifteen and eleven hundred years ago, as western Europe recovered from the disaster of the collapse of its part of the Roman Empire. Understanding how this civilization built on previous human experiences, however, requires our reaching back beyond the fall of Rome to humanity's beginnings. Therefore, this particular book covers prehistory and the West's deep roots in the Middle East and Mediterranean regions. Sometimes coverage overlaps between chapters, and it certainly intensifies the closer it is to the present, because recent events impact our present more directly. Chapter 2 lightly skims over several million years, while chapter 15 rushes through only a few decades.

Covering much of Western history in fifteen chapters requires careful selection of the most resonant information. This narrative touches on all the basic topics of politics, economics, technology, society, culture, and intellectual cultural trends, depending on the historical period. This story does not emphasize the everyday-life aspects of people in the past, such as what children ate or how families lived in their homes. While these aspects are interesting and instructive, they in themselves rarely promote significant change in large societies. Five main topical themes regularly guide the flow: technological innovation, migration and conquest, political and economic decision making, church and state, and disputes about the meaning of life. These topics have significantly affected the past and are still influential in the present.

This book, then, covers a lot of time, over a large part of the world, involving many human events. As a concise history, it necessarily leaves out a great deal. Historians are always making choices about what they want to study, what approach they take, and what stays in. As you learn more about history, you can choose for yourself what to learn. For a beginning, the presentation of this text should ground you in the basics of this civilization called the West.

Review: *How do historians study and divide up the past?*

Response:

WHAT IS TRUTH?

History is a human production. Every idea, institution, painting, document, movement, war, or invention originated with a human being. People believe in, fight for, die for, and kill for ideas. While natural forces such as flood, drought, and disease affect people and may influence the course of history, people choose how to react to those disasters. No "force" by itself works to change history.

True power comes from people joined together. People usually organize themselves so that some lead and others follow. Motivations for forming larger groups could include love, favoritism, hunger, greed, blood loyalty, defense of hearth and home, cruelty, and others. The variety of human experiences guarantees different points of view. The challenge for historians is to sort through those views and reach the best explanation of how history changes and what it should mean to us.

In this book's version of history, choices about what to include or exclude are shaped by the broad culture of the modern West, the personal judgment of recent professional historians and the author. In today's modern culture, factions of people sharply disagree about politics, economics, science, and even the meaning of words. Cultural guardians argue over which sets of facts and interpretations today's citizens and students should be required to learn. Some differences are inevitable. The vast amount of possible information imposes selection, as do individual perspectives and agendas. As people select what goes into their history, the accounts will differ from one another.

Degrees of **subjectivity** versus **objectivity** affect any accurate version of the past. Objectivity is seeing things in an impartial way, while subjectivity involves a view ranging from **bias** (inclination toward a particular point of view) all the way to **prejudice** (dismissal of other points of view). Good historians strive to be objective, but no one can entirely escape being somewhat subjective. All historians, being human, are affected by certain mindsets. The historian Herbert Butterfield referred to the "magnet in men's minds" that attracts only information that already aligns with a person's political and social inclinations. Unfortunately for us all, few people really learn from history; most people use history only to confirm what they already believe.

This lack of perspective has been a phenomenon throughout time, shaping or reflecting the values of whole cultures. Different societies have seen their past according to shared grand concepts. In our Western civilization, the ancient Greeks, Romans, and Germans believed in both the intervention of divine beings and a powerful role of unchangeable fate. The rise and fall of people, or nations, followed according to the will of the gods. The Jews saw themselves as being chosen by one all-powerful god, who reserved for them a special place in history. The Christians of the Middle Ages supposed that they were caught in a battle of good versus evil. They condemned their enemies, even if those enemies were fellow Christians, to hell. Thinking in the Enlightenment reasoned that history conformed to unalterable laws of nature. In reaction, adherents of romanticism and nationalism embraced the jungle's competition of claw and fang and cheered on nations warring against one another for supremacy. All of these versions of history's purpose made perfect sense to people at the time. Their histories usually glorified their own achievements and diminished their own flaws. Nor are we in our time exempt from the limitations of our own points of view, which may one day seem quaint or even wrongheaded.

As for our view of the past today, the historical method gives us much of what actually happened, insofar as it can be known. The trustworthiness of history depends on whether it presents **fact**, **opinion**, or **myth**. Facts are those pieces of historical information that all reasonable people agree upon. They are the data of history, drawn from a serious examination of the sources. Once proved by historians, facts are the most reliable and least arguable information available. They come closest to anything we can call truth.

Although we rely on facts, the information can be manipulated. Facts become what people make them into. They may be blown out of proportion or neglected into nonexistence. To use a metaphor, facts are the bricks of historical work. Hard and rough, they can be used to frame a hearth or build a wall, but they can also be tossed aside or thrown through a window. Because of gaps in historical preservation, many facts will always be missing. A historian contemplating an ancient ruin has little information, since bricks have been lost, destroyed, or perhaps never even made in the first place. In contrast, a historian reviewing recent history may have too much information, piles upon piles of construction materials. Either way, we cannot really see behind the façade of the source. We try to read the minds of people in the past, attempt to see through their eyes, but perfect clarity is impossible.

Historians construct opinions using whatever facts are available. Almost all history writing consists of opinions, which historians form as they challenge one another about interpretations of the past. Opinions reveal the significance of the facts and show how they mattered to people in the past or to us today. Arguments among historians with differing opinions help to keep them honest. To extend the metaphor, a historian may say that one set of bricks belongs to a palace, yet another historian, looking at the same bricks, might say they come from a fortress. Who is correct?

Without conclusive evidence (blueprints, foundations, eyewitness accounts), disputes may remain tangled. Usually the weight of public opinion leans one way or another. People will choose facts and opinions written by respectable historians or adopt positions that flatter their belief systems. Sometimes, new insights might lead to an alternative suggestion, such as a compromise—a palace-fortress. Good historians are ready to change their opinions, given solid evidence and cogent argument. This author might conceivably rewrite and improve every sentence of this book to respond to new information in the future. Every new source provides new nuance. This changeableness is not inconsistency, dodging, or flip-flopping, but rather a result of sound judgment.

To provide some coherence to what would otherwise be only a string of facts, historians build themes around what they think changes the course of history. They explain causation and significance in terms of the rise or decline of societies, crises or stability, the primacy of foreign or domestic policy, sex or power, or any number of drives and choices.

This book's themes of supremacies and diversities help to explain our complex past. Supremacies focus on how the use of power dominates societies. Those who want *supremacy* usually seek stability, order, and consolidation. They also often seek to expand their power over others by using anything from warfare to ideologies. People react to such power by accommodating and transforming themselves in obedience or by resisting in public or covert ways. Power may flow from the top down, from rulers to subjects, or from the bottom up, from the masses to the leaders. *Diversity* reflects the creative impulse that creates new ideas as well as people's efforts to define themselves as different. Those who promote diversity create change, opportunity, and individuality.

These two trends do not necessarily oppose each other. They are not a version of dialectic materialism (see chapter 10). The opposite of supremacy is inferiority; the contrary of diversity is uniformity. Nonetheless, both trends involve people excluding others who do not belong to the group. People who want supreme power usually demand *universalism*, applying the same beliefs and practices to everyone. They would promote **acculturation**, where one ethnic group conforms its culture to another. Likewise, people's frequent tendency toward diversity often encourages *particularism*, requiring that various ideas and activities differ according to location. In addition, the mixture of cultures may result in *syncretism*, where elements of one join or blend with another. A tension thus may arise between the supremacy desire for conformity and the diversity push for variety, or the two may align together. One, or the other, or both intermingle in different societies and ages. This interaction has clearly driven historical conflict and change. Whether applied to politics, culture, or society, supremacies and diversities offer a structure in which to illustrate historical change.

Explanations based on facts and opinions can sometimes mutate into myths, which then complicate a historian's task. Myths are stories that give meaning to a society's existence. Because myths obscure the facts they draw on, they complicate getting at the truth. People embrace myths as true because they make sense of a confusing world. Passed on from generation to generation, myths stubbornly exist beyond rational proof. These stories justify both the worst and the best behavior of individuals, societies, and states. The myths inherent in religion and the so-called lessons of history offer particular problems because they are shaping the meaning of life. Even religion, however, may not always offer clarity. In the Gospel of John (see chapter 6), Pilate asks Jesus, "What is truth?" and does not get an answer.

In the attempt to be objective, many modern historians try not to favor one religion or belief system as being more true than any other. Indeed, the rational and empirical historical method cannot assert any religion's validity or falsity. Religion draws on the **supernatural**, which is beyond the limits of nature, to which historians are confined. This restriction does not deny religious truth but reasonably recognizes that no one religion has ever objectively proved to be real in all its supernatural aspects. Faith is there for those willing to believe, or not. The historian instead examines what the followers of any religion believed and, based on those beliefs, how they affected history.

People also want to believe good things about their own society. Thus, myths are often disguised as lessons learned from history. One should be cautious about them, since such myths are often too full of comforting pride. In particular, historical figures are often mythologized into heroes. Our own society promotes potent myths about figures such as Christopher Columbus or George Washington that resist change in the face of reality. Columbus was not alone in thinking the world was round; there is no evidence that Washington chopped down a cherry tree and confessed it to his father. These men might be notable, but their significance should not be based on stories that mislead.

The best history makes us self-critical, not self-congratulatory. Too often, someone's victory and satisfaction is someone else's defeat and suffering. Everyone joins in to take collective credit for victories, but resulting atrocities are done by isolated others. Cracking open myths and examining their core is essential to learning from history. This text will regularly offer "basic principles," obvious statements of common historical behavior; they often contradict common myths and suppositions. The first basic principle is:

> **There is no such thing as the "good ol' days," except in a limited way for a few people.**

People like to believe that there was once a golden age to which we should aspire to return. Whether in first-century Rome or early nineteenth-century Virginia, social elites have always proclaimed myths of their own supremacy to justify their status and power. Both societies, of course, benefited from slaves who did not enjoy the same luxuries as their masters. Of course, a limited number of people in some places did benefit from so-called good ol' days. Plenty of privileged people have always led lives of comfort and calm. If they lost those privileges, then they could legitimately claim that things used to be better. Yet this good life of the few has often been based on the exploitation of a much larger number of other people.

From a broader perspective, looking at the entire sweep of human history, most people have always faced difficulties. We all face our own mortality. There has probably never been a day when one individual did not kill another somewhere or when one people did not fight against another people. Disease, hunger, weather—these caused and still cause much misery. If people successfully confronted one moral problem, they failed in another. Each age has had its trials and tribulations as well as its ecstasies and excitements.

The challenge for this book is making sense of the Western past for someone unfamiliar with its history through the words of one particular author. As should be clear from the above discussion, no single view can be true for everyone, everywhere, forever. This historical account will regularly note the disputes, gaps, and disagreements of modern historians about specific interpretations. This history, however, cannot help but present an authorial voice, since its narrative follows the ebb and flow of supremacies and diversities. Like a reviewer of a book or film, this text both describes what happens and offers some value judgments. It often criticizes the flaws, failures, and contradictions inherent in the West. As the story unfolds, it points out the diverse options created during centuries of new ideas and practices by the many peoples that make up the West. Generalizations too often obscure detail and disagreement. Further reading and learning in history should reveal where this version is more or less objective, what it has omitted or overinterpreted. In a comparatively few pages, though, it offers a starting point to understand the essential people, events, and ideas of the West.

Historians offer the hope that we can learn from history to improve ourselves. The ultimate challenge for each of us is to form an opinion about history. Ask yourself: What can I learn that can give life more meaning? How can I make better decisions today based on the successes and failures of our ancestors? What knowledge of our heritage should I pass on to our descendants? This book offers some perspectives to help you answer those questions.

Review: *How can we evaluate history?*

Response:

CHAPTER 2

Wanderers and Settlers

The Ancient Middle East to 400 B.C.

Every human society tells stories and myths that explain the dawn of the universe, the world, and human beings. In our society, the beginnings of human history remain controversial. Some people agree with ancient peoples who calculated the history of the world to be only a few thousand years old. Those who agree with the scientific and historical methods explained in the first chapter, however, see the world and humanity stretching back much further into time. First, the scientific-historical viewpoint explains the ways of life of the first human beings who wandered out from our ancestral home in Africa. Later, some people settled on the civilized way of life. Still later, the ancient civilizations in Egypt and Mesopotamia produced knowledge to teach the early Europeans.

THE APES' COUSINS

The first humanlike creatures, called **hominids**, appeared on the earth millions of years ago (see timeline A in the back of the book). One of our earliest direct ancestors, *Australopithecus* ("southern ape"), lived about four million years before us. These hominids shared much of their genetic structure and basic anatomy with their closest ape relatives, whose descendants would eventually evolve into modern chimpanzees and gorillas. The hominid forerunners of *Homo sapiens* did so in distinct ways. These differences gave hominids an advantage in the life-and-death struggles in a dangerous world of predators.

Purely physical differences from other apes helped our ancestors' survival. The erect stance on two legs first distinguished hominids from most other creatures. Two million years ago, the hominids came down from the trees of the jungle and began to walk on two legs across the African savannah. Because they could see and travel farther than other apes, they gained access to wider varieties of food. An opposable thumb allowed hominids to make a fist and grasp **tools**. Although an ape might be able to make a primitive tool from a rock or a stick, hominid hands began to craft much more efficient and useful devices. **Weapons** made up for their lack of claw, fang, and muscle. Knives, needles, hooks, and hatchets fashioned from stone and bone were the sources left behind by the first humans. Using these, our ancestors fashioned protective **clothing** and carrying bags that made them still more mobile. Tools became one of the great driving forces of human history. A larger and more complex brain enabled more advanced thought and speech. The language of human words and sentences allowed more extensive communication than did the squeaks, yelps, and buzzes of other animals.

Another human characteristic is our awareness that we die. Our consciousness of our own mortality leads to another basic principle:

> **Humans know they are going to die; therefore, most people form supernatural beliefs about what their purpose is in this life and what happens after death.**

Religion, the structure we give to a set of supernatural beliefs, may have been the first human invention. Religion answers that most basic of human questions: "What is the meaning of life?" This very question recognizes that for each of us, life ends in death, at least in the natural world. Yet nearly all religions suppose that a "super"-natural world also exists beyond or above our senses. Most humans rely on beliefs about a supernatural realm to help them cope with the everyday troubles in the struggle for survival. Our first ancestors probably practiced some form of simple *animism*: the belief that nature is alive with spirits and ghosts that affect our natural world.

Religion's development depended on another difference between the apes and us, namely our ability for complex verbal and pictorial communication. Gorillas and chimpanzees can be taught some simple ways to form basic words and phrases. As far as science can detect, though, they lack anything approaching our sophistication of narrative language. In human culture, the ideas of religion were conveyed in stories. More important, the knowledge needed for survival was taught through words, games, and role playing. Our ancestors shared still more information through symbols with the first forms of art in **paintings** and small **sculptures**. Cave paintings and artifacts survive that portray what people were interested in, primarily the hunting of animals and sexualized figures of men and women.

Historians call this long period of human evolution, from over two million to ten thousand years ago, the **Paleolithic Age** (from the Greek for "Old Stone Age"), named after the stone tools used then. Instead of being lion food, they ate what lions ate, even if they had to steal carrion from lions rather than kill their food themselves. Then the hominids mastered fire for cooking previously inedible foods and for providing warmth in the coldest places. So our ancestors moved out of the tropical climates in Africa, where they had evolved, to spread over almost the entire planet into almost every environment. About two hundred thousand years ago, the first humans, categorized by scientists as *Homo sapiens sapiens* ("thinking, thinking human"), were born in Africa. Like their ancestors before them, human beings left Africa for Asia about one hundred thousand years ago, reaching Europe about forty thousand years ago and arriving in the Americas by route of Asia and the Pacific probably shortly afterward.

During these migrations, hominids moved in groups or social **communities**. In them, humans created much more layered, involved social hierarchies and bonds. Even the behavior of our ape cousins shows the usefulness of groups for individual survival. Like baboons and gorillas, early peoples formed packs, called tribes, ranging from probably twenty to a hundred individuals. Within the tribe, the **family**, the union of male and female with children, became the simplest social unit. A basic principle expresses family relationships:

> **Only women can bear children; everything else about men and women's social roles is up for argument.**

Since women bear the children, they have throughout history devoted much of their time and energy to raising the young. Men found it easier to get away from their children, whether on the hunt or in the public square.

The interrelationship of men and women and their children varies widely within our historical heritage. Life embodies a cycle of parents having children, who in turn become parents. Yet how those parents and children interact with one another varies widely in specifics. Some people argue that because men on average are bigger, stronger, and more aggressive than women, they should naturally have the superior social role. Yet we know the biggest man can be the gentlest father, while the smallest woman with a weapon can kill the largest man. Scientific studies do seem to show that men are usually more aggressive than women, especially because of the hormone testosterone. This quality has both a positive and a negative side for human society. Too much violence and the community is destroyed from within; too little ferocity and it can be destroyed by outsiders. Hence, male aggressiveness is useful when warriors are trained to kill for their community but harmful when men murder their friends, family, or neighbors. Much of our history has been a harsh tale of coping with this male aggression.

From the beginning, humans have lived in both families and communities, men and women, young and old, each mutually dependent and involved with the other. Individuals without family and friends were sure to die. Nor could one family exist by itself for long. Maybe a half-dozen to a dozen families made up the typical human community for much of the millennia during which our ancestors evolved.

To deal with the inevitable squabbles within and quarrels among these communities, our ancestors formed the first political arrangements. Someone needed to organize and lead, deciding where to camp, when to move, how to punish, and even how to protect the young and to raise them with all the knowledge necessary for survival. Hominids developed increasingly complicated rules of behavior, without which communities would fall apart in anger and jealousy. Thus the choosing of leaders, usually men proved in wisdom or strength who could resolve conflicts, became the first political organization.

Hominids also formed a primitive economic system of **hunting and gathering** that wrung the necessities of life from nature. Hunter-gatherers followed the game and the ripening plants as nomads. Everyone in the community participated in foraging for food and raw materials and in consuming them. Tribes traded and exchanged with other tribes for food, tools, and breeding partners. Migrating out of the original human homeland of Africa, people soon adapted to every climate, from the frigid Arctic to the sweltering jungle.

Choices about sexual partners soon created superficial differences in appearance and behavior among groups of humans in all these different living environments. These variations are described now as **ethnicity**. Inherited physical attributes (skin color, eye shape, hair, height, etc.) and learned culture (language, history, manners) separated groups of humans from one another. Human ethnic communities did not remain separated, however, as different ethnic groups traveled to where others lived. Sometimes the settlement of differing groups of people provoked conflict; other times it created bonds of friendship. Despite this surface multiformity, all human beings belong to the same biological species of *Homo sapiens*.

In sum, the anatomy of human ancestors, their tools and weapons, their creative minds, their social and political bonds, and their economic practices gave them advantages over most other animals. All these attributes allowed humans to survive four great ice ages that lasted for tens of thousands of years. Scientists still do not know why these ice ages happened. We ourselves may just be living in a brief geologic pause between one ice age and another.

The global climate change was catastrophic for many species of plant and animal life. Vast ice sheets covered much of the land masses. Growing seasons shortened. Those living things that could not cope became extinct. The Neanderthals were among those who failed to adapt. These close primate relatives and neighbors to humans were named after the German valley where modern archaeologists found the first skull attributed to the species. By about 25,000 B.C., Neanderthals had become extinct, probably because they could not compete with *Homo sapiens*. About ten thousand years ago, the climate warmed again, the summers lengthened, and the glaciers retreated. Humans survived in a precarious place within the world's ecosystem, poised for greater things.

Review: *What important cultural survival techniques did our ancestors use?*

Response:

BOUND TO THE SOIL

The end of the last ice age allowed what could be considered the most fundamental and radical change in human history, the so-called **Neolithic Agricultural Revolution**. For historians, the term *revolution* represents a major transformation of human politics, society, and culture. People lived different lives after revolutions from those they lived before. This first important human revolution occurred during the Neolithic Age (from the Greek for "New Stone Age"), named after the new kinds of tools used, different from those of earlier hunter-gatherers. Archaeological evidence shows how ten thousand years ago the arrowheads and spear points suitable for hunting began to be replaced by hoes and sickles, the tools for planting and harvesting. Humankind discovered farming, forever changing our way of life. While hunter-gatherers adapted themselves to nature, civilized people began adapting nature to themselves.

The culture of farming, or **agriculture**, the growing of plants and raising of animals, seems so natural to us today that we hardly think of it as a human invention. One can imagine how some person, after gathering grains or fruits, noticed that the seeds dropped on the ground produced those same plants weeks later. The logical next step was to push the seeds into the ground and wait for them to grow instead of wandering around, looking for the plants. If people stored enough to live on during the growing periods, they could simply stay put instead of wearing out their feet walking. So instead of living in mobile tents or temporary huts, people built sturdy **houses** from logs, mud, or baked clay bricks. Homes offered better shelter against the elements.

Domestication of animals was equally as important as finding the right plants to grow. Dogs had first begun bonding with humans during the ice ages. While a few societies have dined on dog, most have viewed them as companions and useful helpers in the hunt. Once people settled down to farm, they reasoned that if dogs could be bred to be tame, why not try it with the beasts that one hunted? Wild oxen became beef and milk cattle; boars became pigs; wild fowl became poultry. With taming of both plants and animals, human communities settled down and became tied to plots of land to raise their food.

One cannot exaggerate the vast change these innovations meant for humans. Before agriculture, everyone had been at the mercy of the environment, depending on nature to provide sustenance. Nature was still, of course, important, and its awesome force remained dangerous. An extended drought or a brief flood could kill many people. Nevertheless, farming meant that humans began to dominate nature, at least in small ways. Soon the people who managed food production even learned to outproduce nature. They selected and bred stronger, hardier crops and animals. They weeded out invasive plants that would steal water and nutrients. They irrigated, digging trenches that led water from distant streams to feed the roots of their seedlings. They chased away the wild creatures that would devour the stalks. They diversified their crops and animals to provide more resources. From all this hard work and innovation, people produced more food, allowing families to grow as fast as hungry infant mouths could be filled. Since women did not have to worry about long treks as nomads, they could more easily endure pregnancies while looking after their other young children at the same time. Farmers soon grew enough extra foodstuffs so that a few people no longer had to work in agricultural production.

Nonfarmers could then devote their time to further improving people's ability to dominate nature. Farming thus led to a whole range of new occupations beyond tilling the soil. Some people could devote their energy to making **clothing**. Weavers wove the fibers of flax and hemp on a loom to produce cloth. Tailors cut cloth into unusual styles and colored it with dyes in patterns never seen on plant or animal. Some fashions promoted comfort, protection from weather, and ease of movement; others emphasized social roles at the expense of proper fit. Cooks mixed, roasted, baked, and boiled increasing varieties of plant and animal stuffs into cuisine. Potters baked clay pots that better preserved food, free from spoilage and vermin. Cart-wrights built wagons on wheels to transport large loads over long distances. Masons stacked bricks and stone into secure buildings, beginning the art of **architecture**.

Especially where land could be turned over by the plow, economic success led to growing communities where hundreds of families could reside. Several families planted themselves into small **villages**. These might contain a few families or numbers up to two hundred people. Villages might grow into **towns**, which might hold a few thousand people. Then great **cities** bloomed, ranging from many thousands to today's huge urban areas of millions of people. This complex life of interconnected cities is called *civilization*. The civilized way of life differed from that of the hunter-gatherers. Urban living provided a rich, creative, evolving dynamic that expanded and intensified human domination of the planet.

The first civilized political organization, the **city-state**, was literally the smallest viable unit of civilization. It included the city itself (made up of homes, businesses, and public buildings) and the surrounding countryside of farmland from which the people of the city fed and supplied themselves. These larger numbers of people confined in a small area required new leaders to organize the increasingly complex human activities.

The first important leaders perhaps made use of religion as a key source of convincing others to obey. Agriculture encouraged new, more complex religions. Most were a form of ***polytheism***, the belief in many gods and goddesses, divine beings who were more actively connected to the new practices of farming (see table 2.1). Storm gods and earth goddesses tended to have more distinct personalities and defined attributes than the vague spirits of animism. **Priests** (and, less often, priestesses) conducted elaborate rituals and prayers intended to appease the gods. People often shared in communal meals to celebrate the goodness of what the gods had provided in nature. Ironically, priests and priestesses who managed the temples as centers of worship actually drew much of their power not from their communication with supernatural beings, but from their practical, more systematic knowledge of nature.

This brings up one of the most important basic principles:

Knowledge is power.

As these ancient religious leaders studied the natural world, looking for evidence of the gods, they found data about seasons, climate, and soil conditions. Priests

Table 2.1.   Comparisons of Gods and Goddesses of Ancient Polytheisms

Attribute	Mesopotamian	Egyptian	Greek	Roman	Norse
Ruler of gods	Enlil, Marduk, Asshur	Ra	Zeus	Jupiter	Odin
Sky/storm	Anu	Nut, Horus	Zeus	Jupiter	Thor
Earth	Ninhursag	Geb	Gaia	Terra/Tellus	Erda
Water/sea	Apsu, Enki	Tefnut	Poseidon	Neptune	Aegir
Sun	Shamash	Ra	Apollo	Apollo	Sunna
Moon	Sin	Thoth	Artemis	Diana	Moon
Wisdom	Ea, Nabu	Thoth	Athena	Minerva	Odin
War	Ninurta/Ishtar	Nit, Menhit	Ares	Mars	Tyr
Magic	Enki	Isis	Hermes	Mercury	Odin
Crop fertility	Dumuzi	Ernutet	Demeter	Ceres	Freyr
Alcoholic drink	Ninkasi, Geshtinanna	Osiris	Dionysius	Bacchus	Byggvir
Technology			Hephaestus	Vulcan	
Trickster		Set	Hermes	Mercury	Loki
Love	Ishtar	Hathor	Aphrodite	Venus	Freya
Fire/hearth	Gibil	Bes	Hestia	Vesta	Frigga
Marriage	Innana	Hathor	Hera	Hymen, Juno	Frigga
Death	Ereshkigal	Osiris	Hades	Pluto	Hel

Note: The deities of ancient religions performed similar functions for agricultural peoples in early civilizations.

observed the heavens and calculated the **calendar**; they measured, added, and divided to plan and build their temples and irrigation canals; they quantified trade and agricultural production; they told stories (usually in the form of epic poems about heroes) that defined for their culture the connections of humans to gods; they invented **writing** to keep track of it all. Thus, the fields of astronomy, mathematics, and literature became basic to the civilized way of life.

The priests passed on their knowledge in **schools**, one of the essential institutions of civilization. Instead of having education provided by parents and community leaders, as in hunter-gatherer societies, children of different families more efficiently learned from professional teachers. Usually, though, elites allowed only boys from prosperous families access to a formal education. The knowledgeable few excluded girls and the poor from higher knowledge, thus restricting education to only a privileged few.

Priests had to share leadership of society with **kings**, who became the dominant political figures. **Monarchy**, the rule of kings, has been the most frequent form of government throughout civilized history. The essential political questions became (first) how many decisions affecting other people's lives the king could make and (second) who might influence or share in making those decisions. Some kings possessed only minimal power, enjoying tightly limited roles as figureheads or mere symbols of authority. Members of the royal family, favorites, and court officials or the upper classes might actually run the kingdom behind the scenes. Kings typically strove to rule according to *absolutism*, the practice that one person should dominate as much as possible in authority and decision making.[1] The acceptance of absolute monarchy allowed a ruler to exercise as much power as human limitations allowed. Attempts by rulers to establish absolute monarchies and resistance to such efforts have driven many political changes in history.

Whether weak or strong, kings held three essential roles. First, they represented the unity of the people. Each was symbolically the father of his country, the head of the most important family of families. The importance of family often eased the creation of a **dynasty**, where political power passed from parent to child. Dynasts justified their monopoly on power by claiming connection to the gods, through ancestry, favor, or promise. Even today, powerful political leaders endowed with charisma are often seen as superior to normal citizens. The people worshiped these "Oriental despots" almost as elaborately as the gods they represented. The gods, however, failed to preserve the lines of descendants. Accident, disease, and infertility might end dynasties, provoking political crises. The preference for male, paternal authority often meant that power went from father to son. While this limited the ability of females to rule, women did sometimes come to hold formal power. Otherwise, their power worked like those of many women through history, influencing the family members of their dynasties.

A king's second role was to preserve peace among his own people. In this role, a king usually acted as supreme judge (which was also a divine attribute). People

---

1. Historians and political theorists most often apply the term *absolutism* to European monarchs of the seventeenth and eighteenth centuries A.D. While queens and kings during those years clearly argued for unlimited authority, the concept does apply to all ages.

petitioned the ruler for redress of wrongs. He settled their disputes over pigs or pottery and punished the wrongdoers. To manage the complex relationships of cities, kings began to establish **laws**. The most famous early law code was that which King Hammurabi of Babylon commanded to be carved onto a black stone pillar around 1700 B.C. A picture above the **Law Code of Hammurabi** shows a god himself handing the laws to the king. Here the king was not going through the priests but mediated himself with the gods, becoming the lawgiver within the cosmic order. Such divine connections inspired legal systems for many early peoples. They believed that keeping the law pleased the gods.

The laws, of course, laid out right and wrong in practical ways, dealing with actual problems. Culture is encoded in a society's laws, which reflect what matters and what does not. One of the most essential rights in societies throughout recorded history has been protecting property. Real estate, or arable land as property, supported an agricultural society. Laws guaranteed that land could not be easily taken away from owners and ensured that after the owner's death it went to the correct heirs. Laws defined which property belonged to whom and ordained punishments for those who damaged or destroyed it.

Another universal legal issue for rulers has been regulating violence among people. While hunter-gatherers often punished crimes with isolation or exile, civilized regimes punished by taking wealth or inflicting physical pain. A fundamental question for all societies has been to categorize the killing of one human by another. Was it the defense of the nation by a soldier or of his family by a parent? Was it capital punishment inflicted by the state for justice? Was it a vicious crime by a murderer? Was it manslaughter by accident? Or did it matter at all? Many ancient laws, like Hammurabi's, punished a wide variety of crimes with death, crimes that today we might consider unworthy of such a high price. Laws also began to regulate drunkenness, after ancient farmers discovered how to manage the fermentation processes for turning grapes into wine and grains into beer. For example, a wine seller not reporting bad characters in his establishment to the authorities might be executed for that oversight. Many other punishments involved mutilation. A son who hit his father, in Hammurabi's Code, for example, deserved having his hand cut off. Fines and banishment also were common, but not prison, because of the high cost of keeping a person confined.

The third role of a king was as war leader against foreign foes. Blunt force and the ability to kill is an obvious form of power. Yet no king could fight on his own, except in legend, such as the superhuman hero Gilgamesh of Sumerian literature (see below). A king needed warriors. One of the basic questions through history is, "Whom do the soldiers obey?" Whoever can convince others to kill for him has real power.

By his nature, the king's command over life and death in peace and war gave him supreme authority within a society. The earliest kings ruled over city-states, the smallest and most cohesive political units. Because city-states were vulnerable owing to their small size and because wealth and power tempted kings, they soon desired to dominate other societies. If a king gained power over similar people in a number of cities, he would rule a **kingdom**. If a king came to govern other peoples who may have differed in ethnicity, religion, language, history, or any number of other ways, he became an **emperor** ruling an **empire**. As kingdoms grew to be larger and more powerful, kings often were tempted to conquer their foreign neighbors. Thus arose the practice of *imperialism*, taking over other peoples in order to build an empire. Empires became the largest political structures of all, although they were inherently unstable because of the diversity of the emperor's subjects. Many successful empire builders united their imperial subjects through acculturation. When voluntary cooperation failed, forced obedience often followed.

Whether organized in empire, kingdom, or city-state, the new culture of civilization derived from farming became the way of life for the majority of human beings in Africa, Asia, and Europe by about 3000 B.C. At first, civilized agriculturalists and their uncivilized neighbors lived side by side. Many peoples stopped just short of civilization and did not live in a society with cities, even until a few centuries ago. Some made their livings as nomadic pastoral herders of animals on the plains and steppes of the Americas, Asia, and Africa. A few groups of hunter-gatherers also continued to flourish. The economic and political expansion of people living in civilizations, however, progressively destroyed nonagricultural societies. The civilized often insulted the noncivilized as *barbarian*. They set up a dichotomy of themselves as generous, refined citizens (what the word *civilized* also means to many people) and the others as selfish, uneducated savages. Of course, virtue does not live only in cities and wickedness among the nomads. Instead, civilizations embraced their power, created by highly structured social hierarchies supported by agriculture, and attacked hunter-gatherers and agriculturalists who lacked cities. Relentlessly, powerful, organized agricultural societies grabbed whatever good land could be found for farming, mining, or building. The dwindling pastoralists and hunter-gatherers retreated to isolated jungles or deserts where farming remained impossible or unprofitable. This trend continues even today, where modern encroaching civilizations may require the last barbarians either to convert to civilization or be killed off.

Review: *What did agriculture cultivate as the key components of civilization?*

Response:

THE PRICE OF CIVILIZATION

While the vast wealth of civilization produced numerous comforts, life in cities clearly had some serious drawbacks. We live with these problems as long as we lead civilized lives. Our lifestyle complicates our relation to the environment and to one another.

First, serious health problems arose with life in cities. Famine could easily strike since, despite the best planning, a drought or flood could destroy all the food available in a particular region. The limited abilities for transportation often meant that little food could be imported. In contrast, hunter-gatherers faced with natural disaster could move on to other hunting grounds. Agricultural people, though, felt compelled to stay, for two main reasons. First, they believed that one day the land would be productive again, and so they stayed to prevent anyone else from taking it over. Second, most other nearby land suitable for farming was already taken. Good farmland is a precious and limited commodity. To find new land, farmers might have had to journey a long distance. Lacking the skills to hunt and gather along the way, many would have perished on the move. Farming peoples stuck out the hard times and, consequently, many died where they stood.

Ironically, another health problem was poor nutrition. The hunter-gatherer almost naturally ate a balanced diet out of what nature provides. In contrast, civilized people chose what they wanted to eat rather than have nature choose for them. They often started to go heavier on the meats, avoided certain roots and vegetables, and devoured sweets. Our "sweet tooth" derives from our body's requirements for carbohydrates and fats. For hunter-gatherers, concentrated sugars are limited and rare in the wild. Agricultural people, however, could reproduce and consume sugars in large qualities, unaware of how obesity risked health and rotted teeth.

Contagious diseases also threatened civilized society. Hunter-gatherers lived in small groups that wandered regularly. Their contact with other groups of people was brief. In contrast, cities opened themselves up for illness, encouraging close and regular contact with travelers and traders from other communities. Widespread outbreaks of disease, called epidemics or **plagues**, regularly devastated human populations. Some epidemics spread by water (dysentery, cholera, typhoid), some by human contact (measles, smallpox), some through fleas and lice (typhus, bubonic plague), and some through the air (influenza, pneumonia). We know now that the causes of all these (as explained in chapter 11) are microscopic bacteria and viruses, which live all around and on us. Harmful germs flourished as civilized people lived in increasingly large groups that dumped their waste all around them. Up until a few hundred years ago, few people knew this or cared much about cleanliness. For instance, until recently, more soldiers died of infections than enemy attacks during wars. Ignorant of the real causes of disease, civilized people could often do little more than suffer through them.

Another negative consequence of civilization, for half the human species, is an increase of *sexism*. Sexism is the belief that one sex (usually the male) is better than the other (usually the female). From birth, we separate humans into these two groups, male and female, with that common first question, "Is it a boy or a girl?" Sometimes, physical or genetic irregularities complicate the answer to that question. Regardless, all societies set expectations about gender behaviors. They use both custom and law to define how individuals should express masculinity or femininity. Studies by modern social scientists and historians suggest that differences are much more complicated than we usually like to think, especially when dealing with issues of sexual attraction and gender identity.

In hunter-gatherer families and tribes, sex roles were much more undifferentiated and fluid than in civilized societies. In a community on the move, where everyone bore his or her own share, men and women tended to be more equal in status. Also, in such small communities everyone knew one another. In civilization, however, sexism began to grant more advantages to males. The acquisition of **property** changed everything. Ownership of farmland led to yet another, and simple, basic principle:

> **Land is wealth; wealth is power.**

Of course, land is not the only means to wealth—later commerce, industry, and finance would provide much more efficient ways to become wealthy. Nor is wealth the only route to power—charisma, military force, ruthless violence, and other methods all can be useful in seizing dominion. When agriculture has dominated the economy, though, land has meant power.

Once civilized through owning land, men effectively excluded women from power by their exclusive control of property. This control by men had nothing to do with our Western, traditional idea that the men are out sweating at work while the women are keeping house. Indeed, in many farming societies women work in the fields as much as or more than men, especially during planting and harvest. One reason for women's exclusion from public roles may be that once people settled down, women had more young children to care for (since only women bear children). With increased food production, more children could be fed. In turn, more children provided cheap labor for farmwork.

Women undoubtedly worked behind the scenes, in the kitchens and bedrooms, at mealtimes and in the fields, influencing the decisions of fathers and brothers, husbands and sons. Nevertheless, men largely monopolized the formal and accepted social roles of status and power that developed in civilization. Women's domestic work freed the men from chores so that they could take the lead in public life. Since mothers usually do most of the child rearing, they may have crucially formed the character of their children (leading to the later cliché, "The hand that rocks the cradle rules the world"). Mothers' influence on grown children and wives' on their husbands certainly affected decisions made by men that changed history. It remains difficult, though, to illuminate their role within families, since so few sources survive. Therefore, women's roles in driving decisive changes in history have only rarely been noticed. Only in the twentieth century did numbers of Western women gain rights comparable with or the same as those that men have long had (see chapter 13). The dominance of men over subservient women became traditional in civilizations.

In most societies, social divisions have gone unquestioned, whether applied to gender or labor. Most civilizations produced **social classes**, groups of people structured around a common cultural and economic status. These first developed out of a **division of labor** or specialization in economic production typical of urban civilizations. Dividing work made farming life more efficient. While all hunter-gatherers hunted and gathered, civilized people might focus on those tasks for which they were most suited or found most enjoyable. Weavers, tailors, potters, cartwrights, smiths, bakers, or masons carried out their crafts with greater efficiency than if everyone wove and sewed cloth, molded pots, built carts, or laid bricks. The kind of occupations different people adopted easily became hereditary and connected to the power structures.

Social classes separated people into groups that reflected rulership, wealth, and influence. Upper classes lorded their status over the lower classes. A tiny minority of people took charge, controlling the knowledge, possessing most of the land, and taking the best goods that society had to offer. They became **aristocrats** at the top with the **nobles** just below, who declared themselves destined to pass on dominance from generation to generation. These **upper classes** organized society. The vast majority of others, the **lower classes** or commoners, did the actual work. A tiny **middle class** formed around **artisans** (who made pots, shoes, and furniture) and **merchants** (who bought and sold goods). The overwhelming majority of people, through most of civilized history, were simple farmers called **peasants**. They worked the land and produced the food so that the aristocrats and artisans did not have to. The hard work of peasants raising food from the land was at first, and often still is, the foundation of civilization. Although they created much wealth, peasants often saw few of its benefits. In even worse condition, at the bottom of the social hierarchy, were the poor, those who lost most social connections and the ability to work.

Seeing society as divided between elites and the masses reflects the social divisions of the past. A few people rose to the top of society and controlled economic, political, and religious decisions. The large numbers of people without power usually went along with these decisions and reinforced the authority of the elites in the marketplace, on the battlefield, and within sacred spaces. The masses had little choice. Throughout most of civilized history, most people remained in the class they had been born into. Social mobility, or the possibility that individuals could rise into a better class, remained rare until modern times. More frequently, attempts by the masses to achieve power alongside the elites drove historical change, often manifesting as class conflict.

At the beginning of civilization, though, the aristocrats took charge. Two changes explain the elevation of a few people to aristocratic supremacy over the peasants. One was the aristocratic role in warfare at the beginning of civilization. In hunter-gatherer groups, most adult males fought. Hunting even provided training in tactics similar to battle, with its organization of killing. Farming techniques, however, did not resemble warfare. Civilized warfare thus became the work of specialists: warriors were freed from the daily grind of farming so that they could dedicate themselves to training for combat. The king as war leader shared with a few associated warriors some of his aura of power. The best weapons became more expensive.

Another change to explain the rise of the aristocracy was stability. In a hunter-gatherer group, the nomadic wandering imposed equality. Any one person could possess only as much property as he or she could carry. Most everyone, from chief to child, did the same kind of work: hunting and gathering. In civilization, however, any one person had as much property as could be accumulated, stored, and defended with the support of others. Leadership soon became held by the few, while followers were many. Through most of civilized history, in most places, only a few powerful families have run entire human communities. In civilization, one's parents usually determined one's status. Born to upper-class parents, one could easily stay upper class. Born to poor parents, one could hardly ever rise in status.

Social mobility was rarely possible because of imposed law and custom. Some customs, such as clothing fashions, made it obvious to any passersby on the street to which class one belonged. Where one lived, in how elaborate a residence, also reflected status. Most important, laws regulated this more complicated social order. The earliest laws of Hammurabi and all laws until the eighteenth century A.D. recognized different classes of people, divided at least into aristocrats and commoners. Even crime and punishment usually depended on one's social status. If an aristocrat stole something, he paid compensation thirtyfold; a commoner paid only tenfold. If a person had no money, however, he paid with his life.

The thought did sometimes cross poor people's minds: "Why should we suffer just because we were born to low-born parents?" Resentful of their imposed inferiority, the lower classes every so often rebelled against their superiors. Mostly they failed. Whether the upper classes opposed, granted concessions, or fell to their social inferiors, class conflict affected the course of civilization. A noted tendency, especially in societies of increasing prosperity, has been to open the upper ranks to more people and add new classes or subdivide old ones. Social divisions could become quite subtle and complex, requiring participants to constantly monitor the proper usage of clothing, speech, and behavior.

With these divisions of labor and class arrived the first **taxes**. Two and a half centuries ago, Benjamin Franklin famously quipped that death and taxes were the only sure things in life. More accurate is the following basic principle:

> **The only certainty in civilization is death and taxes. The only essential questions are these: who pays and how much?**

Not everyone pays taxes. In some civilizations, the privileged are tax exempt. Uncivilized barbarians do not pay taxes either: in their small, self-sufficient groups, hunter-gatherer peoples do not divide up their labor and leadership. Yet civilized society cannot exist without the taxes that pay for the rule keepers, warriors, and infrastructure that have kept human interchanges functioning smoothly. Most of the time, the poorer classes, hard-working peasants, have paid for the privileges of the richer classes, land-owning aristocrats.

The worst class division was slavery, which denied any social status to certain humans as people became mere property. Some persons became slaves to pay off debt (for example, fathers could sell their daughters for such purposes). Others were enslaved as punishment for crime. Many people defeated in conquest became slaves rather than suffer death. The harshness of the slave system—how well the slaves were cared for or how hard they were worked—varied according to the customs of a civilization and either the beneficence or intelligence of the masters.

Whether inhumane or not, slavery has been a key component of almost every civilization until modern times. Slavery among hunter-gatherers was much more difficult to manage. If a hunter-gatherer was enslaved but managed to escape, he could live off the land until he managed to find some friendly people of his own. In contrast, a civilized slave who escaped did not know how to survive in the woods, which plants to eat, or how to make shelter. Thus, the civilized form of slavery was much more hopeless for those trapped in its system.

The slave economy was supported by a final negative consequence of the rise of civilization: the perfection of **war**. Some romantics have suggested that human conflict did not exist among noncivilized peoples, who reputedly lived in some idyllic paradise. It seems, however, that humans have always organized to fight with one another, over land, pride, or power. When hunter-gatherers came under attack, though, they could run away—they knew how to live in the wilds and thus could give up a hunting ground rather than be exterminated. Further, the world was less crowded when more people were nomads. Hunter-gatherers also possessed comparatively little of value to plunder.

Agriculture and cities, though, added a more lethal intensity to human conflict. Once people settled down as farmers, the available space became much more restricted: good farmland was limited to well-watered plains. Farmers would not leave their land when threatened by invaders any more than when threatened by flood or famine. Thus, people stayed and fought with more determination and more destruction. The wealth of cities provided more temptation for invaders to take quickly and easily (they hoped) what others had wrung from the soil by long, hard labor. Agriculture also enabled the building of larger and more complex armies, which in turn could more readily devastate a region.

Ironically, war promotes destruction but also cooperation. First, war is an expensive proposition that requires the material support of many who are not warriors. Many noncombatants, mostly old men, women, and children, provided weapons, equipment, food, and even emotional and ideological support. Warriors defended ideals such as the protection of noncombatants, the companionship of fighters, and the trust of allies. Second, any army must have a system of obedience and command to coordinate many individual soldiers into a killing unit. Third, the nature of battle encouraged people to limit participants to only two opposing sides. The best way to defeat an army was to attack it on its flank (or in the rear) instead of head on. Any more than two participants in a battle exposed the flanks too easily. This battlefield reality led to alliances, where different political units either stood together or would be defeated separately. Thus, kings and emperors started a pattern that has endured throughout the history of civilization: conquest and subjugation.

While history is not merely the record of wars and battles, no history can ignore these events, for they often determined the rise or fall of civilizations. The word *civilization* in this sense describes how numbers of people can be united by common culture, social and economic interaction, or political power. A civilization might be confined to the smallest city-state but could embrace kingdoms, an empire, or several diverse politically organized states and peoples. Most successful civilizations in history have won and defended their supremacy through warfare. Many failed civilizations have dissolved by losing wars. Wars are not simply won or lost by battlefield decisions. Effective cultural, social, economic, and political developments at all levels can strengthen a state in victory or defeat.

Wars have melded or destroyed groups of peoples who become part of one civilization or another. Imperialists, those who support building empires, bring diverse peoples into one state. On the one hand, imperialists usually have confidence in the rightness of their efforts. Imperialists have often believed that their dominance in power proves their superior virtues. On the other hand, the fate and attitudes of the conquered could vary quite a bit. While conquests might destroy a people outright, usually conquerors preserve large numbers of the conquered, if only to use them for labor. Maintaining a separate minority ethnic identity is often difficult, as most rulers encourage uniformity. Once conquered, people have sometimes assimilated, or merged, into the ethnicity of their masters. Sometimes, if the conquered people are numerous enough, they have blended with the conquerors, both creating a new identity. A few times, the conquerors have even been absorbed into the conquered. It has also happened that people might break free again, either through their own power or through allies. Empires have frequently been so large or lasted so briefly that diversity of peoples has survived. A civilization's attributes, in governance, economics, and knowledge can be more enduring than its limited political existence. Our history is built on the success and failures of past civilizations, and civilization and war have been close companions throughout history.

Review: What often-ignored problems did civilization create?

Response:

THE RISE AND FALL OF PRACTICALLY ALL MIDDLE EASTERN EMPIRES

Historians still argue about which civilization was the first. Evidence is too fragmentary to fully determine which people get boasting rights for being number one.

Between seven and six thousand years ago, the first contenders lay along great river systems that provided enough water for agriculture. In South Asia the Indus River nurtured Indian civilization; in East Asia the Hwang Ho (Yellow River) gave rise to Chinese civilization; and in the Middle East the valleys of the Nile and the Tigris and Euphrates fed Middle Eastern civilizations. China and India were too far away to have much influence on the formative West, at least at first.

The Middle East, however, laid the foundations for the later rise of the West (see map 2.1). Westerners coined the name *Middle East* about a hundred years ago as they were defining this region as different from both the Far East of India and China and their own West. Europeans often call it the Near East; some geographers prefer labeling the regions North Africa and Southwest Asia. Whatever the name, the Middle East today includes countries stretching from northwest Africa through the Arabian Peninsula, northward through the Levant (the eastern coast of the Mediterranean), Asia Minor, and Mesopotamia and eastward to Iran. Today, Islam substantially defines the culture (see chapter 6). But long before Islam, the Middle East was rich, cultured, and powerful.

Today we often think of the Middle East as desert. Indeed, thousands of years of human overpopulation, soil exhaustion, deforestation, and water overuse, as well as climatic change, have left much of the area arid today. In ancient times, however, ten thousand years ago, the core of the region deserved the name Fertile

[handwritten margin notes: Near East / Mid-E / Persia / Pakaslan]

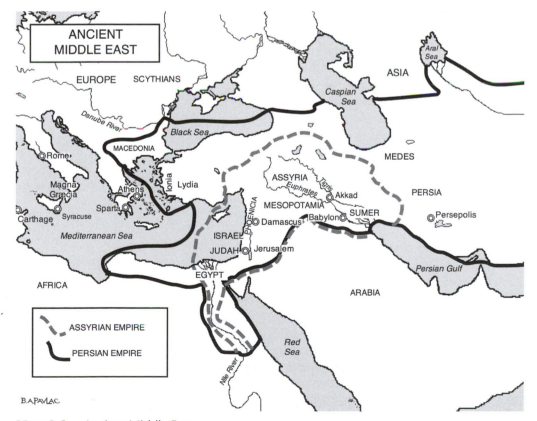

Map 2.1.   Ancient Middle East

Crescent. An arc of agriculturally productive land from the Nile River Valley up through Palestine and down across the Tigris and Euphrates to the Persian Gulf soon fed peoples far more advanced than their neighbors in Europe, Africa, and Asia.

Helping these new agricultural civilizations succeed was their discovery of how to make **metal** tools. Humans had been using wood, bone, and stone for millions of years. Embedded in many stones were ores that, when heated or smelted, could be purified into an elemental metal, such as copper or tin. Thus, the Neolithic or New Stone Age of technology began to end around 4000 B.C. as humans began to mine copper for tools. They soon learned how to make an even better alloy, blending copper and tin into bronze, a stronger metal. **Bronze Age** technology prevailed from about 3000 to 800 B.C. Based on these technologies, two civilizations arose in the Middle East, in **Mesopotamia** and **Egypt**. Each was relatively isolated from the other at first, but both were soon joined in commerce and conquest.

Mesopotamian civilization began around 3500 B.C., when the Sumerians moved into the land of the two rivers of the Tigris and Euphrates (mostly in modern-day Iraq). They founded the earliest significant political units in the form of city-states. The Sumerians were the first of many Mesopotamian peoples who shared a similar culture. As the most important public buildings they built ziggurats: huge step pyramids of baked brick that served as temples for worship of the gods and storehouses for grain. Priests and priestesses celebrated **fertility rituals**. In doing so, they imitated the imagined sexual couplings of the gods, believing such activity sustained the annual cycle of seasons (in other words, sex made the world go round). By studying and learning about the skies, the priests divided the stars into the twelve constellations of the zodiac (creating twelve months), set twenty-four hours to the day, and set seven days to the week. They wrote such knowledge in cuneiform, block symbols formed by a wedge-shaped stylus pressed into clay at different angles (see figure 2.1). On such tablets they composed epic poetry, the most enduring form of literature, popular for thousands of years. Epics are long poems (using verse, rhythm, and often rhyme) composed to tell stories of heroes and gods. The first great epic poem told of the king **Gilgamesh**, transformed from a human ruler into a two-thirds divine hero six hundred years later. After the death of his friend, Enkidu, with whom he had shared many adventures and hardships, the sorrowful Gilgamesh sought the meaning of life. He learned that although the gods failed at wiping out all humankind by a great flood, they still doomed men to death, by wild animals, famine, and plague. Such a gloomy view of existence seemed common in Mesopotamia, despite the riches of the civilization.

The second great Middle Eastern civilization, Egypt, arose in the Nile River Valley of northeastern Africa. Powerful kings called pharaohs united Egypt by around 3100 B.C. These men, and a few women, such as the now-famous Hatshepsut, not only held the power of kings, but were also believed to be actual gods incarnate on earth.[2] They often intensified their bloodline connection to the gods by marrying

---

2. History forgot about Hatshepsut (r. ca. 1479–1458 B.C.) for millennia because her son and heir tried to erase every single mention of her after he came to power. Historians rediscovered her impressive and peaceful reign only about a hundred years ago. To reinforce her status as ruler, she often wore the same artificial long, thin beards that male pharaohs wore. Perhaps to compensate for his "mommy issues," her son started a number of wars.

Figure 2.1. The wedge-shaped lines of cuneiform, the writing of ancient Mesopotamia, scrawl over the sculpture of an Assyrian.

their royal brothers or sisters. As divine beings, pharaohs were exempt from the usual social prohibition against incest. The pharaohs, their officials, and priests wielded power through their abilities to write (in pictographs called hieroglyphics) and calculate (see figure 2.2). With these skills, they controlled agriculture: they accurately predicted the regular annual rise and fall of the Nile floods that nourished the fields. The Egyptian kingdom offered comparative stability and prosperity.

Hence, Egyptians seemed more optimistic about the afterlife than their Mesopotamian neighbors. The Egyptians hoped that, after death, their souls would be judged worthy by the gods, and thus they could spend a luxurious afterlife full of pleasure. According to *The Book of the Dead*, a dead person appeared before the court of Osiris, where a person's spirit was weighed on scales against a feather. The deceased recited a long list of sins not committed and good deeds done. Based on the truth of the declaration and the weight, souls lighter than a feather went to heaven; souls heavier suffered from the Devouress; those equally balanced were servants in the afterlife.

Their belief in some sort of bodily resurrection after death led the ancient Egyptians to mummify their loved ones' dead bodies. So many hundreds of thousands of mummified people (and cats) survived to the nineteenth century that they were ground up for fertilizer or medicine (although Mark Twain joked that mummies were also used to stoke fires for locomotives). For the ancient Egyptians, the most wealth and effort was spent on the bodies of the pharaohs. Several pharaohs commanded tens of thousands of people over decades to build giant pyramids as funereal monuments to house their own mummies and treasure. Sadly for them and for our ability to appreciate the past, most tombs were looted over the centuries, even

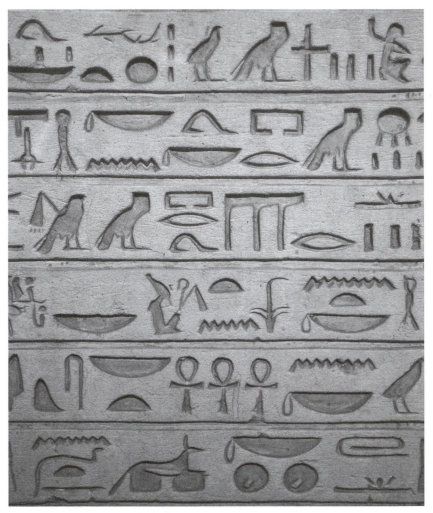

Figure 2.2. The hieroglyphics (pictogram writing) of the ancient
Egyptians decorates the wall of a temple.

when they were buried in the isolated Valley of the Kings. At the height of the
Egyptian civilization, though, the regular pattern of life and death, the flood and
fall of the Nile, the rising and setting of the sun offered Egyptians a comforting cycle
of expectation in this world, while they also hoped for a better life in the next.

One brief exception in Egypt's cyclical history was the Amarna period, created
by the rule of Pharaoh Ahkenaton (r. ca. 1352–1335 B.C.). He came to power with
the traditional name Amenhotep IV but was inspired to transform Egyptian religion
and, thus, his status as pharaoh. Instead of the many gods of traditional Egyptian
polytheism, he encouraged worship of one god, Aton, the sun, with whom Ahkenaton had a special, divine connection, of course. Some historians think this focus on
Aton established the first ***monotheism***, or belief in only one god. Ahkenaton's
ideas, though, did not long outlive him. Whether the priests saw him as a creative
individualistic innovator or an ugly slothful fanatic, they and most Egyptians soon
went back to worshipping according to the traditional patterns. Later pharaohs

erased Ahkenaton's very name from their dynastic records. A brief artistic revolution, though, created lively and fascinating art of the Amarna Period that differed from the static, unchanging forms of most Egyptian painting and sculpture. This art has come down to us in the famous bust of Ahkenaton's wife Nefertiti (see figure 2.3) and in the treasures from the tomb of his successor, the boy pharaoh Tutankhamen (r. ca. 1335–1325 B.C.), or King Tut. Archaeologists discovered Tut's tomb in A.D. 1922. Stories of a mummy's curse that afflicted the tomb's excavators exaggerate the very normal circumstances surrounding the deaths of a few of them.

The curse of warfare, though, nearly killed off both of these early Middle Eastern civilizations. Mesopotamia was particularly vulnerable to attack. Again and again, warriors from the surrounding hills stormed into the fertile valleys to plunder and conquer. Similarly, neighboring kings fought to dominate one another. Mesopotamia, never united for long, offered a dismal and depressing chronicle of slaughter.

After 2500 B.C., various peoples, called Semites by modern scholars, entered Mesopotamia from the Arabian Peninsula. Their name is based upon the similar languages they spoke, supposedly linked to a biblical character. Modern Semitic languages include Aramaic, Hebrew, and Arabic. Soon, the Semitic speakers began

Figure 2.3.   This head of Nefertiti, the wife of Ahkenaton, rests on a swanlike neck in this sculpture.

to dominate the region's politics even as they adopted Sumerian culture. By 2300 B.C., Sargon of Akkad had formed one of the first great empires by conquering Sumer and many of his Mesopotamian neighbors and then installing his relatives as subrulers. His descendants lost their grip on power, and several city-states restored their independence or built new, fragile kingdoms and empires. Throughout, Akkadian remained a common Semitic language to many. In the chaos, the Sumerian civilization died out. King Hammurabi of Babylon (r. ca. 1790–1750 B.C.) expanded the power of his Semitic people, the Amorites, almost to the equivalent of Sargon's. Within a century after Hammurabi's reign, various peoples such as Kassites and Hittites had in turn destroyed his Babylonian empire.

Meanwhile, the Egyptians managed a little more stability, unified by their pharaoh and protected by the desert. Even they, however, eventually suffered invasion. Their impressive Old Kingdom (a long line of dynastic stability) endured for nearly a thousand years, from 3100 to 2200 B.C., until it collapsed in civil disorder. By 2050 B.C., a new dynasty consolidated the Middle Kingdom, which lasted a mere 250 years until foreign invaders brought it down. Finally, the New Kingdom flourished from 1600 to about 1200 B.C. At that time, all over the Middle East, warfare and invasions destroyed civilized states.

Two innovations about this time made war even more destructive. First, the Hittites were the first to figure out how to smelt iron ore and forge iron tools around 1500 B.C. Iron, except for the problem of rust, was stronger and could hold an edge far better than bronze. Iron swords, spear points, and arrowheads became more lethally efficient in killing. Heavy iron helmets, breastplates, and shields likewise offered better protection, although only to those who could afford them or bear their heavy weight. As other people adopted this metal as their key material, the **Iron Age** (1200 B.C.–A.D. 1870) began and endured until just over a century ago. Second, commanders domesticated horses from the steppes of Asia, either as military transportation for individual riders or harnessed to chariots. Both these new warfare techniques enabled ambitious kings to dominate others and build "universal" empires that politically unified Mesopotamia, Egypt, and their neighbors.

The **Assyrian Empire** (ca. 750–600 B.C.) was the first universal empire, a term that means it united most of the peoples of the early Middle East, ranging from the Persian Gulf to the Nile. The Assyrians, with their swift cavalry, iron swords, and utter ruthlessness, were probably the first wholehearted believers in ***militarism***: the idea that virtues such as discipline, obedience, courage, and willingness to kill for the state are the highest values a civilized society can hold. Assyrians loved the hunt and the exercise of their power. Their brutality, however, inspired little affection among the dozens of conquered peoples. If any people dared to resist conquest, the Assyrians punished the defeated populations by burning alive many men, women, and children, mutilating others by hacking off hands, arms, noses, ears, or genitals, and then scattering survivors as slaves. These practices swiftly destroyed many ethnic groups. Many others surrendered rather than resist.

Those survivors, though, organized against their Assyrian conquerors. The Assyrian empire lasted only about 150 years. Two allied peoples destroyed the

Assyrians in 600 B.C.: the Chaldeans (or Neo-Babylonians since they had occupied Babylon) and the Medes from the hills north of Persia (as it was called by the Greeks, but they named their own country Iran, as it is called today). The Neo-Babylonian-Persian alliance completely wiped out the Assyrians, as they themselves had done to so many others. Of the Assyrian civilization only the ruins of their grand monuments to hunting and war survived.

After ridding themselves of the Assyrians, the Neo-Babylonians and Medes lived in an uneasy relationship. Both competed for dominion over weaker societies. During one of the wars, there occurred the first scientifically ascertainable date in history: 28 May 585 B.C.—when a battle between the Medes and the Lydians in Asia Minor was broken off because of a solar eclipse (whose exact date modern astronomers can confirm). After a few decades of intermittent warfare, both Neo-Babylonians and Medes were surprised by the sudden rise of Cyrus "the Great" of Persia. In 550 B.C., Cyrus defeated the Medes and eleven years later took Babylon.

Cyrus established the **Persian Empire** (550–330 B.C.), the second, even larger universal empire: Egypt, the Fertile Crescent, the Medes' lands, and his own Persia. As the shah, the "king of kings," Cyrus ruled over all, venerated like a god on earth. Yet his rule was benevolent compared with that of the Assyrians. He set up satraps (provincial governors) to be his eyes and ears throughout the empire. With broad authority, they kept his various subjects in order. He allowed many of his subject peoples to keep their unique customs and religions. Instead of imposing their own speech on everyone, the Persians encouraged the foreign (to them) Semitic language of Aramaic as a common means for most people to communicate with one another. (A few people today in Lebanon still speak it.) Most of the diverse peoples found the Persian shah's rule to be beneficial.

The Persians encouraged trade, helped by the invention of **money** in their recently conquered province of Lydia in Asia Minor. Money appeared surprisingly late as a means of economic exchange, or at least it might seem so to us who take it for granted. For thousands of years of civilization, though, no one could trust it. Before money, people bartered for goods and services, trading their labor or goods such as pots, cows, or women. Using money meant that specially made lumps of precious metals (usually copper, silver, or gold) could be used instead, creating a more stable and consistent pricing system. One problem, though, with any precious metal was determining how to trust its purity. Money will circulate only when people trust its value. Copper, silver, and gold could be easily degraded with baser metals such as tin or nickel into alloys and thus be worth less than the expected value. Gold could be tested somewhat because of its softness—and thus the custom arose of people biting gold coins to see whether they dented. Silver was a much more common and useful metal for making money, especially after the Lydians figured out how to use a touchstone (a rock on which metals left a specific color streak) to prove the purity of silver coins. The power of government also contributed to the use of money. Rulers put their own faces on the coins and ensured their value by setting purity standards and punishing forgers who debased coins. Hence, out of the Persian Empire came the long-standing practice that the government is responsible for money and therefore always intimately involved in the economy.

The Persians were great and powerful, yet even their empire survived little more than two centuries before another people conquered it. Nevertheless, the Persian Empire represented the high point of Middle Eastern civilization. The diverse peoples of the Fertile Crescent and Nile River basin had developed much of agriculture and architecture, metallurgy and mathematics, literature and law. Their influence on Western civilization was to set an example of these basic practices for other peoples who lived on the fringes of the great empires.

While Bronze Age Egypt and Sumer first reached their high points, various peoples lived without the benefits of civilization in what we now call Europe. The oldest Europeans were probably the Basques, who still live on both sides of the Pyrenees Mountains. Others soon migrated into Europe. We know something about them from archaeological remains of bones and pots. The 1991 discovery in the Alps of a mummy, since nicknamed Ötzi, provided a few insights into the hunter-gatherers of five thousand years ago. The huge ring of stones at Stonehenge in present-day England is impressive, but it tells us little of the people who built it around 1500 B.C. (see figure 2.4). The last prehistoric populations to arrive in Europe came from populations of southern and southwestern Asia. These immigrants shared languages grouped together and designated by scholars as Indo-European.

Early Europeans found an area well suited for human habitation. Flooding was less devastating than along the great rivers of Africa, the Middle East, or Asia, since the major waterways were not nearly so vast. Europe suffered few earthquakes. The temperate climate prevented many insects who bore lethal tropical diseases. The hills contained rich deposits of mineral ores. While dense forests had to be cleared to create farmland, the plentiful wood provided excellent building material and fuel. Many of the native animals were easily domesticated.

Along with these benefits, the Europeans would be enriched by migrations of civilized people and ideas from the Middle East, Asia, and Africa. Political practices, economic systems, social customs, art and literature, religion, and schools were ready-made to be borrowed or stolen. Drawing on the wisdom of ancient Mesopotamia and Egypt, two southern European peoples who had settled on the northern

Figure 2.4.   The mysterious, massive blocks of Stonehenge rise from a meadow in the south of England.

shores of the Mediterranean Sea would build their own civilizations. First, however, an obscure Middle Eastern people, who barely survived the rise and fall of empires, became essential to the West.

Review: What did various Middle Eastern civilizations offer to the early peoples of the West?

Response:

CHAPTER 3

The Chosen People

Hebrews and Jews, 2000 B.C. to A.D. 135

At first, the **Hebrews** or **Jews** seemed insignificant compared with the peoples of ancient North Africa, Mesopotamia, Persia, and Asia Minor who developed the essential practices of civilization upon which the West would build. They borrowed from their greater neighbors. Their tiny political state barely budged the course of history, while numerous vast empires rose and fell around and over them. Amazingly, the Jews survived these cataclysms. Their religion became a key component of the West, and they themselves shared in the civilization, if often from the fringes.

AN OBSCURE HISTORY

The Hebrews were similar to many other pastoral peoples who lived in the Middle East several millennia ago. As they came together into a coherent nation, the Hebrews crafted a meaningful history for themselves. A century ago, modern professional historians enthusiastically accepted and endorsed the Hebrews' version of their own past, since those accounts reinforced the historians' own cultural view of a heroic religious legacy. More recently, historians have doubted the accuracy and legitimacy of much of what the ancient Hebrews wrote about their foundations and origins. Because this history is intimately interwoven with the Hebrew faith of *Judaism*, determining the truth has been all the more complicated. As so often, myths that describe a people's character and purpose seem to outweigh the verifiable facts.

The ancient Hebrews collected their histories into their own sacred scriptures called the Tanakh, an abbreviation for the Torah (first five books), writings of prophets, and other writings. Later Christians included Hebrew scripture as the **Old Testament** of their **Bible**. In the beginning, according to biblical scripture, God created the heavens and the earth. The Hebrews saw their god not only as the creator, but also as the only true deity. The other gods and goddesses of Mesopotamia, Egypt, or any other people were petty demons or fakes in comparison. Since this Hebrew god also came to be revered by most of Western civilization, his name in English is conventionally spelled with a capital G to distinguish him from all other (false) gods. They claimed that God proved his supreme power through the history of the Hebrews.

According to the Hebrew scriptures, God's influence on humanity started with the beginning of all history, in their story about creation. The Hebrews believed that God created two human beings, a man and a woman (although there are two versions of the story offering two contradictory accounts of their formation). They believed that all the rest of humanity descended from these first two people, Adam and Hawwah (Eve in English).

The creation story not only narrated how God created the universe but also described how things went wrong for humans because of bad choices. The archangel Michael threw Adam and Hawwah out of paradise as punishment for eating the fruit of the tree of knowledge of good and evil. As generation begot generation, sins multiplied. At one point, God became fed up with humanity and killed almost everyone with a great flood. Only Noah and his family survived in a large ship, the ark, which also harbored pairs of all living creatures.

Many cultures have similar myths of original couples falling from perfection and of devastating floods covering the entire earth. No valid scientific or historical evidence exists to prove creation or flood myths. No physical location for paradise has been found or is even possible in this world. Building a ship large enough to hold all species of animals and sustenance for them is mathematically and physically impossible. Although stories of origins cannot be literally true, they resonate with miraculous mythic power in our culture.

Generations after mythologized Noah, a more concrete history of the Hebrews began when Abraham and his family left Mesopotamia. They settled in the land of the Canaanites, where Hivites, Perizzites, Girgashites, and Jebusites, among others, also lived. Abraham and his people prospered as herders of livestock. Abraham's grandson, Jacob, also called Israel, had ten sons and two grandsons who formed the twelve "tribes" of Israel. These immigrants claimed the land of the Canaanites for themselves and began to replace the natives by conquest, slaughter, and assimilation, as nations have done before and since. Then, the Bible story goes, in the sixteenth century B.C., during a time of famine, the Hebrews fell under Egyptian domination and moved there.

Egyptian sources do not mention this Hebrew captivity, but the oppression by Egyptians provided a pivotal historical moment for the Hebrews. According to Hebrew scripture and many scholarly estimates, a leader named Moses led his people out of Egypt in the mid-1200s B.C. This event, called the Exodus, is the defining moment of Hebrew history, celebrated ever since in the religious festival of the Passover. The Hebrews wandered in the wilderness (the time length of forty years is probably a mythologized number). Then, the Hebrews once again invaded the land of Canaan and made it theirs by war. The story about their leader Joshua blowing horns to bring down the walls of the ancient city of Jericho is popular in children's Bible stories. Usually, children do not hear how the Hebrews completely destroyed the city and put to the sword all the men and women, whether young or old, and even slaughtered the livestock, sparing only the family of Raban the harlot, who had helped Joshua's spies.

Despite this successful reconquest of Canaan, the Hebrews held a precarious place in a dangerous region. By about 1000 B.C., a new people along the coast, the Philistines (who gave the region its name of **Palestine**), began their own conquest, armed with superior iron weapons. Figures called judges (such as Gideon, Samson, or even a woman, Deborah) led the loose confederation of Hebrews. Their leadership derived both from their military ability and apparent divine sanction. Still, many Hebrews began to insist on having a king, just like their neighboring peoples had. The failures of the first, King Saul, prompted a rebellion by David, son of Jesse. Even after Saul's death in battle against the Philistines, the new King David needed to fight for the loyalty of all Hebrews. He eventually succeeded and established a dynasty, passing the crown to his son, Solomon. Under Solomon the Hebrew kingdom allegedly reached its peak during a weak period for Egypt and Mesopotamia.

The fragile unity achieved by these three kings broke down after Solomon's death. The Northern Kingdom, including ten of the tribes, took the name of **Israel**. The Southern Kingdom of the other two tribes became **Judaea** (or **Judah**), named after one of Jacob's sons. The uneasy rivalry of these kingdoms made them an even more tempting target for neighboring empires. The militaristic Assyrians attacked in 722 B.C. They annihilated the Northern Kingdom: its people disappeared, either killed or enslaved and assimilated, becoming known as the "lost tribes of Israel." The Southern Kingdom narrowly escaped Assyrian conquest in 701 B.C. According to the Hebrews, an angel of the Lord struck down 185,000 Assyrian troops as they slept; according to the Assyrians, the Hebrews bought off the Assyrians with a payment of tribute that included the Hebrew king's daughters. In either case, Judaea's time was limited. In 596 B.C., the Babylonians, who had recently destroyed the Assyrians, picked up where the latter left off. The Babylonians conquered the Southern Kingdom and dragged off many thousands to Mesopotamia as slaves.

The following years between 596 and 538 B.C. became known as the **Babylonian Captivity**, another important turning point for the Hebrew people. Instead of disappearing into the large category of lost peoples of history, the Hebrews endured. They kept their religion; they held their social integrity; they survived despite oppression. After only a few generations of suffering, a rescuer appeared in the person of Cyrus "the Great," the same who destroyed Babylon and founded the new Persian Empire. The magnanimous Cyrus took pity on the Hebrews and allowed them to return to Judaea once again. There they rebuilt their temple in Jerusalem and resumed life under the protection of the shahs of Persia.

The Hebrews' history to that point was indeed remarkable in that they had managed to survive as a people. Many cultures and nations had already become extinct over the millennia, including the Sumerians, Hyksos, Hittites, and Assyrians. All these peoples had been far more powerful than the Hebrews. Yet the Hebrews continued despite multiple migrations: into Palestine, out of Palestine, into Palestine, out, again and again. This achievement would still not have rated the Hebrews much of a mention in history books, however, were it not for their religion.

Review: *How did the history of the Hebrews/Jews contrast with that of other ancient peoples?*

Response:

THE TIE THAT BINDS

During the course of this mythic history, the Hebrews continued claiming that they could see the hand of God regularly revealed. History permeated their religion of Judaism and vice versa. Other Middle Eastern religions emphasized the cyclical nature of creation and destruction, where nothing really changed. The rulers ruled, the people worked, year after year, century after century, millennium after millennium. In contrast, the Hebrews saw a direction to their experiences. Descended from one man and his family, they remained a nation. They optimistically looked toward the future. From the Hebrews' point of view, the whole purpose of history was to illuminate their relationship with their God, who, for unknown reasons, had selected the people of Israel as his special favorites. The Hebrew people sinned and failed as much as any other group of people. Nonetheless, they claimed that a special relationship grew out of the obedience of Abraham, Moses, other kings and prophets, and the people individually and collectively. The Hebrews were to obey the commandments of God, which set them apart from their neighbors and those neighbors' religions.

One main component of this obedience to God was resisting **syncretism**, at least when it came to adopting elements from other religions into their own. The other great Mesopotamian and Egyptian civilizations provided not only knowledge of agriculture, architecture, mathematics, astronomy, metallurgy, and political organization. Along with these other ideas came religion. Many peoples of the ancient world readily absorbed and adapted one another's spiritual beliefs and the rites of their neighbors. The Hebrews tried not to.

The Hebrews repeatedly insisted that their religion was different. They developed monotheism, devotion to one god. God was transcendent, beyond nature, not of this world; rather, he had made it himself. God did not even have a name. He was YHWH, perhaps meaning "I am who I am" (often rendered in English as Jehovah). He was jealous and allowed no other gods. Judaism's almost unique conception of the divine required that the Hebrews reject polytheistic practices, as tempting as fertility cults might be. They excluded Gentiles (non-Jews) from their faith and society in their particularism. In many ways, such as the sacrificial rituals in the temple, the Hebrews' religion resembled those of their neighbors, but they insisted on their own exclusive relationship with God.

At the core of Judaism was the **covenant** that God had concluded with the Hebrews alone. Covenants were political treaties and contracts between greater and lesser peoples. God's contract was laid out not only in the famous **Ten Commandments**, but also in more than six hundred other laws and regulations for everything from murder and debt to food and sex (see table 3.1). The Hebrews believed that if they kept his laws, God would make of the Hebrews a great nation, multiplying them, giving them a land of milk and honey, and cursing their enemies.

The exact nature of this promised land of milk and honey was a matter of dispute. Some Hebrews maintained it to be the land of Canaan/Palestine/Israel/Judaea—a land physically in this world. Others held it to be a metaphysical land in the next world, a heaven after death. Judaism's position on the afterlife was varied. Some Hebrews believed that since God acted in this world, then his promised paradise would happen here—there was no life after death. Others believed that some sort of paradise was attainable after death, with or without a bodily resurrection such as the kind the Egyptians believed in. Judaism has always mainly emphasized living a moral life for God in this world, not the afterlife. Religion and morality are indivisible for Judaism. The Jewish emphasis on morality later influenced its successor faiths of Christianity and Islam.

Besides monotheism, another remarkable feature of Judaism was its organization. God made the covenant with the people without the intervening mediation of kings or priests. A caste of priests maintained the single temple in Jerusalem, but the most important religious figures were the prophets who had a direct relationship with God. They proved their worth through miracles and the validity of their prophecy (although historians would argue that few of the prophecies in the Bible came true in the lifetime of their predictors—they were realized only by reading history backwards). During their lifetimes, prophets often suffered rejection. Both powerful rulers and substantial numbers of the population often ignored and punished the prophets. For example, when the prophet Samuel designated David to replace Saul as king, the multitudes did not listen and rally to his cause. Yet the moral voices of the prophets like Samuel, Ezekiel, Jeremiah, and Isaiah have reso-

Table 3.1. Which Ten Commandments?

Jewish	Orthodox	Most Protestant	Roman Catholic	Exodus 20: 2–17
1		Preface		2 I am the LORD thy God, which have brought thee out of the land of Egypt, out of the house of bondage.
		1		3 Thou shalt have no other gods before me.
	2		1	4 Thou shalt not make unto thee any graven image, or any likeness of any thing that is in heaven above, or that is in the earth beneath, or that is in the water under the earth:
				5 Thou shalt not bow down thyself to them, nor serve them: for I the LORD thy God am a jealous God, visiting the iniquity of the fathers upon the children unto the third and fourth generation of them that hate me;
				6 And shewing mercy unto thousands of them that love me, and keep my commandments.
	3		2	7 Thou shalt not take the name of the LORD thy God in vain; for the LORD will not hold him guiltless that taketh his name in vain.
	4		3	8 Remember the sabbath day, to keep it holy.
				9 Six days shalt thou labor, and do all thy work:
				10 But the seventh day is the sabbath of the LORD thy God: in it thou shalt not do any work, thou, nor thy son, nor thy daughter, thy servant, nor thy maidservant, nor thy cattle, nor thy stranger that is within thy gates:
				11 For in six days the LORD made heaven and earth, the sea, and all that in them is, and rested the seventh day: wherefore the LORD blessed the sabbath day, and hallowed it.
	5		4	12 Honour thy father and thy mother: that thy days may be long upon the land which the LORD thy God giveth thee.
	6		5	13 Thou shalt not kill.
	7		6	14 Thou shalt not commit adultery.
	8		7	15 Thou shalt not steal.
	9		8	16 Thou shalt not bear false witness against thy neighbour.
	10		9	17 Thou shalt not covet thy neighbour's house, thou shalt not covet thy neighbour's wife,
			10	nor his manservant, nor his maidservant, nor his ox, nor his ass, nor any thing that is thy neighbour's.

Note: While people often refer to the Ten Commandments as the foundational laws of our culture, the exact rules are difficult to pin down. Two slightly different versions exist, one, as here, and the other, as in Deuteronomy 5:6–21. Translation challenges lead to different word choices ("kill" or "murder") or archaic phrasing, such as in this, the King James Version. In the original Hebrew, there was no numbering—verse numbers appeared only as late as the twelfth century A.D. Jews, Roman Catholics, Orthodox, and Protestants numbered the commandments in different ways, so where some commandments ended and others began was open to interpretation.

nated through the centuries. Their proclamation of God's word, religion, and his people survived. The prophets called the Hebrews to the path of righteousness and away from worshipping the gods of their neighbors, which many Israelites often did nevertheless.

The Hebrews were likewise unusual in the secular nature of their kings. Unlike monarchs of the Middle East, few Hebrew rulers had a serious connection to the divine. The first man, Adam, was no king (although he would be used by later political writers to argue for kingship through his role as father and husband). The early history of the Hebrews from before Abraham to Moses saw no kings. The judges who reconquered Canaan were not kings. And what happened according to their scriptures once God granted the Hebrews a king? Saul, their first king and allegedly chosen by God, suffered civil war and committed suicide after defeat by the Philistines. The next two, David and Solomon, did much good and lived into old age, but they also sinned mightily. David committed adultery with Bathsheba, the wife of his general, whom he arranged to have killed. Solomon built shrines to the gods of his many foreign wives. Subsequent kings quarreled; the tribes broke apart and were destroyed. What use were kings for the chosen people of God? They did just as much harm as good. Judaism absorbed the lesson that political states were not essential for faith. God made a covenant with the people of Israel, not the kings of Israel.

Thus originated the Western principle of the separation of church and state. This ideal certainly did not mean that the populace lacked religion. On the contrary, the Hebrew people were religious (or not) independent of the status of their government. The emphasis on God's rule did incline them toward *theocracy*, the idea that religion ruled a society through its officials and ministers. Such tendencies, though, never lasted for long. While Hebrew priests played an essential role in ritual and the maintenance of religious laws, the Hebrews insisted on having secular rulers. This practice differed from Mesopotamian kings who claimed divine powers or Egyptian pharaohs who asserted themselves to be gods incarnate. When those states fell, then so did their religions. No one today reveres Ishtar or Osiris. For most of history, however, the Hebrews, the Jews, have done without any state at all. They and their religion survived. God does not care about what constitution a kingdom has, they believed, but how faithful his people are.

Even with God and the prophets to follow, it was difficult for the Hebrews to maintain their distinctive faith with so many nature-worshipping polytheists around and among them. They had little tolerance for the ways of their neighbors, whom the Hebrews feared would seduce them into idolatry and demon worship. The fertility rituals and sex imitation of the gods were tempting. Kings like David or Solomon built up huge treasuries and married many wives. The queens from foreign peoples often lured their royal spouses into allowing other deities to be worshipped in Israel. The scriptures paint Jezebel as one of the worst queens, since she talked her husband, King Ahab of Israel, into promoting her Canaanite fertility god, Baal. The scriptures say that she fell to a miserable death, where the dogs would not even lick her blood. These stories warned political leaders of the dangers of sin despite their royal power.

The Hebrews' failure to have a powerful kingdom like other peoples did not doom them. Their life under the Persian Empire was tolerable. The local governor often gave way to the leadership of priests in local affairs. When the Persian Empire fell in 330 B.C. to Alexander (see the next chapter), Greek kings based in Egypt or Syria ruled the Hebrews for several centuries, again allowing them substantial autonomy.

That conquest by the Greeks began the last great turning point of Hebrew history, the **Diaspora** (dispersion or scattering). Both encouraged by cosmopolitan freedom under other Greek rulers and oppressed in Palestine by their own, the majority of Hebrews left their chosen home for distant lands to live among other peoples. At this point, historians switch from calling them Hebrews to Jews. Within an international cultural and political system dominated by Greeks, many Jews found it easy to leave Palestine and settle in enclaves in distant cosmopolitan cities throughout the Mediterranean and Middle East, even as far as India.

Jews who remained in Judaea found one more brief moment to claim their own worldly kingdom. In 165 B.C., a Greek king desecrated the temple in Jerusalem in honor of his own gods. In reaction, the Maccabee (or Hammer) family led a revolt, winning about a century of independence again for the Jews. Then, in the first century B.C., Roman armies marched into the Middle East (see chapter 5). By 63 B.C., the Romans had easily conquered the weak Jewish kingdom, although keeping order among the Jews proved much more difficult. Recurrent Jewish revolts and rebellions led the Romans to destroy the temple in A.D. 70 and intensify the Diaspora by forcefully ejecting the majority of Jews from Palestine after A.D. 135. From that time until the twentieth century, most Jews lived outside of Palestine and had no political autonomy of their own. They lived in small enclaves in the cities of the kingdoms and empires of other peoples.

The Jews lost their kings, the temple and its priests, and their agricultural base as they moved into foreign cities. Out of necessity, the Jews ceased to be peasant farmers and became urban traders and merchants. Teachers trained in their scriptures, called **rabbis**, came to lead Jewish communities instead of priests or kings. Studies by rabbis were collected into the Talmud, which helped Jews interpret their sacred scripture. Enough tolerance in the Hellenistic and Roman cosmopolitan cities allowed the fragmented Jews to keep practicing their religion across the Mediterranean world.

Toleration went only so far, however. Most states have justified their existence through a divine connection; thus a different faith implied a lack of allegiance. Jews also remained a perpetual irritant for authorities who preferred conformity because they were so often capable at maintaining their distinct religion. Outsiders often resented the Jews' view of themselves as the creator of the universe's specially chosen people. That perspective could be interpreted as excluding all others from divine favor. As the Jews came under Roman rule, they annoyed their new overlords by refusing to make religious sacrifices to the Roman gods, especially the emperor. The Hebrew God was a jealous God and tolerated no worship of other deities. Fortunately, the Romans recognized, in their usual tolerant matter toward religion, that Judaism predated their own rituals. Abraham, Moses, and David had lived centuries before the founding of Rome. So the Romans granted a special license to or exemption for the Jews.

Despite this sympathy for differences, Jewish cultural identity has continuously provoked hostility in their neighbors. Our modern word for this antagonism toward Jews is **_anti-Semitism_**. Scholars coined the term just over a century ago as a polite alternative to "hatred of Jews." Through the centuries, that hatred has ranged from mere dislike for Jews as "different," to discrimination in jobs and housing, to violent persecution, and even to extermination. Had the Jews assimilated, given up any unique clothing, religious practices, and ways of speech or life, then anti-Semitism might have disappeared. But then Jews might have ceased to be Jews. Since many Jews have remained faithful to their conception about how to obey God, they have often faced difficulties with majorities who wanted them to conform or convert.

The Jews survived as a small but significant minority in the ancient world of the Middle East, Europe, and even deeper into South and East Asia. Compared with the rise of the other ancient empires, the political history of the Hebrew kingdoms mattered little. Ancient peoples likewise expressed little interest in the religion of Judaism compared with the other raging currents of faith and superstition in the ancient world. Nonetheless, the Jewish people have endured without a homeland as only a few peoples in world history have done. As residents in the cities of Europe they would contribute from their culture to the growth of Western civilization. Also, out of their religion arose other beliefs that would shake the West and the world to their foundations. Before those moments, however, two other Mediterranean peoples added their own groundwork to Western civilization.

Review: *How did the Jews maintain their cultural identity?*

Response:

CHAPTER 4

Trial of the Hellenes

The Ancient Greeks, 1200 B.C. to A.D. 146

While the ancient Hebrew kingdoms were oppressed on all sides by conquerors, another people, the **Greeks**, were able to prosper far away from dangerous conquerors, at least at first. Later, they would earn the wrath of the most powerful empire of their age. Afterward, the Greeks could have been utterly destroyed like the "lost tribes" of Israel or beaten into political impotence like the last kingdom of Judaea. Instead, for a brief moment in history, the Greeks triumphed to dominate the Eastern Mediterranean and the Middle East. Yet a tragic flaw in their success drove the Greeks into political irrelevance. Nevertheless, the Greeks' cultural achievements made them the second founding people of Western civilization.

TO THE SEA

The Greeks called themselves Hellenes, the descendants of a legendary founder named Hellas. They first came together as a people in the dark time around 1200

B.C., when so many other civilizations had suffered crises at the dawn of the Iron Age. Two of those civilized peoples, the Mycenaeans (who had lived at the southern tip of the Balkan Peninsula) and the Minoans (who had been centered on the nearby island of Crete) survived only through myths and stories of the Trojan War (for the former) and the Minotaur of the Labyrinth (for the latter). At the beginning of these Greek "Dark Ages," the first Hellenes invaded and took over the southern Balkans, displacing, intermarrying, and blending with the surviving indigenous people to become the Greeks. They themselves distinguished three main ethnicities of Dorians, Ionians, and Aeolians.

Although the Greeks remained loosely connected through their language and culture, geography inclined them toward political fractiousness. Greece's sparse landscape seemed inadequate for civilized agriculture, compared with the vast fertile plains of the Nile and Mesopotamian river valleys. The southern end of the Balkan Peninsula and the neighboring islands in the Aegean Sea were mountainous and rugged, with only a few regions suitable for grain farming. Grapevines and olive trees, though, grew well there and provided useful produce of wine and oil for export. Also, numerous inlets and bays where the mountains slouched into the sea provided excellent harbors. Therefore, the Greeks became seafarers, prospering less by farming and more by commerce, buying and selling, as they exchanged what they had for what they needed. And if a little piracy was necessary now and then, they did not mind that either.

The Greeks were so successful that by 800 B.C. the southern Balkan Peninsula and the Aegean islands had become too crowded. In the Greek homeland, the Greeks lived without a king, divided into separate, independent city-states, each one called a **polis** (in the singular; *poleis* in the plural). Elsewhere, though, good farmland lay available for the taking. So the Greeks began a new form of conquest: *colonialism*. In forming colonies, a crowded city-state would encourage groups of families, as many as two hundred men and their dependents, to emigrate. The Hellenes sailed across seas rather than merely crossing plains or rivers to conquer neighboring lands. There, on some other island or distant shore with a good harbor and a hill to build a fort, the emigrants would found a new city-state. Many indigenous peoples were killed, assimilated, enslaved, or driven away. Greek colonization, however, differed from other imperialistic conquests, both in scale and purpose. Greek colonies followed from small invasions, which did not bring in royal or imperial domination. The Hellenes lacked a common king or emperor like most other peoples had. Instead, the Greeks fostered political diversity. The new colonies remained only loosely connected to their founding state. They became free *poleis*, responsible to no higher political authority.

Most of these independent new colonies succeeded. The Greeks occupied all the islands of the Aegean Sea, where they still live today. More Greek populations settled in western Asia Minor (called Ionia), along the shores of the Black Sea, and all around the Mediterranean. Their settlements survived for many centuries, although people of Greek ethnicity no longer live in those places today (see chapter 14). By 500 B.C., more Greeks were actually living in the region of southern Italy and Sicily, called *Magna Græcia* (or Greater Greece), than in the old Greek homeland. The colonies promoted trade networks and encouraged innovation and invention as the Greeks built new homes and thrived in strange lands.

At the same time as the Greeks, the rival **Phoenicians**, a Semitic people, were trading and colonizing in the Mediterranean region. The Phoenicians shipped out from the Levantine coast, the eastern coastline of the Mediterranean that runs from Asia Minor to Egypt. At first, they prospered and expanded more than the Greeks. They clearly dominated the Western Mediterranean in regions untouched by the greatness of Middle Eastern civilizations. Some Phoenicians sailed as far as Great Britain, around the coast of Africa, and perhaps even to the Americas. The Phoenicians gained an early advantage with their invention of the first **alphabet**. All previous and contemporary civilizations, Sumer with its cuneiform and Egypt with its hieroglyphics (or, for that matter, China and India), used written systems composed of thousands of symbols, many of which represented only one word.

Instead, the Phoenicians chose about two dozen symbols to represent sounds. With these few symbols to signify consonants and vowels, they could spell out phonetically (from *Phoenicians*!) any word that could be pronounced. Most neighboring cultures, including the Hebrews, the Hellenes, and even the Egyptians, soon adapted the Phoenician alphabet idea to their own use. Indeed, soon people forgot how to read cuneiform or hieroglyphics, and much of the rich culture of Middle Eastern civilizations remained unknown until Western scholars relearned those writing systems in the nineteenth century (using, for example, the famous Rosetta Stone to translate ancient Egyptian).

Despite their many advantages, the Phoenicians ultimately failed in the competition of civilizations (see chapter 5). Meanwhile, the Greeks succeeded beyond anyone's imagining except, perhaps, their own. The Hellenes had a supreme confidence in their own superiority. They called all non-Greeks *barbarians*, a word derived from what the Greeks thought these foreigners were speaking, namely babbled nonsense. In the Western Mediterranean, the Greeks were often more technologically advanced and sophisticated than natives such as the Celts. The Greeks also labeled as barbarians peoples like Egyptians or Babylonians, who had brought forth great civilizations millennia before the Greeks existed and were still wealthy and mighty compared with the few and scattered Hellenes. Such distinctions were of no matter to the Greeks. They felt themselves to be the only truly civilized people.

Some Greek attitudes seemed rather strange to their neighbors at the time. For one, romantic and sexual relationships between men were more common and accepted in Greece than elsewhere. Many a male teenager was initiated into adulthood through a liaison with an older man. These relationships were not like modern homosexuality and often did not even have a physical sexual dimension. Even Greek men who were not interested in boys exercised in gymnasia or competed in sports while wearing no clothing. The athletes in the famous **Olympic Games** ran, hurled, boxed, and wrestled in the nude for male spectators (although some young virgin girls were allowed to attend, partly to check out prospective husband material). Not only women, but also other non-Greek men were excluded from competing in the Olympics. Our modern Olympic ideal of bringing together all nations of the world in sports was not for the Hellenes. Although famous through the ancient world, the Olympic Games expressed **panhellenism**, the idea that all Greeks were similar. Barbarians were not welcome on the playing field.

While the Greeks shared contempt for non-Greeks, they also separated themselves into smaller units. For a while, the Greeks reversed the trend toward empire so characteristic of the Middle East. Each Greek held allegiance to his own *polis* before and above any allegiance to the people as a whole. This political particularism further intensified into the idea of personhood called **individualism**. The heroic individual mattered more than the family, more than the city or its people. The great epic poem, Homer's *Iliad*, shows how Achilles and his many virtues, called *arête*, were hard to balance against the needs of the larger community. As the hero sulked in his tent, the Greeks were stalemated in their war against the Trojans. Because of the pride of Achilles, many died, including his best friend. Was Achilles to be admired or admonished? In either case, Achilles earned praise for being the best warrior. In everything, from war to theater, the Greeks competed with one another. How the Greeks would deal with this feeling of superiority, exclusiveness, and individuality became their greatest trial.

Review*: How did the Greeks begin as a people and expand through the Mediterranean?*

Response:

THE POLITICAL ANIMAL

As the Greeks built their civilization, they entered a period of political experimentation almost unparalleled in human history. The word *polis* gives us our word *politics*. The Mesopotamian kings and emperors, Egyptian pharaohs, and Persian shahs lacked politics in our modern, Western sense. Their commands were supposed to be unquestioned, endorsed by divine mandate. Only a few select elites, the aristocrats, had any part in the decision-making process that affected tens of thousands of subjects. In contrast, the Greeks originated **democracy** as a form of government. The Hellenic innovation of true politics broadened the decision making to include many people, which is what democracy literally means: rule by the people. More people participated in answering the important question of who pays taxes and how much. In absolutist monarchies, the kings and aristocrats taxed the peasants and made war. In a democracy, people taxed themselves and decided in common to go to war. Despite the difficulties and failures of the Greeks, their politics have continued to inspire us to this day.

The first step toward power for the people came in rejecting the most common political institution of the ancient world: kingship. Instead of allowing their kings to become gods like most other ancient peoples, the Greeks got rid of most of them. The Greeks did not, of course, cast off the gods themselves. They still believed their societies depended upon the favor of deities. At the heart of every city was an acropolis, "the high citadel," in which the people built their temples, held their most important religious ceremonies, and kept their treasures. Yet kings were no longer needed to play mediator, and neither were priests, at least as a special social group. When the Greeks got rid of royal dynasties, they also eliminated the ruling priestly caste. Instead, members of the community shared and alternated in the role of mediators and officiators in religious ceremonies.

Although the Greeks eliminated the political roles of the royal dynasties and priestly castes, they found the next step, breaking the power of the wealthy and well-born families, to be much more difficult. *Aristocracy*, rule of the better born, replaced monarchy at first. Remember that a few well-connected families usually run things. Such happened also in ancient Hellas. The aristocrats supported their power through their wealth in land, control of commerce, and monopoly of leadership in war. The expensive bronze armor and weaponry of the aristocratic warrior, such as Achilles had wielded in myth, made the aristocrats dominant on the battlefield, which in turn secured their monopoly in political counsels.

Politics changed, as it had before and would again, when new military technology and tactics created new kinds of warriors in the seventh century B.C. The rough terrain of the southern Balkans was unsuitable for cavalry, and so foot soldiers became the most important warriors. Then the growing use of iron allowed for new weapons, as it had for the Assyrians. As trade increased and iron metals became more accessible, a new type of Greek warrior appeared: the **hoplite**. The hoplite was lightly protected by a helmet and a large round shield and armed with a long spear and a short sword.

The key to the hoplite's success on the battlefield was fighting in coordination with other hoplites in a **phalanx**. Each phalanx consisted of about four hundred men standing in lines eight ranks deep; each man defended himself with his helmet and large shield that covered both part of him and his neighbor. To attack, soldiers wielded nine-foot-long spears, as they ran together to smash the enemy. The battle often turned into a shoving match, each side pushing until the other started to give way from exhaustion, fear, or the loss of hoplites to wounds. If spears were useless in close combat, then soldiers swung short chopping swords. At the same time, they perfected a new warship for the all-important battles at sea: the trireme. While triremes did have sails, three banks of rowers called *thetes* provided the essential means of propulsion. A large ram on the prow would crash into an enemy ship, aiming to sink it. If that was unsuccessful, armed *thetes* would board the enemy and fight hand to hand to seize the ship. Navies organized ships to fight in groups, like a phalanx at sea.

These two innovations, hoplite and trireme, broke the dominance of the aristocracy in combat and lost them their political monopoly. Repeatedly in history, innovations in military methods have forced changes in political structures. In ancient Greece, a simple peasant could afford the few weapons of a hoplite and then spend several weeks training to march in formation and kill. Anyone with a strong back and limbs could be a *thete*. Once the peasants and merchants realized that they were putting their lives on the line for their "country," they demanded a share of the power and wealth controlled by the aristocrats. Many peasants called for **land reform**, taking away some land from those who had inherited a great deal and giving it to those who had little. Peasants have called for this practice regularly throughout the history of our civilization. Getting the great landowners to surrender power has, however, been more complicated.

The struggle for dominance in Greek city-states reflected the eternal tension between politics and violence. Ideally, politics should mean that people peacefully make a decision after civil discussion. The Greek aristocrats personified warriors of privilege, who believed that their dominance had been granted by the gods. They resisted any land reform, perceiving it as not in their own best interest. The Greek peasants, in turn, were equally as determined to gain their version of justice and fought back. Thus, rebellion and strife have been political tools just as often as laws and votes. The Greeks labeled a situation when all political discourse had broken down into riot as anarchy (from the Greek word for a society without the archons, the appointed administrators). After a struggle, a winning group reasserted the rule of law and order as the winners interpreted it.

A few members of the aristocracy who sympathized with the plight of the peasants assisted the commoners in the seventh and sixth centuries B.C. These leaders seized power from their fellows and won the favor of the masses by pushing through reforms. These popular rulers have been given the name of **tyrants**. To accuse someone of *tyranny* now implies ruthless rule for one's own gain, and indeed that did happen in Greece. More often, though, the tyrants ruled with harshness in order to break the power of their fellow aristocrats and grant rights to the peasants. Greek tyrants were rarely able to establish a dynasty and pass power to their descendants. Instead, the same people who had helped the tyrants subsequently overthrew them, believing, correctly, that they no longer needed the tyrants once the power of the aristocrats was broken. The mechanisms of political power had shifted.

After all this bloodshed and suffering, most Greeks settled on some form of democracy by 500 B.C. Politically eligible citizens were expected to live up to their obligations. The ancient Athenians literally called someone who did not serve in public office or deliberate in civic affairs an "idiot." The Greek democracy nevertheless excluded many people from political decisions, restricting the political rights of **citizenship**, the concept that certain members of the polity have defined rights and responsibilities. First, resident "foreigners" could not participate. A foreigner was defined as anyone not descended from the founders of the particular *polis*, ethnic Greek or not. Second, adult women had no legitimate political role and would not have in the West until the twentieth century. Third, children were excluded, as they are today. Fourth, the large numbers of slaves were, of course, excluded. Fifth, property requirements still kept many of the poor from participation. Greeks often limited democracy to adult male citizens who held a defined amount of wealth, which varied from city to city. So the percentage of people actually engaged in democracy ranged from 30 percent down to only 3 percent of any city-state's population. This percentage was a substantial improvement on the less than 1 percent of people involved in early Greek or most Middle Eastern civilizations at the time. It also compares well with modern democracies, where sometimes only one-third of the population votes in elections.

These restrictions on voting in Greek *poleis* created the first tension within democracy and leads to another basic principle:

Democracy is difficult.

Throughout the brief history of Greek democracy, people not only argued but also killed one another over political principle. Most people cannot easily give up power. Most people cannot peacefully accept that others with whom they disagree should have power over them. Most people cannot resist the temptation to enrich themselves through political office rather than work to improve the community as a whole. The historical record often shows these sad realities. Sometimes, though, people have accepted the rules of democracy and created real and just democratic governments.

A truly functional democracy requires the rule of law and at least two different ideological positions that can both legitimately disagree and compromise with the other. Rules have meant that process, not violent power, should guide change. In ancient Greece, ideology further structured the grounds for debate. The Hellenes developed two basic political directions that are still with us today. One leaned to the past and supported individuals with privileges; the other inclined to the future and wanted to broaden access to status. Factions organized political activity around either appreciating an imaginary past or favoring the imagined future. In ancient Greece, believers in the former became the oligarchs. They promoted **oligarchy**, which limited rule to the few, namely the old aristocrats and the newly wealthy. The proponents of the latter were the democrats (which, like the American political party, are named after the political principle). The ancient Greek democrats favored expansion of political rights to the widest possible number of adult male citizens. Not only did the Greeks have these two distinct democratic viewpoints, but they also had two *poleis* that exemplified each political ideal: **Sparta** and **Athens**.

The city-state of Sparta typified oligarchy. Spartans called themselves Laconians, which has given us the expression "speaking laconically"—using few words to convey great meaning. This city-state was unique among the Greeks because it founded almost no overseas colonies. Instead, the Spartans conquered their neighboring Greeks in the Peloponnesus, the handlike peninsula at the southern tip of the Balkans. Most of the conquered Greeks became helots, subjects who held no political rights and had to surrender half of their agricultural produce annually. The free citizens of Sparta themselves made up only a small subset, perhaps 3 percent of the total population, who ruled over all. Since the unfree helots retained their fiercely independent Greek inclination, the Spartan citizens always feared revolt.

To prevent a successful slave rebellion, the Spartans therefore organized their entire state around militarism and ***egalitarianism***, claiming that these values were an ancient tradition. Egalitarian values meant that all citizens were to be rigorously equal. For example, the government divided up the agricultural plantations in relatively equal portions for each family. Money was made of large iron weights, which were too difficult to store, spend, or steal. Trade and artisanship in luxury goods was discouraged, since it would have increased the display of wealth. The common good (for the elite minority) was seen as better than the individual good.

More famous has been the Spartan commitment to militarism. All men were organized into military service. Male children were taken away from their parents at the age of seven, and from then on they were raised in a military barracks. As part of their training, they were encouraged to be stealthy and steal food from the local population. If an adult caught a boy stealing, he could beat the young one, sometimes so harshly that the boy died. At eighteen, a man who survived was allowed to marry. Even then, a husband ate meals in the warriors' mess until he was sixty. Even on the wedding night, the husband had to return to the barracks after consummation of the marriage. Women were esteemed if they produced male children. Spartan parents often exposed female babies to the elements to die because, as was common in the ancient world, they valued girls less than boys. Likewise, the Spartans also tossed into a chasm any male infant whom a group of elders deemed unfit for growing up to be a proper warrior. The public interest in strong children overrode any parental rights or affections.

Sparta's oligarchic government nevertheless functioned democratically, at least for those few considered full-fledged citizens. No one person could be all-powerful. At age thirty, men became citizens with full political rights. Two traditional kings ruled Sparta as a pair, but they were really figureheads—real power rested with appointed magistrates and a council of elders (about thirty of the leading citizens over age sixty). Generations of Spartans tried to maintain this system with as little change as possible because for them it embodied the virtues of the past and their founding father, Lykurgus. When a political crisis arose, those who promoted a policy always tried to claim, "It's what Lykurgus would have wanted!"

As a contrast in almost every way to Sparta, Athens developed democracy in its purest form. When we think of the civilization of ancient Greece, we usually think of Athens. The Athenians emphasized individualism rather than Sparta's egalitarianism and militarism. Athenian society encouraged its citizens to excel in politics, business, art, literature, and philosophy, according to their talents. Athens' location on a broad fertile plain with easy access to the sea allowed its inhabitants a prosperous economy and a large population. From early on, Athens faced the basic problem of resolving differences among three different constituencies: those of the city, those of the plain, and those of the hills. Each had different priorities and loyalties.

These divisions hindered the formation of a more democratic form of government until a series of tyrants began reforming the system. Draco, one of the first tyrants, became infamous for his set of laws issued in 621 B.C. Many of the laws mandated the death penalty, even for minor crimes. Consequently, his name has become a byword for excessive harshness: *draconian*. A few years after 600 B.C., the tyrant Solon solved so many problems that his name became a byword for political wisdom. To stop unrest, Solon divided the people into classes based on property, canceled farmers' debts outright, and expanded citizenship to the poor. Finally, by about 500 B.C., Cleisthenes left a substantially democratic structure in place.

Cleisthenes' balanced constitutional system served Athens for most of the fifth century B.C. First, Cleisthenes brought all citizens together into a political body called the Assembly. As the supreme legislative body, it included all male citizens over eighteen, about 10 percent of the population. Anyone was allowed to speak and vote, and a simple majority decided most issues. The Assembly declared war, made peace, spent tax money, chose magistrates, and judged capital crimes. Thus every citizen was involved in making the most important state decisions. How was the citizen to make up his mind how to vote in the Assembly? Politicians became orators, speech makers, striving to sway the crowd. If a politician became too powerful, the citizens could impose **ostracism**. The "winner" of a vote made with politicians' names on pieces of broken pottery (ostrakons) was sent into exile. To prevent such votes and hold onto power, politicians built up factions, groups of followers on whom they could rely. In Athens, as in most city-states, one faction tended toward democracy, the other toward oligarchy.

The Assembly met only periodically. Select citizens carried out the day-to-day administration of the city. Interestingly, the Athenians filled most administrative positions by lot: a chance name drawn from a barrel. They reserved actual voting within each tribe (*ethnos*) for elections of generals (*strategoi*, from where we get our word *strategy*). An advantage was that election ensured the generals had the support of their troops. They could hardly disobey someone they themselves had elected. A disadvantage was that soldiers did not always elect the best strategists or tacticians. Popular charisma is not always the best quality in battle. From the point of view of the city's leaders, though, dividing power among ten commanders prevented any one general from possessing too much military power.

Cleisthenes' second innovation aimed to end old feuds between people living in different geographic regions. He broke up loyalties by creating new ties that were not based on blood or status. He divided each of the three regions (city, plain, and hills) into ten districts. One district from each of the three regions was then combined into a new "tribe," artificially forcing the divergent people of city, plain, and hills together. These tribes determined a citizen's role in the rotating administration and military service. Finally, the ten tribes sent fifty representatives each to the Council of 500. This important body prepared bills for the Assembly, supervised the administration and magistrates, and negotiated with foreign powers.

The Athenian democratic idea, as we shall see in later chapters, would endure and continue to inspire change, even violent revolutionary change, up to the present day. Nevertheless, throughout most of Western history, cultural conservatives have attacked democracy and democratic tendencies. Indeed, most Hellenes themselves admired and claimed to prefer the oligarchic Spartans to the democratic Athenians. It seemed less messy to have a more authoritarian system of government. The chaotic debate and passions of the Athenian crowd seemed undignified compared with the stoic calm of Spartan deliberation. As both city-states entered confidently into Greece's **Classical Age** (ca. 500–338 B.C.), this whole argument was nearly lost to history (see timeline 4.1). Just as these early experiments in self-government had begun, the most powerful empire of the age nearly wiped them out.

Review: *How did the Greeks attain degrees of democratic politics?*

Response:

METAMORPHOSIS

The Greeks almost vanished as a people because the emperor of the vast and powerful Persian Empire decided to crush them. Instead the Greeks metamorphosed, their word for transformed, into a political power to be reckoned with. The first stage of this transformation was their defeat of the Persian invasions. After that, however, they nearly defeated themselves. Finally, they regrouped under new leadership to invade and conquer Persia itself.

As seen in the previous chapter, by 500 B.C. Persia's power covered most of Asia Minor, where many Greeks lived. Although the supreme rule of the shah satisfied most of his diverse subjects, the independent-minded Greeks chafed under the absolutist Persian yoke. The Greeks put the conflict in simple terms: freedom versus servitude. In 499 B.C., many Greeks in Ionia rebelled against their Persian imperial masters and burned a provincial capital. The Persians simply saw arson and violent rebellion. In retaliation, Persian troops burned the Greek cities in Ionia and enslaved their residents. Then Emperor Darius found out that the rebels had received help from across the Aegean, from the Athenians and a few of their fellow Greeks. Obviously, these supporters of rebels needed to be smashed, so Darius invaded Greece. Thus began the **Persian Wars** (494–449 B.C.).

In 490 B.C., the Persian forces landed about twenty-four miles east of Athens, near the village of Marathon. The story of a messenger who ran to the Spartans for aid soon grew into the myth of the heroic marathon runner who delivered his message with his dying breath. The distance from Athens to Marathon has given us the modern Olympic race, although the Greeks themselves never ran such a long distance in sport. Surprisingly, the Athenians did not actually need help from the militaristic Spartans. The Athenians and a few allied forces of hoplites managed to push the enemy back from the beaches into the sea, even though the Persian landing force was twice their number.

Ten years later, Darius' successor, Xerxes, decided to avenge his father's defeat, especially after the Greeks sparked a revolt against Persian imperial rule in Egypt. Xerxes amassed the largest army that had ever been assembled, reportedly several hundred thousand troops from all corners of the diverse empire (and including Greeks who had submitted to his authority). To avoid the dangers of a sea-to-land invasion, he built a bridge across the narrow straits of the Dardanelles that separated Europe from Asia. As the Persian army marched into Greece, most Greeks surrendered and begged for mercy.

Others, led by Athens and Sparta, resolved to fight. Athens had built a major fleet of triremes, financed by a recently discovered silver mine. Sparta, of course, had the best hoplites, but a majority of its leaders refused to commit themselves to a common defense. So out of a possible army of eight thousand, only a small force of three hundred Spartans, joined by several hundred hoplites from other city-states such as Thebes and Thespia, advanced to hold off the advancing Persian army in the pass at Thermopylae. Mountains protected the Spartans' left flank, and the Athenian navy supported their right. After a few days of heroic resistance, some Greeks led Persian forces along a mountain path behind the Spartan line. The Persian army surrounded and slaughtered the Spartans. The outnumbered Athenian and allied navy, which had also fought well against the Persians, withdrew.

With the road now clear of opposing armies, all of Greece lay open to annihilation. The Persian army marched into Athens, only to find it abandoned. Xerxes set fire to the city and waited for his fleet to bring essential support to his troops. Then, as the Persian fleet entered the straits of Salamis, the Athenian and allied Greek navy sprang a surprise attack. Crammed into the narrow strait and confused, the Persian captains panicked. One Persian captain, Queen Artemisia of Halicarnassus, attacked her Persian allies in order to retreat. Xerxes had to withdraw. He invaded again the next year, but the Greek phalanxes defeated his army at Plataea. The puny Greeks had beaten the greatest empire in the world.

The Greeks portrayed their victory as the success of liberty and civilized virtue over oppression and barbarian vice. We might, however, exercise some caution in fully embracing their enthusiasm. Remember, the Persians had maintained a relatively tolerant empire. They had allowed the Jews to resettle Palestine. They had created general prosperity and stable rule with which many of their subjects were satisfied. If the Persians had won, some sort of Western civilization still might have developed. Perhaps the Persians could have gone on to conquer the rest of Europe. Or maybe the Romans or Phoenicians could have stopped and reversed the Persian advance. In any case, the Greek triumph did not guarantee success for their versions of liberty and virtue. They would betray those values themselves.

Buoyed by victory for the moment, the Athenians entered their brief Golden Age, which lasted only fifty years, from 480 to 430, less than one lifetime. A new literary genre was invented to celebrate: history. Two famous books frame that age: one describes the war that enabled the Golden Age, the other the war that ended it. Both are early examples of historical writing since they relate how human choices rather than divine intervention drove events. First, Herodotus of Halicarnassus wrote his *History*, a retelling of the Persian Wars, for which he is considered the father of historical writing. Herodotus developed that theme of Europe versus Asia, the Hellenes against the barbarians. Second, Thucydides wrote a history of a civil war fought by Greeks against Greeks, now known as *The Peloponnesian War*. Thucydides was an even better historian than Herodotus, insightfully examining events and evenhandedly assigning fault or merit to the historical players. He also reimagined dialogues and speeches made by leading and representative participants. Such dramatic invention is not like the fact-based writing of modern historians, but it makes for great reading.

Athens vs Everyone

To some extent, the **Peloponnesian Wars** (460–404 B.C.) inevitably followed from Greek particularism. Each *polis* pursued its own aims, usually without regard for the greater good of all Greeks. At the heart of these differences was the contradiction between the ideologies of Athens and Sparta. Democratic Athens looked outward and reveled in culture. Oligarchic Sparta gazed inward and worked at discipline. Could two such different cultures coexist in the same civilization? At first, the necessity of the Persian threat demanded it. After the defeat of the Persians at the Battles of Salamis and Plataea, many Greek *poleis* remained together in an alliance dedicated to the final defeat of Persia and the liberation of the Ionian Greeks. This **Delian League** had its original headquarters and treasury on the Aegean island of Delos. All too soon, however, the Athenians manipulated the Delian League to support their increasing domination. In most of the key battles, the Athenians bore the brunt of the fighting because they had the largest war fleet. For them, this sacrifice fully justified their new supremacy among the Greeks. Athenian culture was enormously expensive and cost far more than what the city-state of Athens produced. Thus, the Athenians extracted tribute from the other *poleis* to pay for the navy and troops. The other states submitted to Athens because they, like most people, were willing to let others fight for them.

Soon Athens had ceased to be a mere city-state—it had become an empire. In 455 B.C., the Athenians ceased all pretense about their own imperial ambitions and moved the league's treasury from Delos to Athens. Even after Persia officially made peace with the Greeks in 449 B.C., the Athenians maintained their supremacy. When member *poleis* tried to withdraw from the Delian League, Athens took over their cities. If nonmember *poleis* threatened Athenian power and prosperity in any way, Athens attacked them. Thus, Athens began to achieve political unity for the Greeks through domination. In their own eyes, they deserved to be the leaders of the Hellenes. Not for the first time would a people practice democracy at home yet imperialism abroad.

The leader of Athens toward the end of this Golden Age was Perikles (b. ca. 490–d. 429 B.C.). Perikles rose to power as the leader of the democratic faction, based on a reputation for honesty and skill in public speaking. He wanted to use the imperial wealth to subsidize the lower classes of Athens. For example, he arranged for jurors to be paid, thus enabling simple laborers to take time off from their jobs to hear cases. Those in the oligarchic faction of well-born gentlemen considered their social inferiors to be a worthless mob. The oligarchs even resented the building of the Long Wall to protect the city and its port. The expensive project may have protected the homes of vulgar commoners, but it left the oligarchs' fields outside the walls defenseless. The oligarchic faction tended to see Perikles as heading toward tyranny for himself. Since they could not attack Perikles directly, they tried to discredit him by bringing corruption charges against those close to him, the sculptor Phidias and his mistress Aspasia (a former *hetaira*, or high-class prostitute/courtesan). Both factions in Athens, though, generally supported Perikles when he proudly rebuilt the city after the Persian devastation with glorious marble temples paid for with the profits of empire.

Other Greeks opposed the Athenian supremacy. Sparta formed a rival Peloponnesian League, which saw Athenian expansionist policies as a threat to liberty as bad as that of the Persians. Corinth, though, began the First Peloponnesian War when it attacked Athens in 460 to stop its expansion. Spartans soon joined in. Neither side, however, fully committed itself to decisive victory because the Spartans were putting down revolts by helots and the Athenians were still fighting the Persians. The two sides signed a thirty-year truce in 445 B.C. It lasted only half that long, as mutual hostility between the Spartan and Athenian alliances continued to grow worse. In 431, when some of the allied states began fighting one another, each side thought the situation serious enough to declare war. Each city-state was confident in the virtue of its vision and its arms.

[handwritten margin note: DIDNT WANT ATHENS EXPANDING (or ITH Sparta)]

These Peloponnesian Wars were the greatest tragedy for Greece. At first, neither side could effectively fight the other. The Spartans dominated with infantry, but they could not breach the high, long walls enveloping Athens. The Athenians ruled the waves, but they could not land enough infantry to defeat Sparta. The strategy backfired early for the Athenians, when plague struck the crowded, besieged city in 430 B.C. It killed Perikles by the next year, and no successor shared his qualities of statesmanship.

In arrogant bids for supremacy, both Athens and Sparta attacked neutral states, thereby forcing all Hellenes to choose sides. Each side basically told other Greeks, "You can have liberty, but only on our terms." In a famous example, the *polis* of Mytiline tried to secede from the Delian League after Athens had been weakened by the plague. In 427 B.C., the recovered Athenians decided to punish the Mytilines by killing every male and selling the women and children into slavery. They had second thoughts, however, and killed only a thousand of Mytiline's men. Such political slaughters by winners on both sides piled upon the casualties from battle and disease. Class conflict also increased as Sparta supported oligarchic factions in various *poleis* and Athens encouraged democratic factions. Rather than solve their disagreements in political dialogue and vote, extremists took to violence, assault, rape, arson, and murder. So Greek political structures were attacked from both without and within.

A truce in 421 B.C. might have ended the war while the Greeks were still strong enough to recover. The Athenians, however, showed themselves to be addicted to power. Thucydides described the Athenian attack on the neutral island city-state of Melos in 416 B.C. The Melians appealed to the Athenians to leave them in peace. The Athenians demanded surrender, defending their supremacy with the harsh reality that stronger societies always dominated weaker societies. As promised, the Athenians defeated the Melian forces. Showing no mercy as they had to the Mytilines, the Athenians killed all the adult males on Melos and enslaved the women and children.

Even worse, the Athenians made a grave mistake by pushing their imperial ambitions too far in a poorly planned and unnecessary attack. Led by the young politician Alkibiades, a majority agreed to outflank the Spartans at sea by establishing power in Magna Græcia, on the island of Sicily. They used the excuse of helping an allied *polis* that had complained of oppression by the great city-state Syracuse, the key to the Western Mediterranean. In 415 B.C., the Athenians landed and found a well-prepared enemy and few allies. Instead of withdrawing or gaining a quick victory by assault, the Athenians tried to build a wall to cut off the Syracusans and starve them out. Meanwhile the Syracusans built a counterwall to isolate the Athenians, who all too soon ate and drank all their supplies. For two years, the Athenians were bogged down in a faraway land until their best warriors were killed and thousands more cruelly enslaved to die digging in quarries. Athens lacked the resources to recover from this defeat. The ostracized Alkibiades fled first to Sparta and finally to Persia. Sparta itself finally counterattacked with its own new navy, built with the help of its old enemy and new ally, Persia. The Spartans cut off supplies to Athens by both sea and land, forcing the city to surrender in 404 B.C.

Sadly, neither peace nor prosperity followed. Persia stoked the mutual suspicions of the Greeks against one another. Sparta began to act as imperialistically as Athens had. The city-states of Thebes and Corinth attacked their former ally Sparta. Then the Greek helot-slaves of Sparta successfully revolted. The once-mighty Sparta declined into an obscure village of no account. Meanwhile, Corinth and Thebes were each too weak to hold new empires of their own. Everywhere, **demagogues** (partisan public speakers) inflamed emotions and manipulated public opinion toward short-term thinking and *factionalism*, or opposing groups' refusal to cooperate with one another. Class warfare worsened. Thus, the Greek *polis* failed politically. Democracy proved to be too difficult.

A political solution to this chaos came from the north: old-fashioned kingship. The kingdom of **Macedon** lay along the mountainous northern reaches of Greek civilization. The southerners had always disregarded the rustic Macedonians as too insufficiently civilized to be true Greeks. The Macedonians did not live in cities; they spoke with poor accents; and they had been weak politically. That changed with King **Philip II** (r. 359–336 B.C.). As a youth, he had been held hostage in the *polis* of Thebes. While classical Greek culture impressed him, its political capabilities did not. He returned to Macedon, reformed the administration of his kingdom, and strengthened his army along Greek lines. He also added cavalry to defend the sides and rear of a more flexible Macedonian phalanx and improved siege machinery to take city walls. Armed with these advantages, Philip began his conquest of Greece, taking city-state after city-state. At the Battle of Chaeronea in 338 B.C., Philip's army crushed the last Greek resistance to his rule on the mainland. He was now *hegemon*, captain-general-ruler of the Greek world (from which we get the word *hegemony* for political supremacy). The **Hellenistic Age** (338–146 B.C.) supplanted the Classical Age of Greece (see map 4.1).

Philip was assassinated at the height of power, perhaps because his wife, Olympia, and his son, Alexander, were behind his murder. The new twenty-year-old King **Alexander** III (r. 336–323 B.C.) soon gained the title "the Great" for his conquest of much of the known world. As one of the greatest generals who ever lived, Alexander carried out his father's proposal to attack the age-old enemy, Persia. His Macedonian and Greek armies routed the Persian forces in Asia Minor, liberated Egypt from Persian imperial power to put it under his own, and then swept through

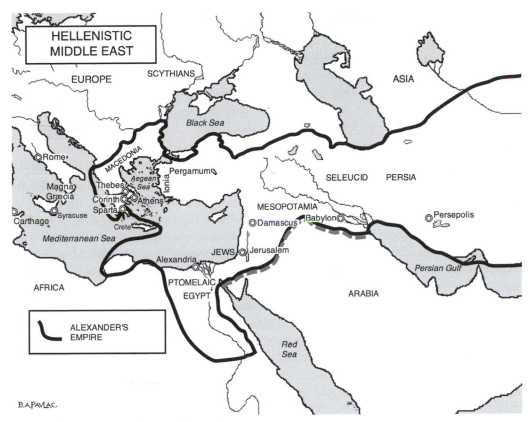

Map 4.1. Hellenistic Middle East

Mesopotamia to take Iran itself. So awed were people, and he himself, by his success that ***deification*** began, the belief that a person became a god. Alexander did not discourage the trend and may have believed in his divinity himself.

Whether Alexander "the Great" was god, emperor, general, or fool, his soldiers followed him farther eastward into the foothills of Afghanistan and into the Indus River valley. Only the fierce resistance by the vast populations of the Indian Subcontinent finally allowed his soldiers to convince the not quite thirty-three-year-old Alexander to turn back toward Greece. On the way, after a night of heavy drinking, Alexander fell into a fever. A few days later, whether from too much alcohol, infection, or poison, the conqueror lay dead.

Review: *How did the Greeks enter a brief Golden Age, and how did it collapse?*

Response:

THE CULTURAL CONQUEST

Opinions about the rise of Macedonian power stir controversy. Critics of Philip and Alexander condemn their use of conquest, destruction of democracy, and overemphasis on the cult of personality. Supporters praise their heroism, reform of government, and unification of Greeks among themselves and with other peoples. Alexander had even encouraged his Greek soldiers to marry Persian women. Regardless, Philip and Alexander's brief reigns changed history for the Greeks and all their neighbors. The Hellenistic Age saw Greek power reach diverse peoples across the ancient world. The great cultures of Egypt, Mesopotamia, and Persia collapsed before the armies of Alexander.

Although the political unity of Alexander's empire died with him, the Greeks stayed on as regional rulers. They founded new *poleis* and colonies of Greeks throughout their kingdoms. Greek became the common language, and Greek practices dominated economics, society, and the arts. The conquered peoples adapted to Greek civilization in a process called **hellenization**. Eventually, being Greek became a cultural attitude, not solely a physical descent from the forefather Hellas.

The classic political democracy, though, was not part of this expansion, since democracy lay in ruins. Ending the give and take of political debate, Alexander imposed absolutism. Like other Middle-Eastern semidivine potentates, the Hellenistic kings employed deification with elaborate rituals emphasizing their similarity to the gods. Thus, the manner of "Oriental despots" entered Western civilization. Alexander's successors were generals who seized power and set up dynasties. In the constant tension between independent local control and centralized authority, the city-state vanished under the Hellenistic monarchs.

Alexander's brief empire fell apart into three great power blocs. One general took Macedon and from there tried to impose Macedonian rule on the Greeks of the south. Another, Ptolemy, seized Egypt, whose rich farmlands and ancient heritage provided the most secure and long-lasting power base. A third, Seleucis, controlled the riches of Asia Minor and ancient Persia. The Macedonian, Ptolemaic, and Seleucid dynasties dominated the Western Mediterranean and Middle East for about two hundred years, until supplanted yet again by other rulers.

While the Hellenistic kingdoms failed to establish enduring political unity, they fostered a cultural success that endured for many more centuries. The Greeks lost political choices, but they gained a role in history that would have amazed even the most optimistic Athenian of the Golden Age. Greek culture became the standard for much of the ancient world as well as the foundation of Western civilization.

Most of that culture reflected Athens and its Golden Age of fifty years after the Persian destruction of 480 B.C. The Athenians rebuilt their ruined city in shining marble. The crowning achievement was the temple atop the acropolis, the Parthenon, dedicated to the city's namesake, Athena, the goddess of wisdom (see figure 4.1). It pleases the eye, perfectly proportioned and harmonious, while its design contains nary a perfectly straight line in the Euclidian sense. The Athenians decorated the Parthenon with the most anatomically correct sculptures done by anyone in the West up to that point (although they usually painted the figures in

Figure 4.1. The remains of the Temple of the Olympian Zeus, with the Parthenon on the Acropolis of Athens looming beyond.

garish colors that would strike us as strange and would horrify later art critics who had learned to admire the shimmering white of marble).[1] The *realism* and *naturalism*, mixed with a poised serenity, characterized the art of the Classical Age.

The effort spent on the temple of the Parthenon demonstrated again how religion was the heart of Greek society. The Greek myths and legends showed the **Olympian gods** to be uninspiring from a moral or spiritual sense. The gods followed *anthropomorphism*; they not only looked like humans but also behaved like them, usually at their worst. For example, the ruler of the gods, Zeus, ruled as a petty tyrant with his thunderbolts. He was notorious for his many affairs with goddesses, mortal women, and even the occasional boy. Likewise, the beauty of Aphrodite, the goddess of love, usually ruined men's lives. The gods' quarrels with one another spilled over into human affairs, and they quickly avenged insults to their divinity. Their divine interference is best recounted in Homer's epic poems, *The Iliad* and *The Odyssey*, mentioned earlier. The latter tells of a Greek king trying to return home after the Trojan War. Because he offends the gods while trying to survive, they throw many obstacles in his way: sirens, cyclopes, sorceresses, and even suitors for his faithful wife, Penelope. The legendary Trojan War itself had

---

1. The Parthenon survived largely intact for almost two thousand years. In A.D. 1687, during a war between Venice and the Ottoman Empire, the Turks stored ammunition in the temple, and a direct hit blew off the roof. In the early 1800s the British Lord Elgin took to England many of the sculptures, which had been neglected by Turkish officials. The Greeks and the British continue to argue about returning the originals.

started because three goddesses fought over who was the most beautiful. Despite, or perhaps because of, this divinely trashy behavior, the Greek myths conveyed a rich and deeply textured heritage. How the human spirit rose above fate and the cruelty of the gods, not the gods themselves, inspires us even today.

The Greeks revered their gods and ancestors by forming restrictive cults that kept outsiders out of each *polis*. Indeed, each city was dedicated to a deity, who might also have been believed to be a parent of semidivine heroic founders. **Civic cults** structured the worship of the city's gods in particular and all gods (out of concern to neglect no divine power). The *polis* organized religious ceremonies as a political responsibility. As mentioned before, the Greeks had no priestly caste or class. Instead, every citizen accepted an obligation to ensure that the civic rites of appeasing and worshipping the gods were performed properly. Consulting the gods through **oracles** provided guidance for everyday activities and major political decisions. The city fathers brought the cultic practices into their own homes by tending sacred fires (of which the Olympic torch is an offshoot) and sharing sacred meals.

Some Classical Greeks soon turned away from the austere formality of civic cults and the lack of spirituality in the Greek pantheon. They instead embraced **mystery cults**, which were centered on rituals of fertility, death, and resurrection. We know little about the worship that focused on deities such as Demeter or Dionysius, since their followers kept most of their activities secret. The cults seemed to promise a conquest of death. Although the cults were popular privately, every citizen still upheld the civic rituals in public. All governing was performed in a religious context.

Little in these religious cults, however, offered much of a guide for the moral or ethical decisions that always have been at the heart of politics. For answers, the Greeks took one important step beyond religion with their invention of philosophy. The word *philosophy* is from the Greek for "love of wisdom." Philosophy began in the sixth century B.C. in Ionia, where some men began to wonder about the nature of the universe. Compared with modern scientific investigation (explained in chapter 11), the Greek theories about how the universe was based on air or water seem rather silly. But they were progress. Instead of relying on myth for explanation, these philosophers began to apply the human mind. The concept that the human mind can comprehend the natural world, *rationalism*, became a key component of Western civilization.

The philosophers who examined geometry or the composition of matter were soon joined by others who speculated about humans. By the fifth century, the so-called Sophists ("wise men") had started to create ideas about moral behavior that are still with us today. They were itinerant teachers who, for a fee, educated Greeks about the ways of the world. Several distinct schools of thought competed for attention. Skepticism doubted knowing anything for certain. **Hedonism** pursued pleasure as the highest good. **Cynicism** abandoned all moral restraints to gain power over other people. Many Sophists seemed to offer methods for becoming wealthy without worrying about moral scruples. Against them, a trinity of Greek philosophers offered alternative views for human action.

First, **Socrates** (b. 469–d. 399 B.C.) argued against the materialism of the Sophists. As he strolled through the streets and plazas of Athens, Socrates constantly asked questions of his fellow citizens. Moreover, through questioning, he tried to give those who would engage in his conversation the chance to learn. This is the Socratic method. Socrates claimed to hold no set of doctrines he wanted to teach; he only desired to seek the truth. Indeed, he said that he knew little at all. When the Delphic Oracle had answered someone's query as to who was the wisest man in Greece with the answer "Socrates," the philosopher was at first puzzled. Then he realized that his self-description ("the only thing I know is that I know nothing") explained the oracle. He concluded that true wisdom was self-knowledge. Therefore, Socrates advocated that every person should, according to the Delphic Oracle's motto, "know thyself."

Amid the conflict of the Peloponnesian Wars, the trial of the philosopher Socrates highlights the Greeks' failure to live up to high ideals. In 399 B.C., as the Athenians tried to recover from their defeat by Sparta, a new democratic leadership charged the oligarchic Socrates with two crimes: blasphemy and corruption of the young. For one day, a jury of five hundred citizens who had been chosen by lot heard the arguments, where plaintiffs and defendants represented themselves. Socrates defended himself of the first charge by openly mocking the nonsense of Greek mythology. How could someone believe in gods who did so many silly and cruel things to humans? He defended himself against the second charge by saying he only encouraged young people to become critical of their elders and society. Socrates gladly saw himself as an annoyance, a gadfly, provoking and reproaching the leaders of Athens. The jury found him guilty. Consequently, when he wryly suggested his own punishment be a state pension, they sentenced him to death. Obedient to the laws of his city, Socrates committed suicide by drinking hemlock, a slow-acting paralytic poison. This political trial illuminated how democracy failed to adapt to changing circumstances.

Second, Socrates' pupil **Plato** (b. 427–d. 347 B.C.) explored new philosophical directions. Since Plato wrote his philosophy in the form of dialogues conducted by his master Socrates, it is sometimes difficult to define where Socrates' views end and Plato's begin. Still, Plato offered the doctrine of ideas, or *idealism*, as an answer for the nature of truth. In his famous allegory of the cave, Plato suggested that our reality is like people chained in a cave who can see only strange shadows and hear only odd noises. But if a person were to break free and climb out of the cave, though blinded by sunlight, he would confront the genuine reality. Actual forms in our world only poorly imitate real universal ideas. How could the person who sees truth then describe it to those still inside the cave, who do not share such an experience? Plato saw the philosopher's task as describing ultimate reality.

Third, Plato's student **Aristotle** (b. 384–d. 322 B.C.) turned away from the more abstract metaphysics of his teacher to refocus on the natural world and people's place in it. Thus, he studied nature and wrote books on matters from zoology to meteorology that would define scientific views for centuries (even if many were ill informed by our modern standards). Aristotle's rules of logic covered politics, literature, and ethics. He used *syllogisms*, called **dialectic logic**, where two pieces of known information are compared in order to reach a new knowledge. It was the most powerful intellectual tool of its day, and indeed long after. Finally, Aristotle promoted the "golden mean" of living a life of moderation.

Altogether, these philosophers helped to establish an idea called ***humanism***. As this book will use it, humanism means that the world is to be understood by and for humans. A phrase by the philosopher Protagoras, that "man is the measure of things," embodies the approach. (And the Greeks usually meant specifically "man," considering females to be an inferior form of the idealized male.) According to humanism, our experiences, perceptions, and practices are important and useful in dealing with life, here and now. This belief has repeatedly offered an alternative to religious ideas emphasizing life after death.

One of the great humanistic triumphs of Greek culture was its literature. Many educated people knew the epic poems of *The Iliad* and *The Odyssey* by heart. Lyric poetry also was quite popular. Then, as today, lyric poetry meant shorter, personal poetry about feelings, rather than stories. In Greece, all poetry was literally said, or sung, while someone played the lyre, a stringed instrument, or a flute. Many Greeks declared Sappho to be one of the greatest lyric poets. Instead, more people now know her name as standing for female same-sex love, ***sapphism***; the alternate term ***lesbianism*** also is connected to Sappho, namely from the island where she had her school, Lesbos. As far as literary historians can tell, though, she loved both men and women. Her poetry has come down to us in only a few fragments (much of it destroyed later by Christians offended by her sensuality).

When the Greeks combined literature and performance, they invented **theater** (see figure 4.2). Like politics, theater had a religious context in Greek culture. Ritual stories of the gods turned into festivals, where actors dramatized the poetry with voice, movement, music, and even special effects. The most famous of the last is the *deus ex machina* (Latin for "god from the machine"), where a tangled plot could be instantly resolved by divine intervention, an actor playing a god lowered onto the stage from above. The most popular and important plays were tragedies, where the protagonist of the story fails, often due to pride (in Greek, *hybris*). The most famous tragedy is *Oedipus Tyrannos* ("Clubfoot the Tyrant," usually called *Oedipus Rex*). By trying to do what is right, the title character causes suffering. During the day on which the play takes place, Oedipus reviews his past. He has left his home of Corinth because he heard a prophecy that he would be responsible for the death of his parents. After killing the monstrous sphinx by answering her question, Oedipus has taken over nearby Thebes, whose ruler was recently killed by bandits. Oedipus discovers in the course of the play that he was actually adopted, had killed his own father, and had married his mother. She hangs herself, and he blinds himself and goes into exile.

Performances of several tragedies would be balanced by a comedy. Some Greek

Figure 4.2.   The theater outside the Greek city of Miletus in Ionia lies poised for the next performance more than a thousand years after its last.

comedies were merely bawdy farces, but others rose to transcendent political satire. For example, *Lysistrata* by Aristophanes, first performed during the Peloponnesian Wars, managed to harpoon both male aggression and ego. The heroine of the title successfully organizes the women of two warring *poleis* to go on a sexual strike until their men stop fighting.

It often happens that enduring culture is produced during brutal war. As rival Greek kings too often fought over their shares of Alexander's empire, the ruling Greek elites fostered a new phase of creativity called Hellenistic civilization (338–146 B.C.). While critics often characterize Hellenistic culture as less glorious than Athens' Golden Age, elites spread that age's classic works along with fostering their own new products. The cities became cosmopolitan, growing vibrant with peoples from many diverse ethnic groups. Alexander founded several and named them after himself, such as the most successful Hellenistic city, Alexandria, located at the mouth of the Nile. Streets laid out on grids connected places of education and entertainment: schools, theaters, stadiums, and libraries. Commerce in the Eurasian-African trade networks supported luxuries. Sculpture conveyed more emotion and character than the cool calm of the Classical Age. Greek philosophers who studied nature gained enduring knowledge in astronomy, mechanics, and medicine.

The two most popular philosophies to come out of the Hellenistic period reflected pessimism about the future, however. *Epicureanism* sought to find the best way of life to avoid pain in a cruel world. Epicureans taught that the good life lay in withdrawal into a pleasant garden to discuss the meaning of life with friends. In contrast, *stoicism* called for action. Stoics accepted the world's cruelty but called on everyone to dutifully reduce conflict and promote the brotherhood of mankind (women not included, as usual). This duty should be pursued even if one failed, which was likely.

The Greeks ultimately failed largely because of fighting among themselves, not because of external enemies. A few of their city-states managed to defeat the world's greatest empire. They briefly held supreme power over masses of Asians and North Africans. The Greeks, however, were too few and too divided to permanently dominate these peoples. Although they contributed many high ideals, they betrayed them just as often. The Greek heritage of art, literature, and philosophy enriched the peoples of the ancient world, as it continues to do for many in the world today. Nevertheless, democracy fell to imperialism; imperial unity fell to particularism; and the intellectual honesty of Socrates fell to fear. The Greeks' cultural arrogance condemned them to become marginalized instead of being the ongoing bearers of history. The next founders of Western civilization would soon conquer most of what Alexander had and add yet more to the foundations of the West.

Review: What Greek culture expanded through the ancient West?

Response:

CHAPTER 5

Imperium Romanum

The Romans, 753 B.C. to A.D. 300

While Greeks quarreled themselves into fragmentation, another people, the Romans, were proving much more adept at power politics. The Romans forged the most important and enduring empire of the ancient world. This achievement is all the more impressive since Rome started out as just another small city-state. Roman success can, perhaps, be attributed to their tendency to be even more vicious and cruel than the Greeks, although, as seen in the preceding chapter, the Hellenes could be fairly nasty themselves. The Romans' empire rose through military supremacy, cultural diversity, and political innovation (see map 5.1). The glory of the *Imperium Romanum*, the **Roman Empire**, still appeals to the historical imagination.

WORLD CONQUEST IN SELF-DEFENSE

The city-state of **Rome** was, at first, small and surrounded by enemies. According to Rome's own mythological history, refugees from the destroyed city of Troy in

Map 5.1. Roman Europe

Asia Minor had fled westward, eventually settling in the province of Latium, which was halfway down the western coast of the Italian Peninsula. It was there, according to the story, that a she-wolf raised two twin brothers, Romulus and Remus. As adults, they argued about the founding of a new city. In one version, in the year 753 B.C. Romulus killed his brother Remus and named the new city after himself. Thus Rome was founded on fratricide. The Romans were proud of their violent inheritance; they themselves later became some of the best practitioners of state-sponsored violence in the history of the world.

Whatever truth may lie in the myth of Romulus, Rome's actual founders took advantage of a good location. The Tiber River provided easy navigation to the sea, yet the city was far enough inland to avoid regular raids by pirates. The city also lay along north-south land routes through central Italy. Hence, the founders had ready contact with nearby stronger societies and began to borrow from them liberally. The early Romans cobbled together a hodgepodge culture, learning much from the Greeks who lived in the cities of Magna Græcia in southern Italy and Sicily. The Romans borrowed the Greek Olympian gods and goddesses, usually giving the deities new names better suited to the Romans' language of **Latin**. Another important influence on Roman culture was the neighbors to the north, the Etruscans (who have lent their name to Tuscany). Actually, for much of Rome's early history, the city itself was so weak that Etruscan kings ruled the Romans.

Roman myth supplied another violent story about winning freedom from the Etruscans. According to the legendary history, Sextus, the son of an Etruscan king, lusted after Lucretia, the wife of a Roman aristocrat. When the husband was away from home one day, Sextus demanded that Lucretia have sex with him. If she did not, he promised to kill both her and a male servant. He promised he would then put them in bed together and report that he had found and rightfully killed them for shameful adultery and violation of class distinctions. So Lucretia gave in to Sextus. When her husband and his companions returned home, Lucretia confessed what had happened before stabbing herself in the heart to remove her shame. The outraged Romans organized a rebellion and threw the Etruscans out of their city. Thus, rape and suicide inspired Roman political freedom.

This charming tale passed down through the generations probably has as little fact behind it as the tale of Romulus and Remus. For the Romans, though, this myth proudly showed once again how violence and honor were woven into their history. Moreover, historical and archaeological evidence indicates that around 500 B.C. the Romans had indeed won freedom from Etruscan domination.

What the Romans then did with their new freedom was something remarkable: they chose a democratic form of government. Technically, the Romans founded a **republic**, where citizens chose other citizens to represent them. So, like the Greeks, they had no kings, although unlike the Greeks, they did not require all citizens to hold public office. The most important government institution was the **Senate**, a council of elders who protected the unwritten constitution and were involved in all major decisions. Initially, the Senate had three hundred members who served for life and were supposed to embody the collective wisdom of the state. As the head of their city-state, the Romans also elected two consuls as administrators. These two ran the city government, commanded the army, spent the money, and exercised judicial power. The two consuls held office at the same time, and each had veto power over the other. The consuls served only a year, and only two terms were permitted for any individual in a lifetime. Many other magistrate positions (praetors, questors, censors, lictors) were similarly limited. Thus, the Senate and People of Rome (using the initials SPQR) began an elaborate system of **checks and balances**, where, according to their constitutional structure, no single individual or family could gain too much power.

Officially, all male citizens voted and held official government positions, while privately, a handful of families actually made the major decisions behind the scenes. Roman society was divided into two main groups: the aristocrats (a few dozen families called **patricians**) and the free-born peasants (called **plebians**). In the early centuries of the Roman Republic, patricians controlled all the political positions. Indeed, someone could hardly hold office without patrician wealth since government service was unpaid. After the Romans reformed their military along lines similar to the Greek phalanx, however, male peasants replaced aristocrats as the essential warriors of Rome. Inevitably, as patricians declined in number and, more especially, in significance on the battlefield, the plebians wanted a larger say in government. Their demands followed the Greek example of political change following military innovation.

A key event that pushed these military changes was Rome's near destruction by the **Celts** or **Gauls**. These peoples spread through primitive Europe from the sixth through the fourth centuries B.C. Many eventually settled in what is now France and the British Isles, retaining their ethnic identity to the present. In the course of their ancient travels, they stormed down the Italian Peninsula, plundering and laying waste. They attacked Rome itself in 390 B.C., occupying and destroying much of the city. Only the last fortress on the Capitoline hill managed to hold out, barely saved from a surprise attack by the honking of disturbed geese. The Romans then regrouped and drove off the Celts. This Celtic invasion wounded the Roman world-view. The Romans decided to make their nation so powerful that it would never be conquered again, however briefly. For eight hundred years they succeeded in this goal—a good run for any empire.

The key military innovation that enabled such success was the Roman **legion**. The Romans improved upon the Greek phalanx, which they must have encountered in Magna Græcia. The legion used smaller, more maneuverable groups of men who marched in formation but threw their spears at the enemy. Then, in the clash of close combat, the legionaries stabbed their foes with their short swords. Supported by cavalry and siege weapons, the Romans replaced the Greeks as the best warriors of antiquity.

So, while the city-state used aggression against its neighbors, its own citizens sought more representative government where disagreements could be worked out peacefully. The military participation by the plebians as troops for the burgeoning empire unlocked their access to power. The peasants threatened to strike rather than fight. The aristocratic patricians, numerically incapable of defending Rome on their own, began to make concession after concession. Patricians created the political office of the **tribunes**, who protected the plebian citizens from aristocratic magistrates who unjustly intimidated plebians. Tribunician authority was one of the broadest and most powerful in the state. Patricians also soon allowed the plebians a major political body of their own: the Assembly of Tribes. By 287 B.C., the Assembly gained the power to make binding laws, declare war and peace, and elect judges. Patricians finally allowed wealthy plebians to become magistrates as well. Thus, more checks and balances perfected the ideal republican government of the Senate and People of Rome (SPQR).

Although the Romans developed republican government at home, they had to decide how to treat their new subject peoples in what had become an empire. By 250 B.C., the Roman legions took over most of Italy, including "foreigners" such as the Samnians, who were actually more native to the peninsula than the Romans were. The secret to Roman success was not pure military force but a good dose of inclusiveness, which had been so foreign to the Greeks. The Romans offered a ***romanization*** policy to many of the survivors in their new conquests. The vanquished were allowed to become more like Romans instead of beaten people. Locals had the option of keeping local government and even their traditional gods and religion. All they had to do was accept Roman control of foreign affairs, contribute taxes, and provide military service. While originally only Roman citizens held the political power of voting and holding important offices, their subject peoples soon gained these privileges as well, especially as they intermarried with Roman families. Slowly, naturally, Roman culture took over as other peoples throughout the Italian Peninsula were romanized. Many peoples gave up their own languages and adopted Latin, accepted the sensible Roman laws, worshipped the Roman deities, and even espoused Roman virtues like responsibility and seriousness.

The city-state of Rome became the model throughout its empire (in fact, if not yet in name). The center of Roman society was the city, even though most people lived and worked in the countryside as farmers. Where cities existed, the Romans transformed them; where cities did not exist, the Romans built them. Most of these cities were small, with only a few thousand inhabitants each. The heart of each city was the **forum**, a market surrounded by government buildings and temples. The public bathhouse was the most essential institution of civilized life—the Romans were clean people. For other entertainment they built theaters for plays, amphitheaters for the brutal slaughter of beasts and gladiators, and, most popular of all, stadiums for the chariot races. Architectural innovations such as the arch and the dome, as well as the use of concrete as a construction material, allowed Roman cities to be built taller, more graceful, and more grand than any other cities in the ancient world. The dome of the Pantheon has inspired architects ever since (figure 5.1). Aqueducts brought in fresh water from distant hills and springs (figure 5.2). The Roman roads were so well designed that some, such as the Appian Way from Rome to Naples, are still being driven on today. While the roads were meant to serve the military first, commerce and civil communication naturally followed and flourished. Roman roads were so well built and widespread that "all roads lead to Rome" became a byword for their civilization.

As the Romans marched along these roads, they bore their laws to other peoples. Roman law not only supported one of the most sophisticated governments of

Figure 5.1.   Light shining through the oculus of the dome of the Pantheon in Rome.

Figure 5.2. Roman civilization relied on clean, fresh water, here brought into Segovia in Spain by a tall aqueduct.

the ancient world but also influenced other legal systems for centuries to come. The founding point was around 450 B.C., when the plebians insisted on a codification of laws, the Twelve Tables. Roman magistrates defined law for everyone's benefit. Clarity about the laws protected citizens against abusive government. Both the patrician and the plebian could appeal arbitrary enforcement of rules by a magistrate.

Roman law became a flexible system that recognized political change. Divine law, such as what Hammurabi or Moses received, could not be changed except by the gods. But the Romans began to invent the idea of **natural law**. This theory accepted that deities designed nature and humans to act in a certain way, but it proposed that human understanding of nature could change as we learn more. Through practice and experience, humans could create laws that were in better harmony with the natural order, consequently shaping a more just society. The Romans thought that if a law did not work, then a new one should be fashioned. Legal decisions and judgments were supposed to be founded on facts and rational argumentation, not divine intervention. As such, Roman law became the basis for many European legal systems today.

The Romans also established that all citizens should be treated equally by the law (with the usual exemption of women, of course). Expanding rights of citizenship broke down the barriers between upper and lower classes, ethnic Romans and others. Citizenship granted important status and political participation (although, of course, while women might be citizens and had some rights over property, the political system shut them out). To manage this growing and complicated system, the Romans also invented professional helpers in the law: lawyers. Roman lawyers had as bad a reputation in their own time as many lawyers have today. They were seen as greedy, loud, and annoying. Regardless, lawyers were essential to the smooth functioning of civil society. The Roman legal and political systems allowed people to have more of a voice and choice in politics than in most other societies in the ancient world. A republican government designed for a city-state, however, found itself strained as it expanded ever further. The romanization policy could not resolve increasing tensions within Rome's imperial rule.

Review: *How did Rome grow from a small city-state to a vast multicultural empire?*

Response:

THE PRICE OF POWER

Despite the admirable legal innovation, civil society in Rome nearly collapsed in the third century B.C. because of the Roman addiction to world domination. Their military success fed the Romans' appetite for conquest. The next hill always hid some possible danger to Rome, and such a threat forever justified another expedition. Soon the Romans decided not to stop at the water's edge of the Italian Peninsula and set their eyes on Sicily. This target, however, led to a life-or-death crisis for Rome.

As seen in Chapter 4, the Phoenicians had been Middle Eastern competitors with the Greeks in forming colonies across the Mediterranean. Their major city had become **Carthage**, located on the north coast of Africa across the sea from Sicily. Phoenician and Greek colonies in Sicily controlled the central Mediterranean, as the Athenians had recognized during the Peloponnesian Wars. Greek cities complaining of Phoenician oppression gave the Romans the opportunity to intervene in the name of defending liberty. The Phoenicians could not allow the Romans expansion onto the island. The Romans were determined. So, from 264 to 146 B.C., several generations of Romans fought the **Punic Wars** (named after the Latin word for the Phoenicians). *Rome & Phoenicians = did not want R. expansion*

The most memorable stage of the Punic Wars was the invasion of Italy by the Carthaginian General **Hannibal**. In 218 B.C., he marched his armies (including war elephants) from Carthaginian territories in the Iberian Peninsula over the Pyrenees and Alps to enter Italy from the north. This brilliant feat of military command and logistics astonished the Romans. Unfortunately for Carthage, Hannibal failed to seize his most important objective, Rome itself. He did rampage up and down the peninsula, causing great fear and considerable damage, but was unable to inflict a fatal defeat on Rome. This delay in capturing Rome gave the Romans the chance to learn from Hannibal's strategy and tactics. They counterattacked by invading Africa in 203. Hannibal returned to defend his own capital city of Carthage. The next year they fought at Zama. The Romans defeated the fearsome Phoenician elephants by frightening them with trumpets or letting them pass through the lines without opposition. The legions surrounded the rest of the Carthaginian army and forced Hannibal to surrender.

The Phoenicians, severely weakened by this defeat, offered no further threat to Roman expansion. Within only a few years, though, demagogues in Rome began to chant the slogan *"Carthago delenda est"* ("Carthage must be destroyed"). The Romans finally carried out that final devastation in 146 B.C., tearing down the city and sowing the fields with salt so that nothing would grow again. The cultural liberties Romans had allowed to other defeated societies were not permitted here. Potential Phoenician contributions to Roman civilization were rejected, its literature and culture erased. Rome wielded undisputed mastery over the Western Mediterranean.

In the same year, coincidentally, the Romans gained a strategic foothold in the Eastern Mediterranean. Since the collapse of Alexander's empire, the Greeks had been fighting among one another. The Macedonian kingdom had continuously tried to dominate the Greeks in the southern tip of the Balkan Peninsula, but supremacy remained elusive. Some Greeks, seeking help against the Macedonians, began to invite the Romans in as mediators, then as protectors. Soon the Romans stayed as rulers. Many Greeks accepted the Romans, who brought order and peace. Those Greeks who resisted were conquered and enslaved. In 146 B.C., the destruction of Corinth, the last independent Greek city-state in the Balkans, marked the end of resistance to Roman rule. The Romans were well on their way to declaring the Mediterranean *Mare Nostrum* ("Our Sea").

The Romans did not notice at first that their victories came at great cost, as expanding an empire so often does. The weak spots in Rome's society grew worse. One great flaw was the classic economic recipe for social disaster: the cliché of "the rich get richer while the poor get poorer." The vast and productive new provinces fell under the exploitation of the aristocrats of Rome. As these patricians plundered the distant lands, discontent spread abroad while envy arose at home. One of the great new sources of wealth was the enslavement of the defeated peoples, who were forced to work on large plantations (called *latifundia*). The plantation owners began to grow cash crops such as olives and wine, which outsold the produce of simple farmers. Before the Punic Wars, the farmer-plebians had been the backbone of Roman society and the army. Afterward, economic competition led rich slave owners who were profiting from slave labor to grow richer while free peasants lost their farms. These unemployed masses, forming the new social class of the **proletariat**, migrated to the cities, especially to Rome itself.

This mass urban migration shredded the social fabric of urban life. To keep the poor occupied, the patricians created an expensive welfare system known as "bread and circuses." They handed out grain (the bread) and provided entertainments (the circuses—meaning chariot races on which people gambled). Many other Romans increasingly complained that traditional values were vanishing. Effeminate Greek ways were becoming more fashionable, especially the Greek custom of older men closely bonding with adolescent boys. Meanwhile the Roman wealthy noble equestrian class (named after its members' ability to afford horses for cavalry service) resented the aristocratic patricians. Despite having become wealthy from the burgeoning trans-Mediterranean trade, their modest family connections and nonpatrician status excluded equestrians from the true mechanisms of power.

By the late second century B.C., these social tensions sparked civil wars that lasted for the next hundred years. In such times of emergency, Roman constitutional law provided for tough solutions. For example, the Senate might appoint a sole dictator, who did not have to worry about another consul second-guessing his decisions during a six-month term. Or the Romans practiced **proscription** to remove overly powerful politicians. When a politician's name was posted on the *rostrum*, the speaking platform of the tribunes, he was declared an outlaw. Anyone could kill him without penalty—a fate rather more harsh than the Athenian ostracism and exile. Meanwhile, the patricians divided into two factions. Those called *optimates* united to preserve oligarchy with as few social or economic reforms as possible. Those called *populares* advocated democracy, a broader political base, and land reform.

Two patrician brothers in the *populares* party, **Tiberius** and **Gaius Gracchus**, tried to help the plebians, as the tyrants had once done in Greece for the commoners. In doing so, the Gracchi brothers used extralegal violence to their advantage. In turn, the rival *optimates* led mobs to kill them both in 133 B.C. Their deaths meant that the previous system of democratic politics, where checks and balances peacefully compensated for class differences, fell to fights over tyranny.

Violence soon became the routine means to solve political problems. A new permanent standing army only fueled bloodshed. Rome had risen to regional supremacy based on the idea of citizen-soldiers, peasants who would serve for set terms in an emergency. Late in the second century, imperial defense and the danger of slave revolts required an army of recruits who served their whole working lives. Many recruits came from newly conquered peoples who had not been fully converted to republican-style politics. This professionalization led to soldiers becoming more loyal to their commanders than to the idea of Rome. Soon, generals such as Marius and Sulla began to fight one another over the wealth and power of the empire, while soldiers and citizens paid with their lives. Dictators stayed in power for the long term instead of only during a crisis. Proscription became a regular practice to eliminate hundreds of enemies rather than a rare tool to maintain a constitutional balance. The ability to intimidate and kill mattered more than the talent to persuade. The Roman Republic staggered from bloody crisis to crisis.

Review: *How did Rome's conquests end in a long civil war?*

Response:

THE ABSOLUTIST SOLUTION

Only the collapse of the democratic-republican government and the establishment of absolutism resolved Rome's political and social crises. One politician and general, **Julius Caesar** (b. 100–d. 44 B.C.), almost succeeded in restoring order. Caesar rose to prominence and popularity as a leader of the *populares*. In 62 B.C. he formed the First Triumvirate, a three-man coalition with two other powerful Romans, Pompey and Crassus. They briefly restored peace to the political system.

Caesar's ambition was to surpass his two partners, who had gained reputations as generals. Pompey already had a solid reputation as a commander, having conquered Hellenistic kingdoms in Asia Minor and the province of Judaea, thus bringing the homeland of the Jews into the growing Roman Empire. Crassus had crushed the revolt led by Spartacus, a free man who had fought in Rome's army only to be enslaved to fight as a gladiator. In 73–71 B.C., Spartacus and his army of rebel gladiators and other slaves killed their masters and escaped. Crassus defeated the slave army and crucified more than six thousand of them along the Appian Way. Caesar sought to outdo his two colleagues by conquering northern Gaul.

Since their near-conquest of the city in 390 B.C., the Gauls had done little to harm the Romans for several centuries. The Celts and Germans who lived in the Gaul of Caesar's time were civilized, comparably prosperous, and even wore pants (while Roman men still wore skirts). They already interacted with the Græco-Roman Mediterranean culture, supplying agricultural products and slaves captured in wars between the tribes. Several tribes had even agreed to defense treaties with Rome. When the Helvetii (ancestors of the modern Swiss) tried to move through a territory of a tribe allied with Rome, those Gauls asked for Roman help.

Caesar seized the opportunity to expand Roman dominion, enhance his reputation, and win wealth (see map 5.1). For eight years, from 59 to 50 B.C., Caesar exploited the fighting among different Celtic tribes to conquer Gaul (and even briefly to invade Britain). Although the integration of the Celtic Gauls into the Roman Empire would take several generations, Caesar wrote a book about his "successful" conquest, *The Gallic War*, to make sure people realized what a good leader he was.

With his fame established, Caesar turned to his real aim: leadership in Rome. He declared his intentions of becoming sole dictator by leading his army from Gaul into Italy in 49 B.C. His crossing of the river Rubicon (now a metaphor for an irrevocable decision) set him at war with his former allies and the Roman constitution itself. Inevitably, might made right. By 46 B.C. Caesar had defeated his rivals and become dictator. He built on his success by adding Egypt to Rome's dominions through his intervention on behalf of its queen, Cleopatra, who had been quarreling with her brother over sharing power. Caesar's sexual and political alliance with Cleopatra gave him control over Egypt, the breadbasket of the Mediterranean.

Like the better Greek tyrants, Julius Caesar did not rule solely to satisfy his own lust for power; he also addressed real problems. He carried out land reform, especially by rewarding his veterans with confiscated property. He extended Roman citizenship to conquered peoples in Gaul and Spain, improved the administration, lowered taxes, and built public works such as aqueducts, baths, and temples. He even made sense out of the seasons through his reform of the calendar. Caesar's **Julian calendar** gave us the basic system of twelve months and a periodic leap year that we use now (although the Roman September through December were their seventh through tenth months, as their Latin translations indicate).

Caesar's enemies either envied his success or feared that he might make himself king. The Romans had disliked kingship ever since they had rebelled against Etruscan kings at the beginning of their republic. For some, a monarchy undermined the core of Roman identity. So a handful of senators plotted to assassinate Caesar. During the ides (the middle of a month) of March in 44 B.C., as he entered the Senate's meeting place, they stabbed him twenty-three times.

Yet this political murder still did not resolve the problem of how to govern Rome. Immediately, another war broke out over Caesar's legacy, about who could inherit his mantle. Caesar's assassins were quickly discredited and killed. Among his allies, the leading candidate was at first Marc Antony, Caesar's lieutenant (known today by the speech that Shakespeare put in his mouth: "Friends, Romans, countrymen, lend me your ears. I come to bury Caesar, not to praise him"). But Marc Antony had fatefully taken up with Caesar's paramour Cleopatra. Many Romans disapproved of the queen of Egypt, who was too Greek and too female. Instead, Caesar's grandnephew and adopted heir, **Octavian**, won the struggle for power. In the course of several years of warfare, Octavian grew into leadership until he had utterly destroyed all rivals, including Antony and Cleopatra. With this takeover, the last Hellenistic kingdom formed by Alexander's generals ended its independent rule. By 27 B.C., Octavian ruled over an empire that came to symbolize Roman greatness. With the civil wars largely ended, the empire entered the period called the Pax Romana—a period of peace and prosperity maintained by Roman power.

Octavian replaced the Roman Republic's form of government with his own version of absolutism, which historians call the **Principate** (27 B.C.–A.D. 284) (see diagram 5.1). The new master of Rome was smart enough not to repeat his late uncle's mistakes. He vigorously professed modesty and a reluctance to assume power. Octavian claimed to restore the order and stability of the old republic and refused the title of king. Instead, he merely accepted the rank of "first citizen" or *princeps* (from which we derive our word *prince*, a powerful ruler, not only the son of a king). The republic's name lived on, since officially the Senate and People of Rome (SPQR) retained their traditional government roles.

Despite his humble platitudes, Octavian really concentrated all power in his own hands. His actions reveal another basic principle:

> **Sometimes politicians do the exact opposite of what they say they are doing.**

He continued to collect titles and offices, such as consul, tribune, and even *pontifex maximus*, the head priest. To make sure he was not assassinated, he assembled an

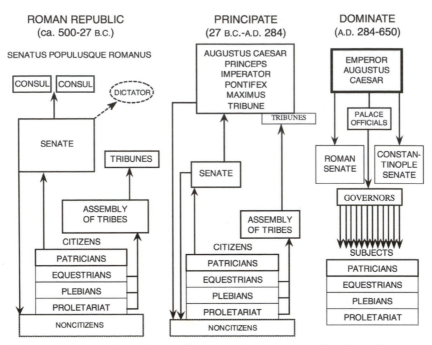

| ROMAN REPUBLIC (ca. 500-27 B.C.) | PRINCIPATE (27 B.C.-A.D. 284) | DOMINATE (A.D. 284-650) |

Diagram 5.1.   Three Phases of Roman Government. After throwing out the Etruscan kings, the Romans first established the Republic. Representatives of the people worked through various governing institutions, calling on a dictator only in case of emergency. Under the Principate, the emperor's power worked through surviving republican institutions. With the Dominate, the overwhelming power of the emperor reduced participatory citizens to obedient subjects.

unprecedented group of soldiers to protect his person, the **Praetorian Guard**. The key to Octavian's power was the office of *imperator*, or commander of the armed forces (and from which we derive the word *emperor*). For the common people, Octavian continued the reforming trends begun by Julius Caesar and set standards of behavior and efficiency for the imperial ***bureaucracy*** (meaning rule by bureaus, cupboards with drawers to store documents and records). Even the census called by him was to promote efficient and fair taxation.

Senators authorized the changes that violated the old constitution. Octavian granted to many of them a cut of the empire, although retaining for himself a large share of the rule and profits of the overseas provinces. The Senators called Octavian the father of the country and granted him the title **Augustus** (r. 31 B.C.–A.D. 14), or "honored one," by which he is often known today. Indeed, both his family name of Caesar and his honorific Augustus became synonyms for the word *emperor*. Even more, he proclaimed the spirit of his "father" Julius Caesar as elevated to godhood. Augustus Caesar, of course, shared in some of that divinity. Therefore, he began the process of deification in Rome; the emperors became gods, as important for worship as the old civic mythological gods had been. The Romans thus imitated the "Oriental despots" of Persia, as Alexander had, harnessing godhood for political stability. And so Augustus became the first Roman emperor.

Augustus' system functioned well, but it possessed one great weakness: it was based on lies. Rome, of course, had been an empire for centuries, based on its rule of many different peoples. The republican labels survived, but the Principate concentrated government in Augustus' hands. Officially, Augustus pretended not to be as powerful as a king or emperor, but everyone knew he was. The names "Caesar" and "Augustus" disguised the face of authority. Since there was officially no emperor, the Romans lacked a legal process for succession. As a consequence, the emperor's death raised problems.

Members of Augustus' family, called the Julio-Claudian dynasty, used the lack of clarity to continue their rule of the empire. Augustus' first heir, Tiberius, brooded in his sex den on the resort island of Capri while his lieutenant Sejanus almost seized power. Just in time, Tiberius had Sejanus, his wife, and their young children bloodily executed. The next emperor, Caligula, was probably insane, believing that he had indeed become a god. Caligula named his horse to be a senator, raped senators' wives, and married his own sister before being murdered by his own Praetorian Guard. Caligula's older uncle Claudius survived to become emperor because until Caligula's death, everyone thought Claudius was an idiot. Although Claudius ruled reasonably well, his third wife, Messalina, was a sex maniac, while his fourth, Agrippina, probably poisoned him. Agrippina's son, Nero, followed as emperor and soon had his helpful mother assassinated. He proclaimed himself the world's greatest actor and forced rich and poor to sit through his awful performances of singing and strumming a lyre. He is infamous for "fiddling" while a good part of the city of Rome burned, although he was probably innocent of that bad behavior. He certainly did not play a fiddle, since it had not yet been invented. In any case, fed-up Romans soon forced him to commit suicide.

Since Nero's death in A.D. 68 meant that all male heirs in Augustus' dynasty had died, the Romans fought a brief civil war in A.D. 69, the year of four emperors. The winner was the new dynasty of the Flavians, who started out well with Vespasian and his elder son Titus. Each ruled briefly, with sense and moderation. Then the younger son Domitian followed. He became increasingly paranoid and violent until he was himself murdered in A.D. 96. That Rome did not collapse into anarchy under so many cruel and capricious rulers was a testament to its own vitality and the success of the reforms made by Julius and Augustus Caesar.

The leaders who followed Domitian from A.D. 96 to 180 have become known as the Five Good Emperors. They secured Rome's everlasting glory. The great eighteenth-century historian of Rome, Edward Gibbon, credited the greatness of Rome to the wise and virtuous reigns of Nerva, Trajan, Hadrian, Antoninus Pius, and Marcus Aurelius. Trajan gained the last major province for Rome, exterminating the people of Dacia, north of the Danube River by the Black Sea. The Romans who replaced them later created the Romanian language.

While Gibbon certainly exaggerated, ancient Rome during this time has always been attractive to readers of history as a Golden Age. Rome flourished by providing a structure for political peace while allowing substantial cultural freedom. The empire of this period stood for universalism—"all is Rome"—but the emperors did not crush particularism. People worshipped diverse gods and deities, wore their own ethnic fashions, and ate their exotic cuisine. The Roman urban culture, fostered by planting colonies of retired Latin soldiers, helped diverse peoples become romanized to various degrees. Their previous cultures gradually and peacefully faded as they adopted Roman social ways and the responsibilities and benefits of citizenship. While some local ways of life faded away altogether, other regional and ethnic diversity remained. The Romans advocated Latin as a language, yet every educated Roman also spoke Greek. Many Greeks, who predominated in the eastern regions of the empire, barely bothered to learn Latin. The protections of Roman law increasingly covered non-Latins as citizens, until virtually everyone born free within the borders of the empire could claim the privilege of Roman citizenship (although it counted more for men than women). Even slaves had opportunities to win their freedom.

Outside the Roman Empire's borders, though, lived many peoples who did not share in its riches and looked on in envy. The Romans had tried to conquer the world in self-defense, but they did not succeed. Two of the empire's borders seemed secure. In the far north, much of Great Britain had been brought under the Roman yoke in the first century A.D. Yet the ferocious Picts in the island's north stopped Roman advancement. Giving up the idea of invading the highlands, Emperor Hadrian built a wall across the island to separate and defend the Roman province from the wild northerners. The Celts on the island of Hibernia (Ireland) were not even considered worth conquering. These two free peoples, though, hardly threatened the empire's interests. Likewise, on the border in the south, the Sahara desert provided a natural barrier to the rest of Africa. Most of Rome's other borders, however, remained dangerously vulnerable. Slow communications meant responses to emergencies took much too long.

The first major threat lay along the empire's border through the heartland of Europe. There the **Germans** or **Goths** dwelt in the dark woods and resisted subjugation by Rome. The Romans categorized the Germans as barbarians. They were, in the sense that the Germans did not live in organized fashion around cities and empire. Instead, they remained in loose and quarreling pastoral and agricultural tribes along Rome's central European borders. They sometimes traded, other times raided to gain Rome's luxury goods. They pursued comparatively egalitarian lives, enjoying hunting and warfare.

Under Augustus, the Germans had already dealt a major defeat to Roman ambition. One memorable German leader, called Arminius in Latin (Hermann in German), knew Roman ways from his life as a soldier who rose through the ranks in the empire. Back in his homeland, Hermann led his people to ambush and slaughter three Roman legions in the Teutoburger Forest in A.D. 9. Consequently, Augustus called for the later Romans to refrain from further expansion in that direction. The Romans eventually built a line of defensive fortifications, the *limes*, along the Rhine and Danube Rivers, trying to fend off what they could not take over.

The second threat to the Romans was the Persians. By the first century B.C., the Romans had conquered the Greeks from the west. At the same time, the Parthians, horse-riding archers from the Asian steppes, seized the Persian Empire from the east, toppling the last of the Seleucid Hellenistic dynasts. The rich Mesopotamian heartland of civilization lured both the Roman and Parthian/Persian empires. Held off by the Parthians at first, the Romans had occupied Mesopotamia by early in the second century A.D. Yet the Romans failed to defeat Persia as Alexander had.

Thus, Rome could no longer expand, limited by the Germans in Central Europe and the Parthian/Persians in the Middle East. Failure to defeat the Germans and Persians marked the Romans' doom. Only the internal rivalries among both the German tribes and Parthian elites as they fought one another postponed for a few decades any catastrophic confrontations with Rome.

During this pause, as the second century A.D. wore on, preservation of the Roman Empire became more necessary than expansion. First foreign threats and then internal weakness brought on crises that threatened to tear the Roman Empire apart, as had almost happened in the civil wars of the first century B.C. The office of emperor finally failed to preserve the functioning of the bureaucracy. The Five Good Emperors also did not solve the problem of finding a successor emperor. The first four of those five emperors, who had no sons, did implement a policy of adoption and designation, which showed promise. The reigning emperor sought out a good, qualified successor and then adopted that person as his heir. This imitation dynasty borrowed the stability of family rule to ensure talented leadership. Tragically, in A.D. 180, Marcus Aurelius' son, Commodus, inherited the empire from his father. This end to the successful policy of adoption and designation was bad enough, but Commodus' insanity (combining paranoia with the belief that he was Hercules incarnate) was catastrophic. Conspirators assassinated him, launching a series of briberies, murders, and war over imperial power. Plague also ravaged the empire, reducing the ability of Rome to recruit and pay for soldiers.

Then, in the late second century, the Germans and Persians attacked. In Central Europe, the Germans invaded across the *limes*. Clumsy Roman interventions in Mesopotamia allowed the native Persian Sassanian dynasty to replace the weakened Parthian rulers of the Persian Empire and revive its power. In the Middle East, the Sassanian-led Persians aggressively pushed the Romans back toward the Mediterranean.

This time, when Rome required capable leadership, it had none. Just as during the collapsing republic of the second century B.C., experienced Roman generals were too busy fighting one another over control of Rome. Unfortunately for political stability, generals have rarely been successful as politicians. Constant violence crippled imperial authority. In the fifty years between A.D. 235 and 284, emperors served an average of two years, with only two dying naturally and peacefully in their beds. The "barbarian" Germans actually cut down one "civilized" emperor in battle, while the Persians captured and enslaved another. Such humiliations deeply shocked the proud Romans. Even worse, rampaging Germans sacked Roman cities. Trade suffered, urban life cracked, and regions looked to local leaders for organization and defense. Many towns hurriedly built walls, believing the far-off emperor could not help. The Roman Empire almost fell apart in the third century A.D.

Then, in A.D. 284, one more general, **Diocletian** (r. 284–305), seized the throne. As the son of a freedman (a manumitted slave), he had worked his way through the army ranks and through the rivals for the empire until he stood alone at the top. Fortunately for Rome, Diocletian proved to be a rare man of talent and vision. His changes created Rome's third system of government, which historians call the **Dominate** (284–ca. 650) because it finally recognized the emperor's domination of Rome. Diocletian kept only traces of the republican system of citizen rule. Instead, based on the style of "Oriental despots," he wanted his subjects to exalt him as mysterious and semidivine. He reinforced deification and emperor worship. More importantly, he implemented practical solutions for the problems in the government. He appointed governors to run the administration for him across the many and varied provinces, and he made them more professional and well paid. He also planted secret informers to report on government abuses. At the same time, the military abandoned the now-outdated legion system. The emperor created a large field army under his direct command, one that relied more on heavy cavalry. Diocletian strengthened border defenses with more ditches and forts.

All these government expenses, especially armies and war, required a great deal of money, so Diocletian raised taxes. To collect sufficient taxes, he needed a good economy. Since economies require stability, he instituted government controls on wages and prices. Indeed, Diocletian went so far as to make professions hereditary. If a man's father was a soldier, the son soldiered; if the father was a baker, then the son baked. These limitations on economic freedom sparked complaints and did not work as well as hoped, but neither did the economy collapse. By expanding the emperor's authority and reducing people's rights, Diocletian lengthened the life of the Roman Empire for centuries. Diocletian's policies show that sometimes the solution is more government, not less.

Diocletian's sole failure (except perhaps the wage and price controls) was his attempt to regulate the imperial succession. He aimed to revive a form of the adoption and designation policy used in the second century A.D. First, Diocletian recognized that the empire was too difficult for one man to govern, so he divided the empire in half on a north-south line along the western edge of the Balkans. Second, for each half, he designated himself and a co-emperor as leaders, each called "Augustus." Each Augustus then designated an assistant, called "Caesar." When the Augustus retired or died, the Caesar would succeed him as Augustus and then designate a new assistant as Caesar. Such a complicated and unnatural system could not last. Yet even though Diocletian's successors altered his model of succession, they largely preserved and expanded his other governmental reforms.

In the year 300, Rome yet reigned as one of the great empires of the ancient world. From the Roman Republic through the Principate, Rome's greatness once more seemed secure under the Dominate. Rome had risen from an obscure city-state. It had survived internal political conflict, invasions by external enemies, and success itself, for which Romans thanked their gods. As a god-emperor, Diocletian particularly hated one religious sect, the Christians. These criminals refused to recognize his divinity or that of any of the gods of Greece and Rome. Diocletian persecuted the Christians but found himself unable to destroy them. These victims of Diocletian's intolerance would, surprisingly, be running the empire within only a few years.

Review: *How did key rulers establish order within the Roman Empire?*

Response:

THE ROADS TO KNOWLEDGE

If Rome's greatness had been based only on its ability to conquer, it would have faded as quickly as had the Assyrian Empire. The Romans, though, believed they were civilizers. Their efforts at romanization succeeded in making diverse peoples loyal to the empire. Likewise, they absorbed much from those they ruled over, laying a foundation of culture that has inspired us ever since. Through the Middle Ages, into the Renaissance of the fifteenth century, through the Enlightenment, and even into the twenty-first century, the culture of classical antiquity fostered by Rome can teach us about ourselves.

Three hundred years ago, some Italians digging a well struck upon a treasure trove of lost history, the buried Roman city of Herculaneum. A few decades later, others found Pompeii. Both cities had been buried in the year 79 by the sudden eruption of the nearby volcano Vesuvius. As the earth shook and a dark mushroom cloud filled the sky, many people started to flee toward the sea; others took refuge where they could. Poisonous overheated gas killed many people (figure 5.3). Hot mud then drowned Herculaneum, while fiery ash, cinder, and stone smothered Pompeii. The bodies of the dead were preserved as gray, rough castings. Their silence still speaks to us of human mortality. Much of the cities themselves and their evidence of the everyday life of Romans was preserved. Their art of frescoes, mosaics, and sculptures depicting gods, heroes, and friends; their taverns, villas, and brothels; their gardens, stadia, and baths; their utensils, furniture, and jewelry all offer invaluable artifacts to help us appreciate the civilized, urban culture fostered by the Roman Empire at its height.

One of the most important cultural attitudes of the Romans was their appreciation of Hellenistic civilization. From their earliest history, the Romans accepted Greek influences, beginning with the stories of most of their gods. Roman polytheism simply renamed and rewrote the Olympian gods and their myths (see table 2.1). Ovid's *Metamorphoses* retold many of the amusing, tragic, and bawdy stories about gods and people changing forms. From the Eastern Mediterranean the

Figure 5.3.   The casts of Romans who died in the eruption of the volcano Vesuvius near Pompeii show their last actions.

Romans also imported various mystery cults, as long as their followers did not disturb the peace. Mithraism was particularly popular among the soldiers of the legions. This religion believed that the son of the sun god born from a rock on 25 December grew up to slaughter a magical bull to provide fertility for the world, died, was reborn, and served as a mediator between heaven and earth. Mithras' followers (men only) were baptized in blood, celebrated with a common meal of bread and wine, and believed they would attain eternal life.

The Romans also loved Greek art. Most of the white marble statues of Hercules or Venus we have today are copies made by eager Roman collectors from Greek originals of Herakles or Aphrodite. Roman architecture drew directly on Greek orders of columns, Doric, Ionic, and Corinthian (the last especially favored by Roman architects). In their own right, Roman artists developed a particular talent for portraiture. Paintings and busts not only capture unique features but underlying feelings of their subjects. The Romans pushed much of their artistic effort into propaganda. The impressive temples of the forums, lofty triumphal arches, and noble statues of emperors reminded people in the cities of their rulers.

Not only art, but also Greek literature flourished under Roman rule. As mentioned earlier, every educated Roman learned Greek and often spoke it in everyday life. Most of the populations in the Eastern Mediterranean who spoke Greek as a common language before Roman rule continued to do so. The Romans read Herodotus about the Persian Wars and Thucydides about the Peloponnesian Wars. Newer Greek writers found patrons in Rome to support them as they wrote their poetry, history, and science. Plutarch's popular collection of biographies, *Parallel Lives*, compared Greek and Roman heroes and villains. Ptolemy's views on astronomy and Galen's on medicine, translated into Latin, would have a long-lasting influence on the West for more than a thousand years after they wrote.

The Romans also produced their own literature in Latin. They especially differed from the Greeks in their plays for the theater. Rather than the tragedies preferred by the Greeks, Romans most enjoyed bawdy comedies or violent melodramas (where a death on the stage might be portrayed by the actual killing of a slave). In rhetoric, or the art of communication, the greatest orator or speech maker was Cicero, who during the fall of the republic opposed Caesar and was killed by Antony's proscription. His writings provide us models of rhetoric and discourses on the duties of citizens. In the next generation, Vergil's epic poem *The Aeneid*, about the founding of Rome by refugees from the Trojan War, celebrated the virtues of Augustus' Principate. Later historians, such as Suetonius and Tacitus, however, insightfully analyzed both the virtues and the vices of emperors.

The Romans appreciated Greek philosophy, although their favorites were Epicureanism and stoicism. Romans particularly found in stoicism a reflection of their traditional values of following rules, performing one's duty, and doing hard work. The stoic philosopher Seneca's failure to satisfy the emperor Nero led to his dutiful suicide. Emperor Marcus Aurelius himself penned a collection of stoic sayings, called the *Meditations*.

Late in the empire's history, some scholars organized the Roman curriculum, or a "running path" to follow toward knowledge. They chose seven subjects, called the **seven liberal arts**, which they split into two parts. The first part was the "three roads," or *trivium* (from which we unfairly derive the word *trivial*). These included grammar, rhetoric, and logic. Second was the "four roads" or *quadrivium* of arithmetic, geometry, music, and astronomy. All seven of these subjects taught the skills (arts) that would enable people to be free (the "liberal" in liberal arts equated to liberty) from the slavery of ignorance. Later generations in the West would draw on this heritage of Rome to emphasize freedom.

Actual freedom in Rome, of course, could be quite limited, despite the rhetoric. The economy relied on millions of slaves drawn from diverse peoples both within and without the empire's borders. Women citizens did not enjoy the same status as their male counterparts. Many peoples were forced into the empire by conquest, not by voluntary choice. The Romans purposefully destroyed the cultures of the Phoenicians and the Celts, ignored the Germans as barbarians, and opposed the Persians as traditional enemies of Europe. At the height of its creative power, though, the mixed pagan culture of Greece and Rome gained a new, unexpected enemy in Christianity. This religion would claim to offer classical antiquity a new kind of freedom.

Review: *How did the Romans bring together the cultural heritage of classical antiquity?*

Response:

CHAPTER 6

The Revolutionary Rabbi

*Christianity, the Roman Empire,
and Islam, 4 B.C. to A.D. 1453*

While the Romans were sorting out the new imperial government of Augustus, in one small part of the Roman Empire called Palestine a series of events began whose effects would outlast the emperor's political reforms. In Palestine, many Jews resented Roman rule. A handful also began an obscure cult that later grew into the major religion called **Christianity**. From its insignificant beginnings among a few believers in Judaea, this new faith triumphed over the whole Roman Empire, thus becoming an essential part of Western civilization.

THE SON OF MAN

Christianity started with **Yeshua** (or Joshua) **benJoseph of Nazareth**. His name has since become better known in its Latinized version, **Jesus Christ**. The Yeshua of history became the Jesus of religion. Later myths settled the date of his birth on 25 December, the year 1 of the "Year of the Lord" (A.D., or in Latin, anno Domini). According to the best modern historians, Jesus was actually born in the springtime, in one of the years between 7 and 4 B.C. Therefore, any celebrations marking events in his lifetime two millennia later have been and will be a bit off the expected dates. As mentioned in the first chapter, medieval historians considered the appearance of Jesus in this world important enough to create the major dividing point in the calculation of the history of the universe, between B.C. ("Before Christ") and A.D.

Historically, Yeshua lived and died a Jew. The only surviving records of his life are from the writings of his followers in biographies called the **Gospels** ("Good News"). The authors of these stories, Matthew, Mark, Luke, and John, were probably not those named in the Gospels themselves as Yeshua's disciples. These Gospels did not always clearly reveal Yeshua's teachings, complicating all interpretations about him ever since. Yeshua often used challenging parables to illustrate his teachings and did not propose an organized set of principles. Therefore, much of what we know about Jesus Christ has to be taken on faith, not facts.

Still, some general trends are easily observable. Yeshua criticized the Jewish religious establishment of his day, which he thought was not teaching people to prepare properly for the Kingdom of God. Our life in this world, he taught, determined our place in the next world, after death. The life after death, the Kingdom of God, was far more important than treasures accumulated in this existence. Yeshua constantly emphasized moral action over strictly following the letter of the Jewish religious laws. He criticized the rich, wanted to help the poor, and preached pacifism and forgiveness. According to the Gospels, he worked miracles (especially in healing the sick) to confirm and reinforce his teachings. To carry his message further, he gathered followers (disciples) and teachers (apostles).

During his three years of ministry, Yeshua generally avoided conflict with the Roman Empire ("Give to the emperors the things that are the emperors', and to God the things that are God's," Mark 12:17). The pressure of certain Jewish leaders to get rid of him swayed the local Roman imperial governor, Pontius Pilate, to convict Jesus of treason on his alleged claim to be the king of the Jews. Instead of resisting, Yeshua surrendered himself to death and ended up more powerful than ever. About the year 27, the Romans executed Jesus in the same way as they did many other condemned criminals: crucifixion. The victims of crucifixion were nailed alive to a large cross and hung on it until dehydration, hunger, exhaustion, or suffocation finally killed them in a painful ordeal that could last for days.

After Yeshua's execution by the Romans, his followers claimed that Jesus was resurrected in the body—that he physically became alive again and walked the earth until he ascended into heaven. Belief in resurrections was not unusual in those times (indeed, Yeshua is recorded as himself raising several people from the dead). Regardless of any debate about the truth of the resurrection, belief in it encouraged his followers. They multiplied from a small, persecuted group of Jews to a force that changed the course of Roman history.

"Who exactly was Jesus?" was the first question faced by his followers after Jesus' departure from this world. During his lifetime, he referred to himself most often as the "Son of Man," but that term's meaning is unclear. A few times he is recorded as using the name "Anointed One" ("**Messiah**" in Hebrew or "Christ" from the Greek). The concept of the Messiah was a recurring theme in Jewish thought at the time. Many people in the first century were awaiting a savior who would rescue them from the troubles of this world. Jewish believers disagreed upon the exact manner of salvation, but they most often imagined a warrior-king. While Jesus certainly did not fit that view, Christians soon considered him to be much more than the Messiah. According to two of the Gospels, Jesus had a human as a mother and God as a father—but what does that actually mean? What is Jesus' connection to God and vice versa? These questions challenged the first Christians and still confuse many Christians today.

His followers' explanation about who Jesus was took four centuries to work itself out. They had to decide what was *orthodoxy*, the genuine position supported by most of tradition, and what was *heresy*, a belief close to, but rejected by, the religious authorities. A large group eventually identified as heretics held to *Gnosticism*. Gnostics believed in secret knowledge that emphasized dualism, considering Jesus' human aspects as bad but his divine as good. Christian leaders eventually concluded that Jesus was not just the Christ, or the Son of God; Jesus was God himself, incarnate, in the flesh, a human being like us. He died on the cross, rose again, and after forty days ascended into heaven. Then, fifty days after his resurrection (commemorated as Pentecost, or the "fiftieth day"), the Holy Spirit came to spread the passion of faith among people. Christians, therefore, have held that the Trinity of God the Father, God the Son, and God the Holy Spirit has ordained a universe where people live and die. After death, humans could end up in either one of two places. Righteous Christians who believed in Jesus' resurrection and behaved morally would be saved to spend eternity in blissful unity with God in heaven. Sinners would be damned to hell, surmised to be a place of horrible suffering, forever.

In coming to these conclusions about Jesus, the Christians worked their way through available sources. It took until the fourth century for Christians to agree that their Bible (which means "book") would include the Hebrew scriptures as an Old Testament and a New Testament of the four Gospels, the Acts of the Apostles, twenty-one letters (epistles), and an apocalyptic text. Some writers who brilliantly expounded on the faith during the first few centuries of Christianity came to be called Church Fathers. They often took the role of apologists, which meant defending Christian viewpoints against those of Judaism, ancient philosophies, and mystery cults. Other writings, like the Gospels of Thomas or of Mary Magdalene, were banned and destroyed as misinformation.

Another early action of the Christians was to organize themselves into an institution called the Church. While all baptized Christians could be considered members of the Church, selected people became the Church's leaders and administrators. Many Christians accepted the idea of *apostolic succession*, the belief that those whom Jesus had charged with his mission could pass on that authority to others, one to the next, and they, in turn, to still others. Thus began a distinction between the laity (normal Christians) and the **secular clergy** (Church officials). Overseers (later evolving into **bishops**) began to manage elders (priests) and servers (deacons). Each bishop had a special church called a cathedral (from the Latin for the

Bishops
priests
deacons

"bishop's chair") from which he administered a territory called a diocese (or a see, or a bishopric). Church **councils**, starting with the first major one described in the Acts of the Apostles, brought the Christian leaders together to debate and resolve important controversies.

Through these discussions and interpretations of the scriptures, the Church leaders established several methods to help people in their heavenly pilgrimage. The Church taught that grace (God's gift of salvation) could be obtained through the beliefs, sacraments, and ceremonies of Christian worship. *Baptism*, performed on all infants, initiated involvement in Church life, which carried through to the last rites before death. Most important was the **mass**: a performance with processions, prayers, readings, songs, and a sermon that culminated in a sacred meal, called Communion or the Eucharist. For most people it became the custom to attend mass on Sunday morning, which the Christians turned into their Sabbath, or Lord's Day. The sacraments became so important that the Church could threaten anyone who strayed from the proper path with *excommunication*. That punishment excluded a sinner from the sacraments until he or she asked for forgiveness. The average peasant rarely worried about excommunication, though. The beliefs and rituals of Christianity did relieve some of the daily grind of life and the fear of death. The Christian calendar of the seven-day week, ending with a day of worship and rest, combined with various holidays ("holy days") such as Easter (the day of Christ's resurrection) or Pentecost (fifty days later, when the Holy Spirit entered Christ's followers), increasingly shaped the living patterns of Christian society for the next few centuries.

In these early formative centuries, Christianity did not appear fully formed and obvious. It rose from discussions and controversy among believers. The early Christians disagreed with one another over what Jesus actually taught either about morality and behavior or about authority and obedience. These same questions confront Christians today, who have splintered into many different sects over these very issues. The solution to these questions was even more difficult in antiquity because the early Christians lived within a culture that was hostile to them.

Review: *How did the new religion of Christianity begin?*

Response:

THE CULTURAL WAR

Not surprisingly, the Jews were the first to attack the Christians, who had themselves all originally been Jewish. From Judaism the Christians had adapted the key belief system regarding Jesus as Messiah and God. For the Jews, however, Christianity was heresy. Many Jews were actively hostile to the new faith, and they had Christians arrested or stoned to death. Foremost among the persecutors was Saul of Tarsus. Then, on the road from Jerusalem to Damascus one day, Saul claimed to have had a vision of Jesus and converted to Christianity. He changed his name to **Paul of Tarsus** and became one of the leading apostles.

Encouraged by Paul's missionary work among the Gentiles (non-Jews) of Asia Minor and Greece, Christians took a decisive step away from Judaism when they opened up Christianity as a universal religion. While theoretically anyone could convert to Judaism, Jews tended to emphasize ethnic inheritance. In contrast, Christians abandoned obligations to many of the Jewish dietary rules and other restrictive laws to make their faith more hospitable to Gentiles. Paul's special success was in converting Gentiles to Christianity. Indeed, almost anyone could easily become a Christian, even among socially disadvantaged groups such as women, lower classes, outcasts, and slaves. Women even took on leadership roles as patrons, deacons, and apostles in the early Church. The Christian message of love and example of charity attracted many who found little care within other ancient religions and philosophies.

Christianity quickly spread outward from Palestine, whether to Jewish communities of the Diaspora or directly into the hellenized and Roman towns and cities of antiquity. At first, Christianity was an urban religion. The Christians relabled polytheism after the peasants of the countryside, using either *paganism* (after the word for farmers) or *heathenism* (after those who live on the heath). Unlike the Jews, Christians regularly used syncretism, adapting foreign customs to Christian practices, such as replacing pagan holidays with Christian ones. For example, the 25 December date of Christmas, the commemoration of Christ's birth, was chosen because it coincided with pagan festivals of the winter solstice. As a belief system, Christianity offered something different from the civic religions, the mystery cults, and the schools of philosophy, all sanctioned and supported by the state. The official myth-based religions were too empty of fervor, the mystery cults were too exclusive and secretive, and philosophy was too intellectually challenging. In comparison, Christianity offered a religion of passion, open to all, Greek or Roman, rich or poor, male or female, slave or free.

The Roman Empire, however, did not make life easy for Christians. As viewed by the imperial authorities, Christianity remained an illegal religion. By the first century A.D., the Romans had unified their empire through a state religion based on sacrifices to the gods of Rome, including their deified emperors. Romans believed that only diligent sacrifices prevented the gods from punishing the state with destruction. The government labeled anyone as a traitor who refused to support the state through sacrifice. Thus, all citizens and subjects were obligated to acknowledge the Græco-Roman gods through a simple act, usually burning incense or sacrificing a bird on an altar.

As explained in chapter 3, the Jews, who regarded such actions as idolatry, were exempted from performing this sacrifice. In contrast, the Romans considered that since Christianity had been founded within living memory, it deserved no special exemption. Many emperors and magistrates therefore persecuted the Christians by arresting and punishing them in various creative ways. Christians were sold for use as slaves in mines, forced to become temple prostitutes, beheaded, or even ripped apart at gladiatorial games by wild animals. Christians who suffered death for the sake of faith were believed to become **martyrs** and immediately enter heaven.[1]

Fortunately for the Christians, these persecutions failed because the Roman emperors could neither apply enough pressure nor maintain the scope of hunting down Christians for very long. The Christians were able to outlast the attention span and strength of the most powerful rulers in the ancient world. Also, the noble death of so many Christians inspired many Romans to consider Christianity more seriously. Hence, despite intermittent official and occasional popular disapproval, Christianity survived. Still, Christians had not convinced a large number of Romans to convert. By A.D. 300, Christians probably made up only 10 percent of the empire's population.

Success and security came only when the emperors themselves co-opted Christianity. In the fourth century A.D., Christians amazingly attained the pinnacles of power out of the depths of persecution. Their speedy and surprising success can be credited largely to one man: Emperor **Constantine** (r. 306–337) (see figure 6.1). His father had become Augustus in Diocletian's system of imperial succession. Upon his father's death in A.D. 306, the troops proclaimed Constantine an imperial successor. Over the next few years, Constantine successfully defeated other claimants to seize the imperial supremacy for himself.

As the sole Roman emperor, Constantine continued the strong imperial government revitalized by Diocletian, adding three improvements of his own. First, he solved the question of succession by creating an old-fashioned dynasty. A son (or sons in the divided empire) would inherit from the father. While this system had the usual flaw of dynasties (sons and cousins might and did fight over the throne), it limited the claimants to within the imperial family rather than ambitious generals proclaimed by legions. Second, Constantine built a new capital for the eastern half of the administratively divided empire. He chose the location of the Greek city of Byzantion, situated on the Bosphorus, the entrance from the Aegean to the Black Sea. Strategically, it was an excellent choice: close to key trade routes, in the heart of the vital Greek population, and easily defensible. He modestly named the new capital after himself, **Constantinople**.

His third improvement reversed Diocletian's religious policy of exterminating all Christians. Instead, Constantine decided to help them. As the story went, Constantine was fighting against a rival who was a great persecutor of Christians. Constantine had a vision and a dream of the Christian symbol of the *labarum* (similar to the letter *P* with a crossbar) in the sun (which held a special connection to his

---

1. Note, however, that one cannot choose martyrdom; it has to be forced on one. Thus Christians were not allowed to simply walk up to Romans and announce their faith, hoping to be executed as a consequence, although it did happen.

Figure 6.1.   The colossal face of Emperor Constantine stares into the future.

family as a patron deity). He won victory over an imperial rival under this sign in a battle at the Milvian Bridge, just to the north of Rome. The victorious emperor then ordered all of the empire to tolerate Christians by issuing the **Edict of Milan** in 313. This law reinforced a previous Edict of Toleration of two years earlier. In this edict, the Christians were exempted from making sacrifices to the emperors. Although Constantine himself probably remained a pagan until his death, as of 313 Christians in the Roman Empire were no longer criminals because of their faith.

Beyond simply tolerating the Christians, Constantine showered his imperial largesse upon them. He favored them with land and buildings. The design of the new public Christian churches, basilicas, was based on the design of imperial meeting halls. Constantine bestowed special privileges on Christians, such as rights of self-government and exemptions from imperial services. He probably thought Christianity, which had proved so resistant to persecution, could help the empire through its prayers and zeal. Overnight, Christianity had moved from being the counterculture to the establishment.

Saints served as new role models for Christian society, since martyrs became a rarity without persecutions (although many martyrs came to be considered saints). Originally, a saint referred to any faithful Christian. Over time, the term *saint* became restricted to those who both lived the virtuous life in this world and proved their divine connection by working miracles after their death. Saints' lives became meaningful not only in stories, but also in their physical remains. The faithful believed that parts of saints' bodies or objects associated with them channeled divine power to work miracles long after the saint's death. The relics of specific saints preserved in and around altars often gave churches their names. For example, the grill on which St. Lawrence was roasted and the headless body of St. Agnes reside at their respective churches located outside the walls of ancient Rome. These churches were being openly built in great numbers to hold all the new relics and the converts they won. They became destinations of regular worship and special veneration.

In one of those amazing ironies of history, just when they reached social acceptance, Christians began to attack one another publicly. Uncertainty raised by Gnostics about the combined humanity and divinity of Jesus burst out into the open. These conflicts threatened Constantine's aim for Christianity to provide stability, so he called the **Council of Nicaea** in 325 to help the Church settle the matter. The majority of Church leaders decided on the formula that Jesus was simultaneously fully God and fully human, embedding this idea and other basic beliefs into the Nicene Creed that is still professed in many Christian churches today. That creed became catholic orthodoxy (the universally held, genuine beliefs). The large majority believed along catholic (universal) orthodox (genuine) lines. Orthodox catholics considered those who disagreed with them to be heretics, no longer Christian.

A large group of heretics, the Arians, remained unconvinced about Jesus' complete combination of divinity and humanity.[2] They continued to spread their version of the faith and tried to convince the majority to change its mind. Over the next few decades they convinced emperors to switch sides. They even succeeded in converting many Germans along and outside the borders of the Roman Empire to their version of the Christian faith. For a long time, heretical **Arianism** looked like it would become the orthodox faith. The Christian leadership, convinced that the Holy Spirit worked through them, persecuted, exiled, or even executed the heretics. By the sixth century, only a few Arian Christians survived in the West, but many, called Nestorians, spread their version of Christ throughout Asia.

Christians also adopted a new relationship with the Jews, whose religion was the undoubted foundation for Christianity. Through the centuries, many Christians have respected the Jews, recognizing their position as God's chosen people. Such Christians tolerated Jews who continued to live as a religious minority within Christian cities and society. Jews maintained their distinct religion and did not have to entirely assimilate to the dominant Christian culture of the West.

Too many Christians, however, turned toward anti-Semitism. Nominal excuses for this hatred ranged from blaming Jews for killing Christ, through disliking Jewish refusal to recognize their truth of Jesus as the Messiah, to resenting Jewish religious obligations that the Christians had rejected. Nonsensical reasons included blaming the Jews for plague or for committing ritual murders. Whatever the excuses, many Christians persecuted Jews once Christianity reigned. Increasingly over the centuries, and particularly in the West, Christians restricted Jewish

---

2. Arians take their name from one of their important theologians, Arius. They are not to be confused with Aryans. That term is a racist-tinged and outdated concept describing European ancestors who originated in India (see chapter 13).

civil rights. Christians limited Jews to certain occupations, had them confined in ghettoes, forced Jews to convert or emigrate, or simply killed them. Christians were, and remain, burdened by these uncomfortable relations with their Jewish brethren.

Besides deciding on orthodox beliefs and how to relate to the Jews, Christians needed to decide their attitude toward Græco-Roman culture, which dominated the Roman Empire during the centuries after Christ. With the famous question, "What has Athens to do with Jerusalem?" some Christians attacked and wanted to reject the classical heritage. Indeed, Christianity threatened to wipe out much of Græco-Roman civilization. Christians thought that pagans like Socrates, Plato, or Aristotle had little to say to the followers of Jesus Christ. What could the histories of Herodotus or Thucydides teach those who followed the greater history of the Hebrew people, the apostles, and saints? When Christianity became the sole legal religion of the Roman Empire in 380, the government banned paganism and many of its works. The Christians toppled temples, destroyed shrines, burned sacred groves, shut philosophical schools that had been started by Plato and Aristotle, silenced oracles, halted gladiatorial contests, and abolished the Olympic Games. A Christian mob murdered the mathematician and polytheist philosopher Hypatia by cutting her down with shards of pottery in the middle of a public street. The murderers and instigators (who may have included the bishop) went unpunished.

Eventually, however, the Christian Church embraced much from classical antiquity. This attitude was an important milestone in the West's cultural development, perhaps the most important. If narrow-minded zealots had won this culture war, Christian-led society would never have been open to *intellectualism* and innovation. Church leaders might have only gazed inward at the Gospels and focused on the Kingdom of Heaven alone, while rejecting human rationalism and empiricism by educated people, or intellectuals. Such *anti-intellectualism* would have allowed civilization to stagnate. To this day, some Christians still condemn knowledge that does not fit in with their conception of what is godly. Christianity partly succeeded, however, because it compromised with the secular world and opened itself up to the voices of others. In doing so, Christianity adapted and prospered in unexpected ways over the centuries and eventually spread around the world. Before that could happen, however, barbarians almost wiped out this newly Christian civilization.

Review: How did conflicts among the Jews, Christians, and pagans lead to the Romans creating a new cultural landscape?

Response:

ROMA DELENDA EST

In another of those amazing ironies of history, just after Christians overthrew the Romans' religion, various Germans triumphed over the Romans' armies. In A.D. 410, the army of the Visigoths (western Germans) sacked Rome, the first time since the Celts had done so in 390 B.C. The Visigoth armies then marched on to plunder other regions, while more Germans crossed the borders and took what they wanted. It seemed the Roman curse *"Carthago delenda est"* ("Carthage must be destroyed") came back against Rome itself. Many Romans who had not been thoroughly Christianized and still maintained their heathen beliefs in the old gods naturally blamed the Christians for this catastrophe. The coincidence of events raised suspicions: first Christianity became the state religion, and then a few years later barbarians plundered the city of Rome for the first time in eight hundred years. Some interpreted the pagan gods to have shown their anger at the rise of Christians by removing their protection from Rome. Calamities seemed a sure sign of divine wrath, as people often still believe in our own time.

To answer this charge against the Christians, Bishop **Augustine** of Hippo (d. 430) wrote the book *The City of God*. This book defended Christianity by presenting Augustine's view of its workings in history. Augustine said that people were divided into two groups who dwelt in metaphysical cities: those who lived for God and were bound for heaven and those who resided in this world and were doomed to hell. Every political state, such as the Roman Empire, contained both kinds of people. While Rome had been useful to help Christianity flourish, whether it fell or not was in the end irrelevant to God's plan. This argument emphasized the separation of church and state. God sanctioned no state, not even a Christian Roman Empire. Instead, individuals ought to live as faithful Christians, even while the so-called barbarians attacked. Indeed, shortly after Augustine's death, German armies destroyed the city of Hippo, near ancient Carthage, over which he was bishop.

How did the Gothic Germans and their allies come to destroy Hippo and so many other cities of the Roman Empire? Historians have proposed a number of explanations, some better than others. Reasons such as the poisoning of the Roman elites by lead pipes are silly. It is likewise absurd, as some cultural critics do, to blame the fall of Rome on moral corruption. When it fell, Rome was as Christian and moral a state as there ever could be. The Christians, such as Bishop Augustine, were in complete control. Many Romans may have been imperfect sinners, but a closer cooperation of church and state could hardly be imagined. Despite this, the great historian of the fall of Rome, Edward Gibbon, blamed much of the Roman collapse on this rise of Christianity, saying that its values of *pacifism* undermined Rome's warrior spirit. The conflicts among orthodox Christians, heretic Arians, and lingering pagans also weakened the empire. Modern historians do not embrace Augustine's eschatology (the study of the end of the world), but neither do they completely agree with Gibbon.

The best explanations of Rome's fall focus on its economic troubles, which remained unsolved by imperial mandates. First, plagues had reduced the numbers of Roman citizens. Rome was no longer strong enough to conquer and exploit new provinces. No expansion meant taxes at home burdened the smaller population.

Second, the shortage of revenues also meant smaller armies. Therefore, the Romans began to recruit the unconquered Germans living on their borders. Troop levels still fell short despite the recruitment of Germans. Transfers of warriors from one part of the border to the other left gaps in the defenses.

Imperial armies soon depended on these cheap barbarians hired to defend Rome from other barbarians. Immigrant Germans never became as integrated or romanized into Roman society as had many earlier conquered peoples. As they increased their power and influence, the Germans tended rather to barbarize the Romans, at least in their systems of politics based on personal relationships rather than complex written laws. Here, as with the Greeks, changes in military structures affected politics and society. Given the wealth of its civilization, though, the Romans stood a good chance of defending the empire against the majority of Germans, who had no serious reason to launch major assaults.

The military situation changed, however, when the **Huns**, a horse-riding people from the steppes of Asia, swept into Europe. The Huns reputedly slaughtered most people in their path, drank blood and ate babies, and enslaved the few survivors. The terrified German peoples in eastern and northern Europe fled from the Huns in the only direction possible: into the Roman Empire. They entered not as an invading army but as entire peoples—with the elderly, the women, and the young. Thus, these movements are sometimes called the **Germanic barbarian migrations**, not merely invasions. The German tribes and nations themselves were in flux, absorbing and reforming as different groups melded together under warrior-kings. Peoples came together under inspiring leaders, as long as they lasted. Some remained a force for decades or even centuries, and others broke up and rapidly reformed with different tribes and nations.

At first, the group called Visigoths by later historians crossed the boundaries of the empire with permission, as refugees from the Hun attack in A.D. 378. Two years later, their quarrels with imperial authorities culminated in the Battle of Adrianople. The Germans crushed the Roman army and killed the eastern emperor. Afterward, the divided and inexperienced Roman emperors and commanders were unwilling to risk another battle against them, so the Visigoths briefly settled along the Danube. But pressure from plundering raids by the Huns continued to push new Goths against the borders, threatening both Romans and Visigoths. The new Visigothic leader Alaric led his people through the empire looking for a place to settle. His army carried out the second sack of Rome in 410. Alaric reluctantly allowed his troops to plunder because the Romans refused to negotiate about a homeland for his people within the borders of the Roman Empire. At least the sack of 410 was not as bad as those to come: the Christian (if heretic Arian) Visigoths especially preserved the churches. Within a few years, Visigoths had settled down into a kingdom that straddled the Pyrenees from the south of Gaul into the Iberian Peninsula.

The example of the Visigoths inspired others to follow. More barbarians poured across Rome's once-well-defended borders. The frozen Rhine River allowed large numbers of Alans (mostly Asians), Alemanni, Sueves, and Vandals simply to walk into Roman Gaul in the winter of A.D. 406. The Vandals passed through the Visigothic kingdom to cross the Mediterranean and conquer North Africa (including Carthage and Augustine's Hippo). From there, the Vandals carried out one of the worst sacks of Rome in 455, lending their name to the word *vandalism*. The emperor left Britain defenseless by withdrawing troops to the mainland. Angles, Saxons, and Jutes who sailed across the North Sea in the mid-fifth century conquered the island, despite a defense by a leader who became the legendary King Arthur. Finally, The long-feared Huns themselves moved into the empire. Actually, they turned out not to be quite as monstrous as the tales spread about them. From their own point of view, they were just one more collection of peoples seeking a place to live and grabbing as much power as they could. The Romans even negotiated with the Huns, surrendering territory along the Danube or even paying tribute rather than fighting them.

For a time, the leader of the Huns, Attila, thought he could conquer the remnants of the Roman Empire. The massive walls of Constantinople made him hesitate to attack eastward. When he moved west into Gaul in 451 and south into Italy in 452, armies drawn from the Germans now living there provided most of the muscle to resist the Hunnic forces. The allied Romans and Germans held off Hunnic conquest (although one story goes that the Bishop of Rome, called Pope Leo, personally convinced Attila to turn back from another sack of his city). The next year Attila died of a nosebleed on his wedding night to his (perhaps) seventh bride. After Attila's unexpected death, no competent ruler followed. The Hunnic Empire dissolved, and the Huns disappeared as a people, retreating back to Asia or blending in among the diverse Europeans.

But the Germans remained. They soon advanced to finish off the Roman imperial administration in the west. The Franks, one of the largest groups of Germans, decisively took charge in Gaul by A.D. 486. By that time, Roman authority in the west had been gone for a decade. German commanders were fighting the battles. In A.D. 476, the Gothic king and Roman commander Odavacar (or Odoaker) seized power by toppling the last Roman emperor in the west, who bore the fitting name Romulus Augustulus (evoking the founder of Rome and the founder of the imperial position together with the belittling diminutive *-ulus*, meaning "small"). This unwarranted deposition annoyed the current Roman emperor in the east, so he commissioned the Ostrogoths (eastern Germans) under their king Theodoric to invade Italy on his behalf. After several years of warfare, Odavacar surrendered. The victorious Theodoric assassinated Odavacar at dinner and then proclaimed himself ruler, backed up by his Ostrogothic warriors. While the emperor in Constantinople recognized Theodoric, he ruled without restriction over an Ostrogothic kingdom in the Italian Peninsula. Although he remained an Arian, he tried to forge a society that tolerated religions and ethnic differences between Romans and Germans. The so-called **Germanic barbarian kingdoms** were ultimately supreme throughout western Europe.

The western half of the Roman Empire fell because its armies could not defend it. It must not be forgotten, however, that the Roman Empire continued for another thousand years. The barbarians' feet had trampled only the western portion of the empire. The eastern half continued to fight on and to preserve Roman civilization. For centuries the new capital of Constantinople was one of the greatest cities in the world. Later historians have designated that part of the Roman Empire as **Byzantium** or the **Byzantine Empire**, named after the Greek city Byzantion that Constantine had made his capital. The emperors maintained their roles as protector and promoter of the Christian Church, in the tradition of Constantine. Historians call this imperial Church leadership **caesaro-papism**. A "sacred" emperor appointed the bishops who worked with the unified Christian state. After the fall of the western half of the Roman Empire, the eastern half increasingly took on a Greek coloring, since ethnic Greeks filled the leadership positions. Once more the Greeks ruled a powerful political state.

The reign of **Emperor Justinian** (r. 527–565) marked a transition from the ancient Roman Empire to the medieval Byzantine Empire. Justinian has been considered both the last emperor of Rome and the first Byzantine emperor. He had several notable achievements. First, he built one of the greatest churches of the world in Constantinople, the Hagia Sophia, or Holy Wisdom (see figure 6.2). Second, he had the old Roman laws reorganized into the Book of Civil Laws, often called the **Justinian Code**. This legal text not only secured the authority of Byzantine emperors for centuries to come, it also helped the west rebuild its governments after the twelfth century (see chapter 8). Justinian's attempt to restore the *Imperium Romanum* was less successful. His armies, led by brilliant generals such as Belisarius and Narses, managed some reconquests, including the Vandal kingdom in North Africa and much of the Ostrogothic kingdom in the Italian Peninsula.

These victories notwithstanding, Justinian's attempt at the revival of Roman power failed. In the short term, Byzantine meddling at the court betrayed the generals. In the long run, the eastern empire also lacked the resources and power to hold onto the old western provinces of Rome. Shortly after Emperor Justinian's death, most of Italy fell back under the control of squabbling German kings. From

Figure 6.2.   Justinian's Hagia Sophia, the Church of Holy Wisdom, rose over Constantinople at the emperor's command. The minarets were added later, when it was converted into a mosque after the fall of the Byzantine Empire in 1453. Today it is secularized as a museum.

then on, the German kings ignored Constantinople, and Byzantium ignored them right back.

Review: How did the Roman Empire fall in the west, yet not in the east?

Response:

STRUGGLE FOR THE REALM OF SUBMISSION

The sudden rise of the Islamic civilization in the seventh century surprised everyone. The new religion of **Islam** (which means "submission" in Arabic) claimed the same omnipotent God as Judaism and Christianity. It originated in Arabia, an arid peninsula that had so far largely remained outside the political domination of major civilizations flourishing around the Mediterranean Sea or the river basins of Nile, Tigris, and Euphrates. Mohammed (b. ca. 570–d. 632), a merchant from the Arabian city of Mecca, became Islam's founder and only prophet. At about the age of forty, he claimed that the angel Gabriel revealed to him the message of God (called Allah in Arabic).

These messages formed the Koran or Qu'ran (meaning "Recitation"), the book containing the essentials of Islam. These are usually summed up as five "pillars." The first is *shahadah*, the simple proclamation of faith that there is no God except Allah and that Mohammed is his last prophet. Second is *salat*, praying five times a day, at the beginning of day, noon, afternoon, sunset, and before bed, always on one's knees and facing toward Mecca, whether in a mosque or not. Third is *zakat*, the obligation to pay alms to care for the poor. Fourth is *sawm*, to fast from sunrise to sunset every day during the lunar month of Ramadan. Last is a pilgrimage (*hajj*) to Mecca that should be undertaken once in one's lifetime. Everyone who keeps these pillars is a Muslim and is promised eternal life after death.

Other issues such as polygamy or restrictions on food or alcohol were less important but added to the discipline of submission to divine commands. Islam was syncretic: it combined the Arab's polytheistic religion centered on the moon (hence the crescent symbol), the Persian dualism of **Zoroastrianism**, a common connection with Judaism via Abraham as a common ancestor, and even a recognition of Jesus as a prophet (although not God incarnate). Scholars over the next decades developed rules of behavior or sets of laws called *shari'a*, based on what they could interpret from what they knew from Mohammed and the Qu'ran. Again, Mohammed's was the last word.

When the residents of Mohammed's hometown refused to listen to his calls for submission to God's commands, he fled to a nearby city in 622. That flight (*Hegira* or *Hijra*) marks the founding year of the calendar still used today in Islam, namely 1 A.H., from the Latin *anno Hegirae*, in the year of the emigration. His refuge became "The City of the Prophet," or Medina, as he gained followers called **Muslims**. Mohammed's followers launched a series of conquests to force their neighbors' submission to the commands of God's prophet.

This was jihad, whose meaning ranges from "struggle" to a Muslim version of holy war. Clearly, his followers interpreted Mohammed's message to mean that Islamic submission to Allah should reign everywhere. When peaceful, voluntary conversions failed, the alternative was war to establish political supremacy over non-Muslims. Starting with Mecca, Mohammed ruled much of Arabia by the time of his death. His successors went on to conquer a third of what had been the Roman Empire (from the Iberian Peninsula, across North Africa, and over Palestine and Mesopotamia) as well as the Persian Empire. Within a hundred years of Mohammed's death, Muslim armies had won territories from the Atlantic Ocean to southern Asia into the Indian Subcontinent.

The Muslim conquest succeeded for several reasons. First, the fanaticism and skill of its nomadic Arab warriors from the desert overwhelmed many an army fighting for uninspiring emperors and kings. Second, both Roman Byzantium and Persia had exhausted themselves from their long and inconclusive wars over Mesopotamia. Third, many Muslim rulers were tolerant of the religious diversity among their new subjects. So long as Muslims ruled, Islam did not compel conversion of those who believed in the same God. Muslim rulers usually allowed Jews and Christians to keep their lives and their religions, burdening them only with paying an extra tax. So, although individuals may have converted to Islam, the Christian, Jewish, and even Zoroastrian or polytheistic communities endured for centuries within Muslim states.

With their conquests, Arabs became a new cultural contender. Islam's conquests prevented those former areas of the Roman Empire in the Iberian Peninsula, North Africa, and Mesopotamia from sharing in the history of the western part of the empire that had fallen to the Germans. The Muslims took the shared Græco-Roman heritage in another direction. They carried out their own *islamicization*, encouraging the faith and practices of Islam, as well as *arabization*, promoting Arabic culture and language. Since the Qu'ran was supposed to be read in the original language in which it was written, namely Arabic, every educated Muslim read that language. In much of Mesopotamia and North Africa, Arabic became the dominant language, replacing the German, Latin, Coptic, Aramaic, and other languages of the conquered peoples. Only in Persia did the natives resist linguistic conversion, although the Persians shared their rich civilized heritage with their fellow Muslims.

Islamic civilization drew on what the Greeks and Romans had united and mixed in Persian and other cultures. While Roman cities in western Europe crumbled under barbarian neglect, Muslim cities blossomed with learning and sophistication.

They had paved streets, plumbing, and libraries. Although their religion prohibited pictures and sculptures of people, they created impressive public buildings, especially mosques with lofty domes and towering minarets, decorated with elaborate calligraphy, patterns, and designs. Communities of scholars investigated both the Qu'ran and other facets of human knowledge. Philosophers explored issues of metaphysics, medicine, mathematics, and science. Al-Khawarizmi, whose name the West borrowed to label both the words *algebra* and *algorithm*, popularized Arabic numbers (although they were invented in non-Muslim India). Mystics called Sufis explored the religious experience of the divine. Pilgrims traveled hundreds of miles without being molested within the Muslim-Arabic Empire. Merchants ventured with their luxury goods of silks, ceramics, carpets, and spices far into Asia and Africa, by land and by sea, to bargain and trade.

This Arabic Empire surpassed Alexander's in size and civilization. It also lasted about as briefly. Mohammed and the Qu'ran left little guidance about who should lead the Muslim community after Mohammed's death. Muslims split over who should be Mohammed's successor, called the caliph or *khalifa* (deputy), the ultimate judge in all matters political or religious. The majority, or Sunni (meaning "traditional"), Muslims were willing to accept any respectable dynasty, whether established, as they would be over the centuries, in Medina, Damascus, Baghdad, or Istanbul. Hence, Sunnis were open to competing rulers and did not worry so much about political divisions among Muslims. A minority, the Shia or Shi'i (meaning "sect"), thought the heirs of Mohammed's family should unite all Muslims in Dar al-Islam (the realm of Submission to God). The last members of his family were soon dead, however. The fourth caliph, Ali, Mohammed's cousin and son-in-law, had been assassinated early in A.D. 661 (or 40 A.H.) and Ali's son, Hussein, died in battle twenty years later while trying to seize the caliphate. Although no physical descendants remained, Shiites believed that a holy figure, the imam, would miraculously unite Muslims again. Also, ethnic differences among Arabs, Berbers, Persians, and romanized Egyptians and Mesopotamians weakened solidarity and loyalty toward any one empire. Shi'ites concentrated in Persia, partly as a result of Iranian ethnic pride. Islam thus lost its political unity and has been unable to regain it ever since.

And since Islam failed to triumph over all Christians, hostile borders separated Muslims from the Christians in western Europe and the Byzantine Empire. In particular, the Byzantine Empire fought off multiple Muslim attacks, helped by the early collapse of the Arabic Empire. Although the Byzantine emperors lost substantial territory south of Asia Minor to Muslims, they managed a few compensatory gains in the Balkan Peninsula. Slavic invaders had settled in eastern Europe and the Balkans after the Hunnic Empire had vanished.[3] By the eighth century, Christian missionaries from the Byzantine Empire had converted most of them in the south. The Cyrillic alphabet, modeled on Greek letters, became the written script of many southern Slavs. The Byzantine Empire then fought to gain direct rule over these Christians in the Balkans. Emperor Basil II, "the Bulgar Slayer" (r. 976–1025),

---

3. Because so many slaves were soon taken from those peoples during the Middle Ages, the word for *slave* in several languages referred to the Slavs.

expanded his dominion over the Albanians, Serbs, and Bulgars (an Asiatic people who had blended with the Slavs). Basil earned his harsh nickname not only by killing many Bulgarians in battle, but also by allegedly blinding thousands of Bulgarian prisoners before sending them home.

The multicultural Byzantine Empire of Greeks, southern Slavs, and other ethnic minorities straddling the Balkans and Asia Minor for a time seemed secure. Then the Seljuk **Turks** seized power in Persia in 1040. The Turks were horse-riding warriors who swept off the Asiatic steppes toward Europe, as the Huns did before and the Mongols would do later. The Seljuk dynasty's conversion to Islam allowed it to win support among non-Turkish Muslims. With surprising swiftness, the Seljuks conquered Mesopotamia and then moved into the Byzantine Empire to confront the "Roman" emperor at the Battle of Manzikert (1071). The decisive Turkish victory gained them Asia Minor, which became a new Turkish homeland, today the country of Turkey.

[margin note: Byzantine overpowered by Turks]

The Greek lands of Asia Minor had been some of the most important and prosperous areas of the Byzantine Empire. Their loss weakened the empire, leaving it less able to resist any further possible attack by the Turks or anyone. Confronted with this new threat, the Byzantines sought reinforcements from the west. That request unleashed the Crusades against the Muslims in the Holy Land (see chapter 8). The Crusades actually further hurt Byzantium, as western forces seized lands for themselves, increased Islamic fanaticism, and even briefly conquered much of the Byzantine Empire itself in the early thirteenth century. These attacks left the empire vulnerable to a renewed Turkish offensive in the fourteenth century led by the new Ottoman dynasty (see chapter 9). By 1453, the last "Roman" emperor died on Constantinople's walls, fighting alongside his handful of imperial troops and volunteers. The Ottoman Turks renamed Constantinople as Istanbul and made it the capital of their own Muslim Empire. The Greeks were a conquered people once more.

[margin note: Crusades]

If the Roman Empire had survived intact or the attempted Muslim conquest of Europe had succeeded, the West as we know it would never have existed. In either case, the civilization would have had a very different geographic foundation, centered, like the Roman Empire, on the Mediterranean. Byzantium or Islam might have bound western Europe together with the Balkans, North Africa, and the Middle East.

Instead, the collapse of Roman power in the west combined with the rise and fall of the Byzantine and various Muslim empires meant that eastern Europe, Africa, and Asia remained outside the main development of Western civilization for the next thousand years or more. Ruling over lands once part of the Roman Empire, the Orthodox Christian Byzantine Empire and the various Muslim realms certainly enjoyed rich and powerful civilizations and drew on the mutual Græco-Roman culture of classical antiquity. Yet Byzantines and Muslims flourished on the other side of a cultural divide after the German conquest of the western portion of the Roman Empire. Only in western Europe did various elements of Græco-Roman, Judeo-Christian, and German cultures meld through many difficult centuries to become Western civilization.

Review: How did Islam rise as a rival civilization?

Response:

CHAPTER 7

From Old Rome to the New West

The Early Middle Ages, A.D. 500 to 1000

The collapse of Rome in the west during the fifth century A.D. marked the end of "ancient" history and the beginning of "medieval" history (see timeline 7.1). The intellectuals after the fifteenth century who coined the term *Middle Ages* (whose Latin form provides *medieval*) saw the thousand years of history between classical antiquity and their own day as one horrible detour for civilization. For the intellectuals of the so-called Renaissance (see chapter 9), the previous thousand years seemed simply barbaric when compared to the glories of Greece and Rome. Even today, "medieval" describes something backward, vicious, or stupid. These meanings do not actually reflect the historical truth. Rather, much changed in the course of the Middle Ages, usually for the better. Historians divide the thousand years between A.D. 500 and 1500 into three periods, hence the use of the plural "ages." First came the **Early Middle Ages** (450–1050), during which Europe rebuilt after the collapse of Rome (see map 7.1). During these centuries, three cultures (Germanic, Judeo-Christian, and Græco-Roman) wove together to become the West. During the first part of the Middle Ages, western Europeans survived the

Map 7.1.   Dark Ages Europe

collapse of Roman civilization and then gave birth to and nurtured the childhood of Western civilization.

GOTHS IN THE GARDEN

The Germans or Goths who had destroyed the western half of the Roman Empire settled amid the remnants of its Christianized Græco-Roman civilization. As the new political masters, they oversaw the formation of a new culture. The term *Gothic* often serves as an alternate term for the medieval period. At the end of the Middle Ages, humanist admirers of classical antiquity proclaimed that svelte Corinthian columns and bleached-white calm nudes were superior to pointed arches and the polychrome tortured crucifixions of late medieval art. They used, and art historians still use, the term *Gothic* for most of the art and architecture of the High and Later Middle Ages. Cultural critics used *Gothic* as an insult, implying that crude barbarian Germans had crushed the simple, clean beauty of Greece and Rome. In contrast, the medieval people often referred to their culture in a fashion similar to the way we refer to our own: "modern."

    That we view the Middle Ages as unmodern, as lacking in sophistication and enlightenment, reflects its beginnings in the ruin of Roman civilization by these alleged barbarians. The uncivilized leaders of the so-called Germanic barbarian kingdoms who replaced the officials of imperial Rome in the west were mostly illiterate and therefore left few written records. Thus, the first few centuries after the fall of Rome might justifiably be called the **Dark Ages**. We are in the dark about much that happened. Sadly, the term *Dark Ages* too often insults the entire Middle Ages as being full of ignorance, cruelty, and superstition.

Although the Germans were uncivilized, they had not intended to destroy all the benefits of civilization. Rome's wealth and comforts had attracted them in the first place. German regimes clumsily tried to continue the Roman system with the remnants of the Roman elites, but barbarians simply did not know how to manage urban life. They feared and avoided the cities. Thus, towns lost populations, sports stadiums sat empty, libraries crumbled, and forums gave way to farmland. Much was lost, unintentionally, from neglect. Ancient technology, such as water mills and glassmaking, was forgotten. Until the ruling elites learned the ways of civilization, the West lapsed into primitive rural conditions.

The barbarian conquest ended with two large groups living side by side, the ruling Germans and the former Romans. The German kings set up their own new elites, taking the best land for themselves. The early Germans preferred woodland and field. Urban life virtually vanished, as agriculture remained the mainstay of the economy and shaped society. The German lords lived in manor halls (large structures that housed warriors and dependents) and small villages throughout the countryside. The conquered Roman natives often became servile dependents, working for the German warriors in charge.

The Germans themselves were diverse, as shown by the numerous names of the tribes who had either settled what had once been Roman land or remained behind in "Germania": Visigoths, Ostrogoths, Alans, Alemanni, Vandals, Suevi, Franks, Angles, Saxons, Jutes, Gepids, Lombards, Frisians, Rugians, Burgundians, Bavarians, and Thuringians. Some were not even Germans, as various peoples entering Europe from Asia attached themselves to successful leaders. Constant warfare left some groups so weak that they either quickly joined a new ethnic conglomeration or disappeared altogether. These tribes spoke in many different dialects and accents, which were almost incomprehensible to one another. In western Europe they separated into many petty realms, regularly trying to conquer one another.

Within the borders of the old empire (except Britain), the Germans were actually an ethnic minority. Gradually, they stopped speaking their German language and adopted the ever-evolving language of the Romans. Thus, Latin slowly turned into vernacular Romance languages: Spanish and Italian named after Roman geography, and French coming from the Germanic Franks. Over centuries, the distinctive German character of the elites disappeared as they intermarried with the conquered ex-Roman peoples.

Initially, though, the Germans brought with them their own laws based on blood and oath, which separated them from the subject Roman populace. The early Germans did not understand the justice of Roman law courts and evidence provided by lawyers, nor the concept that only the government could use violence. They thought of justice as personal, rather than state controlled. Instead of loyalty to some impersonal state, or to abstract ideology, or to the deity of Rome, or to the person of the emperor, Germans were connected to one another through ties of kinship, from the nuclear family of parents and children to extended families, clans, tribes, "folk," and, finally, kingdoms. Families, meanwhile, took justice into their own hands, avenging wrongs by punishing wrongdoers themselves. So if one family member had been robbed, other family members hunted down the robber and exacted punishment (usually death, of course).

Thus, the tendency to emphasize personal punishment soon escalated into larger confrontations. For example, a robber killed in vengeance probably had a family of his own who did not take kindly to his death, perhaps seeing it as murder rather than justice. Thus they might go on to kill one of the killers, and soon, reciprocal vengeance might bring on vendettas or **feuds**, as families were caught in escalating cycles of attacks against one another. The German kings and lords tried to prevent feuds through *wergild* (having guilty parties pay families money in compensation for injuries or robberies). When guilt or innocence was in doubt, the barbarians resorted to **trials by ordeal** instead of the Roman criminal court procedures. For example, an accused would carry a bar of hot iron for nine paces without dropping it. The burned hands would then be wrapped. If after three days the wounds were healing, the accused was innocent; if they festered with infection, the accused was guilty and subsequently hanged. The Germans believed that God blessed the whole procedure through the grace of ministers of the Church and guaranteed a just outcome.

Indeed, the Christian Church itself was the greatest survivor of Rome's collapse in western Europe. Its institutions and beliefs helped to sustain whatever civilization survived. Actually, when the Germans invaded Rome, many of them had already been converted to Christianity. The invaders were usually respectful of holy places. The network of Christian bishops in their dioceses that had coexisted with Roman imperial provinces continued uninterrupted in many places. The Christian order, however, was somewhat complicated by the heretical form of Christianity held by many of the ruling Germans. Arians who rejected the Nicene Creed had converted them (as mentioned in the previous chapter). The Church managed only slowly to bring back many Germans into catholic orthodoxy.

This new society built on the ruins of the Roman Empire often defined itself as a realm of Christians, or **Christendom**. Serious divisions throughout the Middle Ages, however, prevented Christendom from ever becoming more than an ideal. Various leaders dreamed of this ideal, but only one came close to turning the geographic religious unity into a political one. Royal rivalries remained more powerful than cooperation toward any Christian commonwealth. Religious unity also suffered as a rift grew between Western, or Latin-speaking, Christians in western Europe and Eastern, or Greek-speaking, Christians in the Byzantine Empire. The concept of Christendom soon excluded those orthodox Christians still in Byzantium. In addition, kings would soon be fighting with their own bishops and the Bishop of Rome over leadership in the West. The idea of Christendom during the Middle Ages remained attractive but unrealized.

In these dangerous Dark Ages of warfare and cultural collapse, many Christians turned away from the European-wide concepts typical of Christendom to live in a highly localized manner. They began to withdraw from worldly cares so that they could better concentrate on God. A new way of life, called **monasticism**, evolved to organize people who wanted to devote themselves to strict Christianity. The monastic movement had already begun in the late Roman Empire, as some Christians in the East imitated Jesus' wanderings in the wilderness and isolated themselves to live as hermits. As this isolationist ideology migrated to the West, religious leaders promoted cenobitic, or group, monasticism. Its participants, communities of monks led by an abbot (or, for females, nuns under an abbess), gathered together apart from the bustling world to dedicate their life to prayer and meditation.

In the 520s, Benedict of Nursia became the most important abbot when he set up the monastery of Monte Cassino in southern Italy. To guide his flock of monks, he wrote down a special set of rules or regulations to cover those in this special lifestyle. While life under the **Benedictine Rule** was not unduly harsh, it was not particularly comfortable, either. The abbot (or abbess) exercised paternal authority in leading monks (or nuns) in a life of work and prayer. Monks or nuns were to have few changes of clothing. Unless they fell ill, they ate as vegetarians. The brothers slept together in common dormitories and spent their days in constant prayer and work. They sang psalms and farmed the land. Perhaps most important for the future of civilization, they read books. Under the Benedictine Rule, monks and nuns read the pagan classics of Greece and Rome in addition to the Bible and spiritual writings of the Church Fathers. They laboriously copied these texts by hand onto parchment bound into books, thus preserving much of the literature of the ancients in their small libraries. For a while, the monasteries were isolated islands of learning in a sea of barbaric illiteracy. In time, these islands would provide fertilizer and seed for the later regrowth of civilization.

The rise of monasticism divided the ministers of the Church into two groups: first, the monks, known as **"regular" clergy** (abbots and monks guided by regulations and separated from lay communities), and second, the "secular" clergy (bishops and priests involved in the world). Of the two, the monks were the role models of the Early Middle Ages for the laity, the rest of the population of lords and peasants. Cloisters seemed to create a heavenly community here on earth. The lay magnates and lords who wanted to support monastic work donated land to them or sent their extra children (boys whose inheritance might weaken the family patrimony or girls whose marriage might do the same) to join the monastic communities. Even the roughest sinner, when he felt death's hand upon his neck, might join a monastery, renounce the world, and partake in a blessed community that seemed a sure path toward paradise.

The Christian monks and the bishops did much to educate the uncivilized Germans, but they could not easily reduce their warrior habits. Rivalry among the Germans and the desire to attain political supremacy in western Europe meant one kingdom would conquer another, perhaps only to be itself conquered in turn. The Ostrogoths seized the Italian Peninsula; the Lombards soon replaced them. The Visigoths grabbed the Iberian Peninsula only to fall to the Muslims, as did the Vandals who took North Africa. Most German kingdoms briefly rose in power only to soon vanish into history.

The ethnic differences, though, left traces in the **regionalism** that still flourishes in many provinces of Europe today. European regions inherited their diversity both from the original peoples, such as Gauls and Celts romanized to varying degrees after Roman conquest, and from *germanization* following the new German conquerors. The Jews who lived scattered through the decaying cities, though, kept their culture relatively segregated and intact, as usual.

Only two large groups of Germans survived these early medieval centuries to dominate and provide the political and social framework for Western civilization, namely, the Anglo-Saxons and the Franks. Interestingly, both of these German peoples had entered the Roman Empire as pagans (not as heretics, like many other Germans) and were converted directly to orthodox, catholic Christianity.

The first of these groups, commonly called the **Anglo-Saxons, invaded the island of Great Britain**. Originally, the invaders were members of different tribes, mostly Angles, Saxons, and Jutes, who attacked across the North Sea beginning around 450. Since the Roman military had largely withdrawn decades earlier, the Romano-Britons were easily overrun (although some native resistance may have left traces in the myths of King Arthur). By the sixth century, the Germans ruled most of the formerly Roman areas, except for the fringes of Cornwall and Wales. The people who dwelt in the northern third of the island, beyond Hadrian's wall, also fought off the Germans, as they had the Romans. These people soon became the Scots of Scotland, closely tied to the Irish of Ireland (who had likewise never been conquered by Rome, although they had been converted to Christianity by Saint Patrick and others). In the southern two-thirds of Great Britain, though, the Germans soon so outnumbered the Romano-Britons that the latter's Celtic and Latin languages disappeared. These German conquerors established numerous small kingdoms, such as those of the Angles (Anglia), the West Saxons (Wessex), the East Saxons (Essex), and the lands in the north around the Humber River (Northumbria).

Christian missionaries from Ireland soon targeted the pagan Anglo-Saxons for conversion. Irish monk-missionaries arrived to preach throughout the northern realms. Meanwhile, other missionaries from the Bishop of Rome succeeded in converting the king of Kent in the south. Forced to choose between the Irish and Roman versions of Christianity, the majority of Anglo-Saxon kingdoms accepted unity with Rome at the **Council of Whitby** in 663. Energized with faith, Anglo-Saxon missionaries were soon both enforcing church discipline and evangelizing other Germans on the Continent.

While the Anglo-Saxons gained religious unity, political divisiveness almost led to their downfall. Beginning in 835, the **Vikings** began raiding the British Isles. The Vikings, Norsemen, or Northmen were a new wave of Germanic peoples who had settled in Scandinavia (modern Denmark, Norway, and Sweden) outside the orbit of ancient Rome or the moderating influence of Christianity. At first, the Vikings plundered ruthlessly. Soon, however, they conquered and occupied most of the Anglo-Saxon kingdoms (as well as key portions of Ireland and parts of the Continent, as explained below).

Only the Kingdom of Wessex barely survived and came back to defy the invaders under **King Alfred "the Great"** (r. 871–901). As a younger son of a king, Alfred originally wanted to be a monk. After the deaths of his brothers made him king,

Alfred instead found himself at war. He led his armies to fight the Vikings to a standstill. Secure from conquest, Alfred then tried to promote culture and literacy, especially with his translation of part of the Bible into Old English. Alfred's success established the unified kingdom of **England** (taking its name from the Angles). Ancient Celts, Roman immigrants, Anglo-Saxons, and now Vikings in the region called the Danelaw grew together to become the English. In the 990s, another wave of Viking invasions again almost destroyed the kingdom. The Danish king Canute, who had converted to Christianity, even managed to seize the English crown. King Canute (r. 1016–1035) of England preserved the realm, briefly uniting it with his other possessions around the North Sea. After his death, England once more gained a dynasty separate from Denmark. Despite this shaky, vulnerable start, the English melded together from this diverse Celtic/Roman/Anglo-Saxon/Viking heritage. Another invasion and ethnic clash shortly after Canute's death would force England into the High Middle Ages and to a central role in the development of Western civilization.

Meanwhile, on the Continent, the **Franks** had asserted themselves as the second enduring group of Germans. They started out more united than the English by having a royal dynasty called the **Merovingians** after a legendary founder, Merovech. By the end of the fifth century, the Franks had expanded from their base in northern Germania across the Rhine into northern Gaul. **King Clovis** (r. 481–511) won the support of the local Roman population and elites when he (and therefore his people) converted directly to orthodox, catholic Christianity. He then used his blessing from the clergy to conquer many of his neighboring Germans, such as the Aquitainians, the Burgundians, and the Suevi, still heretical Arian Christians who rejected the Nicene Creed. The kingdom that Clovis established was ethnically diverse. It combined the various German tribes with the large population of Roman Gauls. Although Clovis and his successors committed murders, betrayals, and various atrocities, the clerics who wrote histories thought that God specially blessed the Merovingian kings because they championed orthodox, catholic Christianity and political unity. In these uncertain times, it could seem right to honor God through the brutality of warfare.

Like the Anglo-Saxons, the Franks came close to vanishing into history, as they were nearly conquered by Muslims. In 710, a combined Arab and Berber army invaded Europe by landing near the southern tip of the Iberian Peninsula, which then became known as Gibraltar (or "Rock of Tarik," named after the Muslim commander). The Muslim army quickly crushed most of the Visigothic kingdom. Then it crossed the Pyrenees Mountains and attacked the Franks. In October 732, at the **Battle of Tours** or **Poitiers** (there has been some dispute about the location), a Frankish army led by Charles Martel ("the Hammer") stopped and turned back the Muslim invaders. The Muslims (who soon came to be called the Moors or the **Saracens** by the western Europeans) retreated into the Iberian Peninsula, most of which they continued to control for several centuries. But the armies of Islam were not able to conquer more of western Europe. The Franks had halted the Muslim advance into Europe, at least for the moment.

The Franks had been able to stand strong only by dispensing with their other political danger: dividing up kingdoms among heirs. Since the time of Clovis, if the king died with more than one son as heir, the realm was split up among the survivors. Before long, royal brothers and cousins were fighting against one another over the divisions of the fractured Frankish kingdoms. These kings grew weaker as they handed out lands and authorities to the aristocrats and nobles who did their fighting for them. Within a few decades, the Merovingian dynasts gained the nickname of "do-nothing kings." They gloried in their semidivine royal authority but did little to govern for the benefit of the people.

Fortunately for the future of the Franks, ambitious royal servants kept Frankish power intact. Managers of the king's household soon seized the important reins of rulership. These mayors (from the Latin word *major*, meaning "important") of the various royal palaces soon became the powers behind the thrones. One of them, the above-mentioned Charles Martel, managed by 720 to reunify the splintered kingdoms in the name of his Merovingian king. The successes of Mayor Charles Martel helped Western civilization to form in western Europe.

Review: How did German rule combine with the Roman heritage in the West?

Response:

CHARLES IN CHARGE

Charles Martel, who won at Tours/Poitiers, belonged to one of the most important families in Western history. Historians call that dynasty the Carolingians, from Carolus, the Latin version of the name Charles. Members of this family rescued the Franks from infighting and made them a powerful force again. Having beaten back the Moors, Charles handed his power to his two sons (although one quickly gave up and retired to a monastery). The sole heir, Pepin or **Pippin "the Short"** (r. 741–768), soon grew dissatisfied with ruling as mayor in the name of the officially crowned King Childeric III of the Merovingian dynasty. Pippin appealed to the person whom he considered to have the best connection to the divine, the Bishop of Rome, better known as the **pope**.

The institution of the popes, called the **papacy**, played a key role in the rise of the Carolingians and Western civilization. *Pope* comes from *papa*, or "father," a name often used for bishops. A number of bishops called popes or patriarchs had risen to preeminence by the fifth century in Rome, Alexandria, Antioch, Jerusalem, and Constantinople. Together, in Church councils, they and the other bishops declared doctrine and settled controversies. With the division of the Roman Empire into two halves and the collapse of Roman authority in the west, four patriarchs remained under the growing authority of the Byzantine emperors in the east. Meanwhile, the Bishop of Rome claimed the title of pope for himself alone and claimed a superior place (primacy) among the other bishops and patriarchs. The other patriarchs were prepared to grant the Bishop of Rome a primacy of honor, but not authority over them and their churches. In any case, the popes lived too far away to change developments in the eastern Roman or Byzantine Empire. In western Europe, though, religious and political circumstances favored a unique role for the Bishop of Rome.

The figure who embodied the early papacy was Gregory I "the Great" (r. 590–604). The growing importance of the monastic movement is reflected in his being the first pope who had previously been a monk. Much more important, though, were Gregory's three areas of activity, which defined what later popes did. First, the pope provided spiritual leadership for the West. Since the West lacked a literate population in comparison to the East, Gregory's manuals (models of sermons for preachers and advice on how to be a good pastor) filled a practical need. His theological writings were so significant that he was later counted as one of the four great Church Fathers, alongside Ambrose, Jerome, and Augustine, even though Gregory lived nearly two centuries after them. Second, after his literary endeavors, Gregory acted to secure orthodox, catholic Christianity all over the West, far outside his diocese in central Italy. Gregory sent missionaries to the Visigoths in the Iberian Peninsula, to Germany, and, most famously, to the British Isles. Third, the pope was a political leader. He helped organize and defend the lands around Rome from the invading Lombard Germans, helping to found the political power of the popes.

The necessity for papal political leadership increased when later popes disagreed with some Byzantine emperors in the eighth century. The eastern Christians were caught up in the Iconoclastic Controversy, which interpreted literally the Old Testament commandment about breaking graven images. Those in the Church who sought to shatter religious pictures and sculptures convinced some emperors to go along with them. Those with this viewpoint were, literally, iconoclasts (today the word figuratively refers to those seeking to overturn traditional ways). Since the Byzantine emperors sponsored so many bishops with these views, the eastern patriarchs and bishops began to support iconoclasm, and actually destroyed art in churches. When the western popes refused to go along, the Byzantine emperor confiscated lands in southern Italy that had been used to support the papal troops. Meanwhile, the Lombard invaders from the North still seriously threatened Rome.

At this pivotal moment, when the pope needed a new ally in the west, a letter came from the Frankish mayor of the palace, Pippin, son and heir of Charles Martel. In the letter, Pippin coolly inquired whether it was right that the one who had the power of a king should actually be the king. The pope agreed. So the last Merovingian king was shaved of his regal long hair and bundled off to a monastery. Pippin was crowned king, not once, but twice. First, he held a ceremony in 751 only for the Franks; then Pope Stephen II came to France and consecrated him again. In exchange, Pippin marched to Italy and defeated the Lombards in 754 and 756. His victories gave him control of the northern half of the Italian Peninsula (while the southern part remained under nominal Byzantine authority for the next few centuries). In his gratitude Pippin donated a large chunk of territory in central Italy to the pope. This **Donation of Pippin** eventually became known as the **Papal States**. These lands provided the basis for a papal principality for more than a thousand years. The arrangement also began a mutually supportive relationship, profitable to both the pope and Pippin, which historians call the **Frankish-Papal Alliance**.

The cooperation between the papacy and the Carolingians culminated under Pippin's son, Charles. He is known to history as **Charlemagne** (r. 768–814), which means "Charles the Great." As his father had before him, Charlemagne at first inherited the throne jointly with his brother, but the latter soon found himself deposed in a monastery. As sole ruler, Charles continued to support the popes. First, he invaded Italy, utterly breaking the power of the Lombards. A few years later, after political rivals had roughed up the pope, Charlemagne marched to Rome to restore papal dignity.

On Christmas Day A.D. 800, the pope crowned Charlemagne as Emperor of the Romans. The circumstances surrounding this act have remained unclear. People then and historians since have argued about the coronation's significance. Did it merely recognize Charlemagne's actual authority or give it a new dimension? Was the pope, by placing the crown on Charlemagne's brow, trying to control the ceremony and the office? Did it insult the Byzantine emperor, who was, after all, the real Roman emperor (even if some alleged at the time that the eastern throne was vacant, since a mere woman, Empress Irene, ruled after deposing and blinding her son)? In any case, the coronation resulted in a brief revival of ancient Roman ideology. An emperor once again ruled the West in the name of Rome's civilization (see map 7.2).

In most ways, though, Charlemagne resembles his barbaric German ancestors more than a Roman Caesar Augustus. He dressed in Frankish clothing and enjoyed beer and beef (instead of wine and fish as the Romans had). A man of action, he led a military campaign every year to one portion of his empire or another. Thus, he expanded his rulership and conquered the heartland of Europe, which became the core of the European Community more than a millennium afterward. He deposed the Bavarian duke and took over his duchy. He smashed rebellious Lombards as his father had. He also fought the Saxons in northern Germany (cousins of long-since Christianized Anglo-Saxons in Britain). For thirty years, the Christian king tried to convert the pagan Saxons to both religious and political obedience. These Saxons faced two choices: either be washed in the water of holy baptism or be slaughtered in their own blood. Many died; survivors converted. Charlemagne wiped out the Avars (Asian raiders who had settled along the Danube). The emperor successfully defended his empire's borders against Danes in the north and Moors in the south. Charlemagne's empire became bigger than any other political structure in the West since Emperor Romulus Augustulus had lost his throne in A.D. 476.

Charles was more than a bloodthirsty barbarian king. He consciously tried to revive the Roman Empire and its civilization. The government still heavily depended on his person, but he continued the efforts of his predecessors to expand governance into an institution centered on the palace. He had administrators, such as a

Map 7.2.   Europe, 800

chamberlain to help manage finances. He set up ***missi dominici*** (messengers from his household), powerful counts and bishops charged with checking up on local government. He collected and wrote down laws for his various peoples. In one law, called "A General Warning," Charlemagne noted that too many clergy were unlettered and going about carrying weapons, whoring, gambling, and getting drunk. The warning ended with the dire prediction that life is short and death is certain. The Christian emperor wanted an ordered realm in this world so people could gain heaven in the next. Charlemagne's government was the most ambitious western Europe had experienced in three hundred years.

To improve upon his government, Charlemagne and his international advisors, like Paul the Deacon from Lombardy and Alcuin Albinus from Northumbria, consciously sought to revive civilization. Aachen, or Aix-la-Chapelle (today located in northwestern Germany near Belgium), was built as a new capital city: it aimed to be a new Rome, the first city built in stone since the barbarians had taken over the forums. Aachen's centerpiece was a church, small but splendid and harmonious with its high octagonal walls capped by a dome. Aachen soon became an intellectual center. Scribes fashioned a new, legible script, Carolingian minuscule, which invented the lowercase letters you are reading right now. Every work of history and literature that scholars could find was rewritten in this new style, helping to preserve much of the legacy of Greece and Rome.

Charlemagne's intellectuals also revived the Roman educational curriculum of the fifth century: the **seven liberal arts**. The *trivium* of grammar, rhetoric, and logic with the *quadrivium* of arithmetic, geometry, music, and astronomy were taught once more, this time in schools attached to monasteries and cathedrals. This so-called **Carolingian Renaissance** (780–850) hoped to use education to revitalize a way of life that had disappeared in the West since the Germans had swept away Roman rule. The Frankish/German Charlemagne used the liberal learning of Greece and Rome to establish the culture of Western civilization.

Regrettably for the cause of civilization, Charlemagne's revitalization attempt failed. The empire was too large and primitive for the weak institutions of government he could cobble together. First, he faced the difficulty of paying for art, literature, architecture, and schools with a poor agricultural economy that offered no functional taxation. Second, Frankish aristocrats saw little value in book-learning. Third, Charlemagne's own codifications of laws, written for the Alemanni, Burgundians, or Saxons, preserved ethnic differences rather than binding together a new common imperial unity. A final difficulty for Charlemagne was his own mortality. He drove the system along by force of will and sword, but death was certain. Few rulers could measure up to his abilities and achievements.

Charlemagne's vast empire actually held together for a few years after his death because of the good fortune that only one son survived him. Under Emperor Louis "the Pious" (r. 814–840), the Carolingian Renaissance peaked. Then Louis prematurely divided up his empire among his own three sons and invested them with authority during his own lifetime. Not surprisingly, they soon bickered with him and with one another. When Louis tried to carve out a share for a fourth son by another wife, civil war broke out. His heirs first humiliated Louis on the battlefield and then fought themselves to a bloody standstill. The resultant peace agreement shattered the political unity of western Europe for more than a thousand years.

The **Treaty of Verdun** in 843 broke apart Charlemagne's empire into three sections, each under its own Carolingian dynasty. The actual treaty was written in both early French and German, offering clear evidence that a linguistic division was now sealed as a political one. The treaty established a kingdom of the West Franks, out of which grew **France**; a kingdom of the East Franks, out of which rose **Germany**; and a middle realm, Lotharingia (named after Louis' grandson, Lothar). At the time, Lotharingia was the heart of the empire, including not only today's small province of **Lorraine** on the border of France and Germany, but also the Lowlands (modern Belgium, the Netherlands, and Luxembourg), south through Switzerland and over the Alps into northern Italy. This mixed ethnic and linguistic middle realm had no cohesion except its prosperity and its dynasty. Both the West Franks and the East Franks targeted Lorraine after the Carolingian dynasty died out. For the next eleven hundred years, the French and the Germans fought over possession of the middle.

As if all of these political divisions were not bad enough, foreign invaders killed any hope for a unified and coherent empire. From the north, the Vikings or Norsemen sailed in on longships; from the east, the **Magyars** or Hungarians swept out of the steppes of Asia on swift ponies; and from the south, from North Africa and the Iberian Peninsula, Muslim Moors or Saracens raided by land and by sea. None of these invaders was Christian. Only the Saracens were civilized. They all plundered, raped, and burned what they could. The feuding Carolingian kings could do little to stop these marauders. The fragile and young western Christendom might have ended under these attacks.

Thus, Charlemagne's brief success at the revival of civilization crashed in the chaos of jealous children, resentful aristocrats, invading barbarians, and hostile non-Christians. Few empires could have survived such an assault from both within and without. The popes were of little help, too, as petty Roman nobles fought over the papal throne. In 897, a vengeful pope, Stephen VI, even put the corpse of one of his predecessors, Formosus, on trial. Such post-mortem vengeance did little good, since he was himself soon deposed and strangled.

Even as the Carolingian Empire died, its corpse became the fertilizer for the future. The empire left a dream of reunification, reinforcing the longing for the long-lost unity and cultural greatness of the Roman Empire. The political reality that followed, however, divided West Franks and East Franks into France and Germany. These two realms, together with England, formed the core of the West. Despite limited resources, these westerners fought off the assaults from without and established a new order and hierarchy from within. The result was the blossoming of medieval Western civilization.

Review: How did the Carolingian family rise and fall?

Response:

THE CAVALRY TO THE RESCUE

Without a central government, the peoples of the collapsing Carolingian Empire needed to defend themselves. New leaders, whether through their own achievements or using family ancestry, inspired others to follow them. To defend against the Viking attacks, they built military fortresses called **castles** (see figure 7.1). These fortifications were not simply army bases with walls; they were family homes. The quaint saying, "A man's home is his castle," quite literally came from this period. Castles were originally primitive stockades or wooden forts on hills. A castle became the home of a local leader who convinced others to build it and help defend it.

Figure 7.1.   The square block of an early castle dominates the town of Loches in France.

These castles became new centers of authority from which lords ruled over small areas, usually no larger than a day's ride.

Hiding out in castles was not a long-term solution, however. "The best defense is a good offense" is another saying appropriate to the time period. Fortunately for Western civilization, the **knight** rode to the rescue before all could be lost in the onslaughts of Vikings, Magyars, and Saracens. The new invention of stirrups, imported from Asia, secured these warriors firmly in the saddles of their warhorses. Their armor for defense and lance and sword for offense made knights effective heavy cavalry when riding together in a charge. A large group of knights and horses made up of several tons of flesh and iron overpowered all opponents.

Already by 1050, knights had won Europe a respite from foreign invasions. The three external enemies of Christendom, the Vikings, Magyars, and Saracens, ceased to be threats. The Norsemen stopped raiding, converted to Christianity, and set up the Scandinavian kingdoms of Denmark, Norway, and Sweden. The adventurous spirit of the Norse carried some of them across the Atlantic Ocean to settle in Greenland and even, briefly, North America. The Magyars, meanwhile, became Hungarians, as they settled in the plain of Hungary along the middle Danube. Their King Stephen consolidated both his rule and the structure of the Kingdom of Hungary with his conversion and that of his people to Christianity in 1000. Only the Saracens remained hostile and unconverted. Still, they concentrated their efforts on developing their own civilization in the Iberian Peninsula, called Andalusia, rather than conquering their Christian neighbors.

Knights won because they were the best military technology of the age, dominating battlefields for the next five hundred years, long after the threats of Vikings, Magyars, and Saracens had dissipated. As we have seen before, a group with a monopoly on the military can rule the rest of society. In the Middle Ages, knights began to claim authority in the name of the public good and elevated themselves above the masses as a closed social caste of nobles. Their ethos of nobility meant that they lived the good life because they risked their lives to defend the women, children, clerics, and peasants. They lived in the nicest homes, ate the most delicious food, and wore the most comfortable clothing, and everyone else paid for it.

During the political chaos of the invasions, whoever commanded the loyalty of others became noble. Over time, though, nobles closed their ranks and limited the status of nobility to those who inherited it. After 1100, usually only those who could prove noble ancestry could become knights (with the rare exceptions of kings ennobling talented warriors). This closed social group of the nobility reinforced itself through **chivalry**, the code of the knights. The ceremonies for initiation to knighthood were surrounded with elaborate rituals. In their castles and courts, knights practiced courtesy and refined manners with one another, such as using "please," "thank you," and napkins. At **tournaments**, they practiced fighting as a form of sport, entertaining crowds and winning prizes. On the battlefield, they applied rules to fight one another fairly, never attacking an unarmed knight, for example.

While there was much regional variation, the organization of these knights required new structures, or *feudal politics*.[1] The vassal (a subordinate knight) promised loyalty (fealty) and personal service on the battlefield or in the political courts to the lord (a superior knight) in return for a fief (usually agricultural land sufficiently productive for the knight to live from). A lord was as powerful as the number of vassals he could call on. Lords began to take on new titles that reflected the number of vassals each could bind to himself with fiefs. Above the simple knight at the bottom of the hierarchy were, in ascending order, barons, counts (or earls in England), dukes, and, ultimately, the king. Kings were only as strong as the number of vassals they personally controlled. The most important political units in the eleventh and twelfth centuries were the baronies, the counties, or the duchies, rather than the kingdoms. These political constellations also often reflected underlying ethnic differences, whether dating back to the German invasions or the original Roman conquests.

A network of mutual promises of fidelity provided the glue for feudal politics. All governments are ultimately based on whether or not people uphold the rules. Family interests of the knights complicated matters. Originally, fiefs were supposed to revert to the overlord upon his vassal's death. The powerful drive of family, however, where parents provided for their children, soon compelled fiefs to become virtually hereditary. Lords and vassals did break their pledges of service and loyalty, probably as often as many modern married people break their vows. When vassals defied their lords, only fights among the knights could conclusively settle the dispute. Thus, the feudal age has been renowned for its constant warfare. Yet enough lords and vassals did maintain oaths so that medieval society became stable. The web of mutual promises of loyalty, the gathering at court to give advice and pronounce judgments, the socializing at tournaments, and the shared risks of battle all forged a ruling class that held onto power for centuries.

Even the Church could not avoid being drawn into the feudal network, since dioceses and abbeys possessed so much land. Various lords demanded that the

---

1. The term *feudalism* carries too many different meanings to be useful as a historical concept anymore; it is best avoided. Likewise, the phrase "feudal system" makes these arrangements sound more organized than they were. Finally, do not confuse "feudal" politics with feuds or vendettas.

Church contribute its wealth to support the common defense. Rather than have knights seize control and turn Church-owned farms into fiefs, bishops and abbots became feudal lords themselves. Thus, clerics became responsible for building castles, commanding knights in battle, and presiding over courts. Some bishops and abbots even ruled as princes, similar to feudal dukes and counts. These political obligations recognized the Church's real power but often clashed with its spiritual aims.

To compensate somewhat, the Church tried to suggest that certain divinely inspired morality was part of chivalry and the rules of war (see figure 7.2). In some regions, bishops and princes proclaimed the **Peace of God**, which both classified clergy, women, and children as noncombatants and limited the reasons for going to war. Church leaders also tried to assert the **Truce of God**, which limited how often warfare could be conducted, especially banning it on Sundays, holidays, and during planting and harvesting.

Figure 7.2. This sculpture in Magdeburg Cathedral of the ancient martyr and saint Maurice portrays the saint as a black African in twelfth-century armor. The Church thus identified Christian values with knighthood, regardless of ethnicity.

Paying for all the expensive armor, horses, and castles was the agricultural production by peasants. Those who did the farm labor—namely, the vast majority of the population—did not share in the political relationships of the knights. In a connected, yet separate sociopolitical relationship called **manorial economics**, the peasants did the farmwork that provided the food and wealth for the knights.

These medieval peasants are known as **serfs**. A medieval serf had servile status, but not as low as that of a slave. They were legally connected or bound to the land of their knightly and clerical lords. Serfs lost the right to make decisions about their own lives (such as choice of marriage partners or where to live) and owed work, taxes, and service to the landowners. These burdens kept them poor from generation to generation. Nevertheless, serfs did benefit from always being tied to land at least, since it provided food. Parents and their children lived in the same villages and farmed the same lands, season after season, according to law and custom. Neither they nor their descendants could be thrown off the land as long as they performed their customary services.

The harsh conditions of the Early Middle Ages forced many manors to become self-sufficient. Trade had nearly vanished, and the roads were too dangerous to travel. The peasants cooperated in their local communities to produce much of what everyone needed to survive, such as food, clothing, and tools. They depended on their lords for justice and defense and relied on the parish church for salvation.

Then a simple agricultural innovation on these manors soon helped Europe prosper as never before. Beginning in the dark times after the fall of the Carolingian Empire, someone came up with the idea of **three-field planting**. Previously, the custom in European farming had been a two-field system, which left half the farmland fallow (without crops) every year to recover its fertility. The new method involved planting one-third with one kind of crop (such as beans), another third with another crop (such as wheat), and letting only a third lie fallow. The following year they rotated which crop they planted in which part of the field. The result was a larger harvest for less work and an improved diet for everyone.

New technology, much of which had spread to Europe after being invented in Asia, further enlarged what the manorial peasants could accomplish. The horse collar enabled horses to pull plows without strangling. Windmills ground grain into flour without human or animal labor. These and other agricultural and technological advancements added to the wealth of Europe. The craft and farmwork of the peasants continued to produce wealth at the lord's behest. The rule of the knights defended the fragile kingdoms of France, England, Germany, and the rest. The prayers and labors of the clergy made Christianity the sole religion of the West. Western civilization appeared to be secure.

The fall of Rome in the West in the fifth century had initiated a troubled time about which much remains in the dark for historians. In such difficult times, little energy was spent on learning and intellectual endeavors. Survival mattered more than the bare minimum of culture preserved in the rituals of the Church and the epic songs of the Germans. Over the next few centuries after the chaos of the invasions, powerful rulers, such as Alfred in England or Charles Martel among the Franks, consolidated numerous barbarian kingdoms into a few realms. For a while, it looked as if the Carolingian Empire might unify the West as a revived Roman

Empire. Its failure nonetheless left the kingdoms of France and Germany strong enough to hold out against new invasions. A thousand years after Christ's birth, the West was strong and stable. The successful ordered medieval society of catholic clergy, feudal knights, and manorial peasants seemed settled forever as God's plan for humanity. The success of Christendom soon led to change, however. More sophisticated political and social structures, and even ideas, shook up accepted assumptions. New people sought supremacy. As a result, the West passed from the Early Middle Ages into the High Middle Ages in the eleventh century between 1000 and 1100.

Review: How did feudal politics and manorial economics help the West recover?

Response:

CHAPTER 8

The Medieval Mêlée

The High and Later Middle Ages, 1000 to 1500

Christendom had grown up among the ruins of the western part of the ancient Roman Empire during the Early Middle Ages. Thus began a distinct Western civilization, having combined the surviving remnants of Græco-Roman culture and Christianity inspired by Judaism with the rule of the German conquerors. The following **High** or **Central Middle Ages** (1000–1350) represented the culmination of medieval politics and culture. The improved manorial agriculture raised the amount of wealth, while the stable feudal governments provided more security. The medieval kingdoms became civilized, as towns and cities provided new avenues to riches. At the same time, though, there seemed to be constant fighting, from the hand-to-hand mêlée of medieval knightly combat to vast wars of ideology. Institutions and ideas fought with one another over which would master the minds, bodies, and souls of Christendom. New environmental pressures shaped these conflicts in the **Later Middle Ages** (1300–1500). Medieval methods adapted to new times, reflecting the growing success and power of Europe (see map 8.1).

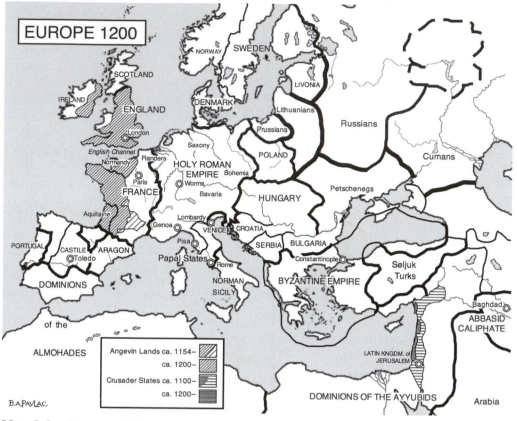

Map 8.1.   Europe, 1200

RETURN OF THE KINGS

After the danger of Vikings, Saracens, and Magyars had passed, the knights of Christendom waged war more and more against one another. These lords ignored the
kings, who represented order and sovereignty. The politics of feudal lords and
vassals decentralized authority. In some areas, the local knight in his castle and
what he controlled were all that mattered to people. Violence increased as private
wars determined public policy. Kings clung precariously to their thrones, often
controlling fewer resources than their greater vassals but still trying to pass on their
dynasties from father to son. When this failed, some other aristocrat placed the
crown on his own head—someone had to be king.

Despite this weakening of real royal power, kings and their special position
became the focus of state building. The traditional roles of the king (warrior, lawgiver, symbol) and the new feudal structure offered certain advantages to kings.
Some kings united their realms, rebuilding the fragmented feudal fiefs into a unified
hierarchical state and moving from the personal oaths of fidelity to the rule of law.
The old Germanic tradition that believed kings were semidivine combined with the
Christian Church's desire for a stable sociopolitical order. Likewise, most kings also
had attained a feudal position of the *suzerain* (supreme lord) over all others, at the

top of the hierarchy of feudal relationships. Kings pulled their unruly dukes, counts, barons, and knights with their fiefs into a coherent political system. Their key difficulty was how to delegate without losing control to feudal competitors. Conflicts between kings and their rival aristocrats and nobles over obedience shaped the various states of Europe.

The first kingdom to experience a reinvigorated royal power was that of the East Franks, which was soon called the Kingdom of the Germans and then grew into a new empire. Local military commanders, the dukes, better defended their various provinces against the Magyars and Vikings than did the distant kings. In the process, the dukes promoted feelings of regional unity under their own rule. Thus the dukes became more powerful than the nominal king. In 911, the last of the Carolingian dynasty, Louis "the Child," died and passed the kingship to the Duke of Franconia—ruler of the heartland of the East Franks. After a troubled reign, that duke in turn handed the kingship over to his strongest rival, the Duke of Saxony. The new king of the Germans was able to found a royal dynasty for Germany, passing power from father to son for several generations. The continuity of these Saxon kings managed to rebuild royal authority.

The most important king of this Saxon dynasty, **Otto I "the Great"** (r. 935–973), originally faced both rebellions and invasions. He managed to quell the revolts begun by his relatives using both successful military campaigns and the support of the bishops, to whom he granted lands and authority. Unlike dukes and counts, bishops had no heirs to whom they could pass on their power, and the king usually had the most important voice in the successors' selection. This arrangement bound together many bishops and kings in Germany. With the support of these prince-bishops, Otto broke the power of the Magyars at the Battle of Lechfeld in 955, allegedly helped by the Holy Lance that had pierced Christ's side. Afterward, the Magyars ceased to invade, settled down to establish the tame kingdom of Hungary, and converted to Christianity. Otto further extended his own rule over Italy. His pretext for invading Italy was the rescue of the young widowed Queen Adelaide, whom a usurper had locked up in a castle. Otto drove out the usurper and rescued Adelaide, making her his queen (which, of course, then supported his own claims to be "king" of Italy).

Otto confirmed his rulership in Italy eleven years later in 962, when he had the pope crown him Emperor of the Romans in the tradition of Charlemagne. This act once again employed the name of the ancient Roman Empire, reviving what had first been lost to the West in the fifth century, what had then failed with the Carolingians in the ninth century, and what technically still continued in Byzantium. The political state ruled by Otto and his successors eventually came to be called the **Holy Roman Empire** (962–1806) by its rulers and later historians. At its height, this empire included all the lands of the Germans, Italy from the Papal States northward, much of the Lotharingian middle-realm territories of Burgundy and the Lowlands, Bohemia, and some Slavic lands on the northern plains of Central Europe. The Holy Roman Empire dominated European politics for the 150 years after Otto.

While the Germans were building the Holy Roman Empire, the Kingdom of England had just managed to survive another onslaught of Vikings in the tenth century. The short rule of King Canute's dynasty from Denmark settled matters briefly. When this dynasty died out in 1066, civil war broke out. First, the native

English earl Harold Godwinson claimed the English throne. Next, Harold fought off a Scandinavian invasion by another claimant in the north. Finally, Harold had to rush to the south to fight an invasion from Normandy. There he fell at the Battle of Hastings, defeated by the army of the Norman duke **William "the Conqueror"** (or "the Bastard" from another point of view). The **Norman conquest** of England changed the course of history.

The Normans were Vikings (Norsemen) who had seized and settled a province of France along the English Channel in the tenth century, calling it Normandy after themselves. They recognized the French king as *suzerain* and soon spoke only French. This combination of Viking and Frankish heritages created a people who were extraordinarily influential in European history. Other Normans later seized southern Italy and Sicily from the slackening grip of the Byzantine Empire and created a powerful and dynamic state there. In that kingdom, unique in Christendom, the Norman-French rulers fostered prosperity and peace among diverse populations of Italians, Greeks, and Arabs. The Normans also played a leading role in the Crusades (see below).

The victorious Duke William crowned himself King William I of England (r. 1066–1087) on Christmas day. William replaced virtually all the local magnates with his own loyal vassals after he crushed several rebellions by English nobles (see figure 8.1). England therefore became less and less involved in the Scandinavian affairs of northern Europe and more tied to France and western Europe. The French-speaking Normans only slowly adopted the language of the majority of English speakers. As a result, a French/Viking influence of the Normans added to the previous Viking, Anglo-Saxon, Roman, Celtic, and prehistoric cultures to create England.

William's military victories enabled him to assert a strong monarchical rule and to bind his new land under his law. One example was his command to have the *Domesday Book* written in 1086. It assessed the wealth of most of his new kingdom by counting the possessions of his subjects, from castles and plowland down to cattle and pigs. William used the knowledge of this book to tax everything more effectively. This assessment was the first such official catalogue in the West since the time of ancient Rome.

William's dynasty ran into trouble, though, when his son Henry I died from eating too many lampreys in 1135. Henry sired over twenty bastards, but his only legitimate male heir had drowned in a shipwreck. The result was, of course, civil war. On one side was Henry's daughter, Matilda, the widow of German Holy Roman Emperor Henry V and current wife of the powerful Geoffrey, Count of Anjou, just south of Normandy. On the other side, most barons of England supported her cousin Stephen of Blois from northern France. Yet Matilda and her husband's forces won Normandy in battle and negotiated a truce stipulating that after Stephen's death the English throne would go to Geoffrey and Matilda's son. The young **King Henry II** (r. 1154–1189) thus founded the English royal dynasty of the **Angevins** (the adjective for Anjou), or **Plantagenets** (after a flower symbol adopted as a badge). The Plantagenets ruled England for the rest of the Middle Ages, from 1154 to 1485. In addition to England, Henry inherited Normandy and Anjou from his mother and father. Moreover, he gained Aquitaine through marriage to its duchess,

Figure 8.1. William "the Conqueror" started building the castle, the White Tower of the Tower of London, after his conquest of England.

Eleanor, who had recently divorced King Louis VII of France. Thus, Henry II reigned over an empire that stretched from the Scottish border to the Mediterranean Sea.

Being crowned king and exercising real power were two different things, however, especially since many lords in Henry's vast territories had usurped royal prerogatives during the chaos of civil war. Henry used the widespread desire of many to return to the peace and prosperity of the "good ol' days" as a way to promote innovations in government, especially in England. In a campaign similar to that of Augustus Caesar to "restore" the republic, Henry claimed he wanted to revive the ways of his grandfather, the last Norman king. By doing so, he really concentrated rule in his own hands. Henry II pursued this through four means. First, he needed military domination, so he attacked and demolished all castles that did not have an explicit license from him. He built others in key locations, using the latest technology imported from the Crusades in Palestine (see the next section). He also preferred paid mercenaries to feudal levies. He asked his knights to pay "shield money" instead of feudal military service.

Second, he began a revision of royal finances to pay for this military might. His own treasurer had written that the power of rulers rose and fell according to how much wealth they had: rulers with few funds were vulnerable to foes, while rulers with cash preyed upon those without. Henry obtained good money through currency reform, creating the pound sterling: 120 pennies equaled a pound's worth of silver. If his minters made bad money, he had their hands chopped off. Circulating coins improved his people's ability to pay taxes. Further, he reinforced old sources of taxation, including the Danegeld tax imposed on the descendants of Viking invaders who had long since become assimilated with the English. He raised crusading taxes to pay for a crusade he never took part in. All these funds were accounted for by the Office of the Exchequer, which took its name from the checkerboard with which officials tracked credits and debits.

Third, in his role as law preserver and keeper, Henry improved the court system. He offered more impartial judges as alternatives to the wide variety of local baronial courts. His judges also earned a better education at new universities in Oxford and Cambridge, where they trained in a revived study of Roman law based on the Justinian Code. These judges traveled around the country (literally on a circuit), hearing cases that grand juries determined to be worthy of trial. The judges often used a **jury** of peers to examine evidence and decide guilt and innocence, rather than relying only on the allegedly divinely guided trial by ordeal. Henry's subjects could also purchase writs, standardized forms where one had only to fill in the blanks of name, date, and the like, in order to bring complaints before the sheriff and, thus, the king. These innovations increased the jurisdiction of the king's law, making it relatively quick and available to many. At the same time, people became involved on the local level, holding themselves mutually responsible for justice. This system is still used today in many Western countries.

Fourth, Henry II needed a sound administration to organize all this activity, of which the Exchequer was a part. Since he spent two-thirds of his time across the English Channel in his French provinces, Henry needed loyal officials who could exercise authority in his name but without his constant attention. The result revived government by bureaucracy. Writs and official records began to be kept, stored, and perhaps even consulted. Permanent bureaucratic officials, such as the treasurer or the chancellor, stood in for the king. London started to become a capital city, as it offered a permanent place for people to track down government officials. New personnel were hired from the literate people of the towns rather than from the traditional ruling class of nobles. These men had the protection of the king, through whom they gained wealth and advancement. The king could hold these officials accountable and hire or fire them at will, unlike nobles, who inherited offices almost as easily as they had fiefs. Henry paid the lower grades of officials with food, money, or even the leftover ends of candles, while he compensated higher-ranked ministers with Church lands and feudal titles. These civil servants made government more responsive both to change and to the will of the governed.

The challenge any king faced in controlling appointed officials came to life in Henry's infamous quarrel with **Thomas Becket** (d. 1172). Becket had risen in Henry's service to the highest office of chancellor, all the while fighting for extended royal rights and prerogatives. Henry had Thomas Becket made Archbishop of Canterbury, the highest-ranking Church official in England, believing that Becket would serve the royal will in both positions. Unfortunately for Henry, Archbishop Thomas experienced an unexpected religious conversion after his consecration. He became one of the reformers who resisted royal intervention in Church affairs (see the next section). Years of dispute ended when four knights bashed Thomas' brains out in front of his own altar. Thomas Becket's martyrdom allowed the English clergy to appeal to Rome in Church matters and to keep benefit of clergy (that clerics be judged by Church courts, not secular ones). Still, many clerics remained royal servants.

Despite bureaucratic innovations, government still remained tied to the personality of the ruler. Rebellions by his sons marked the last years of Henry II's reign. His wife and their mother, Eleanor of Aquitaine, helped to organize the revolts. Henry had committed adulterous affairs and kept Eleanor under house arrest after she showed too much independence and resentment. In return, she and her sons found support among barons who resented the king's supremacy. Nevertheless, the dynastic unity of Henry's lands survived for a few years after his demise, largely due to the solidity of his reforms. His immediate heir, King Richard I "the Lion-Hearted" (r. 1189–1199), was away from England for all except ten months of his ten years of rule, and yet the system functioned without him. In contrast, Richard's heir, his younger brother King John (r. 1199–1216), pushed the royal power to its limit as he quarreled with King Philip II of France, Pope Innocent III, and his own barons, only to lose most of the Angevin territories in France.

In 1215, John's unhappy subjects forced him to agree to the famous ***Magna Carta*** (Latin for "Great Charter"). This treaty between the king, the clergy, the barons, and the townspeople of England accepted royal authority but limited its abuses. In principle, it made the king subject to law, not above it. This policy of requiring the king to consult with representatives of the people became permanent mostly because John died soon after signing it, leaving a child to inherit power. The clergy, barons, and townspeople grew accustomed to meeting with the king and his representatives. In 1295, King Edward I summoned a model assembly of those who would speak with the king, called **Parliament**. This body of representatives of the realm effectively realigned the rights of English kings and their subjects.

Meanwhile, the kings of France, who had started out in the tenth century weaker than those of England, became stronger by the thirteenth century. The founder of the Capetian dynasty (987–1328) had seized the throne from the last Carolingian king. At first, the Capetians held only nominal power, effective only over an area around Paris called the Île de France. With the rise of feudal politics, royal power had almost vanished. Only the king's position as *suzerain*, or keystone of the feudal hierarchy, barely preserved respect for the crown. More powerful than the king were the dynastic magnates, especially the Count of Flanders, the Duke of Normandy, the Count of Anjou, and the Duke of Aquitaine.

Two particular medieval French kings built France's strong monarchy. **Philip II "Augustus"** (r. 1180–1223) gained a significant advantage over the Angevins. At the beginning of Philip's reign, Henry II's Angevin Empire seemed to doom French monarchy, since Henry's territories in France of Normandy, Anjou, and Aquitaine overwhelmed the French king's lands. Fortunately for France, Henry's French possessions collapsed under his son John. Philip fought a war against John, sparked by feudal complaints of the vassals. The Battle of Bouvines in 1214 sealed Philip's victory with the conquest of most of the continental possessions of the Plantagenets except for a sliver of Aquitaine called Guyenne. As conqueror (like William of Normandy in his conquest of England), Philip accumulated overwhelming authority. He then carried out reforms modeled on those of Henry II. His new administrative bureaucratic offices were settled in his chosen capital city, Paris. His only mistake was to break his first marriage to Ingeborg of Denmark and marry Agnes of Meran without permission of the Church. The papal interdict on France lasted four years.

By the reign of his descendant **Philip IV "the Fair"** (r. 1285–1314), the king's power in France was supreme. Philip IV further intensified royal authority with his own representative body, the **Estates-General**. Similar to the English Parliament, the Estates-General included representatives from the clergy, landed nobility, and commons or burghers from towns. These members gave their consent to and participation in enacting new royal taxes and laws. Philip IV also secured royal authority against even the papacy (see the next section).

Thus, the kings in Germany, France, and England had managed to restore authority and create the first three core states of Western civilization. This fragile Christendom might still have been crushed by yet another invasion, that of Mongols or Tartars, polytheist pony-riding warriors who had come to dominate Asia in the early twelfth century under their leader Genghis or Chengiz Khan. In 1241, the Mongol invaders under Genghis Khan's grandson Batu smashed multinational armies of Christians in both Poland and Hungary, paving the way for conquest of Europe. The next year, though, a fight over the Mongol dynasty ended their interest in invading the little western corner of Eurasia. Thus, Christendom survived, led by kings who worked closely with the wealth and influence of the Church, defeated powerful enemies, and promoted the rule of law. The kings had taken primitive feudal authority and brought the nobles into some order and structure, if not full obedience and subjugation. Their rivalries with one another also provided a dynamic of competition, both economic and military. Out of the diversity of these states and others to follow, Western civilization lurched forward in war and peace.

Review: *How did more centralized governments form in western Europe?*

Response:

DISCIPLINE AND DOMINATION

The feudal lords of Christendom struggled to bind people together politically, while the prelates of the Church attempted to unify the faithful religiously. The Christian Church had survived both the fall of the Roman Empire in the West and the fall of the Carolingian Empire. Most people, peasant and noble, labored on in their roles of farming and administering, attending church as best they could. Large numbers also retreated from the cares of the world to the haven of monasteries to become monks and nuns, as during the chaos of the fifth century. Since many regular clergy lacked sincere religious belief, religious dedication slipped. In numerous monasteries, the regulations of Benedict were either unheard or unheeded.

One group of monks in the wild district of Burgundy decided to change that neglectful attitude with the foundation of the new monastery of Cluny in the year 910. First, the monks of the **Cluniac Reform** dedicated themselves to a strict devotion to the Benedictine Rule, including a disciplined practice of the prayers of the Divine Office. Second, in order to maintain reform in their own cloister and in others who imitated it, they held regular meetings to set a proper tone and to correct abuses. Third, they exempted themselves from local supervision of either the nobility or the bishop, because they thought the local nobility would interfere more than they would help. Both the nobility and higher officers of the Church were too compromised by the rough-and-tumble feudal network to be trusted. Instead, the monks placed themselves under the direct supervision of the distant Bishop of Rome, the pope.

This act was done without the knowledge or permission of the pope, but it reinforced a trend with enormous consequences for the Christian Church in the West. According to tradition and **canon law** (legal rules that governed the institutional Church), a local bishop or the king assumed supervision of a monastery. Local nobles might also intrude, using their power of patronage and family connections among the monks and nuns. Charlemagne had also supported the reorganization of the Church into provinces, which united the dioceses of several bishops under the supervision of one who became an "archbishop." To weaken this trend, the supporters of bishops "found" a number of charters that documented an overarching authority by the distant pope in Rome. Later organizers of the canon law accepted these forgeries as genuine. Hence, the pope became increasingly exceptional in the canon law, a unique, superior authority. An appeal to Rome over any matter from ownership of a fishpond to possession of a benefice (a paying Church position) could transform a local fray into a fundamental legal dispute. The popes asserted their unique jurisdiction by binding themselves with clerics throughout the West.

The Cluniacs, meanwhile, had enormous success building new monastic communities and reforming old ones. People chose to abandon the pleasures of aristocratic pursuits and accept a hard life of obedience and discipline, although only aristocrats and nobles really had this choice. Medieval peasants, closely bound to the land as serfs, could not readily leave their obligations to their manorial lord to undertake new ones to the divine Lord. Over the years, so many nobles donated land and children to the cause of monasticism that some worried about the increasing wealth and influence distracting the Cluniacs from properly focusing on divine worship.

In the late eleventh and early twelfth centuries, many male monastics supported a new **Cistercian Reform** that sought to go beyond the dedication of the Cluniacs. In monasteries like Chartreuse, Prémontré, and Cîteaux (which gave its name to the movement), these new monks interpreted the Benedictine Rule as strictly as possible. They journeyed even farther into the hills, forests, and wastelands to build churches and farms to avoid secular temptations and concerns (see figure 8.2). This internal colonization increased the amount of arable land in the West and, therefore, its wealth. The monks often labored with their own hands, although some orders opened up opportunities to laymen, called *conversi*, who were a form of second-class monk. These *conversi* gained the benefits of communal life without being burdened with the obligations of education and prayer required of full monks. The reformed monks also took only converts older than sixteen years, refusing to accept the unwanted children of aristocrats. The new monks believed they had a true calling. They even inspired some diocesan clergy to reform as **canons regular**. As regular clergy, these men lived together in communities of prayer, and at the same time as secular clergy, they served the world as pastors and teachers.

These monastic reforms opened various options for choosing the religious life, either among regular or secular clergy. Benedictine monasteries remained largely class based, requiring members to come from well-connected and wealthy families who could afford to donate land and children. The religious life provided access to influence to nobles not using the sword. The life of Abbess Hildegard of Bingen (b. 1098–d. 1179) illustrates some of the options open even to Benedictine nuns. As the tenth child, her noble family sent Hildegard first to join an anchoress when she was only eight years old. As an adult, she became abbess of the neighboring abbey and collected enough donations to found a new nunnery. She became famous for writings of her visions (perhaps caused by migraines) as well as medicine, theology, and music.

In contrast to the Benedictines, or the reformed and disciplined Cluniacs, the Chartreusians, Premonstratentians, and Cistercians were more open to lower-class seekers. Some orders emphasized contemplation and learning, others activity in hospitals and the care of souls, and still others spirituality and mysticism. Despite such differences, all clergy remained unified in one Church under the pope.

Monks and nuns, whether reformed or not, increasingly relied on the papacy, whose practical power and authority were rapidly expanding. Whereas the Cluniacs in the ninth century could think of Rome as distant, the Cistercians in the twelfth century saw an invigorated papacy all around them. This powerful papacy had first needed to rise out of the depths of degradation. For centuries, the papal office had been the pawn of the rambunctious Roman nobility. One family or another forced its candidate into St. Peter's Chair. Thus, the popes were too often men merely interested in the power that the wealth of the papal office made possible. Many westerners, however, wanted this spiritual leader to be morally worthy. In 1046, when petty Roman squabbles created three popes at once, King of Germany and Holy Roman Emperor Henry III arrived in Rome to restore order. Henry called a

Figure 8.2.   This sculpture of the sin of temptation on Strasbourg Cathedral warns about what lies behind a pretty face: poisonous snakes and toads.

council held at nearby Sutri. The Synod of Sutri dismissed the three popes and then a chose a new, universally recognized pope.

This pope and his successors took inspiration from the Cluniac Reform. They believed that a strong papacy could bring the idea of a religious calling to the secular ecclesiastical hierarchy. Reformed popes could reach throughout the western Church, extending past the other bishops to the lowest cleric and layperson. Just as monks rejected supervision by local nobles, so did the popes. Not kings or emperors, but popes should ultimately be in charge. These attitudes initiated what is called the **Hildebrandine** or **Gregorian Reform** (1050–1150), named after the monk Hildebrand, who became **Pope Gregory VII** (r. 1073–1085).

One immediate tragic consequence of the restored papal authority was a *schism*, or "tearing" or "splitting," of the orthodox catholic Christian Church into two parts: the Latin-speaking hierarchy in the West, which took the term *Catholic*, and the Greek-speaking hierarchy in the East, which has come to be called *Orthodox*. Since the fall of the western half of the Roman Empire, the Church had slowly been separating on organizational, theological, and liturgical grounds. The eastern patriarchs and bishops had kept a close relationship with Byzantine emperors. Although they had lost some dioceses to the Muslim advance in the Middle East and Africa, they had found new missionary success among the peoples of the Balkans and eastern Europe. The distant Roman bishop, however, wanted not only independence from the eastern Roman emperor but a recognition of Roman primacy in authority over all the other patriarchs and bishops. Arguments over relatively minor issues such as the supervision of churches, the addition to the Nicene Creed of the word *filioque* ("and the Son" when mentioning who sent the Holy Spirit), and the use of leavened or unleavened bread in the Eucharist brought on a crisis. In 1054, members of a papal commission to Constantinople aggravated the situation by excommunicating the patriarch there, who, of course, excommunicated them right back. Unity between Christians in East and West has never been able to recover. Christianity has remained fundamentally divided between Eastern *Orthodox Christianity* and Western Catholic Christianity ever since in what is sometimes called the "Great Schism."

For the reforming clerics in the West, though, expanding papal supremacy justified the split. They strengthened the role of **cardinals**, who originally had been created as assistants to run the diocese of Rome. In 1059, a unique election law reformed the election process for the pope. Previously, the pope had been chosen in the same manner as other bishops had been. Officially, the accepted canon law said that any bishop was supposed to be chosen by both the clergy and laypeople of the diocese. Practically, though, powerful men, like a king, actually did most of the choosing in most dioceses. The new papal election law excluded laypersons entirely from the pope's selection as well as most of the clergy. Only cardinals appointed by popes could elect the next pope. This law aimed to remove the pope from being the plaything of the Roman nobility, but it also cut out the German king and emperor of the Romans. It took some centuries for this system to function as intended—the emperor and nobles did not like being shut out—but it remains the basic way popes are elected today.

The reformers in Rome also hoped to encourage a higher quality of cleric by targeting what they considered to be the two worst problems in the Church: **simony** and the sexual activity of clerics. Simony, named after the figure Simon Magus in the New Testament, originally meant the sin of trying to purchase salvation. It had come to mean the crime of paying money, or even using political influence, to acquire a Church office or benefice. The attack on clerical sexual activity was partially related to the opposition to simony. Reformers thought that when clergy had children, the tendency to pass on to their heirs a priestly office (not to mention parish property) compromised the holiness of the priesthood (and the Church's possessions).

Additionally, some reformers were squeamish about women and sex. Already in ancient times the Church had begun to exclude women from leadership. Church authorities then began to restrict married men from offices or sacraments, insisting on celibacy. They adopted misogynist attitudes from pagan philosophers and culture about female inferiority and corrupt sexuality, cringing at the thought that a priest might handle the holy body and blood of Christ in the mass after having touched the impure flesh of a woman. So reformers began a campaign against the many priests who were married and others who kept concubines or "house companions." Of all the reform efforts, people in the local parishes surely noticed this one the most, whether their priests obeyed or not.

To change clerical attitudes, the papacy began to intervene in local Church affairs as never before. The cardinals increased in number and authority. They, with the pope as highest judge, established a court of last resort to solve any disputes within the Church over rights, properties, and privileges. Legal scholars collected and commented on old and new canon law in support of the tighter Church organization. Popes added lawyers and bureaucrats to this papal court called, in Latin, the Curia. The popes often sent cardinals throughout Christendom as legates, the pope's official representatives who had his full authority. The papal scribes issued bulls (named after the lead seal of authenticity hanging from them) in which the popes, on their own authority, codified law and moral issues. To provide a broader base of advice, communication, and acceptance, the popes also began to gather together clergy from all over the West, not just their own diocese or province, in councils claiming to represent the universal Church. Ironically, as a result the pope became less a spiritual leader than the head of a vast bureaucratic machine. While many of the popes over the next centuries were great lawyers and politicians, few had any inclination toward sanctity or sainthood.

One unique right that the popes began to exercise at this time was the calling of **crusades** (1095–1492), the Christian version of holy war. Before the eleventh century, war was sometimes recognized as a necessity but had always been considered sinful. Jesus' clear, explicit commands about nonviolence had even led many Christians in the Roman Empire to be pacifists. Augustine had helped to establish what we call the just war theory, allowing wars if they were defensive, did not involve too much destruction or brutality, and aimed at establishing a more just peace. Although this theory could allow Christians to go to war under many circumstances, every act of killing was a sin that required confession, penance, and reconciliation.

But the concept of crusade turned the sin of war into a virtue. Instead of regretting the killing of another human being, the crusader could glory in it. Killing the enemies of God became a holy act, a good deed. No sin was committed—indeed, one got as much closer to heaven as if one were on a pilgrimage. The crusaders, then, were armed pilgrims. Instead of hiking to Santiago de Compostela to pray, they marched to Jerusalem to slay.

Many regions became the target of crusading activity. The popes first gave their blessing on the crusade to reconquer the Iberian Peninsula, called the *Reconquesta*.

Crusaders struck southward from the northern remnants of early medieval Christian kingdoms against the Islamic Moors of Andalusia. By 1130, crusaders had founded the Christian country of Portugal along the Atlantic coast. They expanded the kingdoms of Leon, Castile, and Aragon southward. These kingdoms would wrangle with one another and the Moors until the end of the Middle Ages, when a united Spain stomped out the last Muslim foothold in western Europe. An even more important result came from the conquest of the city of Toledo, which sparked an intellectual fire in the West (see below).

The most famous crusades, those to liberate the Holy Land, *Outremer* (French for "across the sea"), or Palestine, were based on a misunderstanding. A Turkish victory at the Battle of Manzikert (1071) threatened the Byzantine Empire. Despite the schism, the Byzantine emperor called on the pope to find mercenaries to help him liberate Asia Minor. Instead, Pope Urban II, promoting myths of Muslim atrocities, exhorted knights and infantry to drive the Muslims from the lands of Christians, particularly from Jerusalem.

Surprisingly, or maybe miraculously, the First Crusade (1095–1099) actually succeeded. At first, a ragtag horde of inspired outsiders and peasants shouting, "God wills it!" marched toward Jerusalem. Along the way, the rabble slaughtered some European Jews who refused to convert to Christianity. This mob ended up slaughtered or enslaved by the Turks in Asia Minor before ever reaching Jerusalem. In 1199, a better-organized feudal army under various dukes and counts barely survived a difficult journey through Europe and Asia Minor, suffering battle, thirst, and hunger (the last sometimes solved by cannibalism). Miraculously, these crusaders conquered the Levantine coast, including Jerusalem itself, allegedly helped by the Holy Lance that had pierced Christ's side as well as by fasting and processions. As they sacked the "holy city," the Christian crusaders waded up to their ankles in the blood of slaughtered Muslim men, women, and children in one mosque where they had taken refuge. The crusaders also burned Jews alive in their homes and synagogues. Then the rival crusading leaders set up several small principalities.

To survive for the next two centuries, these crusading princedoms needed more than miracles. The new Western princes and knights in *Outremer* hardly cooperated with either each other or the Byzantine Empire. They did make some efforts at cooperating with the Muslims who were their subjects and neighbors. They needed and received continued reinforcements from Christendom. These zealous and temporary conquerors disliked the civilizations of Byzantium and Islam as something strange, despite their shared Græco-Roman legacy. Their crusading mentality often prevented the Christians who permanently lived in Palestine from working with the pragmatic Muslims and allowing peoples of different heritages to live together in peace.

Also complicating relations was a new form of regular clergy inspired by crusading, namely, military monasticism. The odd figures of **monk-knights** lived Christian lives of chastity, obedience, and prayer like monks, but also fought as warriors on the battlefield against the infidels. These militarized religious orders, like the Hospitallers or the Templars, provided much-needed resources of money, social service, and trained warriors.

The Middle East became a complicated jumble of diverse and competing characteristics. Although the Muslims called all western Christians "Franks," the crusaders were deeply divided (not forgetting the constant attempts of the Byzantines to assert authority). The Franks rarely forgot that they came from England, Scotland, France, various provinces of the Holy Roman Empire, or Norman Sicily, all of whose governments quarreled with one another. Political loyalties, ethnic pride, and religious bickering often weakened their efforts. City-states of northern Italy also built up their own commercial networks in the Levant, either selling to or selling out their fellow Franks, as business required.

In turn, the Franks labeled all their opponents under the blanket term *Saracens*, which ignored the deep religious differences about the choice of a new caliph, such as the divisions of Sunni, Shi'ite, and even Assassin (an unusual Muslim secret sect of alleged hashish smokers that murdered its enemies, giving us the term *assassination*). The Assassin murders of important Muslim leaders helped keep factions divided, terrorized, and at war with one another. Likewise, ethnic differences among Arabs, Egyptians, Persians, Kurds, and Turks long delayed a united Islamic front. For decades, the divisions among Muslims allowed the crusaders to survive a bit longer by playing one group off against the other. The Kurdish Saladin (Salah al-Din Yusuf ibn Ayb), who had taken control of the Egyptian caliphate, almost succeeded in defeating the crusaders in the 1180s. But Richard "the Lion-Hearted's" so-called Third Crusade reestablished a strong Christian foothold, even if Jerusalem remained under Muslim control. Finally, in 1295, unified and zealous Muslims drove the crusaders back to the sea and reclaimed Palestine and the Levant.

The Holy Land had been lost, but other crusades continued. The third-most-important region for crusading, after Palestine and the Iberian Peninsula, was in northeastern Europe, along the southern and eastern shores of the Baltic Sea. The **Teutonic Knights**, named after their common German ethnicity, were the most successful crusaders there. They had started as an order of crusading monk-knights in Palestine. Later, the Teutonic Knights gained a papal license to help the Holy Roman Empire conquer the pagan peoples of eastern Europe, a movement called the *Drang-nach-Osten* ("drive to the east"). They conquered the still-pagan Prussians and then founded their own state, called **Prussia**. These Teutonic monk-knights henceforth ruled over the Prussian peasants, who were slowly converted to Christianity and assimilated into German culture. Heretics within Christendom were the fourth major target of crusaders (see the next section), after the Iberian Peninsula, Palestine, and the Baltic region.

The Crusades flowed from the conviction that Christians held the only answer to the meaning of life, combined with the military power to impose Christian beliefs beyond the heartland of Christendom. The Crusades promoted little cultural exchange or even rivalry. The Muslims who interacted with the Franks considered them uncivilized, even barbaric. With few exceptions, political or intellectual leaders of East and West barely communicated with each other. Many westerners did develop a taste, though, for luxury goods, spices, rugs, porcelain, and silk that came from Muslim merchants. And even though the Crusades failed in Palestine, their success in the Iberian Peninsula, northeastern Europe, and against heretics strengthened the supremacy of the Church.

Thus, the medieval Church had created numerous versions of regular clergy, religious men and women who lived under special rules. The monk-knights fought actual wars against Saracens or ruled countries such as Prussia. Cistercians and their like bowed to the harshest discipline of monastic life. Canons regular served in parishes and cathedrals. Cluniac and unreformed Benedictine houses of men and women continued to dot the medieval religious landscape. Tying them all together was an increasingly influential papacy, eager to spread reform beyond the clergy.

Review: *How did reforms of monks lead to a reform of the wider Church and the creation of the medieval papacy?*

Response:

PLENTY OF PAPAL POWER

The Gregorian Reform created a papacy that, in its administrative effectiveness, became a model for royal governments. Subsequently, however, the popes became rivals to kings. One consequence was the weakening of the Holy Roman Empire. Ever since the Frankish-Papal Alliance under the Carolingians, the popes bound themselves to the revived Roman imperial office in the West, first with Charlemagne in 800 and then with Otto the Great in 962. Otto the Great had also used the bishops of Germany to help him establish a powerful basis of authority and military might. The German empire collected together a variety of peoples, yet regional tendencies resisted the domination of one king over all. Still, Otto's successors generally continued the slow gradual expansion of royal authority, reaching a high point under Henry III, who had cleaned up the disgraced papacy in 1046 by forcing elections of worthy men.

The empire faced a turning point ten years later when Henry III died, leaving as heir his six-year-old son, **Henry IV (r. 1056–1106)**. Many magnates used the long regency until Henry IV came of age to seize what they could from his royal rights and prerogatives. The papacy also, as mentioned above, asserted its independence via its new election law. Further, when a pope tried to crush the Normans in southern Italy and Sicily, the Normans there turned defeat into an alliance with their former enemy. Thus, the popes no longer needed the German emperor's protection. When Henry IV became a ruler in his own right, he wanted to restore the power that his father Henry III had wielded.

Henry IV's attempts revealed a clash between church and state that changed the West. The extreme papal claim for a "plenitude of power" threatened the role of kings across Europe. The radicals in the papal reform movement had expanded the definition of simony to include any lay involvement in the election of bishops, even when no money changed hands. Papal claims to be the highest figure in Christendom took away royal rights not only about choosing clerics and bishops to serve the royal regimes but about having final authority in any political decision. Disagreements between King Henry IV and Pope Gregory VII over who would be bishops in northern Italy sparked the first open fight over papal versus royal power. The **Investiture Struggle**, Contest, or Controversy (1075–1122) takes its name from the religious ceremony of investiture, which formally installs bishops in their office. This conflict fueled a civil war in the Holy Roman Empire.

As German King Henry IV's episcopal candidates clashed with reform nominees, Pope Gregory VII threatened Henry with excommunication. Gregory had already formulated a grander concept of papal prerogatives than all his forebears had. In his proposed schema, the *Dictatus papæ*, he claimed that only the pope could properly use the Roman imperial insignia, that all princes should kiss the pope's feet, and even that the pope could depose emperors. Pope Gregory declared that Henry IV was no longer king, also excommunicating him, after Henry convinced his bishops to withdraw their allegiance to Gregory.

Although the pope's legal claim to depose Henry was doubtful, Henry's enemies in Germany seized the opportunity to rise up against him. Even many of his bishops abandoned him. In a brilliant move, however, Henry rushed to Italy over frozen Alpine passes. The pope fled to the castle of Canossa, fearing an attack. Yet Henry arrived with only a small retinue. Instead of raging in armor and ferocity, the king stood in sackcloth and repentance before the castle gates for three wintry days. Since the pope was in the job of forgiveness, he lifted Henry's excommunication. Although Henry remained, technically, deposed from his kingship, the confusion about his status gave him the opportunity to regroup his military forces and defeat most of his opposition.

Nonetheless, the war in the empire dragged on as each side stuck to its interpretation of the role of bishops and their election. Gregory excommunicated Henry a futile second time. In turn, Henry's armies drove Gregory from Rome into exile with the Normans in southern Italy, where he died. Finally, Henry's own son rebelled against him to become Henry V (r. 1105–1125).

On the one side, supporters of Gregory VII saw him and his successors as heroes for their reformed papacy at the summit of Christendom. In this view, Henry IV and his heirs were corrupt tyrants. On the other side, followers of the German kings and emperors saw Henry IV as the legitimate ruler trying to hold the state together. In such a perspective, Gregory VII divided the empire through his unjustly claimed royal authority. The basic struggle between royal and Church power continued and spread to France and England (for example, in the quarrel of Henry II versus Becket).

Henry V ended two generations of open warfare between church and state when he came to terms with the papacy in the **Concordat of Worms** in 1122. A concordat is an agreement between a state and the Church, while Worms was a city on the upper Rhine River, ruled by a bishop, where the treaty was signed. The treaty compromised on papal and imperial authority. The principle that all bishops were to be elected by the clergy and laypeople of their dioceses was reasserted (except for Rome's bishop, of course). Still, the king could be present at each election in Germany (and thus exert an influence and even decide deadlocked elections). The German king gave up the right of investiture regarding a bishop's ecclesiastical office, but he could grant feudal possessions before a bishop's full consecration (at least within the German, if not in the Burgundian or Italian, parts of the empire). Similar compromises were eventually worked out in France and England.

While the Investiture Struggle was officially over, neither advocates of papal authority nor proponents of royal power remained satisfied with this compromise. The Holy Roman Empire especially suffered from ongoing differences between emperors and popes. Emperor Henry V was unfortunate enough to die without an heir in 1125. As usual when a dynasty died out, a civil war erupted. Two major families took the lead in the competition for support from the magnates: the Welfs and the Staufens. Successive popes, using their influence and their recognized right to crown the German king as Holy Roman Emperor, regularly played one side against the other over the next several generations. Potential German kings/Holy Roman Emperors wanted the riches of Italy and the prestige that influence over the Church granted them. Meanwhile, generations of popes were trying to gain independence in Italy and the Papal States while increasing their own standing in the Church. Kings and their allies used war and propaganda against the popes and their supporters. In turn, the popes applied excommunication, crusade, and interdict (the forbidding of clerics to perform sacraments in a territory until its leader had asked forgiveness).

By 1256, the Staufen dynasty had been extinguished, while the Welfs had shrunk to mere territorial significance. Even worse for German power, the dynastic principle had been broken. Instead, three powerful archbishops, the king of Bohemia, two dukes, and a margrave asserted themselves as the seven "electoral princes" of the German king. As a result, the office of emperor/king with the Holy Roman Empire declined in power, if not prestige, while the actual rule of the local territorial magnates was magnified. Unfortunately for the popes, their obsession with weakening the Holy Roman Emperor led them to ignore two new threats—the kings of England and France.

Review: *How did the popes fight with kings and other religious movements?*

Response:

THE AGE OF FAITH AND REASON

The debates and writings provoked by the protracted conflict over papal authority helped to create a new literature of political theory, where people could speculate about the nature and purposes of government. Many of these new ideas came from an unexpected source, the Muslim-dominated Iberian Peninsula, called Andalusia. When Christian crusaders liberated the city of Toledo in 1085, they found libraries full of books written in Arabic. Rather than burning them in fanatic zeal, they hired Jews who had long lived peacefully among the Arabs in Toledo to translate the books into Latin. In that city and soon in several more, the writings from ancient Greeks and Romans as well as more recent Muslims, such as Ibn Sina (Avicenna) and Ibn Rushd (Averroës), became available to medieval scholars. Most important, the westerners found the writings of Aristotle, whom the Arabs had long appreciated, studied, and interpreted. Aristotle's dialectic logic lit an intellectual fire in the westerners and carried his method to the monastic and cathedral schools that had survived the collapse of the Carolingian Empire. Given their more stable and prosperous civilization, Western Christians leapt at the opportunity to learn.

Some of these schools began to flourish with academic activity, soon blossoming into **universities**. Basic education continued to be the curriculum of the seven liberal arts. The new universities then provided advanced, higher education, where students became "masters" and "doctors" (teachers) by studying canon law, secular law, medicine, theology, or philosophy. A now-familiar kind of person, the scholar, appeared in the West for the first time since the fall of Rome. The whole point of scholars in universities was to profess new knowledge. They brought the light of education to what had been the darkness of ignorance. Secular rulers likewise recognized the necessity for these institutions of higher education and encouraged their foundation in places as diverse as Bologna, Salerno, Paris, Oxford, Cambridge, and Heidelberg.

Although kings often chartered these universities, the Church remained in charge of the educational process. Those who studied in this system were members of the clergy. Therefore, students fell under special laws of the Church or university and not under those of the secular courts. The metaphor of the ivory tower reflects the legal distinctions that separated institutions of higher education from the urban communities in which they were located. Conflicts between townspeople and students were considered (and sometimes still are) "town" versus "gown." Then, as now, youthful enthusiasm for extracurricular activities would sometimes annoy the neighbors. Then, as now, learning was difficult. Then, as now, some students preferred to study varieties of beer and wine rather than versions of Plato and Aristotle.

In the thirteenth century, donors and Church officials organized **colleges** as residential and educational spaces to help the young "bachelors" become more disciplined. The collegians might move on to the higher degrees of master or doctor, but many were satisfied with a "bachelor's degree," as they are today. The word *bachelor* also indicates that only men could study at these new, advanced schools. Women might receive some education in monastic schools, either as nuns or students of the nuns. Formal higher education, though, remained closed to women for centuries. In any case, the Church was the cradle for this growing systematic structure for creating knowledge in the West.

The Church almost strangled that baby in the cradle. Some Christians feared that ideas drawn from pagans were dangerous or irrelevant. These sources of knowledge from anything other than divine revelation frightened them. The use of human reason might lead to error, even heresy. The scholar **Peter Abelard** (b. 1180–d. 1142) seemed the perfect example. Through sheer intellectual *chutzpah,* he had become one of the leading academicians of his day. Then his scandalous affair with his pupil Heloïse almost ruined his career. He had arranged for himself to be employed as her private tutor (since the Church forbade women to attend schools and universities). After she had his illegitimate child, though, instead of properly marrying her, he seemed to want to put her away in a nunnery. Her angry guardian hired some thugs, who castrated Abelard. He recovered to resume his teaching at the university, where his ideas got him into worse trouble. His enduring attitude about wisdom was that we must first doubt authority and then ask questions; questioning will then lead us to the truth. Abelard's questions, though, led him into trouble, just as Socrates' had in ancient Athens. Their experiences suggest another basic principle:

> **Questioning authority is dangerous.**

Abelard's opponents organized to silence him. Those defenders of tradition seized upon his too-subtle explanation of the Trinity to get his ideas condemned at a Church council. They compelled him to stop teaching and even to throw his own books into the flames.

A century later, though, Aristotle's dialectic method emerged victorious. Other clerics, notably **Thomas Aquinas** (b. 1225–d. 1274), used the tools of Aristotelian logic but were careful to make sure their answers were complete and orthodox. Aquinas thought that human reason, properly used, never conflicted with divine revelation. This ***Scholasticism***, or philosophy "of the schools," is clearly expressed in Aquinas' book, the *Sum of Theology*. Therein he used dialectic arguments to answer everything a Christian could want to know about the universe. Aquinas allayed the fears about Aristotle by harnessing his logic for the Church. Eventually Aquinas' logical explications seemed so solid and orthodox that the Roman Catholic Church declared him its leading philosopher.

Despite Aquinas' success, the intellectual debate did not stop. Philosophers continued to argue about realism. Some drew on Plato's idealism that universal ideas shaped reality; others advocated ***nominalism***, which proposed that only particular things in the observable world existed. Another debate among scholars focused on politics. They developed political theories that were coherent proposals about how best to rule human society. Aquinas argued that the pope was the supreme human authority, but many others fought this idea with words and weapons. Kings sought out scholars and founded universities to argue for the supremacy of kingship and the royal connection to the divine, as had been done since the dawn of ancient civilizations.

Within these debates, the institution of the university further strengthened liberty for everyone by promoting new knowledge. Universities were not intended to convey merely the established dogmas and doctrines of the past or of powerful princes and popes. Instead, professors were, and are, supposed to expand upon inherited wisdom. Once the idea of learning new ideas became acceptable, it inevitably led to change. Nevertheless, popes continued to claim the allegiance of all humanity. Kings still tried to bind their clergy to them as servants to enforce the royal will. Neither of these attempts dominated in the West. By the end of the Middle Ages, no single power, whether the pope, king, one's own connection to God, or the independent human mind itself, would rule both the hearts and minds of mortals. Creative tensions between the demands of faith and the requirements of statehood enriched the choices available to peoples of the West.

During time off from intellectual pursuits, some scholars produced literature, which at the time was not studied at universities. Much of the literature of the Middle Ages was written in the language of scholarship, government, and faith, namely, Latin. Student poets called Goliards were famous for their drinking songs, while other clergy produced histories, epic fantasies, mystical tracts, and religious hymns.

Modern universities today usually neglect to teach about this medieval Latin literature. They instead favor studying the literature from vernacular languages, those that people spoke at home and that later evolved into the European languages of today: Romance languages (French, Italian, Portuguese, Spanish, and Romanian), Germanic languages (German, Dutch, Norwegian, Danish, Swedish, and English), Celtic languages (which still survive as Irish Gaelic, Scots, Welsh, and Breton), and even Slavic languages (Polish, Czech, Serbo-Croatian, Bulgarian, Russian, etc.). Most of these languages began their development from literary works written down primarily after the twelfth century.

Romance became one of the most popular genres of vernacular literature. These works of prose or poetry often told of heroic adventures complicated by men and women facing challenges in their love. The most famous work of medieval literature is Dante's so-called *Divine Comedy*, written in Italian. The author had fallen for the ideal girl, Beatrice, but she had died young. In a vision, Dante journeys to hell (*Inferno*), where the Roman poet Vergil guides him through circles of punishment. Then Beatrice helps him through purgatory and finally to paradise to behold the ultimate love of God. Along the way, Dante sees and converses with many people whose stories and fates illustrate his view of good and evil, right choices and wrong choices, made in the Middle Ages.

In religious belief and practice, medieval people did have some choice, however carefully limited. Except for a few Jews and fewer Muslims, everyone who lived in Christendom had to believe in the dogmas of the Western Latin Church and worship in its dioceses and parishes. The structures built for worship, the cathedrals and parish churches, along with abbeys and monastery churches, remain as testimonies to the importance of faith in the Middle Ages. Believers replaced the wooden and few stone churches of the Early Middle Ages with such zeal that almost none survive today. Huge amounts of wealth, effort, and design went into constructing the new stone cathedrals, minsters, chapels, and parish churches of the High Middle Ages.

Church floor plans were usually based on the Latin cross or the ancient Roman basilica, which had a long central aisle (or nave, after the Latin word for "ship") with an altar for the Eucharist at the far end. The people would gather in the nave, while clergy carried out the sacrificial ceremonies around the altar. Music increasingly added decorative sound around the spoken word. We still have records of medieval music because monks invented a system of musical notation (no records of Greek or Roman music have survived). Western music began with a simple plainsong, one simple line of notes called Gregorian chant, and evolved into complex polyphony, many notes sung alongside and around each other in harmony.

Two styles of churches can be recognized as medieval. The first style of stone churches we now call Romanesque, because they inherited many of their design elements from ancient Roman buildings, especially the rounded arch (see figures 8.3 and 8.4). These churches, built between 1000 and 1300, tend to have a blocky appearance, with thick walls necessary to hold up the roof. Still, they could be built quite large, often airy, and full of light. The walls were often decorated with frescoes, and the capitals of columns were carved with sculptures illustrating key ideas of the faith. The second style of churches we now call Gothic (that insulting term mentioned at the beginning of chapter 7), but medieval builders called it the "modern" or the "French" style (see figures 8.5 and 8.6). Gothic cathedrals were built from about 1150 to 1500. The invention of the Gothic or pointed arch allowed architects to build even taller naves and open up the walls to more windows. They

Figure 8.3.   The blocky Romanesque Abbey of Maria Laach sits squarely on the earth, while its towers point to heaven.

Figure 8.4. The bright nave of the Romanesque Abbey of St. Godehard in Hildesheim illuminates the decorated paneled ceiling.

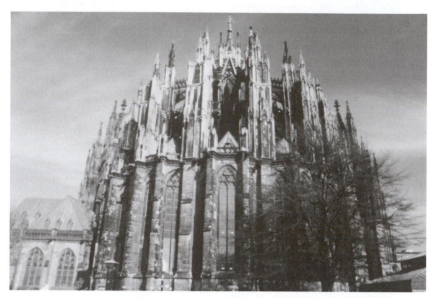

Figure 8.5.   The outside of the Gothic choir of Cologne Cathedral highlights the flying buttresses reaching toward heaven.

filled the windows with stained glass, designed in patterns and pictures of faith, pierced by light from heaven.

All these structures required highly skilled builders and a great deal of wealth. Townspeople competed with their neighbors in other communities to have the best possible church. Sometimes, their efforts to surpass one another led to disaster, when improperly designed churches collapsed. Other times, sponsors ran out of resources, and building remained idle for decades, centuries, or forever. Medieval skylines were sometimes defined by castles, but always by churches, whose steeples one could see and bells one could hear for miles throughout the surrounding countryside.

For the people of Christendom of the High Middle Ages, it made sense to devote much time and energy to the religion of Christianity. The worldview that a moral life in this world prepared one for another life after death gave meaning to the troubles people faced as individuals and as a society. Kings might fight with popes, but that did not cast doubt on the meaning of the Gospels. Cluniac monks might live differently from Cistercians, who in turn did not act like Templars, but all observed rules set to conform their lives to the commands of the Church.

Review: How did medieval culture reflect both religion and rationalism?

Response:

Figure 8.6. The high Gothic nave of Canterbury Cathedral opens a sacred space.

A NEW ESTATE

While kings and popes quarreled over the leadership of the West, a new urban power was growing that would overshadow them both. Townspeople did not fit into the usual medieval classifications, typically divided into three estates: priests to pray for all, knights to fight for all, and peasants to work for all. No sooner had this trinitarian social division established itself in the popular imagination than the shock of economic development shattered its reality. The growing success and stability of medieval society had brought back civilization by the twelfth century. And by definition, towns and cities were civilization.

The growth of these cities sprang directly from improvements in the economy and in political rule. Wealth from three-field farming and from monastic communities now financed those who did not themselves live on and work the land. The peace and order from the kings' supremacy in the feudal hierarchy cleared space for cities to organize. Some cities regrew from Roman cities, especially where cathedrals and their clerics maintained cores of religious communities. Since the time of the ancient Roman Empire, bishops had been obliged to live in their cathedral cities. Although bishops had been tempted to move away while cities were in decline during the Early Middle Ages, boom times in the High Middle Ages made urban life attractive again. New cities also sprang up at the feet of castles, where feudal and manorial lords controlled a ready source of wealth. Some clever ecclesiastical and secular lords who saw the increasing importance of trade even planted new cities at crossroads and river crossings. Thus, cities such as Cambridge or Innsbruck arose, named after the bridges over their rivers.

Cities grew first and fastest in two regions, the Lowlands (modern Belgium, Netherlands, and Luxembourg) and Lombardy in northern Italy (with nearby coastal cities such as Venice, Genoa, and Pisa). Both regions had dense populations and easy access to seaborne trading routes. By the twelfth century, merchants from those areas gathered at **fairs** in the Champagne province of France (long before the invention of the sparkling wine that has taken the province's name). These fairs greatly expanded upon a typical village market day, since merchants from many communities competed with one another about price and quality with products from distant lands. As farmers entered contests for their animals and produce, competition encouraged better and bigger specimens. The festive atmosphere entertained consumers with varieties of new goods to purchase. Today's county fairs across the United States or trade fairs in Europe are descendants of these medieval fairs. Then and now, fairs were engines of economic growth. The triad of the Lowlands, Champagne, and Lombardy became the core of new commerce of the High Middle Ages.

Traders from medieval Europe began to venture even farther abroad. The First Crusade to the Holy Land had founded new Western principalities in the Levant. Traders were right behind the warriors. The Lombard cities of Genoa, Pisa, and Venice exploited the Mediterranean Sea routes, avoiding and soon outselling the Byzantine Empire. As the crusading states failed, the city-state of Venice in particular succeeded in becoming a maritime political power. Venetians continued to oppose

Muslim expansion while exploiting every trade opportunity. They were also behind the brief Western conquest of the Byzantine Empire during the Fourth Crusade in 1204.

Some European merchants even ventured beyond the Mediterranean watershed. Some traveled along the ancient Silk Road through Central Asia, which had long connected the Middle East with China. The most famous merchant was the Venetian Marco Polo (b. ca. 1254–d. 1324), who with relatives and servants lived in the Chinese Empire and East Asia in the second half of the thirteenth century. He wrote a book about his adventures while a prisoner of war held by Genoa. Many people scoffed at his tales (and some are scoff-worthy), but he did accurately describe much of the wealth and glory of China, which far excelled that of Europe at the time.

Still, the Europeans kept gaining ground. Building on wealth produced from commerce, Europeans were starting to use machines to make products, a process called **industrialization**. Historians disagree about which ideas or technology (such as iron plows, horse collars, drills, gears, and pumps) merchants brought back from the comparatively advanced Chinese, Indian, or Muslim civilizations. Years ago, history textbooks credited European inventors with technological innovation. Clearly, though, Asians and North Africans used similar machines decades, if not centuries, before the westerners. The Europeans did invent spectacles or eyeglasses, for which many people who could only with difficulty read this book are assuredly grateful. Whatever the origins of specific technology, after the twelfth century, industrialization further increased the availability of goods to Europeans. The word *manufacture*, which originally meant making something by hand, now described people working with machines.

A boom in textile manufacturing arose from a **cottage industry**, where merchants who traveled from home to home, door to door, were "putting out" goods to be manufactured and then picking up the finished products. Family members in one home might spin the raw wool into thread; down the lane they might weave the thread into cloth; and on the other side of the village they might sew the cloth into a tunic. Peasant wives and children had more time to devote to this new work because of labor saved in the farm fields through iron plows, horse collars, and three-field planting. Peasants thus earned extra income that allowed them to purchase still more new goods. An increasing spiral of growth followed. As some people's work became more specialized, they quit being peasants and became artisans and craftspeople who lived in towns, earning their living from the skills of their minds and hands, not from labor on the land.

These commercial people of towns and cities, however, did not easily fit into the medieval trifold conception of clergy, nobles, and commoners. With no other option, the townspeople became part of that third estate of commoners, yet their social status shared little in common with that of the medieval serf. They gained a new status as burghers, burgesses, or **bourgeoisie** (drawn from the Latin word for castle). Burghers were free men (bourgeois women, of course, remained less free than their fathers, husbands, and sons). Unlike the subservient serfs, burgesses were not bound to the land but could travel freely. Indeed, the bourgeoisie held the freedom of ownership, buying and selling of property, and possessing it in peace. They were not responsible to the manorial courts. Instead, the townspeople exercised the freedom of self-government, creating laws and representative political institutions such as **mayors** and **town councils**. Many burghers even gained the right to bear arms. Towns could be thought of as huge castles, although with a multitude of families living behind high stone walls instead of only one. Townspeople raised their own troops and defended their fortifications. Many town patricians even gained entrance to the nobility and aristocracy, imitating the lords who dominated society. None imagined that the bourgeois way of life would one day dominate Western civilization.

These freedoms did not come easily. The communal self-government of mayors and town councils slowly revived democratic government in the West. Once again, though, democracy was difficult. The townspeople often had to fight to have their liberties and rights respected by the well-born lords of society. They began to organize **communes**, meaning they sought to have the laws recognize them as a collective group of people who could organize their own affairs separately from the rest of nobility-dominated Europe. The kings, dukes, bishops, and magnates often resisted and attacked the communes at first, seeing them as a threat to their authority. Eventually, however, the lords largely accepted the townspeople, recognizing the economic advantages of a flourishing urban life that created new wealth. The lords granted charters of liberty to the burghers, defining and affirming their self-government and civil rights.

Having successfully fought the lords, townspeople next fought one another over a share of the authority and wealth. The politics of medieval cities were filled with violence. The rich and powerful wanted to exclude the poor and the powerless. The elite patricians fought against the middle-class artisans. Both tried to keep down the more numerous commoners. If frustrated by loss in an election or by exclusion from any political participation at all, groups of townspeople might assassinate their rivals or riot to overthrow them.

Institutions called **guilds** often provided a peaceful framework for political, social, and economic action. These organizations allowed owners (the masters) and workers in a craft or trade (baking, shoemaking, cloth dyeing) to supervise the quality and quantity of production. Even universities (whose product was knowledge) structured themselves as guilds. Masters trained the next generations of apprentices and journeymen (day laborers) in the proper skills. Guilds also became the vehicles for social and political cohesion, as they provided social welfare for their members, organized celebrations, and set up candidates for urban elections. Despite some instability that always goes with democracy and economic change, cities and their civilization were a success in the West again. Towns soon began to grow in size and numbers comparable with the contemporary civilized societies of Islam, India, and China.

To minister to these new townspeople, new kinds of monks called **mendicants** began to appear in the thirteenth century. Their name comes from the Latin word for begging, and that is how they were supposed to receive their livelihood. The earlier Benedictine or Cistercian monks drew income from the production of the land. Mendicants were to live from the excess production of town commerce. The townspeople had become wealthy enough to have extra money that they could devote to charity. The mendicants were to preach and teach, living only from alms.

Ironically, the mendicants preached against the popular values of city life. The new urban elites gloried in wealth and ostentation, imitating the nobility. This attitude was *materialism*, valuing goods and pleasures provided by wealth in this world. The most famous medieval Christian opponent of this materialism was the founder of the Franciscans, **Francis of Assisi** (b. 1181–d. 1226). Francis helped to promote the idea of *apostolic poverty*: that the original apostles were poor, and so modern clergy should be also. He set an example of rejecting the wealth of the patricians and reaching out to the new urban poor.

As we have seen with previous monastic reforming groups, the success of mendicant monks led later generations of them to diverge from the original ideals. They acquired endowments, properties, and possessions. The Franciscans were soon split between those who sought apostolic poverty and those who observed obedience to the wealthy and politically powerful papacy. Another main group of mendicants, the Dominicans, focused on education and fighting new heresies that were already appearing in the twelfth century. Serious heresies had not been a problem since the German barbarians who were Arian Christians had converted to orthodox catholic Christianity at the beginning of the Early Middle Ages. Since then, everyone in the West had to be Christian.

Everyone, that is, with the exception of the Jews. Christian authorities allowed Jews to retain their faith, honoring them as the original "chosen people" of their God. The Christian authorities nevertheless carefully and legally discriminated against the Jews, confining them to living in towns (and usually particular neighborhoods), prohibiting them from owning farmland, and allowing them only certain professions, such as money lending. Christians periodically stole their wealth, forced Jews to convert, falsely accused them of crimes, and attacked them when things went wrong, such as during a plague. At any time, a king might expel the Jews from the kingdom, as happened in England in 1290 and France in 1306. Even if it had been allowed, no Christian would have chosen to convert to Judaism.

The new heresies of the High Middle Ages were different from Judaism, since they offered real alternatives to catholic Christianity. They probably arose because of the increasing success of the European economy. More trade with the East (eastern Europe, the Middle East, Asia) opened up merchants and markets to new ideas from those distant places. For too long, much of the hierarchical Church remained mired in ministry to the knights and peasants, with too little thought to growing urban needs. As some merchants became wealthy, enjoying their own materialism, many decided that the Church should not share in their rising economic comforts. Instead, they listened to advocates of apostolic poverty.

One of the first heretics was Pierre Valdès (or Peter Waldo), who lived in the late twelfth century. He might have turned out like Francis of Assisi a generation later, had he been treated differently. Like Francis, Waldo called for poverty and simplicity within the Church. Bishops uncomfortable with his call to poverty tried to silence him. He refused and escaped into the Alps, where he set up small groups, the **Waldensians**, some of which survive to this day. These communities were too isolated, small, and unthreatening for Christendom to expend the effort to wipe them out.

The other major heretical movement was that of the **Cathars** (which probably comes from a word meaning "the pure") or **Albigensians** (named after the southern French town of Albi). These heretics were more dangerous to Christianity because they offered a popular alternative belief system, *Catharism*. The Cathars' *dualism* alleged that God ruled the spirit while the devil claimed material things. Since in this view even the flesh was evil, entirely resisting the pleasures of this world was necessary to gain heaven. Cathars rejected the Western ecclesiastical hierarchy and set up their own counterchurch. As they attracted members from the nobles, townspeople, and peasants, the Cathars broke the monopoly of the official Western Church, especially in southern France.

The Catholic Christians struck back. They tried the preachings of the mendicants first, but words were not enough. So they turned to the justice system and revived the ancient Roman legal procedure known as the **inquisition**, which comes from the Latin word for inquire or ask. Normally, someone has to complain for a crime to be investigated. To maintain public order, however, the Romans occasionally used the inquisition as an alternative. In this procedure, the government would commission a tribunal to uncover crimes committed in a certain region, even if no complaints had been officially registered. Traveling judges were empowered to investigate crimes, arrest people, prosecute alleged criminals, and punish them. Thus the modern legal powers that are today divided among police, district attorneys, judges, and juries were combined into one very effective instrument.

The Church authorities in the thirteenth century thought the situation serious enough to bring this method back. When the majority of people in a region had converted to heresy, no complaints of the crime would come to authorities. So popes and bishops commissioned investigators, often Dominicans, to ferret out heretics. They could enter a province only with the explicit permission of the local political ruler. After finding heretics guilty, the clerical inquisition then handed them over to the secular arm, namely the local political powers, to be executed by burning alive at the stake. The use of torture during the investigations has disgraced the Inquisition in the history of jurisprudence. At times, some historians and critics of religion have exaggerated the Inquisition's excesses of brutality and injustice. Nevertheless, that the "Holy Inquisition" happened at all, with the blessing of Christian leaders, is enough to condemn it thoroughly and stain its legacy.

Surprisingly, even the inquisition could not stamp out heresy. The Church finally resorted to its highest level of violence: a crusade. In 1225, Pope Innocent III sanctioned a Catholic invasion of southern France to destroy the Cathars. The so-called Albigenisan Crusade succeeded. One story goes that in a town in the south of France, everyone was massacred. Those who worried that some Catholic Christians might have been caught in the general slaughter were told that "God will know his own," bringing the righteous into heaven and sending the heretics to hell. The success of the Albigensian Crusade strengthened the French king by giving over confiscated lands to his direct control. The crusade and subsequent royal rule destroyed a flourishing, distinctly southern French culture.

In the next centuries, Church leaders elsewhere in Christendom likewise called other crusades against several rebellious enemies, since by definition defying the Church's authority in any fashion was heretical. Other forces were forming that would challenge the Church and the rest of medieval society. The wealth produced by the successful towns and cities promoted changes that would shift the West out of the High Middle Ages and into the Later Middle Ages.

Review: *How did the revival of trade and towns change the West?*

Response:

NOT THE END OF THE WORLD

The spread of heresy might have threatened people's souls, but the spread of disease surely plagued their bodies. Tragically, trade connections with Asia brought not just spices and silks, but also the disaster called the **Black Death**. In 1347, contagions that had swarmed along trade routes entered the crowded and dirty cities of Europe. For the next several years and regularly thereafter, plague sprawled through both urban and rural Christendom. The exact nature of this epidemic, or epidemics, is unknown. The contemporary descriptions that drew on ancient accounts of plagues or listed various contradictory symptoms have led historians to suggest that more than one disease was at work. Regardless of its origins, the Black Death swept through the population of western Europe to a degree unknown for centuries, killing probably one out of three people. The impact varied, though, since some regions saw almost no sign of disease, while other towns were nearly wiped out. Well into the eighteenth century, less-virulent waves of plague returned to strike down tens of thousands of Europeans, over and over.

Aiding the spread of disease was a general cooling of the climate. What historians call a mini ice age began about 1300 and lasted until about 1700. The climate in Europe became a few degrees cooler. Winters lasted longer, and summers were shorter. This change shortened growing seasons and increased rainfall where it was not needed. The effects sharply reduced food production, and a hungry European population became even more susceptible to illness.

Historians usually see this period between 1300 and 1350 as the transition from the High Middle Ages to the Later Middle Ages. The climatic change and increase in epidemics created what scholars call a demographic catastrophe that sent the gradually rising European population into a sharp decline. The high mortality rates and fear of death led at times to a breakdown of the fragile social order that had been created during the High Middle Ages (ca. 1000–1350). As the Later Middle Ages (ca. 1300–1500) followed, everyone had to cope with rougher natural circumstances, the continued political and social dominance of the clergy and knightly nobility, the increasing competition with townspeople, and dissatisfaction among the peasants. The Later Middle Ages is still very much medieval, but it was a time of increasing unrest and uncertainty.

The reduction in population caused labor shortages that forced economic changes. Peasant farming shifted from lord-serf to landlord-tenant. Now peasants' uncertain livelihood depended on paying rent instead of long-standing customary obligations such as labor services and portions of crops. Post-plague, if a peasant failed to come up with the rent, he and his family could more easily be thrown off the land, left with nothing. Also, landlords tried to focus more on cash crops for export instead of a balanced diet for local consumption. The latter had traditionally been encouraged on the self-sufficient manor, when farmers grew what they needed to eat. While serfdom had limited social and political freedom, being tied to the land allowed serfs a certain economic freedom—they could at least feed their families.

Peasants began to rebel against both the restrictions of serfdom and, ironically, the insecurity caused by its decline. Some even thought of a religious justification, as shown in the rhyme, "When Adam delved and Eve span, who was then the gentleman?"[1] **Peasant revolts** started to happen with some regularity. The most famous are the Jacquerie, a rebellion in France in 1358, and the Wat Tyler Revolt in England in 1381. In the first stage of rebellions, peasants killed a few landlords, burned some buildings and records, and grabbed property for themselves. Sadly for the peasants, virtually all revolts ended in defeat. Within weeks, royal or noble armies reorganized and slaughtered hundreds, if not thousands, of peasants. The traditional landholding clergy and nobility, joined by the bourgeoisie, were too well organized and too powerful. That these rebellions increasingly took place at all, though, showed that something was wrong with the order of society.

In some areas of Europe, the leadership of the clergy likewise eventually found itself challenged anew by kings, although not in Germany. During the High Middle Ages, popes had struggled with the Holy Roman Emperors over leadership in Christendom. The popes seemed to have won. The constant switching of royal dynasty because of elections made the Holy Roman Emperor seem more of a ridiculed annoyance than a respected monarch. In 1356, Emperor Charles IV tried to strengthen royal power by adjusting the succession process with his **Golden Bull** (named after its seal, similar to those for papal documents). It limited those who could choose the king of the Romans to seven electors: The prince-archbishops of Cologne, Mainz, and Trier; the king of Bohemia; the Duke of Saxony; the Count of Palatine by the Rhine; and the Margrave of Brandenburg. The king then expected to be crowned Holy Roman Emperor by the pope in Rome. In the long run, the Golden Bull merely regulated the electoral process, not the empire itself. Territorial

---

1. Or, reworded for modern sense: "When the first human beings worked, Adam dug in the ground and Eve spun thread like peasants; no class distinctions existed as they did when nobles ruled and profited from peasant labor."

princes, dukes, counts, and bishops concerned themselves with their own rule rather than the empire's position as a whole. The German kings of the Holy Roman Empire remained weak compared with either popes or the German princes in territorial duchies and counties.

In contrast, the kings of France and England became strong monarchs with centralized authority over their realms. The kings of both those countries drew on the power of dynasty, military might, and taxes on towns. They also relied on the advice and support of people through elected representative bodies, the Estates-General in France and the Parliament in England. Both kingdoms were expanding. England almost succeeded in conquering Scotland, held off only by the lucky heroics of William Wallace and Robert the Bruce in the early 1300s. The English did, however, increasingly dominate Ireland and Wales. The French, meanwhile, nibbled away at the Western borders of the Holy Roman Empire. Even more important, France and England offered renewed resistance to papal claims of authority.

The new power shift appeared during the reign of Pope **Boniface VIII** (r. 1294–1303). Boniface's papal election had been controversial because he had convinced his saintly predecessor, Celestine V, to resign. As pope himself, Boniface resisted the aims of the kings of England and France, who wanted to tax the clergy to finance a war they were preparing to fight against each other. In his bull of 1296, *Clericos Laicos* (named after the first sentence, which claimed that laypeople have always been hostile to clergy), he forbade kings to tax the clergy without papal permission.

Boniface further insisted on the ancient privilege called benefit of clergy, which allowed clergy accused of crimes to be tried in Church courts rather than those of the king. In 1302, when Boniface issued *Unam Sanctam* (titled after the first words: "One Holy, Catholic and Apostolic Church"), he declared, said, defined, and proclaimed that every human creature needed to be wholly subject to the Roman pontiff in order to obtain salvation.

The pope's declarations notwithstanding, the kings of England and France had other ideas. The kings retaliated by shutting down their borders and forbidding all export of precious metals and revenues to Rome. They convened their representative assemblies (Parliament and the Estates-General) in order to improve their jurisdiction over all their subjects. These bodies even included the clergy, many of whom sided with their nations against the pope. The most extreme reaction was from King Philip IV "the Fair" of France. He sent agents to Italy who tried to kidnap the pope while he was enjoying the summer in Anagni, away from the heat of Rome. Although freed by Anagni's townspeople, the shocked pope died a month later. If a German emperor had tried to do this fifty years earlier, the Church would have proclaimed a crusade against him. In this case, the king of France escaped with impunity.

Indeed, Philip IV tried to grab hold of the papacy for himself and his dynasty. He helped to elect a Frenchman as pope, Clement V (r. 1305–1314), a man who not only favored the French king but also packed up and moved the Curia out of Rome to the city of **Avignon** on the southeastern border of France. There the papacy resided for the so-called **Babylonian Captivity** (1309–1377), named after the real Hebrew exile 1,800 years earlier. Actually, the popes expanded their administration of the Church. They paid for their palace and power by collecting tithes and annates (the first year's income of important ecclesiastical offices such as bishop and abbot). Popes even took over provisions or reservations (the right to name men to Church offices), although these appointments were often done in consultation with, and at the request of, the local princes.

Many Christians were properly aghast at this situation. The pope was, of course, the bishop of Rome, and by canon law a bishop was to reside in his cathedral city. It often seemed, as the number and influence of French-born cardinals increased, that the papacy had become a tool of the French king. Many called for the pope to return to Rome, including the famous inspirational religious figures Catherine of Siena and Bridget of Sweden.

Finally, Pope Gregory XI did return to Rome in 1377, only to die the next year. The cardinals, under pressure from the Roman mob, quickly elected an Italian, Urban VI (r. 1378–1389). To their dismay, the cardinals found him not only difficult to work with, but apparently even insane. Rather than deal with the situation forthrightly, one night the cardinals snuck out under cover of darkness. They then deposed Urban in absentia, elected a new pope of French descent, Clement VII (r. 1378–1394), and blithely returned with him to Avignon. Urban, however, refused to recognize his deposition and continued to reign in Rome. Thus the Church was faced with a unique schism: two popes who had been elected by the same cardinals. Different princes chose allegiance to one pope or the other, often depending on whether they liked the French (and their Avignon puppet) or not.

The division grew worse. Indeed, history books often label it the "Great Schism," even though this conflict did not turn out as divisive as the other "Great Schism" that separated Catholic and Orthodox Christianity back in 1054. At first, this Great Western Schism likewise threatened to go on forever, since both popes created cardinals, and each group elected a papal successor after its pope had died. At one point, the majority of cardinals from both parties decided to end the schism by meeting at Pisa in 1410. In the shadow of the leaning tower, they deposed both the Avignon and Roman pontiffs and elected a new pope. Since the first two refused to recognize their depositions, Christendom now had three popes!

This Great Western Schism was healed by the old practice of *conciliarism*. After first being liberated under Constantine, Christians had originally used Church councils to try to resolve their differences. Important ecumenical councils of all Christians had been held for centuries until the original Great Schism in 1054 between the Catholics and Orthodox ended the possibility of Christian cooperation. As popes revived "universal" councils for the West in the eleventh century, such limited councils became a tool of the monarchical papacy to control the western Church. Now, ironically, Church reformers called for a council to check the papal monarchy. Supported by the Holy Roman Emperor, Sigismund of Bohemia, all parties attended the **Council of Constance** (1414–1417). The council first gained the resignation or deposition of the three popes based in Pisa, Avignon, and Rome, and then successfully elected a new, universally recognized pope, Martin V. The council also tried to guarantee itself a constitutional role within Church governance by requiring new councils to be called at set intervals.

The papal monarchy, although saved from civil war by conciliarism, proceeded to stamp out the idea. The popes delayed and restricted the brief insignificant councils of the following years. Finally, the Council of Basel (1431–1449) successfully, if briefly, defied the pope and reasserted conciliar authority. Yet the council fell into disorder and confusion as the pope exploited an opportunity to end the other schism with the Eastern Orthodox Church. When the Muslim Turks attacked the Byzantine Empire from all sides, some Eastern Orthodox Christians thought unity with the West might provide a lifeline. In the end, however, the Byzantine emperor and Orthodox patriarchs, bishops, abbots, and theologians rejected papal supremacy. The Byzantine Empire fell, while the Christian Church remained divided, Catholic in the West, and Orthodox in the East. The papacy in Rome settled onto its seemingly secure foundations.

Although feudal and Church lords could both claim victory, the changing structures of civilization were ending the Middle Ages and beginning the Early Modern Period. The Middle Ages had fashioned Western civilization in medieval Christendom (see map 8.2). Society was at first divided into three groups: those who prayed (the clergy) and those who both fought (the knights) and ruled over those who worked (the serfs). The successes and struggles within this order transformed the West. Kings struggled to dominate their knights, while nobles strove to keep their independence. Popes strained to rule both their own clergy and the kings, while alternate forms of religious life began to flourish and most kings grew

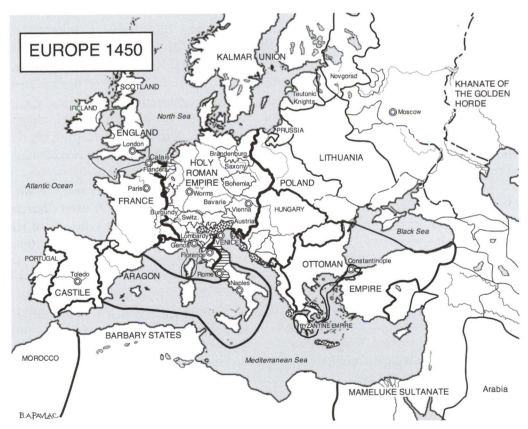

Map 8.2.   Europe, 1450

stronger in their kingdoms. These struggles strengthened institutions of state and Church overall. Meanwhile, food production by peasants helped revive towns and reestablish civilized life. Faith and wealth fostered cultural creativity and economic growth. The townspeople with their economic power asserted their respectable status among the established medieval nobles and clergy. Before long, old ideas and new practices would further fracture Christendom, transforming it into our modern West.

Review: *How do the Later Middle Ages expose the problems of medieval institutions?*

Response:

CHAPTER 9

Making the Modern World

The Renaissance and Reformation, 1400 to 1648

Already in the fifteenth century, some intellectuals had begun to claim that centuries of backwardness had given way to a "modern" age. Ironically, the key to this transition was a new appreciation for antiquity, the culture of classical Greece and Rome. Historians have named that perception the **Renaissance**, meaning a rebirth of attitudes drawn from Græco-Roman culture. Classical antiquity had, of course, been appreciated to one degree or another since its collapse in the West a thousand years before. Beginning around 1400, however, a renewed interest in antiquity intertwined with economic, political, and religious developments. Digging into the deepest recesses of their souls and reaching out to the four corners of the world, the Europeans transitioned out of the Later Middle Ages (ca. 1300–1500) and burst into the Early Modern Period of history (ca. 1400–1815) (see timeline 9.1).

THE PURSE OF PRINCES

As the Europeans recovered from the onslaught of the Black Death, the resurging economics of the towns propelled them into undreamed-of wealth, and success.

Amid plague and peasant rebellion, a dynamic idea later called *capitalism* began to catch on. Capitalism was a new form of economic practice that went beyond the markets of farmers or fairs. The capital of capitalism refers to a substantial amount of wealth that is available, and necessary, for investment. Many businesses require capital to begin operation or maintain themselves. One form of capital is profit, wealth left over after all expenses have been paid. When profits could be obtained, the practice of capitalism dictated what to do with them: reinvest.

In its simplest form, then, capitalism is reinvesting profits gained from investing capital. The usual human inclination is to spend excess wealth on showiness: fine homes, gourmet foods, parties, designer fashions, and grand edifices. One can, of course, give money away or bury it in the ground. Investing profit in one's own operations or in providing start-up and operating funds for another business, however, promoted long-term growth. Successful investments in turn created more profits, which then might be invested still further. Thus, capitalism became an engine for economic progress. Wealth bred more wealth. Likewise, capitalism encouraged innovation. Clever investors looked for a new enterprise, a novel endeavor, which, if successful, would bring an even greater profit.

Only much later did historians and theorists use the exact term *capitalism*. Some historians also argue that other civilizations, either Muslim, Indian, or Chinese, practiced capitalism first, and that westerners learned its techniques from them. Wherever it came from, a bigger problem is that people today often misunderstand the term *capitalism*. Many people often confuse capitalism with free markets. While capitalism requires markets (a space for people to exchange goods and services), they do not have to be entirely free (without restrictions imposed by authorities). This leads to another basic principle:

> **There is no such thing as an entirely free market; all markets have rules and costs.**

One of the key arguments among market participants, then and now, is how many regulations or fees there should be. One of the most important rules determines how much honesty is required between buyer and seller. If the market is an actual place, there are expenses for rent, cleaning, and upkeep. Many fees are taken by middlemen. The number of rules and expenses markets have make them more or less free or fair.

One of the biggest problems about capitalist financial markets occurred when people lost their capital. If a business venture failed, not only was there no profit, but the capital could also disappear as well. Risk has always existed with capitalism—wealth can simply vanish into thin air. On the one hand, luck, creativity, and business acumen can create huge funds from a small incentive. On the other hand, misfortune, stupidity, and economic ignorance can just as easily destroy riches. Poor investors have lost vast assets. For example, a sudden mania for tulips in the Netherlands during the 1630s drove up prices to where one bulb in a flower box cost the equivalent of a major mansion. When the bubble burst, tulip bulbs once again became mere potential flowers. Since early capitalists succeeded more often than they failed, however, the European economy grew better over the long term. Indeed, capitalism helped make Western civilization the most powerful culture the world has ever known, during what historians have called the **Commercial Revolution** (1350–1600).

The encouragement of innovation and the increase in wealth after the Black Death made medieval economic methods obsolete. The guild's hierarchical, regulated structure stifled progress, as measured by the creation of new forms of business. By definition, the guild promoted one kind of industry and opposed others. The masters who ran guilds increasingly seemed to want only to hold on to their power rather than seek improvements. While guilds had served to help medieval towns thrive, they were too inflexible to adapt to capitalism's drive for change.

The Commercial Revolution put in place more modern economic methods. Replacing the guild as the important structure for business was the partnership or firm. Usually this involved a family or several families pooling their resources to provide capital. As a business evolved, different members or alliances would come and go, which also encouraged creativity.

In the fourteenth century, families began to establish **banks**, the premiere capitalist institution. Banks evolved from benches of money changers into organizations that housed money and earned profits through finance. While bankers paid interest to attract depositors, the collection and safeguarding of deposits was merely a means to accumulate capital. Bankers invested assets as loans. A system of banks also allowed money to move more easily from one part of Europe to another without actually lugging around boxes of gold bars and bags of silver coins. Instead, banks issued bills of exchange, the forerunner of the modern check (the idea probably borrowed from Muslim trading partners). Spreading out from Italy, bank branches sprang up in cities all over Europe.

This rise of finance as a major economic activity required some religious reform. The Church had long taught that charging interest was a sin called usury. Thus Jews, as non-Christians, had been the main moneylenders to medieval Christians. By the close of the Middle Ages, however, Church leaders had redefined the sin to allow more lending so that they, too, could borrow to finance palace and church building.

To keep track of all this wealth, money counters invented double-entry bookkeeping. Since ancient times, businesses had simply entered a running tally of incomes and expenses in paragraph form, if they kept records at all. This new method, much like any modern checkbook or bank statement, arranged the moneys into two columns, which could be easily added or subtracted; a third column tracked the running sum of overall credit or debt. Thus a business leader could easily account for how much he had on reserve or owed.

As in most economic revolutions, benefits and costs distributed themselves unevenly among varied social groups. People still earned wealth through agriculture, commerce, and manufacturing, but finance began its rise to predominance. As happens so often, the rich became richer while the poor became poorer. Women were encouraged to work, although in lower-status jobs at lower wages than men were paid for the same work. Women workers' low cost and the ease with which they could be fired helped businesses maintain their profit levels. A growing class of menial laborers piled up at the bottom of the social scale since well-paid family artisans lost out to cheap labor. The wealthiest merchants began to merge with the nobility, becoming indistinguishable from them in their manner of living except for titles and family trees of noble ancestors. As a whole, though, the overall affluence and standard of living in Western society rose.

Princes who took advantage of this economic boom became the monarchs of the Late Middle Ages and Early Modern times. The practice of **public debt**, allowed by the new banking system, financed their expansion of power (see figure 9.1). Before capitalism, a prince's debts were considered his own—he would have to finance them from his dynastic revenues. Although a prince's incomes were often quite substantial, they were limited by agricultural production and a few taxes on trade. The new idea of public debt meant that bankers could finance loans to the princes, and then all of the prince's subjects had to pay the loans off through taxes and duties. Bankers usually supported this growing debt since they made a profit off the loans. Sometimes, a prince reneged on his debts and capital would disappear, followed by business failures and unemployment. More often, however, governments settled up their loans with interest, the bankers got their profits, and the princes became more powerful, while the common people paid.

Figure 9.1.   This woodcut from a legal handbook (ca. 1500) shows the various punishments monarchs inflicted on criminals. Top row: cutting off an ear, preparation for dunking, disembowelment, burning alive at the stake, hanging. Bottom row: flaying, beheading, breaking with the wheel, cutting off a hand.

Princes borrowed money especially for warfare. Wars involved different kinds of risk from capitalism but were always expensive. The **Hundred Years War** (1338–1453) between France and England illustrated the transition from medieval to modern. King Philip IV "the Fair" of France died in 1314, leaving three young sons. Within a few years, they had also died without leaving any male heirs in the Capetian dynasty—a situation France had not faced for more than three hundred years. The French aristocracy, without too much fighting, decided on Philip's grand-nephew, who succeeded as King Philip VI, the first king of the Valois dynasty (1328–1589). Meanwhile, King Edward III of England's Plantagenet dynasty decided to claim the throne of France through his own descent as a grandson of Philip "the Fair" (although through Philip's daughter). Edward also wanted to protect some independence for Flanders and preserve what few English territories remained in the southwest of France. These lands, called Guyenne, were the last holdings of Henry II's empire (most of which his son John had lost in the thirteenth century).

As the name implies, the Hundred Years War took generations to grind its way toward a conclusion. Along the way, war and politics changed decisively. When the war began, methods of warfare were still medieval. For centuries, the knight had reigned supreme on the battlefield. Weapon makers constantly tried to devise better ways of killing knights and storming castles, and armor makers and castle architects kept building better ways to defend them. At the time of the Norman Conquest in 1066, knights wore chain mail (heavy coats of linked iron rings). By the middle of the Hundred Years War, jointed plate armor enveloped knights from head to toe. Castles in the eleventh century had been simple wooden forts on hills. By the fourteenth century, they had become elaborate stone fortresses with massive towers and high walls built in concentric circles and surrounded by deep ditches.

England perfected the use of two medieval weapons in its wars with its immediate neighbors. By the fifteenth century, the English had conquered the Welsh but continued to fight off and on in the north against the Scots. The English experience from these border wars encouraged change in military technology and tactics. The English adopted a unique weapon, the longbow. Originally used by the Welsh, the longbow was as tall as a man and required long training and practice to pull. It could pierce armor at four hundred paces and be reloaded more quickly than its only competitor, the crossbow. English skills with the longbow were so important that in 1349 the king banned all sports other than archery. English knights also had learned from fighting the Scottish William Wallace and Robert the Bruce to dismount from vulnerable horses and defend themselves and their archers with pikes, long spears of two or three times a man's height. Thus, foot soldiers once more returned as a powerful force on the battlefield, as had been the phalanx and the legion.

During the Hundred Years War, the English raided France, devastating the countryside. French knights who tried to stop the raids took a while to realize that they no longer dominated combat. The English archers and dismounted knights wreaked havoc on French armored cavalry in three mighty battles: Crécy (1346), Poitiers (1356), and Agincourt (1415). Each battle turned the tide for the English and nearly led to the destruction of the French monarchy and kingdom. In the Treaty of Troyes (1420), King Henry V of England forced the French king to skip over the legitimate royal heir, the Dauphin, and instead grant the succession to the future child of Henry V and his French princess-bride.

Henry's sudden death, however, saved the French. He left an infant heir, Henry VI (r. 1422–1461)—always a precarious situation. The English advantage might still have prevailed over the divided and demoralized French. Then the unique **Joan of Arc** (b. 1412–d. 1431) arrived to save the French kingdom. This lowborn teenager believed that the voices of saints and angels told her to help the uncrowned French prince, the Dauphin. In 1429, he put her in shining armor at the head of a French army, which she miraculously led to victories over the English. The Dauphin gained his crown as King Charles VII (r. 1429–1461), but Joan was captured in battle. The French did nothing to rescue Joan, while the English put her on trial as a heretic. The crime of wearing men's clothing doomed her. They burned her alive at the stake and scattered her ashes.

Meanwhile, Charles VII cleverly used the ongoing English occupation of northern France to extort power from the French nobles and townspeople. In 1438, they supported him at the Council of Bourges, in which the king claimed broad authority over the Church in France. The Estates-General also gave him the right to regularly collect taxes such as those on salt or hearths. Everyone paid the salt tax, while the rich paid progressively more of the hearth tax, since their larger homes had more fireplaces. These revenues enabled Charles VII to raise a national, professional army paid by the government rather than one composed of the typical loyal retainers, feudal vassals, or hired mercenaries. Such a force had not fought in Europe since the time of the Roman legions. He also invested in the new technology of **gunpowder**, buying guns and cannons. With these cannons, Charles VII's armies pounded English-occupied castles to rubble and finally drove the English out of France.

The English did not cope well with this defeat. They did become more English, as the elites stopped speaking French, their language of choice since the Norman Invasion. Their government, though, briefly spun out of control. When Henry VI turned out to be mentally unbalanced, factions formed to control him. These opposing groups eventually came to blows in civil wars called the **Wars of the Roses** (1455–1487). During these, one aristocratic alliance (Lancaster) lost to another (York), which in turn lost to a third (Tudor) in 1485. King Henry VII (r. 1485–1509) of the new **Tudor dynasty** (1485–1603) provided England with a strong monarchy, exploiting the desire of the English to return to political stability. He restricted the rights of aristocrats to maintain private armies, set special judges against lawbreakers, and negotiated peace abroad. English commerce revived and flourished. Henry VII accomplished all this in alliance with the English Parliament. In Parliament's House of Commons, Henry bonded the English monarchy with the English middle class. The Tudor kings working with Parliament gave England a strong and flexible government, able to adapt to changing times.

While English and French kings reaffirmed their ascendance, the Holy Roman Emperors slipped even further into impotence. Since the end of the Staufen dynasty in 1256, powerful dynasties had fought over who would be Roman king and emperor, a problem the Golden Bull of 1356 had not solved. The election of King Frederick III in 1438 offered some stability, although no one knew it at the time. His **Habsburg dynasty** (1438–1918) began a monopoly on the royal and imperial title that would last, with the briefest of interruptions, until the empire's end in 1806 and beyond.

Realistically, the Habsburgs' power and interests lay with their own dynastic lands: **Austria** and its neighbors. Effective rule of the empire remained beyond their grasp. Frederick III was the last Holy Roman Emperor to be crowned by the pope in Rome. His son and successor Maximilian (r. 1486–1519) found too little success in wars to expand imperial domination. Instead, marriages arranged for and by him added numerous territories to the Habsburg dynasty's collection. His own first marriage gained him parts of Burgundy and the Lowlands, after his father-in-law Duke Charles "the Rash" of Burgundy died in battle with the Swiss. Marriages of his children and grandchildren added Bohemia, Hungary, and even Spain. It was said of his dynasty, "Let others wage war for a throne—you, happy Austria, marry."

Looming on Maximilian's Hungarian border, the new threat of the Ottoman dynasty appeared to unsettle the self-satisfied princes of Christendom. The Ottomans took their dynasty's name from their founder, Othman (and gave their name to our plush, round footstools). In the late thirteenth century, Othman and his *ghazi* (religious warriors) defeated their cousins, the Seljuk Turks, who had earlier seized Asia Minor from the Byzantine Empire in the eleventh century (see chapter 6) but had been weakened by attacks from the Mongols and others. Othman's successors became sultans, a title given to powerful rulers only second in rank to the caliphs. They soon aspired to be caliphs themselves.

With this goal, the Ottoman Turks began an imperialist expansion in all directions. In 1354, Turkish armies crossed the Dardanelles and entered southeastern Europe. Neither the Byzantine Empire nor the small Balkan kingdoms could halt the Muslim advance. Once the Turks had taken the province of Bosnia-Herzegovina, where the Bogomils had built up a heretical kingdom united by the dualistic religion of Catharism, many of the Slavs there converted to Islam. Next the Turks crushed the Serbian kingdom at the Battle of Kosovo Polje (28 June 1389), a site also called the Field of the Blackbirds after the winged scavengers who fed on the innumerable corpses of Christian warriors. In 1396 the Turks repeated their success by defeating a Christian crusading army at Nicopolis on the lower Danube. The Ottoman armies soon relied on young Christian boys taken from the conquered lands and trained to be expert warriors called janissaries. Christendom gained a respite when the Ottomans were attacked by the great conqueror Tamerlane or Timur the Lame of Samarkand (b. 1336–d. 1405), whose reputation for slaughter surpassed that of the Huns or the Mongols. Timur's defeat of the Ottoman armies in 1402 almost ended the dynasty.

Three years later, however, Timur was dead, and his empire crumbled apart. The Ottoman Empire reconsolidated and expanded. Jews, Orthodox Christians, Muslims, Greeks, Turks, Slavs, Arabs, and Armenians were organized into efficient groups that provided troops and taxes. The Ottomans organized interconnected bureaucracies to manage the diverse peoples and widespread territories. The Ottoman sultans took the ancient title of caliph, the religious and political leader of all (Sunni) Muslims. In 1444, the Ottomans routed another Christian crusading army at Varna on the mouth of the Danube. In 1453, Mohammed or Mehmet II "the Conqueror" besieged Constantinople, the last remnant of the once-mighty Roman

Empire. His massive cannons shelled the city for weeks. Defeat was only a matter of time as the walls became rubble. A Byzantine soldier who forgot to close a door through the walls, though, opened the way to a speedy end. The last Byzantine emperor died among his troops, defending the once-impregnable walls. Thus fell the Byzantine or Roman Empire, once and for all.

Mehmet II made Constantinople his new imperial capital, renaming it Istanbul ("the City"). He rebuilt and repopulated it (although no one told the Turks of the many underground cisterns that had been used to supply the city with water since Roman times). The Ottomans expanded their rule over diverse peoples in the Middle East and North Africa. In 1526, the Turks then seized much of Hungary from the Habsburgs. The Ottomans were then ready to advance into the Holy Roman Empire itself and, perhaps, from there conquer all of Christendom.

By 1600, the Ottomans were equal in power, wealth, and creativity to any of the Europeans (see figure 9.2). Their empire proved its success by conquering huge swatches of territory in the Middle East and North Africa. On the one hand, they allowed people to keep their ethnic identities while welcoming conversions to Islam or becoming Turkish. On the other hand, they sometimes exploited the ethnic conflicts to maintain their rule, encouraging minorities to dislike one another rather than the masters. Either way, the Ottoman Empire provided a powerful rival to the West.

These victories of the Ottomans ended any medieval romantic notion of a united Christendom. Meager attempts by the West to undertake a countercrusade and help the Byzantine Empire and other Balkan Christians had failed miserably. Western popes and princes worked against one another rather than against the common enemy. The various monarchs were looking out for their own narrow dynastic interests first. Western civilization clustered around the various principalities, kingdoms, and empires of Europe.

Figure 9.2. The Blue Mosque dominating the skyline of Istanbul reflects the glory of the Ottoman Empire around 1600.

Once Christendom was gone, so was a key component of what had made the Middle Ages. No one precise moment, event, or battle marks the transition from when medieval became modern history. Today, some historians even argue that medieval times lingered into the seventeenth and eighteenth centuries. Transformations in thought and belief, though, would further turn the West away from the medieval construct of priests, knights, and peasants. Indeed, Western civilization would become the most powerful society in world history.

Review: *How did late medieval monarchs concentrate still more power?*

Response:

MAN AS THE MEASURE

Italy led the way in ending the Middle Ages. As the heartland of urban development in the West, Italy's rich cities had been prizes for foreign powers since German kings and emperors such as Pippin "the Short" and Otto "the Great." Cities such as Genoa, Pisa, and Venice had expanded amid the ruins of Roman greatness with the medieval economic revival of the High Middle Ages. They became fat and rich from trade and finance and hard and powerful from politics and warfare. They won independence from both German emperors and Roman popes and even took away commerce from the Byzantine emperors, bargaining with Turks, Arabs, and even Mongols.

Self-government was difficult, however. Strained by economic change, citizens easily fought among themselves over control of elections and laws. Class warfare between the wealthy merchants, prosperous artisans, and the poor tormented the peace of the towns. In desperation for some order, tyrants known as despots seized power in many Italian towns during the Late Middle Ages. These despots started as local nobles, merchants, or even mercenaries, called *condottieri* in Italy. Since these dictators removed one more source of strife—namely, the struggle for leadership—the citizens often tolerated them, just as had happened in ancient Greece and Rome. Some maneuvered themselves into establishing dynasties. Thus, these new Italian princes often cut short the towns' initial experiments in democratic, republican government.

A successful despot might provoke more war across the Italian Peninsula, seeking for his city-state to dominate others. Ambitious princes began to conquer their neighboring towns, urged on by merchants wanting to eliminate competitors. Since the urban revival of the twelfth century, city-states and small principalities had tried to crush one another in wars that gave ready employment to *condottieri* and their mercenary troops. The Peace of Lodi in 1454 granted Italy four decades of relief from warfare. That treaty established five great powers within the Italian Peninsula who substantially upheld a fragile peace among themselves. In the south, the Kingdom of Naples was the largest in area, but it was weakened by the struggles over the throne by the foreign houses of Anjou (from France) and Aragon (from the Iberian Peninsula). In the center of the peninsula, the Papal States were bound loosely under the authority of the pope. Just north of Rome, in Tuscany, **Florence** dominated all its immediate neighbors (see figure 9.3). In the northwest, Milan ruled the plains of Lombardy. Finally, in the northeast, the maritime power of Venice had put down a strong foothold on the mainland, adding to its other possessions stretching along the eastern coast of the Adriatic and into the Aegean Sea. Venice's unique government was an oligarchy of the most powerful merchants who dominated their elected ruler, called the doge.

This balance of power in the Italian Peninsula ended in 1494, when the French king Charles VIII as heir of Anjou invaded to claim the Kingdom of Naples. Charles' invasion sparked decades of war throughout the peninsula (and spread a new, nasty form of the sexually transmitted disease syphilis, which may have come from the Americas). Wars proliferated while French kings, German emperors, Spanish monarchs, and Italian despots fought for supremacy. In the midst of these wars, over several generations, European culture left the Middle Ages and entered the Modern Period of history.

A cultural shift called the Renaissance (ca. 1400–1600) helped push Europe into modernity. The Renaissance started in Florence. While figuring out how best

Figure 9.3.   The Renaissance dome of Florence's medieval cathedral dominates the skyline.

to succeed in their political challenges, the Florentines sought inspiration from the Greeks and Romans of ages past. Their banks generated enough wealth to revive humanism from classical antiquity. At first, humanism had merely meant an interest in "humane letters" or the reading of classical writers. Inspired by the poet Petrarch (b. 1304–d. 1374), intellectuals had begun to scour old monastic libraries for ancient manuscripts. Then they edited what they found, creating the intellectual tool of *textual criticism*—comparing different versions of an author's writings in order to find the best, most accurate text.

Emphasis on the Latin literature of Rome soon led these humanists to appreciate the importance of the Greek language to classical civilization. During the Middle Ages, the knowledge of Greek had been virtually lost. The phrase "It's all Greek to me" came about because medieval readers could not decipher passages of Greek quoted by ancient Roman writers. Drawing on help from scholars fleeing the collapsing Byzantine Empire, the Western curriculum expanded to include the literature of ancient Greece. While today literature in the vernacular (that spoken by the common people), like the Italian poetry of Petrarch, is more highly valued, the ancient classics in "dead" Greek and Latin were the focus of Renaissance intellectuals.

Florence's **Medici** family played a key role in supporting this intellectual revival Greek after they took over that city's leadership. They had risen to power in local government financed through their family banking business. Over time, the Medicis survived urban rebellions, assassination plots, invasions, and banishment to found their own aristocratic dynasty. Along the way, they aspired to be patrons of the arts, those who fostered creative interaction with Greece and Rome.

On an intellectual level, Renaissance Neoplatonic philosophers reinterpreted the ideas of Plato. On a visual level, artists drew inspiration from styles of classical art and created the new painting, architecture, and sculpture of Renaissance art. Artists such as Leonardo da Vinci, Michelangelo, and Raphael pioneered a new naturalism in painting and sculpture that emphasized a realistic view of the world and the human body (see figure 9.4). On a literary level, intellectuals eagerly sought and read authors from classical antiquity.

One such intellectual was Niccolò **Machiavelli**. At the beginning of the sixteenth century, Machiavelli had himself been tortured and exiled from Florence for supporting the wrong political faction. In those times, suspicion of disloyalty to rulers meant having one's arms jerked out of the sockets on a torture device called the *strappado*, modified from a pulley. During his exile from the city, Machiavelli consoled himself every night by communing with ancient writers of Greece and Rome. Inspired by them (and to win the favor of the Medici), he wrote *The Prince* (1513). This book combined examples of classical antiquity and contemporary politics. It offered advice on how a prince should hold on to power in an occupied territory, suggesting that a ruler's primary goal should not be virtue, as political writers had been propounding through the Middle Ages. Instead, a prince was to wield power, using force and fear, lying or largesse, as long as he did not become hated. Many readers claimed to be shocked by this "Machiavellian" advice for amoral political behavior, freed from the constraints of Christianity. In secret, though, most princes and politicians have admired how Machiavelli accurately

Figure 9.4.   In this selection from his fresco the *School of Athens* in the Vatican, Raphael portrays Leonardo da Vinci as Plato in the center left and Michelangelo as the architect leaning on the block in the foreground. The majestic setting and the many other great thinkers from classical antiquity reflect the Renaissance fascination with Greece and Rome.

described brutal power politics. He aimed to end the diversity of Italian principalities by uniting them under one powerful prince. All his practical suggestions were grounded in his humanist scholarship of antiquity.

A major boost to the humanist scholarly enterprise was the invention of the **printing press** in Germany around 1450. Using a few hundred letters of movable type, any imaginable written page could be reproduced much more cheaply, easily, and quickly than with the laboriously handwritten leaf of every single book of Western history up to that moment. The multiplication of books further encouraged the expansion of literacy, since more publications became readily available to read.

This flood of printed matter also helped spur a change in education, giving rise to new kinds of schools. The sons of nobles and wealthy townspeople would, after an education in a primary or "grammar" school, then attend secondary schools. These advanced institutions went beyond the primary education of reading, writing, and arithmetic, but not so far as the serious scholarly study offered by the "higher education" of colleges and universities. In these secondary schools (the forerunners of American high schools), students further refined their knowledge of the classical curriculum of the liberal arts. Through reading ancient Latin and Greek authors, a student was supposed to learn how to be worthy of liberty. The well-rounded gentleman, an individual fit in mind and body, became the Renaissance ideal.

Compared to that of men, the place of women, genteel or not, remained much more restricted. Ladies were to be respected, but few opportunities opened for their advancement. Lack of access to schools and the inability to control property remained the norm. A rare individual like **Christine de Pisan** (b. 1363–d. ca. 1430) could make her living from writing. Widowed and with children to support, she managed to market her books on history, manners, and poetry to rich male patrons in France and England. She remained an isolated example of the successful woman, unfairly forgotten soon after her death. Society still measured success by a man's achieving his material best, crafting for himself a place of honor in this world.

Perhaps the greatest writer of the Renaissance, if not of all time, was the English actor, poet, and playwright **William Shakespeare** (b. 1564–d. 1616). His plays ranged over histories (such as *Henry IV* and *Henry V*), comedies (such as *Twelfth Night* and *A Midsummer Night's Dream*) and tragedies (such as *Hamlet* and *Macbeth*). His writing captures in poetry and action a sense of universal human drama and character, drawing heavily on the classics. The Globe Theater in London, along with other new theaters in European cities, revived plays from ancient writers adapted to new audiences.

With all this focus on success in the world, the humble path of Christ seemed somehow less attractive. Yet, as Renaissance ideas spread from Italy to northern Europe, many scholars in England, the Lowlands, and Germany did bend humanism to a more Christian view. This **Christian humanism** still emphasized the classics, using one's critical mind, and taking action in the world, but it added an interest in the writings of the Christian faith. Thus, along with Latin and Greek, Christian humanists learned Hebrew in order to read both the Old Testament in its original language and the writings of rabbi commentators.

The most famous Christian humanist was **Erasmus** (b. 1466–d. 1536). He sought to promote the best, most pure form of Christianity as he understood it from his reading in the New Testament and the writings of the early Church Fathers. His humanist outlook gave him a mockingly critical attitude to authority. In his *Praise of Folly* (1509), Erasmus satirized all the problems of his contemporaries, especially the hypocrisies and failures of the Church. Questioning authority became an important intellectual tradition, although authorities have never taken kindly to it.

Although Renaissance humanists encouraged a more critical look at the world, Erasmus and many of his contemporaries carelessly accepted dangerous changes in beliefs about witches and witchcraft. Historians have yet to fully understand how and why the fear of witchcraft began during the Renaissance. Prior to 1400, the usual position of the Church had been that witches did not exist. The Church taught that anyone claiming to be a witch was rather a dupe of the devil, and any supposed magic spells were meaningless deceptions. After 1400, many Church authorities changed their opinions to say that a real conspiracy of witches existed, organized by the devil as a vital threat to Christian society. Actually, no reliable evidence remains that any such organized plot existed or that any magic has ever succeeded against anyone.

Regardless, many ecclesiastical and secular leaders began the **witch hunts** (1400–1800), actively seeking out suspected witches, torturing them into confessing impossible crimes, and then executing them. Like the ancient Roman persecution of Christians, the hunts were sporadic, intermittent, and geographically scattered: worst in the Holy Roman Empire, moderate in France, Scotland, and England, and rare in the rest of Europe. Nevertheless, tens of thousands died, with more untold numbers submitting to false accusations, having loved ones persecuted, or suffering from pervasive fear. Authorities most often accused older women living on the margins of society, yet also younger women, men, and even children fell victim to suspicions.

These witch hunts ended once leaders no longer believed in the reality of diabolic magic. Fewer bouts of bad weather, the rising power of the state, improving economies, and more rational attitudes promoted by the Renaissance, the Scientific Revolution, and the Enlightenment (see below and chapter 11) all contributed. By the eighteenth century, most leaders, both religious and political, had once more come to the sensible view that witches and witchcraft were imaginary and no threat.

While scholars studied the classics and certain magistrates hunted witches, religious leaders rethought the givens of medieval faith. European elites had become more modern, embracing the study of ancient Greeks and Romans. The new, more worldly emphasis of humanism, however, contrasted with the basics of medieval Christianity. Humanism prioritized this world; Christianity, the next. Most people in Christendom found meaning and purpose in their faith. The ongoing need of many people for religious certainty would break the unified religious system of the Middle Ages. Just as westerners accepted and fought for separate political states, they would soon embrace and die for divided religious sects.

Review: *How did the Renaissance promote the West's transition into modernity?*

Response:

HEAVEN KNOWS

A religious revolution called the **Reformation** (1517–1648) fractured the medieval unity of the Christian Church in the West beyond recovery. The Reformation first addressed the Church's role in the plan of salvation. Yet the Reformation also reflected the ongoing political, economic, and social changes created by Europe's growing wealth and power. The calls for reform in the western Latin Church had been long and loud since the Great Western Schism had divided the papacy between 1378 and 1415. With the concept of conciliarism crushed, calls for reform went unheeded. The Church leadership's long avoidance of reform made the Reformation more divisive than it might have been.

Some believers did find comfort and hope in many of the rituals and practices of the medieval Church: sacraments from baptism through the mass to final unction, pilgrimages and shrines, saints' days, the Daily Office, hospices, and hospitals. An increasingly popular mysticism (the idea that people could attain their own direct experience of God) led some to question the value of a Church hierarchy. Religious women such as the recluse Julian of Norwich (d. 1416) or the wandering housewife Margery Kempe (d. 1438) continued the practice of Hildegard of Bingen by sharing vivid and novel visions of their interactions with God. The Church's worldly interventions also alienated many. Popes had not lived down the scandals of the Avignon exile and the Great Western Schism.

Even worse, the Renaissance wars over Italy led many to consider the pope to be a typical petty prince rather than a potent moral force and spiritual leader. Christendom watched as the popes deepened their political rule over the Papal States in central Italy. The faithful were scandalized by seeing papal armies commanded first by Cesare Borgia for his father, Pope Alexander VI (r. 1492–1503), and later by a pope himself, Julius II (r. 1503–1513). Popes played power politics and lived in pomp as princes. Thus, many Christians gradually grew disillusioned with papal monarchy. Rome seemed to represent the obstacle to reform.

A successful call for reform rose in an obscure and unexpected place: the small town of Wittenberg in the Holy Roman Empire. There, the simple son of prosperous Saxon peasants, **Martin Luther** (b. 1483–d. 1546), had risen to be a professor at the nearby university of Erfurt. Additionally, he dedicated himself to monastic discipline in a house of Augustinian canons regular (sometimes called Austin Friars). Finally, Luther served as the pastor of a parish.

As a pastor, Luther became increasingly disturbed when his poor parishioners bought **indulgences** from traveling salesmen. Indulgences had originally developed out of the Church's sacramental system of penance. When one committed sin, the Church taught, one had to do penance, such as some good deed, prayers, or a pilgrimage. Toward the Later Middle Ages, some clever clerics suggested that, instead of having a penitent take the time and trouble for a complicated and expensive pilgrimage to Rome, why not just have that person pay the comparable amount of cash instead? Consequently, the Church gained money, which it could use for anything it wished. Granted, the Church did officially insist that indulgences did not forgive sin unless the purchaser was truly contrite. Nevertheless, the sales pitch by indulgence sellers often overlooked that quibble. Encouraged to buy these fill-in-the-blanks forms, people believed that their sins (or those of their dead friends or relatives) would be instantly pardoned in return for some coins.

In Luther's home province of Saxony, the local prince-archbishop of Magdeburg had authorized a vigorous sale of indulgences. The archbishop's share of the profits paid off his debts to the pope, who had suspended canon law so that the archbishop could take possession of more than one prince-bishopric. The pope needed these funds to help build the new Renaissance-style St. Peter's Basilica on the Vatican hill. This new edifice, the largest church building the world had yet seen, designed by the great artist Michelangelo, replaced the crumbling twelve-hundred-year-old structure built under Constantine.

Ignorant of these back-door financial deals, Martin Luther developed his own objections to indulgences. In his own studies of the faith, he began to question the entire concept of indulgences within the plan of salvation. For Luther, sin seemed so pervasive and powerful that he felt any normal means of penance could not erase its stain on the soul. No matter how many good works he undertook or how much he attended church, Luther worried that sin made him unworthy to enter the perfection of heaven. In comparison, he felt like a lump of manure. Luther broke through his dilemma with a revelation upon reading Romans 1:17: "The just shall live by faith." He proposed that a person is assuredly saved, or justified, simply by the belief in the death and resurrection of Jesus Christ. For Luther, worship was to be a moment of faith, not a process of rituals and ceremonies. And if faith alone justified sinners, then the sacraments provided by the ordained priestly hierarchy of the Church were unnecessary. Hence, Luther's declaration of "justification by faith alone" undermined the dominant position of the chief priest, the pope, as an arbiter of salvation.

Luther offered his **95 Theses**, or arguments, about his developing theological point of view. According to tradition, he posted them on the door of the Wittenberg church on 31 October 1517. Publishers printed these theses and spread them with amazing rapidity across Christendom. Luther became the hero and voice for those who wanted to reform the Church.

Not surprisingly, the Church hierarchy reacted slowly. Even once theologians realized how popular Luther's criticisms had become, their debates with this obscure monk only drove him to harden his point of view and write more pamphlets spreading his ideas. When the pope finally excommunicated Luther in June 1520, the defiant reformer publicly burned the bull along with the books of the canon law, thus dismissing the entire structure of the western Latin Church.

To deal with this upstart monk, the pope sought an ally in the newly elected Holy Roman Emperor **Charles V** Habsburg (r. 1519–1556). Charles convened a diet (the German version of Parliament) in 1521 in the city of Worms to consider the situation. At the **Diet of Worms**, Luther refused to recant, putting his faith in his own understanding of scripture, reason, and his own conscience. He held his position with the legendary words, "Here I stand; I can do no other." The emperor allowed Luther to leave the diet alive, whereupon his supporters spirited him away into hiding. Charles concluded the diet by declaring Luther an outlaw and pledging to kill him in order to stamp out his heretical ideas.

Since Emperor Charles V ruled over the most wide-ranging empire in history up to that time, such a threat carried weight. As the head of the Habsburg dynasty, Charles V had inherited the lands of Austria and most of the lands of Burgundy (including much of Flanders) from his grandfather, Emperor Maximilian. From his mother he received Naples and Spain, which by this time also included much of the New World (see below), and soon, possessions in Asia. The sun never set on Charles V's empire.

Yet, ironically, this powerful emperor never concentrated enough power to crush Luther and his allies. The office of Holy Roman Emperor had been wasting away during centuries of conflict with the popes and the German princes. Moreover, the Austrian lands were weakened by wars over claims to both Bohemia and Hungary (since Bohemians and Hungarians opposed Habsburg rule). Even Spain, although rich from its new colonial possessions, rebelled against Charles' authority. The wealthy Burgundian lands yearned for more independence while France grabbed what it could. Indeed, the king of France could not tolerate being hemmed in by the Habsburg dominions and also wanted its share of Italy. France thus helped the Lutherans by starting the Habsburg-Valois dynastic conflict. Even though he enjoyed the title "Most Christian," King Francis I of France even encouraged the Muslim sultan of the Ottoman Empire to conquer Charles' ally Hungary in 1526 and besiege the Austrian capital of Vienna in 1530.

As Charles nonetheless gathered resources to crush Luther, the former monk set up a new Christian denomination called *Lutheranism*. In his hiding place, Luther translated the Bible into simple German. In doing so, he both set the style of modern German and promoted literacy. He simplified the worship ceremonials, emphasizing more preaching, prayer, and music. Then he reined in many reformers who had started to destroy all images and fancy decorations in churches. The bourgeoisie had long wanted more asceticism from the clergy (although the burghers themselves often spent their wealth on conspicuous consumption).

Luther further encouraged simplification by closing monasteries and ending monasticism. That attitude complicated his personal life, however. A nun, Katherine von Bora, and several other nuns were both inspired by Luther's writings and disappointed with religious life. They had escaped from their nunnery in fish barrels. Then Katherine had complained to Luther that since the single, celibate life of a monastic was no longer an option, nuns needed to be married and have children. So he obliged her. He married Katherine and started a family.

Luther's reforming efforts won much popular support. Many German peasants seized on Luther's rhetoric on the defiance of authority and applied it to their social and political obligations. They rebelled against their noble lords in 1525. As was typical of peasant revolts during the Later Middle Ages, the peasants killed a few hundred landlords; the nobles then regrouped and avenged the deaths by hanging many thousands of rebels. Luther disassociated himself from the peasants, calling them "thievish, murderous hordes."

Ultimately, Luther relied on the power of princes. Starting with Luther's own Duke of Saxony, many northern German princes and kings in Scandinavia welcomed the Lutheran Church. The new structures allowed them to act as popes in their own provinces. The rulers administered much of the former Church property and lands for themselves and had a strong hand in appointing the bishops and priests. The Church could devote itself to spiritual matters (which did not involve land reform for peasants).

Consequently, many German princes protected Luther and his fledgling Lutheranism. When the Habsburg Charles V tried to ban Lutheranism at a diet in 1529, Lutheran princes protested. From that event onward, Christians who are neither Eastern Orthodox nor Roman Catholics have usually been called **Protestants**. Once debate failed, the Protestants resorted to weapons, and civil war fitfully raged through the empire. Charles never achieved the military victory needed to crush Luther's princely supporters. With the **Treaty of Augsburg** in 1555, Charles V capitulated to the rights of princes to maintain their Lutheran churches. Despondent, he resigned his throne the next year and died shortly thereafter.

Luther's successful defiance of ecclesiastical and political authority raised a question for Christianity: who had the authority to interpret and define faith? The original, traditional answer had been the Church councils. That was still the position of the Orthodox Churches in eastern Europe, although they had not held a council since long before the Great Schism with the western Latin Church in 1054. The western Catholic Church had rejected conciliarism and instead granted the papacy a monarchical authority to determine the faith.

In contrast, Luther relied solely on his own conscience, as guided by Holy Scripture. Yet how was his conscience necessarily better than anyone else's? Could not anyone claim to be guided by the Holy Spirit and use individual judgment to assert doctrine? Such is what happened. Religious leaders formed new sects and denominations. Success in drawing followers validated divergent religious truths. *Protestantism* became a container for multiple Christian groups, each avowing to have the one true interpretation of Christianity.

A variety of sectarians who enjoyed some success in the sixteenth century were collectively known as Anabaptists. *Anabaptism* was not one movement but consisted of many different groups lumped together by enemies who disagreed with their common refusal to accept infant baptism. For Anabaptists, only mature adults should be baptized. These groups often drew their followers from the lower classes, who rejected religious hierarchy and ecclesiastical wealth.

Both Lutherans and Catholics joined in exterminating most of these Anabaptists through such traditional methods as torture and war. The most famous example was the siege and destruction of Münster in 1535. There the allied Lutherans and Catholics killed thousands of Anabaptists as they retook the city. The victors tortured the survivors, executed them, and then hung their remains on a church tower in cages that remain there today. Only a few groups of Anabaptists survived, often by fleeing to the New World, especially Pennsylvania, which was founded in the late seventeenth century on a principle of tolerance. Their successors exist today in such denominations as the Mennonites, Moravians, Hutterites, and the Amish or Pennsylvania Dutch.

Various reform ideas soon spread to France, one of the most powerful nations in Europe. The kings of the Valois dynasty had little need or interest in supporting any changes. The monarchy had already arranged the Concordat of 1516, which created a convenient royal co-dominion with the Church in France. The agreement authorized the French king to appoint most of the bishops, abbots, and abbesses, while the pope got a large cut of the revenues.

One Frenchman, however, found himself more sympathetic to Luther's reforms than the structures of kings and bishops. **Jean Calvin** (b. 1509–d. 1564) learned of Luther's ideas in school. Inspired by them, he created his own new religious framework, called *Calvinism*, which he solidified after being called to be the leading preacher in Geneva, Switzerland. Geneva became the center of a theocracy, a government based on divine commands. While elected leaders still ran the town council, they passed laws that tried to make the townspeople conform to Calvin's beliefs. From Geneva, Calvin then sent missionaries throughout Europe.

Calvin differed from Luther in two main ways. First, Calvinism focused on **predestination** or *determinism*: the belief that God determined in advance, for all of time, who was saved and who was damned. Nothing any person did could influence God's preordained omniscient decision. This idea went back to Augustine and had a certain logic to it: if God knows everything, then he surely knows who is going to heaven and who is going to hell. While some complained that this belief removed free will, Calvinism called believers to choose to live the exemplary life of saints, participating in baptism and the Lord's Supper. In doing so, they hoped to re-create heaven on earth.

A second difference in Calvinism was its democratic tendency; members of a church were supposed to be involved in running it. The congregation itself approved ministers or appointed the preacher instead of a distant pope or prince from above. Calvinism expanded through much of the West under the title of Reformed churches in the northern Lowlands or the Netherlands and much of the Rhineland. In France, Calvinists were called Huguenots. In Scotland they formed Presbyterian churches, and in Wales, Congregationalist churches. In England and its colonies, the Calvinists were labeled Puritans.

When Luther first called for reform, no one thought that the authority of the pope could be overthrown by religious ideas. Yet Lutherans, Calvinists, small groups of Anabaptists, and other sects successfully defied papal control. Papal supremacy would suffer yet another loss before it reorganized and redefined itself. Amid all this religious diversity, killing for reasons of faith would continue.

Review: *How did Early Modern reforms among Christians culminate in wars over religion?*

Response:

FATAL BELIEFS

Although Calvinism gained popularity in England, the **English Reformation** (1534–1559) originated, uniquely, due to matters of state. The reigning king, **Henry VIII** (r. 1509–1547), had strongly supported the views of the pope against Luther. The pope had even awarded King Henry the title of "Defender of the Faith," still sported by English monarchs today. A higher priority for Henry, however, was the security of the Tudor dynasty, for which, he thought, he needed a male heir. After twenty years of marriage to Catherine of Aragon and six births, only one child, a daughter Mary, had survived. Although a daughter could legally inherit the throne in England, Henry believed, like most monarchs of his time, that he needed a son. So he asked the pope to end his marriage, as many kings before and since have done. Contrary to the common version of history, Henry did not want a divorce (the breakup of a genuine marriage). He actually sought an annulment (the declaration that a marriage never had existed). Catherine steadfastly resisted. Her nephew and Luther's overlord, Emperor Charles V, backed her up. Charles just happened to have an army outside of Rome (although it briefly went out of control and brutally sacked the city in 1527). Fearing the nearby Holy Roman Emperor more than the distant English king, the pope refused to support Henry's annulment.

Still determined to father a legitimate heir, Henry decided to break with the pope. His Parliament declared him head of the **Church of England**, and his bishops willingly annulled his first marriage and blessed his second with his courtier, Anne Boleyn. Although the pope excommunicated Henry and declared his new marriage void, that little bothered the monarch or the great majority of the English people. Both the king and many of his subjects had long disliked what they saw as Roman interference in English affairs. Moreover, many of the members of Parliament profited nicely from the subsequent dissolution of the monasteries, whose properties they bought up at bargain rates. Despite the schism, Henry remained religiously conservative, so Calvinist and Lutheran ideas gained very little influence.

Unfortunately for Henry, he did not achieve his sought-after heir with his second wife, Anne Boleyn; she managed to give birth only to a healthy daughter, Elizabeth. To make way for a new wife, Henry had Anne executed on trumped-up charges of adultery. The third wife, Jane Seymour, gave birth to his heir, Edward VI (r. 1547–1553), but died soon after. Three more marriages followed. Henry had the fourth marriage annulled and the fifth wife legitimately executed for adultery. His sixth wife managed to outlive him. Despite this rather unseemly string of marriages, most of the English people did not oppose their king. Henry had to chop off the heads of relatively few who resisted his religious transformation.

A genuinely distinctive Church of England, or *Anglicanism*, grew after Henry's death. His son, King Edward VI, came to the throne as a child, and his advisors began to push the Church of England further away from the Church of Rome. They began to significantly alter the interpretations of the sacraments and methods of worship to be more in line with simplifications introduced by Calvinist, Lutheran, and other Protestant reformers from the Continent.

These policies abruptly reversed after the young Edward died after a reign of only six years. A brief effort to put his cousin, the Protestant Lady Jane Grey, on the throne failed. Henry's daughter by his first marriage, Mary I (r. 1553–1558), won the day. Her religious policy forced the English church back under Rome. In doing so, she persecuted clergy and laypeople, many of whom, surprisingly, were willing to die rather than go back to obedience to the pope. She burned several hundred "heretics." For these efforts the English have dubbed her "**Bloody Mary**." Her disastrous marriage to her cousin King Philip II of Spain did not help, either. Many English hated him as a Spaniard and a Roman Catholic, and he avoided both the country and his wife. When she died without an heir, Henry's daughter by Anne Boleyn, Queen **Elizabeth I** (r. 1558–1603), inherited the crown.

Elizabeth, who had managed to survive the changes of political and religious policy, now faced a choice herself: should she maintain obedience to Rome or revive the Church of England? In 1559, with the Act of Supremacy enacted in Parliament, she chose the latter course. The English monarch occupied a ceremonial role as head of the Church of England. Henceforward, Anglicanism defined itself as Protestant while still Catholic, trying to maintain the best of both. The *Book of Common Prayer* (1549) laid out how worship was to be carried out, but it said little of belief. One's conscience was up to oneself—a fairly tolerant attitude. Fortunately for Elizabeth, most English embraced her religious compromise.

In fact, Elizabeth became one of England's greatest monarchs. The late sixteenth century saw a number of powerful and effective women on or behind the thrones of Europe. The Calvinist preacher John Knox in Scotland railed against such a "Monstrous Regiment of Women," as he titled a pamphlet against them. Although the others ruled fairly competently, Elizabeth outshone them all. England flourished during her reign, culturally, economically, and politically. Renaissance culture reached its high point with Shakespeare's plays. Meanwhile, the English navy began to help its countrymen explore and start to dominate the rest of the world, taking the first steps toward becoming the British Empire. It is ironic that Henry VIII thought he needed a son, when Elizabeth was "man" enough to surpass her father's accomplishments.

The one force that seriously threatened Elizabeth was *Roman Catholicism*. By the beginning of her reign, Rome had begun what historians call either the "Counter-Reformation" or the "Catholic Reformation." Devoted and energetic popes, recovering from the opulent distractions of the Renaissance, now sought to recover lands lost by the Roman version of Christianity. Having accepted the inevitability of reform, the papacy called the **Council of Trent** (1545–1563). Leaders chose the obscure cathedral city at the southern edge of the Alps for a general council because it satisfied Charles V (it was in the empire), the king of France (it was not German), and the pope (its residents spoke Italian).

Some clergy at the Council of Trent wanted to compromise or adopt some ideas of the Protestants, but the council rejected that path. Instead, the Church of the popes insisted on the value of justification by faith supported by good works, combined with the mediating role of the priesthood and the sacraments. The Tridentine Reform (named after the Latin word for Trent) limited some abuses and corruptions and established seminary schools for a better-educated priesthood. The council affirmed that the Church, through the papacy, had the final authority to define belief and interpret scripture—not Luther's conscience, or Anabaptist interpretations, or Calvin's scholarship, or anyone's literal reading of the Bible. The popes increased their interest in organizing and clarifying the smallest details of belief and practice. The Roman Catholic Church did recognize, however, the importance of tradition. Practice and understanding could change over time.

New monastic orders and reformations of older ones aided the popes in reform. The Ursulines dedicated themselves to the education of girls and women. Most importantly, the Society of Jesus, or the **Jesuits**, gained sway in European affairs. Ignatius Loyola founded the Jesuits after suffering wounds as a warrior in Charles V's Spanish army. During the painful recovery from a shattered leg, he envisioned a new kind of monastic order, one not confined to the cloister. Active in the world, Jesuits dedicated themselves to religious vocation (formed through the Spiritual Exercises), education (becoming teachers and guides), and missionary work (both in Europe and the world). Loyola saw his order as a spiritual army for the Roman Catholic Church, with a so-called fourth vow (after poverty, chastity, and obedience) of absolute dedication to the pope.

The Tridentine Reform set a militant tone for Roman Catholicism during the next two hundred years. Roman Catholicism aimed to recapture the allegiance of lost followers and gain more new ones. A new Roman Inquisition revived in 1542, partly inspired by the Spanish Inquisition of Ferdinand and Isabella. The Spanish Inquisition policed converted Jews and Muslims; this new version hunted Protestants as heretics. An **Index of Forbidden Books** declared the reading of certain authors to be sinful. First issued in 1559 by the Holy Office in Rome and regularly reissued thereafter for four hundred years, the list restricted the circulation of banned works in Roman Catholic countries and forbade Roman Catholics from reading these prohibited books. This censorship even included all the works of Erasmus, so fearful had Rome become of any criticism.

The Roman Catholic vigor also expressed itself in a series of Wars of Religion that lasted until 1648. Traditionally, territorial, dynastic, and economic reasons shaped decisions for fighting wars. In this period, ideological differences between adherents of branches of Christianity became significant motives. For a few decades, people were ready to die, and kill, for Lutheranism, Anabaptism, Calvinism, Anglicanism, or Roman Catholicism. Monarchs thought that their subjects and their neighbors needed to conform to their own dogmas as a matter of both public order and divine virtue. People volunteered for armies in the belief that their neighbors should worship the same way they themselves did. Some also enlisted simply as a way to earn a living—soldiering was a growth industry.

In the vanguard of militant Roman Catholicism was Elizabeth's former brother-in-law, King **Philip II** of Spain (r. 1556–1598). Philip had inherited most of his Habsburg father Charles V's possessions except the Austrian ones, which, along with the elected title of Holy Roman Emperor, went to his brother Ferdinand. Yet Philip got the better share: Spain had one of the world's best armies; Flanders was the textile manufacturing center of Europe; and the Americas poured silver into his treasuries. Philip also briefly united Spain with Portugal, making Spain the sole global power. He built a new, modern capital for himself in Madrid. Although Madrid was not conveniently connected to the waterways that bound Philip's empire together, it was easily accessible from his palace of el Escorial, a massive, gray religious retreat (see figure 9.5). Philip was hard working, but perhaps too focused on small details. He saw himself as a divinely appointed monarch obliged

Figure 9.5.   King Philip II of Spain often retreated to the gray abbey of El Escorial, which served also as a second palace away from Madrid.

to attend to every corner of his empire. At the apex of a vast bureaucracy, he regulated the lace on court costumes, ordered murders of political enemies, corrected the spelling of secretaries, and held autos-da-fé (public burnings of heretics at which he served as master of ceremonies).

Above all, the king of Spain sent armies to fight for his vision of the Roman Catholic faith. His navy's victory over the Ottoman Turks at the Battle of Lepanto (1571) cheered the Christian West, showing that the Ottomans were not invincible. At the time, the Muslim sultan claimed the defeat meant nothing—he would just build another fleet, which he did. Despite this boast, historians have seen the defeat at Lepanto as an obvious turning point toward the long, slow decline of Ottoman dominion. Ironically, Philip's power also began to diminish. His empire, too big for the available means of communication, could not be managed from Madrid. He could not afford his government either, declaring bankruptcy three times and thereby damaging the bankers and merchants he needed so badly.

In particular, some of those capitalists, namely the prosperous Calvinist Dutch in the northern part of the Lowlands, resented paying for Philip's imperialistic and Roman Catholic dreams of grandeur. In 1581, they declared independence from his rule to form the **Dutch Netherlands** (often called Holland after the main province). They even began to construct their own democratic government (see the next chapter). The Dutch would fight off and on for eighty years before they gained full independence for themselves. To stop this rebellion, Philip first sent in the Duke of Parma, whose army earned infamy for its brutality against the civilian population. In turn, Dutch and Huguenot merchants harassed Spanish shipping.

Philip turned his attention to England, which had been supporting the upstart Dutch after the death of his wife Queen Mary I. Hostilities simmered for several years as English sea dogs or privateers (informal pirates with permission from a government to raid shipping) preyed on Spanish possessions. Riches looted by the Spanish from the American natives wound up being plundered by the English instead.

Philip retaliated by instigating plots against Elizabeth's life and throne. The pope declared her an illegitimate, excommunicated heretic and encouraged the faithful to overthrow her rule. Philip and the pope supported Elizabeth's cousin, Mary Stuart, Queen of Scots (not to be confused with Elizabeth's half-sister "Bloody Mary" Tudor, the late queen of England) as the true English monarch. The unfortunate Mary Stuart had lost her Scottish Highlands kingdom through her own folly, falling under a reasonable suspicion of blowing up her first husband. She fled from her own people to England. Elizabeth kept her in comfortable confinement until Mary got herself implicated in a treasonous Roman Catholic plot. Elizabeth finally ordered Mary's beheading, although it took the headsman three whacks of his axe to succeed.

Seizing upon Elizabeth's execution of Mary in 1587 as an excuse, Philip assembled the **Spanish Armada**. This fleet of 130 ships aimed to sail from Spain to the Lowlands and then ferry Parma's troops across the North Sea to invade England. It all went terribly wrong. The most famous English sea dog, Sir Francis Drake, destroyed most of the fleet in its harbor. A rebuilt fleet launched in 1588, but adverse weather slowed its progress. That the commanding admiral had never been to sea was not helpful, either. Easily repulsing the English in the Channel, the admiral did finally anchor his fleet off the coast of the Lowlands, only to be told, quite reasonably, that if troops there were diverted to England, the Netherlands might succeed in their rebellion. Then the English broke up the Armada by pushing fire ships, empty burning hulls, among the fleet. The panicked Spanish broke formation and came under English guns. Storms sank most of the rest.

Philip at first wrote off this defeat much as the Ottoman sultan had his own at Lepanto. Notwithstanding Spain's appearance of strength over the next decades, it sank to a second-rank power. England, however, continued its ascendancy, becoming stronger than ever as its national patriotism became bound with its religion and its burgeoning imperialist ventures.

Meanwhile, France had not been able to help Philip II of Spain fight its traditional enemy England, since France itself almost broke apart in religious warfare. The Huguenots (the name for French Calvinists) had grown to about 10 percent of the population. Their numbers were particularly strong in the productive artisan and business classes. The Valois dynasty might have moved against them once its long conflict with the Habsburgs ended in 1559. But that same year the Valois dynasty plummeted into crisis with the unexpected death of King Henry II, killed during a joust by a piece of splintered lance thrust through his eye into his brain. His three young sons and their mother, Queen Catherine de Medici (b. 1519–d. 1589), were trapped between two powerful aristocratic families: the Huguenot Bourbons and the Roman Catholic de Guises. Fighting over the throne using betrayal, assassination, and war, these powerful families nearly destroyed the monarchy and the country.

The Roman Catholic party almost succeeded with the **St. Bartholomew's Day massacre** (14 August 1572), where they viciously murdered thousands of Protestants, great and small, men, women, and children, in the streets of Paris. Henry of Bourbon survived that slaughter and was soon able to gain military domination over most of the country. After the death of the last Valois in 1589, he became officially recognized as the French King **Henry IV "of Navarre"** (r. 1589–1610), founding the Bourbon dynasty. Hostility to his Protestantism still stood in the way of his acceptance by some Roman Catholics. So, in 1593, he converted to Roman Catholicism, allegedly saying, "Paris is worth a mass." He continued to protect the Protestants, though, with the proclamation of the **Edict of Nantes** (1598). This act mandated a certain level of religious tolerance. It allowed Protestants to worship and to fortify fifty-one cities for their own self-defense. Diversity brought some peace and security.

The last of the religious wars, the **Thirty Years War** (1618–1648), engulfed the Holy Roman Empire and drew in the entire continent. The conflict began in Bohemia, as the Austrian branch of the Habsburgs labored to convert that province back to Roman Catholicism. Leaders in Prague "defenestrated" the emperor's representatives—meaning they tossed them out the window. Habsburg armies quickly crushed the rebellious Bohemians, but other German princes who feared a resurgent imperial power soon took up arms against Austria. As the emperor gained victories through talented generals such as Wallenstein, foreign Lutheran monarchs invaded the empire—first the king of Denmark, then the king of Sweden. Regardless, the Austrian Habsburgs continued to win, fortified by the resources of their Spanish cousins.

Eventually, what began as a religious war ended as a purely political conflict. Roman Catholic France had long feared being surrounded by the Habsburg territories of Spain in the south and the empire in the east. So Roman Catholic France opposed Roman Catholic Austria. Dynastic and national politics overruled religious fraternity. Thus, religion faded as a motive to go to war in the West.

Indeed, the **Peace of Westphalia**, which was signed in 1648, forced Europe into new, modern, international political relationships (see map 9.1). With religious diversity now irreversible, the medieval icon of a unified Christendom was completely broken. Instead, the numerous independent states of Europe lived in an uncertain rivalry. Each became a sovereign state, free from the influence of higher authorities, although able to agree on international principles if necessary. The most important principle maintained a *balance of power*, where the countries would league together against any state that tried again to dominate Europe. This principle kept the great powers in check and left the middle-ranked and small buffer states free to prosper.

The rest of the treaty redrew some political borders to establish this rough balance of power. Spain held onto the southern "Spanish" Netherlands (soon to be known as Belgium) but lost the northern Dutch Netherlands, which everyone recognized as an independent, sovereign state. The Swiss had their independence affirmed. The Holy Roman Empire became a mere geographical expression as a synonym for Germany. The petty principalities of the empire were more sovereign than the empire itself. The Holy Roman Emperor became even less relevant, a still weaker figurehead. While the Austrian Habsburgs kept control of the imperial office, their varied collection of territories on the empire's southeastern borders mattered far more than the office of emperor. France chewed away a few bits of the empire, bringing its border to the upper Rhine River. Of course, the end of these religious wars did not stop war altogether. Despite this reasonable settlement, great powers continued to try to expand at the expense of their neighbors.

Map 9.1. Europe, 1648

The lack of total victory for any one side assured that religious diversity remained part of Western civilization. While nations might continue to fight, hoping for power, pride, or prosperity, religion as a reason for war declined. States became the key binding agent for Europeans. The Reformation weakened the bonds between religion and the state. Many governments continued to impose religious uniformity on their own people. Indeed, many people remained satisfied with whatever tradition they were brought up in. Yet people only had to look across borders to know that others differed on Christianity and that some individuals might even be able to choose their faith, or even no belief at all.

Review: How did Early Modern reforms among Christians culminate in wars over religion?

Response:

GOD, GREED, AND GLORY

Another change from the medieval to the modern in European history was **Western colonial imperialism**, when various kingdoms built empires based on overseas colonies. Historians today argue about what exactly made the Europeans strong enough to take the lead in a new global history after 1500. Answers used to imply, if not outright argue, *Western exceptionalism*, the idea that Europeans were somehow different (and better) than peoples in other civilizations. More recent historians object to that characterization, especially considering the brutality with which Europeans would "civilize" the world. Comparative historians measure the relative accumulation of wealth, strength of government, level of cultural sophistication, status of technological development, and impulse toward creativity of various civilizations around the world over the centuries and note that Europe would not have ranked near the top.

The Europeans benefited from excellent timing as they began their modern history with their "voyages of discovery." These expeditions allowed them to take advantage of existing trade networks that incorporated much of Asia and Africa. The European national governments began to drive toward global supremacy over other empires and peoples across the seas (see map 9.2). Europeans had three desires that fed this drive to go abroad.

The first came from Christianity's own evangelistic and crusading impulses, which had already driven Western culture beyond the borders of Europe. Even before Latin Christianity began to split apart, westerners wanted to spread the gospel of Christ to "heathens," as seen in the Crusades. The Reformation only encouraged the divided Christians to convert the world, to prove their own version of Christianity as the most successful and, therefore, most divinely sanctioned. Some Europeans ventured on a path of world domination in the name of eternal salvation. Would Jesus, the Prince of Peace, have approved that his message come at the

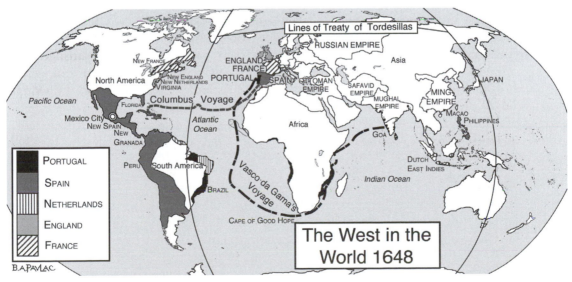

Map 9.2.   The West in the World, 1648

point of a sword and with the price of plundering? His followers thought so, and they had the power to do it.

God provided a spiritual motivation, while money afforded a material one. The capitalism that sprouted from the Commercial Revolution had transformed Europe from a poor offshoot on the fringes of a world trade system centered in Asia to a pillar of economic dynamism. Financial investments from capitalists further pushed these "voyages of discovery" forward. Instead of being barriers, the deep seas and oceans soon became highways much as rivers and coastal waters had long been. These explorers, of course, only "discovered" what other humans and cultures had long known was there. The difference was that Europeans were now able to exploit these "new" lands and foreign peoples as never before in their history.

A second motive for colonialism, then, was the opportunity for profit. Europeans wanted to travel to "the Indies," regions in distant Asia known to possess fantastic wealth. The Europeans knew little about these half-mythical realms except that they were the source of a variety of spices, such as pepper, cinnamon, and nutmeg. What today sits on our shelves in small jars costing pennies was worth its weight in gold in 1500. The increasingly wealthy Europeans could now afford these exotic spices to make their food more palatable in an age before preservatives.

The main trade routes to the Indies had traditionally run through the Middle East. Only a rare merchant from Europe, such as Marco Polo in the thirteenth century, might travel along the Silk Road through Central Asia all the way to the Chinese Empire. During much of the Middle Ages, most western European merchants bought from the merchants of the Byzantine Empire. After the Byzantine Empire's demise in 1453, the Muslim Ottoman Turks took over supply routes. The idea that the Muslims shut down the trade routes is a myth; rather, the western Christians resented paying these "infidel" middlemen. Europeans looked for alternative access to the East.

Pride offered a third motive for imperialism, on both the personal and national levels. At the forefront, monarchs were drawn to the glorification that conquest always brought. New lands meant wider empires and revenues. At the lower social levels, adventuring in foreign lands raised a Renaissance gentleman's reputation and status. Any poor man might acquire treasure or farmland of his own, taken from natives who could not defend it. Thus an obscure man could rise to prominence, whether lording it over foreigners or bringing immense wealth back home to Europe. All these contradictory motives, winning fame, fortune, and souls for Jesus, tempted Europeans out into the world.

Surprisingly, the new imperialism began with the little country of **Portugal**, founded in the twelfth century as part of a crusade during the *Reconquesta* of the Iberian Peninsula (see chapter 8). Over the years, Portugal had fought against the Muslims, but its armies were soon cut off from confronting the enemy by neighboring Castille's successful expansion. Unable to combat the Moors in the Iberian Peninsula, little Portugal sought another outlet for its crusading zealotry. It channeled its expansionism toward Africa, hoping both to convert the Africans and profit from trade on that continent. Prince Henry the Navigator (d. 1460), one of the main proponents of African expeditions, also wished to find enough gold to maintain his court in proper style. His sponsored voyages discovered and colonized the islands of the Azores and the Madieras in the Atlantic. Colonists found the latter islands so heavily forested that they set a fire that burned for seven years, leaving the land covered in ash. From this new, fertile soil they grew a new wine, Madiera. Heavily populated Africa was a different matter. Instead of converting and conquering, the Portuguese could only wrest away small chunks of African coastline, where they built forts to defend trading outposts and harbors.

Explorers soon thought that it might be possible to sail around the continent of Africa to reach the Indies. Yet sailors faced some serious challenges. First, the dangers of ocean travel in the Atlantic surpassed those of the Mediterranean and coastal waters to which the western Europeans had confined themselves since the fall of Rome. The Portuguese adapted sailing technology from Africa and the Middle East to build sturdy ships called caravels, which could handle the high seas. Second, the North Star, so necessary for navigation, disappeared beyond the horizon south of the equator. Improved maps and charts of the heavens for navigation helped with that problem.

Hugging the Atlantic coast, the Portuguese were best located to launch such voyages. The Portuguese explorer Diaz rounded the Cape of Good Hope, the southernmost point of Africa, in 1468. It took another thirty years before **Vasco da Gama** traveled beyond that cape. In 1498, he sailed up the east coast of Africa and then ventured across the Arabian Sea to reach India. He did not have much of value to trade with the Indians then, but the spices he brought back profited his expedition thirty times the amount of its cost. On da Gama's next voyage, Portuguese military technology of guns overpowered the natives. Da Gama plundered foreign merchant cargoes, blew the Arab ships out of the water, shelled cities, exploited rivalries between states, and intimidated princes. Other Portuguese followed. Soon they dominated all seagoing trade and commerce in the Arabian Sea, Indian Ocean, and China Sea.

The Portuguese started an empire that ended only in the late twentieth century, with the loss of its last possessions in Africa and Asia. Portugal was too small to grab and keep large territories. For five hundred years, though, the Portuguese held on to fortified enclaves: Angola, Guinea, Mozambique in Africa; Goa in India; Timor in the Indies; and Macao in China. Only in Brazil, in the Americas, did they establish a large colony with European immigrants. Despite its imperial success, Portugal itself remained on the periphery of European affairs, only rarely participating in the approaching wars between Western states over Europe and the world.

Even before Vasco da Gama had begun exploiting and killing Indians, Portugal's neighbor **Spain** had hoped to beat its rival to the Indies. Spain was a young country then, founded only in 1479 as King Ferdinand came to the throne of Aragon, while his wife of five years, Isabella, ruled the neighboring kingdom of Castille. They united their two kingdoms to create Spain, centralizing power in both their hands while weakening the nobles and other estates. Spain's hold on southern Italy was secured through Ferdinand's wars on that peninsula.

Ferdinand and Isabella rounded out their immediate realm on the Iberian Peninsula by finishing the *Reconquesta* begun in the eleventh century, taking back European territory from the Muslims. In 1492 they defeated Granada, the last Muslim principality in western Europe. Then, to impose uniformity and conformity on their tidy kingdom, they kicked out of the country all Muslims and Jews who refused to convert to Christianity. Spanish authorities worried about the sincerity of conversions by those Muslims and Jews who stayed behind, called respectively Moriscos (after the old term *Moors*) and Marranos (a word for "pig"). The monarchs set up the infamous **Spanish Inquisition** (1478–1834) to deal with their concerns. The Spanish Inquisition investigated and punished cases about people who secretly practiced Islam or Judaism, as well as sodomy or even, allegedly, witchcraft. Over the centuries, the inquisitors ferreted out, tortured, and burned many people to death. Early in the 1600s, Spain simply gave up worrying about the Moriscos and expelled tens of thousands of them to North Africa. Spain's authorities enforced cultural uniformity as they built their new nation.

While Queen Isabella presided over the defeat of Muslim Granada, she gambled on an unusual plan to reach the lavish Indies. An eccentric Italian ship captain, **Christopher Columbus**, proposed sailing across the Atlantic Ocean westward, rather than to the south around Africa (which would not be successful for six more years). Isabella's advisors were correct to warn her that Columbus' voyage should fail. Contrary to a popular, yet incorrect myth, their advice was not based on a mistaken belief that the world was flat—since the time of the ancient Greeks, every educated person knew that the world was round or, more properly, a globe. Instead, Isabella's advisors were correct to point out that Columbus had underestimated the distance from his last supply point in the Canary Islands to Japan. While Columbus thought that he would need to travel a mere 2,400 miles, Isabella's advisors knew, in fact, the distance to be more than 8,000 miles. Columbus would have died at sea had he not stumbled upon the "New World." For too long Columbus believed that what he had claimed for Spain was part of the true Indies of the East, just as he read in Marco Polo's book. Instead, other explorers, like Amerigo Vespucci, quickly recognized that the islands of the Caribbean were the "West" Indies and that new continents lay just beyond. Therefore, mapmakers labeled the continents **North** and **South America**, not Columbia or Christopheria.

Columbus discovered the Americas at exactly the right moment for Europeans to exploit their advantages. There had been, of course, earlier contacts between the Old World of Eurasia and Africa with the New World of the Americas. Information about them can be gleaned from records, most interestingly from the Vikings. In all these earlier interactions, however, the travelers lacked the interest or ability to dominate the "native" Americans who had been living there for tens of thousands of years. In 1492, however, Spain was ready to commit resources for conquest and lucky enough to have them succeed beyond expectation.

Columbus' domination of the natives (mistakenly, of course, called Indians after the East Indies) further tarnishes his legacy. He kidnapped natives and killed to seize land at will. In his desire to acquire gold, Columbus cut off the hands of natives who failed to turn in set quotas of gold. Those who fled he had hunted down with huge dogs. Following Columbus, Spanish conquerors, called **conquistadors**, conquered much of the Americas, supported by a firm conviction in God's blessing for their cause, rich financial backing, and a well-drilled military equipped with horses and guns.

Historians call the European takeover of the Americas and its consequences the

Columbian Exchange. This mutual transfer, however, mostly added up to be in the West's favor. European settlers rushed into the Americas, grabbing control of vast expanses of land and virtually enslaving native peoples. Wealth in precious metals and food products flowed into Europe, having been produced by the native peoples. Europeans ate better with foods from the New World, including peanuts, maize, potatoes, and tomatoes (although tomatoes were originally suspected of being poisonous because of their bright red color). Tobacco smoking provided a new social pastime. In turn, both native and immigrant Americans fed on sugarcane, coffee, rice, bananas, and even the honey of honeybees from the Old World. The American natives gained new oppressive rulers, farm animals, and the faith of Christianity.

The European conquest came surprisingly easily, within a few decades after Columbus' discovery. At first, the Indians of the Americas easily outnumbered the Europeans. But the natives were not united; they were even more diverse than Europeans, with hundreds of different cultures and more than a thousand different languages. Alliances and cooperation against the determined European invaders rarely lasted long.

Natives on the Caribbean Islands could not organize a strong military resistance since they were still at the socioeconomic level of hunter-gatherers or simple agriculturalists. In contrast, millions of American Indians on the mainland were quite civilized and organized. Two recently formed empires maintained societies based in cities as sophisticated as any in the Old World. One of the peoples who ruled the so-called Aztec Empire, the Mexica, gave their name to modern-day Mexico. Their political power reached southward toward Central America. The Aztec capital of Tenochtitlan (today, Mexico City) arguably possessed more comforts, and certainly more people, than any one city in Spain. The Incan Empire based in Peru controlled much of the west coast of South America. Each empire coordinated agriculture, war, and peace for millions of people with armies well trained in conquest. These civilized societies were, ironically, even more vulnerable to conquest. They shared three serious disadvantages for competition with the Spanish: deification, ethnic conflicts, and vulnerable immune systems.

First, deification hurt the natives because they expected too much from their own human rulers, who were considered to be gods. The Aztec practice of sacrificing humans for religious reasons, carving out beating hearts with obsidian knives, also upset many subject peoples who did not believe in the Aztec gods. Even worse, the natives too often incorrectly believed the Europeans were gods themselves. The newcomers' pale skins, shiny armor, and unfamiliar horses contributed to this falsehood, which the lying conquistadors exploited to the utmost. This sham allowed Cortés in Mexico and Pizarro in Peru to get close to, capture, and then execute the native emperors. Therefore, the embodiment of both church and state collapsed with one blow. Murdered emperors left the natives disorganized and doubting.

Second, the diversity of the Native Americans likewise helped the Spanish defeat the native political states. The Incan and Aztec empires, like many empires, centered on specific ethnic groups that dominated others. Enemies of these empires, tribes that remained unconquered or had been recently subjugated, cooperated with the Spanish against the native imperial supremacy. The Spanish played various tribal groups against one another. Then, conquistadors replaced every native civilized political structure that ruled over good farmland. Only on the fringes of the Spanish empire did Indians retain some self-rule. They usually survived as hunter-gatherer societies, protected by mountains, deserts, or jungles.

The third, and worst, problem for the natives was the vulnerability of their bodies to diseases carried from Europe. We understand now how many diseases are caused by germs (see chapter 11). In the sixteenth century, though, many people felt that disease was a punishment from God. Such had been the case with the Black Death, which killed a third of the European population within a few years. Little knowledge existed on how to cure most illnesses. The Spanish, naturally and unintentionally, brought with them various germs from Europe, from diseases as harmless as the common cold to the more lethal measles and chicken pox and the very lethal smallpox. The Europeans bore substantial immunities to these diseases; but the native Americans had never been exposed to them. In contrast, perhaps the only illness that the Europeans brought back from the Americas might have been the sexually transmitted disease of syphilis. It first appeared in Europe at about this time and for the next few centuries would disproportionately afflict sexually promiscuous people, especially prostitutes, soldiers, and aristocrats. The number of sufferers overall, however, was limited.

In comparison, the natives of the Americas were not so fortunate. Millions became sick and died. Spreading rapidly along imperial roads, pandemics (epidemics that range over whole continents and beyond) killed large portions of the population. Large regions were completely depopulated, and native sociopolitical networks broke down.

Through exploitation of political rivalries, military tactics, and disease, Spain quickly came to dominate the Americas, wiping out much of the indigenous cultures and civilization and replacing them with its version of Western civilization. At the time, the Spanish did not realize the complete extent of the devastation or fully comprehend their own role in the plagues. But they knew how to take advantage of the situation. Empty land was theirs for the taking. Those natives who survived disease and slaughter were conquered. Only the low number of colonial settlers prevented the Spanish from expanding farther north than they did.

The Spanish masters exploited the defeated. Natives dug in the silver mines (of which there were plenty, but disappointingly few sources of gold). Or they labored in the fields for long hours under the southern sun. Many died from overwork and lack of care, exploited worse than animals. Only a few voices protested, notably Bartolomé de Las Casas, the first priest ordained in the Americas. He spoke out to claim human and Christian dignity for the Indians. He and others won the argument that Indians had souls and were human, capable of entry into heaven after death. But many continued to die. Within a few decades the native population of the Americas fell from what was probably eleven million to only two and one-half million.

While the depopulation guaranteed European domination, it also threatened the Western exploitation. Who would produce the silver and food that the Europeans desired and needed? How could they replace all the dead miners and peasants?

The Portuguese offered a solution with the **Atlantic-African slave trade**. In the year 1400, slavery hardly existed in Europe. Soon after, the Portuguese had gained an interest in slavery, which they had seen operating among the Africans. They began to buy and sell black Africans, beginning in 1444 with the official excuse of the need to convert Muslim prisoners to Christianity. In reality, they wanted cheap, expendable labor. The new plantations for sugarcane, which everyone's sweet tooth craved, promoted harsh labor practices. The crop required hard, nasty, and dangerous harvesting in dank thickets, where workers hacked away at rough, sharp stalks with machetes. So over the next few centuries, Europeans of various nationalities captured and shipped millions of diverse Africans to work as slaves in the Americas. The first boatload arrived by 1510, not even two decades after Columbus' discovery.

Thus, the new Spanish rulers forcibly converted the native American "Indians" and the imported Africans to the ways of Western civilization, which largely supported and benefited the European masters. Of course, through most of history, in most civilizations, the masses, both free and slave, have supported the few at the top. The institutionalized racism of the Americas, though, has left an especially challenging legacy. "Black" skins were identified as inferior, while "white" skins claimed superiority. The periodic revolts by both the Indian and African slaves always ended with the Western masters victorious.

An improved method of investing capital, the bourse or **stock exchange**, soon financed this slave trade and other colonial investments. First appearing in Antwerp in 1485, the stock exchange provided an alternative to banks as a place for capital to be gathered and invested. Where banks promised some protection of deposits, the bourse offered no such protection. If a business failed, the stock became worthless. But the greater the risk, the greater were the possible profits. At first, members pooled their resources for new investment capital. But collective membership risked all of one's own possessions to pay debts if too many of the collective's investments failed. By 1600, joint stock companies provided a better way to protect investments by restricting losses to only the number of shares any individual owned. This limited liability meant that no one could be ruined who prudently invested only a portion of his wealth through stock in any one venture.

Remember, risk was always part of capitalism. Although the New World looked like a profitable investment, it had a mixed impact on the European economy. American mines added tons of silver bullion to the treasuries of Spain, which then filtered out to the other nations of Europe and even to China through world trade. But so much silver also led to a quick and devastating inflation. A "price revolution" of swiftly rising costs of goods and services hurt the middle and poorer classes of Spain, eventually weakening the Spanish Empire. The history of capitalism is rife with both growth in wealth and suffering caused by crises in investments.

The simple idea of capitalism, reinvesting profits, offered no real guidelines on how to best keep those profits flowing to everyone's benefit. Some intellectuals attempted to figure out how to prevent economic disaster and promote economic growth. As part of the Commercial Revolution, they began to propose one of the first **economic theories**, sets of ideas that offered comprehensive explanations for how people carried out economic activity. Since then, many theories have tried to suggest plans for action on how best to harness capitalism. Unlike scientific theories (see chapter 10), though, no economic theory has as yet sufficiently explained human economic activity.

The early ***economic theory of mercantilism*** linked the growing Early Modern nation-states to their new colonial empires. Theorists emphasized that the accumulation of wealth in precious metals within a country's own borders was the best measure of economic success. Mercantilist theory favored government intervention in the economy, since it was in governments' interest that their economies succeed. The theory argued that a regime should cultivate a favorable balance of trade as a sign of economic success. Since most international exchange took place in bullion, actual gold and silver, monarchs tried to make sure that other countries bought more from their country than they bought from other monarchs' countries. Thus, the bullion in a country's treasury would continue to increase. Monarchs then obsessed about discovering mines of gold and silver, a practically cost-free method of acquiring bullion.

Because of this tangible wealth, governments frequently intervened by trying to promote enterprises to strengthen the economy. State-sponsored monopolies had clear advantages for a monarch. A state-licensed enterprise, such as importing tea leaves from China or sable furs from Siberia, could easily be supervised and taxed. Diligent inspections and regulation ensured that monopolies' goods and services were of a high quality. The government could then push and protect that business both overseas and domestically.

Fueled by this burgeoning capital and developing theory, more explorers sailed off to make their fortune by exploiting the riches of Asia, Africa, and the Americas. Unfortunately for imperialists, the world was fairly crowded already with other powerful peoples. Various kingdoms and states in East Asia (the Chinese Empire, Japan), the Indian Subcontinent (the Mughal Empire), and Africa (Abyssinia) had long histories, rich economies, sophisticated cultures, and intimidating armies. In comparison, from antiquity through the Middle Ages, Europe had remained a minor market on the fringe of the Eurasian-African economy.

Even so, Spain and Portugal boldly divided up the world between them, even before Vasco da Gama had reached the Indies, with the **Treaty of Tordesillas** (1494). The pope blessed the proceedings. The treaty demonstrated a certain hubris in those two states. They claimed global domination, notwithstanding their inability to severely damage the rich, powerful, well-established, and disease-resistant kingdoms and empires of Africa and Asia. The European powers ruled the oceans but could only nibble at the fringes of Asia and Africa.

People of other Western nations did not let the Spanish and Portuguese enjoy their fat empires in peace for long. Outside the law, pirates in the Caribbean along the Spanish Main (the Central and South American coastline) and in the Indies plundered whatever they could. Within the law, a few captains preyed on the Spanish and Portuguese, each other, and the foreign peoples almost like pirates, licensed by governments with "letters of marque." For example, raids by the English Sir Francis Drake and his sea dogs helped provoke the Spanish Armada.

By 1600, the Dutch, the English, and the French had launched their own overseas ventures, with navies and armies grabbing and defending provinces across the oceans. They all began to drive out natives in the Americas, Africa, and Asia. They also turned on one another. In Asia and Africa, the Dutch grabbed Portuguese bases in South Africa and the East Indies. The English, in turn, seized Dutch possessions in Africa, Malaysia, and North America (turning New Holland into New York and New Jersey). The English planted their own colonists along the Atlantic seacoast of North America. The French settled farther inland in Quebec. Likewise, in the Caribbean, India, and the Pacific, the French and English faced each other in disputes about islands and principalities, while the native peoples were caught in the middle.

The slowness and fragility of transportation and communication did mean that the governments in the homelands could not closely supervise the colonies. Westerners both in Europe and abroad comforted themselves that their success justified their dominion, even though it lacked any legal basis except an invented right to seize allegedly empty or neglected land. The new elites of European heritage immigrated to these distant lands and began to forge their own unique cultures, drawing on Western civilization but also able to adapt to local circumstances. The "illegal immigrants" only rarely learned from the native peoples, except, if at all, how to properly farm in new climates and soilscapes, both in the tropics and in temperate zones.

Everywhere they went, the colonizers ravaged the native cultures, often with cruelty (scalping was invented by Europeans) and carelessness (smashing sculptures and pulverizing written works). Priceless cultural riches vanished forever. Land grabbing displaced the local farmers, while slavery (whether in body or wages) and displacement of native peoples by Europeans dismantled social structures. Where social bonds did not snap apart, European immigrants ignored and discriminated, trying to weaken the hold of native religions, languages, and even clothing styles. Robbed of their homes and livelihoods, most non-European subjects found resistance to be futile against the weight of European economic and political decisions.

As a result of the westerners' expansion around the world, "Europe" replaced "Christendom" in their own popular imagination. Nevertheless, these diverse Europeans continued to hurl insults and launch wars against one another, which they promoted through grotesque ethnic stereotypes. While the people of one's own nation were invariably perceived as kind, generous, sober, straight, loyal, honest, and intelligent, they might allege that the Spanish were cruel, the Scots stingy, the Dutch drunk, the French perverted, the Italians deceptive, the English boastful, or the Germans boorish. So Europeans remained pluralistic in their perceptions of one another.

At the same time, the elites recognized their common bonds in how they practiced their gentlemanly manners in ruling over the lower classes, expanded their many governments, grew their increasingly national economies, and revered the Christian religion (no matter how fractured). Some Europeans adopted a notion of the morally pure "noble savage" as a critique on their own culture. Missionaries preached the alleged love and hope of Christianity, while global natives found themselves confronted by new crimes brought in by the westerners, such as prostitution and vagrancy. The West's confidence in its civilization made westerners feel that they deserved superiority over all other peoples. These diverse Europeans insisted that they themselves were "civilized" and that their dominated enemies were "savages." They began to think more in racist categories, "white" Europeans and "colored" others, whether "red" American Indians, "brown" Asian Indians, "yellow" Chinese, or "black" sub-Saharan Africans. All these other "races" by definition were believed to be less intelligent, industrious, and intrepid. Through increasing contacts with other peoples, the rest of the world seemed truly "foreign."

This Eurocentric attitude is reflected in the early maps of the globe. Medieval maps had usually given pride of place in the center to Jerusalem. By the sixteenth century, geographers had a more accurate picture of the globe and could distinguish other continents as connected to one another by at most a narrow isthmus (Panama for the Americas, Sinai between Eurasia and Africa). Nonetheless, they "split" the continent of Eurasia into "Asia" and "Europe," arbitrarily deciding on the Ural Mountains as a dividing point (although these hills hardly created a barrier—as the Huns and Mongols had demonstrated). Westerners saw vast stretches of eastern Europe as hardly civilized at all, a tempting target for building empires. From living in one small corner of the map, Europeans in all their varieties had moved to the center. Certainly, the explorers who led the voyages of discovery showed audacity and heroism, added to the scientific knowledge of Europeans, and allowed some mutually beneficial cultural exchange. But they were also expansionist and imperialist. Wielding a newfound global power, Western civilization was unleashed on the world.

Review: *How did the "voyages of discovery" begin colonial imperialism by Europeans?*

Response:

CHAPTER 10

Liberation of Mind and Body

Early Modern Europe, 1543 to 1815

While people fought over forms of faith, they also pondered man's place in God's creation. Was each person's position ordained and unchangeable, or could people achieve something higher than the status into which they were born? The increasing use of the mind, as advocated by the humanists of the Renaissance, supported the latter attitude. Yet the more time European intellectuals spent examining the writings of the Greeks and Romans about the natural world, the more they discovered flaws and mistakes. If the philosophy of antiquity could be so wrong, then how did one find truth? Western civilization provided a new method with the so-called **Scientific Revolution** (1543–1687), which unleashed an ongoing force for change and power. Ideas that freed people from ignorance about nature would in time lead them to question all of society and then to transform politics.

LOST IN THE STARS

A religious problem, ironically, triggered the invention of modern science. The Julian calendar from 45 B.C. had become seriously out of sync with nature. As mentioned in chapter 5, Julius Caesar had reformed the calendar by adding a leap day every fourth year to compensate for 365 1/4 days of the solar year. According to the Julian calendar, the first day of spring (the vernal equinox, when the hours of day exactly equaled those of night) should occur on 21 March. By the fifteenth century, the vernal equinox fell in early April. The Church feared that this delay jeopardized the sanctity of Easter (which was celebrated on the first Sunday after the first full moon following the vernal equinox). The Counter-Reformation papacy, eager to have its structures improved and reformed, called on intellectuals to come up with both an explanation about the calendar's discrepancy and a solution.

The dominant Aristotelian philosophy hindered a resolution at first. Ever since the victory of Scholasticism in the Middle Ages, most intellectuals accepted Aristotle's logical assertion that the earth sat at the center of the universe. According to Aristotle, the sun, the moon, the other planets, and the stars (attached to giant crystalline spheres) revolved around the earth (which every educated person knew was a globe). The Greek philosopher Ptolemy had elaborated on this idea in the second century A.D. Aristotle and Ptolemy's earth-centered universe was labeled the Ptolemaic or **geo-centric theory**. After the success of Aquinas and the Scholastics, the western Catholic Church endorsed this Aristotelian view. It liked the argument that proximity to the center of the earth (hell's location) corresponded with imperfection and evil, while distance from earth (toward heaven) equaled goodness and perfection.

The geocentric theory was not the only reasonable view of the universe, however. A few other ancient Greeks had disagreed with Aristotle's concept and argued instead that the sun was the center of the universe, with the earth revolving around it (and the moon revolving around the earth). Two planets, Mercury and Venus, were therefore closer to the sun than the earth, while the other planets and stars were farther out. This sun-centered universe was called the **heliocentric theory** (see diagram 10.1).

Many people today misunderstand the meaning of a **scientific theory**, probably because the word *theory* has multiple definitions. In science, a theory does not mean something "theoretical" in the sense of a possible guess that is far from certain. Rather, a valid scientific theory explains how the universe actually works and is supported by most of the available facts and contradicted by very few, if any. If not much is known, then several opposing theories may well be acceptable. After scientists have asked new questions and new facts have been discovered, a scientific theory may either be invalidated and discounted or supported and strengthened. Without any winning evidence either way, Renaissance intellectuals could, at first, reasonably see both the geocentric and the heliocentric as valid scientific theories. Nevertheless, as scientists discovered new information, the geocentric theory soon failed to explain the heavens, while the heliocentric theory won support.

As sixteenth-century astronomers looked at the heavens, they discovered the information that they needed to correct the calendar. They measured and calculated the movement of the stars and planets. They figured out that the year is actually a fraction less in length than the 365 1/4 days used by the Julian calendar. Therefore, a new calendar was proposed, one that did not add a leap day in century years that were not evenly divisible by four hundred. For example, 1900 would not have a leap day, but 2000 would. Pope Gregory XIII adopted these changes in 1582,

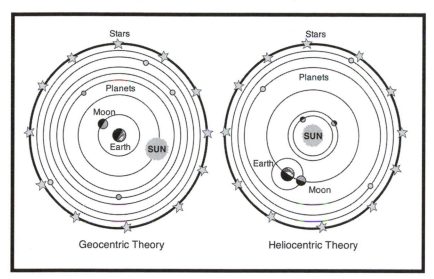

Diagram 10.1. Geocentric vs. Heliocentric Theory. Based on their observations and perspectives, ancient Greek philosophers had first proposed these theories for the structure of the universe.

giving Western civilization the **Gregorian calendar** to replace the Julian. He dropped ten days from that year to get the calendar back on track with the seasons: thus the day after 5 October 1582 became 15 October 1582, at least in those areas that accepted papal authority. Anglican England and Orthodox Russia waited until centuries later to conform to the papal view, partly because they were suspicious about anything that came from the Roman Catholic Church.

Yet the papacy had its own problems with science. Earlier, in 1543, the canon and astronomer Mikolaj Kopernig in Poland (who used the Latinized name **Nicolaus Copernicus**) published a book, *Concerning the Revolutions of the Celestial Bodies*, which argued convincingly for the heliocentric theory. Copernicus knew the controversy that this position would provoke and had waited to publish it until he was on his deathbed. As he expected, the Roman Catholic Church rejected his argument out of hand and put his study onto the *Index of Forbidden Books*. The papacy told astronomers they had to support the geocentric theory because it conformed to their preferred belief system of Aristotle and Scholasticism.

The Roman Catholic Church's beliefs notwithstanding, new evidence continued to undermine the geocentric theory and support the heliocentric theory. The best facts were presented by **Galileo Galilei** (b. 1564–d. 1642) of Florence. In 1609, he improved a Dutch spyglass and fashioned the first functional telescope, which he turned toward the heavens. Galileo discovered moons around Jupiter, mountains and craters on the moon, sunspots, and other phenomena that convinced him that the heavens were far from Aristotelian perfection. His publication the next year, *The Starry Messenger*, supported the Copernican theory. It sparked a sensation among intellectuals, while it also angered leaders of the Roman Catholic Church. Clergy warned Galileo his ideas were dangerous. Therefore, he kept silent until he thought a pope had been elected who would support his inquiries. Cautiously, he framed his next book, *Dialogue on the Chief World Systems* (1636), as a debate in which the Copernican view technically lost but the Aristotelian view looked indefensibly stupid.

The papacy saw through the device. The Roman Inquisition called in the aged man and questioned him, using forged evidence. The Inquisitors threatened Galileo with the instruments of torture, probably including pincers, thumbscrews, legscrews, and the rack. They defined disagreement with the Roman Church as heresy, and thus Galileo was automatically a heretic. Galileo pled guilty, and the Inquisition sentenced him to house arrest for the rest of his life. The aged scientist nonetheless continued experiments that helped lay the foundation of modern physics. His studies increasingly showed that Aristotle was incorrect about many things, not only the location of the earth in the universe.

A person born in far-off England during the year Galileo died, **Isaac Newton** (b. 1642–d. 1727), assured the doom of Aristotle's views about nature. Newton first studied the properties of light (founding modern optics) and built an improved reflector telescope, which he also turned to the heavens. From his studies of the planets, Newton accepted the Copernican/heliocentric theory, but he still wanted to find an explanation for how stars and planets stayed in their orbits while apples dropped from trees to the ground.

Newton started from that inspirational falling apple and continued with the invention of calculus to help him measure moving bodies. He finally arrived at an explanation for how the universe works, published in the book *Principia* (1687). In that treatise, Newton's theory of universal gravitation accounted for the movements of the heavenly bodies. He showed that all objects of substance, everything with the quality of "mass," possess gravitational attraction toward one another. So the moon and the earth, just as an apple and the earth, are being drawn toward each other. The apple drops because it has no other force acting upon it. The moon stays spinning around the earth because it is moving fast enough; its motion balances out the earth's gravitational pull. The delicate opposition of gravity and velocity keeps the heavens whirling.

With the publication of the *Principia*, many historians consider the Scientific Revolution to have triumphed, having created the modern, Western idea of science. Between the years of Copernicus and Newton's books, other intellectuals such as Francis Bacon and René Descartes had worked out basic scientific principles. Traditional authorities, such as Aristotle, were to be doubted until proved. Instead of relying on divine revelation or reason (the big debate of the Middle Ages), trustworthy knowledge could be obtained through a specific tool of reason called the **scientific method**. To solve a problem, one followed careful steps, starting with formulating a hypothesis (a reasonable guess at a solution), continuing through controlled observation and experimentation, moving to the formation of conclusions, and then, most importantly, communicating the whole process to other scientists.

The scientific method also compensated for the human frailties of individual scientists. For example, Newton wrote serious commentaries about the biblical book of Revelation, tried to vindictively destroy the careers of academic rivals, and fudged some of the data in his *Principia*. With the scientific process, however, human scientists applied the method to test his conclusions and produced better information about the natural world than had ever before been available in history. Science had become such an essential part of the Western worldview that it forms another basic principle:

> **Science is the only testable and generally accessible method of understanding the universe; every other means of explanation is opinion.**

The Scientific Revolution had enormous consequences for Western civilization. Science discovered reliable and reproducible answers about the workings of the universe. Assuming that the secrets of nature could be revealed, scientists kept expanding their investigations and creating tools to help them (see figure 10.1).

Figure 10.1.   A seventeenth-century scientist examines a barometer.

One result was the acceleration in the invention of technology, namely the creation of tools and machines to make life easier, safer, and more comfortable. Most people in the world around 1600 lived much the same way as they had for several thousand years. By the late seventeenth century, though, **scientific academies** (such as the British Royal Society) institutionalized scientific inquiry and its application to economic growth. Scientists were not mere theoreticians but innovators and inventors, from thermometers to timepieces, pumps to pins. These inventions were soon translated into the physical power used to dominate the globe. Medical and agricultural advances based on science followed. By 1800, westerners were living much more prosperous and comfortable lives, largely because of science.

The success of the Scientific Revolution was not complete or universal. Its attitudes only slowly spread from the elites through the population. Many westerners rejected the scientific mindset of skepticism toward traditional authorities because of the importance of religion or the grip of superstition. Science does not answer basic questions about the meaning of life and death. Honest scientists cannot proclaim certainty about the permanence of their discoveries: when presented with new information, true scientists should change their minds. And theories can come and go. For example, by the time of Newton, no reasonable scientist supported the geocentric theory because too little evidence supported it and too much contradicted it. Even the heliocentric theory has since been severely modified—while the sun *is* the center of our solar system, it is certainly *not* the center of the universe. In turn, Newton's own theory of universal gravitation was rejected on some important points (see chapter 13). By its nature, because of its many discoveries and regular revisions, science has propelled Western civilization into constant change.

Review: *How did the Scientific Revolution energize economics and society?*

Response:

FROM THE SALONS TO THE STREETS

Historians have decided that 1687, the year of Newton's *Principia*, marks the beginning of a major intellectual movement known as **the Enlightenment** (1687–1789).

During this time, scientific academies and universities adapted and spread many scientific ideas. In addition, a few wealthy and curious women gathered a variety of interesting people to discuss the issues of the day in their **salons** (pleasant rooms in their fine homes). Beginning in Paris, salon hostesses such as Madame Goffrin or Madame Rambouillet guided the witty conversation of clergymen, politicians, businessmen, scientists, and amateur philosophers, writers, and popularizers known as *philosophes*. The *philosophes* took what they learned, especially the lessons of science, and publicized it.

Philosophes made Paris the cultural capital of Western civilization. For about a century, French culture reigned supreme among the elites of the West. The French language took over intellectual life and international communication, replacing the Latin of the Middle Ages and the Renaissance. Europeans who wanted to seem sophisticated imitated French styles of cuisine, clothing, furnishings, luxury goods, and buildings. Salons and *philosophes* spread French taste across Europe. Along the way, these intellectuals explained to society how new science and economics impacted life. Four major concepts summarize their Enlightenment views: **empiricism**, **skepticism**, **humanitarianism**, and **progress**.

The first of these concepts, *empiricism*, came from the starting point of science: observations by our senses were both accurate and reasonable. Knowledge obtained from studies of the natural world could consequently help explain human activities. This effective idea contradicted many past religious authorities, who had depended on divine revelation for their knowledge. Those supernatural, metaphysical, or spiritual answers were too open to dispute, too difficult to prove. Of course, humans do not always draw the correct conclusions from their observations, nor does the natural world always correspond to human experience. Regardless, *philosophes* were convinced that applying the tools of science to human character would help improve society.

One proponent of empirical thinking was John Locke of England. He proposed that the human mind was like a blank slate, or *tabula rasa*, on which all learned information was written. His most famous empirical argument justified England's Glorious Revolution (see below) toward more democratic politics. Locke argued against books such as Thomas Hobbes' *Leviathan*, in which religious perspectives favored absolutism.

Another famous example of an empirical argument became the economic theory called *classical liberal economics*. This theory contradicted the prevailing theory of mercantilism, arguing instead for making capitalism "free-market" or **laissez-faire** (as coined by contemporary French economists). Classical liberal theorists justified their case on their observations of the behavior of peoples and institutions, from smugglers to ministers of state, from banks to empires. They argued against the theory of mercantilism, where government officials made key economic decisions by granting monopolies and raising tariffs. Instead, they theorized that rational individuals looking out for their own "enlightened" self-interest would make better economic choices. The most famous formulation came from the Scotsman Adam Smith in his book *The Wealth of Nations* in 1776. He saw that individual actions would accumulate to push the economy forward, as if collectively by a giant "invisible hand." Like most economic theories, classical liberal economics has serious flaws, as later history showed. For a long time, though, it made more sense than the likewise flawed theory of mercantilism.

The second Enlightenment concept, *skepticism*, followed from Descartes' principle of doubting everything and trusting only what could be tested by reason. A popular subject for skepticism was Christianity, with all its contradictions, superstitions, and schisms. Skepticism soon promoted the fashionable belief of *deism*. This creed diverged from orthodox Christianity. Deists saw God as more of the creator, maker, or author of the universe, not really as the incarnate Christ who redeemed sinful man through his death and resurrection. It was as if God had constructed the universe like a giant clock and left it running according to well-organized principles of nature. Thus, for many deists, Christianity became more of a moral philosophy and a guide for behavior than the overriding concern of all existence.

Many leading intellectuals embraced *agnosticism*, thus going even further down the road of doubt. Agnostics considered the existence of God impossible to prove, since God was beyond empirical observation and experimentation. Agnostics were and are concerned about this life, ignoring any possible afterlife. A few among the elites, such as the Scottish philosopher and historian David Hume, journeyed all the way to *atheism*, denying outright the existence of God. Many agnostics and atheists, moreover, attacked Christianity as a failed religion of misinformation, exploitation, and slaughter.

For the first time since the Roman Empire's conversion, Christianity was not held by all of the leading figures of Western civilization. This trend would only continue. A natural result was that **religious toleration** became an increasingly widespread ideal. The most famous *philosophe*, Voltaire (b. 1694–d. 1778), thought religion useful, but he condemned using cruelty on earth in the name of saving souls for heaven. The spread of *toleration* meant that people of one faith would less often torture and execute others for having the "wrong" religion. Instead of Christian doctrine being compulsory, it increasingly became one more option among many. Religion became a private matter, not a public requirement.

Nonetheless, while many leaders were turning away from traditional religion during the eighteenth century, most of the masses experienced a religious revival. Following a lull after the upheaval of the Reformation, large numbers of westerners embraced their Christian beliefs even more passionately. Furthermore, Christianity continued to fragment into even more branches. During the "Great Awakening" in America, revivalist Methodists broke off from the Church of England, which they considered to be too conservative or moderate. New religious groups such as the Society of Friends, nicknamed Quakers, left Europe to settle in the new American colony of Pennsylvania, founded explicitly for religious toleration. Quakers expressed their faith in meetings of quiet association. In Germany, followers of *Pietism* sought to inspire a new fervency of faith in Lutheranism, dedicating themselves to prayer and charity. Ironically, if one counted believing Christians and compared the numbers to those of nonbelieving rationalists, the Enlightenment remained more an age of faith than of reason. These measures lead to another basic principle:

> **Every religion has elements that are nonsensical to a rational outsider; nonsense or not, belief in some form of religion fulfills a vital need for most people.**

Enlightenment *philosophes* clearly stated the first part of the principle; the historical record proves the second part.

Religious toleration reflected the Enlightenment's third big concept, ***humanitarianism***, the attitude that humans should treat other humans decently. Ostensibly, the Christian faith and Christ's command about loving one's neighbor had a strong humanitarian component. Throughout history, however, Christian society clearly fell short of that ideal, with crusades, inquisitions, witch hunts, slavery, and cooperation with warmongers, for example. Some Christian preachers had even claimed that suffering was a virtue, calling on the faithful to wait until they died before they received any reward of paradise.

Beyond the suffering of hard conditions, active cruelty saturated eighteenth-century Western society. People visited insane asylums to watch inmates as if they were zoo exhibits. Ironically, zoos also started at that time out of scientific interest; they likewise cruelly confined wild animals in unnatural, small, bare cages. Popular sports included animal fights where bulls, dogs, or roosters ripped each other to bloody shreds. The wealthy ignored the sufferings of the poor, worsened through economic upheavals and natural disasters. Public executions frequently offered Sunday pastimes for large crowds, who watched as criminals were beheaded, burned, disemboweled (intestines pulled out and thrown on a fire), drawn and quartered (either pulled apart by horses or the dead body chopped into four pieces after partial strangulation and disembowelment), beaten by the wheel (and then the crippled body tied to a wheel and hung up on a pole), or simply hanged (usually to die by slow strangulation). The corpses dangled for weeks, months, even years, until they rotted to fall in pieces from their gibbets.

With the Enlightenment, the elites began to abolish such inhumanity. This new humanitarianism's virtue did not require divine commandments as its foundation. Instead, this principle of morality simply declared that human beings, simply because they were observably human, should be respected. Rulers passed laws to end the practices of torture and to eliminate the death penalty, or at least to confine it to the most heinous of crimes. Soon, long-term imprisonment became the common, if expensive, method of punishing criminals. Some reformers actually thought that prisons might even rehabilitate convicts away from their criminal behavior.

Even more novel, leaders began to use social reforms to prevent crime in the first place. They reasoned that poverty and ignorance contributed to the motivations of criminals, so by attacking those social ills, crime rates could be expected to decline. The idea of promoting a good life in this world, summed up in Thomas Jefferson's famous phrase, "life, liberty and the pursuit of happiness," came, for some, to be considered a basic human right.

Another radical idea of the humanitarians was the abolition of slavery. In the Enlightenment, for the first time in history, most leaders of society actually began to feel guilty about enslaving other human beings. Soon, Western civilization became the only civilization to end slavery on its own. Some historians argue that growing industrialization (see the next chapter) made traditional slavery less necessary. Still, abolitionists faced great resistance from economic interests and racists. Western powers finally abolished formal, state-sanctioned slavery during the nineteenth century.

In spite of this new recognition of humanity, half of the species, namely women, continued to suffer sexist subordination. A handful of reformers did suggest that wives should not be under the thumb of their husbands. **Mary Wollstonecraft**'s book *A Vindication of the Rights of Woman* (1792) put forth well-reasoned demands for better education of the "weaker" sex. Her notoriously unconventional lifestyle, however, undermined her call for justice and instead convinced many people that women were irrational and immoral. She conducted an unhappy and very public love affair that produced an illegitimate daughter. Long after the Enlightenment, few opportunities opened for women. True women's rights in politics, the economy, or society would have to wait many decades.

The notion that things could grow better, namely ***progress***, was the fourth big concept of the Enlightenment. In contrast, the Judeo-Christian concept of history had direction, but not necessarily any sense that life would improve. Christians thought that at some point, either today or in the distant future, the natural world would end and humanity would be divided into those sent to hell and those united with God in heaven. The *philosophes* argued instead for a betterment of people's lives in this world, as soon as feasible, based on sound scientific conclusions drawn from empiricism. They argued that material and moral development should even happen in their own lifetimes.

Encyclopedias, such as the *Britannica* (first published in 1760 and still going today) or the French *Encyclopedia* or a Systematic Dictionary of the Sciences, Arts and Crafts (begun in 1751 and finished with its first edition in 1780), offered concrete resistance to lapsing back into ignorance. In thirty-five volumes, the French *Encyclopedia* provided a handbook of all human knowledge, indeed a summary of the Enlightenment. According to its editor, Denis Diderot, the project was supposed to bring together all knowledge, especially about technology, so that humanity could be both happy and more virtuous. Progress became reality as more people learned to read and more written materials appeared for them to read. The new literary form of **novels** (which means "new") also entertained people about the possibilities of change. Novels are book-length, fictional stories in prose about individuals who can pursue their own destinies, often against difficult odds. Samuel Richardson's *Pamela, or Virtue Rewarded* and Daniel Defoe's *Robinson Crusoe* told such tales. **Newspapers** also began to be published to inform people of recent developments in politics, economics, and culture. Armed with these foundations of information, society could only move forward.

Progress, humanitarianism, skepticism, and empiricism were agents for change in Western civilization. The *philosophes* wrote about new expectations for human beings in this world, not necessarily connected to traditional Christianity. Building on Renaissance humanism, the Enlightenment offered a rational alternative to the Christian emphasis on life after death. Actions based on reason, science, and kindness could perhaps transform this globe, despite the flaws of human nature. The question was, who could turn the words into action and actually advance the Enlightenment agenda?

Review: *What improvements did Enlightenment thinkers propose for human society?*

Response:

THE STATE IS HE (OR SHE)

Since the late sixteenth century, a series of works by political theorists had been articulating how government could contribute to progress. Some intellectuals suggested rather radical ideas, which are explained in the next section. Most, however, justified the increasing powers of **absolute monarchy**. This idea reflected a new intensity of royal power, the most effective form of absolutism to date.[1] Many political theorists and *philosophes* asked how people should be ruled in a fashion that improved society. Their answer was to concentrate as much power as possible in the hands of a dynastic prince.

While the term *absolutism* is embedded in the seventeenth and eighteenth centuries, the basic concept dates back almost to the beginning of civilization. Rulers had always been naturally inclined to claim as much authority as possible. Yet ancient and medieval rulers lacked the capacity for effective absolutism. A king like Charlemagne sought to correctly order society, but other forces—the aristocracy, the weak economy, the low level of education, as well as foes he needed to slaughter—made society too resistant and slow to feel the power of government.

Early Modern arguments for absolutism relied on two main justifications. The first one, popular from the late fifteenth to the early eighteenth centuries, was rule by *divine right*. This idea drew on ancient beliefs that kings had special connections to the supernatural. Even the early medieval Germanic kings like the Merovingians appealed to their divine blood to justify their dynasty. The Carolingians and Christian dynasties afterward based their views on Old Testament kings like David

---

1. The famous phrase from Lord Acton, "Power tends to corrupt, and absolute power corrupts absolutely," leaps to mind. But he was writing decades later.

and Solomon. It was a comforting thought that God had selected monarchs through royal bloodlines. Kings mirrored the God who ruled the universe: as he reigned in heaven completely, so monarchs on earth had the right to be unconditionally powerful. This dynastic argument was so strong that even women were allowed to inherit the throne in many countries.

With the rising skepticism of the Enlightenment, the justification for absolutism eventually changed. Since deists doubted God's active intervention in our planetary affairs, justifying monarchy by divine selection lost its resonance. Therefore, the second argument sanctioning royal absolutism turned on rational utility. This ***enlightened despotism*** asserted that one person should rule because, logically, unity encouraged simplicity and efficiency. Moreover, this absolute rule should benefit most of the subjects within the state, not merely enhance the monarch's own personal comfort or vanity.

The new absolute monarchs almost wielded enough power to fit their own claims of supremacy. Absolutism depended on more than the destruction of war or confiscation of taxes. Absolute monarchs could wage wars, but usually only within the bounds of a primitive international law defined by rules of warfare. War became more professionalized, and noncombatants (especially women, children, clergy, and the elderly) suffered less. Monarchs could improve the economy, social status, and even the life of the family to greater and greater degrees. By 1600, many were embracing the change.

Historians usually credit France with becoming the first modern European state through its royal revival of absolutism. By ending the civil wars of the late sixteenth century, King Henry IV rode a tide of goodwill and a widespread desire for peace to become an absolute monarch. He revised the taxes, built public works, promoted businesses, balanced the budget, and encouraged culture. He originated that famous political promise that someday, there would be a chicken in every pot. In an age when most peasants rarely ate meat, that was quite a goal. Living well in this world was becoming more important than living well for the next.

Henry's assassination by a mad monk in 1610 threatened France's stability once again. Henry left only a child, Louis XIII, on the throne. As illustrated before, a child ruler has often sparked civil wars as factions sought to replace or control the minor. This consequence highlighted a major flaw of monarchical regimes dependent upon one person: what if the king were incompetent or a child? The system could easily break down since so much depended on the individual monarch.

Appointing competent and empowered bureaucrats to rule in the king's name solved this weakness. Louis XIII gained such a significant and capable minister with **Cardinal Richelieu** (d. 1642). Instead of serving the papacy, as his title would suggest, Richelieu became the first minister to his king. As such, he worked tirelessly to strengthen absolute government in France. As a royal servant, the cardinal ruled in the name of the king. Also, because as a cleric he was required to be celibate, he did not pose a threat in creating his own rival dynasty, as the Carolingian mayors of the palace had done under the Merovingians. When Louis XIII came of age, he continued to relish all the privileges of being a king while Richelieu did all the hard work.

Therefore, the king's minister continued to deepen the roots of monarchical authority. Richelieu strengthened the government with more laws, more taxes, a better army, and a streamlined administration. By executing select nobles for treason, he intimidated all of the nobility. Although he was a Roman Catholic cardinal, Richelieu helped the Protestants during the Thirty Years War because weakening the Habsburg emperors benefited France. He also took away some of the privileges granted to Protestants by the Edict of Nantes, although not because of religious prejudice. The rights of Protestants to self-defense and fortified cities threatened the king's asserted monopoly on force. In the most notorious example, the cardinal manipulated a panic about demon-possessed nuns in order to gain control of the Huguenot town of Loudun.

Both Richelieu and his king died within a year of each other, again leaving a child as heir, **Louis XIV** (r. 1643–1715). Once more, the crown almost plunged into a crisis over a child king. Nevertheless, Louis XIV managed to hold onto the throne under the protection of another clerical minister, Cardinal Mazarin. Once he reached maturity, Louis XIV became the most powerful king France had ever known. Louis XIV differed from Louis XIII in that he himself actually wanted to rule. He took charge, depicting himself as the sun shining over France, "the Sun King." According to Louis' vision, if the land did not have the sunlight of his royal person, it would die in darkness.

Louis XIV's modernizations were numerous. He met with his chief ministers in a small chamber called a **cabinet**, thus coining a name for executive meetings. These cabinet ministers then carried out the royal will through the bureaucracy. Instead of relying on mercenaries, France raised one of the first modern professional armies, which meant that paid soldiers were uniformed and housed in barracks. Since so many troops were recruited from the common classes, this army continued the decline of medieval ways of the nobility. Being a noble no longer meant military service. Instead, modern central governments asserted a monopoly on violence: only agents of the king could kill. To pay for these royal troops, Louis intervened in the economy with the intention of helping it grow. His ministers adopted the economic theory of mercantilism, whose advocacy of government intervention naturally pleased the absolute monarch. The government targeted industries for aid and both licensed and financed the founding of colonies.

Louis XIV's most noticeable legacy (especially for the modern tourist) was his construction of the palace of **Versailles**, which became a whole new capital located a few miles from crowded, dirty Paris. There he collected his bureaucracy and government and projected a magnificent image of himself. Interestingly, the palace was rather uncomfortable to live in. The chimneys were too short to draw smoke properly, so rooms were smoky and drafty. The kitchens were a great distance from the dining room, so the various courses, from soup, fish, poultry, and so on, got cold before they could be consumed. Yet Louis nourished a palace culture, with himself as the royal center of attention. Aristocrats and nobles clamored to reside there, maneuvering to attend to both the intimate and public needs of the most important person in the country. They dressed him, emptied his chamber pots, danced at his balls, bowed down at his entrances, and gossiped behind his back. Naturally, this luxurious life cost huge amounts of money from the nobles and the taxpayers. Likewise, the brilliance of the court did not entirely blind the members of the aristocracy to their long-standing prerogatives; but for a moment, absolutely, Louis was king.

Louis' greatness is qualified by two ambivalent decisions. For one, Louis XIV revoked the Edict of Nantes. He did not comprehend the advantage of allowing religious diversity in his realm. His view was *un roi, une loi, une foi* (one king, one law, one faith). This action raised fewer outcries than it might have decades earlier; many people had transferred their desire for religion into loyalty to the state. Still, outlawing Protestantism in France hurt the economy, since many productive Huguenots left for more tolerant countries, especially the Netherlands and Brandenburg-Prussia (see the next section). For his own purposes, though, Louis XIV achieved more religious uniformity for Roman Catholicism.

The second ambivalent choice of Louis's reign was his desire for military glory, *la gloire*. He thought he should wage war to make his country, and consequently himself, bigger and stronger. He aimed to expand France's borders to the Rhine River. Such a move would have taken territories away from the Holy Roman Empire. The most tempting targets were the rich Lowlands, both the Spanish Netherlands held by the Habsburgs and the free Dutch Netherlands. Louis was no great general himself; he entrusted that role to others. Without risk to his own person, in his desire for glory he committed France to a series of risky wars. Unfortunately for his grand plans, other European powers, particularly Britain and Habsburg Austria, resolutely opposed France, fearing a threat to the balance of power.

By the time Louis XIV died in 1715, France had sunk deeply into debt and lay exhausted. This situation reveals another flaw of absolutism: if anyone disagreed with government policies, little could be done to change the monarch's mind. In France, the Estates-General, the representative parliamentarian body created in the fourteenth century, had long since ceased to convene. At best, people could present a petition. Furthermore, Louis and other absolute monarchs easily tired of criticism. They tended to insulate themselves and obtained advice only from handpicked, obsequious bureaucrats and self-seeking sycophantic courtiers. Despite this problem, Louis set the tone for other princes, kings, and emperors. Any prince who wanted respect needed new palaces, parties at court, and military victories. Princes all across Europe imitated the Sun King.

One of the Sun King's most interesting imitators came from a place that seemed insignificant at the beginning of Louis' reign. Far off eastward, where Europe turns into Asia, a new power called **Russia** was rising. Western Europeans had not taken much note of Russia up to this point. A Russian principality around Kiev had almost started to flourish in the Middle Ages, but then the **Mongols** conquered it. The Mongols were yet another group of Asiatic horse riders, like the Huns and Turks. They invaded eastern Europe briefly in the 1300s, adding Russia to their vast Khanate Empire. During the 1400s, the dukes of Moscow managed to throw off the Mongol yoke and slowly freed their Russian brethren and neighboring ethnic groups from Mongol domination.

By 1600, the Duchy of Moscow had expanded to become the Russian Empire, ruled by the **tsars** (sometimes spelled *czar*, the Russian word for emperor, derived from "Caesar"). Russia was a huge territory by 1613, when the Romanov dynasty came to power. The Romanovs provided continuity and stability after a period of turmoil. Like other imperialist European powers, the Russians started to conquer Asians who were less technologically advanced than Europeans. Unlike the other European powers, though, Russians did not need to cross oceans; they had to cross only the Ural Mountains into Asia. Thus began the notable reversal of a historical trend. Up until 1600, horse-riding warriors from the vast steppes of central Asia, whether Huns, Turks, or Mongols, had periodically invaded Europe. Now Europeans began to invade Asia. By 1648, Russians had already crossed Siberia to reach the Pacific Ocean. Then they pushed southward, taking over the Muslim Turkish peoples of central Asia. Their empire transformed Russia into a great power, although western Europeans did not recognize it at first since Russia was so far away in eastern Europe.

The first ruler who made Europeans take notice was **Tsar Peter I "the Great"** (r. 1682–1725). Peter saw that Russia could become greater by inaugurating a policy of ***westernization*** (conforming local institutions and attitudes to those of western Europe). Thus, Russia became more and more part of Western civilization. Before Peter, the main cultural influences had come from Byzantium and Asia. Since the Byzantine Empire's collapse, Russian tsars had proclaimed themselves the successors of Rome and Constantinople and the protectors of Eastern Orthodox Christianity. Those roles offered little chance for real political advancement. The Enlightenment offered progress, which Peter learned of firsthand, having toured western Europe in 1697 and 1698. In England, France, the Netherlands, and Germany, he saw the power harnessed by the Commercial and Scientific Revolutions and decided to bring economics, science, and even culture to Russia. In pursuit of that last goal, he went so far as to legislate that Russian nobles shave off their bushy beards and abandon warm furs in order to dress like the courtiers of Versailles. Silk knee pants and white powdered wigs were impractical in a cold Russian winter, but if the tsar commanded, no one said "*Non*," much less "*Nyet*."

Tsar Peter's new capital of **St. Petersburg** surpassed even Louis XIV's Versailles. Peter built not only a palace, but a whole city (the city's being named after the saint with whom the tsar shared a name was no coincidence). First, he had needed to conquer the land, defeating Sweden in the crucial Great Northern War (1700–1721). Before the war, Sweden had claimed great power status based on its key role in the Thirty Years War. Afterward, Sweden was no more than a minor power, while Russia's supremacy was assured. Then at enormous expense, forty thousand workers struggled for fourteen years to build a city on what had once been swampland. Thousands paid the price of their lives. Located on an arm of the Baltic Sea, the new Russian capital was connected by sea routes to the world. St. Petersburg perfectly symbolized the Enlightenment's confidence that the natural wilderness could be tamed into order. Peter also considered St. Petersburg his "window on the West," his connection to the rest of Europe. As much as they might wish, Europeans could never again ignore Russia after Peter; by force of imperial will, he had made his empire part of the Western balance of power.

Besides those rulers of France and Russia, many other monarchs aspired to greatness through absolutism. One of most interesting appeared in the empire of Austria, whose rulers of the Habsburg dynasty were also consistently elected Holy

Roman Emperors. The ethnically German Habsburgs had assembled a multiethnic empire of Germans, Czechs, Slovaks, Hungarians, Croatians, Italians, and many other smaller groups. The dynasty alone, not tradition or affection, held these peoples together. In 1740, many feared a crisis when **Maria Theresa** (r. 1740–1780), an unprepared twenty-three-year-old princess who was pregnant with her fourth child, inherited the Austrian territories.

Although her imperial father had issued a law called the Pragmatic Sanction to recognize her right, as a mere woman, to inherit, he had never trained her to be a ruler. Instead, Maria Theresa's husband, Francis of Habsburg-Lorraine (who was also her cousin), was expected to take over Austria as archduke and become elected as emperor. Maria Theresa loved her husband (literally—she gave birth sixteen times), but Francis showed no talent for politics. Other European rulers also knew this. When Maria Theresa's father died in 1740, France, Prussia, and others attacked in the War of Austrian Succession (1740–1748). Her enemies seized several of the diverse Austrian territories and by 1742 crowned the duke of Bavaria as Holy Roman Emperor—the first prince other than a Habsburg in three hundred years.

Surprisingly, Maria Theresa took charge of the situation, becoming one of the best rulers Austria has ever had. Showing courage and resolve, she appealed to honor, tradition, and chivalry, which convinced her subjects to obey and her armies to fight. To support her warriors properly, she initiated a modern military in Austria, with standardized supply and uniforms, as well as officer training schools. She reformed the economy, collecting new revenues such as the income tax and introducing paper money. This last innovation showed a growing trust of government: otherwise, why would people accept money that for the first time in civilization was not made of precious metal? The move boosted the economy, since conveniently carried paper money made it easier to invest and to buy things. Maria Theresa's confident bureaucracy reorganized the administration of her widespread lands. She also devoted attention to social welfare, leading to her declaration that every child should have a basic education, including girls. Thus schools were built and maintained at public expense. Her revised legal codes eliminated torture, stopped the witch hunts, and investigated crime through rational methods (see figure 10.2). Her imposition of uniformity and consistency promoted the best of modern government. Admittedly, Maria Theresa did build an imitation Versailles at Schönbrunn and did live the privileged life considered appropriate to an empress (see figure 10.3). Yet, in the enlightened manner, people were willing to support such a monarchy that also did something for them. In the end, Maria Theresa's competent reign safeguarded Austria's Great Power status and its people's prosperity.

Maria Theresa' great rival was King **Frederick II "the Great"** Hohenzollern (r. 1740–1786) of **Prussia**. The crusading order of the Teutonic Knights had originally conquered the Slavic Prussians who lived along the southern coast of the Baltic Sea. During the Reformation, these German monk-knights converted to Lutheranism and established themselves as a secular dynasty. Soon after, the Hohenzollern dynasty of the March of Brandenburg inherited Prussia. The dynasty slowly built Brandenburg-Prussia up to a middle-ranked power by the early eighteenth century, becoming "kings in Prussia" by 1715. Frederick himself had some reluctance about becoming king, and as a young man he tried to flee the overbearing rule of his royal

Figure 10.2. In the manner of the Enlightenment, reason applied even to torture. A legal handbook written for Maria Theresa shows the most efficient means of questioning someone, using a ladder for torture.

Figure 10.3.   As a typical absolute monarch, Maria Theresa had a new palace, Schönbrunn, built for herself outside Vienna.

father. The king captured Prince Frederick, forced him to watch his best friend shot for treason, and threatened to do the same to Frederick. The young Frederick bowed to the will of his father and became much more serious about his future kingship.

Frederick's father died in the same year as Maria Theresa's. In addition to the royal crown, he inherited from his father a well-drilled army and a well-coffered treasury. Frederick used these to grab the rich province of Silesia from Maria Theresa, thus starting the War of Austrian Succession. His greatest success was having Prussia survive both the War of Austrian Succession and the Seven Years War that followed with the prize of Silesia intact. As the actual general in command of his armies, much of the credit for this went to him personally. Aside from his conquests, King Frederick II also ruled in an enlightened manner: improving finances, justice, administration, and social welfare. Therefore, by the end of his reign, Prussia was a great power, competitive with England, France, Austria, and Russia.

Austria, Prussia, and Russia sealed their enlightened cooperation with the notorious **Partitions of Poland** (1772–1795). Maria Theresa's and Frederick's younger contemporary, Tsar Catherine II "the Great" (r. 1762–1796), a German princess who seized power from her husband, the Russian tsar, asked the others to join her in helping themselves to choice bits of Polish territory. In 1772, Poland was the second-largest European nation, next to Russia. Yet its elected kings had almost no power. The nobility claimed to run the country through their parliament, the Sejm. Nevertheless, their self-confidence had gone too far, since any one noble in the body could veto any attempt at legislation. Consequently, few laws or reforms passed, and Poland could not keep pace with the innovations of its enlightened neighbors. Considering this incompetence of the Polish government, the enlightened argued that it would be better that Austrians, Prussians, or Russians rule the

Poles. Polish forces were unable to defend and resist the occupation of their country, which only proved the point. In several stages, Austria, Prussia, and Russia carved up Poland. By 1795, Poland had vanished from the map. While the Poles objected, reason and power joined to shape a new European destiny. It seemed obvious that through enlightened despotism, monarchies could go on forever.

Review: How did absolutism gain ascendancy in Early Modern Europe?

Response:

> divine right
> enlight despotism
>   Mary

(PROSPEROUS) PEOPLE POWER

Fundamentally, all political debates are about who should decide when and how governments interfere in the affairs of either their own people or those of neighboring states. With absolutism, the prince (or the reigning emperor, king, queen, archduchess, duke, prince-bishop, etc.) represented the entire state, while all people therein were subjects. She reigned above the law, or was in essence the law herself. Everything circled around the ruler.

While absolutism flourished, some began fighting for another view: that power should flow upward from the people. In the Western heritage, the notion that the people should rule themselves, of course, goes back to the democracies of the ancient Greece *poleis* and the Roman Republic. Those systems had failed, but they were not forgotten. Then, in the Middle Ages, elected governments in towns and cities or in communes reasserted democratic principles. Yet self-government had not really expanded beyond the size of a local government.

The one exception was the **Swiss Confederation**. In the late thirteenth century, townspeople and peasants under the Habsburgs had the audacity to claim self-rule, without any aristocracy. The legends of Wilhelm Tell and his archery date to this liberation from Habsburg supremacy. Contemporaries, however, saw the Swiss success as an unusual circumstance brought about by the Swiss pikemen's ability to defend Alpine passes. Few gave Switzerland much respect. After a brief attempt at becoming a dominant regional power, the confederation retreated into neutrality and nonintervention after 1500. Even then, few understood how the Swiss state held together, divided by four languages (German, French, Italian, and Rhaeto-Romansch) and several versions of Christianity (Roman Catholicism, Calvinism,

Zwinglism, Waldensianism, etc.). For all other countries, monarchy based on a sub-servient aristocracy and nobility seemed the superior method of rule.

Around 1600, though, a few countries began to explore democracy as an alternative structure for political power. The two basic components of all modern democracies have been **republicanism** and **constitutionalism**. As in ancient Rome, republicanism was government by elected representatives, where office seekers competed for votes, served limited terms, and then were replaced, even by their political opponents. Constitutionalism meant that law limited government's powers, whether formally written in an explicit document or merely collected as traditions and practices. Constitutional law prohibited government from violating certain specified rights of citizens. For such a democracy to function, therefore, broad obedience to standards of law and willingness to compromise with others of differing ideologies were required.

The **United Provinces of the Netherlands** was the first modern country to give up on kings, after 1581. As seen in the Reformation, the various provinces of the Calvinist Dutch Netherlands (of which the most famous was **Holland**) had declared their freedom from the Roman Catholic Habsburg king of Spain. Fighting for religious freedom for themselves, they also soon extended it to others. The majority of the Dutch were reformed Calvinists, but they also tolerated English Puritans, Mennonites, Lutherans, and even Roman Catholics.

The industrious merchants behind the successful rebellion against the Spanish monarchy created a new form of national government. The Dutch did not simply replace one monarch with another (although the noble dynasty of Orange was interested). Instead, the great merchants, or *Hooge Moogende* (High Mightinesses), pooled their resources and ran the state. The new Dutch regime was an oligarchy or, perhaps, a plutocracy, rule based on wealth. Only male members of the proper-tied classes held political offices, much like the oligarchic patricians in ancient Rome. Although Dutch people sometimes turned to the aristocratic House of Orange for leadership, the elected representatives usually ran the country, making the key decisions in war and peace.

Under this democratic government, Holland became Europe's greatest economic power for several decades in the seventeenth century. Dutch investors and politicians founded the Bank of Amsterdam in 1609 to provide capital. Cheap fly-boats hauled cargo at the best price and speed.

The Netherlands even became a world power, creating a colonial empire to rival those of the Spanish and Portuguese. The Dutch Empire stretched from the East Indies to South Africa, to the Caribbean, to the "New" Netherlands in North America along the Hudson River. A government-chartered monopoly for Asian trade, the United East India Company (using the initials VOC) paved the way for joint stock corporations in 1602 (see figure 10.4). As colonial masters, the Dutch were less harsh than others toward the natives. The Dutch even encouraged a vibrant trading network in East Asia, unlike other Europeans whose trade solely exploited the colonies for the mother country's benefit. Still, Dutch merchants crushed any threats from Asians to their monopoly on power. Not for the first time, the benefits of democracy at home did not extend to colonized native territories around the world.

Figure 10.4. The "VOC" of the Dutch East India Company (Vereenigde Oost-Indische Compagnie) marks a cannon with which the Netherlands took over trade in the East Indies.

Their economic advantage did not last long, however. Dutch economic supremacy ended by 1700. The Dutch were too small in population, too vulnerable to French invasion, and too easily cut off from the Atlantic by the English, who could close the Channel and patrol the North Sea. Even when a prince of Orange became king of England in 1688, the English mostly benefited. The Netherlands gave up supremacy of the seas but maintained its vital role in the international economy. A state did not have to be mighty to prosper. While Holland was no longer a great power after 1700, the Netherlands nevertheless remained richer and freer than most countries of Europe.

By 1700, England had taken Holland's place as the major maritime power. The accession of the Stuart dynasty of Scotland to the throne of England (1603–1714) had helped England surpass Holland. When the Tudor line ended with the "Virgin Queen" Elizabeth, a quick decision by English leaders settled the crown peacefully on her cousin, King James VI of Scotland, who became King James I of England. These combined realms were officially renamed the **United Kingdom of Great Britain** a century later. The unification of these traditional enemies did not always go smoothly, especially because the English certainly dominated the arrangement. Yet the combined British energies (throwing in occupied Ireland) slowly freed efforts toward science, technology, exploration, and profit. Soon, the British controlled the largest empire in world history.

On the path to becoming a world empire, the English stumbled through the **English Revolution** (1642–1689), which democratized their politics. The revolution's roots go back to the Reformation and deep into the Middle Ages. The medieval English kings, like many kings in the West, had established the representative body of Parliament to help them in their rule. Elected representatives from clergy, nobility, and townspeople worked with kings to raise taxes and to facilitate political change. The English Parliament was originally no stronger than any other medieval political body. Then, the English Reformation granted it decisive power. Parliament participated in making the laws that established the Church of England. It also had more continuity than the dynasty, endorsing successions as Henry VIII went through his wives and as his children were crowned and subsequently died. These historic decisions ensured that Parliament's elected representatives enjoyed a real partnership with the royal government.

The new Stuart dynasty at first lacked an appreciation for this development. That was odd, since the first Stuart monarch, James VI of Scotland, had minimal power in his own homeland, being hemmed in by rambunctious nobles who had thrown out his mother, Mary Stuart, Queen of Scots. Yet when James VI of Scotland also became James I of England (r. 1603–1625), he became infatuated with the divine right theories of absolutism. He even tried to lecture Parliament about his God-granted prerogatives. James' heir, Charles I (r. 1625–1649), went even further. He temporarily refused to summon Parliament and tried ruling without them. His effort ultimately failed.

The delicacy of the Anglican compromise actually prevented absolutism in England. The government required that everyone worship in the Church of England, but those within the Church of England disagreed about what should be in *The Book of Common Prayer*. At one end of the spectrum, English Calvinists, called Puritans, wanted a more reformed church. At the other end, supporters of bishops wanted worship and belief similar to Roman Catholicism, although without the papacy.

Nevertheless, belonging either to extreme Protestant sects or Roman Catholicism remained illegal. Some Puritans felt so oppressed by being forced to worship in the Anglican style that they became **separatists**, rejecting not only the English faith but also England itself. One group settled briefly in the tolerant Netherlands before getting permission to settle in the New World; they became the Pilgrims of Plymouth Colony, Massachusetts, in 1620 (the ones who originated the American holiday of Thanksgiving).

The Stuart kings usually tried to support the Anglican compromise, but many Puritans suspected them of being too Roman Catholic. James I's commission of a translation of the Bible into English, the King James Bible, helped to overcome suspicions concerning his religious inclinations (although his favor toward certain male courtiers continued to provoke gossip and anger about his sexual inclinations). Suspicions about the religious reliability of the Stuarts increased under Charles I, James I's son and successor. Charles I had unwisely married a French princess and held Roman Catholic masses for her in the royal palaces. The son believed in absolutism even more than his father had. Even worse, his version could not tolerate religious diversity. As head of the Church of England, Charles insisted that all of his subjects worship the same way. In 1640, he tried to impose the Anglican *Book of Common Prayer* on the Scottish Calvinist Presbyterians. The Scots rebelled.

Charles did not have the funds to fight a civil war with his usual revenues. According to precedent, though, Parliament claimed the right to participate in the decision to raise taxes. Reluctantly, Charles held elections and called Parliament into session. The parliamentarians proceeded to insist on their prerogatives to share in government with the king. By 1642, the king (supported by many of the nobility, great landowners, and conservative and moderate Anglicans) was at war with many of the parliamentarians (supported by lesser gentry and yeomen, the merchant classes, the large cities, and the Puritans). The **English Civil War** (1642–1648) consequently broke out. The country gentleman Oliver **Cromwell** (d. 1658) soon became the commander of the parliamentarians. Cromwell best mastered recruiting, commanding, supplying, and inspiring armies to victory. His New Model Army—using the latest military technology of combining cavalry, pikes, and muskets—reinforced the increasing role of common people in the armed forces at the expense of the nobility. Just as in ancient Greece and Rome as well as in the Middle Ages, military change transformed politics. Parliament's armies defeated the royal forces and captured the king. Parliament tried King Charles I for treason, found him guilty, and had him beheaded on 30 January 1649.

The English then faced running a government without a monarch, having declared themselves a purely republican system, or as they called it, the **Commonwealth**. Of course, democracy was difficult. Cromwell quickly became discouraged with all the infighting and quarreling among the country's leaders. So he took harsh action. He purged the government of those representatives he did not like and took over himself. Basing his authority on the command of the armed forces, he turned the Commonwealth into his own dictatorship, called the Protectorate. Cromwell suppressed Roman Catholics and rebellious sentiment in Ireland by conducting severe reprisals. He then encouraged the settlement of Protestants from Scotland and Wales into the northern counties of Ulster and also led a trade war against the Dutch. Many of the English, though, saw Cromwell as a benevolent dictator.

After Cromwell died, the British had to decide how to secure stability and responsibility without the dictator's strong hand. Cromwell's son and heir lacked the ability of the father, and he willingly resigned. Unable to resist a royal dynasty, Parliament finally recalled the Stuarts, asking for the **Restoration** of the monarchy. King Charles II (r. 1660–1685) eagerly accepted. While he had the same Roman Catholic and absolutist sympathies as his father and grandfather, Charles II was at least clever enough not to let them get in the way of enjoying being king. Instead of fighting political battles with Parliament over power, Charles II relished a sumptuous court life and many mistresses. Despite all his sexual activity, he had no legitimate children, so upon his death the British throne went to his brother James II (r. 1685–1688). James began to insist on absolutism. Even worse, he openly converted to Roman Catholicism and had his son and heir baptized in that faith. The English had had enough.

In the **Glorious Revolution** of 1688, the English established the basic system of republican and constitutional government that still exists today. With little bloodshed, they forced James to flee to France. Parliament then invited James' Protestant daughter Mary to be queen, with her husband, William of Orange, as coruling king. James attempted to win back the throne with an invasion of Ireland but lost at the Battle of the Boyne in 1689. Thereafter the English possessed Ireland, and Irish independence vanished for centuries.

Other Scots, meanwhile, especially those in the Highlands, wanted James' Stuart dynasty back. Large parts of Scotland rebelled in 1715 and again in 1745 in the name of Stuart pretenders to the throne. Following the Battle of Culloden in 1746, the English crushed Scottish hopes for independence. The victorious Parliament generously approved a small measure of toleration for religious dissenters, both Roman Catholics and Presbyterian Calvinists.

Most importantly, Parliament affirmed through the Glorious Revolution that it was in charge, not the monarch, although it took several more decades for Parliament to reach its full authority. The idea of ***parliamentarianism*** meant that an elected representative body ran the government. A cabinet system in which the leaders of Parliament met in a conference room became the location of decision making. More and more often meeting without the monarch, the **prime minister** took on leadership. The British kings and queens faded into figureheads, representing that old ideal of parents of the country rather than actual war leaders and judges. Representatives elected in republican style made all-important decisions and appointed the bureaucrats to carry them out. By keeping a royal dynasty and using it as a stabilizing force, Britain became the most important Western ***constitutional monarchy***.

It is surprising that having suffered so much for the sake of establishing democratic government at home, the British were unwilling to grant it to their fellow countrymen abroad. Once the British acquired an empire, they lost the perspective of the ruled and relished the supremacy of the ruler. By 1763, Britain had the most significant world empire of all the European nations. The first clash among these empires was the **Seven Years War** (1756–1763), which could be considered the first world war. Armed forces fought three simultaneous campaigns in Europe (especially Maria Theresa of Austria versus Frederick II of Prussia), in India (where the British called it the Third Carnatic War), and in the Americas (where the American colonists called it the **French and Indian War**). In the last two theaters, the British victory was decisive. The British drove the French out of India, leaving the British as the only significant Western power there. Likewise, the French lost their North American possession of Quebec and managed to hold onto only a few islands in the Caribbean. For the next two centuries, the British Empire was the greatest empire of the world, surpassing all previous empires.

Nevertheless, wars and empires are expensive. Despite their victory, the British needed to figure out how both to pay for and defend their world empire. One obvious choice for revenue was the American colonists, who had gained security with the loss of the French threat to the north. The British wanted the Americans to contribute their fair share to the economic well-being of the mother country. Many Americans wanted instead to look after their own welfare; and they hardly wanted to pay any taxes. If they did, they at least wanted a voice in parliamentary decisions—thus a slogan of their rebellion became "No taxation without representation." The **American Revolution** (1775–1789) basically was fought about taxes: who pays, how much, and who decides. The English had no idea how to allow the American colonists any representation, even though the Americans were about as sophisticated with their technology, politics, society, and even culture as the English themselves. The American lands were rich with potential, especially since the native "Indian" peoples were so easily and quickly being eliminated after losing their French allies in the Seven Years War.

The American colonists created an adequate institution of national self-government with the Second Continental Congress. More importantly, they organized their own military forces. First, the American minutemen militias skirmished with British troops at Lexington and Concord in April 1775. Then, with proper financing and with George Washington (d. 1799) in charge, the Americans soon had an army almost able to win European-style set-piece battles. On 2 July 1776, the Congress declared independence from Britain. Two days later the adoption of a Declaration of Independence immortalized that independence. In that document, the **United States of America**, as the joined colonies called themselves, provided a clear justification for their actions: resistance to tyranny. Of course, the Americans knew that labeling the king a tyrant was mere propaganda. Ever since the English Revolution, Parliament was actually responsible for the governance of the British Empire. Whether targeting the king or not, the Americans argued that governments were responsible to the governed and that people had a right to change them when necessary, even by force.

Ultimately, force decided the destiny of the United States. Facing the strongest empire in world history, the American revolt seemed doomed to fail. Canadians refused to join, although the United States' forces had tried to invade and conquer British provinces there. Some people, like Thaddeus Kosciuszko and Casimir Pulaski from partitioned Poland, helped Americans because they were inspired by the United States' claims to liberty. Others merely wanted to hurt the British. Those countries whose worldwide empires had all suffered most from British attacks and competition eventually allied with the Americans: the Dutch, the Spanish, and, most importantly, the French. Without the help of these foreign states, the **American War of Independence (1775–1783)** would probably have been lost, and Americans would still be drinking tea with crumpets. Instead, the Americans found themselves free and independent after signing the Treaty of Paris in 1783.

The difficulty of defeating the British then gave way to the challenge of creating permanent institutions of government. Fearing the rabble, people of wealth and property remained in charge in America—there was no argument about that. Nevertheless, they decided against an American monarchy (Washington's lack of legitimate children certainly discouraged dynastic thoughts). Americans needed to construct a political system that recognized the diverse needs of so many different colonies and colonialists. Fearful of the concentration of centralized power, at first the Americans created a weak central government. This attempt, the Articles of Confederation, lasted only a couple of years before the solution proved unworkable.

So, in a rather radical step, the politicians decided to start over. The leaders of the revolution, especially Washington, Benjamin Franklin, Alexander Hamilton, and James Madison, knew that a strong central government was required. They consequently decided upon the principle of *federalism* and the office of the **presidency**, which were embodied in the U.S. Constitution, adopted in 1789. Federalism meant that competing institutions of the federal government, the state governments, and the people shared power. It meant that a strong central regime interacted with strong state administrations, while a Bill of Rights protected the people.

The federal government itself separated its powers into legislative, executive, and judicial branches. The legislature enacted the laws, declared war, made peace, and consented to (or blocked) important bureaucratic and judicial appointments. The American presidency differed from the parliamentarianism of other modern democracies, where the prime minister or chancellor served as both leader of the legislature and chief executive official. As head of the executive branch and independent of the legislature, a president commanded the armed forces and enforced the laws. The judiciary resolved civil legal disputes, convicted criminals, and, through judicial review, came to interpret the laws. The big problem of U.S. history and politics ever since has been the balance between the competing interests of the federal government, state governments, and the rights of the people to be free from government. Nearly every serious issue since the foundation of the American republic has been rooted in this tough balancing act.

Historians have argued about what was really revolutionary about the American Revolution. American society before independence hardly differed from that afterward. Politically, Americans largely imitated the British in spirit, if not in structure. The English Revolution had already clearly dismantled absolutism, replaced with elected representatives in control of the government. In both nations, the well-to-do dominated economic, political, and social affairs. Economically, the wealthy Americans who had been in charge before the revolution were largely still in charge after it—only the threat of domination from across the Atlantic had been eliminated. Politically, most poor white males did get to vote by the early nineteenth century, decades before their British counterparts. Others remained excluded. Women did not gain the vote until 1920, Native Americans until 1924, and most African Americans until 1965. Socially, the Americans did eliminate formal class distinctions more than the British, making inherited nobility illegal.

Many of the advantages for economic expansion came from America's location in the Western Hemisphere. The Atlantic Ocean protected the country from the worst of the warfare European states waged against one another. Meanwhile, advanced sailing ships allowed cultural exchange, so science and ideas continued to develop along paths in America similar to, and borrowed from, western Europe. The United States of America remained firmly connected to Western traditions.

America's greatest advantage, perhaps, lay in its vast unconquered wilderness. So much land offered unique opportunities for farmers, unlike in Europe, where most farmland had been divided up and claimed for centuries. Some historians have argued that America thus provided more opportunities than European states to allow creative and energetic people to gain wealth.

The available land in America, of course, was stolen from the native Indians. In grabbing this land, Americans shared the practices of other Europeans, both absolutist and democratic. Without any sense of irony or embarrassment, the Netherlands, Great Britain, and the United States fought for the right of their own common people to participate in government while using violence to impose their undisputed rule over non-Europeans in Asia and the Americas. These republics obviously long remembered all the advantages of absolutist regimes.

Review: How did democratic forms of government spread in the Early Modern West?

Response:

confederation - broke away from Roman E.
English rev. - parlement
Parliament
American Rev. - Federalism
checks and balances

THE DECLARATION OF LIBERTY, EQUALITY, AND FRATERNITY

The clash of republican and absolutist politics peaked in the **French Revolution** (1789–1815). British and American ideals of liberty inspired the French *philosophes* to criticize their own absolutist government, called the **ancien régime** by historians. If the Americans could overthrow royal "tyranny," then why could not the French? The American War of Independence provided an immediate example to the French. France had helped America partly through a desire to hurt Great Britain. In doing so, France paid enormous sums for military endeavors while acquiring almost nothing in return from the Treaty of Paris in 1783. France won no territories, in contrast to the vast continental possessions allotted to the United States. The huge French war debts helped to drive the French government toward a crisis of bankruptcy. Because of the worsening economic situation, all social classes became dissatisfied with the government. Poor harvests in 1787 and 1788 yielded peasant anger at the government. The middle classes also resented their heavy tax burden and limited social mobility. The nobility and clergy objected to how the absolute monarchy had usurped much of their once-great power, if not privileges.

The growing grumbling targeted the monarch personally. Despite France's role in the Enlightenment, the Bourbon dynasty had never produced an enlightened despot to reform its regime. **King Louis XVI** (r. 1774–1792) was a nice man, but he showed no particular talent for governing. He was actually more interested in being a locksmith than a king. This would not have been a problem if some able bureaucrat had ruled for him, as Richelieu had for Louis XIII. Sadly, Louis XVI was neither able to find competent ministers nor able to support them for long against palace intrigues.

Remarkably faithful in his marriage vows (for a Bourbon), Louis likewise lacked an able woman to rule from behind the scenes, such as Louis XV's mistress Madame Pompadour. Louis XVI's spouse, the notorious **Queen Marie Antoinette**, contributed to the growing contempt for the monarchy. Although Marie Antoinette was the daughter of Maria Theresa Habsburg, she inherited none of her mother's talents for governance. She instead preferred parties, balls, masquerades, and the life of luxury that absolute monarchs enjoyed. She never said something so extreme as, "Let them eat cake [*brioche*]," when she heard that peasants were begging for bread; the quote came from a fictional character in a novel. Yet people readily believed that Marie Antoinette could have said it. Her actions and reputation hurt her royal husband's position. Louis XVI's reign again exposed the great virtue and fatal flaw of absolutism: everything depended on one person.

As Louis confronted his shortage of funds, he naturally thought of the basic ways governments raised money: conquest, loans, and taxes. The first choice of war was risky, and it required money up front to equip the troops. Besides, he had no readily available excuse to attack anyone. As for the second alternative, the French banks were tapped out, while foreign banks did not want to take on the risk of French credit. That left only raising taxes. When Louis tried to raise taxes, however, the nobles who ran the courts, the *parlements*, declared that he could not do so. The nobles hoped to use this financial crisis for their own gain, restoring some of their long-lost influence. They insisted that the king would have to call the Estates-General, as Philip IV had done four and one-half centuries earlier. Certainly, as an absolute monarch, Louis could have just raised taxes. Instead of acting firmly and risking some civil disturbance, the king gave in.

Since no living person remembered the Estates-General (it had last met in 1614), public officials quickly cobbled together a process from dusty legal tomes. Three hundred representatives should be elected from each of the three estates: the clergy, the nobility, and the common people (although only the top 20 percent of the bourgeoisie, such as doctors and lawyers, were actually eligible to run for election). Some members of the Third Estate complained that their vastly greater numbers compared with the size of the other two estates deserved more representation. The king gave in, again, and conceded that they could have about six hundred representatives (see diagram 10.2). While this concession might seem more equitable, it did not challenge the predominance of the first two estates. For one, they were often related to and connected to one another, so they shared the same views. For another, each estate voted in a bloc—thus the three hundred clergy had one vote, the three hundred nobles had one vote, and the six hundred commoners had one vote. Therefore, the Third Estate would probably always be outvoted 2–1.

Shortly after the representatives to the Estates-General arrived at Versailles for the opening ceremonies on 5 May 1789, the Third Estate began to agitate for voting by individual representatives, aiming to at least even out the votes to 600–600. They even tried to declare themselves to be a new legislature called the National Assembly. The king was upset by this wrangling and locked the meeting hall on the morning of 20 June. Many representatives, mostly those from the Third Estate along with a few

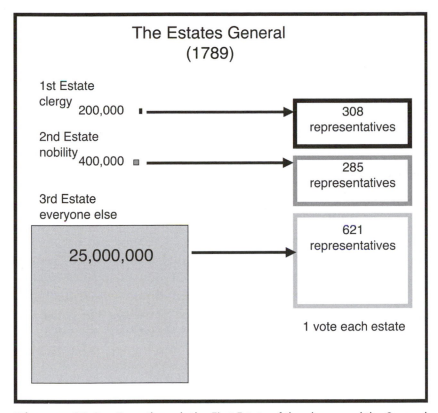

Diagram 10.2.   Even though the First Estate of the clergy and the Second Estate of the nobility had a tiny proportion of the population (the small boxes as compared to the huge box of the Third Estate), each had about an equal number of representatives. Since each estate voted as a unit, the first two could always easily outvote the third. The quarrel over voting by estate versus by representative paralyzed the Estates-General.

sympathizers from the other two, proceeded to convene at a nearby indoor tennis court. They swore the **Tennis Court Oath**, pledging not to go home until they had written a constitution. In fact and in law, a constitution meant the end of an absolute monarchy. Instead of sending in the troops and disbanding this illegal assembly, Louis once more gave in. Thus the bourgeoisie had seized control and begun a true revolution.

Things soon got out of control, as so often happens in political revolutions. While the politicians in Versailles quibbled about the wording of constitutional clauses, the populace of Paris recognized that change was at hand. They naturally feared its destructive potential. To protect themselves and their property, some Parisians began to organize militias, or bands of citizen-soldiers like the minutemen of America. Yet the Parisians lacked weapons. On 14 July 1789, a semiorganized mob approached the Bastille, a massive royal fortress and prison in the heart of the city. The crowd demanded that the Bastille release its prisoners (whom they believed were unjustly held for political reasons) and hand over its arms to the Parisian militias.

The fortress was completely secure from the militia and accompanying rabble, so the name given to this event, the **storming of the Bastille**, is quite exaggerated. In the hope of calming the situation and avoiding too much bloodshed from violence in the neighborhood, the fortress commander opened the gates. The mob rewarded him by beating him to death and parading his head on a pike. While the liberators gained some weapons, they found only a few petty criminal prisoners. Nevertheless, the attack symbolized the power of the people over the monarch. The people had openly and clearly defied royal authority and used violence on their own initiative for their own interests. The citizens of Paris tore down the fortress, stone by stone, actually selling the rubble as souvenirs. A more forceful and ruthless monarch would have mobilized his troops, declared martial law, and snuffed out this attack with notable bloodshed. What did Louis do? Nothing. Again.

Events were soon beyond any possible royal influence. As the peasants in the countryside heard about the storming of the Bastille, they also decided to rise up. The "Great Fear" spread as peasants attacked their landlords. The peasants killed seigneurs and burned the records that documented their social and economic bondage. The National Assembly panicked, since its members owned much of the land that the peasants were appropriating. They acted to calm things down on 4 August 1789, abolishing the ancien régime with its absolute monarchy and feudal privileges. A few weeks later, the National Assembly issued "**A Declaration of the Rights of Man and of the Citizen**." Similar to the American Bill of Rights, this document declared "liberty, property, security and resistance to oppression" for all Frenchmen. It guaranteed liberties to the citizens and restrained government. This document worked as planned: it calmed passions and allowed the forces of order to restore moderation. It also originated the phrase "Liberty, Equality, Fraternity," which became the slogan for the revolution.

Much more would need to be done for these goals to be realized, but the revolution had issued a clarion call for justice. Sadly, these gains did not apply to women, as is illustrated by the masculine term *fraternité* (fraternity/brotherhood). Revolutionary men in France (just as they had in England and America) excluded females from the benefits of Enlightenment ideals. A few months later, Olympe de Gouges proposed "**A Declaration of the Rights of Woman and of the Female Citizeness**," in which she rewrote the original as a document supportive of women. The government soon executed her. A woman might be a "citizeness," but the male citizens enjoyed the real protections and liberties of the law.

The royal family likewise lost their liberty and independence. In October, a mob (mostly of women) marched from the city of Paris out to Versailles. They ransacked the palace and escorted the royal family into guarded custody in the palace of the Tuileries in the heart of the city. The people made Paris once more their capital. This action shattered any remaining independent royal authority. On the first anniversary of the storming of the Bastille, the king swore loyalty to a new constitution.

Louis never reconciled himself to limited authority. In the night of 20–21 June 1791, he and his family fled from their palatial house arrest. A combination of bad luck, incompetence, and the king's own hesitant nature allowed revolutionary forces to catch the royals at Varennes. With the royal family imprisoned and back in Paris, the French decided they needed a monarch no longer. The legislature tried

King Louis XVI for treason, found him guilty (by 361 to 360 votes), and then had his head cut off on 21 January 1793. He met his death on the new, lethally efficient killing machine, the guillotine. Ironically, the king himself had suggested the machine's use of a sharp angled blade as a way to improve capital punishment. In October, Marie Antoinette followed her husband to beheading on the scaffold. While their daughter survived into old age, their son the Dauphin, or Louis XVII, disappeared and was presumed dead. Other relatives fled the country. The Bourbon dynasty seemed to have ended in humiliation.

The elected bourgeois politicians now running France faced other grave problems, not easily solved by chopping off heads. The first problem was how to make political decisions. In a fashion appropriate to democracy, they accidentally established a model of political debate and diversity. When the representatives gathered in the new republic's National Convention, their seating arrangement gave us the terminology of modern political discourse. Those to the **right** of the speaker or president of the body opposed change. Those to the **left** of the speaker embraced change. Those in the middle were the **moderates**, who needed to be convinced to go one way or the other. Extremists on the right were **reactionaries**, and extremists on the left were **radicals** (which today tends to be used for any extremist of any political leaning). This vocabulary of "left" and "right" suggests that all political disagreements are about resisting or accepting change. These labels may have simplified issues, but they enabled politicians to start organizing groups around ideologies and specific policy proposals.

Review: How did the revolutionaries in France execute political changes?

Response:

> French inspired by American/British philosophers
>   Storm of the Bastille
>   Rights of Men
>
>   violence being used
>   constitutions being written

BLOOD AND EMPIRES

The second problem facing the French elected representatives was war. After the French arrested their king, Louis' royal relatives and aristocrats called for an invasion to restore their fellow absolutist to power. The French government declared war before they did. In reaction, an alliance of small and great powers formed against the French. A series of conflicts, called the **Wars of the Coalitions** (1792–1815), burdened Europe for the next generation. Ironically, considering its own revolutionary history, Great Britain became the head of the coalition and France's most determined opponent. Great Britain sought to maintain the traditional balance of power among the states of Europe. England feared the growth of French power more than France's democratic and republican trappings.

Then suddenly, revolutionary France was the most powerful country in Europe. The revolution enabled France to create a new kind of war. During the ancien régime, many of the French officers in the royal army had been "blue bloods," aristocrats and nobles so named because one could see their veins through their fair, pale skin. Many nobles fled the country once revolution began. France's aristocratic enemies then expected that without God-given elite leadership, the rabble republican army would readily collapse. On the contrary, the French were inspired to shed their red blood in defense of their nation more fervently and ferociously than ever before, since it was *theirs* now, not the monarch's. They managed to turn back the first invading forces in a skirmish at Valmy on 19 August 1792. As the war ground on, talented officers rose in the ranks based on their ability, not blue-blooded connections.

The new regime called all the people to war, whatever their status. As ordered by the government, young men fought, married men supported the troops with supplies, young and old women sewed tents and uniforms or nursed the sick, children turned rags into lint for making bandages, and old men cheered on everyone else. Modern "total war" began. Key to victory were the huge new armies of inspired countrymen. The problem of feeding such large numbers of soldiers led to the invention of ways to preserve food. Scientists discovered that food boiled in bottles and tin cans for extended periods would not spoil. This invention for wartime would later free many civilians in peacetime from the danger of starvation.

Under pressure of war and revolutionary fervor, the government became more radical and willing to take extreme steps in changing society. This phase of the French Revolution has earned the name the **Reign of Terror** (June 1793–July 1794), or simply the Terror, an extremist period that lasted only thirteen months. The radical Jacobins (named after a club where they met) and their leader Robespierre decided that they needed to purge the republic of its internal enemies. They formed the infamous **Committee of Public Safety**, which held tribunals to arrest, try, and condemn reactionaries, in violation of previously guaranteed civil liberties. As with other historical national emergencies, the government excused itself for its extreme measures. Actually, the death toll of the Terror was comparatively small (at least compared with the subsequent war casualties). In Paris, fewer than 1,300 people were guillotined. In the countryside, however, death tolls piled higher, with perhaps as many as 25,000 executed in the troublesome province of the Vendée, mostly through mass drownings.

During the Terror, radicals implemented Enlightenment ideals with a vengeance. The radicals' new Republic of Virtue threw out everything that the *philosophes* considered backward, especially if it was based on Christianity. They replaced the Gregorian calendar: a new year I dated from the declaration of the republic; weeks were lengthened to ten days; and the names of the months were changed to reflect their character, like "Windy" or "Hot." Christian churches became "Temples of Reason." Palaces, such as the Louvre, were remodeled into museums. Education was provided for all children at taxpayer expense. Perhaps most radical of all, the government required the metric system of measurements. Tradition and custom were supplanted by the ideas of *philosophes*.

In the end, the Terror gained ill fame because its leaders became too extreme. They began to arrest and execute one another, accusing one another of less-than-sufficient revolutionary passion. Moderates naturally feared that they would be next. So in the "Hot" month called Thermidor in the republican year II (or in the night of 27–28 July 1794), moderates carried out a coup d'état (an illegal seizure of power that kills few) called the Thermidor Reaction. The moderates arrested the radical Jacobin leaders and sent them quickly to the guillotine. The politicians set up a new, more bourgeois government, restricting vote and power to those of wealth. The new regime, called the Directorate, was a reasonably competent oligarchy, but uninspired and uninspiring.

Meanwhile, the military decisions forced change. The republican French armies repeatedly gained victory in battle, due to competent commanders, vast numbers, and inspired morale. Therefore, instead of relying on loans or taxes, the Directorate used conquest to help pay the bills in 1796–1797. In a series of campaigns invading parts of Italy and the Rhineland, one general in particular gained the greatest fame: **Napoleon Bonaparte** (b. 1769–d. 1821). The dashing General Bonaparte soon surpassed the bland politicians in popularity, proving again that people are easily seduced by military successes. While most contemporary monarchs found it safer to stay away from the battle lines, Napoleon's leadership provided that inspirational passion for the French.

Had it not been for the revolution, Napoleon would never have amounted to anything noteworthy in history. As a Corsican and a member of a low-ranked family, he could never have risen very high in the ranks of the ancien régime. The revolutionary transformation of the officer corps and the increased size of the French army, however, provided Napoleon an opportunity to shine. With military insight he maneuvered huge armies, negotiated them through foreign lands, and combined his troops to crush enemy forces in decisive blows. Soon the French dreamed not only of dominating Europe, but also of restoring France's world empire. In 1798, Napoleon sailed off to invade Egypt, aiming to damage British imperial interests in the Eastern Mediterranean and the Middle East. His only success there was the discovery of the Rosetta Stone, whose inscriptions in forms of Greek alphabets and hieroglyphics allowed modern scholars to finally translate ancient Egyptian.

After the British navy decisively crushed Napoleon's hopes for conquest in Egypt, he nevertheless managed to rush back to France before news could spread. Back in Paris he seized control of the government in a coup d'état on 18 Brumaire VIII (or 9 November 1799). Imitating the Roman Republic, Napoleon declared himself the First Consul and proclaimed (with about as much sincerity as Augustus Caesar had) that his leadership would restore the "French Revolutionary Republic." In a brilliant move, he held a **plebiscite** for the French people to endorse his seizure of the state. Named after the ancient Roman plebians, plebiscites are votes with no binding power. So even if the French people had voted against his constitutional changes, Napoleon could have gone ahead anyway. Napoleon's real power was based on his military command. His army could have put down any opposition.

Nevertheless, the French people felt involved merely by being allowed to vote. Many a dictator would later resort to the same method of opinion management. Plebiscites preserved the façade of popular endorsement so well that the trappings of republican government decorated Napoleon's absolutism.

Indeed, Napoleon helped establish a model for the modern dictatorship by weakening the connection between a ruler and a noble dynasty. Napoleon showed that a relatively obscure, simple person could become the leader of a great power through talent, luck, and ruthlessness rather than dynastic birth. People were willing to sacrifice their liberty in exchange for victories against neighboring states. Napoleon's rise was neither unique nor entirely modern. Many an ancient Roman emperor had come from obscurity, especially in the tumultuous third century. In addition, Oliver Cromwell had enforced a benevolent dictatorship over the English.

The lure of dynasty was too powerful for Napoleon to ignore, however. He crowned himself emperor in 1804, abandoning the titles of the republic. A few years later he divorced his wife Josephine, who was too old to bear children, so that he could marry the Habsburg emperor's young daughter Marie Louise. By marrying Marie Louise, the once obscure Napoleon joined the most prestigious bloodline in Europe. Furthermore, the new French empress Marie Louise soon bore her newly imperial husband an imperial heir.

The French experience reaffirms the basic principle that democracy is difficult. In trying to establish a republican government, the French instead unleashed dictatorship, as had the English under Cromwell. They were not the first to experience this; nor would they be the last. Sadly, the human tendency to want simple answers and strong leaders would repeat itself in other revolutions that quickly took the same sharp turns toward authoritarianism.

For a time, Napoleon's political activities as ruler of France helped to cement his positive popular and historical reputation. His foundation of the Bank of France was only the start to growing a strong economy. Napoleon appeased the spiritual desires of many French citizens by allowing the Roman Catholic Church to set up operations again (although without some of its property, power, and monopoly on belief). Napoleon himself felt that his greatest achievement was the **Napoleonic Code**, a legal codification comparable to Justinian's Code in the sixth century. Beyond simply organizing laws as Justinian had, Napoleon's lawyers tossed out the whole previous system and founded a new one based on rationalist principles and the equality of all adult male citizens. These laws were a bit like window dressing, considering Napoleon's dictatorship, and, as usual, women were granted very few rights at all. Nevertheless, Napoleon provided a rationalized system that remained the foundation of French law as well as that of many other countries today in Europe (Holland, Italy), Latin America, and even the state of Louisiana in the United States. On the basis of these reforms, some historians have said that France gained an enlightened despot in Napoleon, at last.

Napoleon's military talent forged a massive empire that could have united the Continent under French power and culture. With his victory at the Battle of Austerlitz on 2 December 1805, he defeated Austria, Prussia, and Russia. He redrew the map of Europe and reduced the size of those three great powers. France bloated into an empire with the annexation of the Lowlands, Switzerland, and much of northern Italy. With other states forced to be allies, Napoleon's empire was virtually the size Charlemagne's had been. The next year, the Holy Roman Empire vanished into history, although the Habsburgs kept an imperial title as emperors of Austria. Bonaparte controlled much of the rest of Europe through puppets, usually his relatives propped up on thrones. He ruled over the largest collection of Europeans up to that point in history.

Great Britain, however, refused to concede Europe to Napoleonic supremacy. Britain's worldwide possessions and growing economy gave it the ability to maintain hostilities with France until a means could be found to break up Napoleon's empire. Napoleon himself recognized the difficulty of maintaining an overseas empire. He had given up substantial possessions in the Americas by selling France's claims to the Louisiana Territory to the United States in 1803 (the indigenous natives who lived there were not consulted, of course). Some weeks before Austerlitz, the British navy decisively crushed the French fleet at the Battle of Trafalgar on 21 October 1805. At that point France could not even control the waters off its own coast. This naval victory notwithstanding, Britain lacked the forces to invade France directly.

Thus, one power dominated the land, the other the sea. Neither could or would end the conflict. Instead, indirectly, the British supported a festering revolt in Spain after 1808. In turn, Napoleon tried to damage the British economy with his "**Continental System**," which established an embargo prohibiting all trade between his empire and any allies of the British Empire. Too many Europeans, however, had become addicted to the products of the global economy (including tobacco and coffee) that often came through British middlemen. Connections between the West and the world were increasingly essential to decisions made in the West. Napoleon's higher prices, heavy taxes, and French chauvinism (arrogant nationalism) alienated many people.

Moreover, the empires of Prussia, Austria, and Russia had merely been defeated, not destroyed. They waited for an opportunity to strike back. In 1812, Russia's refusal to uphold the embargo broke the Continental System. In reaction, Napoleon decided to teach that country a lesson: he invaded with the largest army yet assembled in human history—probably half a million men. Unfortunately for his grand plans, the Russians avoided a decisive battle. Napoleon found himself and his huge army stranded in a burned-out Moscow with winter approaching. As Napoleon retreated, his forces suffered disaster. Only a few tens of thousands survived to return from the Russian campaign.

Although Napoleon rapidly raised another army, his dominance was doomed. Other generals had learned his strategy and tactics too well. Peoples all over Europe rebelled, aided by British money and troops. The insignificant War of 1812 declared by the Americans did not distract the British enough to do Napoleon any good at all. He kept on fighting. The Battle of Nations near Leipzig in October 1813 brought many peoples together against French domination. More than one hundred thousand men died in one of the largest battles in history. Napoleon remained unbeaten but had to retreat from Germany. By March 1814, coalition armies had invaded France and finally forced Napoleon to abdicate.

Incredibly, Napoleon managed to overcome even this major defeat. For a few short months, Napoleon sat in imprisonment on the island of Elba off the coast of Italy. Then one night he escaped, and for "Napoleon's Hundred Days" he once more ruled as emperor of France. The coalition refused to accept Bonaparte as the leader of a great power. British and Prussian forces finally, ultimately, once and for all defeated Napoleon at the **Battle of Waterloo** (18 June 1815) in Belgium. This time the British shipped the captured emperor off to exile on the barren island of St. Helena in the South Atlantic, where he died a few years later of a stomach ulcer.

Everyone knew that an era had ended. Millions of lives and vast amounts of property had been lost in rebellion, repression, and wars, causing the suffering of whole societies. The victors faced the questions of what should be retained and what should be avoided (see map 10.1). The leaders of the French Revolution had proclaimed their inspiration from previous intellectual and political revolutions. The Scientific Revolution granted Europeans new power to understand and control nature. The Enlightenment freed them to play with new ideas that overthrew authority. New governments, both absolutist and democratic, gave Western states still greater abilities to fight with one another and conquer foreign peoples. Revolutions in Britain, America, and France provided examples of how to change regimes. The legacies of scientists, *philosophes*, monarchs, republicans, and radicals worked themselves out on the ruins of Napoleon's empire. Few suspected at

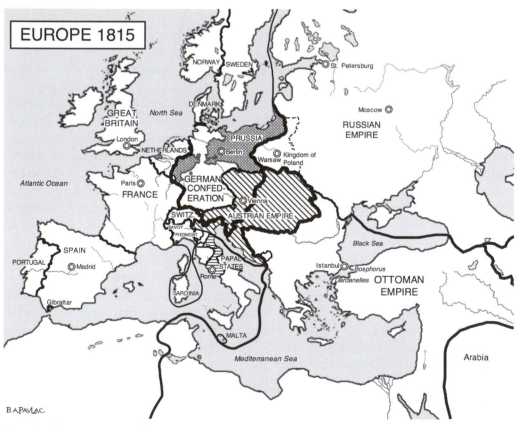

Map 10.1.   Europe, 1815

that time how the next century would transform the West more than any previous century had.

Review: *How did war alter the French Revolution and cause Napoleon's rise and fall?*

Response:

CHAPTER 11

Mastery of the Machine

The Industrial Revolution, 1764 to 1914

Historians call the rough hundred years after the fall of Napoleon the **nine-teenth century** (1815–1914). The period forms a convenient unit framed by the Wars of the Coalition and World War I. Between those two world-wide conflicts Western civilization went through numerous changes in its economic practices, political ideologies, social structures, and scientific ideas. Probably the most important change was the one brought about by the **Industrial Revolution** (1764–1914), or economies dominated by manufacturing via machines in factories. Just as the French Revolution opened up new possibilities, so did the Industrial Revolution. The rise of new technologies and business practices fashioned the most profound economic change in human history since the invention of agriculture. The increasing sophistication of machines both supplied more power to the masters of those devices and dominated the lives of those who worked with them. Machinery also propelled Western civilization to further heights of prosperity and power. Under the leadership of new political ideologies, people increasingly abandoned the quaint agricultural ways of the past and forged the now-familiar industrialized society of our modern world.

FACTS OF FACTORIES

The basic structures of civilization had been fairly stable since the prehistoric Neolithic agricultural revolution. For thousands of years, the overwhelming majority of people, the lower classes, had the assigned task of producing enough food for themselves, plus a little more for their betters who did not farm. Only the few privileged people of the upper classes and middle classes were not involved in tilling the land or raising animals. The environment—insects and rodents, drought, flood, storm, frost—often threatened to destroy the farmers' crops. Whole families labored from dawn to dusk most of the days of the year just to scrape by.

Farming started to become much easier with the **Scientific Agricultural Revolution**. This revolution began around 1650 in England. Science transformed farming life, offering more control over the environment than ever before. Scientists recommended different crops to plant, such as potatoes and maize (corn), because they grew more efficiently and were more nutritious. They developed new kinds of fertilizer (improving on manure) and new methods of land management (improving crop rotation and irrigation), reducing the amount of fallow land. Fences went up as landlords enclosed their fields, consolidating them into more efficient units.

Thus, fewer farmers could produce more food than before. With fewer jobs in agriculture to keep everyone employed, a huge social crisis threatened to overwhelm England. The last traditional protections for peasants of the medieval manor disappeared. Landlords threw tenants off the land that their families had worked for centuries. Long-standing social and economic relationships were severed, with few policies to replace them. The agricultural working class broke up. Even independent family farmers with small plots of land lost out when they could not compete against the improved larger estates.

At the same time, more food and better medical science allowed rapid population growth. As in ancient Rome after the Punic Wars, large numbers of people without land began to move to the cities, hoping for work. Others left England, emigrating to find more farmland, especially in the British colonies of North America. Yet exporting farm laborers could not solve Britain's unemployment rates and a threatening rebellion. Arriving in the nick of time was the Industrial Revolution, which turned many of the landless rural peasants into urban factory workers.

This revolution began in England. The United Kingdom possessed a number of inherent advantages, first being its position at the forefront of the Scientific Agricultural Revolution. Second, Britain's political system of elected representatives quickly adapted to the new economic options. Third, Non-Conformists (mostly firm Calvinists who refused to join the Church of England) put their efforts into commerce, finance, and industry. Lingering religious discrimination excluded them from civil service jobs and universities. So instead, the Calvinists' diligent "Protestant work ethic" (as later coined by sociologist Max Weber) grew the economy.

A fourth advantage for England was its diverse imperial possessions. In the immediate vicinity, England bound Scotland, Wales, and Ireland into the United Kingdom of Great Britain. Across the oceans, Britain held Canada, islands in the Caribbean, Egypt, South Africa, and India. Great Britain ruled the world's largest empire in the eighteenth century, despite the loss in 1783 of the colonies that became the United States. The British navy, so successful in the Wars of the Coalitions against Napoleon, ensured the safety of British merchant ships and their cargos around the globe. Far-flung territories provided many products, from cotton to tobacco. Drinks of imported coffee, tea, and cocoa fueled the schemes of businessmen in cafés.

Financial innovations gave the English yet more advantages over competitors. One innovation was the invention of **insurance,** such as that offered by Lloyd's of London, then and today. Insurance companies would calculate risk to business enterprises, charge according to the odds that those risks would come to pass, and generally make substantial profits. By covering losses caused by natural disasters, theft, and piracy, insurance made investing less risky and more profitable. After 1694, the Bank of England also provided a secure and ready source of capital, which was backed by the government itself. The large number of trading opportunities within the empire minimized capitalist risk. Altogether, Britain possessed the first opportunity to seize upon the new industrial innovations.

Finally, three new developments in energy, transportation, and machinery combined to produce the Industrial Revolution. First, improved energy came from harnessing the power of falling water with water mills. The second development, transportation, overcame the constant problem of bad roads. The technology for paved roads had been neglected since ancient Roman times. Since the fall of Rome, most roads in Europe were dirt paths that became impassable mud trenches whenever it rained. Travel became significantly easier, however, with the building of **canals**, or water roads. During the eighteenth century, many canals were excavated to connect towns within the country. These canals were highly suitable in soggy England because they actually became more passable with rainy weather. Since barges were buoyant in water, one mule on a towpath could pull many more times the tonnage of goods than a horse with a wagon on a muddy path could. While most canals have long since been filled in or forgotten, for a few decades they were the very latest in technologically efficient transport.

The third improvement, machines, vastly increased the power of human beings. The first mechanical devices were invented to make textiles, a huge market considering that all Europeans needed clothing for warmth, comfort, decency, and dignity. At the beginning of the Industrial Revolution, the best technology for making thread was the single spindle on a spinning wheel, as known from fairy tales. Weaving cloth was done by hand on a loom, pushing thread through weft and warp.

A series of inventions through the eighteenth century multiplied the efficiency of one woman at the spinning wheel and loom. The breakthrough of James Hargreaves' **spinning jenny** (1764) used several shuttles to make thread from raw fibers. The name "Jenny" probably came from a version of "engine," not a daughter's name. Hargreaves certainly "borrowed" important concepts from other inventors and businessmen, who, in turn, took his jenny and made money off of it. Richard Arkwright, a former wig maker, combined his own and others' inventions into the best powered spinning and weaving machines.

Inventors protected their inventions with patents, government-backed certificates protecting an inventor's rights. Affording the application process, however, and then defending patent rights in court often proved too costly. The overriding economic benefits to society might also deny an inventor rights to his profits. Various inventors sued Arkwright for patent infringement and won. Nevertheless, Hargreaves died a pauper, Arkwright a wealthy knight. The bold, lucky, and unscrupulous often succeeded in making fortunes, while rightful inventors died in poverty and obscurity.

Women's opportunities in the Industrial Revolution were limited. Men did most of the inventing of and investing in machines. Women lacked the opportunities to enter apprenticeships, gain education and training, or attain jobs that would lead them to develop skills in advanced technology. Likewise, political, economic, and social structures excluded women from positions of authority and influence. Such had been the status of most women since the beginning of civilization. As machines became more important, men even argued that women lacked the ability to be mechanically minded; men alone were suited for tinkering with technology. But machines affected every woman's life, as women worked with them both inside and outside the home. In the nineteenth century, though, men remained masters of both women and the machines.

By combining all three innovations in energy, men like Arkwright therefore launched the Industrial Revolution, transportation, and machinery into the **factory** or (in British) the **mill system**. The alternative had been the cottage industry or putting-out method, functioning since the twelfth century. The merchants brought the raw materials to homes, where families used simple machines (such as the hand loom or spinning wheel) to manufacture (literally from the Latin "to make by hand") them into finished products. By the end of the late eighteenth century, however, merchants brought raw materials to a factory, which hired workers to run the expensive machines. This coordination increased efficiency and lowered prices. And as prices went down, demand went up, since more people could afford the machine-manufactured goods, which ranged from linen tablecloths to teacups. Moreover, as new industrial forms of artificial lighting such as the arc lamp were invented, shifts of workers could labor around the clock to get the maximum use out of the machines. Thus, capitalist industrial manufacturing emerged as investors funded the building of factories for profit.

A second wave of industrialization hit with the invention of steam power. The breakthrough came in 1769 when James Watt and Matthew Boulton assembled an efficient **steam engine**. They had adapted it from machine pumps to remove water from coal and iron mines (see figure 11.1). Coal had emerged as superior to previous materials that people burned for energy, namely plant and animal oils, wood, or peat. With innovation, the coal-fired steam engines vastly increased their energy output while their physical size shrank. By the 1830s, small steam engines on wagons with metal wheels running on tracks called **railroads** were transporting both goods and people (see figure 11.2). Trains on such railways soon eclipsed canals as the most efficient transportation, since they were cheaper to build and could run in places without plentiful water. Water travel remained important, though. Steam engines in ships meant faster, more certain transit across seas and oceans, further tying together markets of raw materials and manufacturing.

Some people resisted the rise of these machines, most famously the **Luddites**.

Figure 11.1. A massive coal breaker looms over an industrial wasteland. Inside, the coal from deep underground was broken down into smaller sizes for transport.

Today, that label applies to anyone who is suspicious of, or hostile to, technology. The term originated from the name of a (possibly) mythical leader of out-of-work artisans. The artisans' jobs of making things by hand were now obsolete. In the cold English winter of 1811–1812, bands of artisans broke into mills, destroyed the machines, and threatened the owners. The government, of course, shot, arrested, or hanged the troublemakers. Great Britain had a war to win against France and was not going to let a few unemployed louts threaten what promised to be enormous profit for the nation.

Nevertheless, the Luddite fear was natural and a foreseeable reaction to a change that left workers vulnerable. At the beginning of the nineteenth century, classical liberal economics (as described by Adam Smith) had increasingly been adopted by both business and government. Industrialization meant that only the entrepreneurial class who controlled large amounts of capital could create most jobs. Neither factory owners nor politicians felt much responsibility for those thrown out of work. Some economists, such as the English banker David Ricardo, told the poor that they should just work harder and be more thrifty. **Ricardo's "iron law of wages"** exploited even those who had jobs. With this economic theory, he advised that factory owners pay workers the bare minimum that permitted survival. Otherwise, he argued, workers might have too many children, only increasing the numbers of the poor and unemployed. The dominant economic theories at the beginning of the Industrial Revolution favored the new industrial capitalists over the new factory workers.

Figure 11.2.   Steam engines on railways (with windmills to pump water from far underground to store in a tank) enabled expansion across the American continent by the mid-nineteenth century.

Review: *How did inventions and capitalism produce the Industrial Revolution?*

Response:

LIFE IN THE BIG CITY

The division of society into capitalists and workers led Western civilization to become more dependent on cities than ever before. The populations of industrialized cities rapidly rose upward in a process called **urbanization**. By definition, cities had been central to civilization since its beginnings, but only a small minority of people had ever lived in them. Most people needed to be close to the land, where they could raise the food on which the few urban dwellers depended. After 1800, the invention of machines helped consolidate more people into urban life. Fewer jobs on the land meant that more people looked for work in the factories. Cities leapt up from villages and expanded into metropolitan complexes. The old culture of the small village where everyone knew everyone increasingly waned.

At first, the cities grew haphazardly, in fits and starts, with little planning or social cohesion. In many sections, people did not know their neighbors, while residents were paid little or had no employment at all. The result was slums of badly built and managed housing. Slums became dangerous places of increased drug use, crime, filth, and disease.

People founded public health and safety organizations to manage these problems. Firefighters became more professional. Likewise, modern **police** forces formed as a new kind of guardian to manage the lower classes. Law enforcement on the scale at which our modern urban police forces function had been unnecessary in earlier rural society. In small, stable rural villages, people had known all their neighbors, and therefore crime was limited by familiarity. In the anonymous urban neighborhood, though, crime by strangers inevitably increased. Of necessity, crime investigations required more care and scientific support. During the 1820s, Sir Robert Peel's "bobbies" (nicknamed after their founder) and their headquarters in Scotland Yard (named after the location) in London were merely the first of these new civil servants. Police forces insisted that only they could use violence within the urban community.

The concentrated numbers of new urban dwellers, which rose from hundreds of thousands into millions, also spewed out levels of pollution unknown to earlier civilization. Streets became putrid swamps, piled high with dumped rotting food and excrement. Major cities had tens of thousands of horses as the main mode of transportation, each producing at least twenty pounds of manure a day. Air became smog, saturated with the noxious fumes of factory furnaces, coal stoves, and burning trash. Infectious diseases such as dysentery, typhoid, and cholera (newly imported from India) plagued Western cities because of unsanitary conditions. Urban populations died by the thousands with new plagues fostered by industrialization.

Since disease was not confined by class boundaries to only the poorer districts, politicians found themselves pressured to look after the public health. Cemeteries were relocated from their traditional settings near churches to parklike settings on the city's fringes (in Paris, for example, the bones emptied from cemeteries were stacked up in huge underground caverns). Regulations prohibited raising certain animals or burning specific materials. The government paved roads, especially with the cheap innovative material of tar and gravel called asphalt or macadam (after its inventor, McAdam). City officials created **sanitation** organizations. People called garbagemen, refuse collectors, or sanitation engineers took trash to dumps. Freshwater supply networks replaced the old-fashioned wells, bringing in clean, drinkable water from reservoirs, while networks of sewers whisked dirty water away as workers hosed down the streets.

In this process, Western civilization perfected the greatest invention in human history: **indoor plumbing**, namely hot and cold running water and a toilet (or water closet). Such mundane items are often taken for granted by both historians and ordinary people. The Romans had public lavatories and baths, some medieval monasteries had interesting systems of water supply, and a few monarchs and aristocrats had unique plumbing built into a palace here or there. But since the fall of Rome, cleanliness had been too expensive for most people to bother with. Whether rich or poor, most people literally stank and crawled with vermin. In the nineteenth century, free-flowing water from public waterworks, copper pipes, gas heaters, valves, and porcelain bowls brought the values of hygienic cleanliness to people at all levels of wealth. Of course, not all worries can go down the drain or vanish with a flush; the waste merely accumulated somewhere else in the environment. Most people, unconcerned, have easily ignored such messy realities. Regardless, more and more nineteenth-century westerners enjoyed the cleanliness and comforts of lavatories. With the new plumbing, plagues like cholera, typhoid, and dysentery began to diminish and even disappear in the West.

As industrialized cities grew in size and safety, their inhabitants accumulated wealth previously unimagined in human history. Some of those riches were spent on culture: literature, art, and music. Some were spent on showing off: bigger houses, fancier fashion, and new foods. Because a few earned so much more than the rest, the Industrial Revolution initiated a major transition of class structures in Western society. At the bottom, supporting the upper and middle classes, was the hard labor of the **working class** (also called the proletariat after the ancient Roman underclass), made up of fewer and fewer farmers and more and more factory workers. The upper classes became less defined by birth once owning land ceased to be the most productive way to gain wealth. A successful businessman could create a fortune that dwarfed the lands and rents of a titled aristocrat. The *nouveau riche* (newly wealthy) set the tone for the upper crust.

Meanwhile, the middle class became less that of the merchants and artisans and more that of managers and professionals: the white-collar worker who supervised the blue-collar workers in the factories. The colors reflect class distinctions: white for more expensive, bleached and pressed fabric, blue for cheaper and darker cloth that showed less dirt. Physicians, lawyers, and professors likewise earned enough to qualify for the "upper"-middle-class way of life. Most people came to idealize middle-class values: a separate home as a refuge from the rough everyday world; a wife who did not have to work outside the home, if at all; the freedom to afford vacations; and comfortable retirement in old age.

Essentially, these middle-class values were new, unusual, and limited only to a very few. These so-called **family values** were not at all traditional, as some social conservatives today would like people to think. Throughout civilized history, most men and women have actually worked at home or close to home on the land. And the entire family worked together: husband, wife, and children, perhaps with a few others in servile status. Most people never thought of vacation trips, only restful religious holidays. Those who survived into old age usually had to keep working to earn their keep. For a model of true traditional family life, look to the Old Order Amish or Pennsylvania Dutch, who live today in communities stretching from Pennsylvania to Illinois. These people have consciously rejected the Industrial Revolution and its technologies. They cannot ignore it, as their young people are tempted toward the ease that the wealth of modern life provides. Nonetheless, their values of hard-working farm families were the family values passed down through the millennia of Western civilization before the Industrial Revolution.

By moving people away from farm communities, the Industrial Revolution generated serious tensions within society that few people wanted to recognize. The domestic sphere was damaged, as people worked outside the home. Social mobility became more volatile, as it was easier to rise but also to fall in class status. One major business failure could send not just the capitalist owner, but also many thousands of workers, into the poorhouse. For workers at the bottom of society there were few protections (see below). Businesses rotated through boom and bust, good times and bad times, hirings and firings. Whole societies became subject to market cycles, which economists have never been able to predict or prevent, despite their professorial proclamations.

Over time, though, the Industrial Revolution did seem to confirm the Western notion of progress. Some people suffered, and still suffer, under the system. But by and large, things for most people usually got better enough to prevent social collapse. The quality of life improved. More people had more possessions. More people became free from ignorance and disease. More people had access to more opportunities than ever before in human history. Before the Industrial Revolution, most people stayed at the level at which they were born. Capitalist industrial manufacturing, it seemed, had unleashed the possibility for anyone to live the good life, as least as far as creature comforts went. The only questions seemed to be: What did those at the bottom need to be able to move up, and how long would they need to wait?

The modern **consumer economy**, where unknown distant workers manufactured most things that people used and purchased, only stoked impatience. Gone were the neighborhood shoemaker, blacksmith, or farmer. Instead, distant capitalists encouraged consumers to buy stuff, even if they did not need it. To accomplish this, **advertising** became a significant tool for economic innovation. It began with simple signs in stores where products were bought. Soon, advertising was on every package and on the side of every road and byway. Advertisers began to create needs to promote consumer purchases and grow the economy. They defined new forms of proper usage for the various classes, in hygiene, fashion, and leisure. By the end of the nineteenth century, majestic department stores served as shopping meccas for the rich and middle classes in urban centers, while the lower classes could buy stuff at the "five-and-dime" discount chains. Even Christian holidays felt the impact, as Christmas (the celebration of Jesus' birth) began to outshine Easter (the celebration of Jesus' resurrection) because its ritual of buying and giving gifts suited consumerism.

Also by the late nineteenth century, a wave of industrial innovation intensified the revolution in new areas. The mastery of electricity and steelmaking allowed cities to grow even larger, not only across the landscape, but also up into the sky. Buildings could be raised to amazing heights and dimensions because of steel girder skeletons, electric elevators, and lightbulbs (1879). Church steeples had been the tallest urban structures since the Middle Ages. Business towers of the modern **skyscraper** now began to define the modern city skyline. Below the earth, subways (London in the 1860s, Paris in 1900, New York in 1904) propelled workers to and from their homes and factories. Communication through telegraph (1829), then telephone (1876), and finally radio (1906) tied the world more tightly together.

All Western economies needed power to function. Coal from the ground gained another competitor in another mineral, petroleum. This "rock-oil" has since become so important to human beings that it has claimed for itself the sole word *oil*. The first **oil** well in Titusville, Pennsylvania, in 1859 led the way in supplying industrial society with a sufficient amount of the material. People first valued oil as a fuel that was refined into kerosene for lamps. Kerosene replaced whale oil, which had replaced other plant and animal oils.

Scientists soon discovered how to easily manipulate petroleum for more than just its burning and lubricating properties. Its associated by-product, natural gas, became a common fuel for lighting, heating, and cooking. Oil's combustible properties likewise beckoned scientists to experiment with it as a fuel source for machines. It began to replace coal.

At the nineteenth century's end came an invention that would transform industrial people's mobility: the **internal combustion engine**. Gasoline, originally considered a waste product from refining oil for kerosene, fueled the most common version. This new engine became a more powerful, smaller, and therefore more mobile motor than the steam engine. The internal combustion engine placed on a frame with pneumatic tires became the **automobile**, which traveled on roadways. When attached to spin a propeller, the gas engine metamorphosed into the **airplane** on large airfoils that flew through the sky. The two Wright brothers who owned a bicycle shop in Dayton, Ohio, assembled and launched the first modern aircraft at Kitty Hawk, North Carolina, in December 1903. Both the car and the plane would revolutionize travel in the twentieth century, outpacing the success of the train.

Oil also became the foundation of a new **petrochemicals** industry. The first businesses made dyes for coloring fabric and then advanced to fertilizers and medicines. By 1900, researchers formulated petroleum into Bakelite, the first plastic. Bakelite could take on new shapes, forms, strengths, and even colors. Plastic continued to unleash waves of inventiveness. At the time, no one worried about how the burning, refining, or disposing of petroleum products might bring their own problems.

Review: How did urbanization develop a modern society?

Response:

> factories
> social revolution
>   plumbing

CLEANING UP THE MESS

Politically, the nineteenth century began not with a leap forward, but with a step backward. By the time the French Revolution was over in 1815, many thought that its ideas of liberty, equality, and fraternity were a thing of the past. The **Romantic Movement** rejected the harsh results of the Enlightenment's rationality and technology's advance. The Romantics produced poetry, stories, and art that expressed a longing for a simpler time, whether a reimagined past or a fantasy fairyland. The French and Industrial Revolutions together brought too much change. A retreat to nature seemed preferable to the dirty, seething cities. Traditional ruling elites seemed better than crude upstarts like Bonaparte. The Corsican's defeat at first comforted traditionalists that all would return to their version of normal.

The victors over Napoleon convened the **Congress of Vienna** (1814–1815) to reorder the chaos left by France's conquest of Europe. Over the course of nine months, hundreds of leaders and diplomats from all of Europe discussed the future (even while dancing and drinking at the many parties). Leading the assembly in its deliberations was Prince **Clemens von Metternich** (b. 1773–d. 1859), the first minister for the absolutist Habsburg emperor of Austria. Metternich and others developed the political concept of *conservatism*, namely, the policy that advocated preserving as much as possible of traditional political, social, and cultural structures. Under Metternich's leadership, the congress allowed only such alterations in the old system as were necessary for European stability. It restored most of the old dynasties to power, dumping Bonaparte's relatives and puppets and sending them into exile or retirement. The restorations ranged from the beheaded Louis XVI's brother as the new king of France to the pope ruling once more over the Papal States. A few citizens protested, but all over Europe princes reaffirmed absolutism by shredding constitutions.

The congress also reasserted the balance of power between the great powers of Europe: Britain, France, Austria, Prussia, and Russia. France had too often tried to conquer Europe. The victors strengthened states on France's borders to help prevent any further aggression. Along the northeastern border of France, the United

Kingdom of the Netherlands combined the Dutch and the Belgians under the aristocratic dynasty of Orange, newly elevated to royalty. Along the southeastern border, the melded Kingdom of Sardinia-Savoy-Piedmont barred the Alpine access to Italy. Austria held sway over the rest of northern Italy. Directly east of France, Prussia acquired a conglomeration of territories in the Rhineland. Prussia and Austria took joint leadership of a new, albeit weakened, German Confederation that reconstituted the hundreds of small principalities of the dead Holy Roman Empire into a few dozen. These measures effectively hemmed in France. No one thought to ask whether the peoples of these newly drawn states wanted their assigned roles in the balance of power.

In an attempt to prevent more warfare and revolutions, the Congress of Vienna tried two new alliance mechanisms. Previously, alliances had lasted for only the duration of wartime. After 1815, nations tried to use alliances to prevent war. First was the **Holy Alliance**, binding together the absolute rulers of Orthodox Russia, Roman Catholic Austria, and Lutheran Prussia in an odd burst of religious cooperation. This agreement called for the promotion of Christian charity and peace, yet it failed due to the power politics of tsar, emperor, and king.

The innovative **Quadruple Alliance** of Austria, Prussia, Russia, and Britain better maintained the reestablished order. For the first time, **collective security** provided an ongoing peacetime mechanism to prevent reckless wars between states. According to the doctrine of balance of power, states organized against one another only when one or more threatened the status quo. Collective security meant that all nations worked together regularly to maintain peace. After 1815, the regular meetings of great powers to produce international harmony became known as the Concert of Europe. The Quadruple Alliance provided the first international peacekeeping structure to solve civil disturbances in the lesser states of Europe and to prevent dangerous unrest among the peoples.

Although the Quadruple Alliance worked relatively well, Britain slowly began to withdraw. As the only great power with a substantial overseas empire, England was uncertain about its growing rivalry with Russia, the dominant Eurasian power. Meanwhile, the restored Bourbon dynasty in France regained its international respectability as it resisted reform and revolution. Thus, France gradually took England's place within the Concert of Europe. Europe settled into a few rare decades of international peace.

No Western ruler even contemplated including the distant United States of America. Yet America's example of republican government also showed to many that an alternative to absolutism was still possible. While strict social hierarchies appeared to be reasserted in Europe, the commoners remembered their access to power under the French revolutionary regime, however brief or illusory. The French proclamation of liberty and equality had not been realized by Napoleon's dictatorship, but the lower classes liked those ideas all the same. The bourgeoisie continued to accumulate wealth and demand more power for themselves. The aristocracy increasingly lost its purposeful social function. Even absolute monarchs had adopted many of Napoleon's and revolutionary France's methods precisely because they were so successful.

The idea of revolution simply would not disappear: people had already seen for themselves that political action could topple incompetent regimes. Those who supported revolutions were usually categorized as liberals. The political concept of **liberalism** stood for embracing change in order to broaden, as much as reasonable, people's political, social, and cultural opportunities. Liberalism appealed to the middle classes rising with the Industrial Revolution. Its ideas encouraged the expansion of their political and economic power and influence.

The beliefs held decades ago by liberals on the left and conservatives on the right of the political spectrum were quite different from what they are today (see table 11.1). The nineteenth-century conservatives embraced absolute monarchy with its strong interventionist bureaucracy, mercantilistic economic theory, distinctions among social classes (with aristocrats at the top), and a close cooperation of state and church (called the union of throne and altar). In contrast, the nineteenth-century liberals called for constitutional and republican government, laissez-faire economic theory, equality before the law for all citizens (perhaps even including women), and separation of church and state with religious toleration. These dichotomies do not necessarily fit well with today's issues and labels. Usually, only the basic attitudes of a leftist acceptance of change and a right-wing resistance to change have remained appropriate. So political identification should always focus on specifics, not labels.

Nevertheless, the basic **political parties** of modern European democracies became organized around these competing ideologies. Political parties offered structure both to win in elections and, once elected, to cast votes in representative bodies. As more people accumulated substantial wealth and property, they wanted to influence political decisions that could affect their ability to make money. Taxation, regulations, and monetary strength became issues of national debate. As a result, the new wealth accelerated the growth of political parties. Over the course of the century both sides in many countries used the methods of parliamentarianism. Liberals tried to reduce government regulations, while conservatives sought to preserve advantageous taxation. In the cities, political parties that controlled the levers of power and patronage operated so smoothly for their constituents that they themselves earned the name "machines." Political parties with their permanent leadership, mass membership, and enforcement of discipline at the polls became essential to the functioning of representative government.

Throughout the nineteenth century, the conservatives retained their dominance in most places. The propertied people of lineage wanted to stay in charge, sharing

Table 11.1. Views of Western Political Parties in the Nineteenth Century

Conservatism	Liberalism
Absolute monarchy	Parliamentarianism
Social class distinctions	Equality of citizens
Aristocratic and upper class support	Capitalist and middle class support
Mercantilism	Laissez-faire/classical liberal economics
Union of throne and altar	Separation of church and state

Note: The issues important in the nineteenth century are not necessarily those that matter today. Then and now, conservatism tends to resist change, while liberalism promotes it.

power with only the new rich capitalists. But politics changed without too much violence in England, which already had basic constitutional and republican structures. Majorities in Parliament bounced back and forth between the first two significant political parties, aptly named Liberals (nicknamed Whigs in England and America) and Conservatives (called Tories even today in Britain). The Whig **Reform Bill of 1832**, for instance, appeased the middle classes by removing some of the worst antiquated structures for parliamentary elections and doubling the electorate to about 20 percent of the population. Working-class citizens then launched the Chartist movement, in which they petitioned, marched, and demonstrated to get representation for themselves. Although the Chartist movement largely failed and vanished after 1848, Parliament slowly legislated reforms to further open up political participation (see figure 11.3). By 1884, the British had reached universal suffrage for men, meaning all adult male citizens had the right to vote. Despite expectations of social revolution, voting and democratic institutions still left the privileged wealthy in charge, much as they always had been since the beginning of civilization. Politics opened the doors of access to power to only a few more people.

On the European continent, meanwhile, liberals resorted to revolutionary action as a force for political change. The revived absolute monarchies allowed very few possibilities for reform through the ballot box. France in particular kept breaking out in revolutionary fervor. Without the same traditions and institutions as Britain had to channel the violence of political change, criticism of the regime all too easily escalated first into riots and then into rebellion. To break conservative dominance, liberals often felt compelled to resort to revolutionary violence. Armed clashes flashed on the barricades, with soldiers on one side and bourgeoisie, workers, and students on the other. This violence recast the regimes, even if it did not always improve them. And once France had erupted into revolution, more outbreaks exploded throughout the rest of Europe in 1830, 1848, and 1870.

Figure 11.3. The British Parliament buildings were built during the nineteenth century in a Romantic style imitating Gothic architecture.

The **Revolutions of 1830** were the first to significantly affect European politics. In July, the French people deposed the absolutist-inclined King Charles X and replaced him with the more liberal King Louis-Philippe. The Dutch and the Belgians took the opportunity to split the united realm into the separate countries of the Netherlands and **Belgium**. The Belgians, in turn, remained themselves divided between French and Dutch (Flemish) speakers. In Austria, the conservative Metternich wanted to invade and force the new countries to reunite, to maintain the Congress of Vienna's decisions. The other members of the Quadruple Alliance would not cooperate. Rather, the great powers recognized Belgium as a sovereign state and signed a treaty that guaranteed its inviolable neutrality. Any country's attack on Belgium would then be a violation of international law and trigger war with the other great powers. In eastern Europe, the Poles, who had been granted by the Congress of Vienna a "kingdom" technically separate but ruled by the Russian tsar, tried to free themselves entirely from Russian domination. Sadly, they lost miserably, and the Russian reprisal erased any political liberty the Polish had enjoyed. Other efforts by Germans and Italians in certain principalities, as well as the Spanish and Portuguese, managed to secure only a handful of meager liberal reforms.

The **Revolutions of 1848** sparked by France were even more widespread and, initially, successful. In February, the French had tired of the Bourbons, with their tendencies to incompetence and tyranny. They tossed Louis-Philippe off the throne and proclaimed the Second Republic (1848–1852). Elsewhere in Europe, many rulers briefly backed down before revolutionary demands. In Austria, Metternich and his mentally deficient emperor, Ferdinand I, both resigned. The new eighteen-year-old Emperor Francis-Joseph I (r. 1848–1916) promised a constitution. Hungarians declared their independence from the Habsburg monarchy. Italians took up arms against their own Habsburg absolutism. The Prussian king accepted a constitution. Many Germans came together at a parliament in Frankfurt to better unify the German people under constitutional authority. Unfortunately for German liberals, a lack of leadership and squabbling over methods and goals slowed progress. Before long, European rulers realized that most of their military remained obedient, while liberal politicians possessed very few armed forces. By the summer of 1849, armies commanded by loyal generals had restored most monarchs to their absolutist thrones at the cost of much bloodshed.

France was not quite done with revolution. First, however, the hastily arranged democracy of the Second Republic quickly degenerated into the Second Empire (1852–1871) under the dictatorship of Louis Napoleon, the nephew of Napoleon Bonaparte. Louis took the name Emperor Napoleon III (by number recognizing the "reign" of Napoleon's son, who had died years earlier as a pampered prisoner in Schönbrunn). One of Napoleon III's few major innovations was to rebuild Paris with broad boulevards. His original intention was that the wide streets would allow his troops to quickly move through the city and, if necessary, break any bourgeois barricades. Its real consequence was to open up Paris for growth and development as one of the leading urban centers in Europe. Napoleon III's imperial rule did not bring lasting peace and stability. It was failed foreign policy rather than domestic insurrection, however, that ended Emperor Napoleon III's reign.

Napoleon III recklessly declared war on Prussia, which began the Franco-Prussian War (see below). France's humiliating defeat led to a brief struggle over the nation's political destiny. Most of the country recognized a moderate-conservative **Third Republic** (1871–1945). At the same time, an organized group of liberals and radicals in the capital proclaimed the **Paris Commune** (March–May 1871). The commune tried to establish a state of complete equality and social justice. Instead, republican forces of moderation and conservatism crushed this effort, using Napoleon III's boulevards to successfully invade the city. The victorious Third Republican government killed or executed more than twenty thousand and exiled another seven thousand Communards. After this reactionary bloodletting, comparable to the radical Reign of Terror a century earlier, the French settled into a functional republican system.

After 1848, both liberalism and conservatism were quite shaken. A new generation of artists and writers offered skeptical and critical portrayals of society called realism and naturalism, replacing the optimistic hopes of the Romantics. Realists described the common social and political problems of the day, while the naturalists focused on the most tragic and harsh aspects of the changing industrialized society. In the second half of the nineteenth century, many conservative princes and politicians accepted both the necessity and inevitability of some change and began to adopt liberal platforms. Also, as will be explained in chapter 12, they learned to use the originally liberal idea of nationalism for their own aims. By taking the lead on constitutions, social reform, and business opportunities, conservatives could regulate what they saw as the inevitable process of progress. The German philosopher Friedrich **Nietzsche** (b. 1844–d. 1900), however, doubted such progress. He proclaimed the doom of Western civilization unless it recognized the moral hypocrisy of its failed doctrines of Christianity. Nietzsche suggested that the human will's desire for power offered the only certain path for the future.

The power of the industrial age certainly made it easier to kill people. Armies could be raised and equipped more quickly and could attack more efficiently. The industrialization of war increased the participation of the lower and middle classes, which made them agitate for greater political participation, as seen many times throughout history since the Greeks. At the same time, industrialization and the resultant wealth produced smaller-scale violence over political disputes. **Guerrilla warfare** (Spanish for "little war," adopted from Spain's resistance against Napoleon) became more common. Guerrillas were irregular forces, neither recruited nor drafted, nor trained and uniformed like the professional soldiers of modern industrial armies. Instead, guerrillas were usually volunteers defending their homeland, moving easily in and out of civilian populations. With their smaller and less-well-equipped numbers, guerrilla bands were too weak and too few to survive open battle against well-armed and drilled armies. They succeeded best in sneak attacks. Guerrillas gained access to more weapons and supplies through the manufacturing capacity and transportation options introduced by the Industrial Revolution.

The other form of political violence enabled by the industrial revolution was *terrorism*. Terrorists used lethal violence to achieve their political ends, usually targeting civilians (mostly because noncombatants are easier to kill than trained, equipped, and alert armed forces). Industrialization enabled terrorists to travel, both to acquire their weapons and training, and then to reach their targets. Civilized regimes resented and feared the terrorists' use of violence, since the modern states considered the use of violence their own unique privilege. Not powerful enough to have armies or even guerrilla forces, terrorists resort to murder and mayhem on a small scale to attain political power, usually to benefit a national group or a political idea. A terrorist without an ideology was a criminal. Yet a terrorist who succeeded could ascend to be a statesman of a body politic.

Bombings and assassinations, consequently, multiplied in the nineteenth century. The most famous terrorists in the nineteenth century were those who believed in *anarchism*, the idea that if the growing industrialized and bureaucratized societies were destroyed, a utopian agricultural society would appear. Anarchists blew up government offices and killed leaders to undermine the structures of political trust and obedience that held societies together. Within a few years of the turn of the twentieth century, anarchists had killed a president of the United States, a prime minister of Spain, a tsar of Russia, a king of Italy, and an empress of Austria. Despite these murderous successes, most people failed to welcome anarchy. Western civilization's basic political divisions of right and left endured, while little today remains of anarchism.

Review: *How did competing political ideologies offer alternatives in the nineteenth century?*

Response:

liberalism
conservalism

Enlightment→ Romantic Movement
↓
Nationalism

FOR THE WORKERS

Conservatives and liberals frequently confused anarchism with *socialism*, although socialism was a very different movement. Many intentionally promoted this confusion, hoping to associate the terrorist anarchists with the socialists and imply that the latter were violent also. Part of the problem was the wide diversity of socialists. There existed, and still exist, many socialisms, although many Americans today often lump them all together as one collective bad thing. Quite simply, socialism in all its forms wanted to improve workers' rights and lives. Socialists tried to awaken a class consciousness, an awareness of what workers under these new conditions shared in common. Different kinds of socialism basically offered workers an alternative organizing principle to those of the liberals of the middle classes and the conservatives of the upper classes. What could be bad about that?

Power to the workers, the possibility of sharing power with the masses, threatened both liberals and conservatives. They feared, to some extent correctly, that giving more wealth, money, and votes to the working classes would mean less for them. If workers had an effective voice, the freedom of middle and upper classes to do what they wanted to do would be hemmed in. They might have to pay higher taxes; they might make fewer profits; they might have to rub shoulders with social inferiors in shops and churches; they might have to ask for the votes of the majority of all adults.

So both liberal and conservative governments of the nineteenth century often supported business leaders in resisting socialism in any form. Governments have protected ownership of real estate since the beginning of civilization, originally to benefit the few who possessed most of the farmland. Meanwhile, peasants called for land reform, since all humanity deserved a share in creation. In the industrial age, factories became the most important places of wealth creation. Factories more obviously belonged to those whose investments financed their construction. Politicians and managers passed laws and used force to intimidate workers, usually calling it "law and order" or "protection of property rights." Workers called for a fair share of wealth, even if they lacked access to capital. Workers organized, demonstrated, and used violence to change the industrial system, calling it "people's justice." For capitalists, the profits generated by the modern industrialized state justified beatings, arrests, and executions. For workers, the exploitation suffered under the factory system excused vandalism, murders, and bombings.

The Industrial Revolution was transforming society regardless. Social roles were in flux and traditional roles based on rural relationships were disappearing. People lost a sense of "knowing their place." Then along came the socialists, advocating social justice and trying to create a more fair society based on a more equal distribution of wealth. Many socialists also argued for granting equal rights to women and for protecting women and children from being harmed by economic necessity. Socialists rejected classical liberal economics and argued for better ways to invest capital and reap profit.

Many workers found socialism more attractive than either liberalism or conservatism because it promised to relieve their misery. Factory owners and managers vigorously exploited workers at the beginning of the Industrial Revolution. Modern lighting and machines meant factories operated around the clock, so workers sweated away in shifts lasting between ten and fifteen hours, with few breaks. Holidays were rare and weekends nonexistent. Lack of education or connections prevented laborers from finding better work than that in factories or mines. Ricardo's "iron law of wages," where owners paid workers as little as possible, resulted in whole families toiling away in factories in order to make ends meet. Also, because women and children were paid less for the same work done by men, factory owners employed larger numbers of them. The lives of worker families focused on the capitalist's factory, not the domestic fireplace. Indeed, the hearth vanished entirely for most, since available housing was in crowded, unsafe, and unsanitary tenements, ramshackle collections of small apartments.

Between the home and factory, wretched homes were often better than the dangerous workplaces. Stale air and loud noise were common health hazards. Whirring gears and belts crushed slow fingers and tore off errant arms. Long days only increased the fatigue and carelessness that allowed accidents. Injuries on the job were the problem of the victim, since worker's compensation or even the ability to sue owners for negligence did not exist. The only alternative to working in a factory was being arrested for the "crime" of poverty and being forced to work in the poorhouse and prisons. Many of the awful conditions faced by the working class are chronicled in that classic holiday chestnut, Dickens' *A Christmas Carol*.

The domination of machines became more relentless at the beginning of the twentieth century. The Industrial Revolution culminated in the perfection of the conveyor belt system and the invention of interchangeable parts. This innovation led to modern mass manufacturing with **assembly-line production**. Henry Ford used it first in the manufacturing of his Model T car in 1905. Workers focused on narrow, repetitive tasks that reduced the time to make a car from a day and a half to an hour and a half. The myth put forward and often believed today is that Ford increased his workers' pay so that they could all afford the cars. In fact, he raised the wages because the workers needed the incentive to work through the mindless repetition of modern production. Ford's policies at his auto factories nevertheless finally began a trend toward increased wages and benefits for workers.

Such concessions were too little too late for workers, many of whom had turned to socialism. Socialists proposed their own solutions to solve the workers' plight, since in the century and a half from the spinning jenny to the Model T, factory owners and capitalists had been unwilling to help workers prosper. A half-dozen separate socialist trends competed against the laissez-faire attitudes of the industrial capitalist manufacturers.

One, *utopian socialism*, called for improvements for workers, often explicitly based on economic facts, historical trends, and even moral visions. Historians have labeled it "utopian" because these socialists dreamed of an ideal society, along the lines described in literature about imaginary states called utopias. The French nobleman Count Henry de Saint-Simon published his call for socialism in 1825, *The New Christianity*, which appealed to the commands of Jesus. In that book, he gave voice to the original phrase of "from each according to his abilities, to each according to his needs." He also called for production to be for the general welfare, not private profit.

Perhaps the most famous utopian socialist was **Robert Owen** (b. 1771–d. 1858), a Scotsman who rose from poverty to become a wealthy capitalist factory owner. The "dark Satanic mills" disturbed Owen. In reaction, he began to argue that employers should treat their workers as humanely as possible. They should provide secure housing, good pay, shorter working hours, schools, banks, and shops. In consequence, he claimed, productivity would increase. Although he continued to make a profit, his attempt at model factory communities, such as at New Harmony, Indiana, were less than successful. Few businessmen or politicians paid attention.

The second variant of socialism, whether called **"scientific" socialism**, *Marxism*, or *communism*, would become enormously influential and creatively destructive. Karl Marx and Friedrich Engels initiated their version in 1848, the year of so many liberal and nationalist revolutions. Their publication of **The Communist Manifesto** began with the phrase "A specter is haunting Europe—the specter of Communism." At the time, few knew what these two were talking about. The *Manifesto* called for a proletarian (working-class) revolution. First, the communist revolutionaries would destroy the current regimes, abolishing capitalist private property and bourgeois sexist laws. Then, workers would control the "means of production" (factories, offices, farms) and construct a society of equality and prosperity.

In subsequent years, Marx expanded on this program and soon conceived a whole new way of understanding history. He expounded upon "scientific" laws that explained the past and the future. Borrowing from the dialectic syllogism applied by the German philosopher Hegel to history, Marx argued that all change in civilization had been the result of class struggle, what he called **dialectical materialism** (see diagram 11.1). In each historical period, a dominant class (such as the patricians in ancient Rome) had controlled the means of production. An opposite, or antithetical, group then rose in response (such as the rebellious class of the plebians). Their clash over economic power generated a new ruling and new subservient class. Marx claimed that this "scientific" study of history could be used in his own contemporary age to understand the dominant bourgeoisie and the exploited proletariat. A violent class conflict was inevitable, but this time the downtrodden would seize control of their destiny. The proletarians were to organize themselves for the forthcoming revolution and guide humanity to a new, more just society. Using "scientific" socialism, Marx claimed that humanity would attain communism, defined as a condition in which the state withered away, economic exploitation vanished, and all people lived in peace and harmony. Technically, then, communism has never yet been achieved.

As an explanation of historical change, Marx's vision was sloppy. Still, his program, whether called "scientific" socialism, Marxism, or communism, held great appeal. As a comprehensive belief system, it made sense of the past, present, and future in distinctly human terms. Marx rejected a belief in the afterlife, seeing God and religion as the equivalent of drugs used to keep the masses of workers tame. Despite Marxism's atheistic attitude, it offered hope to the oppressed and it provided an agenda as an inspirational principle for worker's organizations.

While planning for their revolution, however, Marxist organizers achieved very little for workers' rights. Some communists actually wanted the workers' lot to get worse, hoping to provoke rebellion by driving the workers to desperation. Still, Marxist socialism usually only contained the threat of potential violence. Even though some Marxists did associate with anarchists, these socialists actually carried out very little violence before 1917. They were supposed to wait for the collapse of bourgeois dominance to begin the revolt. In the meantime, workers still suffered.

Some "scientific" socialists began to revise Marxism because they wanted to improve the workers' conditions immediately. These revisionists agreed with Marx's historical analysis but became skeptical of the need for an actual revolution. The experience of France showed that revolutions often veered into uncontrolled violence and destruction.

The revisionists of Marxism offered a third version of socialism, called **social**

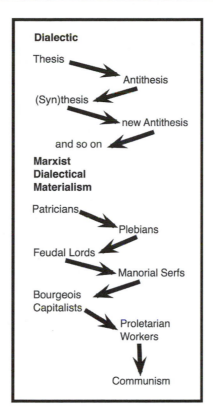

Diagram 11.1.   The dialectic, dating back to Aristotle, combines two pieces of information to create a third. The German philosopher Hegel applied the process to the history of ideas, suggesting that a dominant ideology (a thesis) provoked its opposite (an antithesis) and the two clashed to combine into a new synthesis. That synthesis thus became the new thesis, which generated its antithesis, continuing the process through history. Marx applied the concept to the classes that controlled the means of production. He predicted that the current situation, capitalists against the workers, would lead to a new utopia of communism and the end of history.

democracy or ***democratic socialism***. They argued that the predicted catastrophic class struggle could perhaps be avoided through slow, gradual reforms. Social democrats began to establish political parties to help workers. Since workers were the numeric majority of the electorate in industrialized nations, social democrats worked to get members elected to representative bodies, where they could then pass legislation to incrementally improve conditions for workers. For example, the Social Democratic Party in Germany (founded in 1869) and the British Labour Party (founded between 1881 and 1906) were the results of this revisionist socialism (and both were leading their nations' governments in 2005). Most Western nations, with the notable exception of the United States of America, have prominent social democratic parties.

The atheism of most "scientific" socialists contrasted with the fourth socialist movement, namely ***Christian socialism***. These socialists based their efforts on the

Christian call to "love thy neighbor." Jesus constantly preached about helping the poor and powerless and avoiding the sins of wealth. Pope Leo XIII in *Rerum Novarum* (*Of New Things*, 1891) specifically tried to find a middle ground between the private property absolutists and the more radical socialists. The Roman Catholic Church suggested that while property is a right to be protected, ownership included responsibility to the workers. The pope described the workers as miserably exploited by the unchecked greed of capitalism. He proclaimed that the dignity of human beings requires that workers deserve a just salary (not merely a barely livable one). Christian socialists rejected the utopian dreams of new communities and the atheistic historical views of Marxists and social democrats and instead offered a more moderate, even conservative, alternative. They founded organizations for distributing charity to the poor, for helping workers reach a decent living wage, or even for forming political parties to run for political office.

Some Christian socialists joined in a fifth kind of socialism, which was to organize **labor unions** (trade unions in Britain, syndicalism in France). ***Trade unionism*** originated out of self-help—workers themselves offering care for sick and old workers. They soon tried to demand better working conditions and pay. At first, liberals and conservatives passed laws prohibiting unions from protecting workers' interests. Or, in America, companies hired workers from many different nations so that they could not converse with one another and organize into unions (see figure 11.4).

Workers organized anyway. By the end of the century, unions were trying to use the strike (work stoppage) as a way to force managers into giving them better contracts. Unions carried out tens of thousands of strikes in industrialized nations in the last decades of the nineteenth century. The strikers hoped to gain public sympathy (through marches and picketing), instigate boycotts (refusal to buy the

Figure 11.4. This sign from a Pennsylvania coal mine illustrates the diversity of nationalities brought to build America's industry.

company's products), and prevent companies from hiring replacement workers (called "scabs" by the unionists). The companies, in turn, tried to break these strikes through force and, naturally, this violence provoked more violence. Before 1914 and World War I, the government almost always sided with the capitalist factory owners when fighting erupted.

A sixth variant of socialism finally came from the liberals and conservatives who had so long and so well represented the desires of the capitalists. The liberals in particular worried about keeping votes, as they saw workers flock to the rolls of socialist political parties. Both conservatives and liberals finally took some steps toward meeting the needs of workers at the end of the nineteenth century. The greatest measures were taken by the archconservative Chancellor Bismarck in Germany, who wanted economic stability and political order (see chapter 12). He openly practiced a *state socialism*, where the government helped workers. In the 1880s, while still vigorously opposing the growing Social Democratic Party, Bismarck passed laws providing for health insurance, work accident insurance, and even retirement pensions (social security) for German workers. In turn, England ended its inhumane poor laws and legalized labor unions with their right to strike and picket. Poverty became less of a crime or a private failure and more of a social need to be addressed by legislation.

In many industrialized states, the passing of child-labor laws (prohibiting them from working) also had a revolutionary affect on Western society (see figure 11.5). Ironically, many commoners had actually resisted earlier efforts of enlightened despots to provide universal education. Schooling increased the economic burden of children for their parents. Sending children to school meant they could not contribute to the family labor force until their teen years. Nineteenth-century elites also discouraged education for all people, perfectly aware that workers with education did not often want to do dirty, hard labor. They feared workers would aspire to rise above their "assigned" social level. That is why, even in the West today, a university education is considered a ticket to a middle-class lifestyle. While education was not an immediate cure-all, a compulsory, basic grade-school education at taxpayer expense in state schools soon became the norm in the West. Literacy approached 100 percent in many Western industrialized countries by 1900.

Meanwhile, improved production through worker efficiency and new technology made **corporations** more and more powerful. Until the modern corporation, most businesses had been small, local institutions based on families and the partnerships of a few individuals. The corporation became a business where a multitude of people could pool their capital resources (stockholders) and elect representatives (a board of directors), who then appointed a chief manager (president or chief executive officer) to run the company. The corporation was an artificial legal construction: it could, like a person, own property, incur debt, sue, and be sued. Meanwhile, the people who owned that corporation were immune—only vulnerable for the amount of stock that they held. This legal status granted corporations a huge advantage over mere mortal citizens, since they could theoretically exist forever. This was, of course, blatant hypocrisy by the ruling elites. They could form corporations that represented and united the voice of thousands of stockholders, but they would not allow unions to represent and unite thousands of workers?

Figure 11.5. These boys worked in and around the coal mines rather than going to school. Note that one is missing an arm, probably from an industrial accident.

These corporations, fed by huge flows of capital, soon came to dominate Western economies both within their home nations and around the world.

Corporations were so successful that many quickly bloated into burgeoning conglomerates. Huge corporations combined with others as **cartels** or **trusts**. These associations conspired to establish monopolies, the control of prices and production of whole economic sectors, reducing or completely eliminating competition. Railroads, steel, oil, and even sugar came under monopolistic control in many nations. Critics in the United States called the owners "robber barons," unfairly enriched by exploited workers; the tycoons saw themselves as sharp businessmen justly compensated with unimaginable wealth. Some governments became concerned at this concentration of economic power in a few hands. The dominant "free market" economic theory of laissez-faire (or classical liberal economics) required competition to keep the system fair and efficient. Since cartels crushed competition, governments soon felt compelled to enact antitrust laws to break up the trusts and monopolies. Some capitalists cried that this intervention would ruin economic growth, but governments responded by citing the need to protect their citizens from exploitation.

The question of whether profit-making necessarily excludes fair treatment of workers and consumers has been a challenge faced by citizens of the West ever since the nineteenth century. What actions should citizens or their governments take to regulate or promote the rights of mortal individuals against legal corporations? The bundle of ideas advocated by diverse socialists still provides answers to the world today. Socialism's concept of equality originated in the suffering of the workers early in the Industrial Revolution. Therein lay its appeal, even as versions of socialism underwent varied successes and failures in the twentieth century.

Review: *How did socialists address problems manufactured by the Industrial Revolution?*

Response:

THE MACHINERY OF NATURE

The technology that powered the Industrial Revolution was, of course, based on scientific principles established by the Scientific Revolution. Science continued to advance in areas not focused on profits. Scientists wanted to know how the universe worked. While Newton had supplied many answers about the movements of the planets, scientists began investigating other aspects of the earth itself, life upon it, and even people themselves. How did nature function, especially if science left God out of the equation? Scientists were determined to find out by using observable and experimental data to explain the workings of nature.

First, a new phase of the Scientific Revolution crystallized as the new science of geology developed as a means to study the earth. The traditional Western explanation for the earth's history had been drawn from the biblical Book of Genesis. Jews began their calendar with their calculated date of the beginning of creation, equivalent to

3761 B.C. In the seventeenth century, Irish bishop James Ussher had calculated the earth's age from biblical genealogies: he concluded that God created the world on 24 October 4004 B.C. At first, the influence of scripture inclined scientists to think along the lines of a ***theory of catastrophism*** to explain geology. According to this theory, rare and unusual events of enormous power, resembling divine intervention, explained the features of the earth. While the theory of catastrophism provided some understanding of the earth's past, new discoveries soon called it into question.

Charles Lyell's book *Principles of Geology* provided a new theory in 1829. Lyell proposed the ***theory of uniformitarianism*** to explain the history of the earth, saying that the same (uniform) processes shaping the earth today have always acted to remold the planet. Thus, erosion and deposition, uplift and sinking of land-masses, volcanoes, earthquakes, glaciers, and so on have formed every existing landscape. He concluded that the earth was not fixed, but in flux. Since many of these processes move infinitesimally slowly, the theory required that earth be at least millions of years old.

Many Christian who interpreted the Bible literally opposed this new theory, since these numbers contradicted calculations based on Genesis. Nonetheless, the practice of science increasingly left God out of the equation. Indeed, most scientific evidence collected over the nineteenth century clearly supported uniformitarian-ism, while almost none backed up catastrophism. Uniformitarianism could, by mea-surable natural processes, account for the highest mountain and the deepest valley. Just as with theories of heliocentrism and universal gravitation, scientists embraced the theory of uniformitarianism because it had explanatory power and conformed to the evidence of nature.

Fossils provided much of the evidence for research into the earth's history. Scientists found petrified remains both of contemporary-looking organisms and of strange creatures that did not seem to exist anymore. Excavations for mines, canals, building foundations, and so on in the industrial age unearthed more and more fossils. Scientists began to organize these fossilized bones and called the large crea-tures dinosaurs ("terrible lizards"). As geologists compared layers of rock in which fossils were found, science showed that dinosaurs had lived many millions of years ago before becoming extinct. But how had those monsters, or many other life-forms, died out, while others still seemed to be around?

A second phase of the Scientific Revolution was born as biologists tried to solve that very mystery. The oldest layers of rock showed a few simple living things, such as algae. More recent rock layers showed a connected diversity of life, as evidenced by the appearance of new species (a scientific category of living things that could reproduce with each other). As eons wore on, some species, like the dozens of kinds of dinosaurs, had clearly gone extinct. Others, like ferns, clams, and cock-roaches, had survived into the present with little change. The fossil record showed that overall, life had become increasingly diverse and complex over time. Scientists called this process of biological change ***evolution***.

Christian religious literalists opposed evolution as vehemently as they earlier had denied the age of the earth or, going back to Copernicus, located the earth at the center of the universe. Evolution, the age of the earth, and the earth's noncen-tral place in the universe are, nonetheless, scientific facts. Many nonscientists complained (and still complain) that the idea of evolution is a theory, meaning a mere guess with little supporting evidence. These people apparently misunderstand science. Scientific theories are not just good guesses; they offer comprehensive explanations of the facts. Evolution is a scientific fact, as real as the earth's revolving around the sun. In the mid-nineteenth century, scientists sought a natural mechanism to explain the fact of evolution, how life on earth had become more diverse and complex over the eons.

Charles Darwin (b. 1809–d. 1882) provided a scientific theory to explain the fact of evolution. He pondered the issue for years after investigating the unique species of finches, iguanas, and tortoises on the Galapagos Islands off the western coast of South America, which he had visited during his voyage on the ship *Beagle* in the 1830s. Darwin finally published his book *The Origin of Species* (1859) only when a fellow naturalist, Alfred Wallace, was about to publish on the same subject. Darwin's *theory of natural selection*, also called "survival of the fittest," proposed that the struggle of creatures for food and reproduction encouraged change. As living things adapted to their environment and competed with other living things, certain advantageous characteristics enabled them to survive. Whether by stealth, strength, speed, or size, some organisms outlived others and lasted long enough to pass those favorable characteristics on to their own viable offspring. Over millions of millennia, small, incremental variations slowly separated offspring into more complex and more diverse species. Species that did not compete successfully, especially when a climate changed, became extinct. The theory of natural selection relies on the natural drives for food and sex as a mechanism for diversity. Darwin outlined a means whereby scientists could frame their study of life on earth. While a few modifications of Darwin's theory have since been suggested, all subsequent study has served only to confirm and support the scientific fact of evolution.

This science notwithstanding, some Christians became even more outraged when Darwin's second significant book, *The Descent of Man* (1869), argued that humans were descended from the same apelike ancestors as chimpanzees or baboons. Many Christians were offended by a human connection to beasts and worried what that would imply about the human soul. They preached that this godless view of nature would lead to immorality.

Their point seemed proven when social theorists used humanity's connections to animals to argue that the "survival of the fittest" was how human societies should be run. They called their ideology *Social Darwinism*, even though Charles Darwin had nothing to do with them and Darwinists such as Thomas Huxley disavowed their conclusions. The Social Darwinists argued that human ethics should reflect selfishness, greed, and exploitation of the weak. Thus, the poor deserved their poverty, or the defeated were properly conquered, while the acquisition of wealth proved the superiority of the upper class. This skewed rationalization encouraged nationalism, imperialism, and racism. The millionaire oil magnate John D. Rockefeller himself pronounced that ruthless competition in business was not evil, but instead reflected the laws of nature and God. He himself had risen from a simple farmboy through hard work, frugality, and secret deals. These ideas in turn stimulated materialism and secularism.

Social Darwinism came from an incorrect reading of natural selection and an overblown confidence in human social differences. Social Darwinists falsely saw strength as the only survival virtue and bruising competition as the means. Such views ignored nature's success stories. A despised creature like the cockroach survived with speed, stealth, and the ability to eat garbage. Meanwhile, a dinosaur like *Tyrannosaurus rex* had been the biggest and meanest creature, but it became extinct because it could not adapt. Evolution has no moral direction—it is merely the description of nature's work.

Social Darwinists were only one part of a larger movement to apply science to human activity. A third phase in science during the nineteenth century emerged as intellectuals invented the scholarly subjects of the **social sciences** at the end of the century. These fields sought to analyze human beings and then propose theories and laws to explain them. The subject of history was tossed into this new category after being bolstered with statistical studies. The new subject of political science clarified the multiplying electoral systems of Western democracies. Sociology studied modern societies, while anthropology examined ancient or primitive cultures. The West's new domination of foreign cultures provided new opportunities for social scientists to compare diverse peoples.

Of great consequence was the decision of sociologists and anthropologists to scrutinize Christianity. They noted that Christianity resembled many other faiths and could be compared with them historically. The scholarly schools of ***higher criticism*** even dissected the Bible. Instead of viewing it as a perfect product of instantaneously inspired creation by the Judeo-Christian deity, higher critics applied the techniques of textual criticism begun during the Renaissance. Scholars began to read the Bible as a flawed compilation collected by human beings over hundreds of years. This method reasonably explained many of the Bible's contradictions, inconsistencies, and obscurities. From the Book of Genesis alone, odd passages such as two versions of the creation of humans, different numbers of animals Noah took into the ark, or the unusually long lives of the first humans could be attributed to fallible human records.

The growing explanatory power of science and social sciences weakened the hold of Christianity among the idea makers of Western civilization. In reaction, Christians of all denominations, whether Orthodox, Roman Catholic, or Protestant, began to split into two large groups with different attitudes toward the Bible. Fundamentalists reasserted standard Christian beliefs about the divine Jesus who died to keep believers out of hell. ***Fundamentalism*** developed an interpretation of inerrancy about the Bible, believing it to be divinely created, without error, and able to be clearly understood by using the power of the Holy Spirit. Meanwhile, modernists embraced and learned from a divinely inspired Bible composed by flawed humans, trying to reconcile these attitudes with Christian dogmas. ***Modernism*** accepted science in its worldview and ambiguity in its faith. Thus, Christianity continued its decline as a belief system, although most people in the West remained practicing Christians.

Criticisms of religious belief by the founder of psychiatry, **Sigmund Freud** (b. 1856–d. 1939), focused on its incompatibility with science. Freud abandoned much of his Jewish heritage for a more rational look at culture's interaction with individuals. As a psychiatrist, Freud brought new insights into the debate on the origins of and treatments for mental illness. He famously argued that when a person's subconscious drives (id) conflicted with social expectations (superego) and internalized lessons (ego), then neurosis and even psychosis could result. While this scheme is not broadly accepted today by the psychiatric community, it had enormous impact at the turn of the twentieth century. Freud also shocked the "decent" society of his turn-of-the-century Vienna when he unveiled how the human sex drive (libido) could affect mental health. As a result, sex became a part of our public discourse instead of being confined behind closed doors.

From the mental to the physical world, biological science discovered more practical applications for public health, largely thanks to **Louis Pasteur** (b. 1822–d. 1895) of France. First, Pasteur explained the process of fermentation, which saved the French wine industry. Additionally, his pasteurization process saved milk from spoiling. Finally, his ***germ theory of disease*** helped save lives. Pasteur's science proved that microscopic organisms, such as bacteria and viruses, caused many illnesses. Because it does not yet explain all diseases, such as cancer or those of old age, the germ theory is not perfect. Still, it has led to a huge advancement in medical cures and disease prevention. Pasteur's studies proved immunization through both the old practice of inoculations (giving people a live form of a disease) and new vaccinations (giving a dead form). Antiseptics (which killed germs on the outside of the body) were soon followed by antibiotics (which killed germs inside the body). Modern scientific medicine actually succeeded at improving the health and survival of people to a degree unknown by any previous society.

Finally, physicists were also busy unlocking the secrets of the universe at the smallest level. Scientists such as Pierre and Marie Skłodowska Curie in France and Thomson and Rutherford in England formulated ***atomic theory***. Drawing on ideas of the ancient Greeks, modern physicists consider atoms to be the smallest part of matter that possesses the properties of an element. At the time, no one could have guessed that the atomic force which bound an atom together could be unleashed to enable humans to destroy all civilization.

Overall, the nineteenth century had rapidly multiplied the options open to the citizens of Western civilization. The Industrial Revolution drove the economy, with its varied goods, services, and ideologies available to consumers of the upper, middle, and lower class. Conservatives, liberals, anarchists, and the several flavors of socialists argued for different kinds of political economy and revolution. New scientific ideas and inventions opened the doors to the future, while Romantics and many people of faith found comfort in the past. Christianity continued to fragment. Despite and because of these internal differences, however, Western civilization would soon reign supreme over most other peoples around the globe.

Review: *How did modern science generate new and unsettling knowledge?*

Response:

CHAPTER 12

The Westerner's Burden

Imperialism and Nationalism, 1810 to 1918

By building on the superiority in industrialization and technology achieved during the nineteenth century, Western civilization gained authority over the world as never before. Western advances created a new global domination driven by a revival of colonial imperialism and a new sense of self-identity called nationalism. The West's incursions into diverse world cultures both vindicated and challenged its own cultural assumptions. The British poet Rudyard Kipling's acceptance of ''The White Man's Burden'' illustrates the culture's dialogue with itself. Race, sex roles, and nationalism became still more closely connected with political control over those perceived to be inferiors. Fateful decisions would lead the West on the path toward the most destructive war the world had ever suffered.

''NEW AND IMPROVED'' IMPERIALISM

Western nations had begun having success with colonial imperialism outside Europe in the late 1400s and early 1500s. The ''voyages of discovery'' led to foreign conquests for Portugal and Spain, followed soon by the Netherlands, France, and England. At that time, disease had given the Europeans a decisive advantage in their conquest of the New World since the natives lacked immunities and were killed more often by germs than by guns. Meanwhile, many peoples in the Old World of Africa and Asia offered enough resistance both to disease and to military arms that westerners were confined to mere footholds on the edges of their principalities. Many of these peoples lived in their own civilizations, which for many centuries had been more advanced technologically, politically, and culturally than the West. Asians and Africans mostly governed themselves, as they had since the dawn of human history. By 1830, the Portuguese, Spanish, French, and Dutch controlled only scattered remnants of their once-vast overseas empires in Asia, Africa, or the Americas. Western colonialism's ruling over distant territories seemed destined to decline.

Instead, a revived and more powerful wave of imperialism, or **_neo-imperialism_** (1830–1914), rolled across the oceans. Some Western nations reemphasized imperialism out of jealousy of Great Britain and its empire. The British Empire reigned supreme during the nineteenth century, waving its imperial glory in all the corners of the world, despite the loss of the Americans. Many British saw their imperial rule as benevolent, promoting peace and prosperity at home and around the world (see figure 12.1). Britain's old rival France or new rival Germany (see below) became resentful of this empire on which the sun never set.

Additionally, most westerners were overly confident in their own progress. Because technology had given them increasing dominion over nature, most Europeans thought that their own cultures surpassed those of "primitive," "ignorant,"

Figure 12.1. The Europeans claimed to bring education and civilization, as in this German school in the colony of Southwest Africa. At the same time as African children were being educated, German troops were waging a war of extermination against whole tribes.

and "superstitious" peoples. In their view, Christianity needed to replace native beliefs for the natives' own good. While many Western leaders were personally not very religious, they could appeal to Christian voters by supporting missionary work to convert "heathens." These missionaries naturally needed protection from head-hunters, cannibals, or just fearful natives who held their own religious beliefs. So European governments sent in troops. The West's nationalistic pride, cultural superiority, and international security demanded global empires.

The Scientific and Industrial Revolutions empowered this new burst of Western imperialism. Before 1800, tropical diseases such as malaria and sleeping sickness had easily crippled and killed Europeans who ventured into Africa and Asia. First, scientific medicine enabled westerners to better survive foreign climates. Knowledge about germs and infection, inoculation and vaccination, and the discovery that taking quinine (usually in tonic water with gin) prevented malaria all increased westerners' resistance to previously lethal diseases. Second, modern Western military force and technology outmatched native Africans and Asian armies. In the eighteenth century, many Asians and Africans were armed with bow, spear, and sword; they could not compete with Western soldiers shooting muskets. By 1850, a few thousand well-trained modern troops equipped with quick-loading rifles and artillery could prevail over countless tribal peoples. Third, the new industrial economy compelled westerners to acquire new resources to feed the machines of industry. The round-the-clock factories required raw materials to process, while finished products demanded new markets. Businessmen and the politicians backing them thought that empires would provide both. Additionally, the vast tracts of underused farmland in distant colonies could provide another outlet for the excess population of Europe, easing social tensions at home.

Consequently, economists revised the old economic theory of mercantilism for the new circumstances. While the mercantilism of the seventeenth century had asked for government intervention to foster a favorable balance of trade, the economic *theory of neo-mercantilism* from the nineteenth century restricted itself to asking for government intervention in order to help build empires and open foreign markets. At home, the government was to continue its laissez-faire policy and allow free use of private property. But as merchants wandered into deepest, darkest outlands, they needed the muscle of Western military forces to protect both their persons and their newly "acquired" possessions from the natives. It may seem a bit inconsistent for business leaders to call for government to stay out of economic decisions in one circumstance (domestic) and call for government support in another (international), but they have done so consistently since the nineteenth century.

Supported by technologically advanced armies and navies, the West strode with new determination into the world. Non-Western peoples lost control of their lives. Sometimes, enterprising businessmen simply stole what they wanted. British agents stole tea from China, rubber from Brazil, and cinchona from Peru (to make quinine for fighting malaria). They then grew these plants on plantations in British-controlled South and Southeast Asia. Other times, entrepreneurs used fraud, bribery, or threats to convince native chiefs to sign a treaty surrendering land rights to the Europeans. As a last resort, armies would simply mow down native resistance. As a justification, the imperialists mouthed altruistic intentions of stopping violence and warfare among the natives. They might even protest that they were drawn into empire against their will, forced to make hard, violent, self-interested choices. Further, Europeans often exploited native ethnic differences, exaggerating them to set the ethnic groups against one another. Such tactics revived the classic method of divide-and-rule practice. The westerners almost always profited and prevailed.

The intensity of domination, however, differed in three degrees. First, in **spheres of influence**, the natives were still ultimately in charge. In these areas, one Western state would form an alliance and a close working relationship with the native regime to keep other Europeans out and arrange the best deals for itself. Second, in **protectorates** the native leaders still held a great deal of authority, at least when it came to running their own society. The Western power became decisive only in foreign affairs and in many economic decisions. Third, in complete colonization, native structures and societies were substantially eliminated and Western people moved in and took over.

This had been the case during the colonization of the Latin American states, the United States, Canada, Australia, and New Zealand. Europeans shoved aside the comparatively few natives onto the worst lands. The Dutch colony of **South Africa**, located on the Cape of Good Hope, also saw Europeans drive out the natives from the best farmland. The descendants of the Dutch colonialists named themselves **Afrikaaners**. They saw themselves as Africans, just as the descendants of English colonialists in America viewed themselves as Americans. Meanwhile, the native Africans remained a near-powerless majority of the population.

In most new colonies formed under neo-imperialism after 1830, the natives retained little power and little hope that matters would improve. In most of Africa, the Pacific Islands, and parts of Asia, the minority population of Europeans who possessed the majority of the land and authority restricted the natives to a subservient role—foreigners in their own country. Recent historians, however, see native peoples acting as subalterns, officially subservient to the westerners, yet subversive beneath the surface. Westerners at the time merely interpreted natives' lack of enthusiasm for empire as laziness and stupidity.

Nineteenth-century science supported Western supremacy. Early scientists divided up the human species into several races. The Europeans came to be considered part of the Caucasian race, named both because some scientists considered the people of the Caucasus to be the "prettiest" and because many believed humans first appeared there. Social Darwinism increasingly emphasized racial differences. The dominance of Europeans allegedly proved their racial superiority. To be Western was to be of "white" complexion. Even hard-working and bright colonized peoples could never change their skin color.

The transformation of South Africa opened the door for neo-imperialism. The British seized the colony from the Dutch in 1815. British settlers moved in, creating a mixed society where the Europeans dominated the large numbers of native Africans who still lived there. But the Dutch and English did not get along very well. In 1835, two years after the British outlawed slavery in the South African colony, thousands of Dutch Afrikaaners left the colony on the Great Trek. They journeyed hundreds of miles inland to escape what they saw as British oppression. The Afrikaaners seized new fertile land and enslaved the native black Africans who had survived recent wars among one another. The Dutch Afrikaaners set up the Transvaal and the Orange Free State as two sovereign Western countries in southern Africa. The Western technology and methodology of these farmers (called Boers) made the land prosper as never before.

The South African conflicts focused the attention of Britain's rivals upon the continent. At the beginning of the nineteenth century, only a few European imperial possessions clung to Africa's fringes. Portugal in particular retained its colonial bases gained during the first wave of European colonial imperialism. The French led the new wave. Their neo-imperialism began in 1830 with "the flyswatter incident." When a French diplomat arrogantly refused to discuss repaying a debt owed to Algerians, the Ottoman governor slapped him in the face with a flyswatter. Outraged about an insult to French *honneur*, France conquered the provinces and made them part of France. Thousands of French immigrants then began buying land and settling in.

It took a few more years for European interest to penetrate the rest of Africa, especially the interior south of the Sahara. Europeans called Africa the "Dark Continent" partly because they knew so little about it. By midcentury, missionaries and explorers were bringing back fascinating accounts. Most famous were dispatches from the journalist Henry Stanley as he searched for the humanitarian Dr. David Livingstone, allegedly lost in the Congo in 1871. His dry remark, "Dr. Livingstone, I presume," is a statement of the obvious (finding the only white man amid so many Africans). More important, he published exotic tales of African riches, from gold to ivory. Stanley laid the foundation for the takeover of the Congo River basin by King Leopold of Belgium. Livingstone had wanted to minister to the spiritual and physical needs of the natives; Leopold desired to exploit the region as his own pet colony, plundering it of rubber and ivory. Over the next few decades, the Belgians' brutal treatment of natives reduced the population from more than thirty million to less than ten million.

Western neo-imperialism soon overwhelmed the rest of Africa as other leaders began to follow Leopold's example. The fate of one hundred million Africans changed with the stroke of a pen in 1884. The leaders of Europe convened a meeting in Berlin to discuss the recent Belgian takeover of the Congo. At this Congress of Berlin they defined the ground rules for their **Partition of Africa** (1884–1914). Each interested power was permitted to move in from a specific area of coastline and stake claims to whatever territories it could. During these seizures, the invading nation was to notify other European governments so that they did not stumble into war with one another. The conquest of more than ten million square miles of African lands quickly followed.

Even the traditional rivals France and Britain managed to forget many of their ancient grievances with each other. The French were crossing the continent from east to west, while the British linked a chain of territories from north to south. This competition between Britain and France intersected in the Sudan. The French and British competition there almost sparked a larger war. The French began the **Suez Canal** to build an artificial waterway to link the Mediterranean and the Red Sea. After the French investors ran into difficulties, the British rushed into Egypt in 1882 (see figure 12.2). They wanted to finish the Suez Canal since it offered a much shorter route to British India than sailing all the way around Africa. Then, in 1885, a Muslim revolt led by the "Mad Mahdi" drove the British out of Egyptian-dominated Sudan. The British General Gordon and his troops died defending Khartoum, Sudan's capital. After the French showed some interest in claiming the Sudan, the British invaded again in 1898. They avenged Gordon by killing thousands of Muslims with machine guns and retook the country. But when a small French force confronted the British at Fashoda, the two commanders eventually toasted each other and parted on friendly terms.

While the British ended up with the best share of Africa, they faced an unanticipated challenge to their new supremacy in South Africa again. When the British started to build a railroad from the Cape of Good Hope to Cairo (South Africa to Egypt), the Dutch Boers of the Orange Free State refused to allow the British passage through their territory. So the British tried to conquer the Afrikaaners in the

Figure 12.2.   This cartoon shows a British soldier, with a Turk at his feet, claiming to be the protector of Egypt. No Egyptians are seen, only the Sphinx and pyramids in the distance.

surprisingly nasty **Boer War** (1899–1902). The Boers fought an effective guerrilla campaign until the British defeated them with a new radical measure, the **concentration camp**. The British rounded up large numbers of civilians whose only crime was being the wrong kind of person (in this case, an Afrikaaner) and confined these men, women, and children in barracks under guard and surrounded by barbed wire. The British thus perfected the concentration camp as a technique of social conquest and resorted to its use increasingly thereafter. Tens of thousands of camp residents, young and old, white and black, died from disease and hunger. The British also burned farms and armed native Africans (at least until victory had been achieved). The British won the Boer War, but at the cost of many lives and sharp international criticism. Thus, the Boer War marked the dangerous precedent of westerners fighting other westerners over foreign plots of land.

Despite this crushing defeat, the large population of Afrikaaners still resisted British domination. So the British and the Afrikaaners compromised a few years later with the creation of the **Union of South Africa**. South Africa developed into a Western industrialized nation, although its British and Afrikaaner populations remained a minority. The 80 percent majority of the population, a few immigrants from India, some "coloreds" of mixed heritage, and the large numbers of black Africans slowly tried to organize their own political participation by founding the (South) African National Congress. Joint British and Afrikaaner rule, however, effectively excluded these people of non-European heritage.

In the scramble for Africa, other Western powers managed to grab different slices to appease their appetites for the moment. While Western civilization had ended the international slave trade, many millions of Africans lived under slavelike conditions in their own countries under these European masters. France appeared to hold the next-largest share after England; yet much was the wasteland of forbidding desert or impassable jungle. The Germans won a couple of key colonies, but they grumbled that theirs did not compare well enough with those of the French and English. They nearly exterminated the native Herero and Nama peoples in their colony of Southwest Africa (today Namibia). The success of other states inspired the Spanish and Portuguese to move deeper inland from their own coastal colonies. Even the Italians got a few pieces of Somalia on the eastern Horn of Africa. Regrettably for Italian pride, the poor Italians who tried to invade Abyssinia (also called Ethiopia) had their army decisively trounced by natives armed with arrows and spears at the Battle of Adowa (1896). They were the only westerners to be defeated by Africans during this wave of imperialism. Thus, by 1914, native Africans governed only in Abyssinia and to some extent in Liberia, which was an American protectorate run by Africans whose ancestors had, for a time, been slaves in the United States. Westerners ruled all the rest of Africa.

While Africans succumbed relatively quickly under Western supremacy, the Asians experienced more varied levels of resistance. The first major Asian region to fall was the Indian Subcontinent. Since Britain's victories in the eighteenth century, it had been the supreme foreign power in the land, either directly or indirectly through the East India Trading Company. Still, many princes and rajahs remained independent of the growing British influence. An odd incident in 1857, however, provided the means and opportunity for British imperialists to take over much of South Asia.

A rebellion broke out when the British military introduced the latest Enfield rifle and its cartridges to their native troops, called sepoys. This ammunition was more efficient than the ball and powder of muzzle-loaded muskets. The bullet and explosive charge were wrapped together in greased paper, and a soldier needed only to bite off the paper and load the cartridge in the rifle. Suddenly, the rumor spread among the natives that the grease on the paper was either beef fat or pig fat. The former was abhorrent to Hindus, who believed that cows were sacred, and the latter was repulsive to Muslims, who held that swine were unclean. Thus began the so-called **Sepoy Mutiny** (1857), or as some Indians call it, the "First War for Independence." Sadly for an independent India, the British quickly rallied and used their superior organization and technology to crush the rebels. The British destroyed dozens of temples and mosques and killed and injured thousands of innocent civilians in revenge. One favorite death penalty was to tie a rebel across the mouth of a cannon and blow him to bits. From then on, the British reigned over most of India as an outright colony, while only a few rajahs managed to preserve their states as protectorates. The British also aggravated the traditional differences among religious groups. They set Hindu, Muslim, Sikh, and others against one another. It was the classic divide-and-conquer routine used by imperialists in all ages.

Most of the inhabited islands in the Pacific became colonies in the second half of the nineteenth century. Europeans wanted them as safe harbors to store and provide food, water, and coal for their steamships. Also, many islands were mountains of guano, or bird poop, that was useful as fertilizer. Most islanders could defend themselves with only Stone Age technology and thus quickly lost.

In East Asia, powerful states had much better technology but soon found themselves outmatched by the West. The most powerful Asian state, the Chinese Empire, had endured many invasions and rebellions since its foundation two millennia before in 221 B.C. From the cultivated Chinese point of view, all foreigners were barbarians who lacked the sophistication of Chinese culture. Chinese merchants wanted very little from the outside world, although they were willing to sell their tea, silks, and porcelain for cold, hard Western silver and gold.

The British and the Americans, meanwhile, tried to find a product that the Chinese would be willing to buy. They worried that the neo-mercantilistic balance of trade tilted too much to the Chinese advantage. Ultimately, they found a product that would break open the Chinese markets: illegal drugs, in particular, opium. These narcotics damaged the Chinese economy, health, and morality. Nevertheless, Western merchants smuggled opium into China from the fields of western and central Asia where it was grown. Profits meant more than Chinese law. When the Chinese authorities justifiably confiscated and destroyed these illegal substances, British merchants complained to their own regime about property rights. The British Empire declared war on China to protect the British right to sell illegal narcotics. In the short **Opium Wars** (1839–1842), the Chinese suffered humiliating and decisive defeats by modern British military technology.

The triumphant British imposed treaties that opened up China to Western exploitation. Under the concept of **extraterritoriality**, British people and possessions were exempted from native laws and authority (much as foreign diplomats and embassies still are today). Therefore, British merchants and missionaries could do what they wanted. The treaties also forced the Chinese to hand over parts of several key ports, while British warships and troops could move at will throughout China to defend British citizens and interests. In the next few years, the other Western great powers bullied the Chinese into handing over these same privileges, one by one. Westerners out to make a profit attacked and undermined Chinese society.

By 1900, the United States feared that other Western states might start to carve up the weakened Chinese Empire into distinct economic and political zones. To keep access to markets as free as possible, the United States advocated an "open door" policy throughout China: promising mutual cooperation and no trade barriers between Western imperialists. The open door policy merely meant that China was open to being bought and sold in little bits by westerners rather than all at once. The Chinese imperial government lacked the ability to resist.

Instead, a nativist movement sparked what the westerners called the **Boxer Rebellion** (1900). The name "Boxer" came from an anti-Western society whose symbol was the raised fist. The insurgents attacked foreigners all over China and laid siege to hundreds of diplomats, soldiers, missionaries, and merchants in the foreigners' quarter of the capital city of Peking (today called Beijing). After only fifty-five days, Western armies smashed the revolt and imposed more humiliating treaties on China. Shortly after, in 1903, the incompetent empress who had managed Chinese affairs for decades died, leaving only a child to inherit the crumbling mechanisms of power. Without leadership, the empire fell to a republican revolt in 1911. Western imperialists stayed and provoked terrible consequences in the developing twentieth century, as explained in later chapters.

In Southeast Asia between India and China, **Siam** (modern-day Thailand) managed to negotiate for itself a sphere of influence rather than a more serious takeover. The British had conquered Burma to the west, as the French seized Indochina (what would become Vietnam, Laos, and Cambodia) to the east. Yet neither side was sure how to dominate the powerful little state of Siam, which was likely to put up a fight. Instead, Siam became a buffer between French and British colonies. It learned from both, although the westernizing influence of the governess Anna Leonowens on kings Mongkut (r. 1851–1868) and Chulalongkorn (r. 1868–1910) has been exaggerated by modern musicals and films. Siam's forward-looking kings slowly brought Western ways into the country.

Meanwhile, Europeans confidently predicted that their humanitarian burden of looking after the less-advanced peoples of the world would last far into the future. This "caretaking," however, was two-sided. On the one hand, Europeans could point with pride to the construction of railroads, roads, harbors, large colonial administration buildings, schools, hospitals, and military bases. Their laws and economics brought a Western vision of order and growth to places once considered by Europeans to be violent, barbaric, and stagnant. Christian missionaries were winning converts. And to its everlasting credit, the West ended the international trade in African slaves and did much to stop most other slavery. All humans became more connected, for good or ill, than they ever had been before in history. The Europeans even drew on the culture of the new lands and showed appreciation for some of the art, artifacts, and literature of "Orientals" and Africans.

On the other hand, Europeans blithely ignored the exploitation, cruelty, and hopelessness created by their supremacy. Many native peoples suffered humiliation, defeat, and death. Although their health and standard of living often improved because of participation in global trade, colonial peoples suffered from the consequences of business decisions made in distant lands. These global economic bonds only intensified with time. Natives often felt like prisoners in their own countries as traditional social status and customs vanished. Europeans justifiably outlawed widow burning in India while ignoring how their own policies impoverished many other widows and families. Most of the peoples of the world had been fine without Western colonialism before the nineteenth century. No sooner had they been subjugated than many were working to regain their autonomy. Within a few decades, they would succeed.

Review: *How did the Europeans come to dominate Africa and Asia?*

Response:

FROM SEA TO SHINING SEA

While Europeans added to their empires, a new Western power was rising, unsuspected, in the Western Hemisphere. The United States of America, like Russia before it, initially aimed its imperialism not across oceans, but across its own continental landmass. The peace agreement with Britain after the War of Independence granted the Americans most lands east of the Mississippi River, giving the United States a size comparable to western Europe. Many Americans believed it was their obvious national purpose, or **manifest destiny**, to dominate North America.

Some acquisitions came relatively peacefully. No "Americans" lived west of the Mississippi in 1803. In that year, Napoleon sold the Louisiana Purchase to the United States, giving the new nation its first significant expansion. Neither government in Paris or Washington D.C., of course, consulted with the natives about who owned the land. After a second attempt to conquer Canada in the War of 1812 failed, the Americans peacefully negotiated away any rivalry with Britain over mutual borders in the north of Maine or the Oregon Territory. The United States also bought Florida from Spain.

The newly independent Mexico was another matter. American immigrants who had moved into Mexico's province of Texas successfully rebelled in 1836, after Mexico tried to outlaw slavery. At first, the United States was reluctant to annex Texas. A decade later, though, the activist President Polk did so. Armed troops shooting at one another over disputed borders triggered the **Mexican-American War** (1846–1848). The United States was quickly victorious and briefly considered, but rejected, taking over all of Mexico. Instead, the Yankees only confiscated a third of Mexico's territory, leaving it as the United States' weak southern neighbor.

Meanwhile, the Indians, or Native American peoples, stood in the way of the United States' unquestioned supremacy of America. Most Indians had been killed or removed from the original thirteen colonies before the American War of Independence. In the 1830s, **Indian removals** forced nearly all of those who had remained east of the Mississippi River into reservations on the other side, even though some tried to defend their treaty rights in U.S. courts. Next, Americans migrated westward to the Pacific Coast, crossing the Great Plains, which had been acquired in the Louisiana Purchase, and the Southwest, which had been won from Mexico. Americans rapidly broke all treaties signed with Indian tribes. In a series of **Plains Indian Wars** (1862–1890), superior Western technology and numbers gave the "cowboys" victory over the Indians.

In the popular imagination of Western civilization, images of these conflicts were colored with contradictions. "Noble savages" might seem to be either tragic heroes untainted by the flaws of civilization or barbaric "redskin" murderers. "Civilized" men and women on the frontier might either nobly embody liberty and self-reliance to tame the wilderness or ruthlessly exterminate even women and children to steal Indian land. In the real world, by the end of the nineteenth century, European Americans in both the United States and Canada had killed most Native Americans and confined the remnants to the near-worthless reservations.

As they finished their domination of the natives, some Americans began to consider whether manifest destiny extended beyond the shores of North America. Since 1823, the United States (with the support of the United Kingdom of Great Britain) had upheld the Monroe Doctrine, which prevented the Europeans from reintroducing colonial imperialism to Latin America (see the next section). Increasingly, though, the United States began to see the Western Hemisphere as its own imperialist economic sphere.

The United States gained strength through its industrialization, while Latin America remained largely agricultural. Soon U.S. merchants and politicians applied the dollar diplomacy, or using American economic power, whether through bribery, awarding of contracts, or extorting trade agreements, to influence the decisions of Latin American regimes. Obedience to Western capitalists earned Central American governments the nickname "banana republics." At the end of the nineteenth century, American corporations imported bananas, which originated in Southeast Asia, to cultivate in Central America. Under the American business plan, peasants who had grown corn to feed their families instead became laborers who harvested bananas to feed foreigners. If workers in Caribbean or Central American states resisted, the northern giant would send troops to occupy them and protect American property and trade. American armies in countries like Haiti and Nicaragua then propped up corrupt dictators who exploited their people but maintained friendly relations with the "big brother" to the north.

At the same time, U.S. interests looked to profit in the Pacific. America's first major victim was **Japan**, which almost suffered the same fate as its exploited Asian neighbor, China. The cluster of islands that the Japanese called the Land of the Rising Sun had maintained an isolationist policy for centuries. Since the early 1600s, hereditary military dictators, called shoguns, lorded over a well-ordered, stable, closed society in the name of powerless figurehead emperors. In the first age of imperialism, Japan had tentatively welcomed contact with Western explorers, traders, and missionaries. The Tokugowa dynasty of shoguns, though, had then shut the borders to Western influence by the late 1600s. After that, the Japanese permitted one Dutch ship only once a year to enter the port of Nagasaki for international trade. Otherwise, the Japanese wanted to be left alone.

That isolation ended in 1853 when American warships under the command of Commodore Matthew C. Perry steamed into Tokyo Harbor. Perry demanded the Japanese open trading relations with the United States or else he would open fire with his modern guns. Ironically, the government of the Tokugawa shogun had destroyed most firearms, leaving Japan defenseless. Fearful Japan signed a treaty loaded with extraterritoriality exploitation, just as China had suffered. The British, French, Russians, and all the others soon followed the Americans to share in the spoils.

Despite this forced opening of its borders, Japan ended up doing something few other non-Western countries could: it rapidly westernized. The Japanese replaced the discredited Tokugawa shogun with the figurehead emperor during the **Meiji Restoration** (1868). Then the Japanese traveled out into the world in droves and learned from the West about what made its civilization so powerful. The British taught the Japanese about constitutional monarchy and the navy. The Americans trained them in modern business practices. The French enlightened them about Western music and culture. The Germans drilled them on modern armies. Within a generation, the Japanese revolutionized their country to make it almost like any other Western power.

The name Meiji Restoration is a misnomer, however, since the Meiji dynasty was not so much restored to power as transformed in purpose. Before the restoration, the emperors had drifted through a shadowy, ineffective existence under the shoguns (like the mikado of the contemporary Gilbert and Sullivan operetta). Now, the emperor became a godlike figure who united Japanese religion with Japanese patriotism, much like Alexander or Augustus had done for the Greeks and Romans. This deified monarchy was the only unmodern move made by the Japanese. Otherwise, Japan plunged into a relatively smooth Western revolution, easily crushing the few samurai who resisted. Japan's equivalent of the Commercial, Intellectual, Scientific, Industrial, and English/American/French political Revolutions was all accomplished in short order. The emperor's subjects soon sought to honor him with an empire, imitating what the British had done for their kings and queens. Thus, the westernization of Japan had enormous consequences for the twentieth century.

The United States went on an imperialistic spree at the turn of the twentieth century. The **Spanish-American War** (1898) added Puerto Rico and the Philippines as colonies and Cuba almost as a protectorate. President McKinley partly justified the seizure of the Philippines with the need to convert the native islanders to Christianity. Ignorant Americans apparently did not know that most Filipinos were already Roman Catholic. When many Filipinos fought back with a guerrilla war, U.S. forces ended resistance by resorting to concentration camps. Hundreds of thousands of Filipinos died of disease and malnutrition in the badly managed camps. McKinley also annexed Hawaii, where American pineapple and sugarcane corporations had seized power from the native Queen Liliuokalani. The next president, Theodore Roosevelt, suggested a corollary to the Monroe Doctrine, that the United States would use force on behalf of European economic claims in Latin America (thus keeping the European imperialists out). In 1903, when Colombia refused the American offer to build a canal through its province of Panama, the United States helped provincial leaders stage a rebellion. The new leaders of Panama gave control of a canal zone to the United States. American know-how finished the Panama Canal by 1913, although that extraordinary effort killed over five thousand workers brought in from the Caribbean and Europe.

Such expansionist efforts showed how Americans could behave as badly as the rest of the westerners. Most Americans, however, have usually seen themselves as somehow different, confident in their rugged individualism, creative opportunism, and eager mobility. This concept of moral superiority to our other Western and world cultures is called *American exceptionalism*. It is similar to the common Western exceptionalism that had supported imperialism since the Renaissance. The American version views Americans as better than their fellow westerners. It expresses feelings that manifest destiny reflects a God-given calling and that American motives are more pure and generous than those of contemporary imperialist powers. Some historians have suggested that the United States does indeed differ from European states due to its origins as a society of immigrants seeking freedom and economic opportunities in an empty place with plenty of land and natural resources (although Canada, Australia, and New Zealand offer comparable histories). History shows, however, that American success too often came from brutal means to dominate that land and seize resources, a record which most Americans do not acknowledge. It is no coincidence that the United States began its global imperialism right after the Plains Indian Wars finally ended with the defeat of the Native Americans. Most immigrant Americans were unaware of the consequences of acquiring so much influence over so many peoples, first at home, then abroad; they noticed only the benefits of growing wealth and prosperity. American imperialism made the United States one of the leading Western powers by 1914, poised to become the most powerful country in the world. But with power comes responsibility, and the United States would only slowly come to learn this lesson in the twentieth century.

Review: How did the United States of America become a world power?

Response:

NATIONALISM'S CURSE

While imperialism cobbled together widespread empires, a new idea began to transform politics in Europe. Opposition to the French domination of Europe partly inspired the early advocates of ***nationalism***. This idea decreed that states should be organized exclusively around ethnic unities. Nationalists believed that a group of people, called a nationality, is best served by having its own sovereign state. The Industrial Revolution's empowerment of the masses further affected the choices of definition. Many nationalists argued that the masses of people from the bottom up should define what makes a country, especially since the aristocratic and royal dynasties who ruled from the top down often came from other ethnic groups. Some dynasties, though, took the lead in nationalism, setting the terms for defining nationalist characteristics. Nationalism's earliest proponents hoped that it would usher in an era of fraternal peace as different nations learned to respect one another despite their cultural differences.

Tragically, the emphasis on nationalism instead has more often resulted in increased international conflict. These clashes derive from a basic principle:

> **The greatest difficulty for nationalists was how to define exactly who belonged or not.**

Including some people in a group while throwing others out created tensions. Each ethnic identity varies according to its definers. Ethnicity may be based on geographic location, shared history, ancestry, political loyalty, language, religion, fashion, and any combination thereof. Language was often the starting point, as cultural builders settled on one dialect and collected stories and songs that contributed to a unique identity. In schools and academic institutes, in the theater and novels, nationalists transmitted the supposed identity of a particular nationality. Political history became a victorious story of destined greatness for the winners in state building, or an ongoing grievance for the losers.

By definition, though, including some people in the group meant excluding others. Some extreme nationalists even began arguing for the exclusionary ideologies of *racism*. The ideologies of racism asserted that some communities of humans shared bloodlines (a special, imagined quality inherited from common ancestors) that made them superior to others. Interest groups and political parties soon organized around nationalist and racist ideas, embracing those who belonged and hating those who did not.

At the beginning of the nineteenth century, Metternich's conservative decisions at the Congress of Vienna dismissed nationalist dreams. Hopeful nationalists in turn ignored the difficulties of ethnic diversity. Each of the five great powers included many people who did not fit their "ethnic" name. In the Austrian Empire no one ethnic group was in a majority, as Germans, Magyars, Italians, and Slavs (most importantly Czechs, Slovaks, Croats, and Poles) vied for the attention of the Habsburg emperor. Russia included, among many others, the Asians in Siberia in the east, Turks in the southeast, and Balts in the northwest, as well as the Slavic Poles and Ukrainians in the west. Prussia did have a majority of Germans, but Roman Catholics of the Rhineland felt no sense of "Prussianness," nor did most Danes and the large numbers of Poles and Wends (non-Polish Slavs in eastern Germany). Great Britain locked many disgruntled Scots, Irish, and Welsh into a "United Kingdom" with the English. Even France, which might seem the most cohesive, had Basques in the southwest, Bretons in the northwest, and Alsatian Germans in the east who did not want to learn how to correctly pronounce *patrie* ("fatherland"). Most of the smaller countries of Europe likewise lacked absolute ethnic homogeneity. Nevertheless, nationalists simplistically complained: If the French have France, the English have England, and even the Portuguese have Portugal, why shouldn't our ethnic group have Ethnicgroupland?

Surprisingly, the nationalist spirit first coalesced into reality across the Atlantic Ocean. **Haiti** experienced the earliest nationalist movements. Between 1789 and 1804, slaves of African descent enjoyed a brief independence from French rule. Soon afterward, the upper classes of European descent led the **liberation of Latin America** (1810–1825) from colonial imperialism. The descendants of European conquistadors and colonizers, known as Creoles (or *criollos*), slowly found their interests diverging from the distant imperial mother countries of Spain and Portugal. Many Creoles formed *juntas*, groups of elites who seized power. In 1811, the most famous liberator, Simon Bolívar (b. 1783–d. 1830), began to free Venezuela, uniting it with neighboring Colombia. Meanwhile, José de San Martín, "the Liberator," freed his homeland of Argentina along with Chile and began to fight for Peru. San Martín retired, leaving Bolívar to complete the independence of Peru and Bolivia (later named after him). The success of other freedom fighters helped create Mexico, the United Provinces of Central America, Paraguay, and Uruguay. By 1825, very little remained of what had once been Spain's vast empire in the Americas.

The leaders of these new Latin American nations did not have significant ethnic differences from one another, except for geographic location. They all still spoke the Spanish (or Portuguese in Brazil) of the mother country, wore the same style of clothing, practiced the same politics and economics, and worshipped as Roman Catholics. Among the masses of Hispanic peasants, however, there was much diversity. For example, Mexico had large numbers of *mestizos* (meaning of "mixed" Indian and European lineage), while Brazil had a much larger percentage of descendants of African slaves. Each of the new countries had to deal with these ethnic diversities.

To the north, the United States suffered its own major nationalist ethnic conflict with the **American Civil War** (1861–1865). This war decided whether the United States would survive united as one nation or divide into two or more countries. The country's very name, "United States," revealed the ethnic divisions at its origin. While some citizens called themselves American, more were likely to identify with their state, as a Virginian or a New Yorker. The regional differences concerning slavery sharpened the distinctions. Southerners, even those who were not slave-holders, defended their "peculiar institution" because that was how Southerners defined themselves. Under this pressure, the delicate balance among federal, state, and individual rights broke down. In the war that followed, the northern Union defeated the southern Confederacy because of the North's superior numbers, its technology, and President Abraham Lincoln's determination. Still, the reaffirmed federal unity did not entirely eliminate Southern ethnicity, since resentment still festered more than a century later.

Back in western Europe, nationalism appealed to conservatives and their inclination to look to the past for guidance. Indeed, nineteenth-century historians began to collect and assemble imaginative histories of ethnic groups which they argued were the forebears of modern nationalities. They collected source documents and organized them. Historians in those countries that represented a nationalist victory (for example, England or France) attributed success to cultural or racial superiority. Even historians of ethnic groups excluded from power (for example, the Irish or the Basques) adopted nationalistic perspectives, since they could glorify some distant freedom that had been squelched by political tragedy or unjust conquest. The Romantic movement heavily contributed to these efforts. Nationalism became a key political principle of Western civilization for both liberals and conservatives. After the revolutions of 1848, conservatives adopted nationalism. Conservative leaders used **_Realpolitik_**, or pragmatic power politics, doing whatever it took to achieve one's goals (see table 12.1).

Italy was an early success for nationalism. Of course, there had never before been a country called Italy, at least not like the one envisioned by its nationalist proponents. Italian history began with Rome and its city-state, which quickly became a multi-ethnic empire. In the Middle Ages, no single kingdom ever included the entire peninsula. Since 1494, Italy had been dominated by foreign dynasties—the French, the Spanish, and the Austrians—while the popes clung desperately to their Papal States.

In the wake of the failed revolutions of 1848, many Italian nationalists called for a *Risorgimento* (resurgence and revival) of an Italian nation-state. From 1848 to 1871 the Kingdom of Sardinia-Savoy-Piedmont spearheaded unification. Conservative prime minister **Count Camillo di Cavour** (r. 1852–1861) proposed a scheme for unification to his absolute monarch, King Victor Emmanuel II. First, they would

Table 12.1.   National Unifications in the Nineteenth Century

Kingdom of Sardinia-Savoy-Piedmont		*Kingdom of Prussia*
King Victor Emmanuel II Savoy		King Wilhelm I Hohenzollern
Prime Minister Camillo di Cavour		Chancellor Otto von Bismarck
Austro-Piedmontese War, 1859		
Garibaldi's Red Shirts conquer Kingdom of Two Sicilies, 1860		
Proclamation of Kingdom of Italy in Turin		
		Danish War, 1864
Kingdom of Italy capital to Florence, 1865		
	Seven Weeks War, 1866	
Add Venice		Northern German Confederation
	Franco-Prussian War, 1871–1872	
Add Rome		Add southern German states, excluding Austria
Kingdom of Italy		**(Second) German Empire**

Note: The unifications of Italy and Germany share similar developments and certain wars.

modernize and liberalize Sardinia-Savoy-Piedmont. Then, several well-planned military actions would topple both Habsburgs in the north and the petty regimes in the rest of the Italian Peninsula.

The scheme succeeded. The king graciously granted his own Kingdom of Sardinia-Savoy-Piedmont a constitution and founded a parliament, which, weak as it was, surpassed what most Italians had had before (namely, no legislatures at all). The Piedmontese government built roads, schools, and hospitals. Other Italians began to admire the little northern kingdom. Yet Cavour's sponsorship of the republican mercenary **Giuseppe Garibaldi** almost derailed the plan. In 1861, Garibaldi and his thousand volunteers, the "Red Shirts" (named after their minimalist uniform), were supposed to invade Sicily and cause disturbances that would illustrate the need for Piedmontese leadership in Italian politics. Garibaldi swiftly conquered the island, but he then sailed to the mainland, where he took control of the Kingdom of Naples and even marched on Rome itself. Piedmontese armies rushed south to meet him, and Cavour managed to convince Garibaldi to turn his winnings into a united Kingdom of Italy.

From there, a few more tricks were required to round out the kingdom. Italy bribed France by giving it the provinces of Savoy and Nice. In 1866, Italy, France, and Prussia defeated the Habsburgs and forced them to surrender Lombardy and Venice. The last major obstacle to Italian unity was the papacy. Popes had possessed political power in central Italy since the fall of Rome in the fifth century. In 1870, during the Franco-Prussian War, the French troops protecting the Papal States withdrew. The Italians took control and made Rome the kingdom's capital. The pope resented this new Kingdom of Italy and forbade Roman Catholics to cooperate with it. Nonetheless, Italy soon took its place among the great powers (see map 12.1).

The unification of **Germany** (1862–1871) saw a similar process. Unlike Italy, there had actually been a united Germany back in the Middle Ages, but it had quickly expanded into the Holy Roman Empire, which came to include northern Italy, Burgundy, Bohemia, and the Lowlands. The Wars of the Coalitions had shattered the Holy Roman Empire, but in 1815, a German confederation replaced it. This confederation never functioned well, largely because of the rivalry over leadership between Prussia and Austria. The liberal attempt to create a unified Germany through the Frankfurt Parliament in 1848 failed completely.

The young Prussian aristocrat **Otto von Bismarck** liked neither the Frankfurt

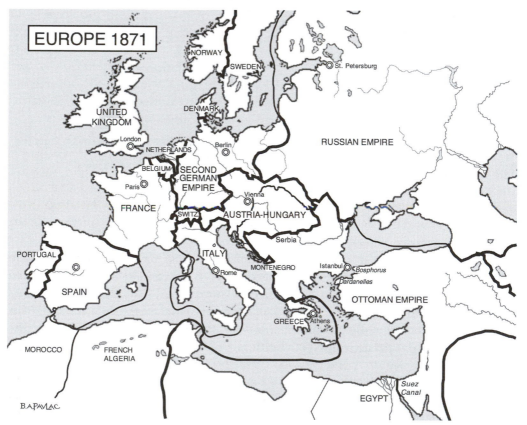

Map 12.1. Europe, 1871

Parliament nor the confederation. From 1862 to 1890, he was prime minister, or chancellor, of Prussia. Imitating Cavour, Bismarck planned and carried out the unification of Germany under the Hohenzollerns of Prussia, thereby excluding the Habsburgs of Austria. He turned Prussia into a more modern, liberal state, albeit with a weak constitution and parliament. His Realpolitik, though, preferred warfare, which he called decision by "blood and iron." Bismarck knew he had to fight, especially against Austria, to overcome the resistance of other great powers to German unity. He therefore tricked his opponents into declaring wars and then defeated them one after another with the most modern army in Europe.

Bismarck's success remodeled Europe. In the Seven Weeks War (1866), the efficient Prussian army with advanced planning and rapid-firing breech-loading rifles quickly defeated Austria. Ousted from any part in a future united Germany, a weakened Austrian imperial government granted political power to the Magyars or Hungarians, transforming the state into the Dual Monarchy of **Austria-Hungary** in 1867. Sadly for the Slavs and others, their nationalistic hopes under the Habsburg's German and Magyar rule remained unfulfilled.

Next, in 1870 the Spanish throne had become vacant, and princes from several dynasties proposed to begin a new dynasty. One day, Chancellor Bismarck received an insignificant report about his king, Wilhelm I, who was vacationing at the spa of Ems. A petty French diplomat had bothered the king in the hope that no prince of the Hohenzollern dynasty would compete for Spain. In a brilliant stroke of Realpolitik, Bismarck reworded the "Ems Dispatch" to make it seem as if the French had insulted the Prussian king. Napoleon III's pride led him to declare war against Prussia. In the Franco-Prussian War (1870–1871), Bismarck drew in the southern German states, and the combined Prussian and German forces swiftly defeated France. In the Hall of Mirrors in Versailles, the German princes acclaimed the Prussian king as German Emperor Wilhelm I Hohenzollern. The Second German Empire (1871–1918) quickly rose to be the most powerful country in Europe.

European nationalism, however, found difficulty including the Jews who had lived in Germany, Italy, and many other older European countries for centuries. Life had not always been easy, since many Christian rulers of the Middle Ages and Renaissance practiced anti-Semitism, whether in the form of lack of civil rights, prohibition from most jobs, confinement in ghettoes, expulsions from countries such as England or Spain, and occasional pogroms (slaughtering of Jewish communities). Renaissance Venice invented the term *ghetto* for a neighborhood in which Jews had to live. With the tolerant humanitarianism of the Enlightenment, Jews actually gained civil rights. They could participate in politics and freely choose professions. Once they were allowed entrance to universities, many Jews rose to prosperity and prominence in law, education, and medicine. Jews themselves had to decide how much to assimilate, or act like their Western neighbors. Some asserted strong cultural identity in language, clothing, and religious worship. Many, though, ceased to keep a distinctly Jewish culture and became "secular."

Ironically, the Jews' sudden success and prominence in the nineteenth century only provoked more anti-Semitism. The most famous example of anti-Semitism from that time was the **Dreyfus Affair** (1894–1906) in France. The French government tried and convicted Captain Alfred Dreyfus, a Jew, of treason in 1894 for turning over secrets to the Germans. They imprisoned him on Devil's Island, a sweltering penal colony located off the coast of South America. Actually, Dreyfus was innocent. Further investigation soon found the real traitor, a well-born aristocrat, Esterházy. Astoundingly, a trial found Esterházy innocent in 1899. The subsequent arguments over Dreyfus' guilt or innocence exposed the fractures in France's unified national façade. After a second trial wrongly convicted Dreyfus again in 1899, only a presidential intervention in 1906 freed him.

As a consequence of the hostility toward Jews that was exposed by this affair, the Jews invented their own nationalism, called *Zionism*. In 1897, the first World Zionist Congress convened in Basel, Switzerland. The delegates faced a real difficulty: how could the Jews have their own country if some people or another already occupied every livable space in the whole world? Although some Jews suggested forming a homeland in South America or Africa, most aimed for the traditional homeland of Palestine, which was at the time a province of the Ottoman Empire. The Ottomans did permit some Jewish immigration at first, since the Jews were a source of revenue. But how many Jews could poor Palestine accommodate, as more arrived?

The issue of the Jews and their attempt at nationalism exposed the most difficult flaw in nationalism: how should nation-states deal with people who did not conform to nationalist standards? Every state had people of other ethnic groups within its borders. Diverse people lived next to one another everywhere, especially since the rise of mobility in modern society. When nationalists gave up on tolerance of ethnic differences, only three choices remained: forcing conformity in outward cultural behavior, imposing confinement to certain parts of the country, or eliminating through exile or death. Any one of these choices, though, provoked conflict. Nationalism has often encouraged domination, but rarely cooperation.

Paradoxically and tragically, nationalism came to mix with imperialism. Just as ideologists were asserting rigidly defined states along ethnic lines, they also encouraged these nation-based states to create multi-ethnic overseas empires. Yet this imperialism was a contradiction. As conquered peoples everywhere learned of nationalism, they then aspired to run their own lives along ethnic principles. While imperialism has since mostly vanished, nationalism has survived as a prevalent concept uniting and dividing people today.

Review: *How did various nationalisms unify and divide Western nations?*

Response:

THE BALKAN CAULDRON

The center of nationalist and imperialist conflict at the beginning of the twentieth century was the Balkan Peninsula, that large triangle of land roughly south of a line drawn from the north of the Adriatic to the north of the Black Sea. The ethnic divisions of western Europe really seemed quite simple compared with those of the Balkans, where multiple ethnicities had vied for dominance for centuries. Along the Adriatic, the Albanians may have been one of the first European peoples. Then the ancient Greeks had been dominant in the very south, and the Romans conquered the area up to the Danube. At the collapse of the western Roman Empire in the fifth century A.D., Germans dominated the peninsula; but most of them eventually left for central and western Europe. The Slavic peoples followed, and soon Serbs, Croats, and Slovenes outnumbered the less-famous Montenegrins, Pomacks, and Torbeshes. In the tenth century, Vlachs, Bulgars, and the Magyars invaded. Romany (or Gypsy folk) wandered through the peninsula. And, as always, there were some Jews in the cities. Finally, as described in chapter 9, the Ottoman Turkish Empire imposed its own order on the region in the Late Middle Ages.

Once a powerful rival to the West, the Ottoman Empire had suffered decline since 1600. The Turks did not experience the commercial, scientific, industrial, religious, and intellectual revolutions of Renaissance, Reformation, and Enlightenment nor the English/American/French political revolutions. The empire's sultans came to power through harem plots, and many of its religious leaders preached against Western ways. Its bureaucracy operated according to complexity rather than efficiency. Its armies practiced tradition rather than innovation. The Ottoman Empire soon lacked the ability to defend itself and earned the nickname "the Sick Man of Europe."

After the failed Turkish siege of Vienna in 1683, the Habsburgs reclaimed all of Hungary, Croatia, and bits of other provinces from the Turks. By the eighteenth century, though, Austria found itself unable to further liberate the Balkans from Turkish rule. While Austria grudgingly accepted the Ottoman Empire as a necessary part of the European state system, in 1815, others saw it as ripe to be challenged.

The first nationalist movement to upset the status quo was that of the founding people of Western civilization, the Greeks. Of course, there had never been a unified state called Greece before. Modern descendants of Spartans and Athenians now decided they wanted their own country, historical precedent notwithstanding. They organized a nationalist rebellion, the **Greek Revolt** (1821–1829).

At first, the Western great powers accepted the Muslim absolute monarchy's war against the Greeks, obedient to the conservative principle of preserving political stability. Many of the common people of Europe, however, saw the Greeks as Romantic heroes, if not fellow westerners, and they sent aid. Some, like the poet Lord Byron, even went off to fight for them (although he died quite unromantically of dysentery). With pressure from their own people, the great powers stepped in to provide a conservative, not a nationalist, solution. The new Kingdom of Greece was provided with an absolute monarch from a German, not Greek, dynasty.

The Greek effort brought a nationalist revolt to Europe, soon imitated by Italy and Germany. Likewise, Greece's Balkan neighbors could not help noticing its example. Many of the peoples in the Balkans began to embrace nationalistic ideas. **Pan-slavism** called for all Slavs to live together. The Russians, as the dominant Slavic group, pushed this the most, by embracing Poles, Ukrainians, and others. A more-focused attitude of nationalism, called **yugo-slavism**, promoted the idea that the southern Slavs of the Balkans should unite. The Serbians, the largest group among these Slavs, favored this policy.

Meanwhile, the expanding Romanov Russian Empire decided to expand southward. Russia targeted the Ottoman Turkish Empire in the name of Orthodox Christian unity, pan-slavism, and imperialism. In a series of wars, the Russians fought their way south to the northern coast of the Black Sea and then around it on either side: in the west toward the mouth of the Danube River in the Balkans, and in the east across the Caucasus Mountains, where they conquered Azerbaijanis, Georgians, and Chechens.

The Russian success alarmed the other Western powers. Britain especially feared that Russian fleets might gain access to the Mediterranean from the Black Sea through the Bosphorus and the Dardanelles, thereby complicating the balance of power. After Russia occupied the Ottoman provinces of Moldavia and Wallachia, Britain and France sided with the Turks in the **Crimean War** (1853–1856) fought on that peninsula in the Black Sea.

This little war is remarkably memorable. First, the traditional enemies England and France cooperated. Second, they learned to overcome the logistical difficulties of fighting so far from their homelands. Third, the work of Florence Nightingale (b. 1820–d. 1910) with the wounded started to promote modern nursing. She taught her male superiors about the benefits of hygiene, rest, and kind attention for soldiers recovering from camp diseases and modern explosive weapons. Fourth, the British poet Tennyson's poem "The Charge of the Light Brigade" tried to stir up courage in the face of futile attacks against deadly cannon fire. And finally, soldiers brought back to Europe the habit of cigarette smoking as a more popular means of consuming tobacco than chewing or smoking cigars or pipes.

While the Crimean War slowed the Russians' advance, they were determined to press on. In 1877, Muslim Ottoman troops slaughtered several thousand Orthodox Christian Bulgarians because of a rebellion against the dynasty. The Russians once again attacked the Ottoman Empire on the pretext of avenging a Turkish massacre. Russia quickly won a resounding victory, and Russian diplomats began to redraw the borders of the Balkans, realizing Russia's pan-slavist hopes. The other great powers, however, again stepped in and brought the Russians to the Congress of Berlin in 1878 (not to be confused with the Congress of Berlin in 1884, which dealt with Africa). This congress forced the Russians to renounce their gains. In doing so, it created the new countries of **Serbia**, **Bulgaria**, and **Rumania**, each stabilized with conservative monarchies.

It seemed only a matter of time until the empire was picked to pieces. The new states of Serbia, Bulgaria, and Rumania were dissatisfied with their new borders. Each looked across its borders into other states and saw people of the same nationality "trapped" in other countries. In Ottoman-ruled Macedonia, some of those people formed one of the first modern terrorist groups, IMRO (Internal Macedonian Revolutionary Organization). Swearing loyalty over a gun and a Bible, its members fought against both Muslim rule and the territory-hungry desires of Serbia, Rumania, and Bulgaria. Austria-Hungary was supposed to preserve **Bosnia-Herzegovina** as a protectorate. Instead, Austrian politicians annexed Bosnia outright in 1908 as a gift for the aged Habsburg Emperor Francis-Joseph's sixtieth anniversary of coming to the throne. Some Turks tried to slow the momentum toward dismembering the Ottoman Empire. A coup d'état by a group of westernizing nationalists called the **"Young Turks"** in 1908 encouraged *pan-turkism*, or using Turkish nationalism to strengthen the empire. Before such a policy could take effect, Italy launched the Italo-Turkish War (1911) to seize the large Ottoman province of Tripoli or Libya, just across the Mediterranean in North Africa (see map 12.2). Interestingly, Italy's venture into modern war provided the first experimental use of both airplanes and poison gas as weapons. Defeating the "Sick Man of Europe" in Africa was a task even Italy's military forces could manage.

Italy's unjustifiable attack upon the Turks encouraged the other Balkan states to imitate its success. In October 1912, Serbia, Rumania, Bulgaria, Montenegro, and Greece pounced on Macedonia, beginning the First Balkan War (1912–1913). The success of the Balkan states in the first war raised the concern of the European

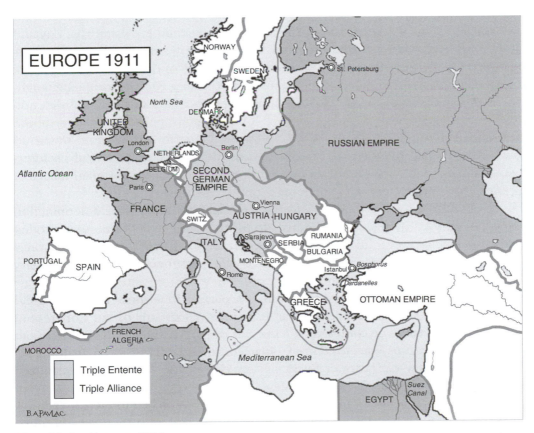

Map 12.2.   Europe, 1911

powers. They convened a conference at London in the spring of 1913 to settle matters. While at the negotiating table, the greedy Bulgarians decided to try to secure what they could on their own. Bulgaria launched a preemptive strike on its recent allies in June, beginning the Second Balkan War (1913).

When the fighting stopped in August 1913, a peace conference set up new borders. Bulgaria had suffered some losses, most importantly its Mediterranean coastline. Rumania and Greece benefited nicely. Serbia ended up with the key chunk of Macedonia. Austria also encouraged the creation of the country of **Albania**. This move followed nationalist principles since the ethnic Albanians were not closely related to the Serbs—they were not even Slavs. Nevertheless, Serbia had wanted to rule over the Albanians, especially to gain a coastline and seaports on the Adriatic Sea.

Consequently, Serbian nationalists felt especially frustrated and focused much of their anger on Austria-Hungary. Elements within the Serbian secret police formed a terrorist organization, the Black Hand, to strike against the Habsburgs. They recruited ethnic Serbian college students from Bosnia. Serbian officials trained these young Bosnians in small arms so that they could carry out an assassination, a method of terrorism made popular by anarchists. The terrorists struck on 28 June 1914, as the heir to the Austro-Hungarian throne, Archduke **Franz Ferdinand**, and his wife, Sophie, visited the Bosnian capital of Sarajevo. The amateurish assassins were less than successful at first. Although a bomb bounced off the archduke's car and injured some soldiers and civilians, security remained lax. Later that day, the archduke's car made a wrong turn and stopped just where Gavrilo Princip was getting a sandwich. The terrorist shot Franz Ferdinand and Sophie at point-blank range. They were dead within minutes, their three young children orphaned.

The political leadership of Austria-Hungary pounced on this incident as a pretext for war against Serbia. Emperor Franz-Josef did not much care for his nephew, and at that time no firm evidence was known linking the Serbian government to the terrorists. But the Austrians thought war would solve their problems with Serbia. Their only ally, the Germans, backed them up with a virtual blank check, a promise to support Austria in whatever action it might take. It took a month after the assassination for the cautious Austrians to send an ultimatum to Serbia, long after the story and sympathy had faded from the front pages of newspapers. The Serbians, as expected, did not accept the whole ultimatum and mobilized their military in preparation for the expected war. On 1 August 1914, Austria-Hungary declared war on Serbia. That lit the fuse for World War I.

Overall, the nineteenth century's experience of nationalism was mixed. It did indeed promote some major peaceful arts. Nationalists identified, categorized, and recorded the language and literature, song and dance, costume and custom of the myriad ethnic groups who resided in Europe. Turning ethnicity into nationality, however, had required wars ranging from such diverse locations as the Alps or the Andes, the Rhine or the Rio Grande, the islands in the Caribbean or the Aegean. Even worse, what should have been no more than a petty third Balkan war between Austria-Hungary and Serbia instead metastasized into the worst conflict in human history up to that point.

Review: How did nationalism and the decline of the Ottoman Empire create instability in the Balkans?

Response:

THE GREAT WAR

Both imperialism and nationalism came together to provide the fuel for the Great War, now known as **World War I** (1914–1918). This first of the three great global conflicts of the twentieth century deserves the global part of its title mostly because of the enormous damage it inflicted and the worldwide reach of its consequences (see timeline 12.1). Although some battles took place in Africa, the South American coast, and the Pacific, the overwhelming bulk of the fighting happened in Europe, in the heart of Western civilization (see map 12.3).

Everyone expected Franz Ferdinand's assassination to spark a war between Austria-Hungary and Serbia, yet few anticipated the conflagration that resulted. Each participant who joined in envisioned a short, sharp war, where the guns of August would be silenced by Christmas. Each nation confidently believed that civilization

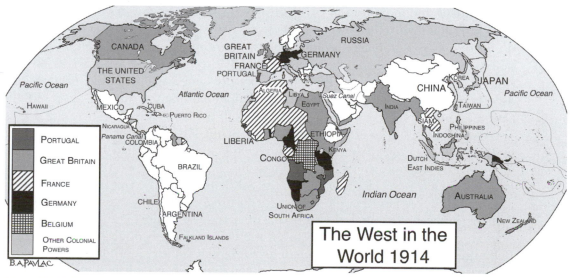

Map 12.3. The West in the World, 1914

and/or God stood with her alone. Each felt aggrieved by the actions of the others. Serbia wanted to dominate the Balkans. Austria wanted a reckoning with Serbia. Russia wanted revenge against Austria. France wanted revenge against Germany. Britain wanted to maintain its international supremacy. The Ottoman Empire wanted to survive. Italy wanted an empire. Few got what they wanted.

Historians have particularly debated about how Germany's war aims shaped the origins of World War I. Many German nationalists had called for an overseas empire to gain the Second German Empire its place in the sun. The clumsy efforts of Kaiser Wilhelm II (r. 1888–1918) to promote German prestige (such as comparing them to the Huns) had other Europeans viewing this latecomer to geopolitics as a bumbling upstart.

Much more responsible for nations declaring the war, however, were the alliances locked in during the previous decades. On one side was the **Triple Alliance,** begun by Chancellor Bismarck to preserve the newly united Germany from French revenge. Therein he bound Austria-Hungary and Italy in a mutual defense agreement with Germany. On the other side was the **Triple Entente**, which France had slowly pulled together in reaction to the Triple Alliance. France carefully balanced itself between Great Britain and Russia, although all three had many traditional and contemporary rivalries among one another. Their combined mistrust and fear of Germany, however, ultimately proved greater than their suspicions about one another. These alliances had originally been intended to prevent war by making conflict too risky. Instead, they turned into mutually supportive military cooperatives, twisting the delicate balance of power into two hostile blocs. Intensifying the alliances were military strategies connected to **mobilization**, or getting armed forces from peacetime standing to wartime footing. The vast armies supported by modern industrialization, transportation, and communication required complex timetables to get their troops where they were needed to either attack or defend. Generals thus pressured politicians to join any fighting in time for mobilization to be effective.

Alliances and mobilization plans escalated the war from a minor Balkan brawl to a clash that involved almost all of Western civilization. After Austria declared war on Serbia, Russia mobilized against Austria, wanting to support its Slavic fellows' defense. Realistically, Russia's claim to mobilize only against Austria was absurd since the Germans knew that Russian plans were aimed against both Germany and Austria. Hence the Germans immediately demanded that the Russians stop mobilization and the French declare their neutrality in the conflict.

The Germans' own strategy (called the Schlieffen Plan after the general who first proposed it) was to defend against an expected slow Russian attack in the east while swiftly striking against Russia's main ally, France, in the west. After taking out Paris within a few weeks, according to the Schlieffen Plan, the Germans would then eliminate the Russian forces at leisure. Accordingly, when the French hesitated to declare themselves neutral, the Germans declared war against France. The German plan to capture Paris, though, required a quick passage through officially neutral Belgium. When German troops began invading that country, both the Belgians and the British objected to the violation of Belgian neutrality established in 1830. Great Britain saw a German occupation of Belgium, which lay at the end of the English

Channel, as too dangerous. When the Germans refused to withdraw, the British reluctantly declared war. So by the end of the first week of August, Russia, France, Great Britain, and Serbia were fighting Germany and Austria-Hungary.

Unfortunately for all the well-made plans, general staffs failed to account for the huge numbers of troops as well as variations caused by both commanders and dumb luck. The British sent troops too quickly to France, Russia invaded too rapidly in eastern Prussia, and France pushed too swiftly in the Alsace. The massive German armies were slowed by unexpected Belgian resistance and then turned southward toward Paris a bit too soon. In response, Parisians rushed enough troops to the front, some in taxicabs, to halt the German advance. Neither side could attack the other's flank since the armies were so huge. So the Germans withdrew a few miles and dug in. Swiftness transformed into slowness as both sides huddled in trenches along a western front stretching from the North Sea to the Swiss border.

Thus, the fighting on the western front unexpectedly developed into **trench warfare**. The Crimean War and the American Civil War had already pointed in this direction, but few commanders had learned from those conflicts. A few soldiers dug in and armed with machine guns could pulverize thousands of approaching enemy troops, especially when assisted by barbed wire, land mines, and distant artillery. Millions of troops faced one another, alternating between aimless boredom in the muddy, filthy, reeking trenches and combat in explosive terror. The German attempt to take Verdun alone cost hundreds of thousands of lives on both sides over several months. Although the French managed to repulse the German attack, the Battle of Verdun weakened the French so much that they could hardly launch any more offensives themselves. The British launched the Battle of the Somme in the north to help relieve the pressure on the French at Verdun. On the first morning, thirty thousand British soldiers were slaughtered in about an hour. Both sides applied new weapons to break the stalemate. But airplanes, poisonous gas, and even tanks (armored vehicles) proved unable to capture victory for either side.

While the western front got most of the press, other fronts also saw massive destruction. Great armies rumbling back and forth across hundreds of miles of territory ravaged Poland and the Balkans. In East Africa, some German forces held out for the entire war. Already in the fall of 1914, the Germans pressured the Ottoman Empire into joining their side. Instead of opening up decisive fronts against Russia, the Ottoman Empire found itself vulnerable. After a disastrous campaign along the Russian-Turkish border in the Caucasus, the Muslim Turks suspected that the Christian Armenians were collaborating with the Christian Russians. Beginning in April 1915, the Turks forcibly relocated the Armenians, marching them hundreds of miles across barren landscapes without proper supplies. These so-called **Armenian massacres** led to hundreds of thousands of deaths from exhaustion, starvation, exposure, drowning, and shooting. These incidents later led to the invention of the word *genocide*—the killing off of an entire ethnic group (although the Turkish government has continued to dispute this interpretation). Whatever one calls these atrocities, the men, women, and children remain dead.

Ultimately, the acquisition of allies became the key to victory. Germany, Austria-Hungary, and the Ottoman Empire became known as the **Central Powers**, surrounded as they were by their enemies. Italy refused to support its Triple Alliance partners and stayed neutral at first. Bulgaria soon joined the Central Powers, still resentful of its losses in the Second Balkan War and willing to crush Serbia. The so-called Allied Powers or **Allies** of Russia, France, Belgium, Great Britain, and Serbia early on outnumbered the Central Powers. Still, German military skill and industrial efficiency might have won the war for its side if the war had been short. The Central Powers' inability to find more allies doomed them in the long run.

The weight of the world slowly massed against the Central Powers as the Allies won more allies to their side. In the fall of 1914, Japan eagerly declared war on Germany and occupied most of its Asian and Pacific possessions. By 1915, the Allies had convinced Italy to attack Austria, tempting it with territory to be confiscated from its former Triple Alliance partner. The Allies enticed the Greeks with possessions to be seized from the Bulgarians and the Ottomans. The British tried to win the support of Arabs in the Ottoman Empire and international Jews at the same time. In the Sykes-Picot Agreement, the British supported the creation of Arab nation-states after the war. By 1917, the British officer T. E. Lawrence (Lawrence of Arabia) had inspired an Arab revolt against the Ottomans in the Arabian Peninsula. At the same time, the **Balfour Declaration** supported a Jewish homeland in Palestine. The Allies did not care that such promises were mutually exclusive.

On the high seas, the British were also hopeful for a decisive blow against the Germans. Short of that, the British hoped that a blockade would starve out the Central Powers. In turn, the Germans tried to blockade the British Isles with another new weapon of war: U-boats or submarines. To neutral nations, submarines seemed more cruel than traditional surface warships, since survivors of an attack could not be rescued by the small, vulnerable vessels.

The Germans especially annoyed the Americans with their submarine warfare. Most notorious was a German U-boat's torpedoing of the passenger ship *Lusitania* (1915), which sank so swiftly that hundreds of people drowned within sight of the Irish coast. Even though the *Lusitania* was a legitimate target that was carrying contraband (weapons and military supplies) in a war zone, the many civilian deaths violated the American sense of fair play. To appease the Americans, the Germans limited their U-boat attacks to warships for a little over a year.

Early in 1917, the Germans further angered Americans with the infamous Zimmermann Telegram. In it the German government tried to convince Mexico to attack the United States even though Mexico could not have launched an offensive, since civil war was then raging. The British intercepted Zimmermann's telegram by tapping into the transatlantic undersea cable and handed over the telegram to the Americans. In April 1917 the United States declared war against the Central Powers (along with a handful of Latin American countries and China).

For three years, the European nations had been exhausting themselves trying to win on their own. Drained of men and resources, the home front became the last crucial area of war efforts toward victory. Out of necessity, most industrialized states had adopted ***war socialism***, under which governments took control of large sectors of the economy, creating a new military-industrial complex. Central planning by government bureaucrats working with leaders of industry ensured access to raw materials and production for the armed forces. Workers gained better wages and benefits to keep up their production of munitions and provisions without striking. Many women entered the public workforce in offices and factories to replace manpower sent to the armies. Consumers tolerated shortages of goods and services in order to help the troops.

To keep up flagging morale, regimes used the modern media for the spread of **propaganda**—information twisted to support a political cause. Lying British propaganda falsely convinced many Allies and Americans that the Germans were monstrous "Huns," despoilers and murderers of innocent women and children. Protestors against the war or activists for women's suffrage ended up silenced and in jail. At the time, U.S. Senator Hiram Johnson insightfully observed that the first victim of war is the truth.

By the autumn of 1918, the peoples of the Central Powers were surprised to discover that they had lost the war, although their governments had always assured them that victory was within grasp. They had briefly hoped for victory when Russia fell out of the war, convulsed by revolution (see the next chapter). America's finances, industrial might, and even its quickly trained armies more than made up for the loss of Russia to the Allies. By late October and early November, the Ottoman Empire, Bulgaria, Austria-Hungary, and, finally, Germany were caught up in their own revolutions, and their armies collapsed. They surrendered, one after the other.

When the killing stopped at 11 a.m. on the eleventh day of the eleventh month of 1918, more than eleven million victims of combat and disease were dead. Millions more had been wounded, some suffering vicious, horrible mutilations made possible only by modern poisonous and explosive chemicals. Billions of dollars of capital had been spent and blown up. Millions of acres of territories had been ravaged; untold thousands of families had been made homeless. Dynasties had been toppled and states shattered: the Romanovs in Russia, the Hohenzollerns in Germany, the Habsburgs in Austria-Hungary, and the Ottomans in Turkey all lost their thrones. Whole populations were demoralized and on the edge of disintegration. Many thought—hoped—that this would be the war to end all wars. Sadly, it was only a prelude to worse conflicts.

Review: *What made World War I more destructive and transformative than all previous wars?*

Response:

CHAPTER 13

Rejections of Democracy

The Interwar Years and World War II, 1918 to 1945

Many people in the West thought they had won World War I in the name of democracy. Western civilization increasingly promoted the idea that most adults in a state should share in rule, making decisions through conflict and compromise within legal and moral boundaries of behavior in established parliaments and other representative bodies. While such participatory politics had been growing in power and influence since the seventeenth century, democracy remained difficult. Democratic governments were undermined by the Great War's loss of life, the economic destruction, high-handed government policies, the shattering of old morals and traditions, and a flawed peace process. The "war to end all wars" led to worse ones.

DECLINE OF THE WEST?

The Scientific Revolution had offered science as the vehicle of humanity's progress toward peace and prosperity. But the modern chemical explosives and machined weapons of the Great War showed how science might instead drive nations toward death and destruction. Nor could science help as a worldwide plague, the **influenza pandemic** (1918–1919), killed perhaps as many as twenty-five million people worldwide, more than twice the deaths caused by the recent war. The flu germs swept around the globe with amazing velocity and lethality. Only the natural mutation of the germ and resistance of the human immune system defeated the plague. But what could prevent another such from striking? Many people no longer had the same confidence that science could make the world a better place.

New scientific views in physics that followed those of Darwin in biology and Freud in psychiatry further weakened confidence that the world could be understood and improved. Einstein's complex **theory of relativity** (1916) replaced the logical simplicity and sensible familiarity of Newton's clockwork universe. According to this new theory, a person's position of observation, or point of view, could affect such facts as the measure of time or distance. Even matter and energy were interchangeable, according to the famous formula $E = mc^2$ (energy equals mass times the speed of light squared). The physicist Heisenberg's uncertainty principle (1927) stated that one could know either the location or the direction of an atom's electron, but not both simultaneously. This atomic theory became a metaphor for an era of increasing doubt.

The future of world peace also grew increasingly uncertain, despite the clear victory of the Allied Powers in the Great War. The American president Woodrow Wilson in particular had proclaimed that the Great War was about making the world safe for democracy. Indeed, many of the new countries created out of the peace settlement of the Paris Peace Treaties declared themselves to be democratic. They actually made reasonable attempts at practicing responsible self-government. Real participation of all adult citizens—with laws and amendments even finally granting the vote to women—reached its high point in most modern industrialized states just after the Great War. Having the structures of republican government, though, did not always result in actual respect for the democratic process.

The Great War's peace process ironically undermined principles of democracy. Negotiations had started off with much optimism in Paris in January 1919. At that time, the Europeans welcomed Woodrow Wilson, the first sitting U.S. president ever to leave the country. Since America's power had won the war for the Allies, the other leaders of the "Big Four" allies (Lloyd George of Britain, Clemenceau of France, and Orlando of Italy) grudgingly accepted his preeminence. A year earlier, in January 1918, while the war was still raging, Wilson had already set the tone for peace proposals with the declaration of his **Fourteen Points.** These ideals proposed a world of international cooperation with open and honest diplomacy, support for nationalistic principles, and avoidance of warfare. The European peoples certainly hoped, based on the sound common sense and decency of the Fourteen Points, that Wilson's American vision would establish a better future for all nations.

Wilson also envisioned a new international institution, the **League of Nations**. This organization was meant to replace the obviously failed practice of sovereign nations facing off in a balance of power, with or without alliances. Instead, the League was to promote collective security in a fashion similar to the Concert of

Europe conducted by the Congress of Vienna a century before. Its ever-present forum of delegates would replace the need for emergency congresses or conferences every time an international crisis threatened to flare into war. The League offered the possibility for diverse nations with divergent interests to work together rather than against one another. Another world war, people rightfully feared, could doom civilization as they knew it.

It was too much to hope, however, that a few months of negotiations could easily overcome the grudges and disagreements amassed during a thousand years of European conflict since the Treaty of Verdun in 847. Complicating matters further were the aspirations of oppressed colonial peoples all over the world. The League's own doom was largely determined by the very place in which it was called into existence, namely Paris, the capital of Germany's bitter enemy. Instead of forging a new beginning for cooperation in Europe, those who wanted to punish the Central Powers outmaneuvered Wilson's good intentions. In the **Treaty of Versailles**, signed in Louis XIV's baroque palace, the Allies forced the Germans to accept the primary blame for the war. That treaty also pointedly excluded Germany from this new organization of "free" peoples. Thus, one of the most important great powers was left out. The victorious Allies also shut out their former great power ally, Russia, because (as explained below) of its new communist government.

The worst blow to League membership was when the United States refused to join. Many Americans had never shared Wilson's vision of world participation; they instead thought the United States should return to an isolationist attitude. These Americans tried to ignore the reality that the United States was inextricably tied up in world affairs with its colonies in the Pacific, its grip on the Caribbean and Latin America, and its worldwide economic reach. Additionally, partisan politics poisoned the process. Wilson was a Democrat, and both houses of Congress were held by Republican majorities. The Republican leaders of the Senate, which constitutionally ratified treaties, suggested a few changes they thought would preserve American independence of action and control over its own armed forces. Wilson refused to compromise and embarked on a whirlwind campaign to win popular support for "his" treaty. The stress of traveling thousands of miles in just a few weeks brought on a stroke, which incapacitated him. His wife, Edith, practically ran the White House for months, as she interpreted the bedridden president's feeble attempts at communication.

Wilson's removal from politics meant that the United States of America signed a separate peace with Germany, without the covenant concerning the League of Nations. So the United States turned its back on the League of Nations. Great Britain and France, nervous about the growing influence of American power, were glad at first to see the Americans leave. For the next two decades, the isolationist United States retreated behind the imaginary shelter of the Arctic, Pacific, and Atlantic Oceans. These bodies of water, however, declined as defensive barriers in an age of iron-hulled motorized ships and aircraft.

Ironically, the United States had become essential to Western civilization even as it withdrew its political interests. Before World War I, most cultural, economic, and social significance came from Europe. After the war, European society seemed stagnant compared to the creativity coming from Americans. During the **Roaring Twenties**, America swelled with the artistic creativity of the Jazz Age. The "Lost Generation" of American writers, disillusioned by both World War I and American materialism, led the literary elites of the West. As the main creditor nation of European war debts, New York replaced London as the capital of finance (see figure 13.1). This cultural and economic shift to the New World remained unthreatening to the Old World because of the United States' reluctance to maintain large armed forces or to throw around its diplomatic weight. American jazz music, however, hit Europe hard, thrilling those who were moved by its African-based rhythms and horrifying those who could not hear its beauty or appreciate its complexity.

Millions first heard jazz music over the new invention of **radio**, which tied the world's cultures together as never before. Although invented before the war, radio

Figure 13.1.   New York. A construction worker on a skyscraper in New York admires the nighttime skyline.

as a medium came into its own in the 1920s. Radio stations were built all over the industrialized nations. Although usage taxes (paid by owners of radio sets) supported public broadcasting in many European countries, advertising mostly financed radio's expansion in the United States. Either way, radio signals reached around the globe, especially thanks to the British Broadcasting Corporation's growth through the British Empire.

When not gathered at home around their radios for entertainment, Western audiences also flocked to the **movies**. Movies, like radio, had started in industrialized countries before the war but became wildly popular afterward. Movie theaters or cinemas, specially built or adapted from performance halls, showed films of current events, works adapted from classic plays and literature, or newly created works. American filmmakers in the sunshine of Hollywood became the most prolific creators of that medium worldwide, soon outproducing the Europeans.

Movies became a dominant feature of Western culture. One of the first movie stars, the British-born Charlie Chaplin with his "Little Tramp" character, became an iconic figure around the globe. For the first few years, movies had no sound except as provided by local musicians in the theaters. The first movie with synchronized sound, *The Jazz Singer* (1929), portrayed the clash of old culture (a Jewish cantor) with his modernized and Americanized son (the jazz singer of the title). It symbolized the new age replacing the traditional past. Because of the success radio and movies had in English-speaking countries, English increasingly became the language of international media and culture.

The new world tied together by radio and movies seemed even smaller because of new innovations in transportation. Airplanes soared across oceans. Lindbergh captured the public imagination with the first solo flight from New York to Paris (1927). His instant fame showed how radio and newsreels spread information and invented personalities. Airlines soon began to fly paying passengers across all barriers of land and sea. The most popular and affordable transport was the motorcar or automobile, symbolic of the movement and force of the twentieth century. As the car became the backbone of industrial production, the demand for paved roads and parking began to radically transform the urban and rural landscape. Affordable automobiles allowed more young people to escape parental supervision, making the "back seat" a byword for sexual opportunity.

The standards of living rose briskly in most of the industrialized West during most of the 1920s. At first, the economic costs and destruction of the Great War had drained the resources of many European nations, so it took a few years to realign their economies back to peacetime production. Then, consumer consumption became the great engine for economic growth of modern economies. More manufacturing meant better pay and benefits for productive workers. While advertising enticed westerners to purchase goods and services, easier access to credit lent them the means to do it quickly and conveniently. A rising level of prosperity nurtured an irresistible tendency toward materialism. Refrigerators and washing machines were soon not just modern conveniences but necessities. Leisure time and vacations came to be expected. By the late 1920s, members of the widening Western middle classes were enjoying themselves as never before.

For some people, that enjoyment included consuming recreational chemicals.

Psychoactive substances such as opium (increasingly purified into morphine and heroin), cocaine, and marijuana became more accessible due to modern agriculture, processing, and transportation. Authorities in Western nations grew concerned over increasing rates of addiction and the resultant social destruction. They began to regulate and outlaw dangerous drugs. The United States went furthest, outlawing the manufacture and selling of alcohol with a law declaring Prohibition (1920–1933). Alcohol was, of course, the most widespread recreational drug since civilization began, whether in the form of beer, wine, or distilled liquor. The American experiment with controlling alcohol consumption was unusual and ultimately unsuccessful. Unsurprisingly, recreational drug use remained prevalent in Western nations despite their official restrictions or prohibitions.

Despite a seeming prosperity, for some the rising materialism, increasing drug use, and spreading popular culture encouraged pessimism. For them, the war had killed or damaged so many promising youths, weakened traditional elites, and led to a decline in churchgoing. Oswald Spengler, in *The Decline of the West* (1922–1926), summed up people's fears. Although his book was more discussed than actually read, Spengler claimed in dense prose that Western civilization had become senile. The events of the 1930s seemed to prove his point.

The troubles began with the **Wall Street crash** (1929), which then triggered the worldwide economic collapse called the **Great Depression** (1929–1941). In the 1920s, the stock exchanges on Wall Street, the financial district of New York, had been pushing people to invest more money in business than ever before. The eagerness to own stock, even in companies that were overvalued, pushed the prices higher. Many people, both rich and middle class, were buying stock on credit, believing that prices would keep rising forever. Thus, billions of dollars in stock values had accumulated out of sheer optimism and greed. One Thursday morning, 24 October 1929, some investors began to doubt the alleged worth of these stocks and sold them while the market was high, hoping to cash out with big profits. The market fell so fast, though, that financial institutions began to collapse, and wealth disappeared. Within a few weeks, the value of the market had fallen by 50 percent, and it continued to fall for the next three years. Billions of dollars of capital simply vanished into thin air.

Since New York had become the pivotal center for the investment of capital, the Wall Street crash smashed other Western economies. Banks called in their loans, but borrowers had little with which to pay back. Even when banks confiscated collateral, such as homes or real estate, they still had too little cash on hand when investors demanded their deposits. Forced into bankruptcy, banks failed, and the life savings of millions of people disappeared. Many businesses could not meet payrolls, saw their capital resources drained, and closed their doors. As consumers had too little disposable wealth to buy goods and services, businesses shut down because new orders dried up. Workers then had no paychecks, further weakening demand and consumption. Governments tried to defend their countries' factories and farms by erecting protectionist trade barriers of high taxes or bans on imports. These measures only damaged international trade and little helped the domestic economies. Even food prices fell, forcing one out of every four farms into foreclosure in the United States. Millions of people went on the move looking for jobs, but few were to be found.

These effects spread through the industrialized West, hitting hardest in the United States, Japan, Germany, and Austria. The worldwide economic depression of the 1930s accelerated the abandonment of parliamentarianism in those countries where they had had too little time to take root. People began to question their government's competency or whether democracy could work at all. Great Britain, France, and a few others clung to their parliamentary democracies, while communist and socialist parties gained in elections in nearly all Western nations.

The only place where organized socialist and communist movements remained weak was in the United States. In America, the administration of President **Franklin Delano Roosevelt** (r. 1933–1945) found other solutions to the economic collapse. When FDR (as he was commonly called) ran for president in 1932, he revitalized the Democratic Party with a coalition of intellectuals, Southerners (both white and black), Jews, farmers, immigrants, and workers—all united in getting the economy moving. Roosevelt's advisors declared that the laissez-faire classical liberal economics was a dead fraud, since its free reign to the capitalists had brought on the economic collapse. Instead, he proposed a "New Deal" for Americans, with massive government intervention in the economy and the society.

The heart of the New Deal program was ***Keynesian economic theory***, which suggested a revision to the long-dominant theory of laissez-faire or classical liberal economics. Laissez-faire theory assumed that capital would always be available for investment. But the economic worldwide collapse of 1929 had eliminated many banks and much capital. To get out of such a serious economic collapse, when private capital was in short supply, British economist John Maynard Keynes recommended that governments spend money they borrowed from themselves. Such government spending could help fuel a recovery, which could then revive private capital investments. The massive public debt created by deficit spending could later be paid off through the normal taxation and borrowing from banks after people were working and investing again. Most Western governments began to adopt and use this deficit spending practice regularly.

Using deficit spending, Roosevelt's administration put Americans to work at government expense at jobs that ranged from planting trees to writing plays, building bridges to digging ditches. Nevertheless, the American economy failed to fully recover during the 1930s. Yet majorities of Americans, cheered by these efforts and FDR's image of cheerful and determined optimism, voted him into office four times, more times than any other U.S. president. Meanwhile, Roosevelt's political and economic enemies hated the growing power of the federal government and accused FDR of socialism and dictatorship.

Leaders of other democracies in the West did not enjoy the kind of popularity FDR had in America, although they did share his inability to end the depression. Those leaders who did gain popular followings actually became dictators and often carried out real socialist policies. One after another, many westerners turned away from enlightened participatory politics of liberal democratic parliamentarianism and handed over their fates to dictators. These dictators then tried to reshape the world into their own visions.

Review: *How did the West suffer cultural confusion in the wake of war?*

Response:

RUSSIANS IN REVOLT

The first great political alternative to the Western democracies arose out of World War I with the **Russian Revolution** (1917–1922). Before the Great War, the Russian Empire had already been playing catch-up as it ponderously industrialized in imitation of its European rivals. In politics, though, the absolute monarchy of Tsar Nicholas II had shown little interest in democratic institutions. Revolution then forced change, as it had in France a century earlier, and with results that were equally as unexpected. The Russian Revolution's overpowering ideology pioneered new forms of government: the modern dictatorships of *totalitarianism* and *authoritarianism*.

These types of dictatorial regimes became commonplace after World War I. Although authoritarianism was perhaps less intrusive and effective than totalitarianism, both types adapted absolutism to a democratic age. As in an absolute monarchy, one person took charge of the state. Yet unlike the monarchies of old, the new dictators did not descend from some special god-linked dynasty but were chosen rather by "historical destiny." Napoleon Bonaparte exemplified this type of charismatic genius who seized power from incompetent politicians. Often, the lower-class birth of a dictator worked to his advantage, allowing him to be portrayed as a man of the people, a member of the masses who had become important and empowered with industrialization. The authoritarian leader's clothing helped to cement this new image. Gone were the crowns, ermine robes, and scepters of kings. Instead, the business suit, antiquated traditional costume, or worker's overalls and cap linked the dictator with average citizens; as an alternative, a military uniform asserted the values of discipline, obedience, and violence.

As opposed to monarchs who relied on tradition, dynasty, nobility, and religion, the modern dictator maintained power through the modern political mechanism of a party—elite followers who willingly and diligently served the leader. The party embodied the "will" of the people, who were asked to participate in only rigged elections and plebiscites. The party structure channeled the will of the dictator down to the local level. Combined with the modern technologies of mass communication, bureaucracy, and law enforcement, the masses could be mobilized to achieve national goals like never before in history.

The twentieth-century authoritarian and totalitarian regimes sprang from both nationalism and socialism that had arisen in the nineteenth century. Karl Marx would have been surprised that the first successful socialist revolution took place in Russia. In 1900, few people, and certainly not Marx, thought Russia was particularly prepared for a proletarian revolution because of its minimal industrialization. The Russian regime had always lumbered on under the sheer weight of its conjoined rule of tsar, Orthodox Church, and landed aristocracy.

Defeat in wars, however, triggered drastic change for Russia. The empire first showed its vulnerability when it lost the **Russo-Japanese War** (1905–1906). The Japanese surprise attack on Russian positions in East Asia expanded its own imperialism at Russia's expense. Nimble Japan successfully humiliated stumbling Russia. In reaction to the defeat of Russian armies and navies, the **1905 Revolution** broke out. The Soviets (or councils) of Workers and Soldiers organized by the socialist Leon **Trotsky** provided some real muscle behind the revolt. At first, Tsar Nicholas II made concessions, at least to middle-class demands for a representative and limited government. After loyal troops returned from the front, however, he realized he had the power to crush the rebellion after all. Consequently, Tsar Nicholas acted on a basic principle:

> **No revolution can succeed against a relatively competent government.**

He broke his promises to liberalize his government, revoked the constitution, and repressed the radicals, executing some and sending many others to Siberia. They and others in exile survived to organize again.

The enormous costs of World War I offered a second chance for revolution as the tsar's system failed in the crucible of that brutal conflict. The Russian front, as mentioned in the previous chapter, is often ignored in histories, which prefer to concentrate on the dreadful trench warfare of the western front. Yet the vast ebb and flow of armies from the mountainous Balkans to the frigid Baltic ravaged eastern Europe more horribly than Verdun or the Somme had western Europe. The Russians did have some successes against the ineffectual Austrians, but as the efficient German high command took over operations on the eastern front, Russia found its troops ground up by modern weaponry. Tsar Nicholas himself went to the front to command the troops, but he lacked any skills beyond his ability to inspire.

Meanwhile, Petrograd (the new name for St. Petersburg) remained in the hands of the tsar's dilettante wife, Tsarina Alexandra. She fell under the spell of the charismatic charlatan Rasputin. That mad "monk" had convinced her that he could cure their son, the Tsarevitch Alexei, of hemophilia (a genetic disease causing uncontrolled bleeding from any bruise or cut, inherited because of the inbreeding of

European royalty). People suspected that Rasputin then exercised a baleful influence over Alexandra, ruling from behind the scenes. Even after a group of nobles brutally murdered Rasputin, the government still seemed adrift. The high casualties among the soldiers and increasing food shortages for the common people made Russia ripe for collapse.

The spark that set fire to the dynastic façade came from the Russian women, or "babushkas" (named after their headscarves). On International Women's Day, 8 March 1917, women trying to provide meals for their families became fed up with government incompetence in bread rationing and took to the streets in protest.[1] Troops sent in to put down the riots with force instead joined the "babushkas." Within a week, Tsar Nicholas was talked into abdication. The Romanov dynasty ended; the first, and brief, Russian Republic (1917) began.

The fate of this new government, founded on liberal democratic parliamentarian principles, was a revolutionary success in itself. Its fate, however, foreshadowed what would happen to so many other regimes after the Great War, as the newly responsible politicians failed to solve their nations' problems. Three serious issues faced Russia's new leader, Alexander Kerensky, a leftist Socialist-Revolutionary. First, the elected government shared power with a shadow regime made up of the revived Soviets of Workers and Soldiers. Second, the wrangling political parties failed to unite on a common policy to solve issues of land reform or energize the economy. Consequently, food shortages worsened. Third, and worst of all, the government continued fighting Germany, after being urged, bribed, and bullied by the other Allied Powers to stay in the war.

A clever move by the Germans guaranteed that Russia's fragile republic would fail. They sent **Lenin** (b. 1870–d. 1924) on a sealed military train from Switzerland to Russia in April 1917. Born as Vladimir Ilyich Ulanov, this revolutionary had taken on the pseudonym Lenin (whose meaning is unclear) and at the turn of the century had become leader of the Bolsheviks, a faction of the Russian Social Democratic Party. **Bolshevik** means the "majority," and Lenin claimed the name for his followers after winning a minor issue during a party congress held in exile in London in 1903. Actually, the other Social Democrats, the Mensheviks, or "minority," were usually in the majority on most issues. Still, Lenin knew the value of a good label. The term *Bolshevism* gave a Russian name to Lenin's strict, hard-line Marxism: the belief that an elite party of dedicated revolutionaries would carry out a violent revolution. Lenin had no patience for the desire of other revisionist Mensheviks and their social democracy to work with the bourgeoisie and change society gradually by applying constitutional methods. Until 1917, Lenin had merely offered words and ideas, having spent some of his adult career in Siberia, the rest in exile in western Europe. By sending Lenin back to Russia, the Germans hoped that his revolutionary activities would destabilize their enemy. Lenin seized the opportunity for the long-awaited proletarian revolution and fulfilled German hopes, to their later regret.

Lenin laid out his program to the masses with beautiful simplicity: "Peace,

---

1. Russia still operated under the Julian calendar, so what the rest of the West counted as taking place in March was called the "February" Revolution by the Russians.

bread, and land!" He promised to end the war, feed people, and let peasants have the land they worked. He was not interested in winning elections. In mid-July, his Bolsheviks tried to seize control of the government. Although that uprising failed, Lenin had converted to his cause Leon Trotsky, who had wavered over the years between Menshevik social democracy, Bolshevism, and his own version of Trotsky-ism. Trotsky then provided more power through the Soviets of Workers and Soldiers. A better-planned revolution succeeded with barely a hitch during the night of 6–7 November 1917.[2] A large number of leftists, including Socialist-Revolutionaries, Mensheviks, and Bolsheviks, seized key public buildings. The warship *Aurora* in the Petrograd harbor fired the shot that launched the assault on the government sitting in the Winter Palace. After a few more shots, the revolutionaries basically strolled right into the palace, which was defended by few soldiers, including some in the grandly named Women's Battalion of Death. Later films showing heroic battles were mere propaganda. Kerensky himself had already left and eventually ended up in New York, where he died in 1970.

On the morning after Lenin's coup, the leftists elected him as head of the provisional government. Now Lenin put into actual practice his version of Marxism, soon called ***Leninism***. Bolshevism moved from theory to practice. First, Lenin's dictatorship began with disbanding the new representative assembly the day after it opened in January. Second, he quickly outlawed and destroyed all the other political parties who had helped in the October Revolution. Terror and violence by secret police and revolutionary-inspired informers kept people in line. Third, Lenin declared a policy of **war communism**, which nationalized business and industry, both domestic and foreign-owned. The land reform went through, at least by taking properties away from the bourgeoisie and the Orthodox Church. Fourth, he reduced the workday to eight hours. Fifth, Lenin relocated the capital from Petrograd to Moscow, seeing Petrograd as too exposed to foreign intervention.

At the time, the forces of opposition were indeed dangerous. The first problem was Germany. Lenin ended Russian participation in World War I with the Treaty of Brest-Litovsk in March 1918. It gave away one-third of the Russian Empire's European possessions, although most of those areas (Finland, the Baltic states, Poland, and the Ukraine) were mostly inhabited by non-ethnic Russians. Then the "Whites" (a loose alliance of nationalists, monarchists, republicans, and socialists) counterattacked the "Reds" (the Bolsheviks and their fellow travelers) from all directions of the compass. The Bolsheviks in turn murdered the imperial family, which had been under house arrest in the distant Ural Mountains. They shot in cold blood the former tsar, his wife, and their five children (including little Anastasia, later pretenders and cartoons to the contrary).

For a while, it seemed as if the "Whites" might succeed in their counterrevolution, especially as they were briefly helped by foreign intervention. The Poles provoked their own war to expand their border to include territories once belonging to the greater Poland-Lithuania. Even more dangerously, Allied armies (British, French, Japanese, and American troops) seized Russian ports in the north along the

---

2. Because of the Julian calendar, Russia's "October" Revolution took place in what the rest of the West called November.

western Arctic coast, in the south along the Black Sea coast, and in the east on the Pacific coast of Siberia. Their ostensible reasons were, first, to help fight Germany; second, to prevent munitions sent to the Russian Republic from falling into Bolshevik hands; and finally, simply to crush the Bolsheviks themselves. At one point five thousand American troops occupied the northwestern ports of Russia, while nine thousand were in eastern Siberia. American soldiers invaded Russia, shot at Russians, and killed some.

Still, the Bolsheviks won the civil war by 1920, despite the Allied intervention. The counterrevolutionary "Whites" lacked any common political program, military coordination, or revolutionary fervor. The "Reds" had better lines of internal communication, the support of many of the peasants, and united, strong resolve under the leadership of Lenin and Trotsky, who had commanded the Red Army.

Following the first Bolshevik victory, the country lay in ruins, with millions dead, millions more threatened with famine and disease, and the economic structures in shambles. Here Lenin showed his true genius by introducing the New Economic Policy in 1921. This policy reversed the extreme nationalization program of war communism. The NEP allowed most businesses to be privately owned and again generate private profits in relatively free markets. By the mid-1920s, Russia had gained stability and caught up with its prewar economic status.

The new success of the country was reinforced in 1922 when Lenin declared Russia to be the **Union of Soviet Socialist Republics,** or **U.S.S.R.** (1922–1991). At the core of this new political structure was the Russian Federative Soviet Republic. It included much of the old Russian Empire, including Siberia. The other socialist republics somewhat reflected ethnic diversity, such as Ukrainians, Belarusians, Uzbeks, Turkmen, or Kazakhs. The collective state of the U.S.S.R. defied, and indeed, superseded nationality with a new ideology based on proletarian revolution. The Communist Party controlled the government bureaucracy and elections, while the Politburo, its highest organ, directed the people in a socialist transition to the utopia of communism prophesied by Karl Marx. Most inhabitants accepted the new stability of their self-proclaimed "worker's paradise."

The victory of the Communists in the Russian Revolution inspired imitators and raised alarm in Western nations. In the chaos of the Great War's end, communists briefly seized power in Hungary and parts of Germany. In 1920, the Party of Institutionalized Revolution settled Mexico's decades of political instability. This Mexican socialist regime carried out land reform of forty million acres and nationalized foreign companies. Even though Mexico found itself too poor to compete with industrialized states, Western nations feared that more socialist revolutions could threaten their own status.

During this **Red scare** (1918–1922), Western politics became dominated by nativism, a fear of foreigners and immigrants. Western nations controlled their borders, suppressed radical political parties, arrested and deported suspected subversives, and fired tainted teachers and civil servants. In 1919, the U.S. government founded a new national police agency, the Federal Bureau of Investigation (FBI), to fight domestic communism. In hindsight, such fears were unrealistic. By the mid-1920s, communism had gained few additional believers.

In Communist Russia, the man who had guided the revolution to its success was also faltering. Lenin ruled in a modest fashion, often out of the public eye. He began to fall ill from a series of strokes in 1922. His wife, Krupskaya, did her best to convey the increasingly debilitated leader's wishes (like Edith Wilson had done for her husband only a few years before). Lenin was dead by January 1924. His mummified corpse, displayed in a glass case within a tomb in Red Square, became the sacred shrine for his Bolshevik revolutionary success. The Bolsheviks now had to replace Lenin without a political mechanism for choosing a successor.

The logical choice was Leon Trotsky, a key figure in the revolutions since 1905. He had much practical experience as an organizer of the Soviets and the Red Army. He was energetic, intellectually brilliant, and rhetorically inspiring. Yet some criticized Trotsky for arrogance, his Jewish heritage, and his ideological impurity: he had only converted late to Bolshevism. Strangely enough, others deemed him too radical as he pushed a program to start communist revolutions around the world.

In the end, Lenin's successor turned out to be someone who had been insignificant up until the early 1920s, a man called **Stalin** (b. 1879–d. 1953). Born Joseph Vissarionovich Dzugashvily in Georgia in the Caucasus Mountains, Stalin played a marginal role in the early revolutionary period. In the new Soviet Union, though, he rose to become general secretary for the Communist Party. In that position, Stalin directed the hard drudgery of bureaucracy necessary for the functioning of any complex modern state. He also found jobs and arranged promotions for his own friends and supporters. Stalin's position of first advocating socialism in one state, Russia, before taking on world revolution, made him appear more moderate.

Stalin quickly secured his own dictatorship. His design of the constitution in 1924 enabled Stalin to take control of both party and state by 1927. He convinced the Politburo to throw Trotsky out of the party and even exile him from Russia. Trotsky fled to socialist Mexico City, where in 1940 an assassin, on Stalin's orders, bashed in Trotsky's head with an ice axe.

Once in complete control, Stalin added his own variant to what Marx and Lenin had done before him. **Stalinism** probably would have horrified both of them. The experimentation of the early years abruptly ended. Instead, Stalin established an absolute personal dictatorship, supported by the cult of his own personality. The dictator eliminated all his rivals, culminating in the **Great Terror (1936–1938)** that echoed the Reign of Terror of the French Revolution. Stalin arrested tens of thousands of "Old Bolsheviks," those who had fought alongside Lenin and Trotsky. All women, who under socialist principles of equality had risen to positions of authority, were removed. He liquidated half of his officer corps. Many of these victims were purged through show trials, where they publicly confessed to crimes of espionage or counterrevolutionary activity of which they could not possibly have been guilty. Stalin had many victims executed; others simply "disappeared." Stalin sent thousands to internal exile, prison labor camps in Siberia called gulags.

The propagandized benevolent image of Stalin tried to counter this campaign of fear. Stalin made sure that his face, his name, and his reputation outshined everyone, including Marx and Lenin. The entire history of the revolution was rewritten to emphasize Stalin's alleged central role. Numerous holidays, ceremonies, and programs were dedicated to Comrade Stalin, who, with paternal caring similar to that of the tsars of old, looked after his proletarian flock.

People put up with this megalomaniacal side of Stalin's regime partly because of his success with another key part of Stalinism: modernization. The Soviet Union had already advanced further than under the tsars, but that achievement was not good enough for Stalin (see figure 13.2). He felt that his state was decades behind other advanced countries and wanted to make up the difference quickly. In 1928, he ended the New Economic Policy, Lenin's experiment with free-market capitalism and private ownership. Instead, a series of **Five-Year Plans** revived central planning of the economy to a degree never before experienced. The government bureaucra-

Figure 13.2.   A poster from the Soviet Congress of 1934 celebrates the revolution, Lenin, Stalin, and the modernization of Russia.

cies transformed the economy to the minutest detail, emphasizing heavy industry. New cities were built in Siberia, such as Magnitogorsk, which went from a population of a few bears to 150,000 people in a few years.

Learning from the large-scale, mechanized, industrial farming done in the United States, Stalin initiated *collectivization* of agriculture in Russia. The state confiscated the peasants' land, and communal groups then farmed the land. Many peasants resisted surrendering the land they had only recently gained. The regime machined-gunned those opponents or sent them to prison camps. In turn, many peasants slaughtered their own animals or burned their own crops in retaliation, thus contributing to a major famine. In all, the application of the Five-Year Plans killed perhaps ten million people and caused suffering for millions more.

In the end, Stalin was successful. The land was cleared; homes grew out of wilderness; factories hummed with production. Stalin's policies also provided access to education and health care for all citizens. The standard of living for most Soviet comrades far surpassed those of the tsar's subjects. Stalin had transformed a weary, second-rate great power into the second most powerful nation in the world, next only to the United States of America. "Nothing succeeds like success," quip the Americans. Many westerners, disillusioned by their own infighting of splintered parties and the failures of capitalism in depression and inflations, admired what Stalin had accomplished. They joined socialist and communist organizations in their own countries, confident that these ideas embodied the future. It was easy to ignore the millions of dead: the pointless World War I, the heartless flu—so many had died in the past decades. At least these Russians, some said, had died for the good cause of progress. Unfortunately, no one could ask the dead for their opinion.

Review: How did the Bolsheviks establish a new kind of state and society?

Response:

LOSING THEIR GRIP

During the years after World War I, the colonial empires of the Western powers began to weaken. Exhausted by the efforts of global war, the European powers did not even realize that the strength of their imperial embrace was wavering. In reality, profits and tax revenues from maintaining empires failed to match the costs of investments and government payments. Leaders came to believe that modern colonialism was not worth the costs, in taxes and lives. Meanwhile, their distant subjects were also growing restless, and stronger.

At war's end, though, the European leaders decided that their own empires should continue, and the new League of Nations helped them with that effort. The League took charge of the colonial territories of the defeated Central Powers and handed them out to the victorious Allies, calling them **mandates**. The British and French empires received most of the former German colonies of Africa and the southern Pacific, as well as much of the non-Turkish regions of the dismantled Ottoman Empire. The Belgians took over Rwanda and Burundi, near King Leopold's original colony of the Congo. The Belgian colonial rulers pitted the very similar Hutu and Tutsi peoples against one another in order to better control the colony. As far as the imperialist designs of Western nations were concerned, it seemed the twentieth century would continue just as the nineteenth had.

Colonial peoples saw this sharing of the spoils as a betrayal of President Wilson's idea of self-determination in the Fourteen Points. The victors callously ignored delegations from colonial areas. The Chinese argued in vain for concessions on extraterritoriality. The Wafd (or "delegation") Party from Egypt could not make its plea for independence heard. The Western powers' insistence on maintaining, and indeed expanding, their empires undermined respect for democratic values. The West believed itself to have exported its glorious Western civilization to peoples who still lived in darkness. Those peoples who lived in the allegedly dark places of the globe did not see it that way.

For the next few decades, westerners remained confident they could hold onto and continue to convert the rest of the world to their way of life. Even though profits from colonial areas were slim to nonexistent, confident investors still hoped to make money. They believed they could adapt those colonial lands to the world economy, mostly to benefit the various mother countries. For example, confident British imperialists thought a handful of Oxford-educated civil servants and trained police officers could handle populations in South Asia that outnumbered them by thousands to one.

This imbalance in numbers ever more tilted against the West. Europe's own prosperity had caused a **population explosion** in the nineteenth century, when the inhabitants doubled in number, even with emigration to the Americas and colonial possessions. By 1914, however, imperialism had brought these industrial and scientific advantages to the four corners of the world. Soon the peoples of Asia and Africa underwent their own population explosions (which to some extent continue still). In contrast, modern industrial society led in the West to smaller families. Compulsory education raised the cost of having children, since they could not contribute to the family's labor resources. Better workers' benefits also reduced the need to have enough children to support parents in their old age. So population growth slowed, stopped, and even began to recede in European countries throughout the twentieth century. Soon the "white" portion of world population began to shrink, as it is still shrinking today, compared with the "colored" portion. Europeans already in the 1920s noticed the trend and began to fear a Yellow Peril, a threat that Asians might regain their independence or even come to dominate the West. These fears found expression in novels about the inscrutable evil genius Fu Manchu or the conquering "Yellow hordes" in the "Buck Rogers in the 25th Century" comic strip.

Contrary to Western stereotypes, the colored peoples of the world were neither stupid nor evil. Certainly, they had not gone through a Commercial Revolution, a Scientific Revolution, or an Industrial Revolution on their own. With imperialism, however, the lessons learned from those tumults were available to everyone with an open mind (and at lower costs). Having their noses rubbed in the cultural ideals of the West, the colonized peoples learned of democracy, heralded by the English, American, French, and even Russian Revolutions. Once they had recovered from the initial shock of the Western invasions and subjugations, the colonized peoples began to wield the westerners' own ideas against them, especially that of nationalism. Self-government was not only for Belgians or Italians but also for Chinese or Congolese. Meanwhile, the Bolsheviks in Russia promoted themselves as the friends of "oppressed peoples" (covering up their own russification of non-Russian subjects). Soviet calls to resist capitalist and imperialist exploitation found willing listeners. Thus, the pressures of the native peoples for self-government grew relentlessly.

The British Empire, which set the example for imperialism in the nineteenth century, led the way in its decline in the twentieth. Immediately after the Great War, its imperial structure began to crumble. The trouble began closest to home as the **"Irish Problem"** flared up for the British. In Ireland, the political party **Sinn Fein** ("Ourselves Alone") had worked toward independence from Britain since the turn of the century. In 1916, the Easter Rising in Dublin had been bloodily crushed. As soon as the war was over, many Irish formed the so-called Irish Republican Army (IRA). At first, the IRA used terrorism, but soon it organized enough to fight a virtual civil war against the special British police troops, the "Black and Tans." The growing violence convinced Great Britain to quit. Both sides agreed to a semi-independent Irish state in 1920. In 1938 this state became the completely sovereign Republic of Ireland.

The fighting did not stop, however, as some Irish thought the victory incomplete. The sore spot remained in the counties of **Northern Ireland**, also called Ulster, which remained part of the United Kingdom of Great Britain. Back in the 1600s, Protestant Scotch-Irish families had settled there and ever since formed the majority. Since they had been in Ireland as long as white people had in North America (or Afrikaaners in South Africa), they considered themselves Irish, even if they identified with the Protestant English and Scots more than the Roman Catholic Irish. The moderate majority throughout Ireland accepted this division of the island, but some few demanded the whole island be under one independent government. So Irish Catholics in the south began killing other Irish Catholics over this disagreement. The Irish Republican Army broke apart in this second civil war. By 1922, the moderate acceptance of a divided island had won. Over the next five decades, only a few underground terrorists occasionally and ineffectively surfaced with a bombing or assassination to protest the ongoing political division of the island.

Of greater consequence to the decline of British power (although less violent) was the breakaway of the empire's four self-governing white **dominions**. Great Britain created the three most important dominions, Canada, Australia, and New Zealand, as they had the American colonies. British immigrants stole the land from the natives, whether called the First Nations and the Inuit of Canada, the Aborigines of Australia, or the Maori of New Zealand. They wrote fraudulent treaties, forced the natives from their lands, confined them to reservations, and discriminated against them in the towns of "white" society. By 1900, white populations had transformed these dominions into Western, modern, industrialized states that were comparable economically and socially to any in Europe. In the fourth significant dominion, the Union of South Africa, the white ethnic British and Dutch Afrikaaners coruled the land, even though they were in minority to the various tribes of black Africans.

All four of these states were tired of being bossed around by a Parliament sitting in London. As mere dominions, they had been automatically drawn into World War I, where too much of their own people's precious blood had been spilled on the battlefields of Europe. They saw too many differences in economic policy as well, especially as the Great Depression overwhelmed the globe. In 1932, these four states negotiated an equal partnership in the newly formed **British Commonwealth**. This new structure offered its members economic cooperation, not political compulsion. As for the United Kingdom, the British Empire clearly dropped in its status as the ranking world power without direct and immediate access to the resources of Canada, Australia, New Zealand, and South Africa.

The British Empire suffered still more setbacks in the Middle East and South Asia. The British finally granted independence to Egypt, a territory they had snatched from the Ottomans in the late nineteenth century. The British kept ownership, though, of the crucial Suez Canal until 1956. To compensate for the loss of Egypt, the British had expanded in the Middle East mandates carved out from the destroyed Ottoman Empire. They constructed the countries of **Iraq** and Transjordan. The British drew arbitrary borders and invented new royal dynasties, using an Arab ally from the Great War, Faisal of the Hashemite dynasty. The British installed him in Baghdad and set up his brother in Transjordan.

The appointed king of a newly constructed Iraq ruled over diverse peoples: a handful of Jews and Christians, the Sunni Arabs in the center of the country, who traditionally hated the Shiite Arabs in the south, and the non-Arab Kurds in the north, who were frustrated that they had not gained their own country of Kurdistan. The British helped Faisal fight insurgencies, using airplanes with poison gas against rebels. But by 1926, they had tired of fighting. The British withdrew, although they kept key military and economic privileges. The next year, petroleum was discovered. Although modern British technology was necessary to pump the oil from the ground and refine it, Iraq was ultimately sole master of this resource, which made it a power to be respected and feared in the region.

Britain's other mandates in the Middle East were as troublesome as Iraq. The British cut the Ottoman province of Jordan into two parts, Transjordan and **Palestine**. The latter was beginning to receive the Jewish immigrants encouraged by the Balfour Declaration of the Great War, which had committed Britain to allowing a Jewish "homeland" there. The native Arabs quickly grew resentful at the growing numbers of Jewish neighbors. By 1936, violence between Jews and Palestinian Arabs had intensified into a near civil war, with the British caught in the middle. By 1939, a fateful year, the British stopped all Jewish immigration in order to keep the peace with the Arab majority.

The "jewel in the crown" of the British Empire, the Indian Subcontinent, was also hostile to continuing English rule. The British mistakenly believed they were doing the Indians a favor. They correctly argued that India's vast area had never really possessed a unified native government before the British had taken over. Often Indians had been ruled by foreign conquerors, of which the British were merely the latest. Instead of being grateful, Indians resisted with their own version of Western nationalism. The **Indian National Congress**, founded in 1886, began as a body to help maintain British dominion but soon worked to get rid of the same.

In 1915, the British Empire was shaken to its roots by the arrival of **Mohandas Karamchand Gandhi** (b. 1869–d. 1948). Gandhi studied law in London. He then tried to practice law in South Africa. Originally, Gandhi had been just one more Indian trying to assimilate into the British Empire. Then the injustice of being thrown off a train because he was not a white European radicalized him. Gandhi learned that for people of color, the Western ideals of liberty and equality were broken promises. First he organized the Indian community in South Africa to fight for civil rights, and then, in 1915, he returned to his native India.

By then, Gandhi had rejected westernization as materialistic, immoral, and godless. He began to transform into a traditional Indian holy man, with enough success to earn him the honorific title "Mahatma" (Great Soul). He discarded Western pinstriped suits, starched collars, and ties and instead wore loose, homespun robes. He cultivated asceticism and simplicity. Certainly, some aspects of his life took on a touch of the unusual, such as his concern with vegetarianism or his practice of resisting sexual temptation by (literally) sleeping alongside naked young women. Most importantly, though, Gandhi took Indian religious ideas and turned them into a political philosophy. He claimed that *satyagraha* (soul force) could defeat the greatest empire in history, and his soul force was based on civil disobedience. Indians, he felt, would wake up British sensibilities with their own ideals of decency and fair play.

A small massacre at Amritsar, boycotts of manufactured goods, protests of taxes on salt, marches against discrimination all worked to Gandhi's advantage. In turn, the British periodically imprisoned him. His nonviolence left him immune to criticism about means, while his fasts, simplicity, and eccentricity made him resistant to personal attacks. News spread by the international press made Gandhi a popular hero around the world. Only the most stubborn of the British, like Winston Churchill, thought that England would hold onto India for much longer.

Meanwhile, the other European imperialist powers failed to recognize the precariousness of the situation. France continued to hope to "civilize" its Caribbean, African, and Asian subjects. Belgium continued to exploit the Congo. The Italian, Dutch, Portuguese, and Spanish outposts limped along. Ignoring calls to recognize humanity in all people, certain westerners began to glorify attitudes of imperialism even more than the many nationalists had in the nineteenth century. These beliefs helped hatch a new ideology based on racism and violence.

Review: *How were the Western empires slowly weakening?*

Response:

FASCIST FURY

The brief spirit of international cooperation seen in the League of Nations was soon overwhelmed by the intensification of nationalism and imperialism. Bolshevism had adapted to nationalism and imperialism under Stalin. A new political ideology, that of *fascism*, now furiously swept across much of eastern Europe as yet another alternative to both communism and capitalism. Like the Bolsheviks, fascists rejected the actual practice of parliamentarian democracy, which seemed more about political opponents quarreling than solving serious problems. Despite this agreement on method, both Marxists and fascists were essentially different from each other. Fascism simplified matters by reducing the options around national unity. Instead of Marx's ideology of how class conflict drove historical change, fascists argued for ethnic conflict.

In the fascist point of view, the stronger people should dominate while the weaker died out. The fascists cited the **eugenics** movement, which twisted scientists' revelations about heredity. Supporters of eugenics called for breeding policies to eliminate undesirables from the human gene pool. In the fascist analysis, the clash of peoples, whether between large races, smaller nations, or tiny tribes, changed the course of the world.

Fascist ideology called for a **corporate state** that unified the leader and people of one ethnic group. Fascists believed that since both workers and property owners belonged to the same ethnic people, they should cooperate in harmony under the beneficial guidance of the leader of the corporate state. Their support of private property, properly used, kept the support of the economic elites, while socialist language won over the workers. Even the old nobility might be welcomed back as guardians of the national heritage.

Fascists also exalted violence. They embraced the superficial gloss of militarism, reflected in their love of uniforms, banners, and parades. Other militaristic virtues such as obedience, discipline, and endurance of hardships replaced liberal ideals such as freedom of conscience or opportunity. Fascism went beyond typical militarism and praised violence as the greatest glory of man, whether applied to the conquest of other peoples or to the forceful repression of domestic differences. Fascist bullies frequently hurt others just to prove their own superiority, even if it disturbed law and order.

The source of this new ideology of hate and hurt was Italy. That country's imperial inferiority complex had combined with a lackluster performance in World War I. At the war's end, Italians found their "victory" to be hollow and bitter. They had never really won any great battles. Their few acquisitions of territory from the dismembered Austrian empire caused more problems than they were worth, since they actually added troublesome ethnic minorities from German South-Tyrol and Slavic Istria. Still, Italy failed to gain anything from the Ottoman Empire, and the papacy, still bitter over the loss of the Papal States, continued to frustrate national politics. Italian politics was bogged down with postwar economic readjustment causing unemployment and strikes, while the traditional socialist, liberal, and conservative parties could not cooperate with one another.

Out of this swamp, a former anarchist and socialist, **Benito Mussolini** (b. 1883–d. 1945), rose to become the first theorist and practitioner of fascism. Mussolini declared that he had the answer to Italy's civil disorders, even while his fascist thugs added to the turmoil. When the fascists staged the massive March on Rome in October 1922, Mussolini waited in the background, ready to flee the country if anything went wrong. He need not have worried. The democratic parties simply walked away from responsibility when confronted by the bold assertions of the fascists, as republicans had done when faced by the Bolsheviks in Russia during 1917–1918. The king readily appointed Mussolini as prime minister. Mussolini used this position to become "Il Duce" (the leader) of both his party and all Italy.

It took several years, however, for the Italian fascists to undermine the republic and consolidate their power. They bullied, assaulted, and murdered their opponents. They stripped Italians of civil liberties and political responsibility. Their propaganda, however, showcased their job programs, swamp drainings, housing construction, and arrests of undesirables. Many people even came to believe that Mussolini made the notoriously late Italian trains run on time. He did not. Yet hopeful Italians and optimistic foreign observers convinced themselves that Italy was on the rise. Mussolini even reconciled the pope to modern Italy by signing a concordat establishing the Vatican City as an independent territory under papal sovereignty. Italians achieved a certain perverse pride in the rise of their national standing again. By 1927, Mussolini could do whatever he wished.

What Il Duce wished was to revive the Roman Empire. His fascist version, though, lacked the original's tolerance for diversity. Instead, Mussolini wanted Italians to impose their culture on all their subjects. On the European continent, he was already forcing Slavs in Istria and Germans in the South-Tyrol to become Italians by forbidding their languages and even translating their family names into Italian. On the continent of Africa, he harshly repressed independence efforts in Italy's colonies in Libya and Somalia. Then some Italian troops in Somalia violated the border of neighboring Abyssinia (more often called Ethiopia) in December 1935. Mussolini could not tolerate black Africans shooting at white Italians. He also sought to avenge the humiliating defeat of Adowa, where Italy had lost to the Abyssinians in 1898. So in the summer of 1936, Mussolini launched the **Italo-Abyssinian War** (1936–1937).

In response, Haile Selassie, the emperor of Abyssinia, appealed to the League of Nations to stop this aggression against one of its own members. The only action the League made in Abyssinia's defense was to impose economic sanctions against Italy in a trade embargo on many products. These sanctions, however, did not include oil, which powered Italy's modern military machines. As a result, using modern trucks, tanks, and planes, the Italian forces decisively defeated Abyssinia's unmodernized forces. By the summer of 1937, with all of Ethiopia occupied, the League lifted the insignificant sanctions, thus essentially endorsing Mussolini's aggression.

Fascism might have remained confined to one country (and its empire), just as Bolshevism had been, without the Great Depression. The apparent failure of democratic leaders compared with Mussolini's obvious success inspired imitators: strong men seized power throughout eastern and southern Europe. These areas were particularly vulnerable to fascism. The Paris Peace Treaties had created many small states out of the former empires of Romanovs, Habsburgs, and Ottomans. This *balkanization* meant that small states struggled with national identity and ethnic minorities, economic competition with neighbors, lack of investment capital, all with little tradition of democracy. Many welcomed the simplistic nationalism of hatred and exclusion sold by fascists.

For example, the **Kingdom of the Serbs, Croats, and Slovenes** founded at war's end soon succumbed to fascist yugo-slavism. Numerous ethnic groups, such as Montenegrins, Bosnians, Germans, Italians, Magyars, Bulgars, Turks, Albanians, Macedonians, Pomacks, Vlachs, and Gypsies (Roma), nestled with the three main groups within the borders of the kingdom. But ancient and new disagreements among these nationalities frustrated effective political action. In 1929, a power-hungry King Alexander dissolved the parliament and suspended the constitution. In his renamed **Kingdom of Yugoslavia**, Alexander enforced a royal dictatorship based on Serbian fascism. Some ethnic minorities were unwilling to meekly accept the new reality, and they organized an opposition. The Macedonians revived the terrorist organization of IMRO, and the Croatians formed the new *Ustashe* (Insurrectionists). Together, they managed to assassinate King Alexander with a bomb on 9 October 1934 while he visited Marseilles, France. His Serbian successor, though, maintained the fascist dictatorship for several more years.

In the far western part of southern Europe, the Iberian Peninsula also knuckled under to fascist dictatorships. Generals seized power in Portugal in 1926, and their military successors continued to rule there until 1974. In contrast, the larger neighbor Spain briefly experienced an expansion of democracy. In 1931, a peaceful revolution had thrown out the capricious and arbitrary king and established the Republic of Spain. At first, liberals and democratic socialists dominated the government. Then anarchists and communists (influenced either by Trotsky or Stalin) won elections and formed a coalition called "The Popular Front." These reform-minded leftists soon encroached on the traditional prerogatives of the Roman Catholic Church and Spanish aristocrats. Conservatives called on Generalissimo Francisco

Franco to overthrow the legitimate government. Franco had won fame and gained experience while crushing colonial rebellions in Africa. He began the **Spanish Civil War** (1936–1939) by leaving his outpost in the Canary Islands and successfully invading Spanish possessions in North Africa, then mainland Spain itself. Franco outmaneuvered his conservative allies and founded a fascist movement under his personal control, which he called the Falange. Fascist Italy and Germany helped him with money, supplies, seventy thousand Italian "volunteer" soldiers, and planes and pilots from the German *Luftwaffe* (air force).

Surprisingly, the legitimate Spanish republican government was able to slow the advance of Franco's fascist armies. A few believers in democracy and socialism, such as George Orwell and Ernest Hemingway, volunteered to aid the republicans, served in their militias, and publicized their cause. The Soviet Union aided the republicans with money and advisors. The help by authoritarian Bolsheviks, however, probably hurt more than it helped the Spanish republicans. No Western democratic government supported the leftist Spanish Republic.

Desperate for support, the republicans made a deal with the **Basques**, a people who have claimed to be the most ancient in Europe. Through centuries of domination by Romans, Visigoths, Moors, and modern Spaniards, the Basques had managed to maintain their language and culture despite having little political power. In October 1936 the Republic of Spain allowed the establishment of the "Republic of Euzkadi," an autonomous region of Basque self-government. To the fascistic nationalists under Franco, such diversity in Spain was intolerable. On 27 April 1937, German bombers unleashed the first successful strategic bombing raid in modern history on the Basque capital. By the end of the day, the city was in ruins, with more than two thousand dead. The terror felt by the people, if not the world, was expressed in Picasso's famous painting, named after the Basque capital: *Guernica*. The Republicans, increasingly divided along ideological and ethnic lines and without allies, could not hold off the fascist onslaught. In March 1939, Franco finally took Madrid and established a dictatorship that would last for the rest of his life, forty-six more years (see figure 13.3).

By 1939, only two countries in southern and eastern Europe remained democratic. The first country was Turkey, on the southeastern fringe of Europe. The Paris Peace Treaty with the defeated Ottoman Empire left only a weak and small Turkish state. Alone among the losers of World War I, however, the Turks resisted the treaty imposed upon them. An army officer, Mustapha Kemal, overthrew the Ottoman sultan and abolished the sultanate on 1 November 1922, ending the one cultural institution that claimed to unite all Muslims. He renamed himself **Atatürk** (b. 1881–d. 1938), which meant "father of the Turks," to symbolize his role as a new founder for the Turkish people. He led Turkish armies to drive out invading Italians and Greeks while the British and French dithered. Atatürk then westernized his nation and set up a secular state.

While Atatürk largely succeeded at founding a stable democratic government, nationalistic resentments led the Turks to solve some ethnic conflicts by expulsion. Turkey expelled most of its Greeks and Bulgarians, while Greece and Bulgaria returned the favor by ejecting many of their Turks. Greeks had been living in Asia Minor since the sixth century B.C. With these forced removals, twenty-five centuries

Figure 13.3.   The Valley of the Fallen. Franco's fascist memorial to the dead of the Spanish Civil War was built with the forced labor of the republican and socialist defeated.

of Greek civilization in the important region of Ionia ended abruptly. Nearly two million people were exchanged with much hardship, although fortunately few slaughters. At the time, few other countries followed this relatively bloodless model of solving ethnic claims.

The brand-new country of **Czecho-slovakia** remained the only other state in southern and eastern Europe to resist authoritarianism. Czecho-slovakia itself seemed like a miniature version of the vast multi-ethnic Habsburg Austro-Hungarian Empire, out of which it had been carved and cobbled together. The rivalry between the two dominant ethnic groups of Czechs and Slovaks mirrored the conflict between Austria-Hungary's Germans and Magyars, while the Sudeten Germans took the place of the Croats as a large third force. A minority of Magyars along the Hungarian border wanted to join Hungary, as Serbs had wanted to leave Austria and join Serbia. Nevertheless, Czecho-slovakia provided democratic representation and relatively fair treatment for all ethnic groups. The Sudeten German fascination with fascism, however, would later destroy Czecho-slovakia (see below).

Thus, by 1939, all of southern and eastern Europe had come under authoritarian or totalitarian regimes: Latvia, Estonia, Lithuania, Poland, Austria, Hungary, Rumania, Bulgaria, Yugoslavia, Albania, Greece, Italy, Spain, Portugal. Those countries that did not have fascist regimes had fascist political parties. Even distant Japan (see below) prostrated itself before a clique of fascist generals. The tide of history clearly seemed to be with dictatorship, not democracy. Soon enough, the most fascistic of all fascists would begin a war intending to dominate Europe, if not the world.

Review: How did fascism spread across the West?

Response:

HITLER'S HATREDS

This most notorious and successful of fascists was, of course, **Adolf Hitler** (b. 1889–d. 1945). In 1933, "Der Führer" (the Leader) transformed Germany into a **Third Reich** (third empire), which followed the first two of the Holy Roman Emperor and the Hohenzollern kaisers. At first, Hitler peacefully extended the borders of his German state to its largest expanse since the fifteenth century. Then, in 1939, he launched a war in the name of his brand of fascism that conquered most of the heartland of Western civilization.

Today it seems incomprehensible that Hitler could have attained such great power so quickly. Indeed, no one who had known Hitler during the Great War would have expected his later achievements. As the son of an insignificant Austrian civil servant, a reject from art school, and a mediocre painter of postcards, Hitler nurtured disgust with the diverse ethnic groups of cosmopolitan Vienna. Ultranationalist ideas of *pangermanism*, that the Germans should unite and dominate, entered his ideology. He fled his native Austria when the Habsburg regime called him to military service, expected of all able-bodied male citizens. Shortly after he arrived in Germany, however, Hitler celebrated the outbreak of the Great War, volunteered, and served on the front lines. Against all odds, he survived four years. During this time, he failed to distinguish himself with any leadership ability and rose only to the meager rank of corporal.

His leadership only had a chance to unfold as World War I ended and revolution threatened to tear Germany apart. During the last few years of the war, the generals Hindenburg and Ludendorff had been military dictators but could not come up with a winning strategy. They had realized the war was irrevocably lost even before the Allied armies broke through German lines in the fall of 1918. Revolutions began breaking out all over the country. The Social Democrats attempted to prevent a Communist takeover by proclaiming a new republic. This republican Germany, governed by its elected representatives, has since come to be known as the **Weimar Republic**, after the city where politicians hammered out its constitution.

Gravely threatening the fragile Weimar Republic were the peace terms imposed by the victorious Allies. As mentioned at the beginning of the chapter, the whole first part of the Treaty of Versailles, which established the League of Nations, was an insult to the excluded Germans. The Germans could have expected to lose Alsace-Lorraine and a few bits of land to Belgium, but they also lost a chunk of territory to Denmark, which had not even participated in the war. In the west, they lost the Saar region to France for fifteen years. In the northeast, the city of Danzig fell under League control as a unique international city. The nearby Polish Corridor cut off the province of East Prussia from the rest of Germany, to give the new state of Poland an outlet to the sea. Even worse, the Germans were to be disarmed: no navy, no air force, and an army of only one hundred thousand men without tanks or heavy artillery.

As intended, such a force was insufficient to defend Germany, much less begin a war. A demilitarized Germany suited France. To further Germany's vulnerability, the left bank of the Rhineland (that side bordering France) was to be permanently demilitarized: devoid of troops and military installations. Thus Germany could not easily invade France and Belgium, while France could march into Germany without trouble. To enforce these provisions, Allied troops were to occupy the Rhineland for fifteen years.

Worst of all, the Allies forced the Germans in Part VIII, Article 231 to accept guilt for the war and responsibility for causing all the war's destruction. As a consequence, the Allies justified making the Germans pay reparations in compensation. The numbers were so huge, though, that it took two years for the Allies to add up and present their bill. In the meantime, under threat of a renewal of armed conflict and with a blockade still starving the country, the Allies forced the reluctant German representatives to sign the treaty on 28 June 1919, five years to the day after the assassination of Archduke Franz Ferdinand of Austria.

Paying close attention to these developments was the former corporal Adolf Hitler. He believed the propaganda that German forces had been stabbed in the back by socialists and Jews. After the war, though, he stayed with the military, working for its intelligence agencies, gathering information on the numerous political parties that were springing up in the new Weimar Republic. One day Hitler attended the disorganized meeting of a group calling itself the German Worker's Party. He soon led the party, changing its name to the National Socialist German Worker's Party, or the **Nazis**. Hitler then reshaped the party's platform into *Nazism* or ***national socialism***, weaving together a powerful fascism with elements from racism, pangermanism, nationalism, socialism, sexism, militarism, conservatism, and many other ideologies.

Hitler's love for Germany inspired a hatred for anything that would weaken it in his eyes. He spelled out his chief goals in his 1924 autobiography, *Mein Kampf* (*My Struggle*). In this book, Hitler argued that cultural diversity endangered Germany. He thought that Jews and Marxists threatened the superiority of the German race, or Aryans (drawn from a pseudoscholarly name for the Indo-Europeans who had settled Europe). To overcome this threat, he needed to destroy parliamentarian democracy and become the dictator of Germany. A true German culture would then unify and strengthen the Germans as never before. Since other nations threatened the German purity, Germany needed to expand into eastern Europe and acquire sufficient *Lebensraum* (living space). In the same book, and in speeches and writings throughout the 1920s and 1930s, Hitler laid out a vision of national revolution and international conquest. Who could not have seen his desire for war?

Yet many in both Germany and abroad did not, even when Hitler's first attempt to seize political power involved force. The opportunity seemed ideal in 1923 and 1924, when Germany was racked by horrible inflation. In 1921, the bill for war reparations totaled 269 billion marks. When the German government stopped paying the reparations in 1923, the French marched across the Rhine and occupied the Ruhr, the industrial heartland of Germany. German workers went on strike, and the Berlin government simply kept printing money to keep the economy functioning. Without either gold reserves or industrial production to back it up, however, the mark fell in value. This disastrous inflation meant that one dollar, which in 1921 had bought four marks, would buy one billion marks in 1923. To stop the disaster, the rich Americans stepped in with the Dawes Plan: U.S. banks would loan the money to recapitalize Germany, which would then pay the reparations to France, which could then use the money to pay back what it had borrowed from the United States during World War I. Thus a circuit of capital flowed through the economic veins of the West. The plan worked, ending the ruinous inflation.

In the meantime, the inflation had provoked political uprisings all over Germany. Among others, Hitler attempted a putsch (German for a coup d'état) organized in a Munich beer hall to take over the province of Bavaria. But the attempted coup failed miserably. And instead of executing Hitler for treason, the conservative court merely sentenced him to five years in prison. He served only nine months, using the time to write *Mein Kampf*. Released from prison with his party banned, nothing more should have been heard of him. He should not even have deserved the merest mention in this history.

Then the Great Depression brought a return of the economic collapse. The American capital necessary for the Dawes Plan disappeared. Economic collapse spread around the world as banks shut down, businesses went bankrupt, and unemployment skyrocketed. Germany suffered worst. Hitler used the disruptions to revive his party and establish it as the center of political discourse. His Nazi party went from the ninth largest in 1930 to the largest in parliament (the Reichstag) by 1932. Soon democracy had ceased to function in the Weimar Republic. One chancellor followed another as each failed to solve the economic crisis. On 30 January 1933, a coalition of nationalists and conservatives appointed Hitler as chancellor.

Hitler then made sure that no remnants of parliamentary democracy would trouble him further. Hitler frightened the parliamentary majority into removing his rivals after a mentally imbalanced Dutch socialist committed arson on the Reichstag building. Hitler's Reichstag first outlawed the Communist Party (which, of course, had nothing to do with the arson, but was the greatest rival to the Nazi Party). In the next few months, the rump Reichstag outlawed every other political party. As for the remaining enemies of the new Nazi order? Within a few months, the Nazis started on their first concentration camp at Dachau, near Munich. Into these camps the Nazis sent political prisoners (communists, socialists, and pacifists), religious prisoners (Roman Catholics, Lutherans, and Jehovah's Witnesses), behavioral prisoners (sex offenders, homosexuals), and racial prisoners (foreigners, Gypsies [Roma], and Jews).

After the communists and other political enemies had been dealt with, Hitler then had the chance to solve his **Jewish Problem**, yet he hesitated. After some initial firings from government jobs, a few boycotts of Jewish businesses, and some assaults on Jews, official Nazi policies did not further harm the Jews for two years after 1933. Many Jews thought that perhaps they had seen the extent of Nazi discrimination. The more fortunate Jews emigrated.

Worse did come. First, in September 1935, new laws that took away Jewish civil rights were issued from the party center of Nuremburg. Jews lost many rights of citizenship. In the next few years, more restrictions took away options for normal lives. The regime exaggerated the Jews' ethnic differences, preventing any possible assimilation. Jewish businesses were marked, then closed; Jewish physicians could not practice on Germans; Jewish lawyers were dismissed from courts; all male Jews had to take on the name "Israel" and female Jews the name "Sarah." During the night of 9–10 November 1938, thereafter called *Kristallnacht* (Night of the Broken Glass), an organized Nazi assault smashed businesses, burned synagogues, looted homes, desecrated cemeteries, and murdered hundreds of Jews (although many of the deaths were officially listed as suicides). Those Jews who still wished to emigrate were allowed—if they could pay and if they could find a place to go. Few other countries wanted Jews. Even the British invitation to Palestine was withdrawn in 1939. The international outcry was minimal. The great powers were more concerned with Hitler's other plans that were slowly becoming more obvious.

Review: How did Hitler rise to power and change Germany?

Response:

THE ROADS TO GLOBAL WAR

World War II can easily be seen as a continuation of World War I. That first great conflict did not resolve the pesky "German problem": How do you cope with a powerful, united Germany in the heart of Europe? Other international problems grew worse. The nationalist aspirations of many peoples in Europe and around the world remained unfulfilled. The harsh competition produced by industrial manufacturing continued to set nations against one another. War still remained a popular solution for resolving differences.

Ironically, many democratic peoples around the world did not want a second world war. The idea of several great powers fighting again for years in vicious futility transformed many thinking people into pacifists: war seemed the worst thing that they could imagine. The two democratic European great powers, Great Britain and France, had been badly frightened by the horrors of that first Great War and the concept of their own fragility.

Meanwhile, westernization in East Asia laid the foundations for a new, greater war. The establishment of the western-style Republic of China in 1911 had ended the rule of two thousand years of emperors. The Western-educated and trained **Sun Yat-sen** (b. 1886–d. 1925) had for years been planting the seeds for a democratic China, organizing the **Nationalist Party** (abbreviated as GMD or KMT).[3] He had designed the party along Western lines by incorporating ideals of nationalism, republicanism, and socialism. After the fall of the imperial regime, Sun returned to nurture the republican government. But democracy had no chance to grow. A few weeks after the new government had begun, a general forced Sun out. The new military dictator could not prevent much of China from falling under the sway of local warlords.

As World War I focused the attention of the other great powers on Europe, Japan took the opportunity to replace Western imperialists in China. The Japanese felt destined to rule East Asia and the Pacific, imitating Western imperialism. Having joined the Allies at the beginning of World War I, Japan took over many extraterritorial privileges in China and began to consider that problematic country its special protectorate.

The postwar period went less well for Japan, as the Western powers sought to rein in its expansion. The Japanese resented the disarmament conference held in Washington, D.C. (1921–1922), which restricted the Japanese navy to being at a lower rank, after the British and American navies. The Japanese were insulted by racist American laws limiting Japanese immigration. Then, the Great Depression struck Japan in 1930 with all the fury that had wiped out businesses in the United States. Many Japanese blamed the resultant unemployment and social dismay on their use of European-style parliamentarianism. Consequently, many Japanese imi-

---

3. Chinese and Japanese names are often in reverse order compared with Western names. Thus Sun was his family name and Yat-sen his personal or familiar name. Also, the difference between GMD and KMT or other names comes from a change in the late twentieth century in how to transliterate Chinese characters into the Latin alphabet. In this text, the more modern is listed first, although the second version is still frequently seen.

tated Western fascism. Fascists wanted to establish a new, revived, glorious Japan, this time with imperial domination of Asia. Intimidation and assassination silenced the critics as the Japanese military gradually came to dominate the government.

Japan's fascists knew their opportunity to dominate China was limited, since China had begun to achieve stability under the leadership of the Nationalists. After being ousted from the presidency, Sun decided to try to build up his own political base against the warlords by using the Nationalist Party and some new allies. One ally was Russia, which Sun's protégé, **Jiang Jei-shei** or **Chiang Kai-shek** (b. 1886–d. 1975), visited in order to learn modern Soviet military organization. The Nationalist Party also allied with the fledgling Chinese Communist Party. Founded in 1921 and inspired by the Bolsheviks, Chinese Communism was another successful Western export. In 1927, after Sun's death, Jiang became leader of the GMD, attacked many warlords, and, unexpectedly, defeated most of them. Along the way, he also attacked his former allies, the Communists, driving the survivors into a distant province in the southeast. By 1928, Jiang began to urge the Western powers to give up their onerous extraterritoriality treaties and recognize China as an equal, sovereign great power.

The interaction of nationalism, imperialism, and communism complicated matters. Having retreated to the southeast of China, **Mao Zedong** (b. 1893–d. 1976) began to adapt communism to the needs of the Chinese peasants, especially focusing on land reform. The communists survived a second attack by Jiang's nationalists through their legendary "Long March" in 1933. At the same time, the Japanese seized the province of Manchuria. After Jiang's government appealed to the League of Nations, an investigatory committee looked into the matter and weakly criticized the Japanese aggression. In reaction, Japan became more belligerent. In 1937, a minor incident at the Marco Polo Bridge in Beijing (named after the medieval Italian traveler to China) prompted the Japanese to launch a full-scale invasion. Japan's attack on the city of Nanking in December 1937 viciously slaughtered almost half the city's population of six hundred thousand. The violation of tens of thousands of Chinese women gave the assault its name: the Rape of Nanking. The rest of the world, and the Western powers, watched and did nothing. They did not realize that this war between two Asian great powers was the beginning of **World War II (1937–1945)**, which was soon to engulf them all.

Britain and France were more concerned with German aggression in Europe, although even there they did little. The French hoped that their Maginot Line, a series of complex and expensive fortifications begun before Hitler came to power, might stop another German attack. In 1934, Hitler violated the Treaty of Versailles and began to rearm Germany. In 1936, he remilitarized the Rhineland, completely ending the imposed restrictions of the Treaty of Versailles. In March 1938, he bullied fascist Austria into agreeing to annexation, or *Anschluß*. When Austria's chancellor tried to hold a referendum to preserve Austrian independence, German troops simply marched into the country. Most people in Austria and abroad accepted the fait accompli. Austrians who openly objected wound up dead or in concentration camps. In the fall of 1938 at the **Munich Conference**, Hitler also got the British, French, and Italians to sign off on his annexation of the ethnic German Sudetenland from Czecho-slovakia. After that agreement, most ethnic Germans in

Europe lived under Hitler's authority. The "rump" Czecho-slovakia meanwhile had lost the ability to defend itself.

The inaction of the great powers concerning the events both in Asia and in Europe has often been attacked as **appeasement**. The word simply describes a policy of giving in to an aggressive government's demands rather than fighting. It has become a term implying weakness and failure because, with hindsight, these actions made Japan and Germany better prepared for war. At the time, though, Western leaders saw appeasement as a reasonable approach. Not every issue is worth a war. When it came to Hitler's demands: why should Germany not be armed as every other nation was? Why should Germany not reasonably occupy and defend its own territory? How could anyone say that Germany should not include all Germans?

After the easy annexation of the Sudetenland, though, Hitler's demands ceased to be reasonable, even under nationalist principles. In the spring of 1939, Hitler occupied Czecho-slovakia after enticing or coercing the Slovaks into declaring independence. For the first time he had annexed substantial numbers of non-Germans, acting as an imperialist instead of a nationalist. This action finally alerted France and Britain to Hitler's plan of expansionism. While France and Britain were not prepared to go to war for Czecho-slovakia, they did pledge their support to Poland, which seemed like Hitler's next target (because of the Polish Corridor and Danzig). Not many noticed or cared about Mussolini's conquest of Albania in April 1939.

Hitler laid the foundation for further acquisitions in eastern Europe in a brilliant diplomatic maneuver. The deadly rivals Nazi Germany and Communist Russia signed a nonaggression pact in late summer 1939. These newfound allies secretly divided eastern Europe into spheres of influence between them. Free from worrying about a possible two-front war, which hurt Germany in World War I, Hitler could now do what he wanted. He invaded Poland on 1 September 1939, beginning the European phase of World War II.

Although Britain and France declared war two days later, there was little they could do to save Poland. Hitler's generals were able to test their **Blitzkrieg** (lightning war) tactics to great success (see diagrams 13.1–13.4). Coordination of air power and tanks solved the problem of maneuvering large armies. These tactics (and Russia's attack from the east) eliminated Polish forces in a matter of weeks.

Germany at first seemed to have all the advantages. Britain and France sat through the "Sitzkrieg" (a word play on Blitzkrieg meaning "sitting war") of the winter of 1939–1940, while Russia defeated plucky Finland to grab key defensive positions. With the spring thaw, Hitler surprised everyone with an attack on Denmark and Norway. Victory came quickly, first because effective use of paratroops enabled the Nazis to seize key locations. Second, native fascists, sympathetic with Nazi Aryan ideology, operated as "fifth columnists" (implying an extra group of troops on the inside) or "Quislings"(named after the Norwegian fascist leader) to help the Nazis into the countries. Hitler thus solved another problem of World War I: Norway's ports on the Atlantic ensured that Germany could not be successfully blockaded, while its U-boats (submarines) could attempt to blockade Britain.

The new British prime minister, Winston Churchill (r. 1940–1945, 1951–1955) was barely in office when German armies attacked Holland, Belgium, France, and Luxembourg. The Germans evaded France's Maginot Line by punching tanks through the ill-defended Ardennes Forest. Like Poland, France fell in weeks. The British and a

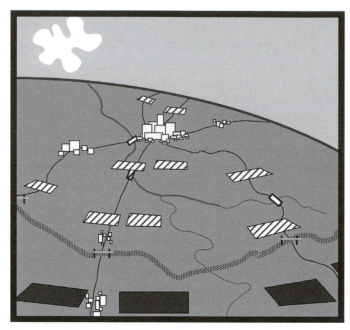

Diagram 13.1. Blitzkrieg, Phase 1. Before the Blitzkrieg-style warfare begins, black and striped military units face each other across a border.

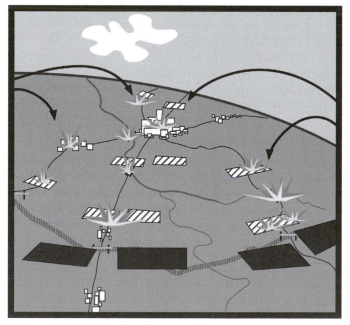

Diagram 13.2. Blitzkrieg, Phase 2. As attacking black ground forces advance, black's bombers strike far behind the lines to break up enemy units, disrupt lines of transportation and communication, and even bomb civilians in the cities, causing panic and confusion.

Diagram 13.3. Blitzkrieg, Phase 3. Attacking black tank forces both confront enemy forces and go around them cross-country. Small commando units seize or build river crossings to enable larger armies to cross.

Diagram 13.4. Blitzkrieg, Phase 4. Aerial bombing, artillery shelling, and flanking and encirclement by black armies have fragmented the defending striped forces. Infantry mops up the remains.

handful of allied forces managed to flee from Dunkirk back to England, leaving much of their weaponry behind. By the fall of 1940, Hitler tried to soften up England for invasion with the **Battle of Britain,** the first decisive air battle in history. Britain won this battle (partly due to the new invention of radar). Since Germany lacked the air cover to protect a sea-to-land assault, Britain gained time to recover and rearm. The prospect of defeating Germany alone, however, seemed bleak.

Meanwhile, Hitler ruled most of Europe, with the largest empire since Napoleon's. If he had remained satisfied with these gains, the course of world history would have been much different. Yet he could not be satisfied with less than German mastery of all Eurasia. Impatient and confident in his previous successes, Hitler betrayed and attacked his ally, the U.S.S.R., on 22 June 1941. His surprise attack was at first brilliantly successful.

Regrettably for Hitler, serious errors slowed his invasion of the Soviet Union. Britain was strong enough to help Russia with supplies. The vastness of Russia, as Napoleon had learned, made it impossible for armies to find and defeat all the Russian forces. With Britain still at his rear, Hitler launched a two-front war. At first, many peoples in Russia actually welcomed the German armies as liberators from the brutality of Stalin. But after the Germans showed that they were Nazis, dedicated to enslaving or killing all non-Aryans, peoples of the Soviet Union learned that there was something worse than Stalinism.

As the German offensive against Russia bogged down in the muddy fall of 1941, several eager Nazis turned their attention to that nagging Jewish Problem proclaimed by Hitler's ideology. They came up with a **Final Solution**: killing all Jews. As a result, the Nazis built several special camps in occupied Poland to which they shipped the Jews from their ghettoes. In camps like Auschwitz, Treblinka, or Sobibor, the Nazis stole the Jews' last possessions, killed them in gas chambers, and burned their corpses in crematoria. The resulting deaths of millions of Jews has been named the **Holocaust** (Greek for burnt sacrifice) or **Shoah** (Hebrew for disaster). Some people these days, calling themselves "revisionist historians," deny the reality of this slaughter. They say it didn't happen; the Nazis did not try to execute all the Jews. Such people are either fools or liars. The Final Solution happened as much as World War II. It is an indisputable fact of history. Given enough time, the Nazis would have killed every Jew they could lay their hands on, followed by other racial and social enemies. The only thing that stopped this Nazi genocide was losing the war.

Germany lost this war because, just as during World War I, its opponents built alliances to outnumber and outfight it. Before the war, Hitler seemed to be the superior builder of alliances. Germany had named itself and its allies the Axis Powers, including hapless Italy, energetic Japan, and reactionary Spain, which, however, stayed out of the war. During the war, the only truly willing allies were the resentful states of Hungary (angry about its small size after World War I), Bulgaria (simmering over its losses in the Balkan Wars), and Finland (having suffered Stalin's attack in 1939). In the end, the lack of cooperation between the Axis Powers doomed them. If Japan had invaded Russia, a two-front war might have brought down the Soviet Union. Instead, Japan decided to attack Great Britain and the United States of America.

Axis attacks made building the Allies much easier. After Hitler attacked Russia, Churchill quickly allied with Stalin, despite his concern about communism. Churchill also successfully cultivated President Roosevelt. Churchill and FDR went so far as to sign the **Atlantic Charter** in the fall of 1941. This document proclaimed their mutual support and set generous goals for a postwar world, even though the United States was not yet in the war. Indeed, most Americans were isolationist, thinking it just fine if communists and fascists and Asians fought each other.

Then, on 7 December 1941, the Japanese launched planes from aircraft carriers and bombed the American military base in Hawaii, **Pearl Harbor**. They also attacked other British and American bases in the western Pacific. The attack on Pearl Harbor, though bold and successful in its immediate goal, was a strategic disaster. Attacking Britain made some sense: England could barely defend itself, much less its worldwide possessions. Bringing the United States into the war, however, doomed Japan. Americans saw the planes flown against Pearl Harbor as unjustified, especially since the bombing had taken place before a formal declaration of war. In the words of one of their own commanders, the Japanese had awakened a sleeping giant. The outraged Americans would never have stopped fighting to avenge the death of 2,600 soldiers and sailors until Japan was utterly defeated.

The entry of the United States into World War II was the beginning of the end. The vast industrial potential of the country and its determination for vengeance for Pearl Harbor guaranteed an Allied victory. A few days after Pearl Harbor, Hitler made the worst mistake of his career. Without any real necessity, he declared war on the United States. This relieved Roosevelt of a huge dilemma. He had wanted to help Britain in Europe but could not really ask Congress to authorize what would be a two-front war. Thus, America entered the European conflict as well.

America was strong enough to fight, and win, a global war with the other Allies (see map 13.1). The United States fully unfolded its vast economic power, helping to equip the Allies and fight major conflicts both in Europe and in Asia, at once. By the summer of 1942, the Japanese were overstretched by the conquest of most British, Dutch, and American possessions in the Pacific. Counterattacking American forces began hopping from island group to island group, learning their own jungle

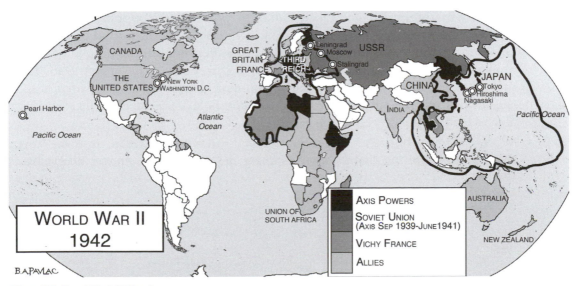

Map 13.1.   World War II

combat and using aircraft carriers to help cut Japanese communications and supplies. The battles in the Pacific were small in scale compared with the hundreds of thousands of men on the Russian front, but the fighting was brutal and nasty. Jungle heat and tropical disease sorely afflicted both sides (Japan is mostly a temperate country). Still, defeat was inevitable, although the Japanese resisted to the last soldier, on almost every island.

In the fall of 1943, the tide turned in Europe, as American forces began to liberate North Africa and the Russians enmeshed the Germans in the Battle of Stalingrad. By early 1944, German armies were in slow, yet inevitable, retreat. D-Day, or the Normandy invasion by the Allies (6 June 1944), saw the largest sea-to-land assault in human history. Axis regimes ran out of fuel and raw materials to produce armaments as well as suffering a lack of workers to use them. Allied heavy bombers, the British by night and the Americans by day, were setting entire cities on fire, sparking firestorms. In one night of bombing, a modern city could be reduced to rubble while tens of thousands of civilians, old men, women, and children, were baked or suffocated to death in their bomb shelters.

Nazi scientists had, for a while, hoped for "wonder weapons" to bring victory. Jets and rockets were applied too little, too late. Another possibility had been a city-destroying device: an **atomic bomb**. German leadership in the study of physics had given the Nazis a great head start. Instead, America built the bomb first. The most brilliant physicist of the century, Albert Einstein, had fled from Nazi Germany to America because of Hitler's persecution of Jews. Einstein wrote to President Roosevelt to encourage America to construct an atomic bomb before the Nazis could. By May 1945, Germany had been conquered. Hitler was dead from suicide, his body only partially cremated in a ditch because his last followers lacked enough gasoline.

After the defeat of Germany, Japan still fought on. In July 1945, American scientists successfully tested their "Trinity" device, applying a divine name to a weapon of mass destruction. On 6 August, America dropped one bomb on Hiroshima; on 9 August, another bomb on Nagasaki followed (see figure 13.4). The bombs accomplished what previously had taken hundreds of bombers dropping thousands of bombs. The two cities were incinerated in a flash: tens of thousands of people killed, many thousands more wounded—and suffering from the little-known phenomenon of radiation. Japan finally offered to surrender on 14 August 1945. Thus, the worst instantaneous destruction in human history ended the worst war in human history. The United States stood at the helm of Western civilization, now able to lead it into the rest of the century.

Review: How did the German and Japanese desire for world empires shape World War II?

Response:

Figure 13.4.   A lonely church on a hill remains from the devastated Nagasaki after the atomic bomb blast.

CHAPTER 14

A World Divided

The Early Cold War, 1945 to 1980

The resounding victory of the Allies in World War II did not lead to a new international stability. Instead, a new kind of conflict, the **Cold War** (1948–1991), dominated most of the latter half of the twentieth century. The Cold War resembled the long geopolitical competition between France and England that had lasted from the fourteenth to the nineteenth century. Two primary enemies, the United States and the U.S.S.R., now wrestled for world domination and threatened everyone as never before. Their ideological points of view made it difficult to compromise or cooperate. During this colossal conflict between different aspects of Western civilization, the Cold War drew nearly every person on the planet into the influence of Western science, politics, economics, and culture.

FROM FRIENDS TO FOES

After the devastation of World War II, the first challenge for all states was the restoration of order and the reconstruction of their economies. Much of Europe and Asia lay in ruins. Among the survivors, tens of millions of people had been displaced as soldiers, prisoners, forced laborers, or refugees. Some nations began to carry out ethnic removals to clean up some of their lingering nationality problems. Millions of Germans who fled or were forcibly ejected from areas subsequently occupied by Russia, Poland, or Czechoslovakia gained little sympathy. Also, Yugoslavia kicked out Italians. Even Bulgaria and Greece seized the opportunity to expel thousands of Turks, even though Turkey had remained neutral during the war. Never before had such numbers of people been forced to migrate. Many displaced persons lacked homes and jobs, although many states became much more ethnically uniform, as nationalistic ideals demanded. The Allied armies that occupied the defeated nations organized the slow rebuilding of their societies and eliminated the fascist policies that had caused the war.

The victorious Allies showcased the defeat of the fascists by conducting trials for war crimes against humanity. The slaughter and genocide of civilians during the war were considered so horrific that the victors undertook the unusual measure of convening international courts. As a result of the **Nuremburg Trials** in Germany, twenty-five captured Nazi leaders were hanged. Over the next several years a few dozen lower-ranking Nazis also faced judgment and execution.

Not all fascist criminals came to justice, however. Some Nazi sympathizers, collaborators, and even high-ranking officials managed to escape, many fleeing to sympathetic fascist regimes in Latin America, sometimes with the knowledge of local governments. In particular, Nazi scientists, especially those responsible for work on rockets and jets, were smuggled to one victor or another. In Asia, the trials for Japanese war criminals were much less thorough. Emperor Hirohito of Japan had declared himself no longer a god, so the American occupiers retained him in office and absolved him of all blame for the war and atrocities committed by Japanese soldiers. Comparatively few Japanese war crimes were exposed or punished, especially since the United States was becoming less concerned about its wartime enemy, Japan, than about its wartime ally, Russia.

That the victorious wartime alliance fell apart so quickly surprised and confused many. Certainly, the victory in World War II created a unique geopolitical situation. The great powers, powerful countries who could assert military action around the world, had dominated international politics since the nineteenth century. By the end of World War II, though, England and its British Empire were clearly exhausted by the effort. France needed to rebuild, as did China, after suffering hard occupations. Of course, Germany, Italy, and Japan lay in ruins and were occupied by the Allies. Only the United States and the Soviet Union remained capable of effective global action. Indeed, they had risen to the status of **superpowers**. They had large populations (over a hundred million), were industrialized, occupied vast continental land masses, were rich in agricultural land and natural resources, and possessed massive military forces. The other declining great powers could not hope to match them.

Equal in power, the United States and the U.S.S.R. were nevertheless divided by opposing ideologies (see table 14.1). The Soviet Union was a totalitarian dictatorship with a secret police, the KGB; the United States worked along more republi-

Table 14.1. Comparison and Contrast between the United States of America and the Union of Soviet Socialist Republics

	Politics	Economy	Society	Culture	Belief
U.S.S.R.	soviet, totalitarian, one party	communism: centralized, state-planned economy	classless society (party elites vs. masses); free public education	rigid censorship, state-controlled press and arts	atheism, persecuted Russian Orthodox Church
U.S.A.	federal, democratic-republican, two parties	mixed economy: laissez-faire capitalism and socialism	upper, middle, and lower classes; private and public education	limited censorship, free press, profit-making arts	religious toleration, separation of church and state, nominally Christian

Note: The U.S.A. and the U.S.S.R. represented different aspects of the Western heritage that competed for people's allegiance during the Cold War.

can and constitutionalist principles. The U.S.S.R. used centralized state planning for its economy (often called communism); the United States practiced capitalism in a mixed economy of some socialistic regulation and competitive, semifree markets.[1] Russia proclaimed itself to have outgrown nationalistic and class divisions (although its party elites led a significantly better life than its common workers); the United States, despite a growing middle class, remained divided into significant economic disparities between rich and poor, often based on sex, ethnicity, and race. The Russian government rigidly controlled and censored its media; businesses, through their advertising dollars, influenced the American media. The Union of Soviet Socialist Republics proudly proclaimed itself to be atheistic (ostensibly believing in the dogmas of Marx, Lenin, and Stalin) and restricted worship by Orthodox Christians; the United States of America asserted religious freedom and toleration, while the majority of citizens attended diverse Christian churches. Communist Russia lost sight of the individual in its mania for the collective—many could suffer so the group could succeed; capitalist America awkwardly juggled individual rights and communal responsibility.

The differences in these practices and ideologies did not necessarily mean that a conflict was inevitable. Both sides could have decided to live and let live. Yet both sides envisioned their own path as the only suitable way for everyone on earth to live. Each state tried to dominate the world with its own vision of order, echoing the clashes of the past, whether between the Athenian creative individualism versus Spartan disciplined egalitarianism of the Peloponnesian Wars, or revolutionary

---

1. As part of this ideological war, the term *capitalism* was transformed to oppose the "communism" of central planning of the economy by government. Thus, today many people define capitalism as the private ownership of the means of production instead of its simpler definition as the practice of reinvesting profits. Soviet-style "communism" likewise differed from Marx's ideal of common ownership.

France against commercial Great Britain during the Wars of the Coalitions. The world split up between them. The United States and its allies often called themselves "the West." The Soviet Union and its allies were often called the "Eastern bloc" because of their center in Eastern Europe or from their association with China in East Asia. A more accurate terminology arose of the "First World" (the nations associated with the United States), the "Second World" (the nations associated with the Soviet Union), and the "Third World" (Latin America and the soon to be newly liberated colonial areas of Asia and Africa).

The splits between these blocs widened during Allied planning conferences as World War II wound down. First, in February 1945 at the Soviet Black Sea resort of **Yalta**, the "Big Three"—Stalin for the Soviet Union, Roosevelt for the United States, and Churchill for Britain—began to seriously plan for the postwar world after their inevitable victory. They agreed in principle that Europe would be divided into spheres of influence, thus applying the language of imperialism to Europe itself. Southern Europe went to the British, while much of Eastern Europe came under the Russian sphere. Under the guidance of the British and Russians, self-government in different nations was supposed to be restored. The only sphere the United States committed itself to was joining Britain and Russia in occupying Germany.

After Germany's defeat, but before Japan's surrender, the "Big Three" met again at **Potsdam** in July 1945, although two of the leaders had been replaced. Stalin still represented the U.S.S.R. In the meantime, Churchill had been voted out as prime minister to be replaced by Labour Party leader Clement Atlee. And **Harry Truman** (r. 1945–1953) had succeeded to the American presidency following the death of FDR in April. These three shaped up plans for German occupation (adding France as a fourth occupier), ***denazification*** and the war crimes trials, restoration and occupation of a separate Austria, and peace treaties for the minor Axis members. While many questions remained open, the settlements still seemed to be going well.

One more hope for a unified future of the world was an organization that had been created by the victorious Allies to prevent new conflict, the **United Nations Organization** (UN). The United Nations charter was first signed in San Francisco on 26 June 1945, as war still raged in Asia. The five victors of World War II (the United States, the U.S.S.R., Great Britain, France, and, generously, China), became the permanent members of the Security Council, with veto power over the organization's actions. The UN could provide some international regulations and help with health-care issues. More importantly, when the Security Council agreed, the organization could quickly and easily commit military forces. Its hope was to use collective security to maintain peace. The UN's peacekeeping role has indeed managed to keep many wars and rebellions from growing worse around the world. From the Congo to Cyprus, peacekeepers have saved some lives, but the UN can solve an issue only when a superpower does not object.

Soon enough, the superpowers diverged, as the temptations of occupation proved too strong for Stalin. Stalin soon began ***sovietization*** of the states in his sphere of influence (Poland, Czechoslovakia, Hungary, Rumania, Bulgaria, and its occupied zones of Germany). Believing it his right to have friendly neighbors in

Eastern Europe, Stalin helped communist parties take over governments, which then claimed to be people's democratic republics. As in the Soviet Union, these regimes lacked opposition parties but still conducted elections. The new communist leaders purged, arrested, and executed not just fascists but also liberals, conservatives, and socialists unwilling to submit. Using the excuse of rebuilding from the war's devastation, communist governments nationalized businesses and property. As the Soviet armies stayed and the new leaders of Eastern European states took direction from Moscow, these satellite or "puppet" states were becoming protectorates rather than merely falling under a sphere of influence. These changes led the retired British prime minister Winston Churchill to use the metaphor of the "Iron Curtain" separating communist oppression from "Christian civilization" (see map 14.1).

At first, Americans ignored Churchill's warning. But growing communist-backed insurgencies in Greece and Turkey led the Americans to accept Churchill's concerns. Soviet intervention in these new areas led Americans to believe Stalin was expanding beyond the provisions of Yalta and Potsdam. President Truman decided to carry out a policy called **containment**, to try to limit the influence of the Soviet Union in several ways. In his speech creating the **Truman Doctrine**, he promised aid to governments resisting hostile seizures of power by foreigners or even by armed minorities of natives. He explicitly contrasted the freedom of the United

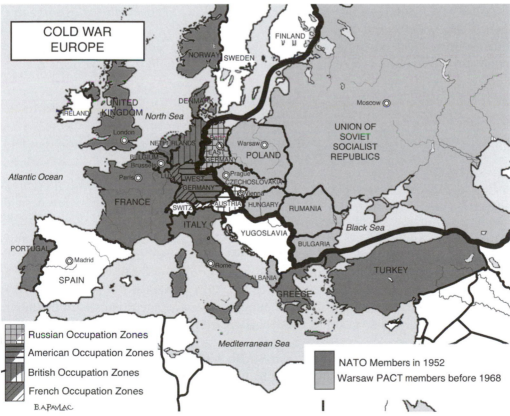

Map 14.1. Cold War Europe

States with the tyranny of Russia. The United States followed up with military aid to the Greeks and Turks, who crushed the insurgencies. Through the Marshall Plan (or European Recovery Program) the United States also provided money to European states struggling with a lack of capital in the wake of the war. A small American investment of seventeen million dollars helped rebuild Europe and weaken the appeal of communism. To further combat communism, a new American **Central Intelligence Agency (CIA)** gathered information and carried out covert operations (including supporting armed intervention, sabotage, and assassination).

Even these heightening tensions only solidified into an enduring dispute centering on occupied Germany. As the war ended, both Germany and Austria had been divided into zones run by the armies of each of the four victorious powers, Britain, France, the United States, and the Soviet Union. They also divided and occupied the capital cities, Vienna and Berlin, located in the middle of their respective Soviet zones. While the four Allies quickly granted some self-government to Austria, they could not agree about Germany. The three Western occupiers wanted Germany to become more independent as soon as possible. Meanwhile, the Soviet Union plundered its East German occupation zone for materials to use in rebuilding its own devastated territories. It also feared that a united Germany could one day invade Russia again.

In June 1948, when the British, French, and Americans took steps to allow a new currency in the Western zones, the Russians initiated the **Berlin Blockade** (1948–1949), shutting down the border crossings, in violation of treaties and agreements. The Allies could have, with legitimacy, used force to oppose these Russian moves. Instead of becoming a "hot" war, with each side unleashing firepower against the other, the war remained "cold." Each side held to a basic principle:

> Nobody wanted World War III because it would mean the end of the world.

With "weapons of mass destruction" of atomic, biological, and chemical technology, the superpowers could exterminate huge numbers of people. Even a small military action against the Russians would have, of course, created a counterattack, with the two superpowers in a shooting war. If it escalated to the use of atomic, biological, and chemical weapons, World War III (a war including several great powers and superpowers against one another) could wipe out all humanity or at least destroy all modern civilized ways of life. Only in fiction did people entertain nuclear war, whether realistically predicting the catastrophic results as in the movie *On the Beach*, or in James Bond movies where evil madmen hoped to spark world destruction.

A nonconfrontational solution, the **Berlin Airlift**, succeeded in the short term. The Western allies supplied the isolated city using airplanes to fly over the Russian barricades. Over nine hundred flights per day provided seven thousand tons of food and fuel to keep the modern city of two million people going for over a year. Enormous sums of money were spent, and men died (in several plane crashes), but no shots were fired. Then one day, the Russians opened the border again. Soon afterward, a new German state appeared in the West, the Federal Republic of Germany, based on the values of the Western Allies. Subsequently, the Russians endorsed the German Democratic Republic in the East, based on sovietization.

Both sides built new alliance systems. The **North Atlantic Treaty Organization (NATO)** bound together most Western European states with Canada and the United States in a mutual defense pact. Sweden and Switzerland retained their neutrality. Russia arranged the **Warsaw Pact** with its satellite states (Poland, East Germany, Czechoslovakia, Hungary, Rumania, and Bulgaria) to better coordinate their military forces in opposition to NATO. These military alliances, ready to fight World War III, faced one another across the barbed wire and barricades that ran through the heart of German field and forest. Still, the divisions solved the "German problem," at least temporarily.

An arms race continued to threaten the world nevertheless. By 1949, the Russians had their own atomic bomb. Then, by 1952, the United States developed the hydrogen or **H-bomb**, on which most modern thermonuclear weapons are based. Each H-bomb can have the explosive power of hundreds of times the Hiroshima and Nagasaki devices (each of which destroyed an entire city). Aided by information gained through espionage, however, the Russians soon tested a nuclear weapon of their own. With or without spying, nuclear proliferation remained inevitable. With enough time, effort, money, and access to supplies, any nation can harness science to build nuclear as well as biological, chemical, and any number of conventional weapons. Throughout the Cold War, both sides kept shortsightedly relying on some technological superiority or another, only to see it vanish with the next application of scientific effort by the other side.

At first, complexity and cost usually meant that nuclear weapons remained in the hands of great powers. The British were next with nuclear bombs in the 1960s, quickly followed by the French. Then the Soviet ally China came next. By the 1990s, India tested its prototype bomb, which prompted Pakistan to produce its own. It is unclear when South Africa and Israel got theirs, probably sometime in the 1970s, although South Africa has given up its technology. Currently, North Korea and Iran are striving to join the "nuclear club."

These states, though, each held only a handful of nuclear weapons. The two superpowers, however, held enough to destroy the world many times over. As technicians perfected **ICBMs** (intercontinental ballistic missiles) by the late 1950s, any target on the globe was vulnerable to vaporization. By 1977, the superpowers had stockpiled tens of thousands of nuclear devices—with the equivalent of about fifteen tons of TNT per person on the planet.

During the Cold War, the superpowers never pressed the button to end human history with the explosion of nuclear weapons. Instead, they relied on **deterrence** (preventing war through the fear that if one side starts nuclear war, the other will finish it). The American policy of deterrence was aptly called MAD, the acronym for "mutually assured destruction." Both sides did play at brinkmanship (threatening to go to war in order to get your opponent to back down on some political point). In reaction to this threat to civilization, some citizens of Western states began calling for nuclear disarmament. Governments also realized that they could not endlessly build risk into global politics. As a result, some areas became off limits for weapons

(Antarctica, the ocean floors, and outer space). Other countries were discouraged from acquiring their own weapons through nonproliferation treaties beginning in 1968; and through the 1960s and into the 1980s the two superpowers negotiated on limits or mutual inspections of numbers and use of arms.

For the next several decades after the Berlin Blockade, the Cold War was on. This third great world war of the twentieth century was unique in the history of politics. Like its predecessors, World Wars I and II, the Cold War cost enormous amounts of money, destroyed a lot of territory, cost many lives, and changed the destinies of nations. But unlike those other two conflicts, the main opponents, the Soviet Union and the United States, did not actually fight each other, despite a string of international crises. Instead, they encouraged other people to do the killing, sometimes supplying intelligence, equipment, advice, and even soldiers. Although the Cold War was an ideological civil war of the West, it weighed on every international and many a domestic decision of almost all countries in the world.

Review: How did the winning alliance of World War II split into the mutual hostility of the Cold War?

Response:

MAKING MONEY

Rather than fight the Cold War, most Americans would probably have preferred blissfully to return to expanding the U.S. economy. But the traditional American isolationism was doomed not only by the events of World War II but by the worldwide economy led by the United States after the war. Some Western economies grew so fast that they needed to import immigrant workers for their factories. Western capitalists regularly took advantage of these workers by paying them less than they would union-organized Western laborers, but even so, such incomes far exceeded what the foreigners could have earned in their native lands. Notably, West Germany's *Gastarbeiter* (guest workers) from the Balkans helped the German economy grow. Their labor helped both West Germany and their home countries. Guest workers typically sent money back to families in their homelands, building capital for those economies. Their lives in Germany remained isolated, however, segregated from the main German culture. For a long time, the Germans thought the workers would go home again, and so they ignored issues of integrating the

Gastarbeiter. Instead, many stayed from one generation to the next. Economic necessity, rather than defeat in World War II, created an ethnically mixed Germany.

Other European nations accepted immigrants from their colonies as cheap labor. So many came to England that the British Parliament restricted holders of British passports from moving from other parts of the Commonwealth to the mother country. Nevertheless, the numbers of foreign-born residents in Western European states began to surpass the number of comparable immigrants in the United States, a nation traditionally much more favorable to immigration. Throughout Europe the guest workers lived in shabby, crowded apartments lacking services and facilities, isolated from the main ethnic groups of the nation. This segregation, however, often allowed foreign workers and their families to maintain many of their own cultural traditions. Nonetheless, many Europeans long ignored these new residents as an invisible underclass, often disregarding either possibilities of integration and acculturation or social disruptions of clashing cultures.

Coming out of World War II, the United States had the strongest internationally oriented economy, with dominant influence in the International Monetary Fund and General Agreement on Tariffs and Trade (GATT). By the 1960s, though, the other great powers, especially Germany and Japan, had recovered from the devastation of the war. They then began to offer serious competition to the Americans. Both Germany and Japan used a socialistic cooperation of government, management, and workers to a degree that the Americans, with their antagonistic interests of owners and unions, could not.

The rapid increase of wealth in the West was a significant victory for socialist ideas. After World War II, social democratic and Christian socialist parties came to power in many Western countries. Their gradual, legal, revisionist, state socialism created the modern **welfare state**. Germany rebuilt itself in record time, using the idea of a social market economy. As in a free-market economy, German businesses were regulated as little as possible. At the same time, the German state enforced socialist theory, which provided workers with protections for illness, health, old age, and joblessness, while labor unions gained representation on the boards of corporations.

For awhile, Great Britain went furthest along the road toward the modern welfare state, although its loss of empire made adjustments difficult. The British swept away poor laws (which had condemned the poor to prison for debt) and instead initiated programs to provide a minimum decent standard of living for most people. Government support and regulation established national health-care programs, pensions, and unemployment insurance. Public education of high quality, through the university level, was available for free or at very low cost. Programs sent aid for housing and food directly to families. Many essential businesses, especially coal, steel, and public transportation, were nationalized or taken over by the government, to be run for the benefit of everyone, not just stockholders. Unfortunately for economic growth, government management did not provide efficiency, and some of these firms could not compete well in the world markets.

All over the West, standards of living rose. The social "safety net" provided more chances for the poor to rise out of poverty. Reliable supplies of electricity and installation of indoor plumbing became nearly universal. The middle class broadened out to include many of the working class, because social welfare legislation and union contracts gave workers decent wages and benefits. More people gained access to labor-saving appliances such as washing machines and automatic dishwashers. Home ownership increased. Meanwhile, the extremely wealthy continued to prosper (even if they disliked paying taxes redistributed to help the middle and poor classes).

This vast increase in wealth also led to an amazing lifestyle change in industrialized nations, especially the United States. Instead of the duality of city and countryside that had marked the living patterns of civilization since its beginning, most people began to live in a novel kind of place, the suburbs. *Suburbanization* meant a new way of life for the growing middle classes. Suburbs are a blend of traditional urban living with rural landscapes. People wanted open space (the yard with lawn) and separate dwellings (the stand-alone home), as well as shopping amenities (the shopping mall). Many jobs, however, continued to be located in the cities (see figure 14.1). Thus commutes multiplied over vast miles of roads. To meet this need, production of motor vehicles in the United States soon reached the equivalent of one car for every man, woman, and child. Huge amounts of new construction catered to automobiles, from superhighways to parking lots. Europe also suburbanized, although more slowly, as it lacked open spaces that could be developed. Both Western and Eastern European societies aimed to provide consumer products, whether through capitalistic or communistic means of production. Europeans also tended to favor mass transportation over commuting by private automobile.

While suburbs had many admirable comforts, their cost tore at the social fabric of the West, especially in the United States. By definition, living in suburbs required

Figure 14.1.   Stockyards in Chicago in 1947 where workers slaughtered meat for America. Better truck transportation would soon allow owners to move these sites outside of cities to rural areas.

a good income. Local zoning laws enforced a middle-class status on suburbs. American inner cities of the East and Midwest to which blacks had migrated from the South before and after World War II became virtual ghettoes as whites fled to live in suburbs. White men, both middle and working class, could earn enough in the 1950s and 1960s to allow middle-class wives to stay home as domestic managers. Yet many stay-at-home women felt isolated in their suburban luxury. The economic shift of the 1970s (see below), however, soon forced women to find jobs, since two incomes were needed to support the suburban lifestyle, and that meant absentee parents. Increasingly, children were left home alone. Television provided mindless entertainment for some. Drugs, consumed behind closed doors, also became widely used among the children of middle-class parents. In dealing with increased drug use, many governments decided to take a criminal direction rather than a medicinal one, leading to larger and larger numbers of incarcerated. By the end of the century, governments such as those of Switzerland and the Netherlands experimented with legalization and toleration.

This expanded middle class and suburbanization had enormous consequences. The incredible affluence of the West led to a cultural revolution, as the children of the post–World War II generation started to come of age. Often called "baby boomers" in the United States, these large numbers of young people had more education, opportunities, and wealth than ever before. They criticized the elites of the "establishment" as hypocritically too interested in power, wealth, and the status quo rather than social justice. In turn, the "establishment" criticized young people as too obsessed with sex, drugs, and rock 'n' roll. The popularity of movies, television, and recorded music indulged trends toward a counterculture. Rock 'n' roll provided a new international youth culture that gained momentum with the British music group **The Beatles** (1962–1970), a worldwide sensation. On the one hand, some Western cultural conservatives worried that the long-haired rockers were as bad as communists. On the other hand, communists condemned the Beatles as sex-crazed capitalists.

A **sexual revolution** arose as part of the new counterculture. Greater freedom in sexual activity became possible with improvements in preventing pregnancy. In the late 1950s, pharmaceutical companies introduced reliable contraceptives in the form of an oral pill. "The Pill" allowed more people to have sex without the risk of pregnancy, while medically supervised abortions could end pregnancy with relative safety for a woman. The revolution also encouraged more sex outside the confines of traditional marriage. Sex became a more noticeable part of literature, instead of being sold under the table. Courts refused to enforce censorship laws against serious novels like Henry Miller's *Tropic of Cancer* or art films like *I am Curious, Yellow*. Everything from girlie magazines like *Playboy* to explicit pornography became more accessible.

This increasing extramarital sexual activity brought unforeseen medical risks. The Pill could have side effects, such as blood clots. Even more serious were venereal or sexually transmitted diseases (STDs). For a few years in the middle of the century, the traditional sexual diseases of syphilis and gonorrhea had become treatable with modern antibiotics, so many thought sexually transmitted diseases could be ignored. But new diseases began to develop, as multitudes of human bodies came into more intimate contact. Acquired Immune Deficiency Syndrome (AIDS) became a worldwide scourge in the 1980s. Since it was spread in the West at first by male homosexual sex, it became a target of cultural conservatives, who saw AIDS as a divine curse. Despite these prejudices, those people attracted to the same sex, gays and lesbians, began to seek acceptance in Western society instead of being confined to the "closet."

The sexual revolution also spurred Western women to claim legal equality with men. As mentioned above, married women were already moving into the workforce again as middle-class standards became more difficult to afford on one income. Women were also progressively more dissatisfied with the title of "housewife," which gained so little respect in the culture at large. The ***Women's Liberation*** movement of the 1960s addressed important issues, such as the right of women to get a good education, to serve on juries, to own property, and to be free from legal obedience to a husband's every command (as many legal systems still mandated well into the 1970s). Despite the notable defeat of the Equal Rights Amendment in the United States, most women in the West achieved substantial equality before the law and opportunity for economic access in the 1970s.

Women's liberation, however, faltered after these initial successes. The women's movement fragmented as women of color, or religion, or class, or different sexual orientation disagreed with the white middle-class women who had first led the reforms. Around the world today, families and societies still deny women education or force them into marriage or prostitution according to long traditions of "civilization." In spite of this subjugation of women, the term *feminism* has often become associated with hatred of men rather than advocating women's access to political, economic, and social power structures.

The inhumane horrors of World War II further motivated some westerners to try to make human rights a permanent part of the social agenda. Eleanor Roosevelt, the widow of FDR, had pushed the United Nations in that direction already in 1948 with the Universal Declaration of Human Rights. Enforcing its noble goals of equality was a different matter. The desire for better human rights had achieved little outside Europe and the United States when Cold War ideology intervened.

In the United States of America, the struggle about **civil rights** for minorities coincided with that about women's rights. The "race issue," oversimplified as "black" vs. "white," divided Americans on who belonged to society. The population of African origin, the former slaves and their descendants, lived under the allegedly "separate but equal" policies, which in reality imposed second-class status on blacks in the United States. Beginning in the 1950s, court challenges, demonstrations, marches, sit-ins, boycotts, and nonviolence of Dr. Martin Luther King, Jr. (d. 1968) challenged the laws. The Civil Rights Acts of 1957, 1963, and 1964 gave blacks real political participation not seen since the Reconstruction period after the Civil War. Sadly, right after these gains, more riots burst out in American cities, and King himself was assassinated. But the possibility for Americans of African heritage to achieve the "American dream" was finally, at least officially, possible.

The Union of South Africa, with its minority of "whites" (those descended from British or Dutch settlers) and a majority of "coloreds" (Indian and mixed ancestry) and "blacks" (native African) offers a contrast. At the beginning of the Cold War, the ruling party had intensified racist discrimination through a legal system called **apartheid** (1948–1993). This set of laws deprived the darker-skinned peoples of their right to vote, choose work, and live or even socialize with anyone of the wrong "race." Fear of the natives' long-standing political organization, the African National Congress, encouraged the South African government to imprison and persecute their leaders, including Nelson Mandela. By the 1970s, in the wake of the American Civil Rights movement, worldwide criticism and boycotts had somewhat isolated the racist regime. Still, many Western governments, in the name of Cold War solidarity, ignored boycotts organized by human rights groups.

Just as some westerners were concerned about the rights of their fellow humans, others focused on the "rights" of the planet itself. Since the beginning of the century, petroleum, usually just called oil, provided the most convenient source of power. Refined into diesel or gasoline, it was cheaper and easier to use than coal. Natural gas, a by-product of drilling for oil, also found numerous uses because of its extreme efficiency in burning. Burning coal or oil, though, added noticeably to a growing problem with air pollution. Petrochemicals were also fouling the waters of rivers and coastlines and killing wildlife. The heavily populated and highly industrialized West produced more waste and garbage than all the humans in all of previous history. A growing awareness of these problems spawned *environmentalism*, or looking after the earth's best interests. Earth Day was first proclaimed in 1971. Political parties usually called **Greens** were organized chiefly around environmental issues, winning representation in governments in some European countries by the end of the century. Meanwhile, many governments responded to environmental degradation with regulations about waste management and recycling. The damage to nature slowed its pace, and in a few areas the environment even improved.

As an alternative to oil, some suggested **nuclear energy**, power based on the same physics that had created atomic and nuclear weapons. Nuclear power plants used a controlled chain reaction to create steam, which drove the turbines and dynamos to generate electricity. Many Western nations began building nuclear power plants, hoping for a clean, efficient, and cheap form of power that did not depend on Middle Eastern oil sheiks. Two disasters helped to reduce enthusiasm for the technology. First, at **Three Mile Island** in Pennsylvania (1979), a malfunctioning valve cut off coolant water to the hot reactor, causing part of the radioactive pile to melt down. If the situation had not been solved, a catastrophic explosion might have created the equivalent of an atomic bomb. Still, today, the hundreds of thousands of tons of highly radioactive debris remain to be cleaned up. Then, at **Chernobyl** in the Ukraine, on 26 April 1986, two out of four reactors at a nuclear complex did explode. Only a handful of people were killed outright, but thousands needed to be evacuated and were forbidden to return to their now-contaminated homes. Hundreds of children also developed birth defects, thyroid diseases, and immune system damage. While neither of these accidents was a worst-case disaster, they were enough to discourage the construction of more nuclear power plants in many Western nations for several decades. The disposal of nuclear waste products, dangerous for generations to come, likewise remains an unsolved problem.

Concern about the physical world mirrored a continued interest in human spirit. Religious divisions, sects, and options multiplied. Perhaps the nuclear arms race, which had created a situation where the world could end with the press of a few buttons, made people appreciate the fragility of human existence. Indian-inspired cults and practices such as yoga, Hare Krishna, or transcendental meditation made their way into Western belief systems. Other leaders reached into the ancient polytheistic religions or combined Christianity with hopes about space aliens. The ability of some cults to convince their members to commit mass suicide regularly shocked most people. The variety of concepts available to communities seeking supernatural answers for the meaning of life reached into the thousands.

At the same time, the established world religions sustained themselves in the West. Muslim immigrants set up mosques in every major city. The first traditional Hindu temple in Europe was dedicated in London in 1995. After being freed from Soviet oppression, many in Eastern Europe sought out Orthodox Christian churches. In contrast, church attendance declined in Western Europe. Religiously inspired laws, such as enforced prayer in schools or no sales on Sunday, disappeared in most Western nations. The Roman Catholic Church, which had once dominated Western civilization, seemed to be drifting toward irrelevance. The second Vatican Council (1963–1965) briefly encouraged many with its new *ecumenism* and liturgy in the language of the people rather than Latin. But soon quarrels over how much the Roman Catholic Church should modernize sapped away momentum. Pope John Paul II (r. 1978–2005) and his compelling personality inspired Roman Catholics and others. The first non-Italian pope since the Renaissance, John Paul II traveled the world and revitalized the international standing of Roman Catholicism. Even his efforts, though, could not reverse the trends in Europe toward unbelief.

In the United States, where religions were most freely practiced and most diverse, large numbers of Western believers still sought out not only churches but also mosques, temples, and meeting halls. Christianity became even more infected with materialism as televangelists took to the airwaves and raised millions of tax-free dollars from people who felt closer to God through their televisions than at the neighborhood church.

In wealth, opportunities, and creativity, the West held its own in the Cold War conflict with "godless communism." The standard of living in communist states seemed meager in comparison, despite the advantages of basic health care, education, and job security for those loyal to the right ideology. Both sides had used their industrialized economies to pay for the ongoing conflict of the Cold War. As it stretched into decades, the decisive question became one of who could afford to "fight" the longest.

Review: How did the postwar economic growth produce unprecedented prosperity and cultural change?

Response:

TO THE BRINK, AGAIN AND AGAIN

The history of the Cold War involved a series of international crises and conventional wars around the world, where East and West confronted each other, fortunately without erupting into a "hot" war, World War III, and the end of civilization. The first major crisis after the Berlin Blockade centered on China. Further putting the seal on the hostility between East and West was the "loss" of China to communism. As World War II ended, everyone expected Jiang's Nationalist Party to rebuild China from the devastation of the war. Because of this expectation, he gained a seat on the Security Council of the United Nations as a great-power victor of World War II.

But westerners did not understand how divided China had become between Nationalists and Communists since the 1930s. Many Chinese reviled Jiang's government as incompetent and corrupt while admiring Mao's Communists as both dedicated guerrilla fighters against the Japanese and supporters of the common peasants. Despite American mediation, civil war broke out in 1947. Most Western observers assumed the Nationalists would win since they controlled far more territory, weapons, and resources. The Communists, not having enough resources at first to engage in open battle, relied on guerrilla warfare. As a model of insurgency for oppressed peoples around the world, they slowly expanded their operations until they could field a national army. The Communists then drove Jiang and his allies to the island of Taiwan (Formosa), where Jiang's followers proclaimed it as **Nationalist China**. Protected by the United States, Jiang ran the small island country as his own personal dictatorship. Meanwhile, on 1 October 1949, Mao proclaimed the state on the mainland as the **People's Republic of China**, a new rival to the West that drew on the Western ideas of Marxism and revolution.

Many Western intelligence analysts had long believed that Mao was merely Stalin's puppet. Instead, Mao began to forge his own unique totalitarian path. With the **Great Leap Forward** in 1958, Mao tried to modernize China, forcing it into the twentieth century and equality with the Western powers. Lacking capital or resources beyond the labor potential of an enormous population, Mao's crude methods turned into a disaster. Instead of investing in Western-style industrial and agricultural technology, he told his people to try to manufacture steel in their backyards and plant more seeds in fields. Chinese peasants obeyed their leader's ignorant suggestions. In the resulting famine, tens of millions died of starvation. Although Communist Party moderates soon ended these catastrophic policies, in 1965 Mao went over their heads to proclaim the **Great Proletarian Cultural Revolution** (1965–1969). He encouraged young people to organize themselves as Red Guards who attacked their elders, teachers, and all figures of authority except for Mao. The Red Guards killed hundreds of thousands and shattered the lives of tens of millions by sending them to "re-education" and prison camps. Although these policies were all aimed to make China's power competitive with the West, China took decades to recover from Mao's mistakes.

China's first major confrontation with the West took place over the division of Korea. The Allies had liberated Korea from Japan in 1945 but had not been able to agree on its political future. So they artificially divided the country: the Russian forces left behind a Soviet regime, the People's Republic of Korea (North Korea), and the Americans installed an authoritarian government, the Republic of Korea (South Korea). Unhappy with this division of their nation, northern forces, with the permission of Stalin and Mao, tried to conquer the south in 1950. The United States convinced the United Nations to defend South Korea, a member state, against aggression, beginning the **Korean Police Action** (1950–1953). In the name of the UN, America provided the bulk of the money and sent the most arms and soldiers, although other Western nations also contributed. An American-led invasion drove back North Korean forces, but then, in turn, hundreds of thousands of Chinese "volunteers" (so named by the Chinese Communist government that claimed no direct involvement) pushed back the UN forces to the original division along the thirty-eighth parallel. Several years of inconclusive fighting later, a treaty reinstated the division of the peninsula between Communist-aligned north and Western-aligned south.

Worried Americans saw the Communists' actions in Berlin, Greece, Turkey, China, and Korea as part of an effort by the Soviet Union to gain world supremacy. A new Red scare tore through the West. This postwar reaction seemed credible, given the power of Stalin's armies and their sway over Eastern Europe. Yet it failed to recognize how divided Communist states were among themselves and how weak Communists were outside of the Russian sphere. Communist Party successes in elections in the West were miserable. In America, the Red scare created *McCarthyism*, a movement named after a senator who used the fear of communism to destroy the careers of people he labeled as "commie pinko" sympathizers. But all the fear and hearings were wasted effort, since communist organizations in the United States were never a serious threat to American security or its way of life.

The military might of the Soviet Union was another matter. After Stalin's death, his successor, **Nikita Khrushchev** (r. 1953–1964), disavowed Stalin's cruelties and called for peaceful coexistence with capitalist countries. That brief moment of optimism ended in 1956, however, when the Hungarians tested the limits of Kruschev's destalinization by purging hard-line communists and asking Russian troops to leave the country. The Russian leadership interpreted these moves as a **Hungarian Revolt**. The tanks of the Warsaw Pact rolled in, and, since Hungary was clearly in the Soviet Union's sphere of influence, NATO could do nothing.

Berlin, for a second time, next focused Cold War tensions. The ongoing four-power occupation of Berlin had turned into a bleeding wound for communist East Germany. Many in the so-called workers' paradise were envious of their brethren in the West. East Germans knew that if they moved to West Germany, they were accepted as full citizens with special benefits. Thousands were soon leaving through Berlin. To stem the tide of emigration, the Russians gave permission to the East Germans to build the **Berlin Wall** (1961–1989) (see figure 14.2). The wall became a militarized barrier to keep East Germans from West Germany. Since preventing the Berlin Wall from being built might have meant World War III, there was little the West could do. The Communists claimed that the Berlin Wall was a necessary bulwark against Western imperialism and capitalism. Many in the rest of the world recognized it as a symbol of the prison mentality of Soviet power. When American

Figure 14.2. The sign at Checkpoint Charlie in divided Berlin, where people could pass through the Iron Curtain, offers only a mild warning.

president Kennedy visited in 1962, he proclaimed that all freedom-loving people should be proud to say, "Ich bin ein Berliner."[2]

Khrushchev's fall from power and replacement by Leonid Brezhnev again suggested to some that the enduring rivalry of the Cold War might calm down. Then Czechoslovakia experienced a virtual repeat of the Hungarian Revolt of 1956. Czechoslovakia and its politicians tested Brezhnev's renewed proclamations of tolerance by initiating broad liberalizing reforms, called the **Prague Spring** in 1968. When the Soviets decided the Czechs had gone too far, the tanks once again lumbered into the country, ending the revolt. Many Czechoslovakians were killed and imprisoned. And again, the West could do nothing without triggering World War III. The new Russian leader proclaimed the Brezhnev Doctrine, clearly stating that once a state had become "communist," its Warsaw Pact comrades would enforce Soviet allegiance to ideology by force if necessary.

In this conflict between superpowers in the name of different ideas, even science became part of the ammunition. An interesting aspect of the Cold War fought by means other than killing was the **Space Race** (1957–1969). Both sides seized on efforts toward the legitimate scientific goals of space exploration to win prestige over each other. The Russians gained the first victory, surprising the technologically superior Americans with the launch of the first functional satellite, **Sputnik** (4 October 1957). The nearly two-hundred-pound ball sent a simple radio signal about as it circled the globe every ninety-five minutes. The Russians then proceeded to beat the Americans by sending the first animal, the first man, and the first woman into

---

2. Literally translated, the sentence means "I am a jelly doughnut." To convey the meaning, "I am a person from Berlin," Kennedy should have said, "Ich bin Berliner." Knowing what he meant, the Berliners cheered anyway.

space. President Kennedy then decided to leap ahead of the Russians. He called on America to land a man on the moon by the end of the 1960s. Just as in a war, large forces were mobilized at high cost, great minds planned strategy, and people died (although in accidents, not by gunfire). In the end, the Americans won the race, as Neil Armstrong became the first person to walk in the lunar dust on 21 July 1969. Hundreds of millions of people watched on live television. Western science proved its ability to move us beyond our earthly home. In the end, the moon turned out not to have much practical value. With the Space Race "won," lunar flights ended by 1972. But the Cold War continued, with other crises and costs, on other foreign fronts.

Review: How was the Cold War fought in the West and around the world?

Response:

LETTING GO AND HOLDING ON

The strains of World War II and the Cold War weakened the great powers of Europe so completely that they were forced to dissolve their colonial empires. The rise of the superpowers of America and the Soviet Union meant that the European ability to dominate the world was definitely finished after 1945. No longer could a European state send its gunboats, at will, to intimidate darker-skinned peoples. The colonies had failed to fuel the European states' economic growth. The costs of building the economic infrastructure and providing order and prosperity in both homeland and colony were finally deemed too expensive. The only motives slowing down the release of colonies were pride that the empires instilled and the sense of responsibility for all the peoples whose native societies had been replaced by European structures.

The colonial peoples of Africa and Asia began to increase their efforts toward independence. Some peoples had to fight for decolonization; others were able to negotiate it; a few had it thrust on them before they were ready. All then faced the difficult challenge of finding prosperity in a world economy run by the nations of Western civilization. A few examples may illustrate the diverse ways imperial colonies became new nations.

The British colony of India led the way, immediately after World War II. As the war ended, the exhausted British gave in to the leaders Gandhi's and Nehru's insistence on decolonization and began a negotiated, peaceful transition to Indian self-government. The British decided to split the colony into two countries, recognizing the legacy of Muslims and Hindus fighting against each other. The bulk of the subcontinent was to be **India**, run by the Indian Nation Congress, while the Muslim League was to control **Pakistan**, a new, artificially drawn country. Pakistan took its name from the initials of several of its peoples (Punjabi, Afghans, Kashmiri, and Sindi, translating as "Land of the Pure"). Pakistan's peoples were united by Islam but divided into two parts, West Pakistan and East Pakistan, separated by a thousand miles and very different languages and traditions.

Immediately upon independence from Britain, after midnight on 14 August 1948, the newly independent nations of India and Pakistan faced serious challenges. Horrible violence broke out as millions of Muslims fled to Pakistan and Hindus escaped to India, each side killing hundreds of thousands in the process. Gandhi himself was assassinated by a Hindu fanatic, angry at some of Gandhi's expressions of tolerance for Muslims. Both states continued to quarrel over Kashmir (from where cashmere wool comes). India became "the world's largest democracy," although electoral violence and assassinations of politicians intermittently continued. Meanwhile, Pakistan's prevailing political system has been military dictatorships. The state fell apart during a civil war in 1971, at which time India helped East Pakistan to become the independent state of Bangladesh, notorious as one of the poorest countries on earth. India and Pakistan remain angry and distrustful of each other, each armed with nuclear weapons in a standoff modeled on the U.S.-U.S.S.R. standoff of the Cold War.

A country that had to fight for its independence was **Algeria**. The native-organized resistance movement, the National Liberation Front (FLN), in 1954 began a campaign of terrorism against French colonists living there. The French colonists struck back with their own use of terror: shootings by the military, torture of suspects, secret executions, mass arrests, and concentration camps. Even in Paris, police allegedly drowned Algerian demonstrators in the Seine. The protracted violence caused a government crisis in France itself, which ended the Fourth Republic in 1958. For the first time, a colonial conflict had brought down a European constitution. The World War II hero Charles de Gaulle subsequently helped France reorganize under the Fifth Republic.

As a newly empowered president, de Gaulle (r. 1959–1969) dismantled France's empire. At first, he tried to organize colonies in a French Community, similar to the British Commonwealth. Violence in Algeria cost hundreds of thousands of deaths until de Gaulle allowed Algerians to vote for independence in 1962. Unfortunately for the Algerians, they could not develop a functional democracy. The FLN set up a one-party state for decades. After experimenting with democracy, a rival Islamic party actually won an election in 1990. But a mysterious group of politicians and generals, called "The Power," seized control. The civil war that followed killed over one hundred fifty thousand people, often hacked to death.

The British colony of **Kenya** showed how a country could win independence by using both violence and negotiation. In 1952, the Kikuyu tribe began the "Mau Mau" revolt against British rule, resentful of exploitation by the colonialists. A few dozen deaths of Western colonists prompted the British to declare a state of emergency. The British crushed the "Mau Mau" revolt by executing hundreds of suspected terrorists and rounding up hundreds of thousands more to live in either in outright concentration camps or "reserves" of impoverished communities on barren land. There, many British and African guards humiliated, raped, and tortured their prisoners, often forcing them into hard labor and depriving them of food and medicine. Tens of thousands died. By 1959, the British ended the campaign.

In 1963, the British handed over rule to the new president, Jomo Kenyatta, a Kikuyu they had until recently held in prison for seven years. Kenyatta practiced a relatively enlightened rule, sharing involvement in government across ethnic lines. Since his death in 1978, his sucessors have been more corrupt, intimidating political rivals and pushing the country more into conflict and decay.

The **Congo** suffered the worst experience of decolonization, simply abandoned by its Belgian colonial rulers in 1960. The country lacked a single native college graduate, doctor, lawyer, engineer, or military officer. It immediately dissolved into chaos. Rebel groups tried to seize different provinces that were rich in minerals. At first, the United Nations had some success in creating stability by sending in troops, but the effort waned the following year after UN Secretary General Dag Hammarskjöld's accidental death in a plane crash. Colonel Joseph-Désiré Mobutu seized power in 1965. Weary of the conflict, Western powers accepted his claim to rulership and supplied him with technology, training, and cash. Mobutu developed a personal and corrupt dictatorship. He tried to discourage tribal identification and instead nourish a Congolese nationalism, *zairianization*. He rejected European names, renaming his country Zaïre, the capital Leopoldville to Kinshasa, and himself Mobutu Sese Seko kuku Ngbendu wa Za Banga. Mobuto's absolutism only ended in 1997, when international pressure after the end of the Cold War allowed a successful rebellion backed by the president of neighboring Rwanda. A major peace agreement in 2004 between Rwanda and the Congo followed by Congo's first-ever election in 2006 seemed to be weakening insurgencies in scattered provinces.

By 1965, almost all of Africa and Asia had been freed of the official imperialism that had been imposed on them since 1900. Many, however, did not reach stability. Sometimes, the former imperialist powers intervened in their former colonies' political affairs. The Commonwealth (which had dropped the adjective "British") and the French Community offered weak structures of unity between former colonies and masters. France in particular had kept many military arrangements with its former colonies, sometimes sending troops to protect the regimes from insurgencies and rebellions, other times toppling dictators (as in Chad in 1975 or the Central African Republic in 1979).

African states faced even more daunting new economic challenges in a world system largely run by Western nations. Economic growth was hindered by minerals and agricultural products fetching low prices in the marketplace, poor decisions by corrupt leaders, and economic aid that benefited industrialized countries more than the African ones. Former colonies often grew cash crops for export to the West, such as bananas or cocoa, instead of staple foods to feed their own people. Farming only a single crop (monoculture) left the population deprived of a varied diet and the crops vulnerable to blight. Further replacing the nineteenth-century colonization was the twentieth-century "Coca-colanization" (a term combining the most famous American soft drink with the word *colonization*, implying a takeover through commerce, not direct imperialism) as Western products were marketed to meet the desires of the world's consumers. Native regional and ethnic drinks, food, and clothing were dumped for American icons such as soda pop, hamburgers, and blue jeans.

From the 1970s on, **global debt** also hampered the worldwide economy, as many countries in Africa, Asia, and Latin America borrowed heavily from Western banks. The loans were supposed to be invested in industrialization but were wasted in corruption or on building from poor designs. As Third World countries could not pay their debts, Western banks threatened to foreclose. An increasing stress between rich nations and poor nations therefore burdened international relations. What little industry existed was still owned and controlled by, and for, Western businesses, who kept the profits. The Third World countries also lacked support systems for sufficient education and health care compared with industrialized nations. What little health and prosperity existed, though, allowed populations to soar, often faster than jobs could be created. The population explosion fueled a cycle of urban poverty and criminality.

The new leaders of new nations also faced political challenges. Too often, leaders seemed less interested in good governance and more involved in **kleptocracy**, using political power to increase their own wealth. The world economy was also skewed so that whenever things went wrong, the military was tempted to seize power. Many regimes alternated from military dictatorship to civilian governments and then back again. The few elected leaders who lasted in power often became dictators themselves. Transitioning to modern statehood so fast, the former colonies continued to prove that democracy was difficult.

The most problematic area of declining colonialism turned out to be in the Middle East, where most colonies had either won independence before or shortly after World War II or had never been completely dominated, like Saudi Arabia or Iran. In the third quarter of the twentieth century, the most accessible oil reserves were located in the Middle East, in nonindustrialized countries that required far less fuel than the energy-hungry West. The desire to control the petroleum reserves in the Arab states kept Western powers intimately involved in Middle Eastern politics. Arab opposition to the new, largely Western state of **Israel**, founded in 1948, also hindered the West's easy access to oil.

Israel grew out of Zionism, the organized movement for Jewish nationalism begun in 1898. The Balfour Declaration during World War I had encouraged Jews to move to Palestine, a British mandate and the site of their ancestral homeland of Judaea. The horror of the Holocaust, the Nazi attempt to exterminate the Jews during World War II, created much sympathy for creating a Jewish state. The British, caught between increasingly violent Jewish and Muslim terrorist attacks, handed over the problem to the United Nations in 1947. A UN commission proposed dividing up the territory into two new countries of roughly equal size: Israel (most of whose citizens would be Jews) and Palestine (most of whose citizens would be

Arabs). The Jews eagerly accepted the proposal and declared their independence on 14 May 1948.

The Palestinian Arabs, however, supported by the Arab League, refused the offer and launched the first Arab-Israeli War (1948–1949). They intended to destroy the new Jewish state. They lost. Victorious Israel seized part of what had been assigned to Palestine, while Jordan and Egypt took control of the rest. The state of Palestine vanished from the map before it even had a chance to begin. Hundreds of thousands of Palestinians who fled Israel thus lived under the rule of Egypt and Jordan, who refused to integrate them, or lived in exile in Lebanon and Syria in internment camps, without rights, seemingly without a future.

Israel organized itself as a Western state, not surprising, since so many Jews had lived in the West. It had a parliamentary government dominated by a socialist party and a conservative party (with other, smaller, liberal and religious parties). Its economy was thoroughly Western, based on markets, investments, private property, and the welfare state. Some Israelis did experiment with socialist living in communes called kibbutzim, but these were more important for building a strong sense of community than for contributing to the overall economy and social structure. Most Israelis believed in Judaism, although the level of devotion varied widely. The government practiced religious toleration, helping the 10 percent of its citizens who were Muslim Arabs. Jews revived the virtually dead language of Hebrew as a living tongue, both to read their scriptures and for daily interaction. Ongoing immigration by Jews from all over the world, including some from non-Western countries in North Africa, Russia, India, and even Ethiopia, increased tensions within the Israeli state, especially between the secularist and traditionalist religious factions.

Ongoing hostility from its Arab neighbors, however, meant that Israel had to fight for its existence, supported by most states of the West. The next war between Israel and the Arabs, the **Suez Crisis** of October 1956, also marked the last time the Europeans acted as independent great powers. In that year, Egypt had nationalized the Suez Canal, violating British property rights and international agreements when they closed it to Israeli shipping. The British and French, in collusion with the Israelis, launched a surprise attack on Egypt. Overwhelmed by the successes of the enemy invaders, Egypt appealed for help from the Soviet Union. The United States feared that the Suez Crisis might escalate to involve the superpowers. The U.S. sent its NATO allies home. The former great powers of France and Great Britain could no longer intervene at will in world affairs.

The ongoing opposition to Israel by Arab states and Palestinians continued, however. By 1964 some Palestinians unified different political factions under the **Palestine Liberation Organization (PLO)**. The PLO began a more aggressive terrorist campaign, intending, ultimately, to destroy Israel. In turn, the Israelis carried out a preemptive strike against their Arab neighbors and won a significant victory in the Six-Day War. Israel conquered the Golan Heights from Syria, the West Bank from Jordan, and the Gaza Strip and the Sinai Peninsula from Egypt. These acquisitions, however, left millions of Muslim Arabs without any rights of citizenship and living under Israeli domination. Israel had no idea what to do about this situation, settling for a military occupation that deprived the Palestinians of civil rights. So Israel's continued oppression made it a target of worldwide criticism, increasingly losing the sympathy that had existed at its founding, handing over that sympathy to the Palestinian cause.

The brief Yom Kippur War in 1973 was the last war so far to attempt Israel's destruction. Attacking by surprise on a Jewish holy day, the Arab states made some significant gains, especially for Egypt in the Sinai. The Arab states also tried to weaken support for Israel among its Western allies using their dominance in the petroleum trade group, the Organization of Petroleum Exporting Countries (OPEC). They imposed an oil embargo on Western states that supported Israel. While this embargo and the resulting fuel shortages did damage Western economies briefly, Israel survived. Subsequent peacemaking efforts, usually mediated by the United States, have failed to fully remove hostility in the region.

The legacy of occupation and ongoing economic and political interests kept Western states involved in Africa, Asia, and the Middle East. The direct imperialism of colonial possessions had largely vanished by 1965. Although neo-imperialism began with noble aspirations and patriotic fervor only a century before, it had obviously failed. The Europeans had used their power around the world to compete with one another, build up their economies, and spread their culture. After letting their colonies go, the West continued to cope with the ongoing political and economic ties of Europeans living in foreign parts and non-Western immigrants moving to Europe, reviving some kind of international order. Since the West controlled the bulk of the world's wealth and power, it could hardly avoid responsibility for some of the legacy of its century of colonialism.

Review: How did the decolonization of Africa and Asia succeed yet force choices between Communist or Third World status?

Response:

AMERICAN HEGEMONY

The unquestioned leadership of the West lay, of course, with the United States of America. Its unique position as the shield against communism led America to expand its global influence in numerous ways. Within the Western Hemisphere, the United States intensified its involvement with Latin America. In reaction, Latin

Americans tended to blame the "Yankees" rather than themselves for their political, economic, and social problems.

Among these problems were great social inequities derived from class and ethnic divisions, dating back to Latin America's westernization as part of the Spanish and Portuguese empires. Creoles, those of European descent, exploited those of Native American or African ancestry. Since the Creole elites feared the results of votes by the alienated poor majorities, they avoided expanding democratic participation beyond their own ranks. Many countries alternated between corrupt civilian leaders and juntas, cliques of military officers ruling as dictators. Meanwhile, the dominant Roman Catholic hierarchy, often drawn from the ruling elites, too often accepted exploitation of the poor. The priests preached to the peasants and the poor to accept their lot as something unchanging, promising rewards after death.

But change was inevitable as Western modernity penetrated the traditional conservative culture. Increased food production and improved health care caused a population explosion among those impoverished by a lack of jobs, as Latin America failed to industrialize. Just outside most urban centers, shanty towns of the suffering poor multiplied. They, as well as dissatisfied members of the middle class, began to listen to communist revolutionary ideas. Some Roman Catholic priests in the 1970s even began to preach **liberation theology**, which called for social justice in this life instead of waiting for the next. The papacy discouraged such speculation and ordered ministers to be silent. The juntas silenced opponents through violence. For example, in 1980 they assassinated Archbishop Oscar Romero of San Salvador while he presided at the Eucharist in a hospital chapel.

The history of **Argentina** reflects many of the tensions between ruling elites holding onto power and the masses seeking opportunity and fairness. As World War II ended, a junta with fascist inclinations ruled Argentina (making it hospitable to fleeing war criminals like Joseph Mengele, the "Butcher of Auschwitz"). But one member of that junta, **Juan Perón** (b. 1895–d. 1975), toyed with socialist ideas. His wife, **Evita Duarte**, who had risen from a broken lower-class family to fame in the movies, helped her husband appeal to the masses, especially the *los descamisados* ("shirtless ones," those too poor to afford even a shirt). Perón seized power in 1945, and for the next ten years he nationalized businesses, increased social welfare benefits, censored the media, criticized the Roman Catholic Church, and used violence and force to maintain power. Evita's death and economic failures encouraged a new junta to drive Perón out in 1955. Succeeding governments that rejected socialism likewise failed to make Argentina prosper. Memories of Perón allowed him to return to power from exile in October 1974, but he died within a year. His second wife tried to rule as his successor, but a coup replaced her in March 1976. A new regime tried to adopt strict laissez-faire policies.

As the economy continued to fail, however, the government launched the so-called **Dirty War** against left-wing political opponents. They secretly arrested suspected radicals, tortured them, and then murdered hundreds, often by dumping victims from helicopters over the Atlantic Ocean. Instead of joining a conspiracy of silence, hundreds of mothers and grandmothers were picketing before the presidential palace, asking for their lost children.

The government then tried to use a patriotic success to distract people's attention, by invading the nearby Falkland Islands possessed by Great Britain, called by the Argentines the Islas Malvinas. The islands' inhabitants were a few thousand British citizens, of British descent, who were outnumbered by their sheep ten to one. Surprisingly, the British decided to fight back. **The Falklands War** (April–June 1982) ended with almost a thousand dead, but a British victory. Argentina's failure led to the collapse of the junta and the exposure of the secrets of its "Dirty War." Since then, successive civilian governments have tried to promote prosperity. Even another experiment with unrestrained laissez-faire capitalism at the end of the century has been unable to make the country truly competitive.

While Argentina remained free of direct political intervention by the United States, other Latin American nations felt the power of their northern neighbor. A case in point is **Guatemala**, where the CIA helped to depose President Jacobo Arbenz Guzman in 1954 when his land reform policies threatened the profits of U.S. banana companies. By 1960, a virtual civil war had broken out between the government, usually run by juntas, and various guerrilla factions, often organized by communists. By the war's end in 1996, military, paramilitary, guerrilla, and terrorist forces had killed perhaps 200,000 Guatemalans. The CIA likewise helped overthrow President Salvador Allende of **Chile** in 1973, as his socialist policies began nationalizing U.S. businesses. A military junta led by Augusto Pinochet killed Allende and several thousand of his suspected supporters. Embracing "neo-liberal" economic policies, Pinochet's government ruled until 1989, when the end of the Cold War made his dictatorship less useful to the United States. Before his death in 2006, various European courts tried to put him on trial for the crimes of human rights abuses and tax evasion. The removal of the president of **Panama** came with the direct intervention of the United States. America did give the Panama Canal to Panama in 1978. But in 1989–1990, American troops literally kidnapped Panamanian president Manuel Noriega in order to bring him to trial for drug trafficking (an activity he claimed to have carried out on behalf of the CIA). France recently found Noriega guilty of tax evasion because of drug money laundering.

The most notorious U.S. intervention was with **Cuba**, which for the most part had been a U.S. protectorate since the Spanish-American War. In the 1950s, Fulgencia Batistá, a semifascist dictator, offered a haven for both legitimate U.S. business interests and criminal organizations. Batistá faced a rebellion led by **Fidel Castro** (b. 1927), the privileged son of a Cuban sugar planter, who at first wanted to play professional baseball. Castro converted to radical politics and began subversive activities all over Latin America. He invaded Cuba in 1956, finally achieving a surprising victory on New Year's Eve 1958. Once in control, Castro set up a one-party socialist state that made him dictator. He arrested his enemies, nationalized most foreign property, tossed out crime syndicates, redistributed land, and provided free health care and education to all the people. Thousands of Cubans fled the island, most settling in the state of Florida. Nevertheless, Castro and the image of Castro's lieutenant Che Guevara symbolized for many Latin Americans a better, socialist future, free of Yankee capitalist exploitation.

The U.S. reaction was to try to get rid of Castro. The CIA organized some 1,500 exiles in an attempted counterrevolution. These Cubans tried to reconquer Cuba with the **Bay of Pigs Invasion** (17 April 1961), named after their landing site. Without open support from the United States or popular backing from the Cuban people, the invasion failed miserably and embarrassed the new administration of U.S. president Kennedy. Castro became worried enough about future U.S. intervention that he began to cooperate even more closely with the Soviet Union. He persuaded the Russians to build missile bases in Cuba.

In October 1962, American U-2 spy planes photographed the missile installations. The resulting **Cuban Missile Crisis** brought the superpowers closer to nuclear war than ever in history. Although Soviet ICBMs located in Russia and on Russian submarines could already target any place they wanted in the United States, the Cuban missile sites seemed a direct threat so close to American shores. From the Russian point of view, though, they were merely imitating American policy: U.S. missiles based in Turkey were just as close and threatening to the Russian border as Cuba was to America.

Kennedy, however, was determined to remove the missiles from Cuba. Nonetheless, he took the moderate step of declaring a "quarantine" of Cuba, meaning that while any military technology bound for Cuba would be stopped at sea by the U.S. navy, other ships could continue. This measure was not quite a blockade, which would have been technically an act of war. The Soviets declined to push the United States into shooting. Instead of forcing the issue, both sides reached an agreement because nobody wanted World War III. The Russian missiles left Cuba. But also, while less publicized, the American missiles left Turkey. The United States also promised never to invade Cuba again. As a result, Castro still rules Cuba today (despite some half-hearted and harebrained attempts at assassination by the CIA, such as exploding cigars). Thus, while both sides gained something, the resolution of the crisis appeared to the public as an American victory.

Cold War rivalries continued in other countries throughout Latin America. Juntas suppressed their opponents in the name of fighting communism. Communists organized revolts in the name of liberating the poor from capitalist oppression. U.S. and European corporations dominated the economy to provide exports for themselves. Middle and peasant classes saw too little profit from that trade. These ideological differences guaranteed that Cold War tensions would find their way into political and social divisions.

Review: *How was Latin America entangled in the Cold War?*

Response:

THE UNEASY UNDERSTANDING

Under the protection of NATO, the Western European nations had managed to create stable parliamentarian, democratic governments that represented most people within each state through fair and competitive elections. Alternating coalitions of conservative, liberal, or social democratic parties, with occasional participation by regional, nationalist, or communist parties on the fringes, governed in most countries. Only tiny states such as Liechtenstein and Monaco remained ruled by princes, although even they were modified with gradual concessions to representation by the people. The last fascist dictatorships, in Greece, Spain, and Portugal, ended in the 1970s with almost no violence during the transition to parliamentary democracies.

The only serious threat to stability broke out in the year 1968. Riots and revolts led by students in cities ranging from Warsaw to Berlin, to Paris, and to Madrid. They protested against war or nuclear weapons, to improve university conditions, to gain civil rights for women, ethnic minorities, or indigenous peoples, or for more democracy. In France, after striking workers joined student riots, the government almost fell. By the end of the year, though, most governments remained firmly in control, enforced by police using clubs and tear gas, sometimes guns, and a few tanks. A "spirit" of 1968 nevertheless continued to inspire young people to question authority. In the next few years, sporadic attacks by terrorist groups, such as Red Brigades in Italy and Baader-Meinhof in West Germany, or by organized criminals, such as the Mafia, caused more feelings of insecurity rather than any actual instability.

European prosperity recovered from World War II, but Europe's standing as a center of military power did not. The Western Europeans had grown used to being the center of world affairs since the neo-imperialism of the nineteenth century. Western Europe found the Cold War duality of the United States versus the Soviet Union hard to deal with. These concerns led them to take a surprising step toward peace and cooperation with one another. For a thousand years, since the collapse of Charlemagne's empire, rival states had been fighting over which share of the European heartland each should reign supreme. The horrors of the last such conflict, World War II, convinced Western European leaders to take a new path.

In the early 1950s, the leaders of West Germany and France began instead to promote international cooperation. They started with the nationalized coal and steel industries, creating an international body to regulate and supervise the joint Coal and Steel Authority of both France and West Germany in 1950. This arrangement succeeded so well that it expanded the next year into the European Coal and Steel Community, bringing in Italy and the Benelux countries (the Lowland nations of Belgium, the Netherlands, and Luxembourg).

Within a few years, these nations integrated their economic and political systems more intensively. They agreed to the Treaty of Rome on 25 March 1957, which founded the **Common Market** or the **European Economic Community**. Soon this international organization aimed at closer political as well as economic union, reflected in its name change to the European Community in 1967. Several neutral countries, such as Sweden, Switzerland, Finland, and Austria, formed themselves into a rival European Free Trade Association. At first, England hesitated to join the Common Market, relying on its special friendship with the United States and the lingering British Empire held together by the economic ties and trade with the Commonwealth. Still, Great Britain gained membership by 1973. Rivalries, political grudges, and inflation in the EC took longer than hoped for to overcome. But slowly, the improving prosperity of the members of the European Community made it a more attractive and serious competitor in the international economy. The European Community's political achievement was another significant achievement. Combined with NATO (after a very weak attempt to recruit a common European defense force), the European Community greatly reduced, if not outright eliminated, the chances of war between members who had literally fought one another every few years for a millennium.

A possible outbreak of World War III remained a concern for Europeans. NATO troops based all over Western Europe provided some reassurance of slowing down a Russian land invasion. The nuclear weapons possessed by the United States, Britain, and France theoretically deterred even that invasion, but would likely destroy the continent if used. President de Gaulle of France remained resentful of American hegemony and vainly tried to assert French leadership by asking U.S. forces to leave France in 1966. NATO headquarters moved from Paris to Brussels, the capital of both Belgium and the European Community. Germany felt most painfully the divisions of the Cold War, separated into its East and West states and aware that it was on the front line of any conventional war. To reduce the possibility of war, Social Democratic leaders of West Germany began a concentrated **Ostpolitik** (East politics) in the early 1970s. They began to talk with the leader of the Social Unity Party in East Germany, hoping to improve relations between communists and capitalists.

The real turning point in Cold War relations resulted from the United States' involvement in the **Vietnam War** (1964–1973). The French had withdrawn from their colonies of Laos, Cambodia, and Vietnam in Indochina in 1956, after being beaten by communist insurgencies, despite secret financial support from the United States. A fragile Vietnam was left divided between the communists, led by Ho Chi Minh, in power in the north, and westernized (and Roman Catholic) elites running the south. The Americans feared, rightly, that Ho Chi Minh would unite the country and make it part of the Communist Bloc. They believed in the domino theory—which asserted that if one state fell to communism, so would its neighbor, followed by the next state, and so on, just like domino blocks knocking one another down. Thus after Vietnam would go the rest of Indochina, then Thailand, the Philippines, and, perhaps, the rest of the world. An alleged attack in the Gulf of Tonkin that killed or injured not a single American provided the U.S. president Johnson with the "justification" to commit combat troops beginning in 1964. Congress gave him a blank check to defend American interests as he saw fit, although without declaring war.

As more troops poured in to protect South Vietnam, it seemed inconceivable that North Vietnam could defeat the strongest empire in world history. Yet the Russians quickly claimed protection of North Vietnam under their nuclear umbrella. A troubling guerrilla war developed, one which the United States could

not win as long as Russia and China both supplied North Vietnam. By 1968, protest-
ers in Europe and, more importantly, a majority of Americans called for U.S. troops
to pull out of Vietnam.

In 1968, **Richard Nixon** (r. 1969–1974) won the U.S. presidential election
partly because he claimed to have a plan to end the fighting in Vietnam. By that
time, the Cold War had been ongoing for twenty years. Again and again, the superpowers had managed to annoy and provoke each other and frighten the globe with
the risk of World War III. Nixon came to power mired in the unwinnable Vietnam
conflict and looking for "peace with honor." The United States' heavy bombings of
North Vietnam had failed. Indeed, the country dropped more bombs on Vietnam
than it had in all of World War II.

Suddenly and surprisingly, Nixon and his foreign policy advisors, especially the
German immigrant Henry Kissinger, came to the realization that they had been
mistaken about the Cold War. They finally figured out that China and Russia were
not allies; the two Communist states had not gotten along for years and were enemies and rivals themselves. Thus, the Americans began a new strategy to exploit
Sino-Soviet tensions and increase the level of peace. Touring ping pong or table
tennis teams paved the way for American and Chinese diplomats to begin talking.
Soon, the former anticommunist crusader Nixon was visiting China, toasting and
treating the former vile despot Mao as a respected equal. Next, Nixon visited Russia,
toasting and treating Brezhnev, who had crushed Czechoslovakia, as a colleague.
These leaders of the three most powerful nations on the planet then agreed to
disagree on many ideological issues but to work together wherever they could to
create order and stability. They called this policy **détente**, using a French term for
a formally cordial, yet distrusting relationship.

Securing the cooperation of China and Russia to manage their North Vietnamese ally, the United States was able to withdraw its armed forces from Vietnam in
1974. When the shooting stopped, more than fifty thousand U.S. troops were dead,
as were several million Vietnamese. Two years later, the Communist north easily
overran the south. When Laos and Cambodia also were seized by communists,
some feared that the domino theory was about to succeed and roll through Southeast Asia and the Pacific. But the stability of Thailand and the quarrels of the communists halted any further progress.

Tragic developments in Cambodia illustrated the worst possible legacy of Western imperialism intensified by Cold War conflict. The totalitarian regime of **Khmer
Rouge** communists there carried certain Western ideas of anarchism and revolution
further than any other modern government. In a wild reaction against capitalism
and industrialized society (and even Marxist ideology), the Cambodian communists
agriculturalized the nation, renamed Kampuchea. Urban populations were driven
into the countryside to become farmers or die trying in the notorious "killing
fields." The Khmer Rouge burned and desecrated all past culture to create their
version of modernity. Exalting equality, they rooted out all traditional or industrial
social differences. They eliminated most scientists, teachers, artists, intellectuals,
and priests. Even families were broken up. The Khmer Rouge slaughtered as much
as a third of its own population in this self-inflicted genocide. By 1979, the Vietnamese were so disgusted that they invaded Cambodia, drove the Khmer Rouge into

the jungles, and installed a satellite regime. The United States, because of its dislike of communist Vietnam, then hypocritically found itself supporting the exiled communist Khmer Rouge in its attempts to throw the Vietnamese out. Once more, Western ideologies confronted and confused one another.

Still, détente continued as a policy between the major states of the world throughout the 1970s. The linkup of a Soviet Soyuz and an American Apollo spacecraft symbolized the high-flying spirit of cooperation. The high point came in the capital of Finland, where the representatives of most European states and the United States fashioned documents to provide a basis for future cooperation. These **Helsinki Accords** (August 1975) finally ended World War II, thirty years after the shooting had stopped. A new body, the Conference for Security and Cooperation in Europe (CSCE) provided a forum for representatives from all European states (along with the United States) to prevent any accidental outbreak of violence or war. The Helsinki Accords also asserted basic human rights of liberty and freedom for all the signatory states. These agreements soon gave people living under communist dictatorships the opportunity to criticize their regimes' failures to live up to such rights.

Détente provided a new way for the industrialized world to live with its ideological differences. Nonetheless, this uneasy truce could not have gone on for the long term. Sooner or later, ideological hostility would have provoked some incident that brought in Russians and Americans to become angry at or even shoot at each other. At its worst, world history could have ended in nuclear annihilation, with all sides losing. Instead, détente's collapse resulted in an American victory in the Cold War.

Review: How did the policies of détente ease Cold War tensions?

Response:

CHAPTER 15

Into the Future

The Contemporary Era, 1980 to the Present

The end of the Cold War startled most intelligence analysts, politicians, and pundits (a new kind of commentator in modern media whose strength was opinion more than analysis). A conflict that had framed international actions and domestic policies for more than four decades came to a close with little warning. Nevertheless, the increasing interaction of the earth's peoples challenged the place of westerners and their wealth as never before. Still, international commerce, science, industry, and politics guaranteed that Western civilization would continue—and go on to change.

A SURPRISE ENDING

The end of the Cold War followed directly from the end of the coexistence policy of détente. The first step came when the Soviet Union sent troops to Afghanistan in December 1979 to prop up a recently installed Communist regime. Afghanistan soon became the Soviet equivalent of Vietnam, as Muslim warriors (mujahedeen) resisted the atheistic communists. Fighting a guerrilla war in difficult terrain and supplied by another superpower (the United States), the mujahedeen kept the Russian occupying forces in turmoil.

Second, a number of labor strikes in Soviet-dominated Poland in late summer 1980 sparked the labor union movement called **Solidarity**. An ordinary worker, the mustachioed Lech Wałesa, became the symbol of the conflict as he organized striking workers from the barricades. The need for workers in a socialist state to form a union for their own self-protection showed the failures of Soviet socialism. The Russians, though, made Polish authorities declare martial law in December 1981, which pushed the movement underground and Wałesa under house arrest. Both actions made the Soviet Union and its system look both oppressive and incompetent.

Third, new leadership in the West became determined to take a harder line against Soviet expansionism. In Great Britain the Conservative Party's new prime minister, **Margaret Thatcher** (r. 1979–1990), disliked socialism in all its forms. She began to scale back the British welfare state, reprivatizing many businesses and industries and breaking unions. She also sharply criticized the totalitarian state of the Soviet Union. In 1981, the former movie star **Ronald Reagan** (r. 1981–1989) became president of the United States. He resolved to resist Soviet expansionism and even threatened the U.S.S.R., which he called an "evil empire," with the possibility of World War III. Some Americans were shocked that the Reagan administration could suggest that a nuclear war with the Soviet Union was winnable, without mutually assured destruction. Reagan also proposed the Strategic Defense Initiative for a new high-tech antimissile system to shield the United States from ICBMs. Since the technology for such a program was decades away from being invented, much less activated, critics named it "Star Wars" after the popular science-fiction film. Even if this antimissile system could have been built, it would have left America's allies in Europe defenseless against Russian mid-range missiles. To counter this threat, Reagan and NATO leaders installed mid-range nuclear weapons in Western Europe. Many Western citizens protested, their resentment of American domination outweighing their fear of Russian invasion.

Reagan also continued the buildup of conventional armed forces of ships, weapons, and soldiers in an effort to prevent possible Russian aggression anywhere. The vast U.S. economy could afford this expensive effort, although the country went deeply into debt to do so. The United States went from being the biggest creditor nation in the world to the biggest debtor nation during Reagan's presidency.

Fourth, America became more concerned about possible Soviet expansionism in Central America, most notably in **Nicaragua**. Since the U.S. Marines withdrew from their last occupation of the country in 1933, the Somoza family had ruled as authoritarian dictators. Left-wing insurgents called Sandinistas stepped up their revolt after the Somoza government mismanaged recovery from a major earthquake in 1979. With Cuban and Soviet support, the Sandinistas drove Somoza from power and created a socialist state.

The Reagan administration disliked communist influence in Nicaragua so much that its officials defied and lied to the U.S. Congress, which did not want to intervene. They began to secretly finance the right-wing Contras to start their own counterinsurgency. Depending on the point of view, one side's terrorists were the other side's "freedom fighters." The Reagan administration financed the Contras' operation by illegally selling weapons to Iran, even though the United States considered that country an international threat. The brief Iran-Contra Affair exposed the secret deals but left Reagan's authority intact. His military also defied international law by mining Nicaragua's harbors, technically an act of war. In the end, the leftist regime fell not from bullets but by the ballot box. In 1990, the Sandinistas allowed free elections supervised by international observers. They lost, they surrendered power, and Nicaragua established a tentative democracy. The Sandinistas remained as a political party, which has since won elections.

The Cold War finally ended in the 1990s after **Mikhail Gorbachev** (r. 1985–1991) became secretary general of the Communist Party in the Soviet Union. He saw the flaws and corruption of the centralized communist system and attempted to reform Soviet society in order to save it. First, he promoted perestroika (restructuring) to allow more free-market competition within the economy. Second, he declared glasnost (openness). The regime reduced censorship, allowed more foreign travel, and imported more Western goods and entertainment. Third, Gorbachev allowed rival political parties to begin to organize, thus creating a true democracy for the first time since the short-lived Russian Republic of 1917.

Despite Gorbachev's reform efforts, his communist state crumbled around him. The people resented their increasingly poor standard of living compared with those of Western Europe. The transition to a market economy created shortages and unemployment. Political reform was clumsy because the Communist Party resisted giving up its privileged position. Finally, the use of force to keep control of the Soviet Union's provinces of Latvia, Lithuania, and Estonia reminded people of the Hungarian Revolt and the Prague Spring.

The Soviet satellite states in Eastern Europe ultimately forced Gorbachev to prove his sincerity about openness as they pushed for an end to Soviet domination. In 1988, Hungary and Poland broke with Communism and launched reforms. In Poland, Solidarity came to power, and Lech Wałesa became president. In 1989, Czechoslovakia withdrew from Soviet control and underwent its Velvet Revolution, so called because the political separation happened so smoothly and with so little violence. The former political prisoner and playwright Václav Havel became president. Rumania rejected the old system in a quick coup that murdered the long-reigning dictator Nicolae Ceaușescu. Even Bulgaria elected a noncommunist government. Gorbachev finally decided against trying to uphold the status quo through force and violence. As a result, the satellite system collapsed without much bloodshed (see figure 15.1).

The most important sign of the Cold War's end was the reunification of Germany in 1990. The East German hard-liners began to lose control as East German citizens began fleeing across the new open border between Hungary and Austria in August 1989. Through Austria they reached West Germany, where they were welcomed as citizens with full and expansive social benefits. At home in East Germany, mass demonstrations organized by churches also began to seek openness. The Communist dictator of many years was deposed, and moderates tried to find new

Figure 15.1.   The statues of communist founders Marx and Engels were relegated to a museum after the Cold War.

directions. When a Communist bureaucrat broadcast on television in the evening of 9 November 1989 that some travel restrictions would be lifted, thousands of hopeful East Germans began to gather at crossing points at the Berlin Wall. They talked the guards into letting them through. By the next morning there was no sealing up the wall again. Indeed, the most potent symbol of the conflict, the Berlin Wall, was soon pounded into rubble as souvenirs for tourists. Within a year, the West German political leadership negotiated unification. On 3 October 1990, the Communist East German state officially disappeared, absorbed into the Federal Republic of Germany.

In 1991, a failed coup by Communist hard-liners in the Soviet Union led to the defeat of Gorbachev, but not of the reforms. By 1992, the Soviet Union was history. The Russian Federation emerged as a state, loosely linked with a few former republics from the U.S.S.R. to lead a so-called Commonwealth of Independent States. This association included new nations in the Caucasus (Azerbaijan, Armenia, and Georgia, for a time), the Turkish states in Central Asia (Kazakhstan, Uzbekistan, Turkmenistan, Kyrgyzstan, and Tajikistan), and Eastern Europe (Moldavia and Byelorussia or Belarus). Ukraine and the Baltic states of Estonia, Latvia, and Lithuania left completely. The Warsaw Pact was soon gone as well. The Cold War was over.

The Cold War's resolution even reached to the Union of South Africa and its repressive regime of apartheid. Over the years, the government had tortured political prisoners from the African National Congress by forcing them to sit on red ants' nests or rubbing poisonous plants into their skin. International pressure through boycotts, absence of a communist threat, and worsening social conflicts all convinced the white racist regime to dismantle apartheid. In 1990, the regime released Nelson Mandela, leader of the African National Congress, who had been in prison since 1962. Mandela and his party won an overwhelming victory in free and fair elections in 1993. President Mandela (r. 1994–1999) passed a law that protected whites' property and advocated forgiveness rather than avenging decades of oppression. A Truth and Reconciliation Commission granted amnesty for the perpetrators of cruelty and violence in return for their honest accounts. South Africans descended from the "white" British and Dutch as well as the "colored" Indians stayed to maintain the Western industrialized culture, although poverty and violence still plagued too many descendants of the "black" native South Africans.

The collapse of communism had not resulted in the pristine victory that the West might have hoped for. During the transition from communism to capitalism, Russia saw much of its wealth fall into the hands of a few well-connected politicians and friends of the elites, since the rule of law and political institutions had been insufficiently established. Pollution, job loss, and military impotence lost the nation its superpower status. Only a few communist dictatorships, such as those in North Korea and Cuba under Castro, still held onto their ideology, despite some economic difficulties without subsidies from the Soviet Union.

Meanwhile, the former Soviet satellite states in Europe tried to become even more Western in the capitalist style. Indeed, in 2004 NATO expanded to include most former Eastern European satellite states, right up to Russia's doorstep. The former Warsaw Pact members of Poland, Hungary, Rumania, Bulgaria, the Czech Republic, Slovakia, and the three former Baltic "republics" of the Soviet Union (Estonia, Latvia, and Lithuania) officially entered the defensive military alliance with the West.

Russian political influence and economic strength collapsed after the end of the Soviet Union. Although Russia no longer posed an invasion threat to Europe, it still wielded the nuclear weapons capable of destroying the world. President Vladimir Putin (r. 2000–2008), a former KGB agent, concentrated power in his hands and boosted Russian pride by promoting nationalistic feelings. The Russian Federation clung to Chechnya, despite continuing rebellion, and resented efforts by the Ukraine and Georgia to join NATO. Russia and Georgia's brief war in 2008 opened the question of whether Georgia would remain under Russian domination or become more a part of the West. Further, too many of the states that have fragmented from the Soviet Empire, especially in Central Asia, established mini-dictatorships of their own. Their new authoritarian rulers commanded with the language of Islam and with nationalism rather than the communist rhetoric of Marx. Thus, ethnic and nationalist hatreds were revived (see below). The world had suddenly become much more complicated, with so many new countries with old grudges and enduring problems.

Review: *How did the Cold War come to an end?*

Response:

SEARCHING FOR STABILITY

As the Soviet Union was splitting apart, Europe was coming together. Europe's ally in the Cold War, the United States of America, remained the world's foremost military and economic nation, the sole superpower. Still, thousands of American troops left Europe, and U.S. military installations shut down, no longer necessary for preventing a Soviet invasion. After a thousand years of warfare in Europe, war between Western states had become inconceivable instead of inevitable. From the fall of Rome in the West in 476 and the failure of the Carolingians in the ninth century to replace it, rival states had quarreled with one another in one bloody conflict after another. The rivalries had contributed to making European states great powers, but World War I, World War II, and the Cold War had shown the risks of mutual destruction. Military interventions by European powers were now subject to NATO and the leadership of the United States.

So the political and economic unification of Europe continued after the Cold War. In 1991, the Maastricht Treaty turned the European Community into the **European Union**. Seeking still further unity, especially because of the economic necessity of competing with the United States and Japan, politicians aspired for the various nations of Europe to become a United States of Europe. In 2002 the Union established its Common Security and Defence Policy (CSDP), which began missions to troubled countries around the world, such as the Congo, Indonesia, and Georgia. Its various operations support police and courts in maintaining law and order, monitor elections, try to prevent smuggling and piracy, and protect refugees and civilians in areas with violent conflict.

The European Union's greatest success remained in economics, drawing on its original concept as the Common Market (see map 15.1). It continued to remove trade and labor barriers between its members. Brussels' subsidies to the poorer member states, such as Ireland and Portugal, helped their economies to grow and compare well with the more prosperous members, such as Germany and Italy. In 2002, a dozen competing monetary currencies from most of the Union countries, from French franc to Italian lire to German mark, vanished into history and were

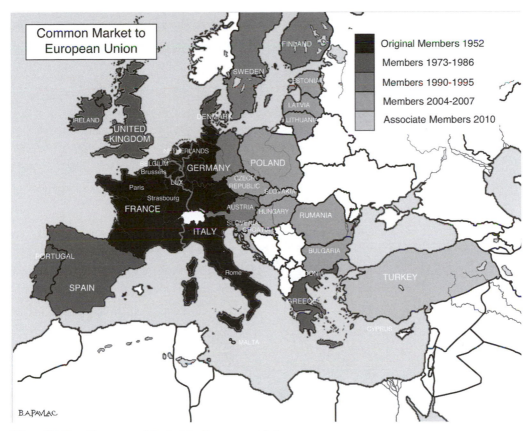

Map 15.1.   Common Market to European Union

replaced by a new common unit, the euro. By 2009, sixteen countries used the euro as a currency, and it remained strong against its international rival, the American dollar.

Ongoing economic success tempted still more countries to join the European Union. First, in 1995, the former neutral nations of Austria, Finland, and Sweden, with their advanced Western economies, were welcomed. Next, many of the newly freed Soviet satellites were eager to join, although they had to develop their market economies and parliamentarian democracies before they could be fully integrated. On 1 May 2004, the former states of communist Estonia, Latvia, Lithuania, Hungary, Poland, the Czech Republic, Slovakia, and Slovenia, along with the island states of Malta and (non-Turkish) Cyprus, became members. Rumania and even Bulgaria entered the Union on 1 January 2007. Serious negotiations finally started to include even the Muslim, yet European, country of Turkey. Some older members of the European Union, however, doubt that Turkey is, or ever will be, "Western" enough.

Other obstacles slowed the path to true European unity. Some "Euroskeptics" saw the dangers of a vast bureaucracy in Brussels that demanded conformity and ignored local differences. Many Europeans wanted to see more *subsidiarity*, where decisions are made at the regional and local levels rather than by the European Commission in Brussels (see figure 15.2). While English grew more popular as a unified lingua franca because of the power of American and British popular

Figure 15.2. The Atomium built for the 1958 World's Fair in Brussels now dominates a park celebrating the European Union, with models of cultural icons from all over Europe.

culture, Europeans continued to speak more than fifty different regional and local languages and even more dialects. Some Europeans only reluctantly accepted the new member states, afraid of the cost of supporting less-developed economies and opening up borders to more immigration, competition from cheap labor, redirection of agricultural subsidies, or lack of "proper" values. Even Germany had trouble integrating Germans from the former East Germany, especially as many businesses in the former socialist state failed to adapt to the new capitalist economy.

The weakening of border controls permitted by the European Union made Europe more diverse than ever, through increased emigration and immigration.

Workers from any member state could get jobs in any other. And the borders continued to be open to many peoples of former colonial Africa and Asia. The wealth of Europe was a magnet to poor people around the world. Foreign workers from the Balkans, North Africa, or former colonies of a Western imperial power were settling into the European cities and forming enclaves of non-Western cultures. Modern communications meant they received newspapers, radio, pamphlets, and television all in their own languages. By 2010 more than fifteen million Muslims resided in Western European urban centers, leading some to label the continent "Eurabia." The call of the muezzin from the minaret competes with the church bells from steeples amid the traffic noise in streets. Benign neglect meant few attempts to assimilate the newcomers, allowing the diverse immigrants to retain their own cultural attitudes. Ironically, the European practice of tolerance, combined with neglect, allowed Muslim extremists to preach intolerance and resistance to assimilation.

In reaction to the growing number of non-Europeans, nationalistic parties and perspectives grew in strength. Politicians such as Jean-Marie Le Pen in France and Joseph Haider in Austria sought both to limit the rights of these foreigners and to resist the control of Brussels along the way. School officials in France, Germany, and Britain called for Muslim women and girls to stop wearing headscarves, symbols of Muslim culture. In counterreaction, the "new Europeans" themselves began to organize politically, either in new parties or by joining traditional parties (usually either Green or Socialist).

Some immigrants, excluded from mainstream culture and meaningful employment, took out their frustration through violence. In November 2005, poor immigrants from North Africa and Portugal rioted over several nights in hundreds of French cities, burning thousands of cars and torching schools around their *banlieues*, the ghettoized districts in which they lived. In the Netherlands, men murdered nationalist political candidate Pim Fortuyn in 2002 and film director Theo van Gogh in 2004 for their alleged anti-Muslim views. Governments in Eastern Europe and Italy passed new laws against the wandering "Gypsies" or Romani people. Nation-states found it difficult to define their populations according to unified ethnicity anymore.

Of course, Europeans had no one to blame but themselves for these immigrants. Europe's colonial empires enabled Asians and Africans to move to the mother countries. Others came to take low-paying jobs that the Europeans offered. Every year millions more arrived because the West provided asylum or refuge from ideologies and cruelties with which other states still oppressed their own resident peoples. Some foreign culture began to weave its way into European sensibilities, especially through cuisine. Curry became as standard for British food as fish and chips, while Germans and Austrians ate *döner kebabs* as an alternative to wurst.

In the homeland of Western civilization, people asked, what does a united Europe mean? Intellectuals, especially Jacques Derrida and Michel Foucault from France, proposed a new technique to interpret Western culture in the 1980s. Their postmodern critique sought to undermine the Enlightenment consensus about individual rights and progress. Postmodernists deconstructed ideas and ideologies to show that they often represent actions of power and exploitation. Prevailing institutions use meanings to preserve their self-serving structures of profit and prestige. Enthusiasm for deconstructionist methods remained mostly confined to academic circles, yet postmodern criticism contributed to uncertainty about whom to trust.

As politicians began writing the Convention on the Future of the European Union in 2002, some tried to enshrine the position of Christianity in the document. Statistically, attendance at Christian churches in nominally Christian Europe had plummeted. Some argued, nonetheless, that the Christian heritage of democracy and freedom should be honored. Others, however, feared the domination of the state by various churches, and the marginalization of the millions of non-Christians (atheists, Muslims, Hindus, Buddhists, and Jews) who now lived in a diverse Europe. In any case, the cumbersome and complicated constitution failed to win endorsement by the French and Dutch voters in spring 2005.

Ethnic minorities from Eastern Europe, former colonies, and all over the world continued to come to Western European nations and settle down. Some were seeking amnesty for political or cultural persecution. Others wanted a job. Since the West had become supreme as a political and economic force in the world, the peoples of the world naturally migrated to prosperous Western states to profit from that power. Would they be integrated, like metal in a melting pot, or stay separated, as fruits in a basket? Would these peoples from Asia and Africa become westernized, or would they change the West?

Review: How did the European Union attempt to provide a new economic and political basis separate from the United States?

Response:

AN UNEXPECTED REVIVAL

At the Cold War's conclusion some pundits predicted that the collapse of communism meant a victory for liberal democracy and the opportunity for prosperity under capitalism. Even while the Cold War drove many Europeans together, some peoples divided over their differences. The claims of communism to unite workers had not weakened ethnic distinctions. Nationalism remained a potent political ideology. While the Cold War's end drained wars of their communist vs. capitalist energy, conflicts were yet empowered by cultural and tribal rivalries.

Two areas of British imperialism illustrate how nationalist conflicts continued during the Cold War. In **Cyprus** the deep divisions between ethnic Greeks (about 80 percent of the population) and Turks (the other 20 percent) degenerated into terrorist attacks, especially by those who wanted unification with Greece. Britain pulled out in 1959, but the new Cyprus was forbidden to unify with Greece. Greeks and Turks never quite managed to live peaceably, relying on UN peacekeepers. In 1967, though, Greece's anti-Communist military dictatorship thought annexing Cyprus would regain it some support lost after shooting student protestors in Athens. In a preemptive strike, Turkish troops occupied the northern third of Cyprus. Tens of thousands of ethnic Greek Cypriots fled to the south. The two NATO allies, Greece and Turkey, just barely managed to avoid war (see figure 15.3). The whole island became a member of the European Union in 2004, but Union authority does not quite apply to the northern third under Turkish rule.

Second, Northern Ireland, which remained under British rule after independence for the rest of Ireland, experienced violence between Protestant and Roman Catholics. Roman Catholics in Northern Ireland saw themselves as oppressed. They often lived in ghettoes, had worse jobs, were paid less, and were allowed fewer political rights than Irish Protestants. So the Irish Roman Catholics began demonstrating against the majority of Protestants and the British government. With a deter-

Figure 15.3.   A sign by peacekeepers of the United Nations marks the division of Cyprus.

mined Protestant majority intent on keepimg its domination, bloodshed escalated. The "**Troubles**" began in 1968 as a splinter group of the long-dormant Irish Republican Army, calling itself the **Provisional IRA**, or Provos, began terrorist attacks. The London government, at first trying to be neutral, eventually sent in thousands of troops to maintain order. The British shooting of more than a dozen Roman Catholic demonstrators on "Bloody Sunday" (30 January 1972) convinced many Catholics to consider them part of the enemy. In the following decades, more than three thousand were killed by all sides. Agreements begun in the late 1990s finally brought the Republic of Ireland, Great Britain, and parties in Northern Ireland toward a permanent, peaceful resolution. In May 2007, a functional coalition government took control in Northern Ireland.

During the Cold War, such ethnic fighting seemed insignificant to people far away from the killing compared with the possibility of World War III. In the meantime, Cold War conflicts had spread modern military technology from the industrialized West to many technologically primitive societies around the globe, whether they were ready for it or not. At first, the superpowers had supplied various dictators, tyrants, juntas, rebels, insurgents, and even terrorists with various kinds of advanced weapons: automatic rifles, grenades, land mines, plastic explosives, antitank rockets, and antiplane missiles. The superpowers had hoped to use these weapons by proxy against one another, whether by making friendly states stronger through armaments or hurting their rival through armed insurgencies. After the Cold War, when the rivals reduced their gifts of arms, international drug trading provided money for weapons. As weapons became cheaper and widespread, more people possessed an easy ability to kill others. The result was increased violence, for reasons of money, ideology, or power.

Much of this violence was nationalist in nature. Terrorists continued to bomb, hijack, kidnap, and murder to create ethnic states and enclaves. Elsewhere in Western Europe, terrorists lashed out in defense of their minorities, including the Basques against Spain, the Corsicans against France, and even some South Tyroleans against Italy. A few Puerto Ricans set off bombs to liberate their island from the United States. In other places of the world, civil wars and massacres broke out, giving the Western powers the choice of either standing by or intervening to stop the killing. After the Portuguese withdrew, East Timor in Indonesia was independent for only nine days (November–December 1975). Then Indonesians moved in and brutalized the native population, killing hundreds of thousands and sending more into exile. Only in 1999 did Australian troops backed by the United Nations begin to stabilize East Timor, creating a sovereign nation by 2002. In 1994, ethnic Hutu regimes in Rwanda and Burundi started a butchering of ethnic Tutsis. By the time they slacked off their massacre because of exhaustion and a small response by the United Nations, eight hundred thousand had died.

Europeans confronted their own massacres in the Balkans of the 1990s. This region, the starting point for World War I, burst into war again after the Cold War. During the Cold War, Soviet troops guaranteed stability in the nations of Hungary, Rumania, and Bulgaria. While Yugoslavia at first looked like it too would become a Soviet satellite, it provided an interesting exception to Russian domination. During World War II, Communist partisans led by Josep Broz, called **Tito** (r. 1945–1980), fought both the Serbian fascist Chetnik insurgents and the Croatian fascist Ustashe regime installed by the Nazis. At war's end, Tito was able to establish a new kind of regime, his own brand of Communist dictatorship.

For his People's Republic of Yugoslavia, Tito maintained a beneficial balance between the rivalry of Communists and capitalists during the Cold War. Officially a Communist state, Tito quite early broke with Stalin and pursued friendship with Western European states. At home, he calmed the ethnic conflicts that had torn apart the Kingdom of Serbs, Croats, and Slovenes. Half-Croat and half-Slovene himself, he deemphasized ethnic identity. He set up a federal system of six states: Slovenia, Croatia, Montenegro, Bosnia-Herzegovina, Serbia, and Macedonia. Each state remained somewhat autonomous from any potential Serbian bullying. Serbian nationalism was further weakened with carving out the two autonomous provinces of Vojvodina and **Kosovo**, with non-Serbian ethnic majorities (Hungarian and Albanian, respectively). With ethnic tensions dissolved, and bargaining for the best from both East and West, Yugoslavia became one of the more prosperous Eastern European countries.

Tito's death in 1980 changed little at first. The presidents of the six republics rotated the presidency. Already in 1981, however, disturbances began in Kosovo, where Albanians, who made up 90 percent of the population, wanted more use of their own languages and better living conditions. As the Cold War ended in 1989, the then-president Slobodan Milosevic decided to use ethnic tensions for his own political gain. A Serb himself, he fueled ethnic resentment of the small Orthodox Christian Serbian minority in the province of Kosovo against the Muslim Albanian majority. He proclaimed that Serbians would not tolerate subservience in their own historic homeland.

With this revival of ethnic divisiveness the leaders of the other federal states worried about a possible Serbian takeover that would repeat the legacy of 1929. In June 1991, **Slovenia** and **Croatia** preemptively proclaimed independence. When an invasion by the Serbian-dominated Yugoslav army failed, both countries were internationally recognized as sovereign states. Nonetheless, Serbian-Croatian warfare was intense, and atrocities became the order of the day. The new term ***ethnic cleansing*** was coined, as both sides used threats, destruction, killing, and rape to drive away rival ethnic groups from villages and districts each wanted to claim as its own.

By early 1992, **Bosnia-Herzegovina** began its own attempt at independence. Unhappily for that state, Bosnia was the most ethnically divided of all, including large numbers of Serbo-Croatian Muslims caught in the middle. Croatia and the shrunken Yugoslavia both attacked it. **Macedonia** used the opportunity to peacefully gain independence, leaving Serbia and Montenegro as the remnant of a Yugoslav Federation. Greek objections to the use of the name "Macedonia," with its Hellenistic heritage from Philip II and Alexander, forced that country to call itself officially the "Former Yugoslav Republic of Macedonia."

Russia's sympathies with its old ally Serbia limited what the United Nations could achieve to stop the violence. Instead, Western powers turned to NATO. The Cold War's end and the dissolution of the Warsaw Pact had robbed that military alliance of much of its original purpose of defending Europe against the Soviet Union. In the 1990s, that Western military alliance system decided as a substitute to become a peacekeeper in Europe. After the Dayton Accords of 1995, NATO sent in thousands of troops to end the fighting in Bosnia. For a few years violence subsided. Bosnia could not survive, however, without the Western occupiers to keep the peace between ethnic groups.

Then, by the late 1990s, a new fight began over ethnic Albanians in **Kosovo**, where the fighting about Yugoslavia had begun. The self-proclaimed Kosovo Liberation Army launched a rebellion in that province on behalf of the Albanian majority. In retaliation for what Serbia saw as Kosovar terrorism, Serbs began ethnic cleansing in January 1999. NATO launched an aerial bombing campaign to stop the killings and expulsions. Soon NATO troops occupied the province and the Kosovar Albanians formed their own self-government. About ten thousand peacekeeping forces from NATO and from other nations, such as Switzerland and the Ukraine, remained. On 17 February 2008, the country's legislative assembly declared independence. Most European states recognized the new states, but many others, including Serbia and Russia, have not. Despite the European Union's efforts to support local police forces with its "Rule of Law Mission in Kosovo" (EULEX), resentment by ethnic Serbs about assimilation and Kosovars about outside intervention has continued to cause trouble (see map 15.2).

Many problems in the world continued to be made worse by nationalism, focusing on ethnic differences instead of any common humanity. Russian domination of

Map 15.2.   Europe, 2010

Chechnya provoked open, nasty, military strikes and terrorism. The ethnic minority of Mayan descent in the Mexican province of Chiapas organized a revolt under the Zapatistas beginning in 1994 that is still simmering today. Other states suffered divisions with less violence but important consequences. In Canada, beginning in the 1960s, the Québecois insisted on their own ethnic French identity, driving millions of citizens of non-French heritage out of the province. When Australia tried to limit immigration by non-European citizens, it sparked riots by resident Lebanese and resentment by its Aboriginal people. The ongoing challenge would be how humanity balanced national and ethnic identity with civil cooperation. Western Europe's apparent easing of nationalism offers one hopeful sign of a revived regionalism. Regional dialects, traditions, and even political structures are flourishing. Perhaps the rule of nations can accept diverse ethnicity.

Review: *How did nationalism resurge after the Cold War?*

Response:

HAVES AND CANNOTS

In the 1970s, the West's economic success began to falter, ending years of unheard-of growth after World War II. The oil embargo by OPEC in 1974 marked a turning point. High fuel prices, international competition, inflation, the cost of good wages and benefits, and environmental regulations weakened profits made from manufacturing in Western nations. Unemployment rates of between 5 and 10 percent burdened Western economies, even if they were well below the levels of the Great Depression. Increasingly, capitalists invested in factories built in Third World nations, where they could pay a fraction of the wages expected by Western workers organized in unions. Many Western nations saw high-wage manufacturing jobs disappear, to be replaced by low-wage service jobs (cooking, cleaning, or clerking). Some economists considered this as mere "creative destruction," as described by the Austrian Joseph Schumpeter. Others worried that this postindustrial economy slowed the rise in standard of living for the lower middle class compared with the upper and upper middle classes.

Different Western governments followed varying economic advice. Sweden and Norway developed the welfare state to the highest possible degree outside Communist regimes. Cradle-to-grave benefits supplied sufficient security and prosperity for many Scandinavians, if not quick economic expansion. Many other countries tried to cut back on some state-managed benefits. Even the socialist leaders in the 1980s of France (Mitterand) and Austria (Vranitzky) trimmed social programs. To compensate for lower wages, Western European regimes increased vacation time, while the Americans encouraged more women and immigrants into the workforce at lower wages.

By the late 1970s the welfare-state concept had come under attack by economists and politicians. Most famously, the "Chicago Boys," led by Milton Friedman, promoted a stronger, renewed laissez-faire attitude, encouraging governments to abandon Keynesian economic theory (see diagram 15.1). According to them, the economy worked best when government did not spend on social programs. Prime Minister Thatcher of Britain led the way, cutting subsidies and reprivatizing nationalized industries. Experiments by Latin American regimes such as Chile and Argentina saw laissez-faire economics fail to bring the predicted prosperity. In the United States, conservatives claimed to adopt similar policies, leading President Reagan to reduce some tax rates. Yet his administration actually spent more on both social and military programs, making up the difference by borrowing money from abroad. By the end of the 1980s, America's singular economic dominance of the West and the world was over.

A new electronics industry based on computers did create new jobs. The Allies had invented computers during World War II in order to break secret codes of the Axis powers, and the computational ability of the computers quickly increased. As new technologies such as transistors and the microchip were invented, computers became cheaper and smaller. The computer revolution accelerated with the invention of the **personal computer**. By the 1980s, desktop or personal computers became a consumer product in the West. First used as advanced typewriters, they soon expanded into drawing, graphics, spreadsheets, and databases, as well as games from simple solitaire to multiplayer strategy and tactics simulations.

Such game players were connected by new global communication networks such as the **Internet** and the World Wide Web. In modern industrialized societies, computers control and regulate our lives more than any human bureaucrat ever could. And, for those who can afford and spend the time to learn to use them, computers help with the acquisition of new knowledge, which is power. Allied with cellular phone technology, which was developed by the end of the twentieth century, personal communications that could connect to a wealth of information became portable and pocket-sized.

The ease with which words and images could be electronically distributed set an example for what capitalists sought for all goods and services. *Globalization* became the slogan of those who wanted to make more money by relying on the worldwide grasp of the modern corporation, cheap transportation and communication, and low or nonexistent trade barriers and regulations. Globalization's advocates suggested that worldwide marketing strategies for material goods would be more important than the nation-state and its politics, while a worldwide trade system would benefit rich and poor nations alike. Recognizing the new situation as early as 1975, leaders of the most important economic powers began to hold annual

MERCANTILISM

LAISSEZ-FAIRE / CLASSICAL
LIBERAL ECONOMICS

SOCIALISM

KEYNESIAN ECONOMICS

SUPPLY-SIDE / TRICKLE-DOWN / REAGANOMICS

Diagram 15.1. Economic Theories of Capitalism. To summarize the various proposals dealing with the challenges of capitalism, these cartoons highlight the alleged role of government (the man with the crown) in dealing with capital (the bag of $) and contracts (the paper): 1. In mercantilism (1600s), the government and businessmen work together by establishing monopolies to benefit the state's balance of trade; 2. In laissez-faire (early1800s), the government takes a hands-off approach, allowing the businessmen to make money according to enlightened self-interest; 3. In socialism (late 1800s), the workers demand a share of the wealth (at first resisted by government and business); 4. In Keynesian economics (1930s), the government steps in with regulations and capital investment to help the economy recover from or to prevent a depression; 5. In supply-side or trickle-down economics or Reagonomics (1980s), a laissez-faire approach allows businesses to make their own decisions with the expectation that profits will spread to government and workers.

summit meetings as the G7 (the United States, Japan, West Germany, Great Britain, France, Italy, and Canada), becoming the G8 in the 1990s with the addition of Russia. These leaders coordinated select economic, social, and political policies as they coped with increasing global trade.

Some economists warned about the negatives of globalization. Citizens began to organize around issues of social justice and human rights in NGOs (nongovernmental organizations), ranging from Amnesty International (to stop torture and cruelty) to Greenpeace (to protect the environment). They saw how Western corporations paid low wages to impoverished natives for their country's natural resources, while charging highly profitable prices to their comparatively wealthy Western customers. Exploitation was simply the price of doing good business. An accidental explosion of an American chemical plant in Bhopal, India, in 1984, for example, killed four thousand and injured tens of thousands of others. Broken wells and wrecked tankers spilled crude oil regularly. Multinational or transnational enterprises seemed to show more loyalty to their managers and stockholders than patriotism or sympathy toward any one country or even general human welfare. Adam Smith's views no longer applied, as customers bought based on price, not country of manufacture.

Inexpensive products also flowed into the West from Asia. Several Asian states modernized their economic policies to adapt to and compete with the dominant Western nations. Japan had led the way in the 1970s with its exports of automobiles and electronics, supported by activist government policies working with major manufacturing cartels. By the 1990s, the so-called Asian Tigers (Singapore, South Korea, Nationalist China/Taiwan, and the British colony of Hong Kong) likewise built on Western values. Leaders encouraged frugality, pushed education, protected investments, and built a socialistic-like cooperation between governments and private enterprise.

At the end of the twentieth century, China had recovered from the mistakes of Mao and was becoming an economic powerhouse by activating a Western-style economy. The regime did not, however, allow Western-style democracy. Calls for representative government were symbolized by a crude reproduction of the Statue of Liberty in 1989 during popular protests in Tiananmen Square in Beijing. The totalitarian, one-party regime dispersed the demonstrators. China's dynamism accelerated after 1997, when the British finally returned to China their colony of Hong Kong, which Britain had held since the Opium Wars in the 1840s. In its own version of the Commercial and Industrial Revolutions, China became an attractive business partner to Western companies, drawing on Western capital to rapidly industrialize. This new Industrial Revolution repeated the exploitation of workers of a hundred years before in the West: child and prison laborers, long hours, high quotas, squalid living spaces. As during the Industrial Revolution in the West, the government forbade workers to organize but was itself slow to protect workers. Still, since workers' wages were superior to those offered by the collapsing rural economy, many Chinese had little choice but to adapt to this new revolution. Westerners could then buy cheap bedding, toothbrushes, clothing, toys, and everything at their discount warehouse stores, all "Made in China."

While science and technology made possible this revolution in manufacturing and consumerism, scientists have also raised questions about its impact on our planet. Chemical emissions seem to have opened a hole over the Antarctic in the ozone layer that protects the earth's surface from destructive ultraviolet rays. Children of European descent in Australia and New Zealand are now mandated to protect their light skin with sunscreen and floppy hats. Other scientific studies suggest that air pollution, energy production, and deforestation have produced a greenhouse effect that is heating up the atmosphere. Millions of acres of arable land in Africa and Asia turned into desert as rivers, lakes, or even the entire Aral Sea dried up. A debate about **global climate change** inclines toward "global warming" melting the glaciers and polar ice caps and then raising water levels to flood coastal areas. Many politicians and economists are reluctant to initiate reforms that might threaten perceived standards of living.

As more people wanted to lead better lives, though, everything became more industrialized, and larger numbers of people moved to bigger urban centers. Even our food supply became mechanized. Modern factories for food crowd thousands of caged pigs or chickens into warehouses. There they dwell in darkness and consume hormones (to speed their growth), antibiotics (to prevent diseases that would normally destroy creatures living so closely together in filth), the recycled remnants of their fellow creatures (as cheap food), and laxatives (to make their excrement more manageable). On the one hand, genetically modified foodstuffs offer the potential to provide still cheaper and more nutritious edibles. On the other hand, they might seriously damage our basic genetic structure and wreak havoc in natural ecosystems unprepared for these artificial strains.

Genetic science has absorbed the building blocks of life into the commercial industrial economy. The biggest leap in the study of life since Darwin was the discovery in 1953 of deoxyribonucleic acid, or DNA. That double helix of molecules is the basic building block of life. DNA science is now used in fighting crime, having replaced fingerprints or dental impressions as the best means for identification of criminals or victims. Its real future, however, lies in scientists tinkering with DNA's molecular structure. In 1988, the U.S. Patent Office granted a patent on a genetically engineered mouse. Since then, synthetic organs, hormones, and compounds of all kinds for humans are being worked on.

Just as with our genes, the sex lives of our bodies became increasingly commercialized. The end of the Cold War brought the West's sexual revolution to the newly liberated Soviet bloc and even to the former colonial regions of the Third World. Business interests using the Internet and globalization provided more access to pornography for more people than ever before in history. Westerners traveled to poor countries in Asia and Eastern Europe for "sex tourism." The demands for the sex trade led organized criminals to virtually enslave women from poor countries to serve in brothels. While much of such commercial sex activity is done behind closed doors and outside the law, new attitudes about marriage of homosexuals came into the open. In 1989, Denmark allowed people of the same sex to enter civil unions, with rights similar to those of marriage. Other Western European countries followed through the 1990s along with several Latin American states after 2001, even allowing legal marriage for same-sex couples.

Other Third World peoples, especially in Africa, resisted more openness about sexuality. Modernists asserted that all people were inherently equal, regardless of sex or sexual orientation. Fundamentalists argued that men and women have different roles while homosexuality was a sin. Although the retired Anglican South African archbishop Desmond Tutu was a notable exception, many African Christians protested the ordinations by Western churches of women and homosexuals. Indeed, societies throughout Africa still opposed mere civil rights for women and homosexuals as part of their hostility toward what they saw as Western imperialism's oppression of native African identities, while many African Christians themselves tolerated polygamy. So Africans formed international alliances with traditionalist Christians in the West. The question for everyone remained whether innovation and wealth or tradition and resistance would hinder or help families and communities to maintain good societies.

That questioning only intensified when the economies around the world suffered deep blows in 2008. Many businesspeople and economists thought that the constant capitalist cycle of boom and bust had been forever broken. Confident that market bubbles and collapse were a relic of history, they deregulated, increased debt, and encouraged incautious investing and rampant profit reaping. Overinflated by risky products called derivatives, the American stock markets suddenly began to fall in 2008 after enough investors began to doubt their worth. The markets fell so fast that financial institutions began to collapse, and vast wealth disappeared over the next year. The trouble in the United States quickly spread abroad because of globalization. The major banks of Iceland failed, ruining that country's economy. Even Dubai on the Persian Gulf, which had been prospering as a haven favorable toward Western investment, slowed its economic expansion. Western governments responded with massive Keynesian spending or careful monitoring and regulation. Which lessons, if any, capitalists would learn from these failures remained open.

Review: How did Western economic practices dominate world trade?

Response:

VALUES OF VIOLENCE

The West's dependence on oil imports forced its attention toward the Middle East. Many people there disliked both Western ideology, with its acceptance of changing social attitudes, and economic exploitation, with its profits flowing out of Arab and Muslim nations. Certain fundamentalist Muslims began to oppose the West with force of their own.[1]

The West could, of course, take much of the blame for the growing opposition of some Muslims. The West did not leave Islam to flourish on its own. When westerners took over much of the Middle East in the nineteenth and early twentieth centuries, they were confident enough in their contradictions to try to force both Christianity and secularism, at the same time, on their imperialist subjects. It was merely unexpected good fortune for many Arab nations that geologists discovered petroleum beneath their desert sands just as the imperialist experiment failed. To more easily exploit this fuel source, Western leaders again propped up despots and dictators with whom they could conveniently make economic arrangements. Meanwhile the common people remained frustrated and powerless.

The tensions between aspects of Islamic civilization and a modern world created by Western civilization were revealed with the **Iranian Revolution** (1978–1980). Through much of the Cold War, the shah of Iran, Mohammed Reza Pahlavi, had ruled as a near-absolute monarch. The CIA had put the shah in power in 1953 by overthrowing the democratically elected but socialist prime minister Mohammad Mossadegh. Serving as a loyal ally of the United States in the region, the shah had been somewhat progressive, carrying out land reform in the 1970s and promoting secular modernization and westernization. By the end of the 1970s, ironically, the rising wealth and education of the middle classes made them disgusted with Iran's secret police and absolutism. From exile in Paris, a religious leader, the Ayatollah Khomeini, orchestrated a revolution that forced the shah into exile in January 1979. Khomeini then created a new dictatorship based on his interpretation of Islam.

The Iranian Revolution kept the science needed to maintain oil wealth and military power, but it rejected most of the rest of Western culture. The revolution even humiliated the United States when Iranian students seized the American embassy in Iran's capital of Teheran. The inability of the United States to bring home these dozens of hostages contributed to the defeat of U.S. president Jimmy Carter in his reelection attempt. In return for the captives' release occurring at the same time as President Reagan's inauguration, the United States promised never to interfere with the Islamist regime. The new Iran championed anti-Western civilization and called on other Muslims to support its expansionist Shi'ite agenda.

While the United States could not take direct action against Iran, it encouraged another friendly and more secular dictator, Saddam Hussein of Iraq, to attack Iran. The resulting Iran-Iraq War (1980–1988) killed hundreds of thousands, reviving trench warfare and even the use of poison gas. After the war ended as a draw, Saddam looked toward Kuwait as a way to pay for the war's costs. In the early

---

1. No one has yet come up with a satisfactory name for collectively describing the wide range of different political agents who have recently combined Islam and terrorism. "Islamofascist" misapplies the nationalistic and state- or corporate-based ideology of fascism. "Jihadist" validates those who believe *jihad* is compatible with slaughter and suicide. "Islamist" may associate the name of the religion "Islam" too closely with those who many perceive to be betraying their faith through indiscriminate killing. But it seems to work as distinct from "Islamic" for those groups that are clearly fundamentalist, as defined in the previous section.

nineteenth century Kuwait had been considered part of Iraq, until the British carved it out as a separate entity. Since then, oil revenues allowed Kuwait's rulers to finance wealthy lifestyles of its male Arab citizens, importing workers and servants from other countries to do manual labor. From Saddam Hussein's point of view, he just wanted to take back what rightfully belonged to Iraq before the Western surge of imperialism. In August 1990 his armies invaded Kuwait.

Kuwait was, however, a sovereign state and a member of the United Nations. Under the leadership of American president George H. W. Bush (r. 1989–1993), the United Nations intervened. During the **First Persian Gulf War** (1990–1991), a half-million American and allied troops liberated Kuwait at the cost of about four hundred lives for the United States and four hundred for its allies, versus probably one hundred thousand Iraqis. The UN forces left Saddam Hussein in power, though, since the organization does not intervene in the internal affairs of its members.

The First Gulf War only helped the new militant version of Islam to grow. Saddam Hussein, though his political base had always been largely secularist, began to portray his conflict as one of Muslims against westerners. Many Muslims in other Islamic countries also had become hostile against their own regimes as well as against Israel, the United States, and Western civilization. Libya, for example, had sponsored the bombing of a PanAm flight to the United States over Lockerbie Scotland in 1988. Muslim separatists in the Philippines kidnapped Western tourists.

Other acts of terror drew their energy from the unending struggle between the Palestinians and Israelis. Israeli governments had failed to implement Palestinian self-government according to the Camp David Accords, while Western governments did little to force them to do so. Instead, Israel continued to dispossess Palestinians and encouraged Jewish settlers to create fortified enclaves within occupied areas. By the 1990s, Palestinians in the occupied territories carried out intifadas (uprisings), consisting of boycotts of Israeli businesses, strikes, demonstrations, and "wars of stones," or rock throwing. The Israelis responded by restricting Palestinian movements (thus preventing them from working), demolitions (bulldozing homes and villages), and force (such as rocket assassination attacks on Palestinian leaders). The Israelis even started to build a fortified barrier to separate the communities, reminiscent of the Berlin Wall or the ghettoes of the Renaissance or Third Reich. By 2001 Palestinian suicide bombers were regularly blowing up themselves and numerous Israelis on buses and in cafes. As both sides continue to use violence, a peaceful resolution seems as distant as ever.

Another nest of hostility to the West developed in Afghanistan. When the Americans had armed the Muslim militant mujahedeen in Afghanistan in the 1980s, they did not foresee what could happen. After the Cold War had ended, some religious students, or **Taliban**, became so disgusted with the ongoing violence that they organized their own attacks on everyone else. Their devotion and discipline helped them to take over the country. They then imposed their own Islamist dictatorship, even harsher in its cultural imperatives than Iran's. Their most notorious actions included forcibly confining women to their domestic roles and iconoclastically destroying priceless ancient sculptures.

The Taliban provided a haven to yet another a new kind of terrorist group, **Al-**

Qaida. A Saudi former oil and construction magnate, Osama bin Laden, financed Al-Qaida to be a secret organization that promoted his version of Islam. He was especially resentful of American intervention in the Middle East, whether in support of Israel or against Saddam Hussein. His Islamist organization launched the boldest terrorist attack in history on 11 September 2001 (**9/11**). Two hijacked airliners hit the twin towers of the World Trade Center in New York City, symbol of Western commerce and capitalism. The resulting fires led to the skyscrapers' collapse. A third plane damaged the Pentagon (the U.S. military's command center in Washington, D.C.), while a fourth crashed into a field in Pennsylvania after its hostage passengers fought back against their hijackers. All told, about three thousand people (mostly Americans, but also dozens from other nations) died on that day from these attacks.

In response, President George W. Bush (r. 2001–2009) declared a "War on Terrorism." Unfortunately for this concept, terrorism is a tactic, not an enemy against whom a state can easily fight using traditional armed forces. Since the end of the nineteenth century, terrorists have used small-scale violence to achieve their political goals. Such terrorist attacks are hard to stop. Armies are ill suited to combat them, since terrorists are so easily part of a civilian population, both before and after they strike. As access to weapons becomes easier and grudges against specific state systems do not fade, terrorism is an affordable substitute for guerrilla war or outright armies. Many former colonies, with their ill-drawn borders, attracted ethnic and religious violence. Even in industrialized Western nations, such as Britain facing the IRA in Northern Ireland or Spain facing the ETA in the Basque regions, authorities could not completely crush terrorist cells throughout the twentieth century. What success they did have may have come from both addressing the root political complaints and using approaches similar to criminal investigations.

Since 9/11, many Western nations have increased investigations by intelligence and police agencies of terrorist organizations. Their lack of training and knowledge of Arabic and Muslim cultures hindered their pursuit of Al-Qaida and others. Many governments passed laws that empowered police agencies. Some laws threatened to remove civil rights and legal due process from both citizens and aliens as they increased surveillance of public places, private computer and phone communications, and even persons' homes. Western states faced issues of balancing security against civil liberty, use of invasive technology versus personal privacy, and ethnic tolerance balanced against economic necessity.

Militarily, the United States and allied troops from NATO first retaliated for 9/11 by invading Afghanistan, where the Taliban had sheltered bases of Al-Qaida. The United States and its allies won a quick victory. Yet most Al-Qaida leaders, including Osama bin Laden, managed to escape. Unfortunately for peace, Afghanistan did not stabilize either, as warlords reasserted their domination against the few American and NATO troops who had remained in the country.

Then, despite being the world's lone superpower, the United States found itself unable to lead the West in dealing with terrorism, despite sympathy generated by the 9/11 attacks. Controversially, President Bush's attention singularly focused on removing Saddam Hussein from power in Iraq. The Bush administration listened to "neoconservative" theorists who promoted a renewed American exceptionalism, believing that the United States could effectively intervene in troubled spots around the world. In this context, the American administration asserted that invading Iraq was part of the wider "War on Terrorism," suggesting that Saddam had connections with Al-Qaida and the attacks of 9/11. Specifically, the United States claimed that Iraq had defied UN resolutions after its defeat in Kuwait about eliminating weapons of mass destruction (**WMD**, a new name for the category "ABC" or atomic, biological, chemical weapons). The failure of UN inspectors to find any evidence of such weapons notwithstanding, Bush pushed toward invasion. Neither the United Nations, nor NATO, nor most of the world's nations supported this action. Many westerners actively protested what they saw as the American rush to war. Nevertheless, the application of new technology and rapid mobile forces won the United States and its "Coalition of the Willing" (with Great Britain as the only serious participant) a quick military conquest in the **Iraq or Second Persian Gulf War** (2003–).

The quick victory did not end the conflict, however, as the occupying American and allied forces faced serious hostility. Iraqi insurgents regularly killed Western and American troops with sniping and IEDs (improvised explosive devices) while terrorizing their own fragile government and weary population with kidnappings and beheadings. Human rights organizations and defenders sharply criticized the American government for its treatment, which inclued torture, of "enemy combatants." New terrorist bombings by Al-Qaida of commuter trains in Madrid on 13 March 2004 or subway bombings in London in 2005 showed that the organization was still active, Osama bin Laden still at large. As President Barack Obama replaced President Bush in 2009, the American and allied occupation in Iraq and NATO's in Afghanistan continued.

Western civilization must decide how it is going to continue to manage its own, and the world's, affairs. Does it follow the lead of a unilateral United States of America? Try to promote international law and multilateral interventions? Is it united at all in the face of geopolitical dangers from varied terrorist groups and rogue nations? Does it turn back to its own religious roots? Are those roots fanatical or tolerant? Can the West spread prosperity with more fairness and less exploitation? Will the rest of the world accept any of this? How will the West continue to adapt to the rapid change created by science, capitalism, industry, transportation, and communication? How will the West adjust to the growing power of Asian nations? Of course, Western civilization is not one single entity, but rather a collection of its individual citizens. All of us, individually and together, must confront each of these questions.

Review: *How did Western and non-Western societies use violence to achieve political and cultural ends?*

Response:

Epilogue: Why Western Civilization?

Several hundred years ago, Western civilization took the lead in the categories of politics, economics, and science and technology compared with other societies around the world. In each of these areas, states and social groups in the West gained more efficiency and effectiveness. On the one hand, westerners used the power from these activities to intimidate and overwhelm other human cultures and civilizations. On the other hand, westerners brought knowledge to those other societies that in turn enabled them to become as powerful as Western civilization. Cultures around the world are still deciding what to keep from the West and what to use against its dominance. Either way, the dynamism generated by the West guarantees that tomorrow will be different from today. Therein lies the dilemma of applying historical understanding. In a changing world, what should we ourselves choose to learn from the past of Western civilization?

A few years ago, students at Stanford University chanted the phrase above in an attempt to transform a Western civilization course requirement in their curriculum. Although the incident was hardly significant, defenders of Western culture sometimes point to this call to deemphasize the importance of Western civilization as a signal of doom. And criticisms of the West go well beyond the lectures of professors in classrooms. Some critics want instead to study history more inclusive of non-Western cultures and more critical of Western power. Such people object to validating Western civilization because they see that it oppressed weaker peoples. Many of these exploited peoples have failed to achieve the high standard of living or political freedoms enjoyed in the West since the collapse of neo-imperialism. Both with words and weapons, Western civilization is under attack today, from both the outside and the inside.

In this rough-and-tumble world, civilization itself has always been under attack. The West has confronted external enemies, from Viking, Saracen, and Magyar hordes plundering the Carolingian Empire to Al-Qaida blowing up commuters in New York, Madrid, or London. The West has also faced internal enemies, from recurrent peasant rebellions to white supremacists blasting a government building in Oklahoma City. All civilizations define themselves by the extent of their supremacy against their neighbors or their control of their subjects. All cultures have, at one time or another, confronted new people and ideas and faced the necessity of either absorbing them or eliminating them. Since Western civilization is so widespread today, it cannot help but provoke opposition from those who do not accept the extent of its reach or agree with its values.

The West exists as long as many of its members and opponents say it exists. Without self-identification or labeling by others, civilizations have no inherent cohesion. As described in this book, Western civilization has been the culmination of a long historical process of human choices. In its belief systems, the West has experienced everything from myths to monotheisms, philosophical speculation to scientific secularism. In its culture, the West has expressed itself in everything from epic poetry to prose history, theatricals and spectacles, novels and newspapers, which have been transmitted on everything from stone and bone, clay and canvas, parchment and paper, to celluloid film and streams of electrons. In its power over nature, the West is rooted with all other cultures in the knife and knapsack of the hunter-gatherers to the plow and pottery of agriculturists. The West progressed further, with the steam engine and steel ship, to today's computers and cars. None of these inventions or attitudes necessarily made the West's culture better or superior. Nonetheless, through the power of its navies, armies, ideas, discoveries, and economies, the West came to reign supreme over world affairs by the nineteenth century.

The West achieved its ascendancy most obviously through political power, supported by its economic wealth and military innovation. In the methods of war and the mechanisms of rulership it rose to world leadership. As leader, however, the West has never spoken with one unified voice. Both a strength and a weakness of Western civilization has been its division into many sovereign states. Individual Western nation-states built their own global empires. Their rivalries with one another spurred innovation and growth as well as destruction and death. This variety also enabled democratic and republican ideals to survive against prevailing absolutism and authoritarianism. The cooperation of individuals and groups in capitalism financed political growth and further fostered responsive government.

Some people believe that the West is based on freedom, but its own history shows an ambivalent interaction with that ideal. Back in the sixteenth century, as representative government began to revive from its Græco-Roman and medieval urban roots, some individual states grew strong enough to create overseas empires. Western guns and galleons gave Europeans a lethal advantage over many other peoples in Asia, Africa, and the Americas. Imperialist Spain and Portugal were joined by France and England, then the Netherlands and Russia, next Germany and Italy, and finally, the United States and even Japan, re-created in the West's own image. The official empires of the West largely collapsed in the twentieth century, partly because the West's power was drained by three world conflicts: World War I, World War II, and the Cold War.

At the end of these conflicts, the United States of America stood above all others as a superpower. The United States has achieved a unique global superiority through its money, media, and military. An economy and financial system allows less than 5 percent of the world's population to consume more than 20 percent of its resources. Since World War II, the United States has wielded an influence without precedent. Its ideas have spread in television, games, and movies, and the power of its armed forces reflects a budget larger than almost all other nations combined.

One of the most fragile aspects of Western civilization today is the extent to which the United States of America will either continue to dominate it or separate from it. Some American exceptionalists have suggested that its hegemony should allow the United States alone to define what the world should be in the future, acting unilaterally. Others wish the United States to work with the nations of Europe, and even the world, funneling war and power through the multilateral international institutions (such as NATO and the UN) created by the West in the second half of the twentieth century.

The study of the West has thus been weakened because of cultural warfare over which aspect of its past (and present) truly represents its traditional values and virtues. Should history remind us of our nobility or convict us of our shame? People want their heroes and villains—although usually we want the heroes to be like us and the villains to be like some "other." It is hard to cope when the roles are reversed. Christianity had Jesus, Saint Francis, and Martin Luther King, Jr., as well as schismatics, crusaders, and inquisitors. Nations had their largely successful King Henry II, King Louis XIV, and Bismarck, as well as their failure-ridden King John, King Louis XVI, and Adolf Hitler. Each has had and will have at least some proponents and some opponents. Historians try to sort out the greatness and the failures that belong to each of us.

More important than the people of the past may have been the different ideologies that informed their choices. Various factions in our culture identify some beliefs as vices, others as virtues, and vice versa. The Enlightenment consensus of reason and science has never completely overwhelmed religious and superstitious viewpoints. The resistance to Darwinian evolution by those who assert a literal interpretation of the Bible illustrates this lack of success. Christianity has not created its "City of God," nor has rationalism built its utopia, because people have never been able to agree on priorities. Some argue that capitalism should sanctify the pursuit of profit only by corporations, while others call for society to embrace all persons as active economic agents. Elites redefine democracy by merely having elections, regardless of whose money gains a greater voice. The masses often seek to be heard but speak in many different voices (quite literally, in the many languages from Bulgarian to Basque still spoken in the European Union). Most people want to win; few people seem willing to compromise.

All these tensions among competing ideas interacted to create Western civilization. Fights over causation, civil rights, capitalism, class, high culture, and Christianity have all driven historical change. Influences from neighboring cultures and civilizations, small and large, from Mesopotamians, Egyptians, Assyrians, Persians, Muslims, North Africans, Byzantines, Slavs, Magyars, East Asians, South Asians, Central Asians, Native Americans, sub-Saharan Africans, Pacific Islanders, and others, helped to shape Western civilization over the centuries.

While advocates of ***multiculturalism*** have attacked Western expressions of power, history shows that the West has always been multicultural. In its earliest phases, Hebrews tried to Judaize their Canaanite neighbors in Palestine; the Greeks began to hellenize the peoples conquered by Alexander; the Romans romanized everyone from the Iberians to the Britains, Germans, Greeks, Mesopotamians, and Egyptians. In the Early Middle Ages, the Church Christianized the ruling Germans and their neighbors. None of these "-izations" succeeded completely—although elements of earlier cultures always survived. The alleged unity of medieval Christendom actually rested on the different "nations" of English, French, Germans, Italians, Spanish, and others. Then, from the Middle Ages into the nineteenth century, the diverse German kingdoms that replaced the western half of the Roman Empire melded into their conquered populations, in the process transforming and spreading a new culture to neighboring peoples. The Germans diversified into the French, the English, the Italians, the Spanish, the Portuguese, the Scandinavians, the Scots, the Irish, the Dutch, the Swiss, the Belgians, and others, including even Luxemburgers, Liechtensteiners, Andorrans, and Austrians. The Slavic states of eastern Europe connected with the West, especially after the fall of Byzantium. As many of these westerners trekked into the world, colonizing and colonized peoples organized as Latin Americans, "North" Americans, Australians, New Zealanders, South Africans, and others. All of them reflect multiculturalism; all of them share in Western civilization.

Does Western civilization have a future? At several moments in its past, Western civilization almost did not. Persia might have conquered Greece. The Romans might have self-destructed in their republican civil wars. The Germans might have resisted Christianity. Invaders might have overwhelmed the Christendom of Charlemagne. The Mongols might have wiped out the West, as they did many societies that opposed them. Muslim or Asian armies might have conquered Europe anytime up to the seventeenth century. Nuclear war might have ended it all during the Cold War (and still may).

Up to now, Western civilization has survived numerous challenges and developed overwhelming power, partly because of the revolutions it has experienced and assimilated. The Commercial Revolution, the intellectual revolutions of the Renaissance and Enlightenment, the religious revolution of the Reformation, the Scientific Revolution, the Industrial Revolution, and the political revolutions of England, America, and France have guaranteed that history would change. These revolutions encourage human creativity and the application of the "new" to improve people's lives.

Change is not common to all historical views. Some cultures, such as the Hindu Indian, see a cyclical turn to history, looking to revive or maintain traditional orders, resisting anything new or different. The Ancient Egyptian and early Chinese civilizations valued the unchanging permanence of a society that mirrored an eternal heavenly order. The monarchs and nobles ruled from their fine palaces, the priests prayed in their gilded temples, the peasants shoveled manure in the fields. So it had been; so it always should be. Any disruptions—an invasion by foreigners, the end of a dynasty and civil war, a natural disaster—were to be overcome so that the elites could restore the right order of things. These attitudes and concepts are also found in Western civilization.

But from the Jews, through the Greeks and Romans, and to the Germans, the West began to embrace change, even when its leaders would not admit it to themselves. The Jews appealed to the eternal law of God but adapted to changing circumstances as they went from wandering tribes, to kingdoms, to a people scattered across the world. Now, some of them are building the national state of Israel and confronting hostility within and without. The Greeks cleverly expanded outward from their homeland and briefly achieved cultural predominance in the Eastern Mediterranean and the Middle East, only to lose it through their divisiveness. They regained a brief ascendancy with the surviving remnant of Rome known as the Byzantine Empire, only to lose that empire to the Turks. The Romans did so well at learning from the Greeks that they passed on an imperialist legacy to the Byzantine East, Islam, and the West. The Germans who inadvertently destroyed Rome in the fifth century A.D. bound the cultures of the Greeks and Romans to their own, tolerated a Jewish presence, and embraced Christianity. Although the Germans failed to unite the West under one government, the common appeal to Christianity, Greece, and Rome combined with the eagerness of the states in western Europe to learn from one another, bred the great revolutions in economics, learning, religion, science, and politics.

The themes of supremacy and diversity reveal this ongoing change. Some leaders and societies have sought supremacy, which bound allegiances into a unity that strengthened. Arguments over what justified supremacy recast societies: a divine mandate (decided upon by whose God?); tradition (choosing which part of the assorted past?); knowledge (as taught by whom?); power (with what degree of violence?). Over time, though, supremacies have often degraded into stifling creativity. They demanded mere obedience, if not outright oppression. At the same time, humans obviously have sought diversity, dividing into smaller unities and striving for what is new. Yet emphasis on too many differences, or focusing too much on them, has fragmented people into mutual hostilities, if not armed camps. The tendency toward diversity has often subverted supremacy.

Today, international and multiregional organizations continue to expand, while nationalistic groups persist in their identities. As the world economy binds peoples together, nationalists want to restrict immigration; local patriotism resists international solidarity among human beings. Most people still fail to empathize with either the exploited or the enemy, although modern media of words, sounds, and images bring them into our living rooms every day. The world seems both smaller and more conflict ridden.

Where does that leave Western civilization? Globalization of all markets and cultures is taking place under pervasive Western methodologies of investment and profit. Superficially, Western culture is everywhere, in the commercial products of food, drink, and clothing, in the machines that make life easier and regulated, in the entertainment of music, games, and visual images. Those countries where Western civilization runs deepest are those whose populations largely descend from western Europe: in North America, both Canada and the United States, and in the South Pacific, Australia and New Zealand. The states of Latin America through the Caribbean, Central America, and South America are all Western, although with large doses of Native American and some African influences. Substantially westernized countries are also in Eastern Europe, including Russia. In the Middle East, Israel is largely Western. Oil riches have brought Western concepts to many other Muslim countries, provoking the hostility behind much modern Islamist terrorism. On the African Continent, South Africa with its British and Afrikaaner minority is most thoroughly westernized. Most other African nations bear the scars and retain some of the benefits of Western colonialism while trying to adapt to a global economy run on Western principles. Japan has become largely a Western nation. Even China has Western capitalist policies, while its current political system originated in Western socialist concepts. In the rest of the world, all former colonial areas of the West, the depth of Western penetration varies. Some nations have strong elements of rejection, while others are eagerly trying to assimilate.

What does it mean to be Western? Take your choice: science or supernaturalism, democracy or dictatorship, socialism or self-interest, class consciousness or ethnic identification, virtuosity or vulgarity, religiosity or rationality. All are rooted in our tradition, and all have flaws, at least according to those who choose one over the other. Perhaps the most significant Western value is ambiguity.

I once found a graffito written on a desk in a classroom where I taught history: "If history is so important, how come it is gone?" The writer, while clever, obviously did not understand the point of studying history. It isn't gone. History is all around us. And not just in dusty museums, crumbling monuments, or misty memories of old-timers. Could you understand your own self without remembering your childhood? The past is in the baggage of our minds, in the frameworks of our institutions, in the complexity of our problems. We cannot escape history. We may ignore it only at our peril, since it frames all events around us. Our common heritage has shaped the institutions and structures within which we live. Every significant event instantly becomes history the moment it is over.

Because of Western developments, more people have more choices to affect their politics, economics, and culture than ever before in history. The ability to choose is, of course, limited by one's position in society. The rich usually have more options than the middle class and the poor. Likewise, legitimate authorities (through law enforcement and war) as well as extralegal organized groups (through crime and terrorism) have the ability to restrict choices of disconnected individuals. Nevertheless, many of us have some freedom to decide our own future.

Our future depends on the choices we make today. Those people who made decisions in the past changed the course of events to restrict our choices. All kinds of people have appeared in the past of the West, whether forward looking or backward leaning, tolerant or closed-minded, humanist or pragmatic, cruel or kind, tyrannical or populist. This diversity allows almost anyone to claim to be defending tradition, whether proposing an innovation or clinging to preservation.

You should understand what you believe, whether inherited from family and society or freely accepted as your own. You should then act according to your beliefs within our global society. This book offers one path to understanding the world's Western heritage. You can learn more on your own or with the help of scholars and teachers, be satisfied with what has been offered here, or forget it all.

You can benefit or not from historical examples of wisdom, stupidity, greatness, and failure. It is ultimately up to you. Choose wisely.

Review: *How should one shape one's own worldview by picking and choosing from the key legacies of Western civilization?*

Response:

Timelines

Note: The timelines present key names, events, ideas, institutions, and inventions in chronological order, roughly according to their first appearance in history. Numbers along each side of the timelines indicate time segments and the name of the general historical period; older dates are at the top, more recent toward the bottom. Additionally, terms placed within the white and shaded boxes between the horizontal lines are in approximate chronological order. The six vertical columns spread across each timeline divide data according to categories explained in chapter 1. In the POLITICS column, information from similar geographic areas tends to be grouped together within the cells, aligned left, center, or right. For example, in timeline C, most of the POLITICS terms aligned at the left all relate to Great Britain. Terms given in all capital letters are states or nations when they first appear, important wars, and regimes. Although some terms in the CULTURE column are not explained in the text, key works, genres, artists, and writers through history are listed to provide context. Book titles are italicized.

Timeline A. The Ancient Middle East and West before 500 B.C.

	SCIENCE & TECHNOLOGY	ECONOMY	POLITICS
Prehistory			
	Paleolithic Age clothing tools	hunter-gatherers	*Homo sapiens*
30,000 Y.A.			
	Neolithic Age	trade/commerce slavery	
7000 B.C.			
	animal domestication agriculture copper Bronze Age	Neolithic Agricultural Revolution property	villages, towns, cities Mesopotamian city states war absolutism monarchy kings kingdoms MIDDLE-EASTERN CIVILIZATIONS Sumerians
2900 B.C.	writing		Egypt
	mathematics astronomy	taxes	pharaohs
	calendar		dynasty
2600 B.C.			
2300 B.C.			empires
2000 B.C.			
			Hebrews
			Middle Kingdom of Egypt Amorites/Babylonians
1700 B.C.			
			New Kingdom of Egypt
1400 B.C.			
			Hatshepsut
			Ahkenaton Exodus "Dark Age"
1100 B.C.	alphabet		Phoenicians Israel & Judea
	Iron Age		colonialism
		money	
800 B.C.			*polis/poleis* Greek Archaic Age Rome
	hoplites-phalanx *thetes*-trireme		ASSYRIAN EMPIRE militarism
			Babylonian Captivity of the Hebrews PERSIAN EMPIRE
500 B.C.			

Ancient History

SOCIAL STRUCTURES	CULTURE	PHILOSOPHY & RELIGION	
nomadic tribes community family	language painting sculpture	animism	
			— 30,000 Y.A.
			— 7000 B.C.
civilization division of labor upper, urban, lower classes sexism	architecture	 polytheism syncretism	
			— 2900 B.C.
aristocrats artisans peasants	 school	priests priestesses fertility rituals	
			— 2600 B.C.
	epic poetry *Gilgamesh*		
			— 2300 B.C.
			— 2000 B.C.
 Law Code of Hammurabi		Judaism Monotheism	
			— 1700 B.C.
			— 1400 B.C.
	Book of the Dead	Moses' covenant Ten Commandments	
			— 1100 B.C.
		oracles anthropomorphism Greek civic cults	
			— 800 B.C.
	Homer, *Illiad*, *Odyssey* Olympic Games		
			— 500 B.C.

Prehistory

Ancient History

Timeline B. The Ancient Middle East and West, 550 B.C. to A.D. 530

	SCIENCE & TECHNOLOGY	ECONOMY	POLITICS
	hoplites-phalanx *thetes*-trireme	land reform	aristocracy- -oligarchy- -tyranny- -democracy *polis* citizenship
			Athenian democracy ostracism ROMAN REPUBLIC
500 B.C.			
	rationalism		PERSIAN WARS Senate, consuls Delian League, Athenian Empire
			PELOPONNESIAN WARS demagogues
400 B.C.			
	Aristotle		Gauls/Celts sack Rome tribunes
	dialectic logic		Philip II of Macedon proscription Alexander III "the Great" ROMAN EMPIRE
300 B.C.	Roman legion Roman roads		Hellenistic kingdoms
200 B.C.			PUNIC WARS
		latifundia	Hannibal ROMAN CIVIL WARS Tiberius & Gaius Gracchus
100 B.C.	Julian calendar		Julius Caesar
B.C.			Antony & Cleopatra
A.D.			PRINCIPATE
			Octavian "Augustus" Caesar *princeps, imperator*, Praetorian Guard
			Pax Romana Goths/Germans natural law, lawyers
A.D.100	geocentric and heliocentric theories		Five Good Emperors adoption and designation
A.D.200		wage/price freeze	DOMINATE Diocletian
A.D.300			Constantine I "the Great"
			Huns Germanic barbarian migrations
A.D.400			Franks, Merovingians Second Sack of Rome
			Anglo-Saxons
			Fall of the Roman Empire in the West
A.D.500			Justinian Byzantine Empire

Classical/Ancient History

SOCIAL STRUCTURES	CULTURE	PHILOSOPHY & RELIGION
GREEK CLASSICAL AGE		
	lyric poetry	
patricians & plebians	Greek Golden Age theater history Parthenon	mystery religious cults philosophy Sophists
		humanism
	Lysistrata Oedipus	Socrates
	Hellenistic Age	Plato idealism Aristotle Jews
Alexandria		Diaspora anti-Semitism
cosmopolitan		Epicurianism stoicism
		rabbis
proletariat		
optimates vs *populares*		
	Gallic Wars Vergil, *Aeneid*	Hebrew scriptures (Old Testament) deification
		Yeshua of Nazareth Christianity martyrs
		Paul of Tarsus gospels councils apostolic succession
		clergy mass saints apologists sacraments excommunication
Constantinople		Edict of Milan Council of Nicaea
		Christian Bible (New Testament) orthodoxy heresy
		Augustine of Hippo *City of God*
		monasticism regular clergy
Justinian's Law Code		

Timeline scale (right axis, Classical/Ancient History):
500 B.C.
400 B.C.
300 B.C.
200 B.C.
100 B.C.
B.C.
A.D.
A.D.100
A.D.200
A.D.300
A.D.400
A.D.500

Timeline C. The Medieval West, 500–1640

Period	Year	SCIENCE & TECHNOLOGY	ECONOMY	POLITICS
Early Middle / Dark Ages				Franks, Merovingians / Clovis Justinian
	600			Justinian's Law Code
			manorial economics	"Do-nothing kings" / Anglo-Saxon kingdoms
	700			CAROLINGIAN EMPIRE
		stirrups		mayors of the palace / Pippin "the Short"
	800		three-field planting	Charlemagne
		horse collars		Vikings, Magyars, Moslems / Alfred "the Great"
				ENGLAND FRANCE GERMANY
				FEUDAL POLITICS
	900	castles		SCOTLAND Otto I "the Great"
		knights		HOLY ROMAN EMPIRE
	1000	reconquest of Toledo		HUNGARY DENMARK NORWAY SWEDEN
High Middle Ages		Arab science in West	Domesday Book	William "the Conqueror"
			commune	Crusades Henry IV
	1100		revival of towns & trade / industrialization	Concordat of Worms
		windmills	putting out/cottage guilds	Henry II PORTUGAL
			master, journeyman, apprentice	Philip II "Augustus"
	1200			John Teutonic knights / Magna Carta
		Scholasticism		
	1300			Parliament Philip IV "the Fair"
		mini ice age begins / pikes		Estates-General / OTTOMAN EMPIRE
		gunpowder, firearms / cannons	COMMERCIAL REVOLUTION	SWITZERLAND / Hundred Years War
	1400		capitalism	Joan of Arc
				Peace of Lodi
		printing press	public debt	AUSTRIA
				Habsburg dynasty Ferdinand & Isabella
		Columbus / Vasco da Gama		SPAIN
				Western European colonial imperialism
Later Middle Ages	1500		Atlantic/African slave trade	Henry VIII Charles V / DUTCH NETHERLANDS
			bourse, stock exchange	
			mercantilism	Elizabeth I St. Bart's Massacre Philip II
				Spanish Armada
	1600			Wars of Religion / Henry IV
				Thirty Years War
				English Civil War Peace of Westphalia

SOCIAL STRUCTURES	CULTURE	PHILOSOPHY & RELIGION	
clan, kin, tribe, people, folk		monasticism Benedictine Rule	
free-unfree	Gregorian chant	caesaro-papism	600
personal justice vendetta/feud	Latin literature	Pope Gregory I Islam: Mohammed Qu'ran	
trial by ordeal customary law			700
	Carolingian Renaissance	Frankish-Papal Alliance Iconoclastic Controversy	800
	minuscule seven liberal arts		
seigneur & serf feudal society	Romanesque art		900
		Cluniac Reform	
	Gothic art	Peace & Truce of God	1000
nobility chivalry courtesy	tournaments rise of vernacular *Chanson de Roland*	"Great Schism" Eastern Orthodox Gregorian Reform Pope Gregory VII Investiture Struggle	
	universities	Crusades ——— 1100 Cistercian Reform canon law	1100
burghers, bourgeois patrician, artisan, common	Romance Goliards	Peter Abelard Thomas Becket	
	colleges	Cathars, dualism Mendicants Francis of Assisi Inquisition Thomas Aquinas	1200
			1300
BLACK DEATH peasant revolts	Dante, *Divine Comedy* Chaucer Christine de Pizan	Pope Boniface VIII "Babylonian Captivity" "Great Western Schism"	1400
	RENAISSANCE textual criticism	mysticism witch hunts	
	humanism	Christian humanism Erasmus	
	Leonardo, Raphael	Spanish Inquisition	1500
	Machiavelli, *The Prince* Michelangelo	REFORMATION Martin Luther Jean Calvin	
	Shakespeare	Anabaptists English Reformation	1600
		Counter-Reformation Council of Trent	
		Loyola, Jesuits Inquisition, *Index*	

Early Middle / Dark Ages

High Middle Ages

Later Middle Ages

Timeline D. Early Modern West, 1540–1914

	SCIENCE & TECHNOLOGY	ECONOMY	POLITICS
Renaissance & Reformation	Copernicus		Wars of Religion
	heliocentric theory astronomy SCIENTIFIC	COMMERCIAL REVOLUTION	RUSSIA
	REVOLUTION		Elizabeth I DUTCH NETHERLANDS Philip II
	Gregorian calendar	mercantilism	REPUBLICANISM divine right CONSTITUTIONALISM ABSOLUTISM
1600		joint-stock company	DUTCH REPUBLIC Henry IV "of Navarre"
	scientific method		GREAT BRITAIN Thirty Years War
	empiricism		Cardinal Richelieu
	Galileo physics		English Civil War Cromwell Peace of Westphalia sovereign nation-state balance of power
	scientific academies	Scientific Agricultural Revolution	PRUSSIA Louis XIV "the Sun King"
	Newton		Glorious Revolution ancien régime Peter I "the Great"
1700	mini ice age ends		cabinet, prime minister
			British Empire enlightened despotism
Early Modern Europe	spinning jenny		Frederick II "the Great" War of Austrian Succession Maria Theresa
	canals	INDUSTRIAL REVOLUTION mill/factory system laissez-faire	Seven Years War American Revolution partitions of POLAND USA federalism, president
	steam engine encyclopedia	Adam Smith classical liberal economics	Louis XVI FRENCH REVOLUTION National Assembly, Bastille, Reign of Terror, Thermidor Wars of the Coalitions
1800			Napoleon Bonaparte guerrilla warfare Battle of Waterloo Metternich Congress of Vienna
		"iron law of wages"	liberalism nationalism conservatism
	railways	Luddites utopian socialism	Monroe Doctrine LATIN AMERICAN STATES
	geology uniformitarianism		British reform bills GREECE Afrikaaners
Nineteenth Century	evolution	consumerism	neo-imperialism Rev of 1830
		corporations	US-Indian removals BELGIUM
	indoor plumbing		Mexico-US War Opium Wars Rev of 1848
	biology	Marxism	Napoleon III Crimean War
	Darwin natural selection	trade/labor unions	Sepoy Mutiny American Civil War Meiji Restoration ITALY Risorgemento Cavour Garibaldi
			Paris Commune Bismark 2nd GERMAN EMPIRE Third Republic
		social democracy	SERBIA, BULGARIA, RUMANIA
		neo-mercantilism	terrorism anarchism
	oil chemicals electricity		US-Plains Indian Wars
	Pasteur, germ theory	state socialism	Dollar Diplomacy pan-slavism yugo-slavism
	internal combustion engine	Christian socialism	Hawaii partition of Africa
			Spanish American War Zionism
1900	automobile airplane atomic theory Freud	cartels, trusts	Boer War SOUTH AFRICA Boxer Rebellion
			Balkan Wars Franz Ferdinand

SOCIAL STRUCTURES	CULTURE	PHILOSOPHY & RELIGION		
		Roman Catholicism		Renaissance & Reformation
estates clergy		Counter-Reformation Council of Trent		
nobility common-peasant	Shakespeare BAROQUE	Wars of Religion	1600	
	orchestra, opera Rembrandt Rubens			
westernization	Rococo art			
	ENLIGHTENMENT *philosophes*		1700	
	novels Bach	humanitarianism skepticism Pietism		Early Modern Europe
		deism agnosticism atheism progress Great Awakening		
	Neoclassicism newspapers			
Wollstonecraft male suffrage *Declaration of the Rights of Man and the Citizen*	Rousseau Voltaire Mozart symphony ROMANTICISM		1800	
upper/middle/lower classes urbanization	Beethoven Mill			
		materialism		Nineteenth Century
police public sanitation	Goethe, *Faust* Turner REALISM			
"family values"	Dickens			
		"higher criticism" Social Darwinism		
	naturalism Richard Wagner impressionism	Christian fundamentalism		
social sciences sociology anthropology	Monet, Rodin, Van Gogh	Christian modernism	1900	
concentration camps		Pope Leo XIII		

Timeline E. The Twentieth Century, 1900–present

SCIENCE & TECHNOLOGY	ECONOMY	POLITICS
telegraph, telephone	neo-mercantilism laissez-faire socialism	neo-imperialism conservative, liberal, socialist political parties
Freud's subconscious	consumer economy trade unions	
auto		terrorism militarism Zionism
airplane	"robber barons" trusts	"open door" policy, Boxer Rebellion Theodore Roosevelt
atomic theory Einstein's relativity	cartels	alliance system
plastic	department stores	progressivism
gas warfare		Balkan crises ALBANIA
U-boats tanks	"war socialism"	WORLD WAR I genocide Russian Revolution USSR Wafd
bombers/fighters		CZECHO-SLOVAKIA ESTONIA LATVIA LITHUANIA HUNGARY AUSTRIA FINLAND
influenza pandemic		KINGDOM OF SERBS, CROATS, and SLOVENES
radio	era of big business USSR: NEP USSR: 5-year plans	IRELAND totalitarianism, authoritarianism League of Nations TURKEY "Red scare" "Yellow Peril"
air conditioning		
Heisenberg's Principle	collectivization	Mussolini fascism Jiang, KMT Mao Zedong
	Wall Street Crash	Stalinism YUGOSLAVIA
	Great Depression	Hitler Naziism FDR
radar	New Deal Keynesian Economics	Spanish Civil War Munich Conference Atlantic Charter WORLD WAR II
jet computer		Blitzkrieg Pearl Harbor United Nations
atomic bomb nuclear bomb	Great Leap Forward	Peron Israel Berlin Blockade apartheid Maoism Nehru COLD WAR
television	baby boomers	NATO CYPRUS McCarthyism Korean Police Action Warsaw Pact
Sputnik space flight Space Race		Treaty of Rome Suez Crisis EEC
ICBMs	shopping malls	Castro decolonization
laser transistor		Kennedy Berlin Wall Congo Crisis Cuban Missile Crisis Johnson race riots Vietnam War
moon landing	German & Japanese economic "miracles"	Northern Ireland troubles Six-Day War PLO
Earth Day	OPEC oil embargo	Nixon Allende détente Helsinki Accords Greens
pocket calculators	G7	Sandinistas Solidarity Iranian Revolution
Three Mile Island personal computer Chernobyl	Reaganomics	Reagan Thatcher Iran-Iraq War Falklands War Gorbachev glasnost End of the COLD WAR
	global debt	
Internet cell phones	globalization	SLOVENIA, CROATIA, BELARUS, UKRAINE, BOSNIA, MACEDONIA MOLDAVIA First Persian Gulf War
	G8	European Union Mandela Chinese Capitalist Revolution
global climate change debate	global recession	9/11 invasion of Afghanistan and Iraq MONTENEGRO, SERBIA, KOSOVO

(Left axis: Twentieth Century; year markers: 1900, 1910, 1920, 1930, 1940, 1950, 1960, 1970, 1980, 1990, 2000)

SOCIAL STRUCTURES	CULTURE	PHILOSOPHY & RELIGION	
industrialization urbanization	advertising	Christian fundamentalism	
	fin de siècle	Christian modernism	1900
suffragettes	ragtime realism, naturalism		
	primitivism cubism expressionism		1910
	abstract art movies		
Ku Klux Klan race riots	dada		
aristocracy depoliticized women's suffrage	Jazz Age sports Roaring Twenties	"Lost Generation" "monkey" trial	1920
Prohibition Lindbergh	surrealism	mass evangelists	
gulags	International School socialist realism Picasso	Gandhi	1930
	abstract expressionism	Holocaust	1940
welfare state	pop art	existentialism	
	television		1950
suburbanization desegregation civil rights movement	"Coca-colanization" rock'n'roll	Islamic fundamentalism	
sexual revolution 1968 student protests	The Beatles op art	Vatican II Martin Luther King, Jr.	1960
women's liberation abortion debate NGOs	rock concerts video games	drug culture cults televangelists	1970
AIDS	music videos	The "Religious Right" Pope John Paul II	1980
ethnic cleansing	postmoderns		1990
homosexual rights			
			2000

Twentieth Century

Common Abbreviations

A.D.   anno Domini, in the Year of the Lord (some historians instead use C.E.,
        Common Era)
b.   born
B.C.   Before Christ (some historians instead use B.C.E., Before the Common Era)
ca.   circa, around or about
cent.   century
d.   died
fl.   flourished
r.   ruled

Glossary

The terms below cover many of the important ideas that Western civilization has either developed on its own, borrowed from others, or interacted with. The terms often end in *-ism* or *-ation*. Some of these ideas have been discredited by dominant attitudes of political institutions, social pressures, intellectual fashions, or religious organizations. Still, all of these diverse ideas, many of which contradict one another, are options to be adopted and practiced.

absolutism: The idea and practice that one person should dominate in authority and decision making within a state. Historians and political theorists most often apply the term to European monarchs of the seventeenth and eighteenth centuries A.D., although the concept does apply to all ages.

agnosticism: The belief that the existence of God or of any supernatural beings is impossible to prove.

American exceptionalism: A point of view that sees Americans as different from their fellow westerners or other peoples, usually as being more virtuous or free. The source of this alleged virtue ranges from a special relationship with God to a unique genius of the Founding Fathers. *See* **Western exceptionalism.**

Anabaptism: A religious belief that rejects infant baptism, an idea that united diverse groups of Christians during the Reformation. *See* **Christianity**; **Protestantism**.

anarchism: A political idea that calls for the destruction of industrialized and bureaucratized societies so that a utopian agricultural society can appear. *See* **terrorism**.

Anglicanism: A branch of Christians formed during the Reformation, first organized as the Church of England, which defines itself as a middle path between Protestantism and Roman Catholicism. British imperialism planted numerous Anglican churches around the world, now loosely connected to one another as the Anglican Communion.

animism: The religious belief that nature is alive with spirits and ghosts that affect our natural world. Animism was probably the first religion, and many remaining hunter-gatherers practice some form of it.

anthropomorphism: The idea that gods and deities look and act like human beings. Much of ancient Greek and Roman art was based on this concept.

anti-intellectualism: The criticism of the thoughts and opinions of educated elites as less useful than those of the "common" uneducated masses.

anti-Semitism: A euphemism for the hatred of Jews. *See* **Judaism**; **racism**.

apostolic poverty: The belief that it is virtuous for Christians to live like the poor, since Jesus and his followers did so. The height of its influence was in the Middle Ages with the Waldensians and Francis of Assisi's monasticism of the mendicants.

apostolic succession: The belief in some parts of Christianity that the true Church requires its leaders (bishops and priests) to be ordained in a direct line from Jesus and his apostles.

arabization: The process of making people conform to Arabic culture, especially Islam and its associated traditions.

Arianism: A religious belief in the third century A.D. that distinguished the human nature of Jesus from the divine. Most parts of Christianity officially defined Arianism as a heresy.

aristocracy: The idea and practice that some people are born to a higher status than others and therefore should rule society.

assassination: The political practice of murdering leaders in order to force change.

atheism: The belief that denies the existence of the supernatural. *See* **supernaturalism**.

atomic theory: The scientific idea that the smallest indivisible part of a unique substance is an atom (Greek for "not able to cut"). Ancient Greek philosophers first suggested the idea, which was scientifically verified in the late nineteenth and early twentieth century.

authoritarianism: The modern political practice of a dictatorship, where a ruler and his party significantly control mass communication and bureaucracy while maintaining order through secret police, paramilitary, and military groups. *See* **totalitarianism**.

balance of power: An idea most popular between 1648 and 1945 that the nations of Europe should league together against any state that tried to dominate the Continent.

balkanization: The practice of carving up larger empires into smaller states, as done after World War I in eastern Europe. Often it is used in a negative sense.

baptism: The religious idea in Christianity that a ritual with water binds one to that belief system.

barbarian: (1) A term used by civilized urban peoples to describe other peoples who are not civilized (living in pastoral or hunter-gatherer economies); (2) a term used by one people to insult another as unjustifiably cruel, regardless of either's level of socioeconomic development.

Bolshevism: The name for the communist movement in early twentieth-century Russia led by Lenin. *See* **communism**; **Leninism**.

bureaucracy: The practice of governing by means of written records and offices that issue, administer, and store them.

caesaro-papism: The practice of the medieval Eastern Roman or Byzantine emperors of helping to organize and supervise the hierarchy and belief system of the Christian Church in their empire. *See* **Orthdox Christianity**.

Calvinism: The belief system held by churches formed during the Reformation that followed the theology of Jean Calvin. Predestination, the belief that God has already chosen who is saved or damned, is its most distinctive doctrine. *See* **Protestantism**.

capitalism: In its simplest form, the practice of reinvesting profits. As part of our modern ideological conflicts, the term often refers to private ownership of the means of production using free markets, as opposed to communism, where the government carries out central planning of the economy. *See* **Marxism**.

catastrophism, theory of: A scientific idea that explains geology or the history and structures of the earth according to rare and unusual events of enormous power, resembling divine intervention. *See* **uniformitarianism, theory of**.

Catharism: The medieval religion that mixed Christianity and dualism and was therefore identified by the Christian Church as a heresy.

Christian socialism: A socialist idea adopted by Christians, especially Roman Catholics, using religious ideology as a basis to improve conditions for workers while still respecting the private property rights of capitalists.

Christianity: The monotheistic religion that asserts that God became incarnate as his son, Jesus of Nazareth. The Romans executed Jesus, but as the Messiah, or Christ, he returned from the dead to offer salvation, or entrance into heaven for his followers. Since the first century, Christians have divided into many groups: a few who did not define Jesus as fully God and human, as well as the vast majority who have. *See* **Anglicanism**; **Calvinism**; **Christianity**; **Lutheranism**; **Orthodox Pietism**; **Roman Catholicism**; **schism**.

civilization: The practice of people living in cities, which supported rich political, social, and cultural lifestyles that could spread over vast territories and many peoples. Distinct governments, social structures, art and literature, and belief systems indicate differences among civilizations.

classical liberal economics, theory of: Also called *laissez-faire*, the idea that the least interference by government provides the best opportunities for economic growth. It was developed in the eighteenth century in opposition to mercantilism.

collectivization: The practice of Stalin during the 1930s, where the state confiscated land from peasants and consolidated the large tracts into communal farms. Communists in other states, such as China and Cambodia/Kampuchea, later undertook similar policies. *See* **Marxism**; **Stalinism**.

colonialism: The action of one state sending out some of its people to settle in another place. A colony may or may not retain close connections with the homeland.

communism: The idea proposed by Karl Marx in the nineteenth century of a perfect society where the means of production would be shared by all. *See* **Leninism**; **Stalinism**.

conciliarism: The idea and practice that Church councils should be the ultimate authority in resolving conflicts among Christians.

conservatism: A political direction, developed into parties during the nineteenth century, that stands for resisting change in order to preserve political, social, and cultural advantages of the elites. Today conservatism often calls for reducing the role of government in the economy.

constitutionalism: The political idea that law limits a government's powers, whether formally written in an explicit document or by the precedent of tradition.

constitutional monarchy: The practice of having a democratically structured government while keeping a royal dynasty as a stabilizing force. *See* **parliamentarianism**; **republicanism**.

cynicism: A philosophy originating among the ancient Greeks advocating the rejection of common social rules and human comforts. Today it often describes a pessimism about people's intentions.

deification: The belief that a human being, usually a powerful leader, can become a god.

deism: The religious belief that God is the creator of the universe, although it deemphasizes the Christian dogma of Jesus' incarnation.

democracy: The political idea and practice that the best form of government involves the largest possible number of citizens making decisions. A democrat is not necessarily to be confused with a member of the modern American political party. *See* **parliamentarianism**; **republicanism**.

democratic socialism: Also called social democracy, the effort of revisionists of Marxism to work through the political process instead of through a proletarian revolution. The various modern labor and social democratic political parties were the result.

denazification: The policy after World War II to purge members of the Nazi Party from leadership positions in occupied Germany.

determinism: A philosophy that asserts humans have very little free will in deciding their fate. *See* **Calvinism**.

dialectical materialism: The theoretical model of history suggested by Karl Marx, where a dominant class conflicts with an exploited class. *See* **Marxism**.

diversity: The term used in this text to describe the creative impulse as a force in history. New ideas and groupings of people create change.

divine right: The political idea that God has placed kings in power as part of his divine order.

dualism: A religious philosophy that sees the universe as divided between two powerful beings, one a good force inspired by spirit and ideas, the other an evil influence based on matter and flesh. *See* **Catharism**; **Gnosticism**; **Zoroastrianism**.

ecumenism: The effort by religions, usually those of Christianity, to tolerate one another, work together, and perhaps unify. It was most influential in the mid-twentieth century.

egalitarianism: The idea that the best society tries to equalize the wealth, influence, and opportunities of all its citizens. It is exemplified by ancient Sparta and much Marxist ideology.

empiricism: The idea that observations by our senses are both accurate and reasonable. It is the starting point of scientific knowledge. *See* **rationalism**; **science**.

enlightened despotism: The political idea and practice that asserted that one person, usually a dynastic monarch, should rule, since unity encouraged simplicity and efficiency.

environmentalism: The idea and practice since the 1960s of reducing human interference with and damage upon the natural world.

Epicureanism: A philosophy that suggests that the best way of life is to avoid pain. The good life lay in withdrawal into a pleasant garden to discuss the meaning of life with friends. Epicureanism originated among the Hellenistic Greeks and was popularized by the Romans.

evolution: The observed scientific phenomenon about the increasing diversity and complexity of life on earth from millions of years ago to the present. Darwin's theory of natural selection is the framework under which most scientists today understand the process of evolution.

excommunication: The practice of various Christian churches of disciplining members by shunning them from society and cutting them off from sacraments.

factionalism: The practice of refusing to cooperate with opposing political and social groups.

fascism: A political ideology, most popular in the 1920s and 1930s, where an extreme nationalist dictatorship seemed the best form of government. Fascist authoritarian and totalitarian regimes offered alternatives to socialism, communism, and parliamentary democracy. Many capitalists were able to accept fascist regimes, since fascism's concept of the corporate state still allowed some private property and profit.

federalism: the political practice in republics of separating governmental power within a country, where a strong central administration competes and shares power with provincial or state and local governments. It contrasts with a confederate system, where the central administration is weaker than the local governments.

feminism: The idea that women are not inferior to men, but rather should have equal access to education, political participation, and economic independence. Today it is often mischaracterized as hostility or sexism against men. *See* **Women's Liberation**.

feudal politics: The system where knights bound one another together by oaths and rituals to rule society after A.D. 1000; use instead of *feudalism*, a term to be avoided because of its many confusing meanings.

fundamentalism: A belief that values traditional, often preindustrial customs and attitudes, especially regarding religion. Fundamentalists reject modern ways of knowing based on the skepticism of literary criticism and the scientific and historical methods. In Christianity, it includes those who support an allegedly literal interpretation of the Bible, rather than an interpretation through higher criticism.

germanization: The policy of making people conform to German culture. Used by some princes in the Holy Roman Empire, bureaucrats in the Second German Empire, and the Nazis of the Third Reich.

germ theory of disease: The scientific theory, argued by Pasteur in the nineteenth century, that microscopic organisms, such as bacteria and viruses, cause many illnesses. While very successful as a means to understand illness, it does not, however, explain all disease.

globalization: The recent practice of the world's economies being tied more closely together, often bypassing the interests of nations, regions, and localities.

Gnosticism: The ancient philosophy or religion that drew on dualism and argued that its followers held secret knowledge about the meaning of life. Gnostics tried to influence early Christianity.

heathenism: A religion of polytheism. It was once a term of insult in late Rome applied to poor peasants who were ignorant of Christianity; since the Early Middle Ages it has meant any non-Christian in or outside Christendom.

Hedonism: A philosophy originating among the ancient Greeks that suggested success came to those who pursued pleasure as the highest good.

hellenization: The policy of making people under Greek authority conform to Greek institutions and culture. Practiced especially by the Greek rulers of the Hellenistic Age, after the death of Alexander "the Great."

heresy: Literally, a "choice" or a "sect," the term with which winners in a cultural debate label the ideas of the losers. *See* **orthodoxy**.

higher criticism: The practice of applying modern scholarly techniques to examining the Bible. *See* **textual criticism**.

history: The idea that the past is a product of human activity that needs to be interpreted. Since the eighteenth century, the historical method practiced by academics has been the most reliable way to produce objective and accurate versions of the past.

humanism: The philosophy begun by the ancient Greeks that the world is to be understood by and for humans.

humanitarianism: The idea that humans ought to treat one another well. It is often incorporated in Christianity and was pushed by intellectuals of the Enlightenment.

idealism: Also known as the doctrine of ideas, a philosophical explanation of reality that proposed that particular things in the observable world are reflections of universal truths. It is famously formulated by Plato in his "Allegory of the Cave."

imperialism: The practice of taking over different peoples in other countries and communities in order to build an empire. Empires surpass kingdoms or nations in the diversity of their subject peoples.

individualism: The idea that political and social policies should favor opportunities for single human beings over those in collectives or groups. *See* **collectivization**.

intellectualism: The idea that educated elites should be privileged.

Islam: The religion begun by Mohammed in Arabia. Muslims believe that the one, true God has established a special relationship to those who submit to his will, as explained in the Qu'ran.

islamicization: The policy of making people conform to Islam and live as Muslims.

Judaism: The religion begun by the ancient Hebrews. Jews believe that the one, true God has established a special relationship with them, as revealed in their sacred scriptures (called by Christians the Old Testament). *See* **anti-Semitism**.

Keynsian economic theory: The economic theory that massive government spending can rescue a nation's economy from a depression. It is named after its creator, twentieth-century British economist John Maynard Keynes.

Leninism: The ideological and political program put in place by Lenin through the Russian Revolution. He established a dictatorship enforced by secret police, had the state take over substantial portions of the economy (a policy called war communism), and carried out land reform.

lesbianism: The practice of women being sexually attracted to and involved with other women. The term comes from the island where Sappho, the ancient Greek poet, had her school (although she herself was not strictly lesbian). *See* **sapphism**.

liberalism: A political direction that developed into parties during the nineteenth century. It generally stands for changing laws in order to broaden political, social, and cultural opportunities for the middle classes. Today liberalism often calls for accepting a role of government in the economy.

liberation theology: A religious idea in Latin America of the twentieth century that called for Christianity to look after the poor in this world and not merely preach about salvation for the next.

Lutheranism: The version of Christianity that originated with Martin Luther during the Reformation.

manorial economics: The economic system in which serfs worked the lands of their seigneurial lords in exchange for the use of farmland for themselves; use instead of *manorialism*, a term to be avoided.

Marxism: The socialist ideology developed by Karl Marx in the mid-nineteenth century that advocated a proletarian revolution to overthrow bourgeois capitalist society. Marx called it "scientific socialism" because of its alleged empirical support. Since then Marxism has been used as a synonym for communism. *See* **Bolshevism**; **Leninism**; **socialism**; **Stalinism**.

materialism: The idea that the physical goods and pleasures in this observable world should take priority over any possible spiritual virtues or destinies.

McCarthyism: A belief usually characterized as a paranoid and unfair attempt to persecute innocent people for their allegedly dangerous political views. It is named after a U.S. senator who during the 1950s wanted to purge alleged communists from the government, politics, and the media.

mercantilism, economic theory of: The idea that government intervention provides the best opportunities for economic growth, especially in establishing monopolies and a favorable balance of trade. It was developed in the sixteenth century in order to manage early capitalism.

militarism: The idea and practice that virtues such as discipline, obedience, courage, and willingness to kill for the state are the highest values a civilized society can hold. It is exemplified by the ancient Assyrians, the Spartans, and the Prussians.

modernism: A belief that accepts changes wrought by the Enlightenment and the Commercial and Industrial Revolutions toward a more secular and materialistic society. In Christianity, it includes those who support interpretation of scripture through higher criticism.

monasticism: A religious way of life in which people live in a cloistered setting under strict rules, usually involving renunciation of property, physical pleasure, and freedom of choice.

monotheism: The religious belief that only one God exists and should be worshipped.

multiculturalism: The idea that knowledge of and appreciation for diverse ways of life is beneficial for society.

nationalism: The political idea that asserts that states should be organized exclusively around ethnic unities.

naturalism: (1) The movement in classical sculpture and art since the Renaissance to portray objects exactly as they appear in nature, rather than with an abstract interpretation; (2) the movement in literature since the late nineteenth century to focus on suffering caused by modern society. *See* **realism**.

natural selection, theory of: Also called "survival of the fittest," Darwin's explanation for how evolution took place. The theory proposes that the struggle of creatures for food and reproduction encouraged change as living things adapted to their environment, competed with other living things, and then passed on useful characteristics to offspring.

Naziism or **national socialism**: The uniquely German version of fascism. Formulated by Adolf Hitler and brought into action during the Third Reich (1933–1945), it fulfilled many Germans' need for nationalistic pride. Its extreme germanization, however, aimed for the Nazi domination of Eurasia and the enslavement or extermination of non-German peoples, especially Jews.

neo-imperialism: The political practice of Western industrialized states that built up overseas colonial empires between 1830 and 1914.

neo-mercantilism, theory of: The economic idea in Western industrialized states between 1830 and 1914 that combined neo-imperialism abroad with laissez-faire practices at home. *See* **mercantilism, economic theory of**.

nominalism: The medieval philosophy that proposed that only particular material things in the observable world exist, while collective ideas and categories are mere "names" created by the human mind. *See* **idealism**.

objectivity: The attempt to remain neutral or interpret disagreements from an unbiased point of view.

oligarchy: The political idea that states are best run by the economic and social elites.

Orthodox Christianity: The version of Christianity originally centered in the Byzantine Empire. It became unique after the schism with Catholic Christianity in 1054.

orthodoxy: Literally, the "right teaching," it is the label adopted by groups whose ideas win a cultural debate. *See* **heresy**.

ostracism: The political practice in ancient Athens of exiling politicians who were considered too dangerous. Today it often means a social practice of shunning. *See* **excommunication**.

pacifism: The political idea that wars are not a proper activity of states. Some Christians and Christian groups promoted the idea in Western civilization.

paganism: A religion of polytheism. It was once a term of insult in late Rome levelled at poor peasants who were ignorant of Christianity; since the Early Middle Ages it has meant any non-Christian in or outside Christendom.

pangermanism: The ideology that all German peoples should be ruled together. As a policy of Adolf Hitler and his Third Reich, it had some success in the 1930s, until Hitler showed his determination to rule non-Germans also.

panhellenism: The idea that all Greeks should be united, at least culturally.

pan-slavism: The political idea that called for all Slavs to live together in one nation-state. The Russians, as the dominant Slavic group, were most behind this movement. *See* **yugo-slavism**.

pan-turkism: A version of Turkish nationalism that sought to promote unity among diverse Turkish peoples. It often became an attitude that encouraged all peoples in the Ottoman Empire to become more like Turks.

parliamentarianism: The political idea and practice that elected representatives with limited terms are the best means of governing a state. Structurally, the person who leads the majority in the parliament, usually called a prime minister or a chancellor, is the most powerful political official in the government. *See* **constitutionalism**; **democracy**; **republicanism**.

particularism: The political and social idea that local variations in institutions and beliefs are the best way to organize the state and society. *See* **diversity**; **universalism**.

philosophy: Literally, "love of wisdom," any intellectual system that proposes explanations for the nature of the universe and the purpose of human beings. While a philosophy may or may not have a supernatural dimension, it should rely on rationalism.

Pietism: A form of Christianity that arose during the eighteenth century, especially among Lutherans, in which believers dedicated themselves to prayer and charity.

polytheism: The belief in many gods and goddesses. Divine beings usually reflected the values and needs of farming communities. *See* **heathenism**; **paganism**.

progress: The idea that people should work to improve political, social, and living conditions in this world. It has been an important Western idea since the Enlightenment.

Protestantism: Any version of Christianity that appeared after Luther's Reformation and its break from Roman Catholicism and Orthodox Christianity; the name originates with those who protested the imperial attacks upon Luther. *See* **Anglicanism**; **Calvinism**.

racism: The social and political belief that some "races" are superior to others. Racism developed as a political ideology in the nineteenth century.

rationalism: The concept that the human mind can comprehend the natural world.

realism: (1) The movement in art since the Renaissance to make paintings and sculptures portray objects as human eyes see them; (2) the movement in literature since the late nineteenth century to focus on social problems. *See* **naturalism**.

Realpolitik: The political practice of both pragmatically making compromise and using force to achieve desired ends, usually the strengthening of the state. It was most promoted by conservative nationalists in the nineteenth century.

regionalism: The political idea that people are best organized within smaller geographic areas rather than the typical large nation-state or centralized empire.

religion: From the word "to bind," a belief system that proposes a supernatural explanation for the nature of the universe and the purpose of human beings.

republicanism: The political idea and practice that elected representatives with limited terms are the best means of governing a state. Republicanism paired with constitutionalism are the foundation of most modern democratic states. In its strict form, a republic elects all significant political figures, thus excluding constitutional monarchy. A republican is not necessarily to be confused with a member of the modern American political party. *See* **democracy**; **parliamentarianism**.

Roman Catholicism: The version of Christianity that originally centered in the western portion of the ancient Roman Empire. It is characterized by being under the authority of the bishop of Rome, eventually called the pope. It defined itself as uniquely Roman after the schism from Orthodox Christianity in 1054 and with the rise of Protestantism in the sixteenth century.

romanization: The process carried out by ancient Romans of conforming their subject peoples, institutions, and attitudes to those of the Roman Empire.

Romantic Movement: The intellectual movement begun in the nineteenth century that appreciated nature, admired the Middle Ages, and emphasized emotion as a reaction against the rationalism of the Enlightenment.

sapphism: The practice of women being sexually attracted to and involved with other women. The term comes from Sappho, the ancient Greek poet (although she herself was not strictly lesbian). *See* **lesbianism**.

schism: Literally, a "rip," usually used to describe one religious group splitting away from another.

Scholasticism: The medieval philosophy "of the schools," which applied Aristotle's dialectic logic to better explain Christianity. *See* **syllogism**.

science: The idea that knowledge of nature can best be gained through rigorous experimentation and observation according to the scientific method. Scientific theories provide coherent explanations for the facts of natural phenomena. Science's many successes have made it the dominant modern methodology. *See* **empiricism**.

sexism: The belief that one sex (usually the male) is better than the other (usually the female).

skepticism: The intellectual idea of doubting everything and trusting only what can be tested through reason.

Social Darwinism: The idea of understanding human society through perspectives influenced by the debate over evolution. Social Darwinists usually rationalized the supremacy of rich European elites over the impoverished masses in the West or the rest of the world. *See* **natural selection, theory of**.

socialism: Several ideas and practices that have developed since the Industrial Revolution to address the political, social, and economic inequalities between capitalists and workers. In principle, socialism stands for helping the workers. Over time, socialist theories and systems have developed in many directions. *See* **Christian socialism**; **communism**; **democratic socialism**; **Marxism**; **state socialism**; **utopian socialism**; **war socialism**.

sovietization: The practice of the Soviet Union during the Cold War of transforming states under their influence to conform to Stalinism.

Stalinism: The developments in the early Soviet Union that both modernized state and society and created a totalitarian dictatorship based on Stalin's cult of personality. *See* **Leninism**; **Marxism**.

state socialism: The practice of conservative governments legislating practices to improve the condition of workers.

stoicism: A philosophy that calls for people to do their duty in difficult circumstances. It originated among the Hellenistic Greeks and was popularized by the Romans.

subjectivity: The inclination to take sides or interpret disagreements from a biased point of view.

subsidiarity: The political idea and practice that decisions should be made at the regional and local levels rather than by a distant national, imperial, or global authority.

suburbanization: The process of moving people to live in areas around cities that mixed traditional urban dwellings with rural landscapes. It became common in the late twentieth century with the increasing use of automobiles.

supernaturalism: The belief that another realm exists apart from the reality that can be empirically observed and sensed. Forces or beings in the supernatural realm are often believed to have influence or power within the natural world.

supremacy: A term used in this text to indicate historical change through the enforced domination of ideas or those with power.

syllogism: An element of dialectic logic as developed by the ancient Greek philosopher Aristotle, where two pieces of known information are compared in order to reach new knowledge. *See* **Scholasticism**.

syncretism: The process in which elements of an idea, philosophy, or religion are blended with those of another.

terrorism: The political idea and practice of using small-scale violence, usually against civilians, to achieve specific political ends. Large-scale violence becomes guerrilla war, rebellion, or actual war. *See* **anarchism**.

textual criticism: The intellectual tool developed during the Renaissance of comparing different versions of an author's writings in order to find the best, most accurate text. *See* **higher criticism**.

theocracy: The political idea and practice that religious leaders should rule the state.

toleration: The idea that people and society should accept other people who believe in different worldviews, philosophies, or religions.

totalitarianism: The modern political practice of a strong dictatorship, where a ruler and his party substantially control mass communication, bureaucracy, and the economy and maintain order through secret police and a strong military. *See* **authoritarianism**.

trade unionism: The practice of organizing labor unions (trade unions in Britain, syndicalism in France) to help workers. At first illegal, unions often successfully improved conditions for workers to the point that the much of the working class blended into the middle class during the twentieth century. *See* **socialism**.

tyranny: The practice of one person seizing power in a government. While today the term is used in a negative way, tyrants among the ancient Greeks often opened politics to become more egalitarian and democratic.

uniformitarianism, theory of: A scientific theory to explain the history of the earth. It states that the same (uniform) processes that are shaping the earth today have always acted to mold the planet. *See* **science**.

universalism: The attitude that the same beliefs and practices should be applied or open to everyone. *See* **particularism**; **supremacy**.

urbanization: The process of moving rural people to live in ever-larger cities, carried out after the Industrial Revolution. Today most people live in urban areas.

utopian socialism: The first version of socialism, which called on capitalists to improve conditions for workers.

vandalism: The practice of writing on or damaging property, either out of spite or to make a statement. It is unfairly named after the Vandal sack of Rome in A.D. 455.

war socialism: A common policy during World War I and World War II where governments took control of large sectors of the economy, creating a new military-industrial complex. In doing so, they often had to appease workers to prevent strikes. *See* **socialism**.

Western exceptionalism: A point of view that sees Europeans as better than peoples in Asia, Africa, or the Americas. The source of this alleged virtue ranges from the success of Western imperial colonialism, through superior moral upbringing, to divine favor.

westernization: The process of conforming non-European institutions and attitudes to those of Western civilization.

Women's Liberation: A movement in the 1960s and 1970s that promoted the rights of women to education, political participation, and economic independence. It was largely successful in Western industrialized states. *See* **feminism**.

yugo-slavism: The political idea that called for all southern (*yugo*) Slavs to live together in one nation-state. The Serbs, as the dominant group of southern Slavs, were most behind this movement.

zairianization: A political idea of Congolese nationalism, where the authoritarian ruler Mobuto in the 1960s rejected European culture and tried to readapt his country to more native African ways.

Zionism: The idea of Jewish nationalism that Jews, like any other nationality, should have their own nation-state. Zionism culminated in the modern state of Israel in 1948. Ever since, the term has sometimes been used to describe the alleged racist and imperialist policies of Israel against Arab Palestinians and thus may be a version of anti-Semitism.

Zoroastrianism: A dualistic religion in ancient Persia founded by the legendary Zoroaster or Zarathustra. *See* **dualism**.

Suggested Readings

1. HISTORY'S STORY

Jacques Barzun and Henry F. Graff, *The Modern Researcher* (1957): Two American scholars lay out basic methodology for students of history.

Marc Bloch, *The Historian's Craft/Apologie pour l'histoire, ou Métier d'historien* (1949): A French historian, killed by the Nazis before he could finish this book, explains the use of history.

John Tosh, *The Pursuit of History* (1984): In the first and more recent revised editions, the author reviews strengths and weaknesses of using theory to organize historical study.

2. WANDERERS AND SETTLERS: THE ANCIENT MIDDLE EAST TO 400 B.C.

Anon., *Gilgamesh* (before the seventh century B.C.): In this epic poem, the king of Uruk seeks the meaning of life.

Anon., *The Book of the Dead* (before the thirteenth century B.C.): A collection of hymns, stories, and speeches reveal much of Egyptian mythology.

3. THE CHOSEN PEOPLE: HEBREWS AND JEWS, 2000 B.C. TO A.D. 135

The Old Testament of the Bible/Hebrew Scripture, especially Genesis, Exodus, Joshua, Judges, Samuel, Kings (before the second century B.C.): These books cover much of the history that Jews used for self-understanding; every person wanting to be educated should read the entire Bible, since it is foundational to Western culture.

Josephus, *Antiquities of the Jews/Antiquitates Judaicae* (ca. A.D. 94): A pro-Roman Jewish scholar offers his own summary and interpretation of Jewish history.

4. TRIAL OF THE HELLENES:
THE ANCIENT GREEKS, 1200 B.C. TO A.D. 146

Arrian, *The Campaigns of Alexander/Anabasis Alexandri* (A.D. second century): This account focuses on Alexander's impressive military exploits.

Herodotus, *History of The Persian War* (mid-fifth century B.C.): "The father of history" offers a wide-ranging description of the ancient world as well as the Greek victory over the Persians.

Ovid, *Metamorphoses* (A.D. early first century): This collection of tales presents many of the classic myths of Greece and Rome.

Thucydides, *History of the Peloponnesian War* (late fifth century B.C.): The first great historian insightfully covers the conflict between Athens and Sparta.

5. *IMPERIUM ROMANUM:*
THE ROMANS, 753 B.C. TO A.D. 300

Julius Caesar, *The Gallic War/Commentarii de bello Gallico* (ca. 50 B.C.): The general not only praises his own victories but provides details on his enemies.

Livy, *From the Foundation of the City/Ab Urbe Condita* (late first century B.C.): The chronicler generously covers many stories of Roman history.

Plutarch, *Parallel Lives/Bíoi Parállēloi* (first century A.D.): A Greek writing for Romans compares and contrasts heroes and villains of the ancient world.

Suetonius, *The Twelve Caesars/De vita Caesarum* (A.D. 121): Brief biographies cover both the noble and scandalous activities of the rulers of Rome.

6. THE REVOLUTIONARY RABBI: CHRISTIANITY,
THE ROMAN EMPIRE, AND ISLAM, 4 B.C. TO A.D. 1453

The New Testament of the Bible, especially The Gospel according to Luke and the Acts of the Apostles: These two books cover the life of Jesus and the formative years of the early Church; every person wanting to be educated should read the entire Bible, since it is foundational to Western culture.

Augustine, *Confessions/Confessiones* (ca. A.D. 400): The author of *The City of God* tells his story of conversion.

Eusebius Pamphili (of Caesarea), *Ecclesiastical History/Historia Ecclesiastica* (ca. A.D. 325): The biographer of Constantine sums up Christianity's conquest of Rome.

Josephus, *The Jewish War/Bellum Judaicum* (ca. A.D. 75): A pro-Roman Jewish scholar offers his own summary and interpretation of recent events leading to the destruction of Jerusalem.

7. FROM OLD ROME TO THE NEW WEST:
THE EARLY MIDDLE AGES, A.D. 500 TO 1000

Bede, *Ecclesiastical History of the English People/Historia Ecclesiastica Gentis Anglorum* (early eighth century): The author views English history through its Christian development.

Benedict of Nursia, *Rule/Regula Benedicti* (sixth century): The founder of Western monasticism outlines regulations for the ideal life.

Einhard, *Life of Charlemagne/Vita Karoli Magni* (early ninth century): This short biography offers a lively summary of its hero's life.

Gregory of Tours, *A History of the Franks/Historia Francorum* (late sixth century): The author promotes the Franks as the protectors of Christianity.

8. THE MEDIEVAL MÊLÉE: THE HIGH AND LATER MIDDLE AGES, 1000 TO 1500

Peter Abelard, *Story of My Misfortunes/Historia Calamitatum* (1132): This confident teacher in the early universities covers the high and low points of his career.

Anon. *The Song of Roland/La Chanson de Roland* (ca. 1000): This epic poem conveys the rough life of early knights within a crusading ideology.

Balderich, *The Deeds of Albero/Gesta Alberonis* (mid-twelfth century): The biography of Trier's warrior-bishop conveys the complexities of church/state issues during and after the Investiture Struggle.

Geoffrey Chaucer, *The Canterbury Tales* (late fourteenth century): This collection of colorful tales from many points of view illustrates medieval society.

Jean Froissart, *Chronicles/Chroniques* (ca. 1380–1400): This French knight who also served in England conveys firsthand the stories of the Hundred Years War and its background.

9. MAKING THE MODERN WORLD: THE RENAISSANCE AND REFORMATION, 1400 TO 1648

Erasmus, *In Praise of Folly/Moriae Encomium* (1509): The author mockingly dissects his contemporary society.

Olaudah Equiano, *The Interesting Narrative of the Life of Olaudah Equiano, or Gustavus Vassa, the African Written by Himself* (1789): A victim of slavery writes an account of his experiences.

Bartolomé de Las Casas, *A Short Account of the Destruction of the Indies/Brevísima relación de la destrucción de las Indias* (1552): The first priest in the Americas criticizes the Spanish occupation.

Niccolò Machiavelli, *The Prince/Il Principe* (1532): The Florentine politician offers enduring and pragmatic advice to Renaissance rulers.

Giorgio Vasari, *Lives of the Artists/Le Vite delle più eccellenti pittori, scultori, ed architettori* (1550/1568): In this long collection, the author offers detailed portraits of many Renaissance artists.

10. LIBERATION OF MIND AND BODY: EARLY MODERN EUROPE, 1543 TO 1815

Edmund Burke, *Reflections on the Revolution in France* (1790): A British conservative comments on the mistakes of the French.

Glückel of Hamelin, *Memoirs/Zikhroynes* (1699–1719): A Jewish merchant describes the challenges she faced.

John Locke, *The Second Treatise of Government* (1690): Written just after the Glorious Revolution, this long tract argues in support of democratic and republican constitutions over and against monarchy.

Michel de Montaigne, *Essays/Les Essais* (1580): These perceptive pieces range widely across social issues of the late Renaissance in France.

Jean-Jacques Rousseau, *Confessions/Les Confessions* (1781/1788): The philosopher reveals the personal behind the polemical.

Duc de Saint-Simon, *Memoirs/Mémoires de Saint-Simon* (1788): A noble participant in the courts of Kings Louis XIV and XV of France collected gossip-filled stories and descriptions.

Voltaire, *Candide* (1759): This novel about an innocent satirizes contemporary events and eternal cruelties.

Mary Wollstonecraft, *A Vindication of the Rights of Woman* (1792): This manifesto calls for the education and equality of women.

11. MASTERY OF THE MACHINE: THE INDUSTRIAL REVOLUTION, 1764 TO 1914

Charles Darwin, *The Descent of Man* (1871): This follow-up to his *Origin of Species* offers a nineteenth-century perspective on science and humanity, applying to human beings his theories of natural selection and sexual selection.

Friedrich Engels, *The Condition of the Working Class in England/Die Lage der arbeitenden Klasse in England* (1844): One of the founders of communism describes the exploitation of workers during the early Industrial Revolution.

John Stuart Mill, *On Liberty* (1859): The author makes the case for nineteenth-century liberalism.

Émile Zola, *Germinal* (1885): This novel about French coal miners vividly portrays their miserable working and living conditions.

12. THE WESTERNER'S BURDEN: IMPERIALISM AND NATIONALISM, 1810 TO 1918

Erich Maria Remarque, *All Quiet on the Western Front/Im Westen Nichts Neues* (1929): The author realistically portrays his actual experiences in the German trenches of World War I.

Henry M. Stanley, *How I Found Livingstone* (1871): The journalist tells the sensationalized experiences of his African expedition.

Alexis de Tocqueville, *Democracy in America/De la démocratie en Amérique* (1835/1840): A French aristocrat studying prison reform contrasts the new American republic with his own country.

Jules Verne, *Around the World in Eighty Days/Le tour du monde en quatre-vingts jours* (1873): A novel shows the Europeans' increasing awareness of and interaction with the rest of the globe.

13. REJECTIONS OF DEMOCRACY: THE INTERWAR YEARS AND WORLD WAR II, 1918 TO 1945

Winston Churchill, *While England Slept* (1938): Churchill's warning against appeasement policies toward Nazi Germany; also, his multivolume *History of the Second World War* (1948–1954) offers his unique voice and perspectives on the conflict.

Sigmund Freud, *Civilization and Its Discontents/Das Unbehagen in der Kultur* (1930): The psychiatrist analyzes the value of civilization, applying his theories of guilt.

Adolf Hitler, *My Struggle/Mein Kampf* (1925/1926): The Nazi leader's manifesto outlines his racial views, which more of his contemporaries should have read more carefully and taken more seriously.

George Orwell, *Animal Farm* (1945): A fantasy novel about farm animals who create their own totalitarian society reflects contemporary developments.

John Reed, *Ten Days That Shook the World* (1919): The journalist offers his eyewitness account of the Russian Revolution.

William L. Shirer, *Berlin Diary: The Journal of a Foreign Correspondent, 1934–1941* (1941): An American reporter presents a firsthand account of Nazi Germany.

Elie Wiesel, *Night/La Nuit* (1958): A survivor of the Nazi "Final Solution" relates his experiences.

14. A WORLD DIVIDED: THE EARLY COLD WAR, 1945 TO 1980

Aimé Césaire, *Discourse on Colonialism/Discours sur le colonialisme* (1950): The author, raised under French colonial rule, indicts imperialism.

Betty Friedan, *The Feminine Mystique* (1963): The housewife-turned-scholar dissects American consumerism to understand women's issues.

Václav Havel, *The Power of the Powerless* (1978): The Czech playwright and future president explains how people can live under communist regimes.

George F. Kennan ["X"], *The Sources of Soviet Conduct* (1947): This article influenced the subsequent policy of containment by the United States toward the U.S.S.R.

Robert S. McNamara, *In Retrospect: The Tragedy and Lessons of Vietnam* (1996): One of the key planners of the war gives his view of what went wrong.

Alvin Toffler, *Future Shock* (1970): The author reviews how modern technological society seems to be accelerating out of control.

15. INTO THE FUTURE: THE CONTEMPORARY ERA, 1980 TO THE PRESENT

Timothy Garton Ash, *History of the Present: Essays, Sketches, and Dispatches from Europe in the 1990s* (1999): Essays by the author of *The Magic Lantern: The Revolution of '89 Witnessed in Warsaw, Budapest, Berlin and Prague* (1990) further illuminate postcommunist Europe.

Tony Judt, *Postwar: History of Europe since 1945* (2005): A contemporary historian pulls together a masterly analysis of recent decades.

Tina Rosenberg, *This Haunted Land* (1995): Interviews reflect on the fall of communism in Czechoslovakia, Poland, and East Germany.

Index

Note: Page numbers in italics followed by a letter indicate the following: d = diagram; f = figure; n = note; t = timeline; tb = table. Terms in **boldface** designate a person.

About the Author

Brian A. Pavlac is the Herve A. LeBlanc Distinguished Service Professor and chair of the Department of History at King's College in Wilkes-Barre, Pennsylvania. He is the author of *Witch Hunts in the Western World: Persecution and Punishment from the Inquisition through the Salem Trials* and articles on Nicholas of Cusa and excommunication as well as the translator of Balderich's *Warrior Bishop of the Twelfth Century: The Deeds of Albero of Trier*.